The Playbill® Broadway Yearbook

Third Annual Edition
2006–2007

Robert Viagas
Editor

Amy Asch
Assistant Editor

Kesler Thibert
Art Director

Aubrey Reuben   Ben Strothmann
Photographers

David Gewirtzman
Production Coordinator

Melissa Merlo
Photo Coordinator

The Playbill Broadway Yearbook: Third Annual Edition, June 1, 2006–May 31, 2007
Robert Viagas, Editor

All PLAYBILL® covers in this book are from the magazine's archives.

ISBN-978-1-55783-732-5
ISBN-1-55783-732-5
ISSN-1932-1945

Published by PLAYBILL® BOOKS
525 Seventh Avenue, Suite 1801
New York, NY 10018
Email: yearbook@playbill.com
Internet: www.playbill.com

Printed by WALSWORTH PUBLISHING COMPANY
Commercial Book Group
389 Piedmont Street
Waterbury, CT 06706

Exclusively distributed by APPLAUSE THEATRE & CINEMA BOOKS/Hal Leonard Corporation.

Applause Theatre & Cinema Books
19 West 21st Street, Suite 201
New York, NY 10010
Phone: (212) 575-9265
Fax: (212) 575-9270
info@applausepub.com
www.applausepub.com

Page 1 Photo Credits: Joan Marcus, Paul Kolnik, Carol Rosegg, Catherine Ashmore, George Holz, Michael O'Neill and Craig Schwartz.

Special Thanks

Special thanks to Amy Asch, David Gewirtzman, Melissa Merlo, Kesler Thibert, Aubrey Reuben, Ben Strothmann, Pam Karr, Greg Kalafatas, Kristen Luciani, Julie Cohen, Maria Somma, Natasha Williams, Jim Ayala, Matt Blank, Andrew Gans, Kenneth Jones, Phil DiChiara, Jenny Shoemaker, Nathan Stufflebean, Bill Blackstock and other stage doormen, and Catherine Ryan whose help, advice and guidance made this project possible.

We also thank the Third Edition *Yearbook* Correspondents who shared their stories with such wit and insight:

Uzo Aduba, Carey Anderson, Lucie Arnaz, Steven Beckler (for the second time), Mary Birdsong, Dan Bittner, Nicole Bocchi, Christian Borle, Mary-Mitchell Campbell, Billy Carter, Matt Cavenaugh, Marcus Chait, Donna Lynne Champlin (for the second time), Victoria Clark, Heather Cousens (for the second time), Luther Creek, Martha Donaldson, Ali Ewoldt, Kathy Fitzgerald, Michael FitzGerald, Jane Grey, Jason Butler Harner, Billy Hipkins, cast members of *Inherit the Wind*, Troy Britton Johnson, Jon Krause, Stephen Kunken, Mary MacLeod, Krisha Marcano, Antoinette Martinez, Linda Marvel, Kenny Mellman, Cass Morgan (for the second time), Naturi Naughton, Kris Koop Ouellette (for the third time), Jill Paice, Heather Parcells, Jacqui Polk, Matt Rauch, Daniel Reichard, Greg Reuter, Tom Alan Robbins, Laila Robins, Michelle Robinson (for the second time), John Scherer, Thom Sesma, Bobby Steggert, Barclay Stiff (for the second time), Jessica Stone, Josh Strickland, Eric LaJuan Summers, Jason Viarengo (for the second time), James A. Williams, Robert Witherow and Alissa Zulvergold.

Also the Broadway press agents who helped set up interviews and photo sessions: especially Chris Boneau, Adrian Bryan-Brown, John Barlow, Michael Hartman, Pete Sanders, Richard Kornberg, Marc Thibodeau, Philip Rinaldi, Springer Associates, Sam Rudy, Origlio/Miramonte, Shaffer-Coyle and their staffs.

Plus Joan Marcus, Paul Kolnik, Carol Rosegg and all the fine photographers whose work appears on these pages.

And, most of all, thanks to the great show people of Broadway who got into the spirit of the *Yearbook* and took time out of their busy days to pose for our cameras. There's no people like them.

Preface to the Third Edition

Welcome to the third annual *Playbill Broadway Yearbook*, the book that takes you behind every stage door on Broadway and introduces you to the thousands of everyday magicians who cast the spell of live theatre.

At more than 520 pages, the third edition is the most comprehensive yet. We enjoyed greater participation than ever from the people of Broadway. There were more than 7,000 names in the first edition, 9,000 in the second and we're pushing 10,000 in this one as we continue to strive for our goal of publishing photos of every person who works in theatre on The Great White Way.

We especially loved working with the Correspondents from each show, hearing about all the joys and sorrows working behind the scenes in our stardust industry. Among those you'll meet are Cass Morgan, the Bird Woman in *Mary Poppins*, who says the ghost of the New Amsterdam is alive (sort of); and Bobby Steggert, who tells the secret of looking hot but staying cool in *110 in the Shade*. Michelle Robinson records her memories of the special tenth anniversary performance of *Chicago*, in which a dozen each of Velmas, Billys and Roxies had to be traffic-managed across the stage. Antoinette Martinez shares her wonderful candid photos of hijinks in the hallways and dressing rooms of *Phantom of the Opera*.

Of special note this year: several long-running shows closed and their correspondents chose to focus on their memories of their final performances. See the chapter on *The Producers* for a touching account from one of the dancers whose little girl had grown up with that show. Legend Lucie Arnaz not only reflects on the closing of *Dirty Rotten Scoundrels*, but shares wisdom on the subject passed down to her from her considerable showbiz family. Victoria Clark left the audience in tears with her closing night speech at *The Light in the Piazza*, and she not only allowed us to reproduce it, but included commentary on what it felt like to deliver it.

Yearbook User's Manual

Which Shows Are Included? *The Playbill Broadway Yearbook 2006-2007* covers the Broadway season, which ran, as per tradition, from June 1, 2006 to May 31, 2007. Each of the sixty-seven shows that played at a Broadway theatre under a Broadway contract during that time got a chapter in this edition. That includes new shows which opened during that time, like *Spring Awakening*; shows from the previous season that ran just a few performances into the new season, like *The Odd Couple*; older shows from seasons past that closed during this season, like *The Producers*; and older shows from seasons past that ran throughout this season and continue into the future (and into the next *Yearbook*) like *The Lion King*.

How Is It Decided Which Credits Page Will Be Featured? Each show's credits page (which PLAYBILL calls a "billboard page") changes over the year as cast members come and go. We use the opening-night billboard page for most new shows. For most shows that carry over from previous seasons we use the billboard page from the first week in October. Occasionally, usually at the request of the producer, we use a billboard page from another part of the season, especially when a major new star joins the cast.

What Are "Alumni" and "Transfer Students"? Over the course of a season some actors leave a production; others take their place. To follow our "Yearbook" concept, the ones who left a show after the date of the billboard page are listed as "Alumni"; the ones who join the cast are called "Transfer Students."

What Is a Correspondent and How Is One Chosen? We ask each show to appoint a Correspondent to record anecdotes of backstage life at their production. Sometimes the show's press agent picks the Correspondent; sometimes the company manager, the stage manager or the producer does the choosing. Each show gets to decide for itself. They bring a richness of experience to the job and help tell the story of backstage life on Broadway from many different points of view.

Who Gets Their Picture in the *Yearbook*? Everyone who works on Broadway can get their picture in the *Yearbook*. That includes actors, producers, writers, designers, assistants, stagehands, ushers, box office personnel, stage doormen and anyone else employed at a Broadway show or a support organization. PLAYBILL maintains a database of headshots of all Broadway actors and most creators. We send our staff photographers to all opening nights and all major Broadway-related events. We also schedule in-theatre photo shoots at every production. No one is required to appear in the *Yearbook*, but all are invited. A few shows declined to host a photo shoot this year or were unable to schedule one before our printing deadline. We hope they'll join us in 2008.

Reviews

The *Yearbook* appears every Labor Day, and while we were assembling this third edition, the second edition arrived on store shelves. Among the reviewers was Naomi Plume at BroadwayWorld.com, who gave us five stars out of five and wrote: "The Second Annual Edition is beautifully designed and handsomely put together, in both concept and content. Essential for any theatre buff's collection or school library. This book is the 'bang for your buck' event of the year! Chock full of info—shows, actors, backstage, front-of-house....It's all here...and more. And photos, photos, photos! This book is CRAZY!"

We thank her for her discernment and excellent taste.

Farewell to Melissa Merlo

The staff of *The Playbill Broadway Yearbook* also bids goodbye and continued success to an original member of its first-edition staff, Melissa Merlo, who began as an intern and eventually staked out the job of scheduling, tracking and gathering caption information for the hundreds of photos of backstage crew and service organizations that have become such an important part of the *Yearbook*.

Melissa Merlo

Sometimes she even took the photos herself. Along the way she got to know the entire Runyonesque parade of stage managers, company managers, stage hands and press agents who make Broadway tick. She showed a unique ability to soften the hearts of Broadway's legendarily crusty stage doormen.

Merlo did all this while a Sociology student at Columbia University. She did well enough in her studies that she was offered a job as a paralegal at one of New York's top law firms on her very first interview after graduation. They will benefit enormously from her organizational skills and her winning personality.

The entire PLAYBILL staff is pleased and proud, and hopes she always remembers her three years at PLAYBILL as a life adventure.

Robert Viagas
June 2007

TABLE OF CONTENTS

Timeline 2006-2007

Opening Nights, News Headlines and Other Significant Milestones of the Season

Broadway broke some records and said some significant hellos and goodbyes in the 2006-2007 season. Here are the headlines, day by day.

May 31, 2006—Broadway closes its books on its most lucrative season to date. A record 12 million seats were occupied and a record $861.6 million worth of tickets were sold, 12 percent more than in 2004-05.

June 11, 2006—The 2006 Tony Awards ceremony is broadcast from Radio City Music Hall. It's *Boys'* night out as *Jersey Boys* wins Best Musical and *The History Boys* is named Best Play.

June 13, 2006—After more than eight years at the New Amsterdam Theatre, Tony-winning musical *The Lion King* moves to the Minskoff Theatre to make way for Disney's latest musical, *Mary Poppins*, which will open later in the year.

June 2006—The north half of Times Square becomes a construction zone as the building at the corner of 46th Street and Seventh Avenue, which for decades housed a Howard Johnson's restaurant and the Off-Broadway Duffy Theatre, is torn down and the 1974-vintage TKTS discount ticket booth in Father Duffy Square is dismantled. TKTS moves to temporary space in the ground floor of the Marriott Marquis Hotel. The landmark statue of George M. Cohan is encased in plywood for the duration.

June 19, 2006 —Mayor Michael Bloomberg is on hand to help open a branch of Brooklyn landmark Junior's restaurant on the east side of Shubert Alley.

June 27, 2006—Despite high hopes from the producers and cast, it is announced that the Kennedy Center's revival of *Mame* will not be coming to Broadway, but not before many musical theatre fans hop Amtrak to Washington, DC to see it.

July 6, 2006—The 2005 Tony Awards broadcast is nominated for two Primetime Emmy Awards. Host Hugh Jackman is nominated for Individual Performance in a Variety or Music Program. Elliot Lawrence is nominated for Outstanding Music Direction.

July 2006—Charlotte St. Martin is named head of The League of American Theatres and Producers, succeeding retiring Jed Bernstein.

Summer 2006—The practice of selling a limited number of "premium" orchestra seats at prices up to $250 ($251.25 with theatre improvement surcharge) becomes widespread, as producers try to get a share of inflated prices being charged by speculators on auction services like eBay (and to offset widespread discounts for subprime seats). Not all shows are able to sell these seats, however.

August 15, 2006—*Kiki & Herb: Alive On Broadway* features downtown cabaret performers Justin Bond and Kenny Mellman and their patented mixture of pop tunes and political barbs.

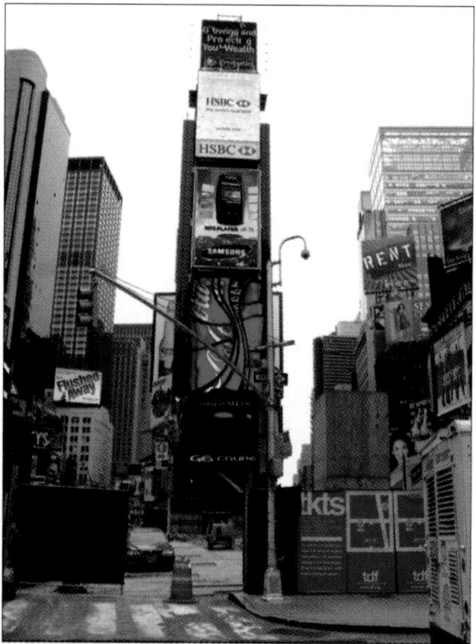

Photo by David Gewirtzman

Why was the north end of Times Square under construction, and who's inside that plywood box? See June 2006.

August 17, 2006—Comedian Martin Short spoofs autobiographical solo shows with *Martin Short: Fame Becomes Me*, a pseudo-autobiographical musical that makes fun of his own celebrity. Among the highlights are a supporting cast of accomplished comedians (including songwriter Marc Shaiman) and a segment in which Short appears in his character of alternately unctuous and insulting talk-show host Jiminy Glick, interviewing a roster of guest stars that changes each night.

August 22, 2007—Pop star Usher takes over the role of lawyer Billy Flynn in *Chicago* and quickly returns the long-running revival to sellout status.

September 24, 2006—Patrick Quinn, new executive director of Actors' Equity Association dies of a heart attack at age 55, less than five weeks after being appointed to the position.

September 28, 2006—Ventriloquist Jay Johnson narrates his lifelong passion for puppetry, and shares the stage with his wood-and-cloth collaborators, in the not-quite-solo show *Jay Johnson: The Two And Only.*

October 5, 2006—Opening night for the first Broadway revival of the Tony- and Pulitzer-winning musical *A Chorus Line*, directed by original co-director Bob Avian and choreographed by original cast member Baayork Lee, r ecreating much of Michael Bennett's original production.

October 11, 2006—Swoosie Kurtz plays Hesione Hushabye and Philip Bosco plays Captain Shotover in Roundabout Theatre Company's revival of George Bernard Shaw's *Heartbreak House*, directed by Robin Lefevre.

October 12, 2006—Matthew Arkin and Mark Linn-Baker star as estranged half-brothers who are forced to confront their past and reveal long-hidden family secrets in *Losing Louie,* a comedy import from London hosted by Manhattan Theatre Club and directed by Jerry Zaks.

October 13, 2006—The film version of *The History Boys* opens in London.

October 22-23, 2006—The sixth annual "The 24 Hour Plays on Broadway" event features Liev Schreiber, Jennifer Aniston, Julianna Margulies, Wallace Shawn, Rachel Dratch, Terrence McNally, David Ives, Julia Cho and two dozen others who write, stage and perform a program of plays within a single 24-hour period at the American Airlines Theatre.

October 24, 2006—The annual audience survey by The League of American Theatres and Producers, "The Demographics of the Broadway Audience 2005-2006," reveals that the number of international visitors to Broadway continued to rebound to pre-September 11, 2001 levels. Attendance by international visitors climbed to 1.32 million for 2005-2006, more than doubling the post-9/11 fallout when admissions hit an all time low of 525,834 (2001-2002).

October 24, 2006—Cynthia Nixon, the 2006 Tony winner as Best Leading Actress in a Play, hosts the annual Tony Honors for Excellence in the Theatre. Honors go to the BMI Lehman Engel Musical Theatre Workshop; *Forbidden Broadway* and its creator, Gerard Alessandrini; Samuel ("Biff") Liff, senior vice president of the William Morris Agency; and Ellen Stewart, founder/director of La MaMa Experimental Theatre Club.

October 25, 2006—In a revival of Simon Gray's *Butley*, Nathan Lane plays an embittered middle-aged college professor who uses angry humor to confront the facts that his ex-wife is remarrying, his male lover is abandoning him and his job is on the line.

October 26, 2006—In *The Times They Are A-Changin',* director/choreographer Twyla Tharp follows up her Billy Joel hit *Movin' Out* by weaving the songbook of folksinger Bob Dylan into an allegorical story about a y oung man coming of age in a traveling circus ruled with an iron hand by the tyrannical ringmaster, his father. Stars Michael Arden, Thom Sesma and Lisa Brescia.

November 2, 2006—The oddball and sad story of real-life Hamptons cat ladies Edith and Edie Beale makes an unlikely hit musical, *Grey Gardens,* which transfers to the Walter Kerr Theatre from a sold-out Off-Broadway run at Playwrights Horizons. Christine Ebersole gets some of the best reviews of her career with her bittersweet performance as the mother in Act I and the grown-up daughter in Act II, with Mary Louise Wilson taking over as her now-elderly mom. The show was written b y Doug Wright

Timeline 2006-2007

(book), Scott Frankel (music) and Michael Korie (lyrics).

November 3, 2006—To accommodate increasing pedestrian crowds in Times Square, lanes of traffic along Broadway and Seventh Avenue are narrowed so sidewalks can be widened.

November 8, 2006—A classic children's book is turned into a holiday musical with the season's longest title: *Dr. Seuss' How The Grinch Stole Christmas! — The Musical.* Patrick Page stars as the greedy green title character, and Tony-winner John Cullum plays his faithful pooch.

November 9, 2006—Trevor Nunn and John Caird recreate one of the longest-running musicals in Broadway history, *Les Misérables*, for a revival starring Alexander Gemignani, Norm Lewis, Daphne Rubin-Vega and Gary Beach.

November 12, 2006—Broadway press agent Bob Fennell dies after a brief illness at age 48. Among his clients were *Wicked* and *The 25th Annual Putnam County Spelling Bee.*

November 13, 2006—Julie White draws a scathing portrait of a stop-at-nothing talent agent in Douglas Carter Beane's comedy *The Little Dog Laughed*, co-starring Tom Everett Scott, Ari Graynor and Johnny Galecki.

November 14, 2006—*Chicago* celebrates its tenth anniversary on Broadway with a special benefit performance that reunites some three dozen stars who appeared in the show over the years playing each scene with multiple actors.

November 16, 2006—Producing powerhouses Cameron Mackintosh and Disney team up for *Mary Poppins*, a musical adaptation of P.L. Travers' story of a magical nanny. Starring Ashley Brown, Gavin Lee and Rebecca Luker, the show closely tracks the 1964 Disney film classic, including most of the score by Richard M. and Robert B. Sherman, with new material from George Stiles and Anthony Drewe.

November 23, 2006—Betty Comden, lyricist and/or librettist (primarily with partner Adolph Green) on Broadway and Hollywood classics *On the Town, Singin' in the Rain, Bells Are Ringing, The Will Rogers Follies, Wonderful Town* and many others, dies today at age 89.

November 27, 2006—Lincoln Center Theater hosts the U.S. premiere of *The Coast of Utopia*, Tom Stoppard's sprawling trilogy of plays following Alexander Herzen, a real-life 19th century Russian revolutionary who suffers the tragedy of being born a half century too soon. I n the course of three plays lasting a total of nine hours, Stoppard charts Herzen's youthful resolve (*Voyage*), the increasing obstacles he encounters in mid life (*Shipwreck*), and the later-life usurpation of his dream by younger, more radical revolutionaries like Karl Marx (*Salvage*). Jack O'Brien directs a cast that includes Brían F. O'Byrne, Billy Crudup, Ethan Hawke and Amy Irving. *Voyage* opens today, with the other two parts joining it in December and February when all three will be performed in rotating repertory.

November 29, 2006—Tony-winning director John Doyle brings his innovative staging of Stephen Sondheim and George Furth's *Company* to Broadway, starring Raúl Esparza as Bobby and Barbara Walsh as Joanne. Like Doyle's Tony-nominated 2005 revival of *Sweeney Todd*, the cast doubles as musicians.

November 30, 2006—Julianne Moore and Bill Nighy star in *The Vertical Hour*, David Hare's London drama about a former American war correspondent, now teaching Political Studies at Yale, who is transformed by her visit to her incipient father-in-law in Britain.

December 5, 2006—*Joaquín Cortés: Mi Soledad*, a revue of flamenco and other Latin dance, is cancelled just weeks after the limited run at the Palace is announced. The move is blamed on an illness in the Cortés family.

December 7, 2006—Walter Bobbie directs *High Fidelity*, a musical based on the film and novel of the same title, about the owner of an esoteric record shop and how he decides which of his Top Five loves will be his Number One. Will Chase and Jenn Colella star in David Lindsay-Abaire's show with an eclectic pop score by Tom Kitt and Amanda Green.

December 10, 2006—Transfer of the Atlantic Theater Company's Duncan Sheik-Steven Sater rock musical *Spring Awakening*, based on the 1891 troubled teen drama by Frank Wedekind. Jonathan Groff, Lea Michele and Stephen Spinella star in the innovative show, which earns headlines for its semi-nude teen sex scene.

December 14, 2006—Brian d'Arcy James and Kristin Chenoweth play the first couple on Earth to Marc Kudisch's Snake in *The Diary of Adam and Eve* segment of Roundabout Theatre Company's revival of Bock & Harnick's *The Apple Tree.* Gary Griffin directs the triptych of one-act musicals that also includes *The Lady or the Tiger?* and *Passionella.*

December 15, 2006—A film adaptation of Michael Bennett's Broadway musical *Dreamgirls*, starring "American Idol" finalist Jennifer Hudson, Beyoncé Knowles and Eddie Murphy, opens at the Ziegfeld Theatre in New York in a special engagement charging a $25 top price.

December 21, 2006—Opening night for *Shipwreck*, part two of *The Coast of Utopia.*

January 1, 2007—Broadway closes the books on its most financially rewarding year in history, selling more than $900 million worth of tickets. The figure was achieved mainly through higher ticket prices, since attendance was down slightly from 2005's record of 12 million seats sold. *Wicked* was by far the top-grossing show on Broadway in 2006 at $73.1 million, according to the League of American Theatres and Producers.

January 1, 2007—*Jersey Boys* raises its top price for regular (non-"premium") seats to $120, a new high for Broadway.

January 4, 2007—Vincent Sardi, Jr., operator of the landmark Times Square eatery that was founded by his father and bears his name, dies at 91.

January 5, 2007—*The New York Times* reports that theatergoers will now be permitted to bring food to their seats at certain theatres. Later in the season, a group of actors will attempt to organize a petition campaign to stop the practice. Shubert Organization Chairman Gerald

Photo courtesy of *Grease*

David Ian, Kathleen Marshall and composer Jim Jacobs choose the cast of the upcoming Broadway *Grease* revival on a competitive TV show. See January 7.

Timeline 2006-2007

Schoenfeld reiterates that eating at seats is still banned at Shubert theatres.

January 7, 2007—An estimated 11.6 million viewers tune in for the debut of "You're the One That I Want," an NBC program along the lines of "American Idol," but designed to cast the leads for a summer 2007 Broadway revival of *Grease.* On-air judges (director Kathleen Marshall, producer David Ian and *Grease* co-creator Jim Jacobs) narrow the field and then viewers vote on their favorites. Over the next few months, another would-be "Sandy" and "Danny" will be voted off the show weekly. In the first two days of sale, $1.3 million worth of tickets for the revival are sold.

January 25, 2007—A star-crossed love between an Irish girl and a British surveyor come to map (and Anglicize) Irish place-names in the early 19th century forms the basis of Brian Friel's drama, *Translations.* Directed by Garry Hynes, the revival stars Niall Buggy, David Costabile and Geraldine Hughes.

February 11, 2007—The Grammy Award for Best Musical Show Album goes to the original cast CD of *Jersey Boys*.

February 18, 2007—Opening night for *Salvage*, part three of *The Coast of Utopia*.

February 22, 2007 —Revival of *Journey's End*, R.C. Sherriff's drama about life in the trenches of World War I. David Grindley recreates his London staging, with a cast that includes U.S. stars Boyd Gaines and Jefferson Mays.

February 25, 2007—The film version of *Dreamgirls* wins two Oscars, Best Featured Actress (Jennifer Hudson) and Best Achievement in Sound Mixing.

March 8, 2007—In a revival of Craig Lucas' *Prelude to a Kiss*, Annie Parisse and Alan Tudyk play a young couple full of joy on their wedding day—until a mysterious old man (John Mahoney) asks to kiss the bride, and their lives slip into "Twilight Zone" territory.

March 11, 2007—Liev Schreiber stars as a late-night talk-show shock jock in Eric Bogosian's *Talk Radio*, which makes its Broadway debut. Robert Falls directs the drama, which originated Off-Broadway with its author as star in 1987.

March 22, 2007—In *Curtains*, with a score by John Kander, Fred Ebb and Rupert Holmes, David Hyde Pierce plays a detective trying to solve a murder backstage at a musical trying out in Boston. Scott Ellis directs a cast that also includes Debra Monk, Edward Hibbert and Karen Ziemba.

March 25, 2007—Viewers of the TV show "You're the One That I Want" vote Max Crumm and Laura Osnes as the leads in the summer 2007 Broadway production of *Grease*.

March 29, 2007—Vanessa Redgrave stars in *The Year of Magical Thinking*, based on J oan Didion's first-person book about the death of her husband, and the decline of her daughter's health.

Photo courtesy Paramount Pictures

Who is this "American Idol" finalist, and in what film adaptation of a Broadway hit did she star? See December 15.

April 5, 2007—The producers of *Riverdance* team up with the composers of *Les Misérables* to present a swashbuckling musical slice of Irish history in *The Pirate Queen*, starring Stephanie J. Block, Hadley Fraser and Linda Balgord.

April 9, 2007—Kevin Spacey, Eve Best and Colm Meaney star in a transfer of London's Old Vic revival of Eugene O'Neill's *A Moon for the Misbegotten*.

April 10, 2007—"American Idol" winner Fantasia Barrino takes over the leading role of Celie in *The Color Purple*.

April 12, 2007 —Tony-winners Christopher Plummer, Brian Dennehy and Denis O'Hare show that the debate between Creationism and Evolution is still a timely one in a revival of Jerome Lawrence and Robert E. Lee's 1955 courtroom drama *Inherit the Wind*, based on the famous Scopes "Monkey" trial of 1925.

April 16, 2007—The Pulitzer Prize for Drama goes to David Lindsay-Abaire's *Rabbit Hole*, which appeared on Broadway last season.

April 22, 2007—With the historical record and his reputation on the line, former President Richard Nixon (Frank Langella) agrees to an interview with British celebrity reporter David Frost (Michael Sheen) in Peter Morgan's post-Watergate drama, *Frost/Nixon*.

April 22, 2007—Also today, Max Bialystock chases Ulla around the couch one last time as *The Producers* closes after 2,502 performances. The Mel Brooks musical won more Tony Awards than any show in history: 12.

April 24, 2007—*Journey's End* and the national touring company of *Jersey Boys* take top honors in the 21st Annual BC/EFA "Easter Bonnet" Competition.

April 29, 2007—Laura Bell Bundy stars in *Legally Blonde*, a new musical by Nell Benjamin, Laurence O'Keefe and Heather Hach, based on the Amanda Brown novel and MGM film about a seemingly ditzy sorority girl who is determined to get into Harvard Law School. Also featuring Christian Borle, Orfeh and Michael Rupert.

May 2, 2007—Two young men who share a love of music find themselves embroiled in issues of class, family and a dreadful crime in *Coram Boy*, a new drama from London by Helen Edmundson, based on the novel by Jamila Gavin. Melly Still directs a cast that features Jan Maxwell, Bill Camp and Wayne Wilcox.

May 3, 2007—Twenty-one-time Tony-winner Harold Prince directs Manhattan Theatre Club's debut of *LoveMusik*, a new musical by Alfred Uhry using the songs of Kurt Weill and based on the composer's letters and life with his wife/muse Lotte Lenya. With Michael Cerveris as Weill and Donna Murphy as Lenya.

May 6, 2007—Two grande dames of American theatre, Tony winners Angela Lansbury and Marian Seldes, return to Broadway in Terrence McNally's new play, *Deuce*, about the relationship between two retired tennis stars.

May 8, 2007—Kenny Leon directs *Radio Golf*, the final chapter in August Wilson's epic cycle of ten plays about African-American life in the 20th century. Completed just before Wilson's death, the drama stars Tonya Pinkins and Harry Lennix in the story of a powerful black politician and his dealings with real estate developers who are seeking to tear down the home once owned by recurring Wilson character, Aunt Esther.

May 9, 2007—Audra McDonald plays Lizzie, a lonely woman in a drought-stricken Texas town in a Roundabout Theatre Company revival of *110 in the Shade*. Her life is turned upside down with the arrival of Starbuck, a man who promises that he can make it rain again. Lonny Price directs this Harvey Schmidt, Tom Jones and N. Richard Nash musical based on Nash's play *The Rainmaker*.

May 31, 2007—Broadway closes its books on the 2006-2007 season, which saw thirty-five openings including 12 new musicals, 11 new plays, five musical revivals, and seven play revivals. Financially, it was Broadway's most bountiful season ever. A record 12.3 million tickets were sold, grossing $939 million, up 8.9 percent from 2005-06.

Head of the Class

Trends, Extraordinary Achievements and Peculiar Coincidences of the Season

Most Tony Awards to a Musical: *Spring Awakening* (8).

Most Tony Awards to a Play *The Coast of Utopia* (7, a record).

Catchphrases and Memorable Quotes: "You'll not see their like again," *Deuce.* "Omigod you guys," *Legally Blonde.* "You're gonna be my bruise," *Spring Awakening.* "It's my—what do you call it?—my sobriquet," *Grey Gardens.*

Awards They Should Give: #1 Best New Showtune. Our Nominees: "Anything Can Happen" in *Mary Poppins.* "The Bitch of Living" in *Spring Awakening.* "Show People" in *Curtains.* "Omigod You Guys!" from *Legally Blonde.* "Nine Percent Chance" in *High Fidelity.* "Around the World" in *Grey Gardens.* "I'll Be There" in *The Pirate Queen.*

Class Is Now in Session: Shows with teachers and/or students as major characters: *Butley, History Boys, Journey's End, Spring Awakening, Legally Blonde, Translations, Vertical Hour, Coram Boy, Doubt, Inherit the Wind, Wicked, How the Grinch Stole Christmas!, The 25th Annual Putnam County Spelling Bee.*

Omigod You Guys!: Shows with pre-teen, teenage or barely post-teen girls as major characters. *Legally Blonde, Wicked, Hairspray, The Color Purple, Spring Awakening, Spelling Bee.*

Teenage Pregnancy Will Wreck Your Life: *Spring Awakening, Coram Boy, Mamma Mia!, Talk Radio.*

Awards They Should Give: #2 Best Special Effects. Our Nominees: Bert walking upside down on proscenium in *Mary Poppins.* The appearance of a magical movie set in *Curtains.* The imaginative dispatch of an important character at the end of Act I in *Curtains* (we can't say more; the cast threatens to shoot anyone who gives away secrets). The thunderstorm in *The Pirate Queen.* The transformer-like set changes in *High Fidelity.* The shipwreck in *Tarzan.* The drowning scene in *Coram Boy.*

Tuning In: *Radio Golf, Talk Radio, High Fidelity.*

Awards They Should Give: #3 Hottest Couple. Our Nominees: Melchior and Wendla in *Spring Awakening.* Robert and Amy in *Company.* Hanschen and Ernst in *Spring Awakening.* Grace and Tiernan in *Pirate Queen,* Lt. Frank Cioffi and Niki Harris in *Curtains.* Paulette and the UPS Guy in *Legally Blonde.* Peter and Rita in *Prelude to a Kiss.*

Stressful Weddings, Which Is To Say, Weddings: *Drowsy Chaperone, Legally Blonde, Company, The Pirate Queen, Mamma Mia!, The Color Purple, Grey Gardens, Prelude to a Kiss, LoveMusik, The Threepenny Opera, Light in the Piazza, The Wedding Singer, Tarzan.*

Left at the Altar (Guys and Gals Who Just Can't Commit): *Company, High Fidelity, Translations, Apple Tree, 110 in the Shade, A Chorus Line, Grey Gardens, The Wedding Singer, Dirty Rotten Scoundrels.*

Awards They Should Give: #4 Best New Rendition of an Old Song in a Revival or Jukebox Musical. Our Nominees: "Sing!" in *A Chorus Line.* "Being Alive" in *Company.* "Raunchy" in *110 in the Shade.* "What Makes Me Love Him" in *The Apple Tree.* "Master of the House" in *Les Misérables.*

Minor Historical Figures as Subjects of Shows: Grace O'Malley in *Pirate Queen.* Alexander Herzen in *Coast of Utopia.* Big Edie and Little Edie Bouvier in *Grey Gardens.* The Four Seasons in *Jersey Boys.* Gary Coleman in *Avenue Q.* David Frost in *Frost/Nixon.*

Broadway's Farm Team #1: TV's "Frasier" provided stars for several Broadway and concert productions: David Hyde Pierce and Edward Hibbert in *Curtains* and *The Drowsy Chaperone,* John Mahoney in *Prelude to a Kiss,* Bebe Neuwirth in *Chicago.* Honorary mention: Kelsey Grammer in a concert version of *My Fair Lady.*

Coolest Juxtaposition of Shows Titles that Didn't Come Off Because Both Productions Got Postponed, Darn It: *Xanadu* and *Zanna, Don't!*

Broadway's Farm Team #2: "American Idol" Contestants on Broadway: Fantasia Barrino in *The Color Purple,* Diana DeGarmo in *Hairspray,* Josh Strickland in *Tarzan,* Frenchie Davis and Tamyra Gray in *Rent.*

Broadway's Longest Runs

By number of performances.
Asterisk (*) indicates show still running as of May 31, 2007.

**The Phantom of the Opera* 8066
Cats 7485
Les Misérables 6680
A Chorus Line 6137
Oh! Calcutta! (Revival) 5959
**Beauty and the Beast* 5397
**Rent* 4630
**Chicago* (Revival) 4383
Miss Saigon 4097
* *The Lion King* 4015
42nd Street 3486
Grease 3388
Fiddler on the Roof 3242
Life With Father 3224
Tobacco Road 3182
Hello, Dolly! 2844
My Fair Lady 2717
The Producers 2502
Cabaret (revival) 2378
Annie 2377

Movies Into Musicals: *Beauty and the Beast, Dirty Rotten Scoundrels, Grey Gardens, Hairspray, High Fidelity, Legally Blonde, The Lion King, Mary Poppins, The Producers, Spamalot, Tarzan, The Wedding Singer.*

And Vice Versa: *Dreamgirls, Phantom of the Opera, Chicago,* and soon, *Hairspray.*

Awards They Should Give: #5 Best Showstopping Moment in a New Production of a Musical. Act I finale in *Spring Awakening.* "Bend and Snap" in *Legally Blonde.* "A Big Black Lady Stops the Show" in *Martin Short: Fame Becomes Me.* "Step in Time" in *Mary Poppins.*

Star Drops: Night falls, and the back of the stage fills with thousands of points of light. It's a star drop! So pretty! So frequently used! *Curtains, Grey Gardens, Les Misérables, The Lion King, Mamma Mia!, Mary Poppins, The Pirate Queen, Prelude to a Kiss.* Extra credit: *Beauty and the Beast* (with meteor!), *The Coast of Utopia* (three-dimensional stars formed by lights on wires!), ditto *Spring Awakening.*

Mount Rushmore (Eminences Grise on Broadway This Season): John Cullum, Brian Dennehy, Frank Langella, Angela Lansbury, Christopher Plummer, Hal Prince, Vanessa Redgrave, Marian Seldes.

Awards They Should Give #6: Best Opening Number. Our Nominees: "Omigod You Guys," *Legally Blonde.* "Mama Who Bore Me," *Spring Awakening.* "Wide Open Spaces," *Curtains.* "The Last Real Record Store on Earth," *High Fidelity.*

Life Is... "Life is random and unfair/Life is pandemonium," *Spelling Bee.* "Life's a bitch," *Spring Awakening.* "Life's a rum go, Guv'nor, and that's the truth," *Mary Poppins.* "Life is fraught-less," *Wicked.* "Life is for the alive, my dear," *Sweeney Todd.* "My whole life's like some test," *Spring Awakening.* "Real life's getting more like fiction each day," *Rent.* "Life's too short, babe," *Rent.* "Life is really up to you," *Spamalot.* "Life is quite absurd and death's the final word," *Spamalot.* "Life's a piece of shit, when you look at it," *Spamalot.* "Life is easy pickings," *Les Misérables.* "Without love, life is like the season with no summer/Life is rock and roll without a drummer/Life is my dad without his Bromo/Life is making out with Perry Como," *Hairspray.* "Life is tit for tat," *Chicago.* "Life is a school," *Chicago.* "Life is a game," *Chicago.* "Life is so unnerving for a servant who's not serving," *Beauty and the Beast.* "Life is hard to bear," *The Apple Tree.* "Life is exactly what I wished for," *The Apple Tree.* "The Circle of Life," *The Lion King.* "Your life is a routine that repeats every day," *Avenue Q.* "Everything in life is only for now," *Avenue Q.*

Autographs

Shows • Events • Faculty • In Memoriam • Index

The Playbill Broadway Yearbook 2006 • 3 • 2007

Shows

The Apple Tree

First Preview: November 29, 2006. Opened: December 14, 2006.
Closed: March 11, 2007 after 18 Previews and 99 Performances.

PLAYBILL

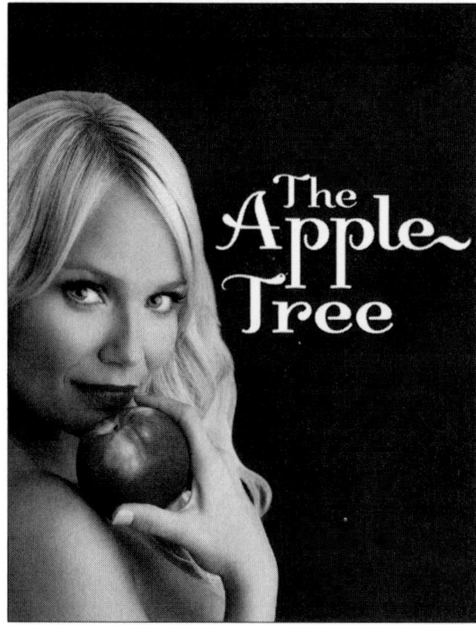

CAST

(in order of appearance)

PART 1
The Diary of Adam and Eve
Based on "The Diary of Adam and Eve"
by Mark Twain

Adam .... BRIAN d'ARCY JAMES
Eve .... KRISTIN CHENOWETH
Snake .... MARC KUDISCH

PART 2
The Lady or the Tiger?
Based on "The Lady or the Tiger?"
by Frank R. Stockton

Balladeer .... MARC KUDISCH
King Arik .... WALTER CHARLES
Princess Barbára .... KRISTIN CHENOWETH
Prisoner .... MIKE McGOWAN
Tiger .... SEAN PALMER
Prisoner's Bride .... SARAH JANE EVERMAN
Nadjira .... LORIN LATARRO
Captain Sanjar .... BRIAN d'ARCY JAMES
Guards .... MIKE McGOWAN, DENNIS STOWE
King Arik's Court .... MEGGIE CANSLER, JULIE CONNORS, SARAH JANE EVERMAN, JUSTIN KEYES, LORIN LATARRO, MIKE McGOWAN, SEAN PALMER, DENNIS STOWE

Continued on next page

STUDIO 54

ROUNDABOUT THEATRE COMPANY
TODD HAIMES, Artistic Director
HAROLD WOLPERT, Managing Director
JULIA C. LEVY, Executive Director

Present

Kristin Chenoweth

Brian d'Arcy James Marc Kudisch

in

Book, Music & Lyrics by Jerry Bock & Sheldon Harnick
Additional book material by Jerome Coopersmith
Based on Stories by Mark Twain, Frank R. Stockton & Jules Feiffer

With Walter Charles

Meggie Cansler Julie Connors Sarah Jane Everman Jennifer Taylor Farrell Justin Keyes
Lorin Latarro Mike McGowan Sean Palmer Eric Santagata Dennis Stowe

Set Design John Lee Beatty *Costume Design* Jess Goldstein *Lighting Design* Donald Holder *Sound Design* Dan Moses Schreier

Hair & Wig Design Charles LaPointe *Music Coordinator* Seymour Red Press *Production Stage Manager* Peter Hanson

Casting Jim Carnahan, C.S.A. *Technical Supervisor* Steve Beers *General Manager* Sydney Beers *Press Representative* Boneau/Bryan-Brown

Director of Marketing & Sales Promotion David B. Steffen *Director of Development* Jeffory Lawson *Founding Director* Gene Feist *Associate Artistic Director* Scott Ellis

Orchestrations by Jonathan Tunick
Music Direction & Vocal Arrangements by Rob Fisher
Choreographed by Andy Blankenbuehler

Directed by Gary Griffin

Original production directed by Mike Nichols
Originally produced on the Broadway Stage by Stuart Ostrow
This production is based on the 2005 New York City Center Encores! Concert Revival of *The Apple Tree*
Roundabout Theatre Company is a member of the League of Resident Theatres. www.roundabouttheatre.org

12/14/06

Brian d'Arcy James as Captain Sanjar and Kristin Chenoweth as Princess Barbára.

Photo by Joan Marcus

The Apple Tree

MUSICAL NUMBERS

PART 1
The Diary of Adam and Eve

Time: Saturday, June 1st
Place: Eden

"Eden Prelude" .... The Orchestra
"Here in Eden" .... Eve
"Feelings" .... Eve
"Eve" .... Adam
"Friends" .... Eve
"The Apple Tree (Forbidden Fruit)" .... Snake
"Beautiful, Beautiful World" .... Adam
"It's a Fish" .... Adam
"Go to Sleep Whatever You Are" .... Eve
"What Makes Me Love Him" .... Eve

PART 2
The Lady or the Tiger?

Time: A Long Time Ago
Place: A Semi-Barbaric Kingdom

"The Lady or the Tiger Prelude" .... The Orchestra
"I'll Tell You a Truth" .... Balladeer
"Make Way" .... King Arik and his Court
"Forbidden Love (In Gaul)" .... Princess Barbára and Sanjar
Reprise: "The Apple Tree" .... Balladeer
"I've Got What You Want" .... Princess Barbára
"Tiger, Tiger" .... Princess Barbára
Reprise: "Make Way" .... King's Court
"Which Door?" .... Sanjar, Princess Barbára, King Arik and his Court
Reprise: "I'll Tell You a Truth" .... Balladeer

PART 3
Passionella
A Romance of the '60s

Time: Then
Place: Here

"Passionella Mini-Overture" .... The Orchestra
"Oh, to Be a Movie Star" .... Ella
"Gorgeous" .... Passionella
"(Who, Who, Who, Who,) Who Is She?" .... The Company
"Wealth" .... Passionella
"You Are Not Real" .... Flip and the Company
"George L." .... Ella and George

Cast Continued

PART 3
Passionella
A Romance of the '60s
Based on "Passionella" by Jules Feiffer

Narrator .... MARC KUDISCH
Ella and Passionella .... KRISTIN CHENOWETH
Mr. Fallible .... WALTER CHARLES
Producer .... WALTER CHARLES
Newsboy .... JUSTIN KEYES
Director .... DENNIS STOWE
Film Critic .... JULIE CONNORS
Stage Hand .... MIKE McGOWAN
Flip, The Prince, Charming .... BRIAN d'ARCY JAMES
Subway Riders, El Morocco Patrons, Fans, Flip's Following, Movie Set Crew .... MEGGIE CANSLER, JULIE CONNORS, SARAH JANE EVERMAN, JUSTIN KEYES, LORIN LATARRO, MIKE McGOWAN, SEAN PALMER, DENNIS STOWE

UNDERSTUDIES

For Eve, Princess Barbára, Passionella:
SARAH JANE EVERMAN
For Adam, Sanjar, Flip, King Arik:
MIKE McGOWAN
For Snake, Balladeer, Narrator:
SEAN PALMER

Swings:
JENNIFER TAYLOR FARRELL,
ERIC SANTAGATA
Dance Captain:
LORIN LATARRO

Production Stage Manager:
PETER HANSON
Assistant Stage Manager:
JON KRAUSE

ORCHESTRA

Conductor: ROB FISHER
Associate Conductor: SAM DAVIS
Violins: MARILYN REYNOLDS, SYLVIA D'AVANZO
Viola: DAVID BLINN
Cello: ROGER SHELL
Woodwinds: JAMES ERCOLE, SEAN FRANK, MARK THRASHER
Trumpets: DOMINIC DERASSE, CHARLES PORTER
Trombone: CLINT SHARMAN
French Horn: ROGER WENDT
Harp: SUSAN JOLLES
Keyboard: SAM DAVIS, Associate Conductor
Bass: JOHN BEAL
Drums/Percussion: PAUL PIZZUTI

Music Copying: EMILY GRISHMAN MUSIC PREPARATION/KATHARINE EDMONDS, EMILY GRISHMAN

Synthesizer Programmer: BRUCE SAMUELS
Music Coordinator: SEYMOUR RED PRESS

The Apple Tree

Kristin Chenoweth
Eve, Princess Barbára, Ella and Passionella

Brian d'Arcy James
Adam, Sanjar, Flip

Marc Kudisch
Snake, Balladeer, Narrator

Walter Charles
King Arik, Employer, Producer

Meggie Cansler
Ensemble

Julie Connors
Ensemble

Sarah Jane Everman
Ensemble

Jennifer Taylor Farrell
Female Swing

Justin Keyes
Ensemble

Lorin Latarro
Ensemble

Mike McGowan
Ensemble

Sean Palmer
Ensemble

Eric Santagata
Male Swing

Dennis Stowe
Ensemble

Sheldon Harnick and Jerry Bock
Book and Lyrics; Book and Music

Jerome Coopersmith
Additional Book Material

Gary Griffin
Director

Andy Blankenbuehler
Choreographer

Rob Fisher
Music Direction and Vocal Arrangements

Jonathan Tunick
Orchestrator

John Lee Beatty
Set Design

Jess Goldstein
Costume Design

Donald Holder
Lighting Design

Dan Moses Schreier
Sound Design

Seymour Red Press
Music Coordinator

Todd Lundquist
Assistant Director

Joanne Manning
Associate Choreographer

Jim Carnahan
Casting

Jack Viertel
Artistic Director, New York City Center Encores!

Gene Feist
Founding Director, Roundabout Theatre Company

Todd Haimes
Artistic Director, Roundabout Theatre Company

Laura Schutter
Ensemble

The Apple Tree

ORCHESTRA
Front Row (L-R): Sean Carney, Susan Jolles (Harp), Rob Berman, Marilyn Reynolds (Violin), Paul Pizzuti (Drums/Percussion).

Back Row (L-R): Roger Shell (Cello), Kathy Venable, John Beal (Bass), Clint Sharman (Trombone), Dominic Derasse (Trumpet) and Roger Wendt (French Horn).

WARDROBE AND HAIR
Front Row (L-R): Elias Aguirre, Nadine Hettel (Wardrobe Supervisor), Robin Cook (Dresser).

Back Row (L-R): Danny Mura, Jay Woods (Dresser), Kurt Keilman (Dresser) and Daryl Terry (Hair and Wig Supervisor).

Photos by Ben Strothmann

FRONT OF HOUSE STAFF
Front Row (L-R): Stella Varriale, LaConya Robinson (House Manager), Jonathan Martinez (House Staff), Nicholas Wheatley (House Staff).

Back Row (L-R): Elicia Edwards (House Staff), Franco Roman (House Staff), Jose Cuello, Katherine Longosky (House Staff) and Ana Bak-Kvapil.

The Apple Tree

STAGE MANAGEMENT
Front Row (L-R): Nancy Mulliner (Company Manager), Peter Hanson (Production Stage Manager).
Back Row (L-R): Katie McKee (Asst. Company Manager), Jon Krause (Asst. Stage Manager) and Tim Semon.

Photos by Ben Strothmann

BOX OFFICE
(L-R): David Carson (Ticket Services), Adam Owens (Ticket Services), Krystin MacRitchie (Ticket Services), Scott Falkowski and Jaime Perlman (Box Office Manager).

CREW
Front Row (L-R): Pitsch Karrer (Production Sound Engineer), Joscelyn Smith, Jean Scheller, Erin Delaney, John Wooding (Head Follow Spot Operator/Assistant Production Electrician).

Middle Row (L-R): Larry Jennino (House Properties), Bill Lombardi, Dorian Fuchs (Follow Spot Operator), Dan Hoffman (Production Carpenter/House Carpenter), Paul Ashton (Automation Operator).

Back Row (L-R): Jess Stevens, Steve Jones (Flyman), Larry White, and Dan Schultheis (Local One IATSE Apprentice).

ROUNDABOUT THEATRE COMPANY STAFF

ARTISTIC DIRECTOR .... **TODD HAIMES**
MANAGING DIRECTOR .... **HAROLD WOLPERT**
EXECUTIVE DIRECTOR .... **JULIA C. LEVY**
ASSOCIATE ARTISTIC DIRECTOR ... **SCOTT ELLIS**

ARTISTIC STAFF

DIRECTOR OF ARTISTIC DEVELOPMENT/ DIRECTOR OF CASTING .... **Jim Carnahan**
Artistic Consultant .... Robyn Goodman
Associate Artists .... Scott Elliott, Doug Hughes, Bill Irwin, Joe Mantello, Mark Brokaw, Kathleen Marshall
Consulting Dramaturg .... Jerry Patch
Artistic Associate .... Jill Rafson
Casting Director .... Mele Nagler
Senior Casting Associate .... Carrie Gardner
Casting Associate .... Kate Schwabe
Casting Associate .... Stephen Kopel
Artistic Intern .... Jill Valentine

EDUCATION STAFF

EDUCATION DIRECTOR ... **Margie Salvante-McCann**
Director of Instruction and Curriculum Development .... Renee Flemings
Education Associate .... Jennifer DeBruin
Education Program Manager .... David Miller
Administrative Assistant for Education ..... Allison Baucom
Education Interns .... George Keveson, Christina Neubrand
Education Dramaturg .... Ted Sod
Teaching Artists .... Phil Alexander, Tony Angelini, Cynthia Babak, Victor Barbella, Brigitte Barnett-Loftis, Caitlin Barton, Joe Basile, LaTonya Borsay, Bonnie Brady, Lori Brown-Niang, Michael Carnahan, Stella Cartaino, Joe Clancy, Melissa Denton, Joe Doran, Katie Down, Tony Freeman, Aaron Gass, Katie Gorum, Sheri Graubert, Adam Gwon, Susan Hamburger, Karla Hendrick, Lisa Renee Jordan, Alvin Keith, Rebecca Lord, Robin Mates, Erin McCready, Jordana Oberman, Andrew Ondrecjak, Laura Poe, Nicole Press, Jennifer Rathbone, Chris Rummel, Drew Sachs, Anna Saggese, Robert Signom, David Sinkus, Derek Straat, Vickie Tanner, Olivia Tsang, Jennifer Varbalow, Leese Walker, Eric Wallach, Diana Whitten, Gail Winar

The Apple Tree

ADMINISTRATIVE STAFF

GENERAL MANAGER .... **Sydney Beers**
Associate Managing Director .... Greg Backstrom
General Manager, Steinberg Center .... Rebecca Habel
General Counsel .... Nancy Hirschmann
Human Resources Manager .... Stephen Deutsch
MIS Director .... Jeff Goodman
Facilities Manager .... Abraham David
Manager of Corporate and Party Rentals .... Jetaun Dobbs
Office Manager .... Scott Kelly
Database Manager .... Dollye Evans
Assistant to the General Manager .... Maggie Cantrick
Management Associate .... Tania Camargo
MIS Assistant .... Micah Kraybill
Receptionists .... Dena Beider, Elisa Papa, Allison Patrick, Monica Sidorchuk
Messenger .... Robert Weisser
Management Intern .... Jen McArdle

FINANCE STAFF

DIRECTOR OF FINANCE .... **Susan Neiman**
Assistant Controller .... John LaBarbera
Accounts Payable Administrator .... Frank Surdi
Business Office Associate .... David Solomon
Financial Associate .... Yonit Kafka
Business Interns .... Li Shen, Richard Patterson

DEVELOPMENT STAFF

DIRECTOR OF DEVELOPMENT .... **Jeffory Lawson**
Director, Institutional Giving .... Julie K. D'Andrea
Director, Individual Giving .... Julia Lazarus
Director, Special Events .... Steve Schaeffer
Manager, Donor Information Systems .... Tina Mae Bishko
Corporate Relations Manager .... Sara Bensman
Manager, Individual Giving .... Kara Kandel
External Affairs Associate .... Robert Weinstein
Institutional Giving Associate .... Sarah Krasnow
Individual Giving Associate .... Kate Bartoldus
Patrons Services Assistant .... John Haynes
Development Assistants .... Jillian Brewster, Christopher Taggart
Individual Giving Intern .... Christopher DeRoche
Special Events Intern .... Erica Rotstein

MARKETING STAFF

DIRECTOR OF MARKETING AND SALES PROMOTION .... **David B. Steffen**
Marketing/Publications Manager .... Margaret Casagrande
Assistant Director of Marketing .... Sunil Ayyagari
Marketing Assistant .... Stefanie Schussel
Website Consultant .... Keith Powell Beyland
DIRECTOR OF TELESALES SPECIAL PROMOTIONS .... **Daniel Weiss**
Telesales Manager .... Anton Borissov
Telesales Office Coordinator .... J.W. Griffin
Marketing Intern .... Darra Messing

TICKET SERVICES STAFF

DIRECTOR OF SALES OPERATIONS .... **Jim Seggelink**
Ticket Services Manager .... Ellen Holt
Subscription Manager .... Charlie Garbowski, Jr.
Box Office Managers .... Edward P. Osborne, Jessica Bowser
Group Sales Manager .... Jeff Monteith
Assistant Box Office Managers .... Andrew Clements, Steve Howe, Robert Morgan
Assistant Ticket Services Managers .... Robert Kane, Ethan Ubell, Carlos Morris
Customer Services Coordinator .... Trina Cox
Ticket Services .... Rachel Bauder, Solangel Bido, Jessie Blum, Jacob Burstein-Stern, William Campbell, Lauren Cartelli, David Carson, Nisha Dhruna, Adam Elsberry, Lindsay Ericson, John Finning, Catherine Fitzpatrick, James Graham, Tova Heller, Dorothea J. Kenul, Bill Klemm, Alexander LaFrance, Krystin MacRitchie, Elisa Mala, Mead Margulies, Chuck Migliaccio, Nicole Nicholson, Bekah Nutt, Adam Owens, Ethan Paulini, David Pittman, Thomas Protulipac, Kate Regan, Jackie Rocha, Heather Siebert, Lillian Soto, Farra Ungar, Pam Unger, Tiffany Wakely, Thomas Walsh
Ticket Services Intern .... Heather Forman

SERVICES

Counsel .... Paul, Weiss, Rifkind, Wharton and Garrison LLP, John Breglio, Deborah Hartnett
Counsel .... Rosenberg & Estis
Counsel .... Andrew Lance, Gibson, Dunn, & Crutcher, LLP
Counsel .... Harry H. Weintraub, Glick and Weintraub, P.C.
Immigration Counsel .... Mark D. Koestler and Theodore Ruthizer
House Physicians .... Dr. Theodore Tyberg, Dr. Lawrence Katz
House Dentist .... Neil Kanner, D.M.D.
Insurance .... DeWitt Stern Group, Inc.
Accountant .... Lutz & Carr CPAs, LLP
Sponsorship .... The Marketing Group, Tanya Grubich, Laura Matalon, Anna Rippey, Erik Gensler
Advertising .... Eliran Murphy Group/ Denise Ganjou, Kara Eldridge
Events Photography .... Anita and Steve Shevett
Production Photographer .... Joan Marcus
Theatre Displays .... King Displays, Wayne Sapper

MANAGING DIRECTOR EMERITUS .... Ellen Richard

Roundabout Theatre Company
231 West 39th Street, New York, NY 10018
(212) 719-9393

GENERAL PRESS REPRESENTATIVES
BONEAU/BRYAN-BROWN
Adrian Bryan-Brown   Matt Polk
Jessica Johnson   Amy Kass

CREDITS FOR *THE APPLE TREE*

GENERAL MANAGER .... Sydney Beers
Company Manager .... Nancy Mulliner
Production Stage Manager .... Peter Hanson
Assistant Stage Manager .... Jon Krause
Assistant Director .... Todd Lundquist
Assistant Choreographer .... Joanne Manning
Assistant Technical Supervisor .... Elisa R. Kuhar
Associate Set Designer .... Matt Myhrum
Assistant Set Designer .... Yoshinori Tanokura
Associate Costume Designer .... China Lee
Assistant Costume Designer .... David Withrow
Associate Lighting Designer .... Mike Jones
Assistant Lighting Designer .... Catherine Tate
Assistant Sound Designer .... Phillip Peglow
Production Carpenter .... Dan Hoffman
Production Electrician .... Josh Weitzman
Assistant Production Electrician .... John Wooding
Production Properties .... Denise Grillo
Assistant Production Properties .... Kevin Crawford
Wardrobe Supervisor .... Nadine Hettel
Hair and Wig Supervisor .... Daryl Terry
Make-up Design .... Angelina Avallone
Production Sound Engineer .... Pitsch Karrer
House Carpenter .... Dan Hoffman
House Electrician .... Josh Weitzman
House Properties .... Lawrence Jennino
Automation Operator .... Paul Ashton
Follow Spot Operator .... Dorian Fuchs
Flyman .... Steve Jones
Moving Light Programmer .... Eric Norris
Head Follow Spot Operator .... John Wooding
Properties Running Crew .... Erin Delaney
Deck Sound .... Valerie Lamour, Larry White
Local One IATSE Apprentice .... Dan Schultheis
Dressers .... Jay Woods, Kurt Keilman, Robin Cook
Assistant Company Manager .... Katie McKee
Production Assistants .... Lindsay Ericson, Jenna Gottlieb
Physical Therapy .... PT Plus
Scenery Constructed, Automated, and Painted by .... Hudson Scenic Studio, Inc.
Lighting Equipment Provided by .... PRG, Production Resource Group
Props Built by .... Paragon Props & Craig Grigg
Soft Goods Provided by .... RoseBrand
Sound Equipment Provided by .... Sound Associates
Costumes by .... Carelli Costumes, Inc.; Tricorne, Inc.; Studio Rouge; and Brian Hamesath
Shoes made by .... Capezio
Hats made by .... Lynne Mackey Studio
Tiger Mask by .... Scott Coppock
Hosiery and Undergarments by .... Bra*Tenders

Special thanks to New York City Center.

STUDIO 54 THEATRE STAFF

Theatre Manager .... Matthew Armstrong
Box Office Manager .... Jaime Perlman
House Manager .... LaConya Robinson
Associate House Manager .... Jack Watanachaiyot
House Staff .... Elicia Edwards, Jason Fernandez, Jen Kneeland, Kate Longosky, Latiffa Marcus, Nicole Marino, Jonathan Martinez, Dana McCaw, Nicole Ramirez, Anthony Roman, Nick Wheatley, Stella Varriale
Security .... Gotham Security
Maintenance .... John Franzoza, Maman Garba
Lobby Refreshments by .... Sweet Concessions

The Apple Tree
Scrapbook

Photos by Aubrey Reuben

1. (L-R): Brian d'Arcy James, lyricist Sheldon Harnick, Kristin Chenoweth, composer Jerry Bock and Marc Kudisch.
2. The ensemble on opening night at Studio 54.
3. (L-R): Kudisch, Chenoweth and James take curtain call on opening night.
4. (L-R): Kudisch, Chenoweth and James at the cast party.

Correspondent: Jon Krause, Stage Manager

The Transfer from "Encores!" to Broadway: A lot of the same people did both productions, including Gary Griffin the director, Andy Blankenbuehler the choreographer, scenic designer John Lee Beatty, costume designer Jess Goldstein, music director Rob Fisher, even the same stage mangers, Peter Hanson and I. Kristin Chenoweth was only cast member who came over with us. The fact that we were all available and it came up quickly was a great surprise. We had so much fun at "Encores!" It was really one of the most pleasant experiences I've ever had in the theatre. We're all having fun. Kristin could not be nicer, and Brian d'Arcy James has got to be the nicest man in show business.

Special Guest: It's such a kick that Alan Alda, from the original 1966 cast, agreed to be our "Voice of God." He and Kristin know each other from last season in "West Wing." He came to see our production with his family in January.

Blessed Event: We did have one baby born: the choreographer and his wife gave birth to a little boy, named Luca Stefano Blankenbuehler. We were all going to name him "Sanjar."

Who Got the Gypsy Robe: The Gypsy Robe went to Lorin Latarro, who had won a few times before. But when the Robe Ceremony began, she said to the committee, "I don't know if this has been done before, but may I pass it on to the next deserving ensemble member?" Terry Marone, who administers the Robe, said "This is a first," and then said, "Why not?" So Lorin passed it to Dennis Stowe, who was very surprised. He's going to put an apple tree on it, with 14 apples, each with the face of one of our cast members.

Memorable Ad-Lib: In Act I, *The Diary of Adam and Eve*, they have this clothesline. One evening Brian d'Arcy James was futzing with it and one end came undone and the whole thing fell to the ground. Just then, Eve (Kristin) made her entrance and Brian ad-libbed, "Eve, will you take care of this?" Kristin smiled, tilted her head and said, "Oh, Adam, you're so handy!" It got such big applause we thought we'd have to leave it in.

Practical Joke: In one scene Kristin has to eat some yogurt onstage. We asked her what her favorite flavor was, and she said strawberry-banana, so we made sure that's always what she had. One night the head prop man, Larry Jennino, came running in to say he couldn't find any strawberry-banana, just strawberry. We went up to Kristin and asked her if that would be OK, and of course she said it would be fine. But then we began to think, hmm, maybe we'll have some fun with Larry. So that night she comes storming off the stage saying, "Who is in charge of the yogurt!!" Larry turns white as a ghost. And Kristin throws a little temper tantrum, "You know, I ask for *one* thing…!" We all contained our laughter as long as we could. Finally Larry catches on and says, "Oh, you guys!" It's all the funnier because Kristin is the opposite of a prima donna—but she knows how to play one.

Avenue Q

First Preview: July 10, 2003. Opened: July 31, 2003.
Still running as of May 31, 2007.

CAST

(in order of appearance)

Princeton, Rod .... HOWIE MICHAEL SMITH
Brian .... EVAN HARRINGTON
Kate Monster, Lucy & others .... MARY FABER
Nicky, Trekkie Monster, Bear & others . RICK LYON
Christmas Eve .... ANN SANDERS
Gary Coleman .... HANEEFAH WOOD
Mrs. T., Bear & others .... JENNIFER BARNHART
Ensemble .... JONATHAN ROOT, MATT SCHREIBER

PLACE: an outerborough of New York City
TIME: the present

UNDERSTUDIES

For Princeton/Rod:
JONATHAN ROOT, MATT SCHREIBER
For Brian:
MATT SCHREIBER
For Kate Monster/Lucy:
JENNIFER BARNHART, AYMEE GARCIA
For Nicky/Trekkie/Bear:
JONATHAN ROOT, MATT SCHREIBER;
For Mrs. T./Bear:
MINGLIE CHEN, CARMEN RUBY FLOYD, AYMEE GARCIA
For Christmas Eve:
MINGLIE CHEN, AYMEE GARCIA
For Gary Coleman:
CARMEN RUBY FLOYD

Continued on next page

GOLDEN THEATRE
A Shubert Organization Theatre
Gerald Schoenfeld, *Chairman* **Philip J. Smith,** *President*
Robert E. Wankel, *Executive Vice President*

Kevin McCollum Robyn Goodman Jeffrey Seller
Vineyard Theatre and The New Group
present

Music and Lyrics by
Robert Lopez and Jeff Marx

Book by
Jeff Whitty

Based on an Original Concept by
Robert Lopez and Jeff Marx

with
Jennifer Barnhart, Mary Faber, Evan Harrington, Rick Lyon, Ann Sanders, Howie Michael Smith, Haneefah Wood

Puppets Conceived and Designed by
Rick Lyon

Set Design
Anna Louizos

Costume Design
Mirena Rada

Lighting Design
Howell Binkley

Sound Design
Acme Sound Partners

Animation Design
Robert Lopez

Music Director/Incidental Music
Gary Adler

Music Coordinator
Michael Keller

General Manager
John Corker

Technical Supervisor
Brian Lynch

Production Stage Manager
Robert Witherow

Press Representative
Sam Rudy Media Relations

Casting
Cindy Tolan

Associate Producers
Sonny Everett
Walter Grossman
Mort Swinsky

Music Supervision, Arrangements and Orchestrations by
Stephen Oremus

Choreographer
Ken Roberson

Directed by
Jason Moore

Avenue Q *was supported by a residency and public staged reading at the 2002 O'Neill Music Theatre Conference of the Eugene O'Neill Theater Center, Waterford, CT*

10/2/06

Barrett Foa with Rod.

Photo by Nick Reuchel

Avenue Q

Cast Continued

DANCE CAPTAIN:
Aymee Garcia

AVENUE Q BAND
Keyboard/Conductor:
GARY ADLER
Keyboard/Associate Conductor:
MICHAEL PATRICK WALKER
Reeds:
JIMMY COZIER
Drums:
MICHAEL CROITER
Bass:
MARYANN McSWEENEY
Guitars:
BRIAN KOONIN

Photo by Nick Reuchel

Stephanie D'Abruzzo with Kate Monster.

Jennifer Barnhart
Mrs. T., Bear & Others

Mary Faber
Kate Monster, Lucy & Others

Evan Harrington
Brian

Rick Lyon
Nicky, Trekkie Monster, Bear and Others, Puppet Design

Ann Sanders
Christmas Eve

Howie Michael Smith
Princeton, Rod

Haneefah Wood
Gary Coleman

Minglie Chen
u/s Christmas Eve, Mrs. T, Bear

Carmen Ruby Floyd
u/s Gary Coleman, Mrs. T., Bear

Aymee Garcia
u/s for Kate Monster, Lucy, Mrs. T., Bear, Christmas Eve

Jonathan Root
Ensemble, u/s for Princeton, Rod, Nicky, Trekkie, Bear

Matt Schreiber
Ensemble, u/s for Princeton, Rod, Nicky, Trekkie, Bear, Brian

Robert Lopez and Jeff Marx
Music and Lyrics, Original Concept

Jeff Whitty
Book

Jason Moore
Director

Ken Roberson
Choreographer

Stephen Oremus
Music Supervision/ Arrangements/ Orchestrations

Anna Louizos
Set Design

Mirena Rada
Costume Design

Avenue Q

Howell Binkley
Lighting Designer

Tom Clark, Mark Menard and Nevin Steinberg,
Acme Sound Partners
Sound Design

Gary Adler
Music Director/ Conductor/ Incidental Music

Michael Keller
Music Coordinator

Brian Lynch,
Theatretech, Inc.
Technical Supervisor

John Corker
General Manager

Kevin McCollum
Producer

Robyn Goodman
Producer

Jeffrey Seller
Producer

Scott Elliot
Founding Artistic Director,
The New Group
Producer

Sonny Everett
Associate Producer

Mort Swinsky
Associate Producer

Becca Ayers
u/s for Kate Monster, Lucy, Mrs. T., Bear

Natalie Venetia Belcon
Gary Coleman, Dance Captain

Barrett Foa
Princeton, Rod

Sala Iwamatsu
u/s Christmas Eve

Jasmin Walker
u/s Gary Coleman

Christian Anderson
Nicky, Trekkie Monster, Bear and Others

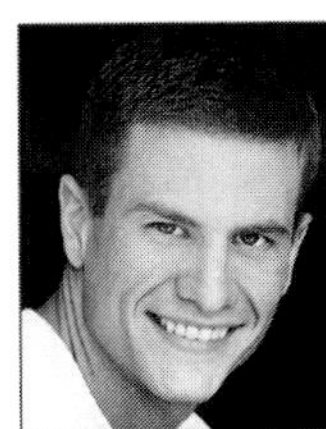
Leo Daignault
Ensemble

Sala Iwamatsu
Swing

Robert McClure
Nicky, Trekkie Monster, Bear and Others

Kelli Sawyer
Kate Monster, Lucy & Others

Jasmin Walker
u/s Gary Coleman

Avenue Q

Staff For *AVENUE Q*

GENERAL MANAGER
John Corker

GENERAL PRESS REPRESENTATIVE
Sam Rudy Media Relations
Sam Rudy
Dale Heller and Robert Lasko

DIRECTOR OF MARKETING
Scott Moore

CASTING
Cindy Tolan Casting
Adam Caldwell, Casting Associate

COMPANY MANAGER
Nick Lugo

PRODUCTION STAGE MANAGER .... **Robert Witherow**
Technical Supervision .... Brian Lynch/ Theatretech, Inc.
Stage Manager .... Christine M. Daly
Assistant Stage Manager .... Aymee Garcia
Resident Director .... Evan Ensign
Assistant Director .... Jen Bender
Associate Conductor .... Mark Hartman
Dance Captain .... Aymee Garcia
Production Assistant .... Alexis Prussack
Assistant to Mr. Corker .... Kim Vasquez
Management Assistant .... Andrew Jones
Management Intern .... Elizabeth Irwin
Associate Set Designer .... Todd Potter
Assistant Costume Designer .... Elizabeth Bourgeois
Associate Lighting Designer/ Programmer .... Timothy F. Rogers
Assistant Lighting Designers .... Douglas Cox, Ryan O'Gara
Production Carpenter .... Bill Garvey
House Carpenter .... Charles Zarobinski
Flyman .... Tom Anderson
Production Electrician .... Craig Caccamise
House Electrician .... Sylvia Yoshioka
Head Electrician .... Rebecca Morris
Video Programmer .... Paul Vershbow
Sound Board Operator .... Elspeth Appleby
Follow Spot Operators .... Joe Pfifferling, A.J. Gigerich
Deck Electrician .... Gretchen Metzloff
Production Properties Master .... Vanessa Gifford
House Properties .... Stephen McDonald
Wardrobe Supervisor .... John A. Robelen III
Dresser .... Jill Heller
Puppet Wrangler .... Phoebe Kreutz
Puppet Builders .... The Lyon Puppets
Rick Lyon, Andrea Detwiler, Vanessa Gifford, Deborah Glassberg, Michelle Hickey, Michael Latini, Adam Pagdon, Laura Parè, David Regan, Sara Schmidt Boldon, James Vogel, James W. Wojtal, Jr., Entirely Different Design, Tim Hawkins, Susan Pitocchi
Music Copying .... Emily Grishman/Alex Lacamoire
Keyboard Programmer .... Mark Hartman
Synthesizer Program Consultant .... Andrew Barrett
Costume Draper .... Karl Ruckdeschel
Assistants to Set Designer .... Heather Dunbar, Donyale Werle
Puppet Wig Consultant .... John James
Makeup Consultant .... Danielle Arminio
Sound and Video Design Effects .... Brett Jarvis
Animation/ Video Production ...... Noodle Soup Productions, Inc./ Jeremy Rosenberg
Advertising .... SpotCo/ Drew Hodges, Jim Edwards Pete Milano, Lauren Hunter
Web Design .... Situation Marketing/ Damian Bazadona
Concessions .... Max Merchandising, LLC/ Randi Grossman
Legal Counsel .... Levine, Plotkin, Menin LLP/ Loren Plotkin, Susan Mindell
Accounting .... FK Partners/Robert Fried
Bookkeeper .... Joseph S. Kubala
Insurance .... D.R. Reiff & Associates/ Sonny Everett, Dennis Reiff
Banking .... JP Morgan Chase
Payroll .... CSI Payroll Services, Inc/ Lance Castellana
Production Photographers .... Nicholas Reuchel Carol Rosegg
Theatre Displays .... King Displays Inc.

The Producing Office
Kevin McCollum, Jeffrey Seller
John Corker, Debra Nir
Ryan Hill

Aged In Wood
Robyn Goodman
Associate Producer: Stephen Kocis
Assistant: Josh Fiedler

Vineyard Theatre
Douglas Aibel, Artistic Director
Jennifer Garvey-Blackwell, Executive Director External Affairs

The New Group
Artistic Director: Scott Elliott
Executive Director: Geoffrey Rich
Assoc. Artistic Director: Ian Morgan
Assoc. Executive Director: Amanda Brandes

Credits

Puppets built by The Lyon Puppets. Scenery by Centerline Studios Inc. 59th Street Bridge Photograph from ***Panoramic New York*** used with special permission by Richard Berenholtz. Stage portals by Atlas Scenic Studios. Lighting equipment by Fourth Phase. Sound equipment by ProMix Inc. Chain motors provided by Hudson Scenic. Christmas Eve wedding dress electrified by International Robotics/Mannetron. Ricola natural herb cough drops courtesy of Ricola USA, Inc. Props built by Prism Productions Services, Inc., Tom Carroll Scenery and Ken Larson. Animation operating system provided by Scharff Weissberg.

Avenue Q has not been authorized or approved in any manner by The Jim Henson Company or Sesame Workshop, which have no responsibility for its content.

Quote from "Something's Coming" (Bernstein/ Sondheim) by permission of Leonard Bernstein Music Publishing Company LLC. (ASCAP).

Special Thanks

Amanda Green, Amy Kohn, Arthur Novell, Bobbi Brown Cosmetics, BMI Lehman Engel Musical Theatre Workshop, Brett Jarvis, Brian Yorkey, Chelsea Studios, Cheryl Henson, Craig Shemin, Doug Aibel, Ed Christie, Jana Zielonka, Jane Henson, Jean Banks, Jennifer Silver, Esq., Jodi Peikoff, Esq., John Buzzetti, Julia Sullivan, Kai Production Strategies, Kristen Anderson, Lara McLean, Manhattan Theatre Club, Maury Yeston, Nicole Rivera, Paulette Haupt, Peter Franklin, Pro-Mark Drumsticks and Mallets, Scott Elliott, Seth Goldstein, Splashlight Studios, Steven Greenberg, Teresa Focarile, The York Theatre, Lee Johnson.

Any donations received during this performance will be given to Broadway Cares/Equity Fights AIDS.

WARNING: This production employs machines that create fog and smoke effects, and strobe lighting.

SHUBERT ORGANIZATION, INC.
Board of Directors

Gerald Schoenfeld, Chairman
Philip J. Smith, President

Wyche Fowler, Jr.
John W. Kluge

Lee J. Seidler
Michael I. Sovern

Stuart Subotnick

Robert E. Wankel
Executive Vice President

Peter Entin, Vice President, Theatre Operations
Elliot Greene, Vice President, Finance

David Andrews, Vice President, Shubert Ticketing Services
John Darby, Vice President, Facilities

D.S. Moynihan
Vice President – Creative Projects

House Manager .... Carolyne Jones

Avenue Q
Scrapbook

Photo by Aubrey Reuben

At the annual "Broadway on Broadway" event in Times Square (L-R): Evan Harrington, Mary Faber, Howie Michael Smith, Haneefah Wood, Sala Iwamatsu, Aymee Garcia and Rick Lyon.

Correspondent: Robert Witherow, Production Stage Manager.
Most Exciting Celebrity Visitor: Probably Frank Oz for obvious reasons. We had every celebrity here you can imagine. Other favorites: George Lucas, Ben Folds, Kate Winslet and Dame Judi Dench. Dame Judi sent a gift basket the following week to congratulate us on the Tony Award.
"Carols for a Cure" Carol: This year it was an original song called "Holi-daze" by Michael Patrick Walker (our associate conductor) and Phoebe Kreutz (our puppet wrangler). It was performed by various cast and crew members.
Actor Who Performed the Most Roles in This Show: Jen Barnhart for sure. She second-hands Nicky and Trekkie, performs Mrs. Thistletwat and the Bad Idea Bear as well as understudies Kate Monster, Lucy the Slut and others. Each night she also animates Rod, Princeton and Kate while other people do the voices. With the exception of The Newcomer, she puppeteers every character in the show. Off-Broadway she had to animate Nicky and Trekkie by herself while Rick Lyon did the voice offstage after he fell off the stage and sprained his ankle.
Who Has Done the Most Shows in Their Career: Ann Sanders, who plays Christmas Eve.
Special Backstage Rituals: We celebrate every cast, crew and orchestra member's birthday. We have a cake and we sing our own original birthday song written by Stephanie D'Abruzzo.
Favorite Moment During Each Performance: "I Wish I Could Go Back To College."
Favorite In-Theatre Gathering Place: Probably the Girls' Dressing Room. We don't have much space in this small theatre, so we'll congregate anywhere—the stage management office, the Boys' Dressing Room. We've stacked up the water bottles in the hallway and put a tablecloth over them to be our table. We put snacks there and birthday cakes. On birthdays we line up along the staircase and in the hallway to sing.
Favorite Off-Site Hangout: Kodama.
Favorite Snack Food: Cake.
Mascot: We have a lot of mascots, as you can imagine: Trekkie, Kate, Rod, Nicky and Lucy.
Favorite Therapy: Ricola, Throat-Coat Tea and Emergen-C. Not necessarily in that order.
Fastest Costume Change: Haneefah Wood, who is currently playing Gary Coleman, only has a couple minutes to change into a tuxedo and do a mic change. She also has to run up two flights of stairs to do it.
Heaviest/Hottest Costume: Ann Sanders as Christmas Eve wears the heaviest costume (it's not really hot). It's a wedding dress that weighs 35 lbs. There are lights in it and a computer program that makes the lights twinkle. The battery pack is also part of the costume.
Who Wore the Least: Ann Sanders also wears a red marabou negligee in the song "Loud as the Hell You Want."
Catchphrase Only the Company Would Recognize: "Burp alert."
Orchestra Member Who Played the Most Instruments: Our percussionist Michael Croiter plays drum set, bell tree, finger cymbal, slapstick, wood blocks, penny whistle and a bunch more.
Orchestra Member Who Played the Most Consecutive Performances Without a Sub: Brian Koonin, our guitarist.

Awake and Sing!

First Preview: March 23, 2006. Opened: April 17, 2006.
Closed: June 25, 2006 after 27 Previews and 80 Performances.

PLAYBILL

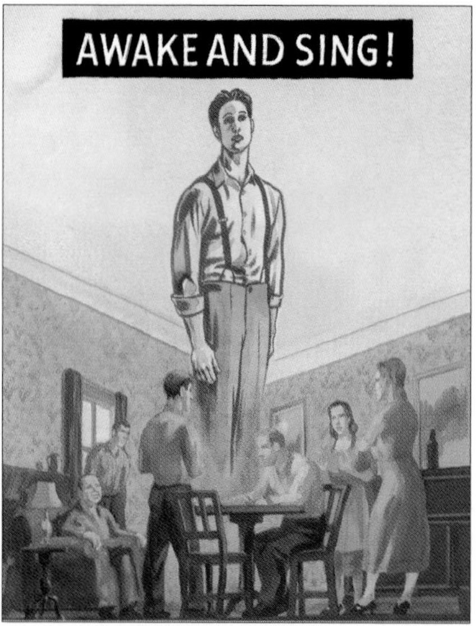

CAST

(in order of speaking)

Ralph Berger .... PABLO SCHREIBER
Myron Berger .... JONATHAN HADARY
Hennie Berger .... LAUREN AMBROSE
Jacob .... BEN GAZZARA
Bessie Berger .... ZOË WANAMAKER
Schlosser .... PETER KYBART
Moe Axelrod .... MARK RUFFALO
Uncle Morty .... NED EISENBERG
Sam Feinschreiber .... RICHARD TOPOL

Time: The mid 1930s
Place: An apartment in the Bronx, New York City

Act I:
A winter evening

Act II, Scene 1:
One year later, afternoon

Act II, Scene 2:
Later that night

Act III:
A week later

Assistant Stage Manager .... DENISE YANEY

Continued on next page

BELASCO THEATRE
111 West 44th Street
A Shubert Organization Theatre
Gerald Schoenfeld, *Chairman* **Philip J. Smith,** *President*
Robert E. Wankel, *Executive Vice President*

LINCOLN CENTER THEATER
under the direction of
ANDRÉ BISHOP and **BERNARD GERSTEN**
presents

AWAKE AND SING!

by **CLIFFORD ODETS**

with (in alphabetical order)
LAUREN AMBROSE NED EISENBERG BEN GAZZARA
JONATHAN HADARY PETER KYBART MARK RUFFALO
PABLO SCHREIBER RICHARD TOPOL ZOË WANAMAKER

sets **MICHAEL YEARGAN** costumes **CATHERINE ZUBER** lighting **CHRISTOPHER AKERLIND**
sound **PETER JOHN STILL** and **MARC SALZBERG** stage manager **ROBERT BENNETT**
casting **DANIEL SWEE** general press agent **PHILIP RINALDI**
director of development **HATTIE K. JUTAGIR** director of marketing **LINDA MASON ROSS**
general manager **ADAM SIEGEL** production manager **JEFF HAMLIN**

directed by **BARTLETT SHER**

LCT gratefully acknowledges generous support in memory of Robert J. Blinken.
The Blanchette Hooker Rockefeller Fund has provided a major grant for this production.
Additional support is provided by the David Berg Foundation.
AWAKE AND SING! is supported by the Doris Duke Charitable Foundation Endowment Fund at LCT.
Special thanks to the New York City Department of Cultural Affairs and the Council of the City of New York.

American Airlines is the official airline of Lincoln Center Theater.
Merrill Lynch is a 2006 LCT season sponsor.

LCT wishes to express its appreciation to Theatre Development Fund for its support of this production.

Get your copy of the Lincoln Center Theater Review on AWAKE AND SING!
available at stands near the exit doors, featuring a rare interview with Clifford Odets.

6/25/06

Photo by Paul Kolnik

(L-R): Ned Eisenberg, Zoë Wanamaker, Jonathan Hadary, Richard Topol and Lauren Ambrose gather around the dinner table.

Awake and Sing!

Cast Continued

UNDERSTUDIES

For Myron Berger and Uncle Morty –
TONY CAMPISI

For Jacob and Schlosser –
STAN LACHOW

For Hennie Berger –
ANNIE PURCELL

For Ralph Berger –
CHARLES SOCARIDES

For Moe Axelrod and Sam Feinschreiber –
ED VASSALLO

For Bessie Berger –
LORI WILNER

Photo by Paul Kolnik

Zoë Wanamaker and Ned Eisenberg as Bessie Berger and Uncle Morty.

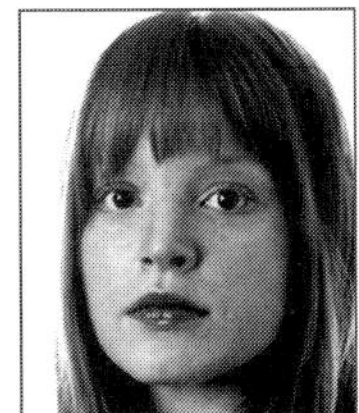

Lauren Ambrose
Hennie Berger

Ned Eisenberg
Uncle Morty

Ben Gazzara
Jacob

Jonathan Hadary
Myron Berger

Peter Kybart
Schlosser

Mark Ruffalo
Moe Axelrod

Pablo Schreiber
Ralph Berger

Richard Topol
Sam Feinschreiber

Zoë Wanamaker
Bessie Berger

Tony Campisi
Understudy for Myron Berger and Uncle Morty

Stan Lachow
Understudy for Jacob and Schlosser

Annie Purcell
Understudy for Hennie Berger

Charles Socarides
Understudy for Ralph Berger

Ed Vassallo
Understudy for Moe Axelrod and Sam Feinschreiber

Lori Wilner
Understudy for Bessie Berger

Clifford Odets
Playwright

Bartlett Sher
Director

Michael Yeargan
Sets

Catherine Zuber
Costumes

Christopher Akerlind
Lighting

Awake and Sing!

Peter John Still
Sound

Marc Salzberg
Sound

William Berloni
Animal Trainer

Robert Bennett
Stage Manager

Denise Yaney
Assistant Stage Manager

André Bishop
Artistic Director, Lincoln Center Theater

Bernard Gersten
Executive Producer, Lincoln Center Theater

FRONT OF HOUSE STAFF
Front Row (L-R):
Dexter Luke and Eugenia Raines.

Second Row (L-R):
Gwendolyn Coley, Meaghan McElroy, Terry Lynch.

Third Row (L-R):
Elisabel Asencio, Kathleen Dunn, Daniel Rosario.

Back Row (L-R):
Tina Bashore and David Josephson.

Photos by Ben Strothmann

STAGE CREW
Front Row (L-R):
Susan Goulet (House Electrician), Rodd Sovar (Dresser), Dylan Foley (Properties), Heidi Brown (House Properties), George Dummitt (House Carpenter), Nichole Amburg (Dresser).

Back Row (L-R):
Denise Yaney (Assistant Stage Manager), Cyrille Blackburn (Production Assistant), Neil B. McShane (Electrician), Valerie Spradling (Sound Operator), Paul Ludick (Dresser), Greg Husinko (Electrician), Rob Cox (Animal Handler), Patrick O'Connor (Properties), John Weingart (Production Carpenter), Al Toth (Deck Carpenter) and Joseph Moritz (House Flyman).

Awake and Sing!

BOX OFFICE
(L-R): Thomas (Tommy) Sheehan (Treasurer) and Jules Ochoa.

LINCOLN CENTER THEATER

ANDRÉ BISHOP, ARTISTIC DIRECTOR
BERNARD GERSTEN, EXECUTIVE PRODUCER

ADMINISTRATIVE STAFF

GENERAL MANAGER ..... ADAM SIEGEL
Associate General Manager ..... Melanie Weinraub
General Management Assistant ..... Beth Dembrow
Facilities Manager ..... Alex Mustelier
Assistant Facilities Manager ..... Michael Assalone
GENERAL PRESS AGENT ..... PHILIP RINALDI
Press Associate ..... Barbara Carroll
PRODUCTION MANAGER ..... JEFF HAMLIN
Associate Production Manager ..... Paul Smithyman
DIRECTOR OF DEVELOPMENT ..... HATTIE K. JUTAGIR
Associate Director of Development ..... Rachel Norton
Manager of Special Events and Young Patron Program ..... Karin Schall
Grants Writer ..... Neal Brilliant
Coordinator, Patron Program ..... Sheilaja Rao
Development Associate ..... Chris Chrzanowski
Assistant to the Director of Development ..... Marsha Martinez
Development Assistant/ Special Eevents ..... Nicole Lindenbaum
DIRECTOR OF FINANCE ..... DAVID S. BROWN
Controller ..... Susan Knox
Systems Manager ..... Stacy Valentine-Thomas
Finance Assistant ..... Kellie Kroyer
DIRECTOR OF MARKETING ..... LINDA MASON ROSS
Marketing Associate ..... Denis Guerin
Marketing Assistant ..... Elizabeth Kandel
DIRECTOR OF EDUCATION ..... KATI KOERNER
Associate Director of Education ..... Dionne O'Dell
Assistant to the Executive Producer ..... Barbara Hourigan
Office Assistant ..... Kenneth Collins
Messenger ..... Esau Burgess
Reception ..... Andrew Elsesser, Daryl Watson

ARTISTIC STAFF

ASSOCIATE DIRECTORS ..... GRACIELA DANIELE, NICHOLAS HYTNER, SUSAN STROMAN, DANIEL SULLIVAN
DRAMATURG and DIRECTOR, LCT DIRECTORS LAB ..... ANNE CATTANEO
CASTING DIRECTOR ..... DANIEL SWEE, CSA
MUSICAL THEATER ASSOCIATE PRODUCER ..... IRA WEITZMAN
Artistic Administrator ..... Julia Judge
Casting Associate ..... Camille Hickman

In Loving Memory of
GERALD GUTIERREZ
Associate Director 1991-2003

SPECIAL SERVICES

Advertising ..... Serino-Coyne/Jim Russek, Christin Seidel
Principal Poster Artist ..... James McMullan
Poster Art for *Awake and Sing!* ..... James McMullan
Counsel ..... Peter L. Felcher, Esq.; Charles H. Googe, Esq.; and Rachel Hoover, Esq. of Paul, Weiss, Rifkind, Wharton & Garrison
Immigration Counsel ..... Theodore Ruthizer, Esq.; Mark D. Koestler, Esq. of Kramer, Levin, Naftalis & Frankel LLP
Auditor ..... Douglas Burack, C.P.A. Lutz & Carr, L.L.P.
Insurance ..... Jennifer Brown of DeWitt Stern Group
Photographer ..... Paul Kolnik
Travel ..... Tygon Tours
Consulting Architect ..... Hugh Hardy, Hardy Holzman Pfeiffer Associates
Construction Manager ..... Yorke Construction
Payroll Service ..... Castellana Services, Inc.

STAFF FOR *AWAKE AND SING!*

COMPANY MANAGER ..... MATTHEW MARKOFF
Assistant Director ..... Sarna Lapine
Assistant Set Designer ..... Mikiko Suzuki
Assistant Costume Designers ..... David Newell, Michael Zecker
Assistant Lighting Designer ..... Ben Krall
Production Carpenter ..... Bill Nagle
Production Flyman ..... John Weingart
Production Propertyman ..... Mark Dignam
Production Electrician ..... Neil McShane
Production Sound Engineer ..... Valerie Spradling
Moving Light Programmer ..... Steve Garner
Props Coordinator ..... Christopher Schneider
Dialect Coach ..... Ralph Zito
Wardrobe Supervisor ..... James Wilcox
Dressers ..... Nichole Amburg, Paul Ludick, Rodd Sovar
Wig Designer ..... Tom Watson
Ms. Wanamaker's Wig ..... Campbell Young
Hair Supervisor ..... Susan Schectar
Makeup Designer ..... Angelina Avallone
Production Assistants ..... Jason Hindelang, Cyrille Blackburn
Animal Handled by ..... Robert Cox

Technical Supervision by
Walter Murphy and Patrick Merryman

Animal Trained by
William Berloni Theatrical Animals, Inc.

CREDITS

Scenery constructed by PRG Scenic Technologies. Costumes by Angels, The Costumiers; John Cowles; Carelli Costumes; Eddie Dawson; and Brian Hemesath. Sound by PRG Audio. Lighting by PRG Lighting. Shoes by LaDuca Shoes. Special thanks to Bra*Tenders for hosiery and undergarments. Telephone bellset courtesy of Boise Contemporary Theater. Natural herb cough drops courtesy of Ricola USA, Inc.

THE SHUBERT ORGANIZATION, INC.
Board of Directors

Gerald Schoenfeld, Chairman
Philip J. Smith, President

Wyche Fowler, Jr.
John W. Kluge
Lee J. Seidler
Michael I. Sovern
Stuart Subotnick

Robert E. Wankel
Executive Vice President

Peter Entin, Vice President, Theatre Operations
Elliot Greene, Vice President, Finance

David Andrews, Vice President, Shubert Ticketing Services
John Darby, Vice President, Facilities

D.S. Moynihan
Vice President – Creative Projects

House Manager ..... Carol Flemming

Beauty and the Beast

First Preview: March 9, 1994. Opened: April 18, 1994.
Still running as of May 31, 2007.

PLAYBILL

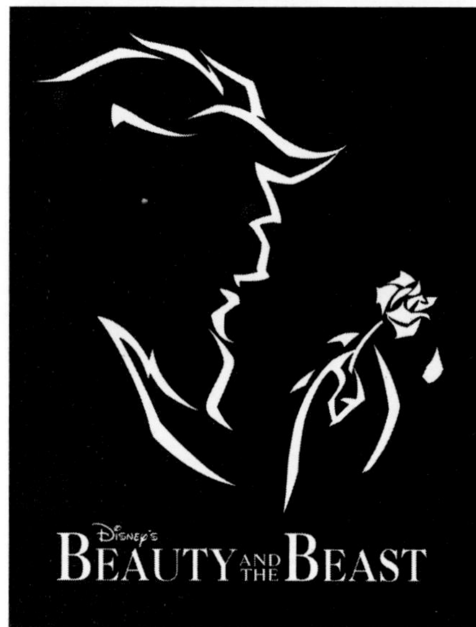

LUNT-FONTANNE THEATRE

UNDER THE DIRECTION OF
JAMES M. NEDERLANDER AND JAMES L. NEDERLANDER

Disney Theatrical Productions
presents

SARAH URIARTE BERRY STEVE BLANCHARD
in

DISNEY'S BEAUTY AND THE BEAST

Music by ALAN MENKEN
Lyrics by HOWARD ASHMAN & TIM RICE
Book by LINDA WOOLVERTON

with
CHRISTOPHER DUVA JEANNE LEHMAN STUART MARLAND JAMIE ROSS

TREVOR BRAUN ALDRIN GONZALEZ MEREDITH INGLESBY
MARLON SHERMAN MARY STOUT

ANA MARIA ANDRICAIN KEITH FORTNER CONNOR GALLAGHER
TRACY GENERALOVICH ALISA KLEIN DAVID E. LIDDELL STEPHANIE LYNGE
GARRETT MILLER BILL NABEL BRYNN O'MALLEY ELIZABETH POLITO
ROD ROBERTS DARIA LYNN SCATTON BRET SHUFORD DAVID SPANGENTHAL
ROB SUTTON ANN VAN CLEAVE ELISA VAN DUYNE BILLY VITELLI TIA MARIE ZORNE

and
DONNY OSMOND
as
GASTON

Scenic Design STANLEY A. MEYER
Costume Design ANN HOULD-WARD
Lighting Design NATASHA KATZ

Sound Design JONATHAN DEANS
Hair Design DAVID H. LAWRENCE
Illusion Design JIM STEINMEYER, JOHN GAUGHAN
Prosthetics JOHN DODS

Associate Producer/Company Manager MARK ROZZANO
Production Supervisor HARRIS PRODUCTION SERVICES
Production Stage Manager JOHN BRIGLEB

Casting BINDER CASTING/MARK BRANDON
Press Representative BONEAU/BRYAN-BROWN

Fight Direction RICK SORDELET
Dance Arrangements GLEN KELLY
Music Coordinator JOHN MILLER

Orchestrations DANNY TROOB
Musical Supervision & Vocal Arrangements DAVID FRIEDMAN
Music Direction & Incidental Music Arrangements MICHAEL KOSARIN

Choreography by
MATT WEST

Directed by
ROBERT JESS ROTH

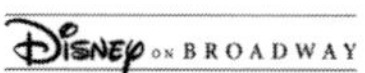

10/2/06

CAST

(in order of appearance)

Young Prince .... CONNOR GALLAGHER
Enchantress .... ELIZABETH POLITO
Beast .... STEVE BLANCHARD
Belle .... SARAH URIARTE BERRY
Bookseller .... BILLY VITELLI
Lefou .... ALDRIN GONZALEZ
Gaston .... DONNY OSMOND
Three Silly Girls .... TRACY GENERALOVICH, ELISA VAN DUYNE, TIA MARIE ZORNE
Maurice .... JAMIE ROSS
Wolves .... ANA MARIA ANDRICAIN, CONNOR GALLAGHER, ELIZABETH POLITO, BRET SHUFORD
Cogsworth .... CHRISTOPHER DUVA
Lumiere .... STUART MARLAND
Babette .... MEREDITH INGLESBY
Mrs. Potts .... JEANNE LEHMAN
Chip .... TREVOR BRAUN
(Tues., Thurs., Sat. Eve., Sun. Mat.)
MARLON SHERMAN
(Wed. Eve., Fri., Sat. Mat., Sun. Eve.)
Madame de la Grande Bouche .... MARY STOUT
Salt and Pepper .... GARRETT MILLER, BRET SHUFORD
Doormat .... CONNOR GALLAGHER
Cheesegrater .... ROD ROBERTS
Monsieur D'Arque .... BILLY VITELLI

Continued on next page

Photo by Joan Marcus

Sarah Uriarte Berry as Belle

Photo by Bruce Glikas

Donny Osmond as Gaston

Beauty and the Beast

MUSICAL NUMBERS

ACT ONE

Overture
Prologue
"Belle" .... Belle, Gaston, Lefou, Silly Girls, Townspeople
"No Matter What"* .... Maurice, Belle
"No Matter What"* (Reprise) .... Maurice
"Me"* .... Gaston, Belle
"Belle" Reprise .... Belle
"Home"* .... Belle
"Home"* (Reprise) .... Mrs. Potts
"Gaston" .... Lefou, Gaston, Silly Girls, Tavern Patrons
"Gaston" (Reprise) .... Gaston, Lefou
"How Long Must This Go On?"* .... Beast
"Be Our Guest" .... Lumiere, Mrs. Potts, Cogsworth, Madame de la Grande Bouche, Chip, Babette, Enchanted Objects
"If I Can't Love Her"* .... Beast

ACT TWO

Entr'acte/Wolf Chase
"Something There" .... Belle, Beast, Lumiere, Mrs. Potts, Cogsworth
"Human Again" .... Lumiere, Madame de la Grande Bouche, Cogsworth, Mrs. Potts, Babette, Chip, Enchanted Objects
"Maison des Lunes"* .... Gaston, Lefou, Monsieur D'Arque
"Beauty and the Beast" .... Mrs. Potts
"If I Can't Love Her"* (Reprise) .... Beast
"A Change In Me"* .... Belle
"The Mob Song" .... Gaston, Lefou, Monsieur D'Arque, Townspeople
"The Battle" .... The Company
"Transformation"* .... Beast, Belle
"Beauty and the Beast" (Reprise) .... The Company

*Music by Alan Menken and lyrics by Tim Rice.
All other lyrics by Howard Ashman and music by Alan Menken.

ORCHESTRA

Conductor: MICHAEL KOSARIN
Associate Conductor: KATHY SOMMER
Assistant Conductor: JOSEPH PASSARO
Assistant Conductor: AMY DURAN

Concertmaster:
SUZANNE ORNSTEIN
Violins:
LORRA ALDRIDGE, EVAN JOHNSON, ROY LEWIS, KRISTINA MUSSER
Cellos:
CARYL PAISNER, JOSEPH KIMURA
Bass:
JEFFREY CARNEY
Flute:
KATHY FINK
Oboe:
VICKI BODNER
Clarinet/Flute:
KERIANN KATHRYN DIBARI
Flute/Clarinet:
TONY BRACKETT
Bassoon, Contrabassoon:
CHARLES McCRACKEN
Trumpets:
NEIL BALM, JAMES DE LA GARZA
French Horns:
JEFFREY LANG, ANTHONY CECERE, ROBERT CARLISLE
Bass Trombone/Tuba:
PAUL FAULISE
Drums:
JOHN REDSECKER
Percussion:
JOSEPH PASSARO
Harp:
STACEY SHAMES
Keyboards:
KATHY SOMMER, MADELYN RUBINSTEIN
Music Coordinator: JOHN MILLER

Cast Continued

Townspeople, Enchanted Objects .... ANA MARIA ANDRICAIN, KEITH FORTNER, CONNOR GALLAGHER, TRACY GENERALOVICH, ALISA KLEIN, DAVID E. LIDDELL, STEPHANIE LYNGE, GARRETT MILLER, BILL NABEL, BRYNN O'MALLEY, ELIZABETH POLITO, ROD ROBERTS, DARIA LYNN SCATTON, BRET SHUFORD, DAVID SPANGENTHAL, ROB SUTTON, ANN VAN CLEAVE, ELISA VAN DUYNE, BILLY VITELLI, TIA MARIE ZORNE
Voice of Prologue Narrator ..... DAVID OGDEN STIERS

UNDERSTUDIES

Enchantress/Silly Girls:
ALISA KLEIN, DARIA LYNN SCATTON
Young Prince:
KEITH FORTNER, DAVID E. LIDDELL
Beast:
DAVID SPANGENTHAL, ROB SUTTON
Belle:
ANA MARIA ANDRICAIN, BRYNN O'MALLEY
Bookseller:
KEITH FORTNER, DAVID E. LIDDELL
Lefou:
KEITH FORTNER, CONNOR GALLAGHER
Gaston:
DAVID SPANGENTHAL, ROB SUTTON
Wolves:
KEITH FORTNER, ALISA KLEIN, DAVID E. LIDDELL, DARIA LYNN SCATTON
Maurice/Cogsworth:
BILL NABEL, BILLY VITELLI
Lumiere:
BILL NABEL, BRET SHUFORD
Babette:
TRACY GENERALOVICH, ALISA KLEIN
Mrs. Potts/Madame de la Grande Bouche:
STEPHANIE LYNGE, ANN VAN CLEAVE
Salt/Pepper/Doormat/Cheesegrater:
KEITH FORTNER, DAVID E. LIDDELL
Monsieur D'Arque:
BILL NABEL, DAVID SPANGENTHAL

SWINGS

KEITH FORTNER, ALISA KLEIN, DAVID E. LIDDELL, DARIA LYNN SCATTON

DANCE CAPTAIN

DARIA LYNN SCATTON

Beauty and the Beast

Sarah Uriarte Berry
Belle

Steve Blanchard
Beast

Donny Osmond
Gaston

Christopher Duva
Cogsworth

Jeanne Lehman
Mrs. Potts

Stuart Marland
Lumiere

Jamie Ross
Maurice

Trevor Braun
Chip at certain performances

Aldrin Gonzalez
Lefou

Meredith Inglesby
Babette

Marlon Sherman
Chip at certain performances

Mary Stout
Madame de la Grande Bouche

Ana Maria Andricain
Ensemble

Keith Fortner
Ensemble/Swing

Connor Gallagher
Young Prince, Doormat, Ensemble

Tracy Generalovich
Ensemble/Silly Girl

Alisa Klein
Ensemble/Swing

David E. Liddell
Fight Captain/ Ensemble/Swing

Stephanie Lynge
Ensemble

Garrett Miller
Ensemble/Pepper

Bill Nabel
Ensemble

Brynn O'Malley
Ensemble

Elizabeth Polito
Enchantress/ Ensemble

Rod Roberts
Ensemble/ Cheesegrater

Daria Lynn Scatton
Ensemble/Swing/ Dance Captain

Bret Shuford
Ensemble/Salt

David Spangenthal
Ensemble

Rob Sutton
Ensemble

Ann Van Cleave
Ensemble

Elisa Van Duyne
Silly Girl/Ensemble

Billy Vitelli
Ensemble/ Bookseller/ Monsieur D'Arque

Tia Marie Zorne
Ensemble/Silly Girl

Alan Menken
Composer

Howard Ashman
Lyricist

Tim Rice
Lyrics

Beauty and the Beast

Linda Woolverton
Book

Robert Jess Roth
Director

Matt West
Choreographer

Stanley A. Meyer
Scenic Designer

Ann Hould-Ward
Costume Designer

Natasha Katz
Lighting Design

Jonathan Deans
Sound Designer

Jim Steinmeyer
Illusions

John Dods
Prosthetics Designer

Binder Casting/
Mark Brandon
Casting

Rick Sordelet
Fight Director

John Miller
Music Coordinator

Danny Troob
Orchestrator

David Friedman
Music Supervision/ Vocal Arrangements

Michael Kosarin
Music Direction/ Incidental Music Arrangements

Thomas Schumacher
Disney Theatrical Productions

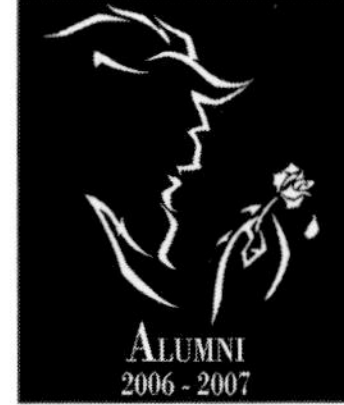

Gina Carlette
Ensemble/Swing

Brian Collier
Doormat, Wolf, Young Prince, Ensemble

Christopher DeAngelis
Salt, Wolf, Ensemble

Gina Ferrall
Madame de la Grande Bouche

Sarah Litzsinger
Belle

Michelle Lookadoo
Silly Girl, Ensemble

Grant Norman
Gaston

Brian O'Brien
Ensemble

Glenn Rainey
Bookseller, Monsieur D'Arque, Ensemble

Alexander Scheitinger
Chip at certain performances

Jennifer Shrader
Ensemble

Jacob Young
Lumiere

Stephen R. Buntrock
Gaston

Christopher DeAngelis
Salt, Ensemble

David deVries
Lumiere

Jonathan Freeman
Cogsworth

Steve Konopelski
Cheesegrater, Ensemble

Beauty and the Beast

Deborah Lew
Belle, Ensemble

Ann Mandrella
Babette

Jennifer Marcum
Silly Girl, Ensemble

James Patterson
Ensemble

Glenn Rainey
Cogsworth

Jennifer Shrader
Ensemble

John Tartaglia
Lumiere

Anneliese van der Pol
Belle

STAGE MANAGEMENT
(L-R): Michael Biondi, John Salvatore, Angela Piccinni and Elizabeth Larsen.
Not Pictured: Margaret Howard, John Brigleb.

Photo by Sanford Kaplan

DRESSER
Michele Reisch

HOUSE PROPERTYMAN
Dennis Sabella

Photos by Ben Strothmann

(L-R): Keith Cooper (Associate Company Manager), Tracey Malinowski (House Manager), Mark Rozzano (Associate Producer), Joe Olcese (Treasurer).

Beauty and the Beast

WARDROBE CREW
Front Row (L-R):
Michael Piatkowski, Teresia Larsen, Rose Keough, Barbara Hladsky.

Back Row (L-R):
Eric Rudy (Assistant Wardrobe Supervisor), Suzanne Sponsler, Joan Weiss, Claire Verlaet, Billy Hipkins, Rita Santi and James Cavanaugh.

Photos by Ben Strothmann

FRONT OF HOUSE
Front Row (L-R):
Evelyn Fernandez (Ticket Taker), Lauren Banyai (Usher), Angalic Cortes (Usher), Barry Jenkins (Porter).

Second Row (L-R):
Carlo Mosarra (Usher), Hector Aguilar (Usher), Paul Perez (Bag Checker), Melody Rodriguez (Usher), Madeline Flores (Directress), Joey Cintron (Usher).

Back Row (L-R):
Stephanie Martinez (Usher), Jessica Vargas (Usher), Honey Owens (Directress), Marlon Danton (Usher), Marisa Perez (Usher), Mildred Villano (Usher), Wil Pacheco (Usher), Roberto Calderon (Usher), Jessica Gonzales and Susan Martin (Head Usher).

STAGE CREW
Front Row (L-R):
Jan Nebozenko (Sound), Eddie McGarry (Spot Operator), David Brickman (Spot Operator), Eric Levy (Spot Operator).

Second Row (L-R):
Ned Hatton (Sound Effects Engineer), George Dignam (Sound), Gerald Schultz (Assistant Electrician/Vari Lite Operator), William C. Horton, Sr. (Assistant Electrician/Special Effects Technician), Peter Byrne (Head Electrician).

Back Row (L-R):
Mark Hallisey (Assistant Carpenter), Mitch Christenson (Spot Operator), Andrew D. Elman (Automation Carpenter), Dana McDaniel (Automation Carpenter).

Beauty and the Beast

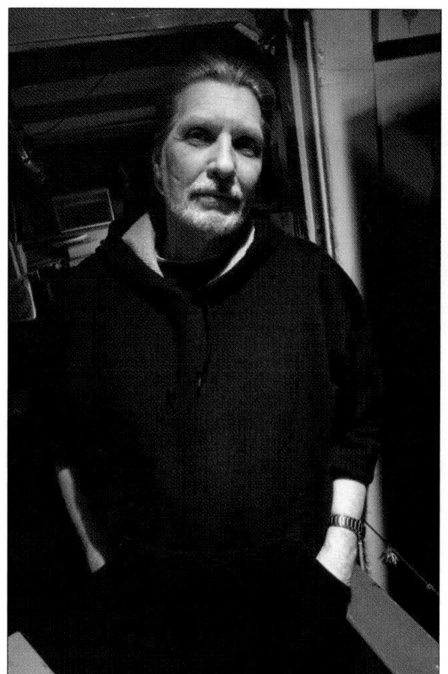

EVENING DOORMAN
Bob Garner

WIG CREW
Front Row (L-R): Amy Uhl, Elizabeth Mathews.
Second Row (L-R): Jennifer Mooney, Rene Kelly.
Back Row (L-R): Armando Licon, Mark Adam Rampmeyer (Hair Supervisor).

Photos by Ben Strothmann

BOX OFFICE
Joe Olcese (Treasurer) and Christine Desavino (Box Office).

STAFF FOR DISNEY'S *BEAUTY AND THE BEAST*

Company Manager .... MARK ROZZANO
Assistant Company Manager .... Keith D. Cooper

Production Supervision .... Harris Production Services

General Press Representative .... Boneau/Bryan-Brown
Chris Boneau/Jim Byk/
Juliana Hannett

Production Stage Manager .... John Brigleb
Stage Manager .... M.A. Howard
Stage Manager .... Michael Biondi
Stage Manager .... Elizabeth Larson
Dance Captain .... Daria Lynn Scatton
Fight Captain .... David E. Liddell

Puppet Design Consultant .... Michael Curry

Special Effects Consultant .... Jauchem & Meeh, NYC

Associate Production Supervisor .... Tom Bussey
Production Manager .... Elisa Cardone
Associate Scenic Designer .... Dennis W. Moyes
Principal Set Design Assistant ...... Edmund A. LeFevre, Jr.
Set Design Assistants .... Stephen Carter,
Judy Gailen, Dana Kenn, Sarah Lambert
Associate Lighting Designers .... Gregory Cohen,
Dan Walker
Assistant Lighting Designers .... Rob Cangemi,
Maura Sheridan
Automated Lighting Programmers .... Aland Henderson,
Richard W. Knight
Associate Sound Designer .... John Petrafesa, Jr.
Original Pyrotechnic Designer .... Tylor Wymer
Automated Lighting Tracker .... John Viesta
Projection Effects .... Wendall K. Harrington
Associate Costume Designer .... Tracy Christensen
Assistants to Ms. Hould-Ward .... David C. Paulin,
Markas Henry, Mark Musters,
Fabio Toblini
Assistant to Mr. Lawrence .... Linda Rice
Synthesizer Programming .... Dan Tramon,
Bruce Samuels

Production Carpenter .... B.B. Baker
Production Flyman .... Peter H. Jackson III
Production Electrician .... Todd Davis
Production Property Master .... Joseph P. Harris. Jr.
Production Sound Engineer .... Scott Anderson
Production Wardrobe Supervisor .... Sue Hamilton
Production Hair Superviso .... Wanda
Gregory,
Mark Adam Rampmeyer
Production Prosthetics Supervisor .... Angela Johnson

Head Carpenter .... B.B. Baker
Flyman .... Frank Frederico
Assistant Carpenter .... Mark Hallisey
Automation Carpenters .... Andrew D. Elman,
Hugh M. Hardyman
Head Electrician .... Tom Brouard
Assistant Electrician/Front Light .... Peter Byrne
Assistant Electrician/
Special Effects Technician .... William C. Horton, Sr.
Assistant Electrician/Vari*Lite Operator ..... Gerald Schultz
Sound Effects Engineer .... Ned Hatton
Head Propertyman .... David L. Bornstein
Assistant Propertyman .... John Lofgren
Wardrobe Supervisor .... Julie Ratcliffe
Assistant Wardrobe Supervisor .... Eric Rudy
Ms. Berry's Dresser .... Erin Byrne
Mr. Blanchard's Dresser .... Rita Santi
Wardrobe Crew .... James Cavanaugh, Joseph Davis,
Dan Foss, Billy Hipkins,
Barbara Hladsky, Rose Keough,
Theresia Larsen, Michael Piatkowski,
Suzanne Sponsler, Claire Verlaet,
Joan Weiss
Makeup/Prosthetics Supervisor .... Eve Morrow
Hair Supervisor .... Mark Adam Rampmeyer
Assistant Hair Supervisor .... Paula Schaffer
Wig Crew .... Jeffrey Knaggs, Anita Lausevic,
Jennifer Mooney, Kevin Phillips

Additional Orchestrations .... Michael Starobin,
Ned Ginsberg
Music Preparation Supervisor .... Peter R. Miller,
Miller Music Service
Assistant to Mr. Menken .... Rick Kunis
Assistant to Mr. Rice .... Eileen Heinink
Assistant to John Miller .... Matthew P. Ettinger
Rehearsal Pianists .... Glen
Kelly,
Madelyn Rubinstein, Amy Duran

Web Design Consultant .... Joshua Noah
Advertising .... Serino Coyne, Inc.
Press Associates .... Adrian Bryan-Brown,
Brandi Cornwell, Jackie Green,
Hector Hernandez, Jessica Johnson,

Beauty and the Beast

Kevin Jones, Eric Louie,
Shanna Marcus, Aaron Meier,
Joe Perrotta, Linnae Petruzzelli,
Matt Polk, Matt Ross,
Heath Schwartz, Susanne Tighe

Press Interns .... Megan Gentry, Cait Ruegger, Elyse Weissman

Casting Associates .... Jack Bowdan, C.S.A., Mark Brandon, Megan Larche, Assistants: Rachel Shapiro-Cooper, Nikole Vallins

Payroll Manager .... Cathy Guerra

Production Assistants .... Bari Kartowski, Mika Hadani, Alison Miller

Production Photography .... Joan Marcus, Marc Bryan-Brown

Production Travel .... Jill Citron

Children's Tutoring. .... On Location Education

Child Wrangler .... Alissa Zulvergold

Theatre Displays .... King Displays

Safety & Health Consultants .... CHSH, Inc., New York City

Originally Produced by

Robert W. McTyre .... Producer

Don Frantz .... Associate Producer

Based on the Disney Film Disney's
BEAUTY AND THE BEAST,
directed by Kirk Wise and Gary Trousedale.
Produced by Don Hahn.
Special thanks to all the artists and staff at
Walt Disney Feature Animation.
Tom Child, Initial Conceptual Development. Anthony Stimac/Musical Theatre Works, Inc.

CREDITS

Scenic & Transformation Effect
Motion Control Featuring
Stage Command Systems™
by Scenic Technologies.

Scenic construction, sculpting and scenic painting by Scenic Technologies. Additional scenery by Variety Scenic Studios; Hudson Scenic Studios, Inc.; Draperies by Showbiz Enterprises and I. Weiss & Sons, Inc. Lighting equipment by Four Star Lighting. Automated lighting by Vari-Lite, Inc. Pani Projection by Production Arts Lighting Inc. Sound furnished by Sound Associates Inc. Custom built props by Seitzer and Associates. Table cloths by Decor Couture Designs. Window treatments, hand and table linens by O'Neil. Costumes executed by Barbara Matera Ltd. Foliage by Modern Artificial. Costumes executed by Grace Costumes, Inc. Dying, screening and painting by Fabric Effects Incorporated. Surface designs and costume crafts by Martin Izquierdo Studios. Prosthetics by John Dods Studio. Millinery by Douglas James, Arnold S. Levine, Janet Linville and Woody Shelp. Footwear by Capezio and J.C. Theatrical. Vacuform costume sculptor by Costume Armour, Inc. Wigs created by Bob Kelly Wig Creations, Inc. Opticals by Fabulous Fanny's Myoptics. Gloves by LaCrasia Glamour Gloves. Beast muscle system by Andrew Benepe Studio. Costume harness and supports by J. Gerard. Additional supports by Danforth Orthopedic. Special Adhesives by Adhesive Technologies, Inc. Illusions by John Gaughan and Associates. Invention and Magic Mirror by Tom Talmon Studio. Pyrotechnical special effects materials supplied by MP Associates, Inc. Pyrotechnical Equipment supplied by LunaTech. All sound recording by Sound Designers Studio, New York City. Emer'gen-C super energy booster provided by Alacer Corp. Throat lozenges supplied by Ricola, Inc.

Cover Art Design © Disney

BEAUTY AND THE BEAST
originally premiered at
Theatre Under The Stars
Houston, Texas
December 2, 1993

Inquiries regarding the licensing of stock and amateur productions of *Beauty and the Beast* or Elton John and Tim Rice's *Aida* should be directed to Music Theatre International, 421 W. 54th St., New York, NY 10019. Tel: 212-541-4684; www.MTIshows.com

---

NEDERLANDER

Chairman .... **James M. Nederlander**

President .... **James L. Nederlander**

Executive Vice President
Nick Scandalios

Vice President
Corporate Development
Charlene S. Nederlander

Senior Vice President
Labor Relations
Herschel Waxman

Vice President
Jim Boese

Chief Financial Officer
Freida Sawyer Belviso

STAFF FOR THE LUNT-FONTANNE

House Manager .... **Tracey Malinowski**

Treasurer .... Joe Olcese

Assistant Treasurer .... Gregg Collichio

House Carpenter .... Terry Taylor

House Electrician .... Dennis Boyle

House Propertyman .... Dennis Sabella

House Flyman .... Mike Walters

House Engineers .... Robert MacMahon, Joseph Riccio III

DISNEY THEATRICAL PRODUCTIONS

President .... Thomas Schumacher

SVP & General Manager .... Alan Levey

SVP, Managing Director & CFO .... David Schrader

Senior Vice President, Creative Affairs ..... Michele Steckler

Senior Vice President, International .... Ron Kollen

Vice President, International Marketing ..... Fiona Thomas

Vice President, Operations .... Dana Amendola

Vice President, Labor Relations .... Allan Frost

Vice President, Domestic Touring .... Jack Eldon

Director, Domestic Touring .... Michael Buchanan

Vice President, Theatrical Licensing .... Steve Fickinger

Director, Human Resources .... June Heindel

Manager, Labor Relations .... Stephanie Cheek

Manager, Human Resources .... Cynthia Young

Manager, Information Systems .... Scott Benedict

Senior Computer Support Analyst .... Kevin A. McGuire

Production

Executive Music Producer .... Chris Montan

Vice President, Creative Affairs .... Greg Gunter

Vice President, Physical Production .... John Tiggeloven

Senior Manager, Safety .... Canara Price

Manager, Physical Production .... Karl Chmielewski

Purchasing Manager .... Joseph Doughney

Staff Associate Designer .... Dennis W. Moyes

Staff Associate Dramaturg .... Ken Cerniglia

Marketing

Vice President, Broadway .... Andrew Flatt

Managers, Broadway .... Michele Groner, Leslie Barrett

Website Manager .... Eric W. Kratzer

Assistant Manager, Communications .... Dana Torres

Sales

Vice President, Ticketing .... Jerome Kane

Manager, Group Sales .... Jacob Lloyd Kimbro

Assistant Manager, Group Sales .... Juil Kim

Group Sales Representative .... Jarrid Crespo

Business and Legal Affairs

Senior Vice President .... Jonathan Olson

Vice President .... Robbin Kelley

Director .... Harry S. Gold

Attorney .... Seth Stuhl

Paralegal/Contract Administration .... Colleen Lober

Finance

Director .... Joe McClafferty

Senior Manager, Finance .... Dana James

Managers, Finance .... Justin Gee, John Fajardo

Production Accountants .... Joy Brown, Nick Judge, Barbara Toben, Jodi Yaeger

Assistant Production Accountant .... Darrell Goode

Senior Financial Analyst .... Tatiana Bautista

Analyst .... Liz Jurist

Controllership

Director, Accounting .... Leena Mathew

Manager, Accounting .... Erica McShane

Senior Analysts .... Stephanie Badie, Mila Danilevich, Adrineh Ghoukassian

Analysts .... Ken Herrell, Bilda Donado

Administrative Staff

Dusty Bennett, Jane Buchanan, Craig Buckley, Lauren Daghini, Jessica Doina, Cristi Finn, Cristina Fornaris, Dayle Gruet, Gregory Hanoian, Jonathan Hanson, Jay Hollenback, Connie Jasper, Kerry McGrath, Lisa Mitchell, Ryan Pears, Flora Rhim, Roberta Risafi, Bridget Ruane, Kisha Santiago, David Scott, Andy Singh

BUENA VISTA THEATRICAL MERCHANDISE, L.L.C.

Vice President .... Steven Downing

Merchandise Manager .... John F. Agati

Operations Manager .... Shawn Baker

Assistant Manager, Inventory .... Suzanne Jakel

Associate Buyer .... Violeta Burlaza

Retail Supervisor .... Mark Nathman

Disney Theatrical Productions
1450 Broadway, New York, NY 10018
guestmail@disneytheatrical.com

Beauty and the Beast
SCRAPBOOK

Correspondent: Billy Hipkins, Dresser for "Lumiere."
Most Exciting Celebrity Visitor: Donny Osmond visited us as "Gaston" for three months and was the nicest man on earth. And dreamy too.
"Gypsy of the Year" Sketch: "We Are Working on That" by Connor Gallagher and Michael Piatkowski.
"Carols for a Cure" Carol: "The Key to Christmas" by Michael Weiner and Alan Zachary.
"Easter Bonnet" Sketch: "The Corkscrew: Unplugged" by Alisa Klein and Bill Nabel.
Actor Who Performed the Most Roles: Rod Roberts' track has the most costume changes but I'm sure our Swings have done the most, often several tracks at a time.
Actor Who Has Done the Most Performances in This Show: Well, Bill Nabel has been with this show since Day One in Houston and has done several other long-running shows so he may hold a record for the most performances on Broadway.
Special Backstage Rituals: People knock on wolf heads as Theresia carries them back to their pre-set; some of the crew watch "Cops" religiously; Scrabble games are much more serious than mere rituals; We have a special cha-cha-cha clap that happens in the music of the battle, swings that can't learn it are abused then fired; Dollar Sunday feels ritualistic too, almost like a stoning.
Favorite Moment During Each Performance: Hearing Maurice get attacked by wolves is hilarious.
Favorite In-Theatre Gathering Places: The cross-under for Birthdays, Happy Trails, and any baked surprises people bring in. Our green room is way up top so it's mostly used for stretching and napping.
Favorite Snack Food: We take that "Be Our Guest" thing to heart and dive into anything left on any surface, complaining through mouthfuls about how bad we're being and thanking/cursing the bringer of sweets.
Mascot: Aldrin Gonzalez. The little brother you never wanted. The neighbor's dog that got loose in your flowerbed. That nightmare you had that came to life. But funny, funny, funny.
Favorite Therapies: We love our Ricolas and our P.T. staff. And a lot of us are now drinking Mona Vie (Contact Beth Polito to learn more!)
Memorable Ad-Lib: Ann Arvia sang: "Set to sacrifice our children badda kadda budda kah!" And the more lost she got, the louder she got.
Cell Phone Issues: We don't get a lot of rings but we *do* see people holding up their phones so the folks back home can hear the pretty music too. That, and chatty children.

Photos by Alissa Zulvergold

Memorable Stage Door Encounters: Mr. Osmond has a lot of loyal fans, several of them clutching porcelain Donny dolls.
Fastest Costume Changes: Turning plates into napkins is a pit crew adventure. And it seems like all of Belle and Beast's changes get faster and heavier as the night goes on.
Busiest Day at the Box Office: We do a brisk walk up business and our weekends are pretty solid. We're closing in July anyway.
Who Wore the Heaviest/Hottest Costumes: If it's enchanted, it's heavy. And bald caps, latex head pieces and beast fur are hot (Looking and to wear.)
Who Wore the Least: The men's ensemble in the cross-under after "Be Our Guest."
Catchphrases: "Boop-boop-a-doo...(The when-you-lose-on-"Price-is-Right" theme). "What is WRONG with him?" Poster Nazi. Dinner Belle. "They treat me like #*@! And I'm sick of it!" "Oh Mountain Dew!"
Best In-House Parody Lyrics: Most are far too filthy to repeat but here's a favorite from the tour: Instead of "Sweep up the years of sadness and tears and throw them away" they created "Fill up my rear with pretzels and beer and have a buffet." Cute.
Company In-Jokes: Wardrobe: "I'm workin' here!" or "Do you know what I do for a living?" Wigs: "We're going back to the original design." All: "Isn't anyone leaving or

1. Backstage birthday party for Trevor Braun ("Chip," center) with (clockwise from left) Rod Roberts, Beth Polito, Connor Gallagher, Stephanie Lynge, David Liddell and David Spangenthal.
2. Meredith Inglesby in costume as "Babette" holding a "Flat Stanley" doll sent by a fan.

Beauty and the Beast
Scrapbook

having a Birthday today?" Advice to the Young Prince: "Just take the Rose!"

Company Legends: Daria Scatton, our dance captain. She taught at least forty-seven people this show this year.

Understudy Anecdote: Speaking of Daria, she brushed up on Madame's role just in case she was called on in an emergency while another understudy was out. And sure enough, that night she went on and was magnificent. Now if only both of our Chips would call out so Tia could go on....

Nicknames: Blanche, Ritsies, Visa, Betty Louise, Spanky, Tracy G, EVD, Rod Roberts Porn Star, Jay Schray, Megadeath, Soap Boy, Granny, Gay Gay, Judy Junior, Test Tube Baby, Sho Sho, The Dirty Chaperone and Pyro Bill.

Sweethearts: Every one of us loves everyone. Always. Honest.

Embarrassing Moments: At the top of the show when the Young Prince and the Hag are in their tableau and the "Once Upon a Time..." track doesn't come on. Awkward. Even more so when the "Ladies and Gentlemen, Welcome..." track comes on instead.

Ghostly Encounters: We don't see a lot of the Ghost upstairs but we do have a tape-stealing Troll on hand.

Superstition That Turned Out To Be True: If you say any former cast member's name three times they re-join the cast.

Coolest Thing About Being in the Show: The paycheck was pretty cool. And steady, too, for a long time. And we know that we've been a lot of people's (especially kids') first Broadway experience. That includes the audiences and the company. It has been a rare treat and great honor to be part of such an amazing family and we will miss the daily togetherness and cherish our memories. "Tale as Old as Time" indeed.

Photos courtesy of Alissa Zulvergold

Photo by Aubrey Reuben

1. The cast in costume for an imagined musical of Disney's *Pocahontas* in the "Gypsy of the Year" skit, "We Are Working on That."
2. Child wrangler Alissa Zulvergold with Trevor Braun.
3. Jonathan Freeman ("Cogsworth") and John Tartaglia ("Lumiere") make things hot for a Flat Stanley doll.
4. Curtain call for the 5000th performance, June 20, 2006.

Bridge & Tunnel

First Preview: January 13, 2006. Opened: January 26, 2006.
Closed: August 6, 2006 after 16 Previews and 213 Performances.

PLAYBILL®

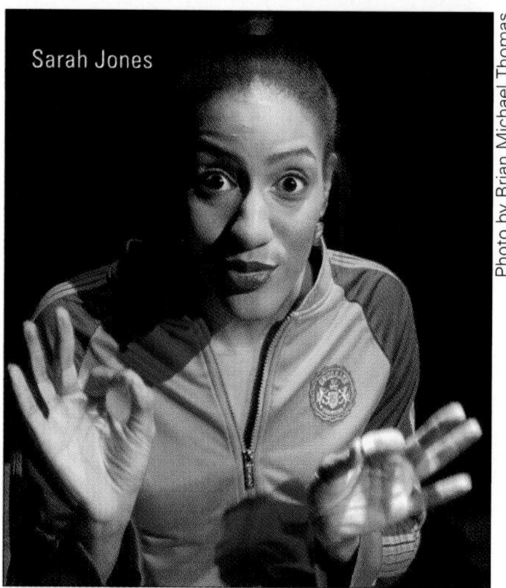
Sarah Jones

Photo by Brian Michael Thomas

THE HELEN HAYES THEATRE

MARTIN MARKINSON DONALD TICK

Eric Falkenstein Michael Alden Boyett Ostar Productions
present

BRIDGE & TUNNEL

written and performed by
SARAH JONES

scenic design **David Korins** lighting design **Howell Binkley** sound design **Christopher Cronin**

press representative **Pete Sanders Group** marketing **Nancy Richards Marcia Pendelton**

assistant director **Steve Colman** production stage manager **Beverly Jenkins**

technical supervision **Aurora Productions** associate producer **Tom Wirtshafter** general management **Richards/Climan, Inc.**

directed by
Tony Taccone

Originally Produced at The Culture Project, NYC
Developed at Berkeley Repertory Theatre, Berkeley, CA

The producers wish to express their appreciation to the Theatre Development Fund for its support of this production.

8/6/06

Howell Binkley
Lighting Design

Christopher Cronin
Sound Design

Asa Taccone
Music

Sarah Jones
Playwright/Performer

Tony Taccone
Director, and Artistic Director, Berkeley Repertory Theatre

Steve Colman
Assistant Director

David Korins
Scenic Designer

Bridge & Tunnel

Beverly Jenkins
Production Stage Manager

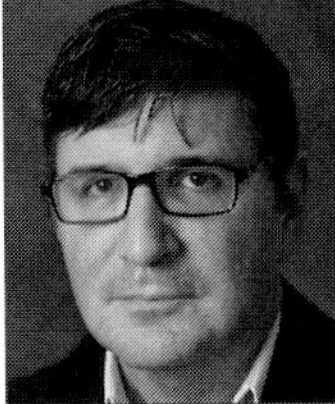
Pete Sanders, The Pete Sanders Group
Press Representative

Nancy Richards
Marketing

David Richards and Tamar Climan, Richards/Climan, Inc.
General Manager

Eric Falkenstein
Producer

Michael Alden
Producer

Bob Boyett
Producer

Bill Haber, OSTAR Enterprises
Producer

Pat Flicker Addiss
Associate Producer

Marcia Roberts
Associate Producer

Elvera Roussel
Associate Producer

FRONT OF HOUSE STAFF
Back Row (L-R): Matt Kuehl, Yuri Ivanov, Alan Markinson (House Manager) and John Biancamano (Head Usher).
Front Row (L-R): Frank Biancamano, Berdine Vaval, Linda Maley and Harry Joshi.

Robert Seymour (Doorman)

Photos by Ben Strothmann

STAGE CREW
(L-R):
Ron Mooney (House Carpenter), Roger Keller, Jr. (House Props), Laurie Goldfeder (Stage Manager), Robert Seymour (Stage Door), Bob Etter (Sound), Trevor McGinness (Wardrobe), Joe Beck (Electrician) and Chris Morey (Company Manager).

Bridge & Tunnel

SCRAPBOOK:
(L-R): Steve Colman and Sarah Jones on the day her caricature was hung in Sardi's restaurant.

STAFF FOR *BRIDGE & TUNNEL*

GENERAL MANAGEMENT
Richards / Climan, Inc.
David R. Richards Tamar Haimes
Laura Cronin

PRESS REPRESENTATIVE
The Pete Sanders Group
Pete Sanders Shane Marshall Brown
Glenna Freedman

COMPANY MANAGER
Jolie Gabler

TECHNICAL SUPERVISION
Aurora Productions
Gene O'Donovan W. Benjamin Heller II
Bethany Weinstein Hilary Austin

PRODUCTION STAFF FOR *BRIDGE & TUNNEL*

Assistant Director .... Steve Colman
Associate Set Design .... Rod Lemmond
Assistant Set Design .... Lawrence Hutcheson
Associate Lighting Design .... Sarah E.C. Maines
Music .... DJ Rekha, Asa Taccone
Wardrobe Supervisor .... Trevor McGinness
Production Carpenter .... Joe Lavaia
Production Electrician .... Joseph Beck
Production Props .... Roger Keller
Production Sound .... Robert Etter
Follow Spot Operator .... Greg Fedigan
Vocal Coach .... Andrea Haring
Production Assistant .... Michelle Dunn
Assistant to the General Manager .... Amanda E. Berkowitz
Assistant to Sarah Jones .... Caitie Bradley
Advertising .... Serino Coyne, Inc./ Jim Russek, Christin Seidel, Jill Jefferson
Marketing .... Nancy Richards, Marcia Pendelton
Audience Development .... Kojo Ade
Promotions .... Uptown Movie Network
Banking .... Commerce Bank/ Barbara Von Borstel, Ashley Elezi
Accounting .... FK Partners/ Robert Fried, Elliott Aronstam
Insurance .... DeWitt Stern Group/ Anthony Pittari, Peter Shoemaker
Legal Counsel .... Franklin, Weinrib, Rudell & Vassallo P.C./ Jason Baruch
Payroll Service .... Castellana Services Inc.
Pre-Production Photography .... Bob Handelman
Production Photography .... Paul Kolnik
Additional Photography .... Bruce Glikas
Producer Associates .... Don McAlarnen, Ian Smith, Megan Hart, Diane Murphy, Theresa Pisanelli, Andrew Cleghorn, Mark Marmer
Press Assistant .... Clifton Guterman
Production Interns .... Mara Klein, Brendan Wattenberg
Press Intern .... Ann Burke

Scenery by Center Line Studios
Lighting equipment by PRG Lighting
Sound equipment by One Dream Sound

Makeup Provided by
M*A*C

Sarah Jones would like to thank Meryl Streep, Michael Alden, Eric Falkenstein, The stellar Bridge & Tunnel Team, The Culture Project, Allan Buchman, Berkeley Rep, The Nuyorican Poets Café, Jayson Jackson, Caitie Bradley, Kori Wilson, National Immigration Forum, Frank Sharry, Karen Paul-Stern, Muzzafar Chishti, Ancy Louis, Margie McHugh, Judy Mark, Ford Foundation, Taryn Higashi, WK Kellogg Foundation, Terri Wright, Henri Treadwell, Frank Taylor, Equality Now, Gloria Steinem, Jessica Neuwirth, Taina Bien-Aime, Pam Shifman, Bryn Mawr College, The United Nations International School, Marjorie Nieuwenhuis, New York Civic Participation Project, SAKHI, Lois Smith, Ken Sunshine, (Frankfurt, Kurnit, Klein, and Selz), Lisa Davis, Mark Merriman, CAA, Kevin Huvane, George Lane, Jeffery Spiech, Olivier Sultan, Gloria Feliciano, Fiduciary Management Group, Ivan Thornton, Thomasina Thornton, John Howell, Rumzi Araj, Hala Araj, Emily Sklar, Breakthrough, Art Start, The Ghetto Film School, Joe Hall, Sky Nellor, Bao Phi, Sadie Nash Leadership Project, Juan Jose Guttierez, Erica Portela, Kirk Nugent, CHIRLA, Michele Andrews, Wei Wah Chan, Mr. And Mrs. Mark Lii, Museum of Chinese in the Americas, Lev Ortenberg, Mr. Borsh, Nancy Hirsch, Leslie Farrington, Hannah Jones, The Farrington Family, The Jones Family, The Griggs Family, Penny Colman, Linda Hickson, Bob Colman, David Lewis-Colman, Crystal Lewis-Colman, Jonathan Colman, Katrin DeHaen, Renee Harris, Mariana Kirby, Naveed Alam, Bruce and Karolyn Gould, Bethann Hardison, David Skurnick, Felicia Noth.

SPECIAL THANKS
Meryl Streep,
Cass Almendral, Dana Beck, Allan Buchman, Chez Josephine, Lisa K. Davis, Toni Hahn Davis, Robert Dragotta, David Drake, David Glass Desserts, Chad Gracia, Johanna Haan, Hamptons Vodka, Megan Hart, Jayson Jackson, Sandra Johnson, William Johnson, Lori Machens, David Marcus, Mark Marmer, Scott Morfee, Marjorie Nieuwenhuis, Origin Wine, Tony Origlio, Marcia Roberts, John G. Rubin, Sand Dollar Cookies, Elyse Singer, Tamara Lovatt Smith, Ken Sunshine, Kip Vanderbilt, Tom Wirtshafter, Kori Wilson

Natural herb cough drops supplied by
Ricola USA Inc.

Throat Coat provided by Traditional Medicinals.

Emer'gen-C provided by Alacer.

THE HELEN HAYES THEATRE
owned and operated by
MARTIN MARKINSON and DONALD TICK

General Manager .... SUSAN S. MYERBERG
Associate General Manager .... Sharon Fallon

STAFF FOR THE HELEN HAYES THEATRE

HOUSE MANAGER .... ALAN R. MARKINSON
Treasurer .... David Heveran
Assistant Treasurers .... Charles Stuis, Andrew Chen
Engineer/Maintenance .... Hector Angulo
Head Usher .... John Biancamano
Stage Door .... Jonathan Angulo, Robert Seymour
Accountant .... Chen-Win Hsu, C.P.A., P.C.
House Carpenter .... Joe Lavaia

Butley

First Preview: October 5, 2006. Opened: October 25, 2006.
Closed: January 14, 2007 after 21 Previews and 94 Performances.

PLAYBILL

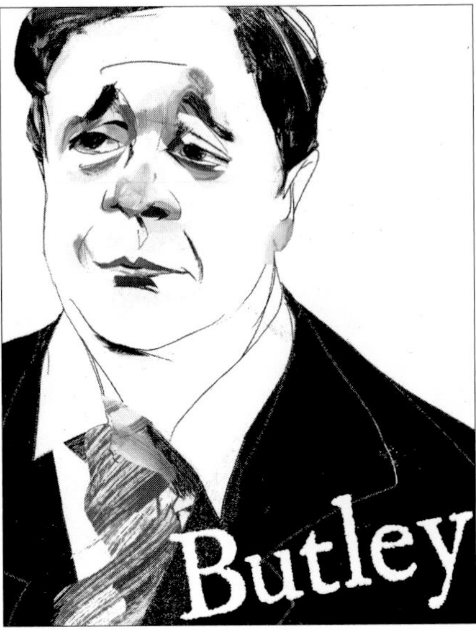

BOOTH THEATRE
222 West 45th Street
A Shubert Organization Theatre
Gerald Schoenfeld, *Chairman* **Philip J. Smith,** *President*

Robert E. Wankel, *Executive Vice President*

Elizabeth Ireland McCann
Stephanie P. McClelland Chase Mishkin Eric Falkenstein Debra Black
Barbara Manocherian/Larry Hirschhorn Barbara Freitag Jeffrey Sine/Frederick Zollo
Joey Parnes
Executive Producer

Present the
Nicholas Martin, Artistic Director — Huntington Theatre Company Production — Michael Maso, Managing Director

of

Nathan Lane

in

Butley

by

Simon Gray

with

Julian Ovenden

Pamela Gray Roderick Hill Darren Pettie Jessica Stone

and

Dana Ivey

SCENIC DESIGN Alexander Dodge
COSTUME DESIGN Ann Roth
LIGHTING DESIGN David Weiner
SOUND DESIGN John Gromada

WIG & HAIR DESIGN David Brian Brown
CASTING Jay Binder/ Jack Bowdan
DIALECT COACH Stephen Gabis

PRODUCTION STAGE MANAGER Michael McGoff
COMPANY MANAGER Kim Sellon

PRESS REPRESENTATIVE Boneau/Bryan-Brown
MARKETING TMG The Marketing Group
ASSOCIATE PRODUCER Tommy Demaio

DIRECTED BY
Nicholas Martin

THE PRODUCERS WISH TO EXPRESS THEIR APPRECIATION TO THEATRE DEVELOPMENT FUND FOR ITS SUPPORT OF THIS PRODUCTION.

LIVE BROADWAY

10/25/06

CAST

(in order of appearance)

Ben Butley .... NATHAN LANE
Joseph Keyston .... JULIAN OVENDEN
Miss Heasman .... JESSICA STONE
Edna Shaft .... DANA IVEY
Anne Butley .... PAMELA GRAY
Reg Nuttall .... DARREN PETTIE
Mr. Gardner .... RODERICK HILL
Students .... MARGUERITE STIMPSON, CHAD HOEPPNER

Stage Manager:
ELIZABETH MILLER

An office in a college of London University, 1971.

UNDERSTUDIES

For Ben Butley:
JOHN LEONARD THOMPSON
For Reg/Joey:
ANTHONY CRANE
For Miss Heasman:
MARGUERITE STIMPSON
For Edna/Anne Butley:
GLORIA BIEGLER
For Joey/Mr. Gardner:
CHAD HOEPPNER

Nathan Lane as Ben Butley

Photo by T. Charles Erickson

SIMON GRAY ON BEN BUTLEY'S OFFICE:

"When we produced this play in London, I was teaching in a basement office at Queen Mary College [part of the U of L]. I shared the office with another professor – our relationship wasn't like Butley and Joey's, but the set for *Butley* was a spot-on reproduction of that office. It was surreal and a little unnerving to come directly from Queen Mary's, where I'd been working all day, to the theatre, and see the room I'd just left."

Butley

Nathan Lane
Ben Butley

Julian Ovenden
Joseph Keyston

Dana Ivey
Edna Shaft

Pamela Gray
Anne Butley

Roderick Hill
Mr. Gardner

Darren Pettie
Reg Nuttall

Jessica Stone
Miss Heasman

Chad Hoeppner
Student

Marguerite Stimpson
Student

Gloria Biegler
Understudy for Anne and Edna

Anthony Crane
Understudy for Reg, Joey

John Leonard Thompson
Understudy for Ben Butley

Simon Gray
Playwright

Nicholas Martin
Director/ Artistic Director, Huntington Theatre Company

Alexander Dodge
Scenic Design

Ann Roth
Costume Design

John Gromada
Sound Design

Stephen Gabis
Dialect Coach

David Brian Brown
Wig/Hair Design

Jay Binder C.S.A.
Casting

Jack Bowdan C.S.A.
Casting

Elizabeth Ireland McCann
Producer

Stephanie P. McClelland
Producer

Chase Mishkin
Producer

Eric Falkenstein
Producer

Debra Black
Producer

Barbara Manocherian
Producer

Larry Hirschhorn
Producer

Barbara Heller Freitag
Producer

Joey Parnes
Executive Producer

Michael Maso
Managing Director, Huntington Theatre Company

James McMenamin
Mr. Gardner

Butley

FRONT OF HOUSE STAFF
Front Row (L-R):
Teresa Aceves (Usher),
Marjorie Glover (Usher),
Bernadette Bokun (Usher),
Catherine Coscia (Usher)

Back Row (L-R):
Marco Malgiolio (Usher),
Nadine Space (Usher),
Laurel Ann Wilson (House Manager)

Not Pictured:
Chrissie Collins (Head Usher),
Nirmala Sharma (Director),
Timothy Wilhelm (Ticket-Taker)

Photos by Ben Strothmann

CREW
Kneeling (L-R):
Michael McGoff,
Elizabeth Miller,
Sandy Binion,
Dave Rogers

Standing (L-R):
Jimmy Keane,
Ron Fogel,
Kenny McDonough,
Wayne Smith,
Ken Brown,
Ron Burns, Sr.

Butley

Photo by Ben Strothmann

BOX OFFICE STAFF
(L-R): Marshall Kolbrenner and Vinnie Whittaker

Photo by T. Charles Erickson

Nathan Lane as Ben Butley

STAFF FOR *BUTLEY*

GENERAL MANAGEMENT
JOEY PARNES

GENERAL PRESS REPRESENTATIVES
BONEAU/BRYAN-BROWN
Chris Boneau Jackie Green Matt Ross

CASTING
JAY BINDER CASTING
Jay Binder C.S.A.
Jack Bowdan C.S.A., Mark Brandon, Megan Larche
Assistants: Nikole Vallins and Allison Estrin

ASSISTANT PRODUCER
S.D. WAGNER

ASSISTANT GENERAL MANAGER
JOHN JOHNSON

PRODUCTION PHOTOGRAPHER
JOAN MARCUS

Company Manager ....Kim Sellon
Assistant Company Manager ....Kit Ingui
Production Stage Manager ....Michael McGoff
Assistant Stage Manager ....Elizabeth Miller
Assistant to the Director ....Michael Matthews
Assistant Set Designer ....Kevin Judge
Assistant Lighting Designer ....Stephen Boulmetis
Assistant Costume Designer ....Michelle Matland
Assistant Sound Designer ....David Baker
Assistant Wig Designer ....Carole Morales
Production Carpenter ....Larry Morley
Production Electrician ....Steve Cochrane
Production Props Supervision ....Mike Smanko
Production Sound ....Wayne Smith
Head Carpenter ....Ken McDonough
Head Electrician ....Jeff Turner
Head Props ....Jerry Marshall
Wardrobe Supervisor ....Dave Olin Rogers
Hairdresser ....Diana Sikes
Star Dresser ....Ken Brown
Dresser ....Sandy Binion
Production Assistant ....Stephanie Atlan
Assistant to Nathan Lane ....Andrea Wolfson
Literary Manager ....Gaydon Phillips
Management Intern ....Madeline Felix
Advertising ....SpotCo/
Drew Hodges, Jim Edwards, Jim Aquino
Website Design/
Online Marketing ....Situation Marketing LLC
Accounting ....Rosenberg Neuwirth & Kuchner/
Mark A. D'Ambrosi, Patricia M. Pederson
Banking ....JP Morgan Chase Bank/
Stephanie Dalton, Richard Callian,
Michele Gibbons
Insurance ....AON/Albert G. Ruben/
George Walden, Claudia B. Kaufman
Payroll ....Castellana Services Inc./
Lance Castellana, James Castellana,
Norman Sewell
Legal ....Loeb & Loeb/Seth Gelblum, Richard Garmise
Opening Night
Coordinator ....Tobak Lawrence Company/
Michael P. Lawrence,
Joanna B. Koondel
Production Physician ....Dr. Barry Kohn, MD

CREDITS

Scenery and props constructed by the Huntington Theatre Company. Additional construction by ShowMotion Inc. Lighting equipment from PRG Lighting. Sound equipment from PRG Audio. Costumes built by the Costume Depot. Natural herb cough drops by Ricola.

Rehearsed at the New 42nd Street Studios

www.butleyonbroadway.com

SPECIAL THANKS

Alaine Alldaffer, Benedick Bates, James Calleri, Stephen Kaus, Austin Lysy, Gilbert Medina, Angela Thornton, Justin Waldman, Jake Weber, Christopher Wigle, Julian Christenberry, Jane Pfeffer, Brian Mahoney, Keith Marsden

House Manager ....Laurel Ann Wilson

Butley
Scrapbook

Photos by Aubrey Reuben

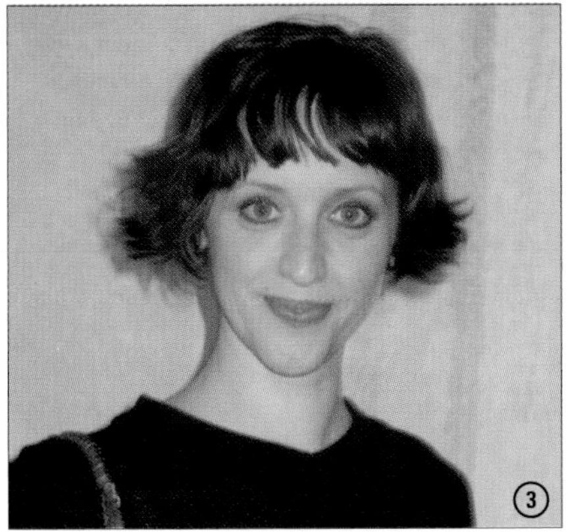

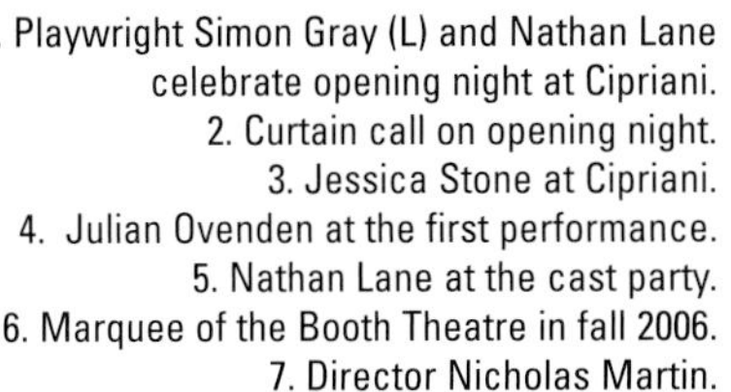

1. Playwright Simon Gray (L) and Nathan Lane celebrate opening night at Cipriani.
2. Curtain call on opening night.
3. Jessica Stone at Cipriani.
4. Julian Ovenden at the first performance.
5. Nathan Lane at the cast party.
6. Marquee of the Booth Theatre in fall 2006.
7. Director Nicholas Martin.

Photo by David Gewirtzman

Chicago

First Preview: October 23, 1996. Opened: November 14, 1996.
Still running as of May 31, 2007

PLAYBILL

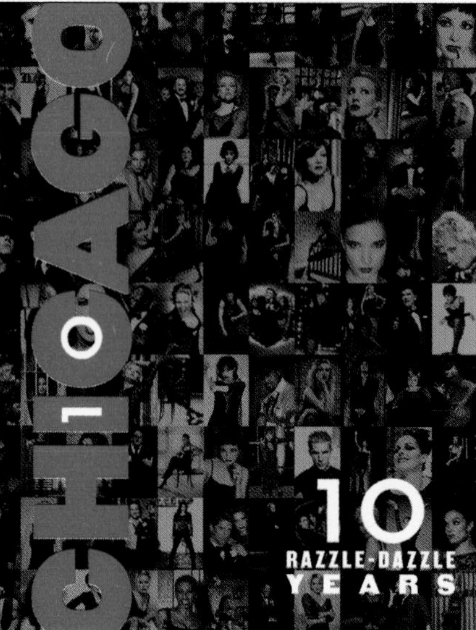

AMBASSADOR THEATRE

A Shubert Organization Theatre
Gerald Schoenfeld, *Chairman* **Philip J. Smith,** *President*

Robert E. Wankel, *Executive Vice President*

Barry & Fran Weissler
in association with
Kardana/Hart Sharp Entertainment
present

Michelle DeJean Brenda Braxton
Christopher McDonald
Rob Bartlett

in

CHICAGO

Lyrics by **Fred Ebb** Music By **John Kander** Book by **Fred Ebb & Bob Fosse**

Original Production Directed and Choreographed by **Bob Fosse**
Based on the play by Maurine Dallas Watkins
with
Roz Ryan R. Lowe
and
Donna Marie Asbury Gregory Butler Mindy Cooper
Bernard Dotson Bryn Dowling Shawn Emamjomeh Gabriela Garcia
Denis Jones David Kent J. Loeffelholz Melissa Rae Mahon
Sharon Moore Denny Paschall Josh Rhodes Matthew Risch
Michelle M. Robinson Mark Anthony Taylor Jennifer West Eric Jordan Young

Supervising Music Director **Rob Fisher**
Music Director **Leslie Stifelman**

Scenic Design **John Lee Beatty**
Costume Design **William Ivey Long**
Lighting Design **Ken Billington**

Sound Design **Scott Lehrer**
Orchestrations **Ralph Burns**
Dance Music Arrangements **Peter Howard**

Script Adaptation **David Thompson**
Musical Coordinator **Seymour Red Press**
Hair Design **David Brian Brown**

Casting **James Calleri C.S.A.**
Original Casting **Jay Binder**

Technical Supervisor **Arthur Siccardi**
Dance Supervisor **Gary Chryst**
Production Stage Manager **David Hyslop**

Associate Producer **Alecia Parker**
Presented in association with **Live Nation**

General Manager **B.J. Holt**
Press Representative **The Pete Sanders Group**

Based on the presentation by City Center's Encores!℠

Choreography by
Ann Reinking
in the style of Bob Fosse

Directed by
Walter Bobbie

Cast Recording on RCA Victor

11/14/06

THE CAST

(in order of appearance)

Velma Kelly	BRENDA BRAXTON
Roxie Hart	MICHELLE DeJEAN
Fred Casely	GREGORY BUTLER
Sergeant Fogarty	MATTHEW RISCH
Amos Hart	ROB BARTLETT
Liz	MICHELLE M. ROBINSON
Annie	JENNIFER WEST
June	DONNA MARIE ASBURY
Hunyak	GABRIELA GARCIA
Mona	BRYN DOWLING
Matron "Mama" Morton	ROZ RYAN
Billy Flynn	CHRISTOPHER McDONALD
Mary Sunshine	R. LOWE
Go-To-Hell Kitty	MELISSA RAE MAHON
Harry	SHAWN EMAMJOMEH
Doctor	BERNARD DOTSON
Aaron	DENIS JONES
The Judge	BERNARD DOTSON
Bailiff	DENNY PASCHALL
Martin Harrison	ERIC JORDAN YOUNG
Court Clerk	DENNY PASCHALL
The Jury	SHAWN EMAMJOMEH

THE SCENE

Chicago, Illinois. The late 1920s.

Continued on next page

Pop star Usher (center) performs "All I Care About Is Love" with the women's chorus.

Photo by Paul Kolnik

Chicago

MUSICAL NUMBERS

ACT I

ALL THAT JAZZ	Velma and Company
FUNNY HONEY	Roxie
CELL BLOCK TANGO	Velma and the Girls
WHEN YOU'RE GOOD TO MAMA	Matron
TAP DANCE	Roxie, Amos and Boys
ALL I CARE ABOUT	Billy and Girls
A LITTLE BIT OF GOOD	Mary Sunshine
WE BOTH REACHED FOR THE GUN	Billy, Roxie, Mary Sunshine and Company
ROXIE	Roxie and Boys
I CAN'T DO IT ALONE	Velma
MY OWN BEST FRIEND	Roxie and Velma

ACT II

ENTR'ACTE	The Band
I KNOW A GIRL	Velma
ME AND MY BABY	Roxie and Boys
MISTER CELLOPHANE	Amos
WHEN VELMA TAKES THE STAND	Velma and Boys
RAZZLE DAZZLE	Billy and Company
CLASS	Velma and Matron
NOWADAYS	Roxie and Velma
HOT HONEY RAG	Roxie and Velma
FINALE	Company

ORCHESTRA

Orchestra Conducted by
LESLIE STIFELMAN
Associate Conductor:
JEFFREY SAVER
Associate Conductor:
SCOTT CADY
Woodwinds:
SEYMOUR RED PRESS, JACK STUCKEY, RICHARD CENTALONZA
Trumpets:
JOHN FROSK, DARRYL SHAW
Trombones:
DAVE BARGERON, BRUCE BONVISSUTO
Piano:
SCOTT CADY
Piano & Accordion:
JEFFREY SAVER
Banjo:
JAY BERLINER
Bass & Tuba:
RONALD RAFFIO
Violin:
MARSHALL COID
Drums & Percussion:
RONALD ZITO

Photo by Paul Kolnik

Usher (L) dances with a member of the chorus.

Cast Continued

UNDERSTUDIES

For Roxie Hart:
BRYN DOWLING, MELISSA RAE MAHON
For Velma Kelly:
DONNA MARIE ASBURY, GABRIELA GARCIA
For Billy Flynn:
BERNARD DOTSON, ERIC JORDAN YOUNG
For Amos Hart:
DENIS JONES, ERIC JORDAN YOUNG
For Matron "Mama" Morton:
DONNA MARIE ASBURY, MICHELLE M. ROBINSON
For Mary Sunshine:
J. LOEFFELHOLZ
For Fred Casely:
DAVID KENT, MATTHEW RISCH, MARK ANTHONY TAYLOR
For Me and My Baby:
DENNY PASCHALL, MARK ANTHONY TAYLOR, DAVID KENT

For all other roles:
MINDY COOPER, DAVID KENT, SHARON MOORE, JOSH RHODES, MARK ANTHONY TAYLOR

Dance Captains:
GREGORY BUTLER, MINDY COOPER, BERNARD DOTSON

Tap Dance Specialty Performed by
BERNARD DOTSON, DENIS JONES, DENNY PASCHALL

"Me and My Baby" Specialty performed by
DENIS JONES AND ERIC JORDAN YOUNG

"Nowadays" Whistle performed by
GABRIELA GARCIA

Original Choreography for "Hot Honey Rag" by
BOB FOSSE

Chicago

Michelle DeJean
Roxie Hart

Brenda Braxton
Velma Kelly

Christopher McDonald
Billy Flynn

Rob Bartlett
Amos Hart

Roz Ryan
Matron "Mama" Morton

R. Lowe
Mary Sunshine

Donna Marie Asbury
June

Gregory Butler
Fred Casely/ Dance Captain

Mindy Cooper
Swing/ Dance Captain

Bernard Dotson
Doctor/The Judge/ Dance Captain

Bryn Dowling
Mona

Shawn Emamjomeh
Harry/The Jury

Gabriela Garcia
Hunyak

Denis Jones
Aaron

David Kent
Swing

J. Loeffelholz
Standby Mary Sunshine

Melissa Rae Mahon
Go-to-Hell Kitty

Sharon Moore
Swing

Denny Paschall
Bailiff/Court Clerk

Josh Rhodes
Ensemble

Matthew Risch
Sergeant Fogarty

Michelle M. Robinson
Liz

Mark Anthony Taylor
Swing

Jennifer West
Annie

Eric Jordan Young
Martin Harrison

John Kander and Fred Ebb
Music; Book/Lyrics

Bob Fosse
Book

Walter Bobbie
Director

Ann Reinking
Choreographer

John Lee Beatty
Set Design

William Ivey Long
Costume Designer

Ken Billington
Lighting Designer

Rob Fisher
Supervising Music Director

Peter Howard
Dance Music Arranger

Chicago

Seymour Red Press
Music Coordinator

David Brian Brown
Wig/Hair Design

James Calleri
Casting Director

Arthur Siccardi, Theatrical Services Inc.
Technical Supervisor

Barry and Fran Weissler
Producers

Morton Swinsky/ Kardana Productions
Producer

N. Adams
Understudy for Mary Sunshine

Obba Babatundé
Billy Flynn

Raymond Bokhour
Amos Hart

Kevin Chamberlin
Amos Hart

Gary Kilmer
Understudy

Dan LoBuono
Harry, The Jury

Bianca Marroquin
Roxie Hart

Kevin Neil McCready
Doctor, The Judge, Tap Dance Specialty

Michelle Potterf
Go-To-Hell Kitty

Angel Reda
Annie

Tracy Shayne
Roxie Hart

Steven Sofia
Aaron, Me and My Baby Specialty, Tap Dance Specialty

Julie Tolivar
Go-To-Hell Kitty

Usher
Billy Flynn

Lillias White
Matron "Mama" Morton

Rita Wilson
Roxie Hart

Julio Agustin
Fred Casely, Sergeant Fogarty

Raymond Bokhour
Amos Hart

Philip Casnoff
Billy Flynn

Emily Fletcher
Hunyak

Robyn Hurder
Mona

Jillana Laufer
Hunyak

Joey Lawrence
Billy Flynn

Huey Lewis
Billy Flynn

Bebe Neuwirth
Roxie Hart

Solange Sandy
Annie

Chicago

Steven Sofia
Understudy

Carol Woods
Matron "Mama" Morton

Amra-Faye Wright
Velma Kelly

BOX OFFICE
(L-R): Jim Gates, Tom McNulty and Tom Sheehan.

STAGE MANAGEMENT
(L-R): David Hyslop (Production Stage Manager), Terry Witter (Stage Manager) and Mindy Farbrother (Stage Manager).

Photos courtesy of David Hyslop

ORCHESTRA
Front Row (L-R):
Bruce Bonvissuto, Dave Bargeron, John Johnson, Jay Berliner.

Second Row (L-R):
Ann Leathers, Mort Silver, Leslie Stifelman (Conductor), Ron Raffio.

Back Row (L-R):
Stu Satalof, John Frosk, Scott Cady, Ron Zito, Jack Stuckey and Rick Centalonza.

Chicago

STAGE CREW
Front Row (L-R):
Luciana Fusco, Dennis Smalls, Eileen MacDonald, Vince Jacobi, Jimmy Werner, Charlie Grieco.

Second Row (L-R):
Joe Mooneyham (Standing), Bob Hale, Lizard, Mike Guggino.

Top:
William Nye.

Photos by Ben Strothmann

DOORMAN
Pat Green

FRONT OF HOUSE STAFF
Front Row (L-R):
Charlene Collins (Usher), Michael Kinsey (Theatre Refreshments), Gerry Belitsis (Usher), Bill Daniels (Theatre Refreshments), David Gamboa (Dewynters).

Second Row (L-R):
Lottie Dennis (Usher), Carol Bokun (Usher), Jorge Velasquez (Usher).

Third Row (L-R):
Yunus Caskun (Usher), Jason Parris (Usher), Dorothea Bentley (Directress).

Back Row (L-R):
Bobbi Parker (Usher), Danielle Banyai (Usher) and David Loomis (Dewynters).

Not Pictured: Samuel A. Morris (Education).

Chicago

Photo by Ben Strothmann

HAIR & WARDROBE DEPARTMENT
Front Row (L-R): Paula Davis, Kevin Woodworth.
Back Row (L-R): Jo-Ann Bethell and Justen Brosnan.

STAFF FOR ***CHICAGO***

GENERAL MANAGEMENT
B.J. Holt, General Manager
Nina Skriloff, International Manager

PRESS REPRESENTATIVE
THE PETE SANDERS GROUP
PETE SANDERS
Shane Marshall Brown Glenna Freedman

CALLERI CASTING
James Calleri, Paul Davis, Erica Jensen, Duncan Stewart, Rebecca Atwood

Production Stage Manager ....David Hyslop
Company Manager ....Hilary Hamilton
Associate Company Manager ....Jean Haring
Stage Managers ....Terrence J. Witter, Mindy Farbrother
General Management Associate ....Stephen Spadaro
Associate General Manager ....Michael Buchanan
Assistant Director ....Jonathan Bernstein
Associate Lighting Designer ....John McKernon
Assistant Choreographer ....Debra McWaters
Dance Captains ....Gregory Butler, Mindy Cooper, Bernard Dotson
Assistant Set Designers ....Eric Renschler, Shelley Barclay
Wardrobe Supervisor ....Kevin Woodworth
Costume Assistant ....Donald Sanders
Personal Asst to Mr. Billington ....Jon Kusner
Assistant to Mr. Lehrer ....Thom Mohrman
Production Carpenter ....Joseph Mooneyham
Production Electrician ....Luciana Fusco
Front Lite Operator ....Michael Guggino
Production Sound Engineer ....John Montgomery
Hair Supervisor ....Justen Brosnan
Production Propman ....John Cagney
Dressers ....Jo-Ann Bethell, Kathy Dacey, Paula Davis, Ronald Tagert, Eric Concklin
Banking ....Chase Manhattan, Stephanie Dalton
Music Prep ....Chelsea Music Services, Inc./ Donald Oliver & Evan Morris
Payroll ....Castellana Services, Inc.
Accountants ....Rosenberg, Newirth & Kuchner/ Mark D'Ambrosi, Marina Flom
Insurance ....Industrial Risk Specialists
Counsel ....Seth Gelblum/Loeb & Loeb
Art Design ....Spot Design
Advertising ....SpotCo: Drew Hodges, Dale Edwards
Education ....Students Live/Amy Weinstein www.studentslive.org
Marketing/Promotions ....HHC Marketing/ Hugh Hysell, Michael Redman
Merchandising ....Dewynters Advertising Inc.
Displays ....King Display

NATIONAL ARTISTS MANAGEMENT CO.

Director of Marketing ....Darby Lunceford
Director of Business Affairs ....Daniel M. Posener
Dramaturg/Creative Consultant ....Jack DePalma
Chief Financial Officer ....Bob Williams
Accounting ....Marian Albarracin
Assistant to Mrs. Weissler ....Brett England
Assistant to the Weisslers ....Suzanne Evans
Assistant to Ms. Parker ....Emily Dimond
Martketing Manager ....Ken Sperr
Receptionist ....Michelle Coleman

SPECIAL THANKS

Additional legal services provided by Jay Goldberg, Esq. and Michael Berger, Esq. Emergen-C super energy booster provided by Alacer Corp. Dry cleaning by Ernest Winzer Cleaners. Hosiery and undergarments provided by Bra*Tenders.

CREDITS

Lighting equipment by PRG Lighting. Scenery built and painted by Hudson Scenic Studios. Specialty Rigging by United Staging & Rigging. Sound equipment by PRG Audio. Shoulder holster courtesy of DeSantis Holster and Leather Goods Co. Period cameras and flash units by George Fenmore, Inc. Colibri lighters used. Bible courtesy of Chiarelli's Religious Goods, Inc. Black pencils by Dixon-Ticonderoga. Gavel courtesy of The Gavel Co. Zippo lighters used. Garcia y Vega cigars used. Hosiery by Donna Karan. Shoes by T.O. Dey. Orthopaedic Consultant, David S. Weiss, M.D.

THE SHUBERT ORGANIZATION, INC.
Board of Directors

Gerald Schoenfeld, Chairman
Philip J. Smith, President

Wyche Fowler, Jr.
John W. Kluge

Lee J. Seidler
Michael I. Sovern

Stuart Subotnick

Robert E. Wankel
Executive Vice President

Peter Entin
Vice President
Theatre Operations

Elliot Greene
Vice President
Finance

David Andrews
Vice President
Shubert Ticketing Services

John Darby
Vice President
Facilities

D.S. Moynihan
Vice President – Creative Projects

House Manager ....Patricia Berry

Chicago

The 10th Anniversary Performance Scrapbook, November 14, 2006

AMBASSADOR THEATRE

A Shubert Organization Theatre

Gerald Schoenfeld, *Chairman* Philip J. Smith, *President*

Robert E. Wankel, *Executive Vice President*

Barry & Fran Weissler
in association with
Kardana/Hart Sharp Entertainment
present

CHICAGO

Lyrics by **Fred Ebb** Music By **John Kander** Book by **Fred Ebb & Bob Fosse**

Original Production Directed and Choreographed by **Bob Fosse**

Based on the play by Maurine Dallas Watkins

with

Donna Marie Asbury Brent Barrett Rob Bartlett Hinton Battle Roy Bean PJ Benjamin Sandahl Bergman Ray Bokhour Jim Borstelman Wayne Brady Brenda Braxton Greg Butler Kevin Carolan Caitlin Carter Lynda Carter Kevin Chamberlin Chuck Cooper Mindy Cooper Charlotte d'Amboise Paige Davis Michelle DeJean Denny Paschall Bernard Dotson Bryn Dowling Mamie Duncan-Gibbs Shawn Emamjomeh Gabriela Garcia Joel Grey Melanie Griffith Gregory Harrison Marilu Henner Ruthie Henshall Denis Jones David Kent Mary Ann Lamb Sharon Lawrence Huey Lewis Marcia Lewis Bryan Jeff Loeffelholz Ryan Lowe Melissa Rae Mahon Bianca Marroquin Christopher McDonald Gerry McIntyre Terra C. MacLeod Sharon Moore James Naughton Bebe Neuwirth Caroline O'Connor John O'Hurley Ron Orbach Destan Owens Ron Raines Ann Reinking Kevin Richardson Matthew Risch Chita Rivera Michelle M. Robinson Roz Ryan David Sabella Ernie Sabella Brooke Shields Ashlee Simpson Mark Anthony Taylor Rocker Verastique Jennifer West Rita Wilson Bruce Winant Carol Woods Tom Wopat Amra-Faye Wright Eric Jordan Young Karen Ziemba Leigh Zimmerman

Supervising Music Director **Rob Fisher**
Music Director **Leslie Stifelman**
Scenic Design **John Lee Beatty**
Costume Design **William Ivey Long**
Lighting Design **Ken Billington**
Sound Design **Scott Lehrer**
Orchestrations **Ralph Burns**
Dance Music Arrangements **Peter Howard**
Script Adaptation **David Thompson**
Musical Coordinator **Seymour Red Press**
Hair Design **David Brian Brown**
Casting **James Calleri C.S.A.**
Original Casting **Jay Binder**
Technical Supervisor **Arthur Siccardi**
Dance Supervisor **Gary Chryst**
Production Stage Manager **David Hyslop**
Associate Producer **Alecia Parker**
Presented in association with **Live Nation**
General Manager **B.J. Holt**
Press Representative **The Pete Sanders Group**

Based on the presentation by City Center's Encores!™

Choreography by **Ann Reinking**
in the style of Bob Fosse

Directed by **Walter Bobbie**

Cast Recording on RCA Victor

LIVE BROADWAY

CHICAGO 10

TIME LINE

November 14, 1996	**CHICAGO** opens at the Richard Rodgers Theatre on Broadway
February 4, 1997	**CHICAGO** moves to The Shubert Theatre on Broadway
April 16, 1997	First National American Touring Company opens at Washington D.C.'s National Theatre
June 1, 1997	**CHICAGO** wins six Tony Awards including Best Musical Revival, Best Direction & Best Choreography
November 18, 1997	London Company opens at The Adelphi Theatre, The Strand
December 12, 1997	Second National American Touring Company opens at Barbara B. Mann Theatre in Ft. Myers, Florida
February 15, 1998	**CHICAGO** in London wins two Laurence Olivier Awards including Outstanding Musical Production
February 25, 1998	**CHICAGO** wins the Grammy Award for Best Musical Show Album
July 4, 1998	Australian Company opens at Her Majesty's Theatre in Melbourne
September 23, 1998	First German Language Company opens at Theatre An Der Wien in Vienna, Austria
February 17, 1999	First Swedish Language Company opens at Eriksberg Hall in Gothenberg, Sweden
May 9, 1999	First Dutch Language Company opens at The Beatrix Theatre in Utrecht, Holland
January 23, 2001	First Spanish Language Company opens at The Teatro Opera in Buenos Aires, Argentina
September 14, 2001	First United Kingdom Tour opens at The Opera House in Manchester, UK
October 17, 2001	Second Spanish Language Company opens at The Centro Cultural Telmex in Mexico City, Mexico
October 4, 2002	First Russian Language Company opens at The Estrada Theatre in Moscow, Russia
December 27, 2002	Miramax film version of CHICAGO opens
January 29, 2003	**CHICAGO** moves to the Ambassador Theatre on Broadway
June 10, 2003	Third National American Touring Company opens at Washington D.C.'s National Theatre
July 17, 2003	First French Language Company opens at Theatre Maisonneuve Place des Arts in Montreal, Quebec
January 26, 2004	First Italian Language Company opens at the Teatro Nazionale in Milan, Italy
March, 2004	Second French Language Company opens at Au Casino de Paris in Paris, France
April 28, 2004	First Portuguese Language Company opens at the Teatro Abril in Sao Paulo, Brazil.
April 28, 2005	South African Company opens at The Nelson Mandela Theatre in Johannesburg, South Africa.
July 20, 2005	South African Company opens at Artscape Opera House in Capetown, South Africa
May 4, 2006	**CHICAGO** touring company plays at Madinat Jumeirah Arena in Dubai, United Arab Emirates.
September 14, 2006	**CHICAGO** surpasses MISS SAIGON to become the 8th longest running show in Broadway history.
October 3, 2006	Masterworks Broadway release a 10th Anniversary Box Set edition of the **CHICAGO** cast album recording.
November 14, 2006	**CHICAGO** celebrates its 10th Anniversary with an star-studded benefit performance featuring the original cast members and celebrity alums.

CHICAGO 10

EXHILARATING.

A MUSICAL FOR ALL AGES.

**Who would have thought there could be such bliss?
If there's any justice in the world, audiences will be exulting
in the parade for many, many performances to come.**

-Ben Brantley, The New York Times

DID YOU KNOW that **CHICAGO** has been performed in English, Dutch, German, Swedish, Spanish, Portuguese, Russian, Italian and French?

DID YOU KNOW that there are cast recordings of **CHICAGO** in English (U.S. and U.K.), German and Dutch?

DID YOU KNOW that **CHICAGO** has given the opportunity for the stars of foreign productions to make their Broadway debuts including Bianca Marroquin (Mexico), Denise Van Outen (U.K.), Terra C. Macleod (France and Canada), Petra Nielson (Sweden), Ute Lemper (U.K. and Germany), Ruthie Henshall (U.K.), Anna Montanaro (Germany and Austria), Pia Dowes (Holland), Marti Pellow (U.K.), Caroline O'Connor (Australia)?

DID YOU KNOW that **CHICAGO** received 6 Tony Awards (including Best Musical Revival), 5 Drama Desk Awards, 5 Outer Critics' Circle Awards, 1 1998 Critics Circle Award, 1 Grammy Award (for Original Cast Recording), 2 Astaire Awards, 1 Drama League Award, 2 Bay Area Theatre Critics Circle Awards, 2 L.A. Drama Critics Circle Awards, 2 L.A. Ovation Awards, 1 Helen Hayes Award, 1 Black Theatre Alliance Award, 7 E.W. Awards, 2 Joseph Jefferson Awards and 1 Elliott Norton Award for the Broadway and National Touring Companies?

DID YOU KNOW that **CHICAGO** received 1 Olivier Award (Best Musical Production), 3 ACE Awards, 3 El Heraldo Awards, 3 Asociacion Mexicana de Criticos de Teatro Awards, 2 Helpman Awards, 4 Guldmasken Awards, and 2 Premio Qualidade Brasil Awards for its international productions?

DID YOU KNOW that **CHICAGO** has played worldwide since its opening in 1996 in the following countries: England, Belgium, The Netherlands, Austria, Germany, Ireland, Scotland, Switzerland, Italy, France, Portugal, Greece, Israel, Russia, South Africa, China, Japan, South Korea, Canada, Mexico, Argentina, Brazil, Australia, Singapore and Dubai?

DID YOU KNOW that **CHICAGO** has grossed over $300 million on Broadway since it opened in 1996, and grossed $915 million worldwide?

DID YOU KNOW that **CHICAGO** has played over 16,000 performances worldwide?

DID YOU KNOW that an estimated 18 million people around the world have seen **CHICAGO**?

**And now CHICAGO celebrates its
10TH ANNIVERSARY AS BROADWAY'S LONGEST RUNNING REVIVAL!**

"STILL THE BEST DAMN SHOW IN TOWN!"

- Liz Smith, Syndicated Columnist

10TH ANNIVERSARY

Special thanks

Actors' Equity Association
Theatre Authority
Ambassador Court Hotel
Ambassador Theatre Staff:
Patricia Berry, House Manager
Ambassador Theatre Box Office Staff:
Jim Gatens
Tommy Sheehan
John Lee Beatty
Sandahl Bergman
Ken Billington
Jay Binder
Walter Bobbie
John Breglio
David Brian Brown
Bryant Park Hotel
Ralph Burns
Carelli Costumes
Crown Plaza Hotel
Darren DeVerna for PRG
Expedia.com
Mindy Farbrother
Scott Faris
Rob Fisher
John M. Fowler
Mariska Hargitay
Andi Henig
Drew Hodges and staff at Spot Co
The Holman Group
Peter Howard
David Hyslop
James Calleri Casting
Jet Blue
Beverly Jenkins
David Kalodner
King Displays
Paul Kolnik
The League of American Theatres Producers
Scott Lehrer
Lighting and PRG Audio
William Ivey Long
Carmine Lucariello
Masterworks Broadway
John McKernon
Net Jets
Playbill
Ann Reinking
Rouge Makeup Studio
Seymour Red Press
The Shubert Organization:
Mary Breilid
Carina Burrell
Phil Catalfo
Joe Cabrera
Lorraine Danza
Arthur Siccardi
The Spoon Group
Leslie Stifelman
David Thompson
Target
Taste Caterers
Telecharge:
Marissa Benetsky
Paul Moss
Joseph Pirolli
Scott Traugott
Nancy Elizabeth West
W Hotels
Terrence J. Witter

Chicago
Scrapbook

Correspondent: Michelle M. Robinson, "Liz"

Memorable Event: On November 14, 2006 we celebrated our tenth anniversary on Broadway with a special performance. Many of the actors who appeared in the show over the years returned to perform a scene or part of a song. We had multiple Roxies, multiple Velmas and lots of Billy Flynns, Mama Mortons, Amoses, et cetera. And we did it all as a benefit for Safe Horizon.

It was an awesome night. And it was special for me because I remember all the stars who have come through. I'm the only cast member who's stayed with this production since opening night.

We didn't find out about the idea to incorporate the past performers until about two weeks prior to the actual event. Getting ready was a lot of work for the ensemble. We had a lot of cleanup rehearsals, of course. And then we had a couple of rehearsals with a few of the principals. Because so many extra people were going to be taking part, we also had to rehearse how all those people were going to get on and off the stage. We'd rehearse the event by day and do the show by night. We were all exhausted.

But when the actual day came, and we knew the audience was out there, the fatigue just went away. It was amazing.

A lot of what went on backstage was traffic control. We had something like ten Roxies, seven or eight Velmas, seven or eight Billys, plus six or seven Amoses and four Mama Mortons.

You'd think that having so many people backstage would be stressful, but it really generated an excitement of its own. When I tell my friends about that night, I talk about the energy and the dynamic of seeing some of the original cast members and having the opportunity to dance jazz with them again. Ann Reinking was here and Bebe Neuwirth was here.... At one point I took a moment to glance over into the wings, and there were those faces. I got an incredible warm, familiar kind of feeling. It was electrifying. Time goes on, but I relished that moment a lot.

Dressing rooms were a challenge, as you can imagine. They tried to house all the Velmas and Roxies here at the theatre, with the remaining characters at the hotel across the street. They were shuttled over twenty minutes before their appearance on stage. Here at the theatre, the wardrobe room was used as a green room, so we all got to hang out with everybody.

Considering how many people were moving around backstage, the evening ran extremely smoothly. If there were any disasters or close calls, I wasn't privy to them. And it was amazing, considering that just hours prior to the event, we were still in rehearsals and there were some performers who hadn't even arrived in town yet.

As they came in, they were shuttled off to rehearsal studios and caught up. But when it came to that evening, you never would have known they had just learned the choreography.

Some of the guest stars traveled long distances. Leigh Zimmerman flew in from London. Caitlin Carter's health wasn't too good for a while, but she felt the need to be here, and there she was.

One of the few people I hadn't worked with was Chita Rivera, who was the star of the original 1975 production. She's a bunch of fun, an amazing woman. And her commitment is consummate. We had the little run-through with her the afternoon of the event or the day before. Of course you always expect Chita to rise to the

Photos by Aubrey Reuben

1. A murder of Roxies at curtain call (front row, L-R): Paige Davis, unknown, Ashlee Simpson, Bianca Marroquin, Karen Ziemba, Melanie Griffith, Brooke Shields.
2. Bebe Neuwirth and Joel Grey at the 10th anniversary.
3. Original 1996 cast members Caitlin Carter (L) and Leigh Zimmerman at the "All That Jazz" afterparty for the 10th anniversary.

Chicago
Scrapbook

Photos by Aubrey Reuben

1. Front Row (L-R): Marilu Henner, director Walter Bobbie, Chita Rivera, Ann Reinking, Bebe Neuwirth and Brenda Braxton.
2. Usher (center) flanked by (L) Bianca Marroquin and (R) Brenda Braxton at Usher's debut party at Nikki Beach in fall 2006.

occasion and she did exactly that. She was cooperative, worked well with everyone. And she looked fabulous.

She sang the opening number, "All That Jazz," and when we rehearsed it, we just kind of marked it through. But I have the original 1975 cast album and in the actual performance, hearing her sing and seeing her dressed in that costume and interacting with us, I felt just like I was in the original production. That was special and I will never forget it.

That Velma entrance is the best entrance on Broadway, and for it to be done once more by Chita, well, I have seen that entrance over maybe three thousand times now and I have always loved it, but I never loved it as much as that night.

So that was a very big moment. So was seeing Bebe Neuwirth and Ann Reinking together again. Then to watch the people who have learned from them as the evening went on, to see people rotating into those roles and performing their take on it and showing what they may have learned from the person that did it before them—it was an amazing experience and a major moment in my life.

There was one thing that I have to say went almost magically well. "Razzle Dazzle" is a slightly intricate number—there are lifts and such. We were working with seven or eight Billys, as I mentioned. And, if my memory serves me correctly, most of them were not at the rehearsals. So we were a little bit concerned. But the guys surprised me and "Razzle" went rather smoothly.

Of course, not everyone was there. Gwen Verdon, the original Roxie from the first production, isn't with us any longer, but I did my own personal salute to her by dancing my ass off.

And then, of course, there's Fred Ebb, the lyricist, whom we lost two years ago. Without them, there'd be no this. Acknowledgement was given by the producers Fran and Barry Weissler at the end of the show, and it got the biggest applause that was received for the evening. Had it not been for them and their hard work and paving the way, this project that has now been running for ten years would not have been in existence. We all paid homage to that in our hearts.

Afterward there was an excellent party over at the Dodgers' Theatre. There was lots of dancing, lots of flowing Champagne, and lots of hors d'oeuvres… It was a well put-together evening. All of the stars came, and it turned into a lovely night of mingling, and reminiscing and photo-taking and just being together. It was really quite beautiful. It was a walk down memory lane for me in a matter of two hours—a dance down memory lane. Dance, stroll, chat, conversation, hugs, kisses, jokes, laughs. Yeah, all of that.

When Fosse and Verdon and Chita were putting together the show in 1975, they all thought they were creating one of the biggest hits in history. I think they were disappointed when *A Chorus Line* won all the awards and *Chicago* ran only two years. Ironically, when we were doing the revival at "Encores!" we thought it was just going to be a limited engagement. My favorite line about *Chicago* is "Who knew?" I always say that when I come out every night. I look out and see the audience packed with people just really ready to see this piece of work that has been going for ten years, and that's when I say it: "Who knew?"

A Chorus Line

First Preview: September 18, 2006. Opened: October 5, 2006.
Still running as of May 31, 2007.

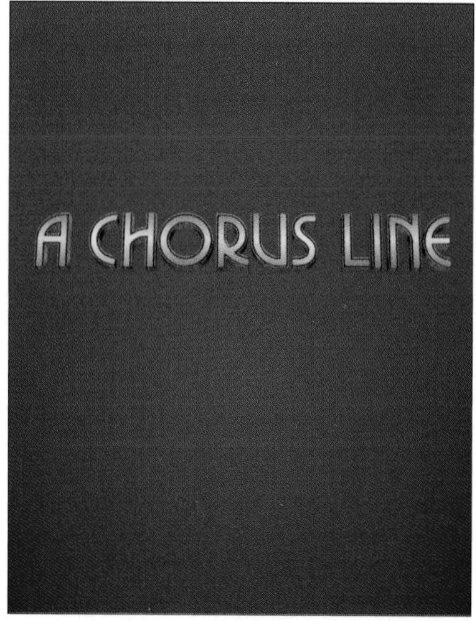

CAST

(in alphabetical order)

Bobby .... KEN ALAN
Don .... BRAD ANDERSON
Tricia .... MICHELLE ARAVENA
Roy .... DAVID BAUM
Zach .... MICHAEL BERRESSE
Tom .... MIKE CANNON
Butch .... E. CLAYTON CORNELIOUS
Diana .... NATALIE CORTEZ
Cassie .... CHARLOTTE d'AMBOISE
Maggie .... MARA DAVI
Val .... JESSICA LEE GOLDYN
Sheila .... DEIDRE GOODWIN
Larry .... TYLER HANES
Lois .... NADINE ISENEGGER
Richie .... JAMES T. LANE
Vicki .... LORIN LATARRO
Mark .... PAUL McGILL
Judy .... HEATHER PARCELLS
Greg .... MICHAEL PATERNOSTRO
Bebe .... ALISAN PORTER
Mike .... JEFFREY SCHECTER
Connie .... YUKA TAKARA
Paul .... JASON TAM
Frank .... GRANT TURNER
Kristine .... CHRYSSIE WHITEHEAD
Al .... TONY YAZBECK

SWINGS

JOEY DUDDING, PAMELA FABELLO,
LYNDY FRANKLIN

Continued on next page

GERALD SCHOENFELD THEATRE
236 West 45th Street
A Shubert Organization Theatre
Gerald Schoenfeld, *Chairman* Philip J. Smith, *President*
Robert E. Wankel, *Executive Vice President*

Vienna Waits Productions

presents

A CHORUS LINE

Conceived and Originally Choreographed and Directed by
Michael Bennett

Book by
James Kirkwood & Nicholas Dante

Music by
Marvin Hamlisch

Lyrics by
Edward Kleban

Originally Co-Choreographed by
Bob Avian

with

Ken Alan Brad Anderson Michelle Aravena David Baum Michael Berresse
Mike Cannon E. Clayton Cornelious Natalie Cortez Charlotte d'Amboise Mara Davi
Joey Dudding Pamela Fabello Lyndy Franklin Jessica Lee Goldyn Deidre Goodwin
Tyler Hanes Nadine Isenegger James T. Lane Lorin Latarro Paul McGill
Heather Parcells Michael Paternostro Alisan Porter Jeffrey Schecter
Yuka Takara Jason Tam Grant Turner Chryssie Whitehead Tony Yazbeck

Scenic Design by
Robin Wagner

Costume Design by
Theoni V. Aldredge

Lighting Design by
Tharon Musser
Adapted by
Natasha Katz

Sound Design by
Acme Sound Partners

Music Direction & Supervision by
Patrick Vaccariello

Orchestrations by
Jonathan Tunick Bill Byers & Hershy Kay

Vocal Arrangements by
Don Pippin

Choreography Re-Staged by
Baayork Lee

Directed by
Bob Avian

The original production of A CHORUS LINE was produced by The Public Theater, in association with Plum Productions.

10/5/06

The Ensemble performs the Finale, "One."

Photo by Paul Kolnik

A Chorus Line

MUSICAL NUMBERS

"I Hope I Get It"	Company
"I Can Do That"	Mike
"And"	Bobby, Richie, Val, Judy
"At the Ballet"	Sheila, Bebe, Maggie
"Sing!"	Kristine, Al
"Hello Twelve, Hello Thirteen, Hello Love"	Company
"Nothing"	Diana
"Dance: Ten; Looks: Three"	Val
"The Music and the Mirror"	Cassie
"One"	Company
"The Tap Combination"	Company
"What I Did for Love"	Diana, Company
"One" (Reprise)	Company

Michael Berresse (center) with the Ensemble.

Photo by Paul Kolnik

ORCHESTRA

Conductor:
PATRICK VACCARIELLO
Associate Conductor/Keyboard 2:
JIM LAEV

Woodwind 1:
TED NASH
Woodwind 2:
LINO GOMEZ
Woodwind 3:
DAVID YOUNG
Woodwind 4:
JACQUELINE HENDERSON
Trumpet 1:
JOHN CHUDOBA
Trumpet 2:
TREVOR NEUMANN
Trumpet 3:
SCOTT WENDHOLT
Trombone 1:
MICHAEL SELTZER
Trombone 2:
BEN HERRINGTON

Bass Trombone:
JACK SCHATZ
Bass:
BILL SLOAT
Keyboard 1:
GREG ANTHONY
Keyboard 3:
MAGGIE TORRE
Percussion:
DAN MCMILLAN
Drums:
BRIAN BRAKE

Music Coordinator:
MICHAEL KELLER
Synthesizer Programmer:
BRUCE SAMUELS
Rehearsal Pianist:
JOHN O'NEILL

Music Copying:
EMILY GRISHMAN MUSIC PREPARATION/
KATHARINE EDMONDS, EMILY GRISHMAN

Cast Continued

UNDERSTUDIES

For Al:
DAVID BAUM, MIKE CANNON
For Bebe:
MICHELLE ARAVENA, LYNDY FRANKLIN
For Bobby:
DAVID BAUM, TYLER HANES
For Cassie:
JESSICA LEE GOLDYN, NADINE ISENEGGER, LORIN LATARRO
For Connie:
MICHELLE ARAVENA, LYNDY FRANKLIN
For Diana:
MICHELLE ARAVENA, LORIN LATARRO
For Don:
E. CLAYTON CORNELIOUS, GRANT TURNER
For Greg:
DAVID BAUM, GRANT TURNER
For Judy:
PAMELA FABELLO, LORIN LATARRO
For Kristine:
PAMELA FABELLO, LYNDY FRANKLIN,
For Larry:
E. CLAYTON CORNELIOUS, GRANT TURNER
For Maggie:
MICHELLE ARAVENA, LYNDY FRANKLIN
For Mark:
MIKE CANNON, JOEY DUDDING
For Mike:
DAVID BAUM, MIKE CANNON
For Paul:
E. CLAYTON CORNELIOUS, JOEY DUDDING
For Richie:
MIKE CANNON, E. CLAYTON CORNELIOUS
For Sheila:
PAMELA FABELLO, LORIN LATARRO
For Val:
PAMELA FABELLO, NADINE ISENEGGER
For Zach:
TYLER HANES, GRANT TURNER

AN AUDITION

TIME: 1975
PLACE: A Broadway Theatre

"This show is dedicated to anyone who has ever danced in a chorus or marched in step…anywhere."
—Michael Bennett

A Chorus Line

Ken Alan
Bobby

Brad Anderson
Don

Michael Berresse
Zach

Natalie Cortez
Diana

Charlotte d'Amboise
Cassie

Mara Davi
Maggie

Jessica Lee Goldyn
Val

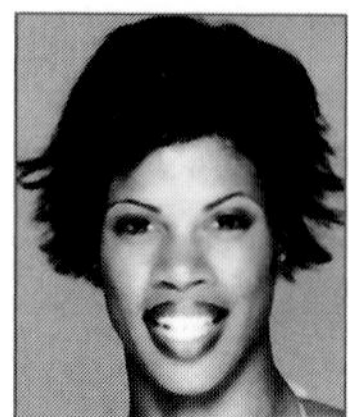
Deidre Goodwin
Sheila

Tyler Hanes
Larry

James T. Lane
Richie

Paul McGill
Mark

Heather Parcells
Judy

Michael Paternostro
Greg

Alisan Porter
Bebe

Jeffrey Schecter
Mike

Yuka Takara
Connie

Jason Tam
Paul

Chryssie Whitehead
Kristine

Tony Yazbeck
Al

Michelle Aravena
Tricia

David Baum
Roy

Mike Cannon
Tom

E. Clayton Cornelious
Butch

Joey Dudding
Swing

Pamela Fabello
Swing

Lyndy Franklin
Swing

Nadine Isenegger
Lois

Lorin Latarro
Vicki

Grant Turner
Frank

Michael Bennett
Conception, Original Director/ Choreographer

Marvin Hamlisch
Music

Baayork Lee
Choreography Re-Staging

Robin Wagner
Scenic Design

Natasha Katz
Lighting Design

A Chorus Line

Tom Clark, Mark Menard and Nevin Steinberg, Acme Sound Partners
Sound Design

Patrick Vaccariello
Music Direction and Supervision

Michael Keller
Music Coordinator

Jonathan Tunick
Orchestrator

Arthur Siccardi
Production Manager

John Breglio, Vienna Waits Productions
Producer

Jay Binder, C.S.A.
Casting

Alan Wasser Associates
General Manager

Aaron J. Albano
Swing

Dylis Croman
Swing

Lisa Ho
Connie

Courtney Laine Mazza
Swing

Jessica Lea Patty
Swing

Josh Walden
Swing

(L-R): Charlotte d'Amboise, Mara Davi, Jeffrey Schecter and Tony Yazbeck perform "Hello Twelve, Hello Thirteen, Hello Love."

Photo by Paul Kolnik

Tony Yazbeck and Chryssie Whitehead perform "Sing!" as Jessica Lee Goldyn watches.

A Chorus Line

WARDROBE
(L-R):
Libby Villanova, Leo Namba,
Hector Lugo, Rory Powers,
Caitley Symons and Shana Albery.

Lype O'Dell (Doorman)

Photos by Ben Strothmann

Adam J. Miller (Associate Company Manager)

CREW
(L-R): Tim McWilliams, Tom Phillips, Fred Ricci, Breffny Flynn, Evan Gelick, Leslie Ann Kilian, Fritz Fritsell, Mary McGregor, Beth Berkeley, Scott Sanders, Peter Guernsey, Eric Norris and Steve Long.

A Chorus Line

ORCHESTRA
Front Row (L-R):
Jacqueline Henderson, Ben Herrington, Ralph Olsen, William Sloat.

Middle Row (L-R):
Michael Seltzer, Jack Schatz, Ted Nash, Jim Laev, David Young.

Back Row (L-R):
John Chudoba, Earl "Bird" Gardner, Patrick Vaccariello and Dan McMillan.

Photos by Ben Strothmann

BOX OFFICE
(L-R):
Greer Bond, Manny Rivera and Vigi Cadunz.

FRONT OF HOUSE STAFF
Front Row (L-R):
Paula Raymond, Raya Konyk, Francine Kramer, Giovanni LaDuke, Gillian Sheffler, Roz Nyman.

Back Row (L-R):
Janet Kay, Matt Blank, Jennifer Jimenez, David Conte, Michael Garro, Nancy Barnicle, Maurice Duggan, Lisa Boyd and Kathleen Spock.

A Chorus Line

STAFF FOR *A CHORUS LINE*

GENERAL MANAGEMENT
ALAN WASSER ASSOCIATES
Alan Wasser Allan Williams Aaron Lustbader

GENERAL PRESS REPRESENTATIVE
BARLOW•HARTMAN
John Barlow Michael Hartman
Wayne Wolfe Andrew Snyder

CASTING
JAY BINDER CASTING
Jay Binder, C.S.A.
Jack Bowdan, C.S.A. Mark Brandon
Megan Larche

PRODUCTION MANAGER
Arthur Siccardi

PRODUCTION STAGE MANAGER
William Joseph Barnes

COMPANY MANAGER
Susan Bell

Associate Company Manager ....Adam J. Miller
Stage Manager ....Laurie Goldfeder
Assistant Stage Manager/Dance Captain/
Assistant Choreographer ....Michael Gorman
Assistant Director ....Peter Pileski
Assistant Scenic Designer ....David Peterson
Associate Costume Designer.................Suzy Benzinger
Assistant Costume Designer ....Patrick Wiley
Wardrobe Consultant ....Alyce Gilbert
Associate Lighting Designer...................Yael Lubetzky
Assistant Lighting Designer....................Aaron Spivey
Assistant Sound Designer ....Michael Creason
Automated Lighting Programmer ....Matthew Hudson
Music Coordinator ....Michael Keller
Synthesizer Programmer......................Bruce Samuels
Production Carpenter.........................Curtis Cowley
Assistant Carpenter...............................Tim Welch
Production Electrician ....Jimmy Fedigan
Head Electrician ....Eric Norris
Assistant Electrician ....Roger Desmond
Production Sound Engineer ....Scott Sanders
Advance Sound ....John Dory
Wardrobe Supervisor...........................Rory Powers
Prop Coordinator ....Heidi Brown

Advertising ....Serino Coyne/
Greg Corradetti, Ruth Rosenberg,
Andrea Prince, Ryan Greer

Website Design & Online Marketing
Strategy ....Situation Marketing LLC/
Damian Bazadona, Sara Fitzpatrick,
Steve Tate

Marketing Services ....TMG – The Marketing Group/
Tanya Grubich, Laura Matalon, Bob Bucci

Legal Counsel ....Paul Weiss Rifkind Wharton
& Garrison, LLP/Deborah Hartnett
Accounting ....Rosenberg, Neuwirth & Kuchner/
Chris Cacace,
Mark D'Ambrosi
Production Associate ....Deborah Hartnett
Administrative Assistant to Mr. Breglio ...Helene Gaulrapp
Associate General Manager ....Aaron Lustbader
General Management Associates ....Jake Hirzel,
Thom Mitchell, Connie Yung
General Management Office.............Christopher Betz,
Christopher D'Angelo,
Jason Hewitt, Jennifer Mudge
Press Office Manager ....Bethany Larsen
Press Associates ....Leslie Baden,
Dennis Crowley, Carol Fineman,
Ryan Ratelle, Gerilyn Shur
Casting Assistants............................Nikole Vallins,
Allison Estrin
Production Assistant ....Annette Verga-Lagier
Production Photographer........................Paul Kolnik
Insurance ....Ventura Insurance Brokerage/
Janice Brown
Banking ....Commerce Bank/
Barbara von Borstel,
Ashley Elezi
Payroll..............................Castellana Services, Inc.
Merchandising ....Max Merchandising/
Randi Grossman
Study Guide ....Peter Royston
Travel Services ....Road Rebel
Entertainment Touring
Assistants to Ms. Lee ....Steven Eng,
Cassey Kivnick
Lighting Intern ....JP Nardecchia
SSDC Directing Intern ....Jillian Loyas
Opening Night Coordination ....Tobak Lawrence Co./
Suzanne Tobak, Michael P. Lawrence

Hair Styling ....Anthony & Rivka Salon
Group Sales ...Theatre Direct International/Broadway.com

www.achorusline.com

CREDITS AND ACKNOWLEDGEMENTS

Scenery built and electrified by Hudson Scenic Studio Inc. Automation equipment provided by Hudson Scenic Studio, Inc. Electric truss built by Scenic Technologies. Lighting equipment provided by PRG Lighting. Sound equipment provided by PRG Audio. Finale costumes by Barbara Matera, Ltd. Costumes by Lynne Baccus; Euro Co Costumes, Inc.; Rick Kelly; D. Barak; Catherine Stribling. Leotards by Bal Togs Industries. Custom shirts by Cego Custom Shirts. Custom knitwear by C.C. Wei. Fabric dyeing and painting by the Craft Show. Footwear by T.O. Dey, J.C. Theatricals. Rehearsal hats by Arnold S. Levine, Inc. Ms. d'Amboise's hair by Paul Labrecque. Mike Costa's shirts provided by Lacoste. Men's socks provided by Gold Toe Brands, Inc. Finale top hats by Rodney Gordon, Inc. Finale shoes by Capezio. Ricola natural herb cough drops courtesy of Ricola USA, Inc. Emergen-C super energy booster provided by Alacer Corp. Cover photography by Walter Iooss. Physical therapy provided by Sean Gallagher. Rehearsed at 890 Broadway.

House Manager ....David M. Conte

The Ensemble

Photo by Paul Kolnik

A Chorus Line
Scrapbook

Photo courtesy Heather Parcells

Photo by Aubrey Reuben

Photo by Aubrey Reuben

Image drawn by Justin Robertson

Correspondent: Heather Parcells, "Judy"
Memorable Opening Night Fax: The entire original surviving 1975 cast sent a telegram/fax from Western Union with all their good wishes.
Opening Night Gifts:
Heather and Mara: Black yoga mats with a *Chorus Line* logo in gold.
Yuka and the Performing Arts Physical Therapy: Foot rollers, back double ball rollers, (physical therapy stuff).
Bob Avian: Crystal engraved star.
Alisan: Rubber engraved bracelets.
Baayork Lee: Engraved star.
Clayton, Grant, James, Stage Management, Joey Dudding: Embroidered towels.
Charlotte: Aroma heating packs.
Tyler: *ACL* caricatures t-shirt.
Marvin Hamlisch: Tiffany bracelets with *ACL* charms and Tiffany clocks.
Paul: "Nothingz" comfy shoes.
David: Caricature in the style of Al Hirschfeld.
Shecky: He drew his own version of all the line members from their childhood.
Patrick Vaccariello: Wine.
Jason: Wine.
John Breglio: Silver picture frame.
Deidre: A personalized notebook with quotes from the show.
Chryssie: Christopher Reeve Foundation dog tags.
Mike, Lyndy, Michelle: ACL hat.
Celebrity Visitors: Antonio Banderas, Bernadette Peters, Rosie O'Donnell, Joy Behar, Rod Stewart, Clay Aiken (sat with his feet against the stage), Melanie Griffith, Jeb Bush, Michael Caine, Joel Grey, Laurence Fishburne, Jessie Spano (a.k.a. Elizabeth Berkley), Karen Ziemba, almost ALL of the original line members, Hillary Clinton, Joan Rivers.
Who Got the Gypsy Robe: Lorin Latarro.
"Carols for a Cure" Carol: "O Come All Ye Faithful" with our own arrangement, Andrews Sisters style, sung by Heather Parcells, Yuka Takara, Mara Davi and Chryssie Whitehead. They got to perform the carol live on ABC's "Good Morning America."
Actors Who Performed the Most Roles in This Show: Lyndy Franklin, who has been on so far for Kristine, Bebe, Connie, Lois, Tricia and Vicki. Michelle Aravena is a close second. She

1. At a GMHC event. Kneeling (L-R): Jason Tam, Yuka Takara, Heather Parcells, Natalie Cortez, Michael Paternostro. Standing (L-R): Ken Alan, Chryssie Whitehead, Deidre Goodwin, Michael Berresse, unknown, Donna McKechnie, Mara Davi, Paul McGill, Tony Yazbeck and Jessica Lee Goldyn.
2. Original cast members Thommie Walsh and Donna McKechnie arrive at the Schoenfeld Theatre for the premiere.
3. Charlotte d'Amboise with her father, Jacques d'Amboise at Gilt.
4. Caricature of the company drawn by Justin Robertson, given as an opening night gift by David Baum.

A Chorus Line
Scrapbook

has been on for: Diana, Maggie, Bebe, Connie and Tricia.

Who Has Done the Most Shows in Their Career: Charlotte d'Amboise (11 including *Carrie*...'nuff said). She is closely followed by Michael Berresse (10) and Deidre Goodwin (10). But we should give a special award to Grant Turner for being offered the most Broadway shows, but couldn't take them until this year because he didn't have his Green Card yet.

Special Backstage Rituals: 1. "Scrunchy Scrunchy" in the third wing stage right before the show.
2. Natalie and Jason's breathing exercises upstage facing the wall during "At the Ballet."
3. Shecky's jumps before the show with Beth (sound) and Lyndy joining in.
4. Tyler and Ali's ass grabbing.
5. Brad and the vibrating roller.
6. "Do do's" before the first girl's ballet group in the opening.
7. Sixth floor dressing room, a.k.a. "The Treehouse" or "Café Cannon."

Favorite Moments During Each Performance:
1. Tyler does something different to entertain the line when Connie starts "4'10"."
2. Michael Gorman dancing to "Tits and Ass" while he is calling the show from the stage manager console.
3. Paul McGill's 1975 opening impression.
4. Shecky's favorite moment: He gets to watch the ladies enter for the finale..."Entertaining is an understatement."
Getting to leave before the Cassie dance—hell, just being offstage PERIOD.

Favorite In-Theatre Gathering Place: 1. "Peep Stairs" where the covers hang during "Nothing."
2. "Rory's Hut."
3. Staircase outside SM's office.
4. The Booth; not the theater...the singing booth.

Favorite Off-Site Hangout: Our own BEDS. We don't hang out. We have to freaking stand on stage for two hours. Try doing that with a hangover?

Favorite Snack Food: We have the infamous "FG" (Fat Girl) drawer in the stage manager's office that everyone contributes to by stocking it with cookies, chocolate, doughnuts, etc.

Mascot: Latice, the doll. However, she was kidnapped by the wardrobe staff and we are

Photo by Aubrey Reuben

Photo courtesy Heather Parcells

Photo by Aubrey Reuben

Photo by Aubrey Reuben

1. Arnold Scassi (L) with members of the original 1975 cast outside the Schoenfeld Theatre on the opening night of the revival.
2. Recording the cast album (L-R): Mike Cannon, James T. Lane, Joey Dudding, E. Clayton Cornelious, Paul McGill, David Baum, Ken Alan and Grant Turner.
3. Chryssie Whitehead and Tony Yazbeck on opening night.
4. (L-R): Natalie Cortez, Ken Alan and Jessica Lee Goldyn at Gilt.

A Chorus Line
Scrapbook

currently searching for her. Her likeness can be seen on an America's Choice milk carton. If you have any information regarding the kidnapping please call the Chorus Line stage manager's office. Thank you. Stats: Ethnicity: African American. Age: Twenty si…five. Height: 3'10". Weight: 1 1/2 lbs. (come on, she *is* plastic).
Favorite Therapies: Ricola, Ben-Gay, Tiger Balm, ICE!!!!, acupuncture.
Memorable Ad-Libs: 1. Grant Turner as Greg: "…and my professional name is, Sydney Perry."
2. Michael Paternostro: After Connie's line about getting off her diet he said: "She's on a diet?" Also, when he introduces himself: "And I'm 24." "AWWWWW COME ON!!!" "I can't wear a dance belt anymore…my ass says NO!"
3. Sung: "Shit, when am I gonna grow tits?"
4. "Yes Judy, I did."
5. Zach: "When I call out your name, I'll tell you where you're gonna be in the formation." Judy: "Oh God, I don't remember my number."
Memorable Fans: 1. Neil—His favorite seat is the last seat house left in the front row in the center section.
2. Tom Bernagozzi—He gave us Christmas gifts: hats, socks, and headbands, Valentine's day cards; "Acorn" socks.
3. Ryan.
Fastest Costume Changes: ALL of us, at the end for the finale of "One." Ken Allen has the fastest. He is the first person who gets the job to be onstage for the finale.
Heaviest/Hottest Costume: I would have to say Ken Alan. He wears wool high-waisted pants with suspenders, a silk long sleeve shirt, and a sweater. But David Baum gives him a run for his money with his wool sweater, wool pants and turtleneck.
Who Wore the Least: Either Heather, Deidre or Chryssie. To figure that out, you would have to measure the material. Estimated guess: Heather.
Catchphrases Only the Company Would Recognize (Company Jokes): 1. "Tippin Like Tyler Hanes"
2. "10 & Out"
3. Boy/Man Cassie
4. "Hi Hectaaaaa!"
5. "Yeow"
6. Joey Dudding's Carol Channing as Cassie
7. Greg: "Bingo" Heather to Ali: "But it's Yellow??"
8. Greg: "Bingo" Ali to Heather "Was his Name-o."
9. "Watermelon Little Peanut"
10. "It's Grant"
11. "Where is my turban?"
12. "Smells like curry"
13. In between shows the cast gets onstage and warms up with either dance class in front of the mirror, or with pirouette contests. Put dancers in front of a bunch of mirrors, and it never stops!!!
Best In-House Parody Lyrics: 1. "Sometime I dance because I want to/ Sometimes I dance because I have to./ This time I dance because I'm paid to."
2. "Gee, I'll never wear pantyhose."

Photo by David Gewirtzman

Marquee of the Gerald Schoenfeld Theatre.

3. "Tits & Ribs."
4. "Mother always said I'd be very attractive, if I threw up, if I threw up…"
5. "Give me a chance in my woolly jazz pants!"
6. "Now that I'm old I wear a hairnet."
Nicknames: 1. Jeffrey Schecter – "Shecky"
2. Tyler Hanes – "Tigra or La Tigra or Tiger"
3. Alisan Porter – Balenciaga
4. Jason Tam – "Tamu"
5. Yuka Takara – "Crunku"
6. Clayton Cornelious – "Boo"
7. Lisa Ho – "HO" or "Don't rent a Ho, Lisa Ho"
Sweethearts Within the Company: Jessica and Tony.
***A Chorus Line* Engagements:** 1. July 12, 2006 – Two days before leaving for San Francisco, Paul A. Schaefer proposed to Heather Parcells.
2. January 1, 2007 – New Year's Day, Aaron Gaines proposed to Mara Davi.
3. By the time this book is published – Jeremy Smith will have proposed to Lyndy Franklin.
Funniest Things to Happen During a Show:
1. Grant's "Sydney Perry"
2. Ali & Brad's Slap Fights
3. Michael Paternostro snot globule landing downstage of the "Line" and remaining completely intact until the Cassie dance
4. TAG
5. One of Charlotte's extensions falling out onstage and remaining there during the entire "Ones" through the tap combination.
6. Heather's boob pads falling out as she ran offstage for the finale and being kicked around like a hockey puck during the finale.
7. Michael Berresse forgetting his opening speech to the Line.
Funniest Quotes: Baayork: 1. "One TWO"
2. "SEVEN!"
3. "Lunch Lunch"
4. "Crotchez -vous"
5. "If you drop the hat, you owe me 5 dollars!"
6. "And CRUNCH"
Gorman: "I want to you to know that I know that you know."
"Gypsy of the Year" Sketch: The West Side Five, a.k.a. the five male swings/cut dancers. (Joey Dudding, Mike Cannon, Clayton Cornelious, David Baum, and Grant Turner) wrote, recorded, and performed their original song "Ten and Out" with members of the Line, with lyrics in the style of 1980s monster ballads:

Walking through that door again,
but I don't know what for
Will it be the same old track or maybe
something more?
I run up to the callboard but much to my dismay
It never seems to say what I want it to say

Tonight I'm ten and out
Ten more minutes in the spotlight
Ten and out
Then I have to exit stage right
Send my prayer right up to God
Man I really need this job
(ten and out, ten and out)

I can do some bad arms, I look right
at the floor
I got a green mesh shirt on and I can
count aloud to four
Every day I step kick kick leap touch
and my hunger grows
When will I get to stand in my logo pose
AHHHHH tell me

Cause I'm ten and out
I'm singing in the wings like a chump
Ten and out
What I'd give to be in Larry's clump
Send my prayers right up to God
Damn, I really need this job
(ten and out, ten and out yeah)

I'm still ten and out
Ten more minutes in the spotlight
Ten and out
Then I have to exit stage right
Send my prayer right up to GOD
Man I really need this job!

The Coast of Utopia

LINCOLN CENTER THEATER AT THE VIVIAN BEAUMONT

UNDER THE DIRECTION OF
ANDRÉ BISHOP AND BERNARD GERSTEN
IN ASSOCIATION WITH
BOB BOYETT
PRESENTS

THE COAST OF UTOPIA

VOYAGE ~ SHIPWRECK ~ SALVAGE

A TRILOGY BY TOM STOPPARD

WITH (IN ALPHABETICAL ORDER)
BILLY CRUDUP RICHARD EASTON JENNIFER EHLE
JOSH HAMILTON DAVID HARBOUR JASON BUTLER HARNER
ETHAN HAWKE AMY IRVING BRÍAN F. O'BYRNE MARTHA PLIMPTON

BIANCA AMATO MIA BARRON LARRY BULL DENIS BUTKUS
MICHAEL CARLSEN AMANDA LEIGH COBB ANTHONY COCHRANE
PATRICIA CONOLLY DAVID CROMWELL ADAM DANNHEISSER MATT DICKSON
AARON KROHN FELICITY LAFORTUNE JENNIFER LYON DAVID MANIS
ANDREW MCGINN KELLIE OVERBEY SCOTT PARKINSON DAVID PITTU
ANNIE PURCELL ERIKA ROLFSRUD BRIAN SGAMBATI ROBERT STANTON
ERIC SHEFFER STEVENS BAYLEN THOMAS DAVID CHRISTOPHER WELLS

TOLAN AMAN MICHAEL D'ADDARIO EVAN DAVES AUGUST GLADSTONE
VIVIEN KELLS BECKETT MELVILLE KAT PETERS SOPHIE RUDIN

SETS BOB CROWLEY & SCOTT PASK COSTUMES CATHERINE ZUBER
LIGHTING (*VOYAGE*) BRIAN MACDEVITT (*SHIPWRECK*) KENNETH POSNER (*SALVAGE*) NATASHA KATZ
ORIGINAL MUSIC & SOUND MARK BENNETT
PRODUCTION STAGE MANAGER ROBERT BENNETT CASTING DANIEL SWEE
DRAMATURG ANNE CATTANEO GENERAL PRESS AGENT PHILIP RINALDI
DIRECTOR OF DEVELOPMENT HATTIE K. JUTAGIR DIRECTOR OF MARKETING LINDA MASON ROSS
GENERAL MANAGER ADAM SIEGEL PRODUCTION MANAGER JEFF HAMLIN

DIRECTED BY JACK O'BRIEN

LINCOLN CENTER THEATER GRATEFULLY ACKNOWLEDGES THE CONTRIBUTORS
WHOSE EXTRAORDINARY GENEROSITY HAS MADE THE COAST OF UTOPIA POSSIBLE:

BRUCE KOVNER • DEBRA AND LEON BLACK • THE ANDREW W. MELLON FOUNDATION
THE PETER JAY SHARP FOUNDATION'S SPECIAL FUND FOR LCT
THE BLANCHE AND IRVING LAURIE FOUNDATION • THE NORMAN AND ROSITA WINSTON FOUNDATION
THE BLANCHETTE HOOKER ROCKEFELLER FUND
THE DORIS DUKE CHARITABLE FOUNDATION ENDOWMENT FUND AT LCT
LILA WALLACE AND DEWITT ACHESON WALLACE ENDOWMENT FUND
THE COAST OF UTOPIA: PART 3, *SALVAGE* IS SUPPORTED IN PART BY AN
AWARD FROM THE NATIONAL ENDOWMENT FOR THE ARTS.

2/18/07

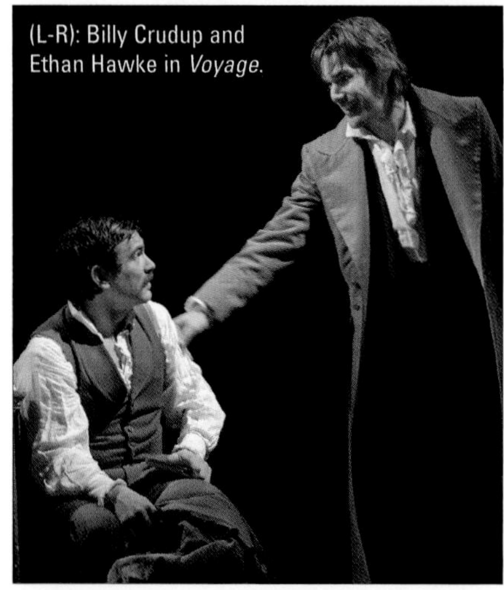
(L-R): Billy Crudup and Ethan Hawke in *Voyage*.

Amy Irving in *Shipwreck*.

(L-R): Josh Hamilton, Kat Peters, Brían F. O'Byrne, Martha Plimpton and Ethan Hawke in *Salvage*.

Photos by Paul Kolnik

The Coast of Utopia, Part One: Voyage

First Preview: October 17, 2006. Opened: November 27, 2006.
Closed: May 13, 2007 after 31 Previews and 45 Performances.

SCENES

ACT ONE All at Premukhino, the Bakunin estate 150 miles northwest of Moscow	ACT TWO Moscow and St. Petersburg
SCENE 1 ...... Summer 1833	
	March 1834 .... **SCENE 1** – The Zoo Gardens
	March 1835 .... **SCENE 2** – A Soirée at Mrs. Beyer's
	March 1835 .... **SCENE 3** – At Mrs. Beyer's
SCENE 2 .... Spring 1835	
	July 1835 .... **SCENE 4** – The Telescope office
SCENE 3 ...... Autumn 1835	
	May 1836 .... **SCENE 5** – The Telescope office
SCENE 4 .... Spring 1836	
SCENE 5 ...... Autumn 1836	
SCENE 6 ...... Autumn 1836	
	November 1836 .... **SCENE 6** – A music room
	November 1836 .... **SCENE 7** – Belinsky's room
	January 1837 .... **SCENE 8** – Engelhardt Hall
SCENE 7 .... January 1837	
	February 1837 .... **SCENE 9** – Belinsky's room
	Spring 1838 .... **SCENE 10** – Belinsky's room
SCENE 8 .... Spring 1838	
	June 1840 .... **SCENE 11** – By the Neva, St. Petersburg
	July 1840 .... **SCENE 12** – A street in St. Petersburg
SCENE 9 ...... Autumn 1841	
	February 1843 .... **SCENE 13** – A Fancy-Dress Ball
	Autumn 1844 .... **SCENE 14** – (Premukhino)

CAST

(in order of speaking)

Alexander Bakunin .... RICHARD EASTON
Varvara, *his wife* .... AMY IRVING
Liubov, *a daughter* .... JENNIFER EHLE
Varenka, *a daughter* .... MARTHA PLIMPTON
Tatiana, *a daughter* .... KELLIE OVERBEY
Alexandra, *a daughter* .... ANNIE PURCELL
Miss Chamberlain,
their English governess .... BIANCA AMATO
Baron Renne,
betrothed to Liubov .... ANDREW McGINN
Semyon, *senior household servant* ..... DAVID MANIS
Masha, *a maid* .... FELICITY LaFORTUNE
Michael Bakunin .... ETHAN HAWKE
Dyakov, *betrothed to Varenka* .... ANTHONY COCHRANE
Nicholas Stankevich,
a young philosopher .... DAVID HARBOUR
Vissarion Belinsky,
a literary critic .... BILLY CRUDUP
Ivan Turgenev .... JASON BUTLER HARNER
Alexander Herzen .... BRÍAN F. O'BYRNE
Nicholas Ogarev, *his friend* ...... JOSH HAMILTON
Nicholas Sazonov,
another friend .... AARON KROHN
Nicholas Ketscher,
a young doctor .... BAYLEN THOMAS
Nicholas Polevoy,
editor of The Messenger .... DAVID PITTU
Mrs. Beyer .... PATRICIA CONOLLY
Natalie Beyer, *her daughter* .... MIA BARRON
Peter Chaadaev, *an essayist* .... DAVID CROMWELL
Stepan Shevyrev,
a professor and editor .... ROBERT STANTON
Katya, *Belinsky's mistress* .... JENNIFER LYON
Pushkin, *a poet*/Cat .... ADAM DANNHEISSER
Serfs, Servants, Party Guests,
Musicians, etc. .... LARRY BULL
DENIS BUTKUS
MICHAEL CARLSEN
AMANDA LEIGH COBB
MATT DICKSON
SCOTT PARKINSON
ERIKA ROLFSRUD
BRIAN SGAMBATI
ERIC SHEFFER STEVENS
DAVID CHRISTOPHER WELLS

Assistant Stage Managers .... DIANE DiVITA, JENNIFER RAE MOORE, JASON HINDELANG

UNDERSTUDIES

For Katya: BIANCA AMATO
For Dyakov, Pushkin/Cat: LARRY BULL
For Natalie Beyer, Tatiana, Alexandra: AMANDA LEIGH COBB
For Semyon, Nicholas Polevoy, Stepan Shevyrev: ANTHONY COCHRANE
For Michael Bakunin: ADAM DANNHEISSER
For Miss Chamberlain, Mrs. Beyer, Varvara Bakunin: FELICITY LaFORTUNE
For Masha: JENNIFER LYON
For Nicholas Ogarev: ANDREW McGINN
For Peter Chaadaev, Alexander Bakunin: DAVID MANIS
For Vissarion Belinsky, Nicholas Sazonov: SCOTT PARKINSON
For Liubov, Varenka: ERIKA ROLFSRUD
For Baron Renne: ROBERT STANTON
For Alexander Herzen: ERIC SHEFFER STEVENS;
For Ivan Turgenev: BAYLEN THOMAS
For Nicholas Stankevich, Nicholas Ketscher: DAVID CHRISTOPHER WELLS

The Coast of Utopia, Part Two: Shipwreck

First Preview: December 5, 2006. Opened: December 21, 2006.
Closed: May 13, 2007 after 12 Previews and 45 Performances.

SCENES

ACT ONE

Scene 1	Garden of Sokolovo, outside Moscow	1846 Summer
Scene 2	Salzbrunn, a German spa town	1847 Early July
Scene 3	Place de la Concorde, Paris	Late July
Scene 4	The Herzens' apartment, rue Marigny	September
Scene 5	Place de la Concorde, Paris	1848 March
Scene 6	The Herzens' apartment, Paris	May 15
Scene 7	A boulevard in Paris	Early June
Scene 8	A street in Paris	June 21
Scene 9	The Herzens' apartment, Paris	June 27
Scene 10	The Herzens' apartment, rue Marigny	1847 September

ACT TWO

Scene 1	The Herzens' apartment, Paris	1849 January
Scene 2	Maria Ogarev's studio, Paris	April
Scene 3	A prison in Saxony	May
Scene 4	Montmorency, outside Paris	June
Scene 5	The Herzens' house in Nice at this time an Italian town	1850 September
Scene 6	The Herzens' house in Nice	November
Scene 7	The Herzens' house in Nice	1851 January
Scene 8	The Herzens' house in Nice	November
Scene 9	The deck of a cross-Channel steamer	1852 August
Scene 10	The garden of Sokolovo	1846 Summer

Assistant Stage Managers ....DIANE DiVITA, JENNIFER RAE MOORE, JASON HINDELANG

UNDERSTUDIES

For Natasha Tuchkov: MIA BARRON
For Karl Marx, Jean-Marie: LARRY BULL
For Benoit, Rocca, Leonty Ibayev: ANTHONY COCHRANE
For Rosa, Marianne: AMANDA LEIGH COBB
For Sasha Herzen, Kolya Herzen: MICHAEL D'ADDARIO
For Konstantin Aksakov, Michael Bakunin: ADAM DANNHEISSER
For Policeman: AARON KROHN
For Madame Haag, Maria Ogarev: FELICITY LaFORTUNE
For Nurse: JENNIFER LYON
For Franz Otto: DAVID MANIS
for Nicholas Ogarev, Nicholas Sazonov: ANDREW McGINN
For Vissarion Belinsky: SCOTT PARKINSON
For Natalie Herzen, Emma Herwegh: ERIKA ROLFSRUD
For Alexander Herzen: ERIC SHEFFER STEVENS
For Ivan Turgenev, Beggar: BAYLEN THOMAS
For Timothy Granovsky, Nicholas Ketscher, George Herwegh: DAVID CHRISTOPHER WELLS

(L-R): David Harbour and Jennifer Ehle.
Photo by Paul Kolnik

CAST

In Sokolovo, Russia:

Alexander Herzen ....BRÍAN F. O'BYRNE
Natalie Herzen, *his wife* ....JENNIFER EHLE
Sasha Herzen, *their son* ....BECKETT MELVILLE
Kolya Herzen, *their younger son* ....AUGUST GLADSTONE
Nurse, *a household serf* ....MIA BARRON
Nicholas Ogarev, *a poet* ....JOSH HAMILTON
Ivan Turgenev, *a writer* JASON BUTLER HARNER
Timothy Granovsky, *a historian* ....ANDREW McGINN
Nicholas Ketscher, *a doctor* ......BAYLEN THOMAS
Konstatin Aksakov, *a Slavophile* ....SCOTT PARKINSON
Policeman ....DAVID MANIS

In Paris:

Vissarion Belinsky, *a literary critic* ..BILLY CRUDUP
Madame Haag, *Herzen's mother* ....PATRICIA CONOLLY
Jean-Marie, *a French servant* ..DAVID CROMWELL
George Herwegh, *a German poet* ....DAVID HARBOUR
Emma Herwegh, *his wife* ....BIANCA AMATO
Shop Boy ....TOLAN AMAN
Nicolas Sazonov, *a Russian émigré activist* ....AARON KROHN
Michael Bakunin ....ETHAN HAWKE
Marianne on the Barricades ....FELICITY LaFORTUNE
Karl Marx ....ADAM DANNHEISSER
Natasha Tuchkov, *Natalie's friend* ....MARTHA PLIMPTON
Benoit, *a French servant* ....DAVID PITTU
Beggar ....SCOTT PARKINSON
Maria Ogarev, *Ogarev's estranged wife* AMY IRVING

Franz Otto, *a lawyer in Dresden, Saxony* ....ROBERT STANTON
Leonty Ibayev, *Russian Consul General in Nice* ....RICHARD EASTON
Rocca, *an Italian servant* ....DAVID PITTU
Rosa, *the Italian maid* ......FELICITY LaFORTUNE

Serfs, French Servants, Revolutionaries, Italian Servants ....DENIS BUTKUS, MICHAEL CARLSEN, ANTHONY COCHRANE, AMANDA LEIGH COBB, MICHAEL D'ADDARIO, MATT DICKSON, JENNIFER LYON, KELLIE OVERBEY, ANNIE PURCELL, ERIKA ROLFSRUD, BRIAN SGAMBATI, ERIC SHEFFER STEVENS, DAVID CHRISTOPHER WELLS

The Coast of Utopia, Part Three: Salvage

First Preview: January 31, 2007. Opened: February 18, 2007.
Closed: May 13, 2007 after 13 Previews and 34 Performances.

England and, much later, Geneva
Time: 1853-1868

CAST

Herzen's Household:

Alexander Herzen .... BRÍAN F. O'BYRNE
Sasha, *his son* .... MATT DICKSON
Sasha, *as a child* .... EVAN DAVES
Tata, *his daughter* .... ANNIE PURCELL
Tata, *as a child* .... KAT PETERS
Olga, *his daughter* .... AMANDA LEIGH COBB
Olga, *as a child* .... KAT PETERS
Olga, *as a young child* .... VIVIEN KELLS
Maria Fomm, *their German nanny* .... FELICITY LaFORTUNE
Malwida von Meysenbug, *their German governess and tutor* .... JENNIFER EHLE
Mrs. Blainey, *an English nanny* .... PATRICIA CONOLLY
Rose, *a parlormaid* .... MIA BARRON
English Servants .... TOLAN AMAN, AMANDA LEIGH COBB, MATT DICKSON BRIAN SGAMBATI

The Émigré Circle in London

Count Stanislaw Worcell, *leading figure of the Polish opposition in exile* .... RICHARD EASTON
Arnold Ruge, *radical German editor, and activist of 1848* .... DAVID CROMWELL
Gottfried Kinkel, *radical German poet and activist of 1848* .... DAVID MANIS
Joanna Kinkel, *his wife, a composer, writer and women's rights activist* .... BIANCA AMATO
Karl Marx, *author of the Communist Manifesto* ... ADAM DANNHEISSER
Ernest Jones, *radical English Chartist politician, lawyer and poet* .... ROBERT STANTON
Emily Jones, his wife .... JENNIFER LYON
Giuseppe Mazzini, *Italian nationalist leader in exile* .... BRIAN SGAMBATI
Louis Blanc, *French socialist politician, former member of the 1848 Assembly* .... DAVID PITTU
Alexandre Ledru-Rollin, *French republican politician, former member of the 1848 Assembly* .... LARRY BULL
Alphonse de Ville, *his aide* ...... BAYLEN THOMAS
Lajos Kossuth, *first President of independent Hungary, in exile* ...... ANTHONY COCHRANE
Teresa Kossuth, *his wife* .... ERIKA ROLFSRUD
Captain Peks, *his aide* .... DENIS BUTKUS
Zenkowicz, *Chief of Staff to Count Worcell* .... DAVID CROMWELL
Tchorzewski, *a Polish bookshop owner* .... MICHAEL CARLSEN
Czerniecki, *a Polish printer* .... AARON KROHN
Polish émigré at the celebration of the new Tsar .... DENIS BUTKUS
Michael Bakunin .... ETHAN HAWKE
Nicholas Ogarev .... JOSH HAMILTON
Natasha Tuchkov Ogarev, *his second wife* .... MARTHA PLIMPTON
Ivan Turgenev .... JASON BUTLER HARNER
Mary Sutherland, *Ogarev's mistress* .... KELLIE OVERBEY
Henry, her son .... TOLAN AMAN

Russian Visitors: The "New" Generation

Nicholas Chernyshevsky, *a radical, author of "What Is to Be Done?"* .... ANDREW McGINN
Doctor at the Seashore (Bazarov) .... DAVID HARBOUR
Perotkin .... DAVID CHRISTOPHER WELLS
Semlov .... BRIAN SGAMBATI
Lt. Korf .... DENIS BUTKUS
Vetoshnikov .... DAVID PITTU
Sleptsov .... SCOTT PARKINSON

In Geneva

Waiter .... ERIC SHEFFER STEVENS
Teresina, *Herzen's Italian daughter-in-law, Sasha's wife* .... MIA BARRON
Liza, *daughter of Herzen and Natasha Ogarev* .... KAT PETERS

Ensemble .... BECKETT MELVILLE, SOPHIE RUDIN

Pianist .... DAN LIPTON
Guitarist .... AARON KROHN

Assistant Stage Managers .... DIANE DiVITA, JENNIFER RAE MOORE, JASON HINDELANG

UNDERSTUDIES

For Teresina: BIANCA AMATO
For Sasha, as a child: TOLAN AMAN
For Tata, Natasha Tuchkov Ogarev: MIA BARRON
For Karl Marx, Czerniecki: LARRY BULL
For Sasha, Lajos Kossuth: DENIS BUTKUS
For Giuseppe Mazzini, Lt. Korf, Sleptsov: MICHAEL CARLSEN
For Emily Jones: AMANDA LEIGH COBB
For Count Stanislaw Worcell, Zenkowicz: ANTHONY COCHRANE
For Michael Bakunin: ADAM DANNHEISSER
For Captain Peks, Polish émigré: MATT DICKSON
For Nicholas Chernyshevsky, Doctor: AARON KROHN
For Mrs. Blainey: FELICITY LaFORTUNE
For Maria Fomm, Rose: JENNIFER LYON
For Count Stanislaw Worcell: DAVID MANIS
For Gottfried Kinkel, Nicholas Ogarev: ANDREW McGINN
For Henry: BECKETT MELVILLE
For Arnold Ruge: SCOTT PARKINSON
For Joanna Kinkel: ANNIE PURCELL
For Olga, Malwida von Meysenbug, Mary Sutherland: ERIKA ROLFSRUD
For Tata as a child, Olga as a child, Olga as a young child, Liza: SOPHIE RUDIN
For Waiter: BRIAN SGAMBATI
For Alexander Herzen, Perotkin, Semlov: ERIC SHEFFER STEVENS
For Ernest Jones, Alexandre Ledru-Rollin, Ivan Turgenev: BAYLEN THOMAS
For Louis Blanc, Alphonse de Ville, Vetoshnikov: DAVID CHRISTOPHER WELLS

(L-R): Richard Easton and Brían F. O'Byrne.
Photo by Paul Kolnik

The Coast of Utopia

Tolan Aman
Shop Boy, English Servant, Henry

Bianca Amato
Miss Chamberlain, Emma Herwegh, Joanna Kinkel

Mia Barron
Natalie Beyer, Nurse, Rose/Teresina

Larry Bull
Company, Alexandre Ledru-Rollin

Denis Butkus
Company, Captain Peks/ Lt. Korf

Michael Carlsen
Company, Tchorzewski

Amanda Leigh Cobb
Company, Olga Herzen

Anthony Cochrane
Dyakov, Company, Lajos Kossuth

Patricia Conolly
Mrs. Beyer, Madame Haag, Mrs. Blainey

David Cromwell
Peter Chaadaev, Jean-Marie, Zenkowicz/Arnold Ruge

Billy Crudup
Vissarion Belinsky

Michael D'Addario
Company

Adam Dannheisser
Pushkin/Ginger Cat, Karl Marx

Evan Daves
Sasha Herzen - Child

Matt Dickson
Company, Sasha Herzen-adult

Richard Easton
Alexander Bakunin, Leonty Ibayev, Stanislaw Worcell

Jennifer Ehle
Liubov Bakunin, Natalie Herzen, Malwida von Meysenbug

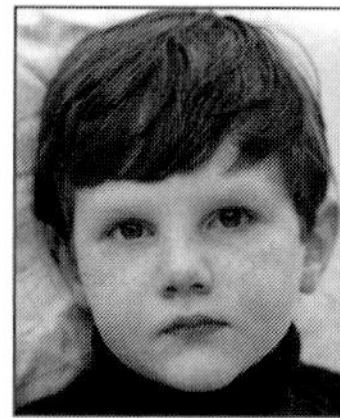

August Gladstone
Kolya Herzen

Josh Hamilton
Nicholas Ogarev

David Harbour
Nicholas Stankevich, George Herwegh, Doctor

Jason Butler Harner
Ivan Turgenev

Ethan Hawke
Michael Bakunin

Amy Irving
Varvara Bakunin, Maria Ogarev

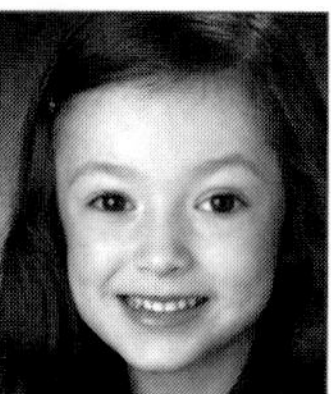

Vivien Kells
Olga- Young Child

Aaron Krohn
Nicholas Sazonov, Czerniecki

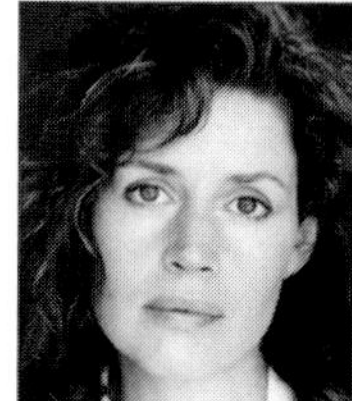

Felicity LaFortune
Company, Marianne/Rosa, Maria Fomm

Jennifer Lyon
Katya, Company, Emily Jones

David Manis
Semyon, Policeman, Gottfried Kinkel

Andrew McGinn
Baron Renne, Timothy Granovsky, Nicholas Chernyshevsky

Beckett Melville
Sasha Herzen, Ensemble

Brían F. O'Byrne
Alexander Herzen

Kellie Overbey
Tatiana Bakunin, Company, Mary Sutherland

Scott Parkinson
Company, Konstantin Aksakov, Sleptsov

Kat Peters
Tata, Olga, Liza

David Pittu
Nicholas Polevoy, Benoit/Rocca, Louis Blanc/Pavel Vetoshnikov

The Coast of Utopia

Martha Plimpton
Varenka Bakunin, Natasha Tuchkov, Natasha Ogarev

Annie Purcell
Alexandra Bakunin, Company, Tata Herzen

Erika Rolfsrud
Company, Teresa Kossuth

Sophie Rudin
Ensemble

Brian Sgambati
Company, Semlov/ Giuseppe Mazzini

Robert Stanton
Stepan Shevyrev, Franz Otto, Ernest Jones

Eric Sheffer Stevens
Company

Baylen Thomas
Nicholas Ketscher, Alphonse de Ville

David Christopher Wells
Company, Perotkin

Tom Stoppard
Playwright

Jack O'Brien
Director

Bob Crowley
Sets

Scott Pask
Sets

Catherine Zuber
Costumes

Brian MacDevitt
Lighting–Voyage

Kenneth Posner
Lighting–Shipwreck

Natasha Katz
Lighting–Salvage

Mark Bennett
Original Music/ Sound

Benjamin Endsley Klein
Associate Director

Michele Reisch
Dresser

Seth Sklar-Heyn
Assistant to the Director

Elizabeth Smith
Voice, Speech Consultant

Bob Boyett
Producer

André Bishop and Bernard Gersten, Lincoln Center Theatre

William Connell
Company

Maximillian Sherer
Company

Photo by Ben Strothmann

WARDROBE
(L-R): Jane Rottenbach (Dresser), Meghan Bowers (Dresser), Elizabeth Stader (Dresser), Linda McAllister (Dresser), Liam O'Brien (Dresser), Lynn Bowling (Wardrobe Supervisor), Jerome Parker (Dresser).
Not Pictured: Susan Cook, James Nadeaux, Virginia Neininger, Rosie Wells.

The Coast of Utopia

STAGE MANAGEMENT
Front Row (L-R): Jason Hindelang (Assistant Stage Manager), Steve Henry (Production Assistant).
Back Row (L-R): Diane DiVita (Assistant Stage Manager), Jennifer Rae Moore (Assistant Stage Manager) and Robert Bennett (Production Stage Manager).

Photos by Ben Strothmann

RUNNING CREW
Front Row (L-R): Victor Seastone (Automated Light Programmer), Andrew Belits (Rail Carpenter), Fred Bredenbeck (Deck Carpenter).
Second Row (L-R): Ray Skillin (Deck Carpenter), Jeff Ward (Follow Spot), Pat O'Connor (Deck Carpenter), Marc Salzberg (Production Soundman).
Third Row (L-R): Frank Linn (Automated Light Technician), John Weingart (Production Flyman), Kevin McNeill (Rail Carpenter), John Ross (Props), Karl Rausenberger (Production Propertyman), Mark Dignam (Props).
Back Row (L-R): Matthew Altman (Follow Spot), Gary Simon (Deck Sound), Bill Burke (Projection Technician), Greg Cushna (Rail Carpenter), Bill Nagle (Production Carpenter), John Howie (Deck Carpenter), Nick Irons (Follow Spot), Juan Bustamante (Deck Automation), Pat Merryman (Production Electrician), Joe Pizzuto (Follow Spot), Rudy Wood (Props), Scott Jackson (Props).
Not Pictured: Bruce Rubin (Conventional Light Programmer/Operator).

USHERS AND SECURITY
Back Row (L-R): Officer Douglas Charles (security guard) and ushers James Dittami, Roberto De Barros, Nick Andors, Kim Mills.
Second Row (L-R): Ruby Jaggernauth, Margareta Shakeridge, Patrick Cottington, Christine Owen, Margie Blair, Judith Fanelli.
Third Row (L-R): Mim Pollock (Chief Usher), Beatrice Gilliard, Jeff Goldstein.
Front Row (L-R): Lydia Tchornobai and Kevin Costigan.

HAIR AND WIGS
(L-R): John McNulty (Hair Assistant), Jamie Stewart, Mary Kay Yezerski (Hair Supervisor).

Not Pictured: Cindy Demand (Hair Assistant).

The Coast of Utopia

LINCOLN CENTER THEATER

ANDRÉ BISHOP — **ARTISTIC DIRECTOR**
BERNARD GERSTEN — **EXECUTIVE PRODUCER**

ADMINISTRATIVE STAFF

GENERAL MANAGER ... ADAM SIEGEL
Associate General Manager ... Jessica Niebanck
General Management Assistant ... Meghan Lantzy
Facilities Manager ... Alex Mustelier
Assistant Facilities Manager ... Michael Assalone
GENERAL PRESS AGENT ... PHILIP RINALDI
Press Associate ... Barbara Carroll
PRODUCTION MANAGER ... JEFF HAMLIN
Associate Production Manager ... Paul Smithyman
DIRECTOR OF DEVELOPMENT ... HATTIE K. JUTAGIR
Associate Director of Development ... Rachel Norton
Manager of Special Events and Young Patron Program ... Karin Schall
Grants Writer ... Neal Brilliant
Manager, Patron Program ... Sheilaja Rao
Assistant to the Director of Development ... Marsha Martinez
Development Assistant/ Special Events ... Nicole Lindenbaum
Development Associate ... Raelyn Richards
DIRECTOR OF FINANCE ... DAVID S. BROWN
Controller ... Susan Knox
Systems Manager ... Stacy Valentine-Thomas
Finance Assistant ... Megan Wildebour
DIRECTOR OF MARKETING ... LINDA MASON ROSS
Marketing Associate ... David Hatkoff
Marketing Assistant ... Kristin Miller
DIRECTOR OF EDUCATION ... KATI KOERNER
Associate Director of Education ... Dionne O'Dell
Assistant to the Executive Producer ... Barbara Hourigan
Office Assistant ... Kenneth Collins
Messenger ... Esau Burgess
Reception ... Rhonda Lipscomb, Michelle Hamill

ARTISTIC STAFF

ASSOCIATE DIRECTORS ... GRACIELA DANIELE, NICHOLAS HYTNER, SUSAN STROMAN, DANIEL SULLIVAN
DRAMATURG and DIRECTOR, LCT DIRECTORS LAB ... ANNE CATTANEO
CASTING DIRECTOR ... DANIEL SWEE, CSA
MUSICAL THEATER ASSOCIATE PRODUCER ... IRA WEITZMAN
Artistic Administrator ... Julia Judge
Casting Associate ... Camille Hickman
Education/Lab Assistant ... Jill MacLean

IN LOVING MEMORY OF
GERALD GUTIERREZ
Associate Director 1991-2003
WENDY WASSERSTEIN
Playwright

HOUSE STAFF

HOUSE MANAGER ... RHEBA FLEGELMAN
Production Carpenter ... William Nagle
Production Electrician ... Patrick Merryman
Production Propertyman ... Karl Rausenberger
Production Flyman ... John Weingart
Production Soundman ... Marc Salzberg
House Technician ... Linda Heard
Chief Usher ... M.L. Pollock
Box Office Treasurer ... Fred Bonis
Assistant Treasurer ... Robert A. Belkin

SPECIAL SERVICES

Advertising ... Serino-Coyne/Jim Russek Roger Micone, Jill Jefferson
Principal Poster Artist ... James McMullan
Counsel ... Peter L. Felcher, Esq.; Charles H. Googe, Esq.; and Carol Kaplan, Esq. of Paul, Weiss, Rifkind, Wharton & Garrison
Immigration Counsel ... Theodore Ruthizer, Esq.; Mark D. Koestler, Esq. of Kramer, Levin, Naftalis & Frankel LLP
Auditor ... Douglas Burack, C.P.A. Lutz & Carr, L.L.P.
Insurance ... Jennifer Brown of DeWitt Stern Group
Photographer ... Paul Kolnik
Video Services ... Fresh Produce Productions, Frank Basile
Travel ... Tygon Tours
Consulting Architect ... Hugh Hardy, Hardy Holzman Pfeiffer Associates
Construction Manager ... Yorke Construction
Payroll Service ... Castellana Services, Inc.

STAFF FOR *The Coast of Utopia*

COMPANY MANAGER ... MATTHEW MARKOFF
Assistant Company Manager ... Jessica Perlmeter Cochrane
Associate Director ... Benjamin Endsley Klein
Assistant Director ... Caitlin Moon
Assistant to the Director ... Seth Sklar-Heyn
Associate Set Designer ... Frank McCullough
Assistant Set Designers ... Jeffrey Hinchee, Lauren Alvarez
Associate Costume Designer ... Michael Zecker
Assistant Costume Designer ... Michele K. Short
Assistants to the Costume Designer ... Court Watson, Holly Cain
Associate Lighting Designer ... Aaron Spivey
Assistant Lighting Designer ... Kathleen Dobbins
Moving Light Programmer ... Victor Seastone
Associate Sound Designers ... Leon Rothenberg, Anthony Smolenski
Assistant to the Composer ... David Ganon
Vocal Music/Instrumental Coach ... Dan Lipton
Projections Designer ... William Cusick
Associate Projections Designer ... Ryan Hosopple
Hair and Wig Designer ... Tom Watson
Ms. Ehle's Wig ... Paul Huntley
Make-Up Designer ... Angelina Avallone
Props ... Scott Laule
Wardrobe Supervisor ... Lynn Bowling
Dressers ... Susan Cook, Linda McAllister, James Nadeaux, Virginia Neininger, Liam O'Brien, Jerome Parker, Jane Rottenbach, Elizabeth Stader, Rosie Wells
Hair Supervisor ... Mary Kay Yezerski
Hair Assistants ... Jamie Stewart, Cindy Demand, John McNulty
Choreographer ... Michele Lynch
Production Assistant ... Steve Henry
Children's Guardian ... Christine Rudakewycz
Children's Tutoring ... On Location Education

Voice, Speech Consultant ... Elizabeth Smith

Musicians for Part One - *Voyage*

Josh Camp – accordion
Marshall Coid – violin
Kevin Kuhn – balalaika, mandolin
Dan Lipton – piano
Alissa Smith – viola
Bruce Wang – cello

Musicians for Part Two - *Shipwreck*

Dominic Derasse – trumpet
Dan Lipton – piano
Sarah Schram – oboe
Jake Schwartz – guitar
Andrew Sterman – clarinet, flute

Mark Bennett, Dan Lipton – Music Directors

Curtis Moore – Arranger: "Émigré Nightmare" ***(Salvage)***

Music recorded at Second Story Studios, Scott Lehrer, engineer.

Actor vocal effects recorded at John Kilgore Studios, John Kilgore, engineer.

CREDITS

Scenery constructed by Hudson Scenic Studio, Inc., Showman Fabricators and Cigar Box Studios. Show control and scenic motion control featuring stage command systems by PRG Scenic Technologies, a division of Production Resource Group, LLC, New Windsor, NY. Scenery fabrication by PRG Scenic Technologies, a division of Production Resource Group, LLC, New Windsor, NY. Costumes by Parson-Meares, LTD., Angels The Costumiers, Peerless Softgoods, John Kristiansen New York Inc., and Brian Hemesath. Costumes and millinery by Carelli Costumes, Inc. Softgoods by Rosebrand. Sound equipment by Masque Sound. Lighting equipment from PRG Lighting. Natural herb cough drops courtesy of Ricola USA, Inc.

Special thanks to Ken Berkeley, Gina Davidson, Alex Hawthorn, Bridget O'Connor, Jane Shaw, Yamaha Pianos, Waves Audio and Dr. Cynthia Harden, MD, and Helene Quinn, RN, from the Comprehensive Epilepsy Center at New York Presbyterian Hospital.

Visit www.coastofutopia.com

For groups of 20 or more:
Caryl Goldsmith Group Sales
(212) 889-4300

Lobby refreshments by Sweet Concessions.

The Coast of Utopia
Scrapbook

Correspondent: Jason Butler Harner, "Ivan Turgenev"
Memorable Opening Night Note: Flowers from my Dad with a note that said "You Did It!" (This is my long awaited Broadway debut.)
Opening Night Gifts: A friend hand-painted a set of nesting dolls with Turgenev on the first one and more and more personal references as you got further inside. Incredible gift. And Josh Hamilton gave me a beautiful edition of Turgenev's "On the Eve."
Most Exciting Celebrity Visitors: Too many to comment on, but Bill Clinton's pre-second act standing ovation from the audience was a lot of fun—as was me rounding the corner with my big whitened head of hair after a marathon and finding Meryl Streep. She was very, very generous. I thanked her and told her my coif was an homage to Diana Vreeland for her.
Actor Who Performed the Most Roles in This Show: With a cast this big, the understudies really worked their butts off. I think Erika Rolfsrud had a hefty amount of covering. So did Scott Parkinson, with Scott going on for Billy Crudup in a marathon performance with an 8 AM notification to do a show from 11AM to 11 PM. That's amazing. I think a lot of the company reached the maximum number of covers Equity allows, in fact.
Actor Who Has Done the Most Shows: I'm sure it's a draw between Richard Easton, Patricia Conolly, and David Cromwell. All three of them are spectacular actors and even better human beings.
Special Backstage Rituals: We have a few. At 'five minutes' an impromptu group meets in the greenroom to hold hands. Someone 'gets the spirit' and says something intended to inspire, regroup or guffaw—whichever feels the most necessary on that particular night. I always do a warm-up with Mia Barron when we do *Voyage*. There are "under the china silk" rituals for each show while we make the waves, before the big reveals. Aaron Krohn and I have a dance (which varies) for Jenn Lyon and Bianca Amato in *Voyage*. Annie Purcell always has to smell my Coriander Kiehl's Lotioned hands under the silk before *Shipwreck*. And I have to touch Jenn Ehle and Patricia Conolly in the free-for-all dance off under the silk for *Salvage*.
Favorite Moments During Each Performance (On Stage or Off): There are so many. I'm not an exclusive definition of 'favorite' kind of guy. I mean, I have two 'best' friends. But I digress. Some moments of mine that I love doing: in *Voyage*, I love ending the act and walking through the serfs with Kellie Overbey. In *Shipwreck*, I really love the moment I share with Bianca Amato where I tell her her husband is having an affair, as I love the moment with Billy Crudup when he says I'm going to be a great writer, as I love my direct address monologue to the audience (the only time that happens at all in all three plays), and I most especially adore

seeing this scene change happen backstage in the second act. It's beautiful. A private moment I get to have standing on stage while the audience is on the other side of a scrim watching Ethan Hawke and Robert Stanton. In *Salvage*: I enjoy sitting on that bench with Brían O'Byrne and smoking, as much as I enjoy stretching out on that chaise in the scene with just Martha, Josh, Brían, Ethan and myself. I really like that scene of old friends dealing with histories. Then there are scenes I love sneaking a peak at. The voms at Lincoln Center are the best gift to letting you watch your fellow actors. When understudies have gone in, the voms are teeming with actors watching and sending support.
Favorite In-Theatre Gathering Place: Ethan Hawke and Josh Hamilton's dressing room is a favorite crash pad, but the intermission gathering at the stage door with the ladies to see the day or night is a particular favorite.
Favorite Off-Site Hangouts: We have toured the somewhat expensive and lonely Upper West Side hangouts. We started at O'Neals A LOT, with later nights at Peter's, but then Angus' top floor became the marathon ritual place. Café Des Artistes is sort of favorite for the boiled eggs, and our smoking cast members are allowed to smoke inside. I think Café Des Artistes is probably my favorite. It's cozy and quiet.
Favorite Snack Food: Roasted almonds, unsalted. Blueberries. And the occasional Twix.

Photos by Aubrey Reuben

1. (L-R): Amy Irving, playwright Tom Stoppard and Martha Plimpton at the opening night party of *The Coast of Utopia Part Three: Salvage* at the Firebird Restaurant.
2. (L-R): Billy Crudup, director Jack O'Brien and Josh Hamilton at the premiere of *Coast of Utopia Part One: Voyage.*
3. (L-R): Richard Easton, Ethan Hawke and Martha Plimpton at the Firebird.
4. (L-R): David Pittu and Patricia Conolly.

Mascot: One of the creepily life-like rehearsal babies has found its way all over backstage, most notably in the fridge.
Favorite Therapies: Bikram has been a godsend. Those Grether's pastilles are helpful, and then a saltwater nasal douche or two has helped with two of the four seasons we've passed through. Oh yes.
Memorable Ad-Lib: Richard Easton in an early preview: ". . . . . Well, what are we going to do now? . . . . ."
Record Number of Cell Phone Rings During a Performance: We've been BIZARRELY lucky. Maybe two rings was the worst. People have managed to turn their phones off for our Russian epic for the most part. The later in the run we got, however, the more ding dongs due to ding dongs we did have.
Memorable Stage Door Fan Encounters: The students who saved up the dough and invested in this event have been as enthusiastically, memorably appreciative as the cultivated theatregoers in their senior years. That has been fantastic. BUT . . . there was one of those index card autograph seekers who ask for a nice, clear "insert name here." I was rushing out at the end

The Coast of Utopia
Scrapbook

Photos by Aubrey Reuben

1. (L-R): Ethan Hawke, Brían F. O'Byrne, Josh Hamilton and Jason Butler Harner at the opening night party of *The Coast of Utopia Part Three: Salvage* at the Firebird Restaurant.
2. (L-R): Martha Plimpton and Vivien Kells at the premiere of *The Coast of Utopia Part Three: Salvage.*

2006-2007 AWARDS

Tony Awards
Best Play (Tom Stoppard)
Best Direction of a Play (Jack O'Brien)
Best Featured Actress in a Play (Jennifer Ehle)
Best Featured Actor in a Play (Billy Crudup)
Best Scenic Design of a Play (Bob Crowley and Scott Pask)
Best Costume Design of a Play (Catherine Zuber)
Best Lighting Design of a Play (Brian MacDevitt, Kenneth Posner and Natasha Katz)

New York Drama Critics' Circle Award
Best Play

Drama Desk Awards
Outstanding Play
Outstanding Director of a Play (Jack O'Brien)
Outstanding Featured Actress in a Play (Martha Plimpton)
Outstanding Set Design of a Play (Bob Crowley and Scott Pask)
Outstanding Costume Design (Catherine Zuber)
Outstanding Lighting Design (Brian MacDevitt, Kenneth Posner and Natasha Katz)
Outstanding Music for a Play (Mark Bennett)

Outer Critics Circle Awards
Outstanding New Broadway Play
Outstanding Director of a Play (Jack O'Brien)
Outstanding Featured Actress in a Play (Martha Plimpton)
Outstanding Set Design (Bob Crowley and Scott Pask)
Outstanding Costume Design (Catherine Zuber)
Outstanding Lighting Design (Brian MacDevitt, Kenneth Posner and Natasha Katz)

Drama League Award
Distinguished Production of a Play

of the show and index card guy kept yelling "Josh" at me. Appreciative though I was, I insisted four times I was not Josh, each time getting aggressively more reprimanded by the Sharpie-armed signature seeker. Finally the guy held up a picture of Josh and said, "Josh, I know it's you." I need to mention at this point that there are ten 8- by 4-foot portraits of the leads down by the stage door at Lincoln Center, and there is one of Josh and one of myself in that bunch. So, he held up the picture and said as if he'd reeeallly caught me . . . "Josssh." And I walked up right next to the picture and stared at him and said, "See?" And then walked away. I got to the street when the guy yelled, "Are you in the show?" at me. "Yes," I said. "Oh, can I have your autograph?" he asked back. "No," I said over my shoulder as I glided on home.

Fastest Costume Change: The girls have it bad with wigs and corsets and all sorts of 19th century accoutrements. Twenty seconds. I have 23 seconds to run from the stage, exiting stage right, down three flights of stairs, through the scene shop, up a flight of stairs and into the trap room to come up through the floor for a scene change. That's always a little fun.

Busiest Day at the Box Office: We sold a record amount of tickets for Lincoln Center when the box office initially opened—much to the delight and surprise of many. Stoppard and his Russian thinkers are a far cry from average Broadway fare.

Who Wore the Heaviest/Hottest Costume: That would probably have to be Adam Dannheisser as The Ginger Cat who has operawear with cape, a cat head with top hat, and a big bushy tail that would make Mae West give a double "Onh."

Who Wore the Least: Too easy. Jennifer Ehle undresses in *Shipwreck* when we recreate the Manet painting. She's gorgeous with a beautiful body, none of this sticks-and-bones nonsense. Beautiful, voluptuous, heavenly Jennifer—dressed and undressed.

Catchphrases Only the Company Would Recognize: Pasudee.

Memorable Directorial Note: Jack had a million of them, but "Show me what you got" was one of his more memorable dares to being as versatile and brilliant as possible.

Company In-Jokes: All words Russian mean new things American. Who knew Hegel and Kant could become punchlines? (Well, I'm sure Kant has been a punchline.)

Understudy Anecdote: Scott Parkinson. Scott Parkinson. Scott Parkinson.

Embarrassing Moments: This group doesn't embarrass easily.

Ghostly Encounters Backstage: I think one of the old toilets is haunting my bathroom because when I don't use my new oscillating pulsating bidet-ed toilet, the sink in dressing room 9 clogs up.

Coolest Thing About Being in This Show: Forty-five stunning actors for nine months running in rep on Broadway with words like these . . . it simply doesn't get better than this. (The marathon curtain call is a world of it's own making.)

Also: We have had an incredible go of it. We were blessed with a dynamic, solid-hearted company that was in constant support of each other on and off stage. And the closing weekend was no exception in its fullness. We just received the Utopia yearbooks we made which are STUNNING with old-world posed portraits by Benjamin Endsley Klein and hilarious backstage and nights-out candids. Our softball team is currently undefeated. We have had a cabaret night with a full band and a hootenanny with guitars and beer. We have spanned four seasons in New York City together. We have rehearsed three huge plays and teched three plays in remarkably short time. We have had one baby born (Horatio Hamilton) and another due any minute ("Showbiz" Sheffer Stevens). We have been in the presence of an actor at his most vulnerable but most valiant. Essentially, it is simple: we have been given a gorgeous gift in our careers, but most notably the pleasure of each other's company, vast life experience, and estimable talent in one hell of an elegant theatre. And we're still laughing.

The Color Purple

First Preview: November 1, 2005. Opened: December 1, 2005.
Still running as of May 31, 2007.

PLAYBILL

BROADWAY THEATRE
1681 Broadway
A Shubert Organization Theatre
Gerald Schoenfeld, *Chairman* **Philip J. Smith**, *President*
Robert E. Wankel, *Executive Vice President*

OPRAH WINFREY
SCOTT SANDERS ROY FURMAN QUINCY JONES
CREATIVE BATTERY ANNA FANTACI & CHERYL LACHOWICZ INDEPENDENT PRESENTERS NETWORK
DAVID LOWY STEPHANIE P. McCLELLAND GARY WINNICK JAN KALLISH
NEDERLANDER PRESENTATIONS, INC. BOB & HARVEY WEINSTEIN
ANDREW ASNES & ADAM ZOTOVICH TODD JOHNSON
Present

The Color Purple

BASED UPON THE NOVEL WRITTEN BY ALICE WALKER
AND THE WARNER BROS./AMBLIN ENTERTAINMENT MOTION PICTURE

Book by
MARSHA NORMAN

Music and Lyrics by
BRENDA RUSSELL ALLEE WILLIS STEPHEN BRAY

Starring
JEANNETTE I. BAYARDELLE
ELISABETH WITHERS-MENDES FELICIA P. FIELDS
BRANDON VICTOR DIXON DARLESIA CEARCY KRISHA MARCANO
and ALTON FITZGERALD WHITE

with KIMBERLY ANN HARRIS MAIA NKENGE WILSON VIRGINIA ANN WOODRUFF
LARRY MARSHALL CAROL DENNIS
JAMES BROWN III ERIC L. CHRISTIAN LaTRISA A. COLEMAN BOBBY DAYE DOUG ESKEW LaVON FISHER-WILSON
BAHIYAH SAYYED GAINES ZIPPORAH G. GATLING MONTEGO GLOVER CHARLES GRAY GAVIN GREGORY
STEPHANIE GUILAND-BROWN JAMES HARKNESS FRANCESCA HARPER CHANTYLLA JOHNSON KENYA UNIQUE MASSEY
CORINNE McFARLANE JC MONTGOMERY ANGELA ROBINSON KEMBA SHANNON LEVENSKY SMITH
RICKY SMITH JAMAL STORY

Scenic Design JOHN LEE BEATTY
Costume Design PAUL TAZEWELL
Lighting Design BRIAN MacDEVITT
Sound Design JON WESTON
Casting TELSEY + COMPANY
Hair Design CHARLES G. LaPOINTE
Production Managers ARTHUR SICCARDI, PATRICK SULLIVAN
Production Stage Manager KRISTEN HARRIS
Press Agent CAROL FINEMAN/BARLOW•HARTMAN
Marketing APEL, INC.
General Management NLA/AMY JACOBS
Music Director LINDA TWINE
Dance Music Arrangements DARYL WATERS
Additional Arrangements JOSEPH JOUBERT
Music Coordinator SEYMOUR RED PRESS
Orchestrations JONATHAN TUNICK
Music Supervisor & Incidental Music Arrangements KEVIN STITES

Choreographed by
DONALD BYRD

Directed by
GARY GRIFFIN

World Premiere Produced by Alliance Theatre, Atlanta, GA
Susan V. Booth, Artistic Director Thomas Pechar, Managing Director

LIVE BROADWAY

11/6/06

Elisabeth Withers-Mendes, Fantasia (center) and company sing "Push Da Button."

Photo by Paul Kolnik

CAST

(in order of appearance)

Young Nettie, Mister Daughter ...... CHANTYLLA JOHNSON
Young Celie, Mister Daughter, Young Olivia, Henrietta ...... ZIPPORAH G. GATLING
Church Soloist ...... CAROL DENNIS
Church Lady (Doris) ...... KIMBERLY ANN HARRIS
Church Lady (Darlene) ...... VIRGINIA ANN WOODRUFF
Church Lady (Jarene), Daisy ...... MAIA NKENGE WILSON
Preacher, Prison Guard ...... DOUG ESKEW
Pa ...... JC MONTGOMERY
Nettie ...... DARLESIA CEARCY
Celie ...... JEANNETTE I. BAYARDELLE
Mister ...... ALTON FITZGERALD WHITE
Young Harpo, Young Adam ...... RICKY SMITH
Harpo ...... BRANDON VICTOR DIXON
Sofia ...... FELICIA P. FIELDS
Squeak ...... KRISHA MARCANO
Shug Avery ...... ELISABETH WITHERS-MENDES
Ol' Mister ...... LARRY MARSHALL
Buster, Chief ...... GAVIN GREGORY
Grady ...... JC MONTGOMERY
Bobby ...... JAMES BROWN III
Older Olivia ...... BAHIYAH SAYYED GAINES
Older Adam ...... LEVENSKY SMITH

Continued on next page

The Color Purple

MUSICAL NUMBERS

ACT ONE

Overture	Orchestra
Huckleberry Pie	Young Celie and Nettie
Mysterious Ways	Church Soloist, Church Ladies and Company
Somebody Gonna Love You	Celie
Our Prayer	Nettie, Celie, Mister
Big Dog	Mister and Field Hands
Hell No!	Sofia and Sisters
Brown Betty	Harpo and Men, Squeak
Shug Avery Comin' to Town	Mister, Celie and Company
Too Beautiful for Words	Shug Avery
Push Da Button	Shug Avery and Company
Uh Oh!	Church Ladies, Sofia, Squeak
What About Love?	Celie and Shug Avery

ACT TWO

African Homeland	Nettie, Celie, Olivia and Adam, Villagers
The Color Purple	Shug Avery
Celie's Curse	Mister
Miss Celie's Pants	Celie, Shug Avery, Sofia and Women
Any Little Thing	Harpo and Sofia
I'm Here	Celie
The Color Purple (Reprise)	Celie, Nettie and Company

Brandon Victor Dixon and Felicia P. Fields.

Photo by Paul Kolnik

ORCHESTRA

Conductor:
LINDA TWINE
Associate Conductor:
JOSEPH JOUBERT

Trumpets:
BARRY DANIELIAN, BRIAN O'FLAHERTY, KAMAU ADILIFU
Trombones:
LARRY FARRELL, JASON JACKSON
Woodwinds:
LES SCOTT, LAWRENCE FELDMAN, JAY BRANDFORD
Keyboards:
JOSEPH JOUBERT, SHELTON BECTON
Drums/Percussion:
BUDDY WILLIAMS, DAMIEN BASSMAN

Guitars/Harmonica:
STEVE BARGONETTI
Bass:
BENJAMIN FRANKLIN BROWN
Violins:
PAUL WOODIEL, MINEKO YAJIMA
Viola:
DAVID CRESWELL
Cello:
CLAY RUEDE
Music Coordinator:
SEYMOUR RED PRESS
Copyists:
EMILY GRISHMAN MUSIC PREPARATION
KATHARINE EDMONDS/EMILY GRISHMAN
Synthesizer Programmer:
BRUCE SAMUELS

Cast Continued

ENSEMBLE

JAMES BROWN III, LaTRISA A. COLEMAN, CAROL DENNIS, DOUG ESKEW, BAHIYAH SAYYED GAINES, ZIPPORAH G. GATLING, CHARLES GRAY, GAVIN GREGORY, JAMES HARKNESS, FRANCESCA HARPER, KIMBERLY ANN HARRIS, CHANTYLLA JOHNSON, KENYA UNIQUE MASSEY, JC MONTGOMERY, ANGELA ROBINSON, LEVENSKY SMITH, JAMAL STORY, MAIA NKENGE WILSON, VIRGINIA ANN WOODRUFF

SWINGS

ERIC L. CHRISTIAN, BOBBY DAYE, LaVON FISHER-WILSON, STEPHANIE GUILAND-BROWN, CORINNE McFARLANE, KEMBA SHANNON

UNDERSTUDIES

For Celie:
DARLESIA CEARCY, MONTEGO GLOVER
For Shug Avery:
FRANCESCA HARPER, ANGELA ROBINSON
For Sofia:
CAROL DENNIS, KIMBERLY ANN HARRIS
For Nettie:
LaTRISA A. COLEMAN, BAHIYAH SAYYED GAINES, MONTEGO GLOVER
For Mister:
CHARLES GRAY, JC MONTGOMERY
For Harpo:
JAMES BROWN III, GAVIN GREGORY
For Squeak:
LaTRISA A. COLEMAN, FRANCESCA HARPER
For Ol' Mister:
DOUG ESKEW, CHARLES GRAY
For Young Harpo, Young Adam:
CORINNE McFARLANE

Dance Captain:
STEPHANIE GUILAND-BROWN
Assistant Dance Captain:
JAMAL STORY

SETTING

The story takes place in Georgia between 1909 and 1949.

The Color Purple

Jeannette I. Bayardelle
Celie

Felicia P. Fields
Sofia

Alton Fitzgerald White
Mister

Elisabeth Withers-Mendes
Shug Avery

Brandon Victor Dixon
Harpo

Darlesia Cearcy
Nettie

Krisha Marcano
Squeak

Kimberly Ann Harris
Church Lady [Doris]/ Ensemble

Maia Nkenge Wilson
Church Lady [Jarene]/Daisy/ Ensemble

Virginia Ann Woodruff
Church Lady [Darlene]/Ensemble

Larry Marshall
Ol' Mister

Carol Dennis
Church Soloist/ Ensemble

James Brown III
Bobby/Ensemble

Eric L. Christian
Swing

LaTrisa A. Coleman
Ensemble

Bobby Daye
Swing

Doug Eskew
Preacher/ Prison Guard/ Ensemble

LaVon Fisher-Wilson
Swing

Bahiyah Sayyed Gaines
Older Olivia/ Ensemble

Zipporah G. Gatling
Mister Daughter/ Young Olivia/ Henrietta/Ensemble

Montego Glover
u/s Celie, Nettie

Charles Gray
Ensemble

Gavin Gregory
Buster/Chief/ Ensemble

Stephanie Guiland-Brown
Swing/ Dance Captain

James Harkness
Ensemble

Francesca Harper
Ensemble

Chantylla Johnson
Young Nettie/ Mister Daughter/ Ensemble

Kenya Unique Massey
Ensemble

Corinne McFarlane
Swing

JC Montgomery
Pa/Grady/Ensemble

Angela Robinson
Ensemble

Kemba Shannon
Swing

Levensky Smith
Older Adam/ Ensemble

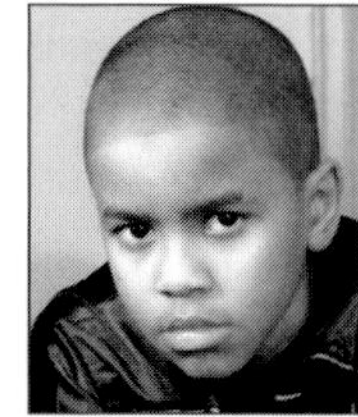
Ricky Smith
Young Harpo/ Young Adam

Jamal Story
Ensemble/ Assistant Dance Captain

The Color Purple

Alice Walker
Original Author

Marsha Norman
Bookwriter

Brenda Russell, Stephen Bray, Allee Willis
Composer/Lyricist

Gary Griffin
Director

Donald Byrd
Choreographer

John Lee Beatty
Set Design

Paul Tazewell
Costume Designer

Brian MacDevitt
Lighting Design

Bernard Telsey, Telsey + Company
Casting

Jonathan Tunick
Orchestrations

Linda Twine
Music Director

Angelina Avallone
Make-up Design

Joseph Joubert
Additional Arrangements

Seymour Red Press
Music Coordinator

Arthur Siccardi
Production Management

Oprah Winfrey
Producer

Scott Sanders, Creative Battery
Lead Producer

Roy Furman
Producer

Quincy Jones
Producer

Stephanie P. McClelland
Producer

James L. Nederlander, Nederlander Presentations, Inc.
Producer

Bob Weinstein
Producer

Harvey Weinstein
Producer

Andrew Asnes
Producer

Adam Zotovich
Producer

Todd Johnson
Producer

Susan V. Booth, Alliance Theatre
Original Production

Sima Bissette
Young Celie, Mister Daughter, Young Olivia, Henrietta, Ensemble

Anika Ellis
Ensemble

Grasan Kingsberry
Older Adam, Ensemble

LaChanze
Celie

Kingsley Leggs
Mister

Kenita R. Miller
Understudy for Celie and Nettie

The Color Purple

Lou Myers
Ol' Mister

Daniel J. Watts
Swing

Shelby Braxton-Brooks
Ensemble

Deidra H. Brooks
Swing

Leilani N. Bryant
Church Lady (Jarene), Daisy

Ruby E. Crawford
Ensemble

Charlotte Crossley
Church Lady (Doris), Ensemble

Fantasia
Celie

Rosena M. Hill
Church Lady (Darlene)

Ashley Reneé Jordan
Swing

Maria McReynolds
Older Olivia, Ensemble

Kenita R. Miller
Celie

Jenny Mollet
Young Celie, Mister Daughter, Young Olivia, Henrietta, Ensemble, Swing

Chaz Lamar Shepherd
Harpo

Teresa Stanley
Swing

Daniel J. Watts
Bobby, Ensemble, Swing

NaTasha Yvette Williams
Sofia

Marion Willis III
Older Adam, Ensemble, Swing

Yolanda Wyns
Church Lady (Doris), Ensemble, Swing

2006-2007 AWARD

THEATRE WORLD AWARD
Outstanding Broadway Debut
(Fantasia Barrino)

Photo by Paul Kolnik

Fantasia in costume as Celie.

The Color Purple

Photos by David Gewirtzman

USHERS AND FRONT OF HOUSE
Front Row (L-R): Michael S.R. Harris, Lori Bokun.

Second Row (L-R): Mattie Robinson, May Park, Alfredo Rosario, Freddy Matos, John Hall, Nathaniel Wright, Santiago Ulises, Selina Nelson.

Third Row (L-R): William Phelan, Jorge Colon, Linda Engh.

Back Row (L-R): Tony Massey, Amy Wolk and Ji Ming.

BOX OFFICE
(L-R): Bob Belkin, Debbie Giarratano

DOORMAN
Fernando Sepulveda

COMPANY MANAGEMENT
(L-R): Tony Magner, Doug Gaeta

The Color Purple

STAGE CREW
Front Row (L-R): Neveen Mahmoud, Lisa Dawn Cave, Kenneth McAliece, Sonya Suzuki.

Second Row (L-R): Sabrena Armstrong, Shazia Saleem, Maureen George, Dora Bonilla, Dora Suarez, Betty Gillispie, Jay Woods, Kelly Stillwell, Thea Yatras.

Back Row (L-R): Kristen Harris, Timothy Harvey, Mia Neal, Peter Becker, Bob Beimers, David Grevengoed, Carin Ford, Valerie Frith, Charles Rasmussen, Renee Brunson, Declan McNeil and Richard DalCortivo.

STAGE MANAGEMENT
(L-R): Neveen Mahmoud, Kristen Harris, Lisa Dawn Cave, Kelly Stillwell.

Photos by David Gewirtzman

ORCHESTRA
First Row (L-R, kneeling): Mineko Yajima, Steve Bargonetti, Ben Brown.

Second Row (L-R): Buddy Williams, Jon Berger, Stu Satalof, Linda Twine (conductor), Shelton Becton.

Third Row (L-R): Clay Ruede, Scott Shachter, Kenny Rampton, Larry Farrell and Jason Webb.

The Color Purple

STAFF FOR *THE COLOR PURPLE*

GENERAL MANAGER
NINA LANNAN ASSOCIATES
Amy Jacobs

COMPANY MANAGER
KIMBERLY KELLEY
Assistant Company Manager ....Doug Gaeta

GENERAL PRESS REPRESENTATIVE
BARLOW•HARTMAN
Michael Hartman John Barlow
Carol Fineman Leslie Baden

CASTING
Telsey + Company, C.S.A.:
Bernie Telsey, Will Cantler, David Vaccari,
Bethany Knox, Craig Burns,
Tiffany Little Canfield, Stephanie Yankwitt,
Carrie Rosson, Justin Huff, Joe Langworth

Associate Director ....Nona Lloyd
Assistant to the Choreographer ......Ruthlyn Salomons

PRODUCTION
STAGE MANAGER ....KRISTEN HARRIS
Stage Manager ....Glynn David Turner
Assistant Stage Manager ....Neveen Mahmoud
Assistant Stage Manager ....Kelly Stillwell
Associate Scenic Designer ....Eric L. Renschler
Assistant Scenic Designer ....Yoshi Tanokura
Associate Costume Designer ....Michael F. McAleer
Assistant Costume Designers ....Dennis E. Ballard, Christine Field
Assistant to the Costume Designer .....Jacob A. Climer
Associate Lighting Designers ....Mark T. Simpson, Jennifer M. Schriever
Assistant Lighting Designer ....Benjamin Travis
Associate Sound Designer ....Jason Strangfeld
Automated Lighting Programmer ....David Arch
Fight Director ....J. Steven White
Fight Captain ....James Brown III
Dialect Coach ....Deborah Hecht

Make-up Design ....Angelina Avallone

Production Carpenter ....Patrick Sullivan
Head Carpenter/Automation ......Charles A. Heulitt III
Assistant Carpenter/Flyman ....Brian Hutchinson
Assistant Carpenter ....Ryan Ensser
Production Electrician ....James J. Fedigan
Head Electrician ....Michael E. Cornell
Assistant Electrician ....Gary Marlin
Production Sound ....Carin Ford
Production Properties ....Michael Pilipski
Head Properties ....Rob Presley
Wardrobe Supervisor ....Deborah A. Cheretun
Assistant Wardrobe Supervisor ....James Hall
Star Dresser ....Betty A. Gillispie
Dressers ....Dora Bonilla, Renee Brunson, Fred Castner, Christina Dailey, Suzanne Delahunt, Tracey Diebold, Valerie Frith, Maureen George, Allison Goodsell, David Grevengoed, Lizz Hirons, James Hodun, Jay Woods
Hair Supervisor ....Mia Neal
Assistant Hair Supervisors ....Joy Marcelle, Timothy Harvey
Hair Dresser ....Joshua First
Rehearsal Musicians ....Damien A. Bassman, Shelton Becton, Joseph Joubert, Daryl Waters, Buddy Williams
Additional Music Copyists ....Singing Potato/Eidco
Production Assistants ....Kelly Stillwell, Angelique Villegas
Child Wrangler ....Bridget Walders
Children's Tutoring ....On Location Education
Teachers ....Abigail Dyer, Maryanne Keller
Advertising ....SpotCo/Drew Hodges, Jim Edwards, Tom Greenwald, Tom McCann, Lauren Hunter
Marketing, Sponsorship & Outreach ....Apel, Inc./ David Sass, Harry Spero, Cherine Anderson, Mathew Farkash, Jessica Stock
Website Design & Online Marketing Strategy ....Situation Marketing LLC/ Damian Bazadona, Ian Bennett, Sara Fitzpatrick
Legal Counsel ....M. Graham Coleman, Esq. and Robert J. Driscoll, Esq./ Davis Wright Tremaine LLP
Comptroller ....Sarah Galbraith
Accounting ....Fried & Kowgios CPA's LLP/ Robert Fried, CPA
General Management Associate ....Katherine McNamee
Press Associates ....Dennis Crowley, Jon Dimond, Rick Miramontez, Gerilyn Shur, Andrew Snyder, Wayne Wolfe
Press Office Manager ....Bethany Larsen
Production Photographers ....Joan Marcus, Paul Kolnik
Insurance ....Albert G. Ruben Company Inc./ Claudia Kaufman
Banking ....City National Bank/Gregg Santos
Payroll ....Castellana Services, Inc.
Study Guide ....Camp Broadway
Merchandising ....Dewynters/James Decker
Travel Agent ....Tzell Travel/ The "A" Team, Andi Henig
Assistant to Ms. Norman ....Brian Tucker
Assistant to Mr. Bray, Ms. Russell & Ms. Willis ....Richard Todd Loyd
Assistant to Mr. Sanders ....Scott Pyne
Assistant to Mr. Furman ....Eileen Williams
Assistant to Mr. MacDevitt ....Jessica Burgess
Music Dept. Assistant ....Nathan Kelly
SSDC Directing Intern ....Malinda Allen
Opening Night Coordination ....Tobak Lawrence Company/ Michael P Lawrence

ALLIANCE THEATRE STAFF
Artistic Director ....Susan V. Booth
Managing Director ....Thomas Pechar
Associate Artistic Director ....Kent Gash
General Manager ....Max Leventhal
Director of Marketing ....Virginia Vann
Director of Finance ....Sallie Lawrence
Director of Development ....Andrea Dillenburg
Production Manager ....Rixon Hammond

www.colorpurple.com

CREDITS AND ACKNOWLEDGEMENTS
Scenery construction and automation equipment provided by Hudson Scenic Studio Inc. Costumes executed by Tricorne, Inc.; Barbara Matera Ltd.; Donna Langman Costumes; John Kristiansen New York. Custom millinery by Lynne Mackey Studio. African headdresses by Arnold S. Levine and Marie Schneggenburger. Custom shirts by the Shirt Store and DL Cerney. Custom eyewear by J. Kirby Harris. Custom Knitting by C.C. Wei. Custom shoes by T.O. Dey; JC Theatrical; Capezio. Fabric painting and distressing by Hochi Asiatico. Lighting equipment by PRG Lighting. Musical instruments provided by Yamaha Drums, Zildjian Cymbals Company, Aquarian Company. Sound equipment by PRG Audio. Marty at Latin Percussion. Props provided by Spoon Group; Cigar Box Studios Inc.; Paragon; Centerline Studios; Ellen Pilipski; The Alliance Theatre. Rehearsed at the New 42nd Street Studios and 37 Arts. Natural herb cough drops supplied by Ricola USA Inc. Makeup provided by M*A*C Cosmetics. Hair products provided by Motions Salon Products. Key art illustration by Peter Sylvada. Emergen-C super energy booster provided by Alacer Corp.

Theatre Manager ....Michael S. R. Harris

The Color Purple
SCRAPBOOK

Photo by Aubrey Reuben

(L-R): Composers Brenda Russell and Allee Willis with actress Jeannette Bayardelle (Celie) and LaChanze (the original Celie) with a celebratory cake at the first anniversary party, at Remi.

Correspondent: Krisha Marcano, "Squeak"

Anniversary Party and Gift: On our first anniversary the producers and the creative team threw us a big party with a cake. We all got these beautiful plush *Color Purple* robes.

Most Exciting Celebrity Visitors and What They've Said: We've had Mary J. Blige, Fantasia Barrino, Blair Underwood, Ralph Fiennes and lots more. They usually address the whole group and they're usually in tears. Among the phrases a lot of people use is that it was very moving, and that we're blessed to be doing a show that isn't just entertaining, but is changing people's lives every day.

Actor Who Performed the Most Roles in This Show: JC Montgomery plays Pa at the top of the show, one of Mister's men in the ensemble, Grady in the second act and a bartender in the juke joint.

Special Backstage Rituals: We have a prayer circle stage right every night. When La Chanze was in the show, we also used to have dancing after the prayer. At intermission while the curtain is down, the kids come on the stage and practice their tumbling.

Favorite Moments During Each Performance: I look forward to my first entrance, it's always a surprise. I could be very tired, but when I make my entrance as Squeak, I instantly come alive. It's just the best feeling. I also love the song "Hell No!" It's not my number but I feel the pain of every woman who has been there. "I may be poor, I may be black, I may be ugly, but I'm here!" Those are the moments in the show that have never lost their feeling.

"Gypsy of the Year" Sketch: "When, Where, Why Will I Go?" by "All things purple and divine." Winner: Best sketch and top fundraiser.

"Carols for a Cure" Carols: Medley of "Bring a Torch, Jeanette Isabella," "Joy to the World" and "Go Tell It on the Mountain."

"Easter Bonnet" Sketch: "Pretty Ladies Who Beautifully Lunch," choreographed by James Brown III.

Favorite In-Theatre Gathering Places: Everyone used to gather to meet and eat in Felicia Fields' dressing room before she left. Now, we all meet on the fourth floor where there's a very small common area. But our favorite place to go between shows is the lower lobby where there is a piano. We have vocal rehearsals there, and every time we have a potluck or a Christmas party, we definitely do it in the lower lobby. It's the most comfortable place.

Favorite Off-Site Hangouts: Two places where we see a majority of the cast: Every Tuesday we go to Café Wha? in the Village and every Thursday it's The Sugar Bar. Most people will get up and sing pop, gospel, r&b, but definitely nothing from the show. It's our chance to sing other stuff.

Favorite Snack Foods: We love popcorn and mini chocolates, like mini Snickers. We keep a bag of that randomly in places. Icebreakers mints in every conceivable flavor and combination. Altoids in all the combinations you can imagine. But our favorite food of all was gooey butter cake made by Kim Harris, who has now left the show. Mother of God, it was the devil incarnate! We all lament the loss of the *Color Purple* signature dessert.

Favorite Therapies: Emergen-C is very popular as are ginger tea, Arnica homeopathic gel and massage.

Memorable Stage Door Fan Encounters: Across the board, people at the stage door are extremely moved. Sometimes they will actually break down in the arms of the actors. I was witness to somebody breaking down in the arms of Sophia, and telling her, "It's time for *me* to say 'Hell no!'"

Memorable Directorial Advice: "Try not to act; try to *tell the story*. You don't have to do anything else but be true to what's in the story. Trust the story."

Ghostly Encounters Backstage: I've heard that this theatre has a lot of ghosts, mainly from some of the people who did *The Wiz* here. The actors in *Color Purple* haven't had any encounters like that, but the musicians say they feel a presence in the pit, like something is standing next to them.

Also: We started a tradition that I hope will be picked up by every theatre: Dresser Appreciation Day. We throw a party for the dressers and they get to sit down while the actors serve them.

Coolest Thing About Being in This Show: I have never seen reactions from an audience like this, and I don't know that I ever will again. When the lights come up at the end and everyone is standing, it feels like we're all equal and all taking the same journey. That's the way it should be all the time, but this is the first time it's really happened to me. We're still brought to tears, even now, at the audience reaction. You can't bottle that, you can't sell it. It's really what makes me come to work every day.

Company

First Preview: October 30, 2006. Opened: November 29, 2006.
Still running as of May 31, 2007

PLAYBILL

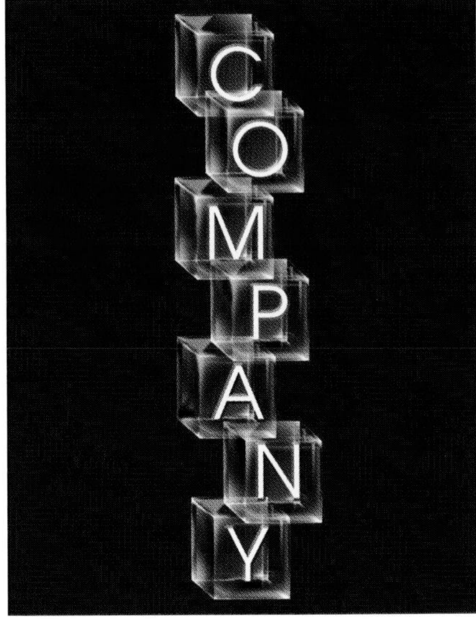

ETHEL BARRYMORE THEATRE
243 West 47th Street
A Shubert Organization Theatre
Gerald Schoenfeld, *Chairman* **Philip J. Smith,** *President*

Robert E. Wankel, *Executive Vice President*

Marc Routh Richard Frankel Tom Viertel Steven Baruch
Ambassador Theatre Group Tulchin/Bartner Productions
Darren Bagert and Cincinnati Playhouse in the Park

present

Raúl Esparza

in

COMPANY
A MUSICAL COMEDY

Music and Lyrics by
Stephen Sondheim

Book by
George Furth

with
Keith Buterbaugh Matt Castle Robert Cunningham Angel Desai
Kelly Jeanne Grant Kristin Huffman Amy Justman Heather Laws
Jane Pfitsch Leenya Rideout Fred Rose Bruce Sabath Elizabeth Stanley
Renée Bang Allen Brandon Ellis David Garry Jason Ostrowski Jessica Wright Katrina Yaukey

and
Barbara Walsh

Set Design
David Gallo

Costume Design
Ann Hould-Ward

Lighting Design
Thomas C. Hase

Sound Design
Andrew Keister

Hair & Wig Design
David Lawrence

Make-Up Design
Angelina Avallone

Casting
Telsey + Company

Associate Director
Adam John Hunter

Production Stage Manager
Gary Mickelson

Resident Music Supervisor
Lynne Shankel

General Manager
Richard Frankel Productions, Inc.
Jo Porter

Press Representative
Barlow·Hartman

Production Management
Juniper Street Productions, Inc.

Musical Supervision & Orchestrations by
Mary-Mitchell Campbell

Direction and Musical Staging by
John Doyle

Proudly Sponsored by Fidelity Investments
The Producers wish to express their appreciation to the Theatre Development Fund for its support of this production.
This production of Company was originally produced by Cincinnati Playhouse in the Park
Edward Stern, Producing Artistic Director Buzz Ward, Executive Director

11/29/06

CAST

Robert .... RAÚL ESPARZA
Percussion
Joanne .... BARBARA WALSH
Orchestra Bells, Percussion
Harry .... KEITH BUTERBAUGH
Trumpet, Trombone
Peter .... MATT CASTLE
Piano/Keyboards, Double Bass
Paul .... ROBERT CUNNINGHAM
Trumpet, Drums
Marta .... ANGEL DESAI
Keyboard, Violin, Alto Sax
Kathy .... KELLY JEANNE GRANT
Flute, Alto Sax
Sarah .... KRISTIN HUFFMAN
Flute, Alto Sax, Piccolo
Susan .... AMY JUSTMAN
Piano/Keyboards, Orchestra Bells
Amy .... HEATHER LAWS
French Horn, Trumpet, Flute
Jenny .... LEENYA RIDEOUT
Violin, Guitar, Double Bass
David .... FRED ROSE
Cello, Alto Sax, Tenor Sax
Larry .... BRUCE SABATH
Clarinet, Drums
April .... ELIZABETH STANLEY
Oboe, Tuba, Alto Sax

Continued on next page

Raúl Esparza (center) with the cast.

Photo by Paul Kolnik

Company

MUSICAL NUMBERS

ACT ONE

"Company"	Robert and Company
"The Little Things You Do Together"	Joanne and Company
"Sorry-Grateful"	Harry, David, Larry
"You Could Drive a Person Crazy"	April, Kathy, Marta
"Have I Got a Girl for You"	Larry, Peter, Paul, David, Harry
"Someone Is Waiting"	Robert
"Another Hundred People"	Marta
"Getting Married Today"	Amy, Paul, Susan and Company
"Marry Me a Little"	Robert

ACT TWO

"Side by Side by Side"	Robert and Company
"What Would We Do Without You?"	Robert and Company
"Poor Baby"	Sarah, Jenny, Susan, Amy, Joanne
"Barcelona"	Robert, April
"The Ladies Who Lunch"	Joanne
"Being Alive"	Robert

Cast Continued

STANDBYS

For Robert:
FRED ROSE

For Sarah, Joanne:
RENÉE BANG ALLEN
Flute, Alto Sax, Tenor Sax, Orchestra Bells, Percussion

For David, Paul:
BRANDON ELLIS
Cello, Drums, Double Bass, Guitar

For Harry, Larry, Paul:
DAVID GARRY
Trumpet, Trombone, Clarinet, Drums, Alto Sax, Tenor Sax

For Peter:
JASON OSTROWSKI
Piano/Keyboards, Double Bass

For Amy, Jenny, Susan:
JESSICA WRIGHT
Flute, Violin

For Marta, Kathy, April:
KATRINA YAUKEY –
Alto Sax, Flute, Oboe, Tuba, Trumpet

Dance Captain:
NEWTON COLE

(L-R): Elizabeth Stanley, Kelly Jeanne Grant and Angel Desai

Photo by Paul Kolnik

Raúl Esparza
Robert

Barbara Walsh
Joanne

Keith Buterbaugh
Harry

Matt Castle
Peter

Robert Cunningham
Paul

Angel Desai
Marta

Kelly Jeanne Grant
Kathy

Kristin Huffman
Sarah

Amy Justman
Susan

Heather Laws
Amy

Company

Jane Pfitsch
Amy

Leenya Rideout
Jenny

Fred Rose
David

Bruce Sabath
Larry

Elizabeth Stanley
April

Renée Bang Allen
u/s Joanne, Sarah

Brandon J. Ellis
u/s Paul, David

David Garry
u/s Larry, Harry, Paul

Jason Ostrowski
u/s Peter

Jessica Wright
u/s Amy, Jenny, Susan

Katrina Yaukey
u/s April, Kathy, Marta

Stephen Sondheim
Music & Lyrics

George Furth
Book

John Doyle
Director

Mary-Mitchell Campbell
Music Supervision and Orchestration

David Gallo
Scenic Design

Ann Hould-Ward
Costume Design

Angelina Avallone
Makeup Design

Bernard Telsey, Telsey + Company
Casting

Guy Kwan, John Paull, Hillary Blanken, Kevin Broomell, Ana Rose Greene, Juniper Street Productions
Production Manager

Marc Routh
Producer

Richard Frankel
Producer

Tom Viertel
Producer

Steven Baruch
Producer

Darren Bagert
Producer

Raúl Esparza as Robert.

Photo by Paul Kolnik

Company

STAGE CREW
(L-R): Al C. Galvez (Carpenter), Philip W. Feller (House Prop Head), Dawn Makay (Head Properties Master), Jim Bay (Sound), Penny Davis (Wardrobe Supervisor), Chip White (Mr. Esparza's Dresser), Lolly Totero (Wardrobe), Tom Lawrey (Electrician), Vanessa Anderson (Hair Supervisor), Mike Wojchik (Sound), Jason Blair (Wardrobe) and Dan Landon (House Manager).

DOORMAN
Peter Condos

STAGE MANAGEMENT
Front: Claudia Lynch (Assistant Stage Manager). Back (L-R): Newton Cole (Assistant Stage Manager) and Gary Mickelson (Production Stage Manager).

Photos by Robert Viagas

FRONT OF HOUSE STAFF
(L-R): Doris Buber (Head Usher), Cindy Acevedo (Usher), Angeline Montauban (Usher), Monica Orellana (Porter), A. John Dancy (Usher), Fran Barbareth, John Barbaretti (Ticket Taker), Aileen Kilburn (Usher), Michael Reilly (Usher), Dan Landon (Theatre Manager) and Peter Cooke (Concessions).

Company

STAFF FOR *COMPANY*

GENERAL MANAGEMENT
RICHARD FRANKEL PRODUCTIONS
Richard Frankel Marc Routh Jo Porter
Laura Green Rod Kaats Joe Watson

COMPANY MANAGEMENT
Company Manager .... Sammy Ledbetter
Associate Company Manager .... Jason Pelusio

GENERAL PRESS REPRESENTATIVE
BARLOW•HARTMAN
John Barlow Michael Hartman
Leslie Baden

CASTING
TELSEY + COMPANY, CSA
Bernie Telsey Will Cantler David Vaccari
Bethany Knox Craig Burns
Tiffany Little Canfield Rachel Hoffman
Stephanie Yankwitt Carrie Rosson
Justin Huff Joe Langworth Bess Fifer

Production Stage Manager .... **Gary Mickelson**
Stage Manager .... Newton Cole
Assistant Stage Manager .... Claudia Lynch
Production Manager .... Hillary Blanken
Production Management
Associates .... Guy Kwan, Kevin Broomell, Ana Rose Greene, Elena Soderblom
Action Arrangement .... Drew Fracher
Associate Scenic Designer .... Mary Hamrick
Assistant Scenic Designer .... Josh Zangen
Scenic Model Builder .... Frank McCullough
Associate Costume Designer .... Sidney Shannon
Associate Lighting Designer .... Paul Miller
Assistant Lighting Designer .... Bradley Clements
Assistant Sound Designer .... Michael Bogden
Production Carpenter .... Fred Gallo
Advance Carpenter .... Jack Anderson
Production Electrician .... Jonathan Lawson
Lighting Board Operator .... Mike Pegler
Sound Engineer .... Michael Wojchik
Production Property Master .... Joseph P. Harris, Jr.
Head Property Master .... Dawn Makay
Wardrobe Supervisor .... Penny Davis
Mr. Esparza's Dresser .... Raymond Panelli
Dressers .... Kevin O'Brien, Laura Totero
Hair & Wig Supervisor .... Vanessa Anderson
Assistant to Mr. Sondheim .... Steven Clar
Assistant to Mr. Baruch .... Sonja Soper
Assistant to Mr. Viertel .... Tania Senewiratne
Creative Director for Mr. Bagert .... Russell Owen
Operations Manager for Mr. Bagert .... Rob Fortier
Company Management Assistant .... Tanase Popa
Production Assistants .... Lauren Roth, Heather Weiss, Rachel Sterner
Advertising .... Serino Coyne, Inc./ Sandy Block, Greg Corradetti, Craig Sabbatino, Karen Girty
Press Associates .... Dennis Crowley, Carol Fineman, Ryan Ratelle, Andrew Snyder, Wayne Wolfe, Gerilyn Shur
Press Office Manager .... Bethany Larsen
Production Photography .... Paul Kolnik
Advertisement Photography .... Chris Callis
Cincinnati Photography .... Sandy Underwood
Web Design .... Bay Bridge Productions
Theatre Displays .... King Displays
Music Copying .... Kaye-Houston Music/ Anne Kaye, Doug Houston
Synthesizer Programming .... Randy Cohen
Insurance .... DeWitt Stern Group, Inc./ Peter Shoemaker, Mary E. De Spirt
Legal Counsel .... Patricia Crown, Esq./ Coblence & Associates
Banking .... Chase Manhattan Bank/Michele Gibbons
Payroll Service .... Castellana Services, Inc.
Accounting .... Fried & Kowgios Partners, CPAs, LLP
Exclusive Tour Direction ...... On the Road/Simma Levine
New York Rehearsals .... New 42nd Street Studios
Opening Night Coordinator .... Jill Van Denburg

Group Sales .... Show Tix (212) 302-7000

RICHARD FRANKEL PRODUCTIONS STAFF
Finance Director .... **Michael Naumann**
Assistant to Mr. Frankel .... Jeff Romley
Assistant to Mr. Routh .... Rachel Kiwi
Assistant to Ms. Porter .... Myriah Perkins
Assistant Finance Director .... John DiMeglio
Information Technology Manager .... Roddy Pimentel
Management Assistant .... Heidi Schading
Accounting Assistant .... Heather Allen
Accounting Assistant .... Nicole O'Bleanis
National Sales and Marketing Director .. **Ronni Mandell**
Marketing Manager .... Melissa Marano
Marketing Coordinator .... Kate Carillo
Director of Business Affairs .... **Michael Sinder**
RFP Casting .... Sara Schatz, The Casting Department
Office Manager .... **Lori Steiger-Perry**
Office Management Assistant .... Stephanie Adamczyk
Receptionists .... Kathleen Kiernan, Risa Binder
Interns .... Kristi Bergman, Ashley Berman, Kevin Condardo, Yie Yoong, Annie Grappone, Julie Griffith, Christina Macchia, Anthony Nunziata, Will Nunziata, Kimberly Jade Tompkins, Philip Wilson

AMBASSADOR THEATRE GROUP LTD.
Chairman .... Sir Eddie Kulukundis, OBE
Deputy Chairman .... Peter Beckwith
Managing Director .... Howard Panter
Executive Director .... Rosemary Squire
For ***Company*** New York:
Associate Producer .... Angela Edwards

CINCINNATI PLAYHOUSE IN THE PARK
Producing Artistic Director .... Edward Stern
Executive Director .... Buzz Ward
Production Manager .... Phil Rundle
Stage Manager .... Suann Pollock
Technical Director .... Stirling Scot Shelton
Costume Shop Manager .... Gordon DeVinney

Piano by Steinway & Sons

CREDITS AND ACKNOWLEDGEMENTS
Scenery constructed by Showman Fabricators, Inc., Long Island City, NY. Lighting equipment from PRG Lighting, Inc. Sound equipment from Sound Associates. Costumes by Tricorne; Scafati, Inc.; Jennifer Love. Custom knitwear by Adele Recklies. Wigs by Bob Kelly Wig Creations. Hosiery and undergarments by Bra*Tenders. Natural herbal cough drops courtesy of Ricola USA, Inc. Thanks to Duke at Sam Ash, Don Robinson, Suann Pollock.

THE SHUBERT ORGANIZATION, INC.
Board of Directors

Gerald Schoenfeld
Chairman

Philip J. Smith
President

Wyche Fowler, Jr. **John W. Kluge**

Lee J. Seidler **Michael I. Sovern**

Stuart Subotnick

Robert E. Wankel
Executive Vice President

Peter Entin
Vice President
Theatre Operations

Elliot Greene
Vice President
Finance

David Andrews
Vice President
Shubert Ticketing Services

John Darby
Vice President
Facilities

D.S. Moynihan
Vice President – Creative Projects

Staff for The Ethel Barrymore
House Manager .... Dan Landon

2006-2007 AWARDS

TONY AWARD
Best Revival of a Musical

DRAMA DESK AWARDS
Outstanding Revival of a Musical
Outstanding Actor in a Musical
(Raúl Esparza)
Outstanding Orchestrations
(Mary-Mitchell Campbell)

OUTER CRITICS CIRCLE AWARDS
Outstanding Revival of a Musical
Outstanding Actor in a Musical
(Raúl Esparza)

DRAMA LEAGUE AWARD
Distinguished Revival of a Musical

Company
Scrapbook

Photos by Aubrey Reuben

Photo by David Gewirtzman

Correspondent: Mary-Mitchell Campbell, orchestrator.

Memorable Opening Night Notes: "From your good and crazy not-so-legally married friends." From Joan Rivers, with earrings: "For Kristin, who didn't have her opening night earrings yet. And some everyday earrings for the other girls in the cast."

Opening Night Gifts: Personalized puzzles from Stephen Sondheim. Heather's baby face cards. Leenya's "I (Heart) Bobby"-bag-carrying-Statue of Liberty. Engraved silver ring pendants from Raúl. People donating funds to ASTEP and BC/EFA. George Furth's card with a comb on the front that said, "So you will always have a good part."

Most Exciting Celebrity Visitors: Judy Collins: "This production is important and poignant. It comes alive in a way it never has." Jerry Stiller told Jason Ostrowski (understudy for Peter) that he was great in the show even though he wasn't in it.

"Carols for a Cure" Carol: "Auld Lang Syne" arranged by Matt Castle.

"Easter Bonnet" Sketch: *A Chorus Line* audition spoof by Fred Rose and Amy Justman.

Who Has Done the Most Shows in Their Career: Barbara Walsh.

Special Backstage Rituals: Tuning together, eating Jelly Bellies together in Raúl's dressing room, singing "Dick in a Box," Easy-Bake Oven, visits from Gary Mickelson, every duet combo imaginable. Kristin Huffman: "Playing a high A on my flute over and over so it doesn't wiff when I have to play the answering machine sounds!" Lolly, our dresser, sprays Kelly's lower regions to eliminate static cling :).

Favorite Moment: The opening number, where we are all on and all playing and singing and swirling. Leenya: Sitting behind Fred on a Lucite box and leaning against his warm back. Understudy dance during "Company," "Side by Side." The moment when Bobby says "STOP!" at the end of the show. It moves us every time. Both the end of "Company" and the end of "Being Alive"—after putting out such a huge amount of energy to play each song and then hearing that audience applause. The other night, it almost sounded like a baseball game where someone had just hit a home run.

1. Barbara Walsh on opening night.
2. Librettist George Furth arrives at the cast party at Copacabana.
3. Director John Doyle at the opening.
4. Orchestrator Mary-Mitchell Campbell.
5. Window card outside the Barrymore Theatre.
6. Bruce Sabath.

Company
Scrapbook

Photos by Aubrey Reuben

1. Raúl Esparza on opening night.
2. (L-R) Elizabeth Stanley, Kelly Jeanne Grant, Angel Desai, Leenya Rideout and Heather Laws at the opening night party.

Favorite In-Theatre Gathering Place: Raúl's outer dressing room. It's stocked with M&M's, pretzels and flavored jellybeans for us!
Favorite Off-Site Hangouts: Cafe Un Deux Trois, Sosa Borella, Cincinnati. :)
Favorite Snack Food: Jellybeans, M&M's, pretzels, Nerds, pear-flavored jellybeans in Raúl's dressing room.
Mascot: Samantha Laws Kono, our very own Broadway baby! During warmups Heather straps her on the front of her and we all play and goo-goo around her.
Favorite Therapy: Grether's Pastilles, Emergen-C, Airborne, lots of stretching, Ben Gay, Bikram Yoga, physical therapy, the amazing women doing chair massages at Ivy Nails and Spa, lots of sleep, Alexander Technique with the incredible Ann Rodiger.
Most Memorable Ad-Libs: "A person like Bob doesn't have the bad things and he doesn't have the bad things, but he doesn't have the good things." (Robert Cunningham).
Unexpected Audience Interaction: Someone said, "Are they really singing, or is that fake too?" when Kelly told Raúl to "shut up!" in the middle of their scene.
Cell Phone Incident: Cell phone ringing right through the silence after Raul's "STOP!" It was so infuriating, and as soon as the show ended someone stood up and shouted at the person, "You owe us all $100!!"
Memorable Press Encounters: Opening night, a photographer showing Leenya a picture he had just taken of her sticking her tongue out with Raúl. Also, the Vogue photo shoot for Raúl, Angel, Elizabeth and Kelly.
Memorable Stage Door Fan Encounters: A man with a box of labeled Ziploc bags, each with every Playbill and possible memorabilia from every show any of us had ever done, ready for our signatures. A fan calling "Elizabeth! Elizabeth!" after Jane Pfitsch as she exited the theater, then running to catch her, looking her in the face and saying "Elizabeth! Hello!" She said, apologetically, "I'm not Elizabeth!"
Catchphrases Only the Company Would Recognize: "It's a crap idea." "I don't play the clarinet but I know people who do." "Just an exercise." "Take it from the top of the story." "That's delightful." "Death." "It was nice where I was." "Nerd." "We're playing for candy!" "One, you cut a hold in the box." "Good times!" "Tacet Walk." "Whoooop!"
Cast Members Who Played the Most Instruments: Jane Pfitsch (violin, piano, string bass, guitar, trumpet, French horn, flute, orchestra bells). Katrina Yaukey (oboe, flute, clarinet, alto sax, tenor sax, tuba, piano).
Best In-House Parody Lyrics: "Bobby's Babies, Bobby's boobies." "Pure baby." "Barely Alive" (about audiences). "She has a cold sore" in "Poor Baby" done *à la* Barb Walsh.
Memorable Directorial Notes: "Do it again but a bit more talented," from John Doyle. "That's candy worthy," from Mary-Mitchell Campbell. "That was a crap idea and I don't care if I ever see those cell phones again," regarding John's idea of using cell phones in a number. "To be honest, I'm not very good at staging heterosexual sex." "Rob, don't go home and slit your wrists or anything but…"
Company In-Jokes: Monkey Band.
Understudy Anecdote: When Jane Pfitsch first stood up to cover for Heather Laws she had been watching her so carefully that she felt like she needed to walk like a pregnant woman.
Nicknames: M&M, Miss Ohio, Lizard, Tin Lizzie, Babs, Katraihyna Yankley, Giant Bobby, Larry-Bruce, Blah Blah, Mer Mitchell, Stew.
Embarrassing Moments: Jane Pfitsch falling off the cube two days in a row (once during "Side by Side" and once at the end of "Not Getting Married Today.") Kristin Huffman: Burning eggs on the stove of the Vernon Manor in Cincinnati on the very first day of rehearsal and having industrial size fans greet me as I walked in that night. Having to call the hotel manager and apologize for almost burning down the hotel. Forgetting three measures in the middle of "Company." :)
Superstitions That Turned Out To Be True: Katrina's mom telling her she'd be on for Marta within a few weeks of opening.
Coolest Thing About Being in This Show: The supportive, talented, amazing cast members and directors; always feeling like your back is covered; the "magic" of thinking and breathing as one; shared dorkiness, jam sessions, playing instruments, sitting in rehearsal when Steve Sondheim was in the room and thinking, "Oh my God, I'm sitting here at the piano, playing and singing music that this man wrote!" Not only being lucky enough to be in a Broadway show, but to be in one that I can wholeheartedly recommend that people come to!
Also: Referring to John Doyle as the "Actor Whisperer" for his uncanny ability to "tame" any actor. Amy Justman: The memory of sitting in the restaurant at the Cincinnati Playhouse and hearing that we were officially going to Broadway—the tears just started streaming down my face. Later, I drove back to the hotel and Elton John's "Mona Lisas and Mad Hatters" was playing on the radio, and I thought to myself, "My life will never be the same."

Coram Boy

First Preview: April 16, 2007. Opened: May 2, 2007.
Closed May 27, 2007 after 17 Previews and 30 Performances.

PLAYBILL

IMPERIAL THEATRE
249 West 45th Street
A Shubert Organization Theatre
Gerald Schoenfeld, *Chairman* **Philip J. Smith,** *President*
Robert E. Wankel, *Executive Vice President*

Boyett Ostar Productions The Shubert Organization Roy Furman Lawrence Horowitz
Stephanie McClelland Debra Black/Daryl Roth Eric Falkenstein/Ralph Guild Elan McAllister/Allan S. Gordon
In association with
Jamie deRoy Jam Theatricals/CPI
Harriet Leve/Ron Nicynski/Laurence Braun Bill Rollnick/Nancy Ellison Rollnick
Present
NT The National Theatre of Great Britain's
production of

Coram Boy

Adapted By
Helen Edmundson
From The Novel By
Jamila Gavin

Jolly Abraham Uzo Aduba Jacqueline Antaramian Bill Camp Dashiell Eaves Xanthe Elbrick Tom Riis Farrell
Brad Fleischer Karron Graves Laura Heisler Angela Lin David Andrew Macdonald Quentin Maré Jan Maxwell
Kathleen McNenny Cristin Milioti Charlotte Parry Christina Rouner Ivy Vahanian Wayne Wilcox

Philip Anderson John Arbo Sean Attebury Renée Brna Charlotte Cohn Sean Cullen Katie Geissinger
Zachary James Tinashe Kajese bj Karpen Katherine Keyes Evangelia Kingsley Eric William Morris Daniel Neer
Nina Negri Mark Rehnstrom Martín Solá Samantha Soule Alison Weller Gregory Wright

Set & Costume Design
Ti Green & Melly Still
Original Lighting Design
Paule Constable
Original Sound Design
Christopher Shutt
Lighting Design Recreated By
Ed McCarthy
Sound Design Recreated By
Acme Sound Partners
U.S. Hair & Wig Design
David H. Lawrence
U.S. Fight Director
Thomas Schall
Additional Vocal Arrangements
Derek Barnes
Music Coordinator
John Miller
Casting
Stanczyk/Cherpakov Casting
Press Representative
Boneau/Bryan-Brown
Marketing
HHC Marketing
General Management
101 Productions, Ltd.
Production Stage Manager
Kim Vernace
Technical Supervisor
David Benken & Juniper Street Productions

Music
Adrian Sutton
Music Director & Principal Conductor
Constantine Kitsopoulos
Directed by
Melly Still

The producers wish to express their appreciation to Theatre Development Fund for its support of this production.

LIVE BROADWAY

5/2/07

CAST

Act I, 1742

Meshak Gardiner .... BRAD FLEISCHER
Angel .... IVY VAHANIAN
Dr. Smith .... QUENTIN MARÉ
Young Thomas Ledbury .... CHARLOTTE PARRY
Young Alexander Ashbrook .... XANTHE ELBRICK
Otis Gardiner .... BILL CAMP
Mrs. Lynch .... JAN MAXWELL
Miss Price .... ANGELA LIN
Mr. Claymore .... TOM RIIS FARRELL
Lady Ashbrook .... CHRISTINA ROUNER
Isobel Ashbrook .... KARRON GRAVES
Mrs. Milcote .... KATHLEEN McNENNY
Melissa .... IVY VAHANIAN
Edward Ashbrook .... LAURA HEISLER
Alice Ashbrook .... CRISTIN MILIOTI
Lord Ashbrook .... DAVID ANDREW MACDONALD
Adult Alexander Ashbrook .... WAYNE WILCOX

Act II, 1750

Mrs. Hendry .... JACQUELINE ANTARAMIAN
Philip Gaddarn .... BILL CAMP
Toby .... UZO ADUBA
Aaron .... XANTHE ELBRICK
Molly .... JOLLY ABRAHAM
Handel .... QUENTIN MARÉ
Adult Thomas Ledbury .... DASHIELL EAVES

CHOIR

PHILIP ANDERSON, JOHN ARBO,
SEAN ATTEBURY, RENÉE BRNA,

Continued on next page

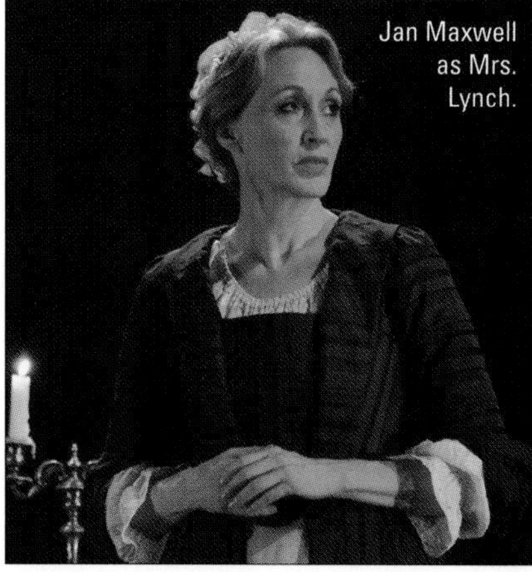
Jan Maxwell as Mrs. Lynch.

Xanthe Elbrick as Young Alexander Ashbrook.

Photos by Joan Marcus

Coram Boy

Cast Continued

CHARLOTTE COHN, SEAN CULLEN, KATIE GEISSINGER, ZACHARY JAMES, TINASHE KAJESE, bj KARPEN, KATHERINE KEYES, EVANGELIA KINGSLEY, ERIC WILLIAM MORRIS, DANIEL NEER, NINA NEGRI, MARK REHNSTROM, MARTÍN SOLÁ, SAMANTHA SOULE, ALISON WELLER, GREGORY WRIGHT

Other parts played by members of the Company.

UNDERSTUDIES

For Meshak Gardiner, Adult Thomas Ledbury, Adult Alexander Ashbrook:
ERIC WILLIAM MORRIS
For Angel/Melissa, Isobel Ashbrook, Alice Ashbrook:
SAMANTHA SOULE
For Young Thomas Ledbury, Young Alexander Ashbrook/Aaron, Edward Ashbrook:
RENÉE BRNA
For Otis Gardiner, Lord Ashbrook, Mr. Claymore, Philip Gaddarn, Dr. Smith/Handel:
SEAN CULLEN
For Mrs. Lynch, Lady Ashbrook, Mrs. Hendry, Mrs. Milcote:
ALISON WELLER
For Miss Price, Toby, Molly:
TINASHE KAJESE

ORCHESTRA

Conductor/Keyboard:
CONSTANTINE KITSOPOULOS
Associate Conductor/Keyboard:
CHIP PRINCE
Violin:
DALE STUCKENBRUCK,
ELIZABETH LIM-DUTTON
Viola:
MAXINE ROACH
Cello:
DEBORAH ASSAEL
String Bass:
JUDITH SUGARMAN
Music Coordinator:
JOHN MILLER

2006-2007 AWARD

THEATRE WORLD AWARD
Outstanding Broadway Debut
(Xanthe Elbrick)

Jolly Abraham
Molly

Uzo Aduba
Toby

Jacqueline Antaramian
Mrs. Hendry

Bill Camp
Otis Gardiner/ Philip Gaddarn

Dashiell Eaves
Adult Thomas Lebury

Xanthe Elbrick
Young Alexander Ashbrook/Aaron

Tom Riis Farrell
Mr. Claymore

Brad Fleischer
Meshak Gardiner

Karron Graves
Isobel Ashbrook

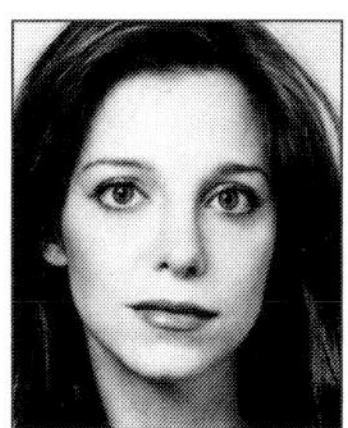
Laura Heisler
Edward Ashbrook

Angela Lin
Miss Price

David Andrew Macdonald
Lord Ashbrook

Quentin Maré
Dr. Smith/Handel

Jan Maxwell
Mrs. Lynch

Kathleen McNenny
Mrs. Milcote

Cristin Milioti
Alice Ashbrook

Charlotte Parry
Young Thomas Ledbury

Christina Rouner
Lady Ashbrook

Ivy Vahanian
Angel/Melissa

Wayne Wilcox
Adult Alexander Ashbrook

Coram Boy

Philip Anderson
Choir

John Arbo
Choir

Sean Attebury
Choir

Renée Brna
Choir

Charlotte Cohn
Choir

Sean Cullen
Choir

Katie Geissinger
Choir

Zachary James
Choir

Tinashe Kajese
Choir

bj Karpen
Choir

Katherine Keyes
Choir

Evangelia Kingsley
Choir

Eric William Morris
Choir

Daniel Neer
Choir

Nina Negri
Choir

Mark Rehnstrom
Choir

Martín Solá
Choir

Samantha Soule
Choir

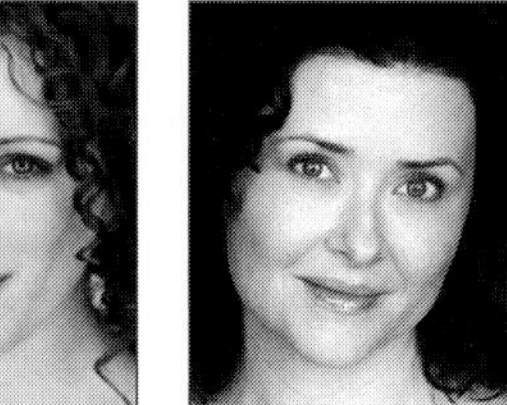
Alison Weller
Choir

Gregory Wright
Choir

Melly Still
Director/ Co-Designer

Helen Edmundson
Playwright

Jamila Gavin
Author

Constantine Kitsopoulos
Music Director & Principal Conductor

Ti Green
Co-Designer

Paule Constable
Lighting Design

Tom Clark, Mark Menard and Nevin Steinberg, Acme Sound Partners
Sound Design Recreation

David Benken
Technical Supervisor

Guy Kwan, John Paull, Hillary Blanken, Kevin Broomell, Ana-Rose Greene, Juniper Street Productions
Technical Supervisor

Stephen Gabis
Dialect Coach

John Miller
Music Coordinator

Nicholas Hytner
Artistic Director, National Theatre

Bill Haber, OSTAR Enterprises
Producer

Coram Boy

Bob Boyett
Producer

Gerald Schoenfeld, Chairman, The Shubert Organization
Producer

Roy Furman
Producer

Lawrence Horowitz, M.D.
Producer

Stephanie P. McClelland
Producer

Debra Black
Producer

Daryl Roth
Producer

Eric Falkenstein
Producer

Elan V. McAllister
Producer

Allan S. Gordon
Producer

Jamie deRoy
Co-Producer

Harriet Leve
Co-Producer

Ron Nicynski
Co-Producer

Laurence Braun
Co-Producer

Photo by Ben Strothmann

CAST
Front Row (L-R): Laura Heisler, Samantha Soule, Ivy Vahanian, Cristin Milioti, Kathleen McNenny, Xanthe Elbrick, Wayne Wilcox, Jolly Abraham.

Second Row (L-R): Tinashe Kajese (yellow), Charlotte Parry, Angela Lin.

Third Row (L-R): Martín Solá, Renée Brna, Karron Graves, Tom Riis Farrell, John Arbo, Jacqueline Antaramian, Brad Fleischer, Quentin Maré.

Fourth Row (L-R): Uzo Aduba, bj Karpen.

Fifth Row (L-R): Nina Negri, Alison Weller, Charlotte Cohn, Eric William Morris, David Macdonald, Christina Rouner, Bill Camp, Katie Geissinger, Daniel Neer, Sean Attebury, Dashiell Eaves.

Sixth Row (L-R): Philip Anderson, Evangelia Kingsley, Katherine Keyes, Sean Cullen, Zachary James, Mark Rehnstrom and Gregory Wright.

Not Pictured: Jan Maxwell

Coram Boy

STAGE AND COMPANY MANAGEMENT
(L-R): Matthew Melchiorre, Paul J. Smith, Thom Clay and Kim Vernace.

Photos by Ben Strothmann

ORCHESTRA
Front Row (L-R): Chip Prince, Dale Stuckenbruck.
Back Row (L-R): Maxine Roach, Liz Lim-Dutton, Debbie Assael, Judy Sugarman and Constantine Kitsopoulos (Conductor).

FRONT OF HOUSE STAFF
First Row (L-R): Jerry Bell, Kay Lynn Beatrice, Jenny Fernendez, Fran Barbaretti.
Second Row (L-R): Stephanie Rivera, Tim Young (Bartender), Lois Fernandez, Christopher Caoili, Dennis Norwood.
Third Row (L-R): Martin Werner, Judy Gilbert, Victor Perez (Porter), Honey Ann Glynn.
Back Row (L-R): Michael Knowles, Tracy Barnett and Joe Pullara (Manager).

DOORMAN
Kevin Kennedy

WARDROBE DEPARTMENT
Front Row (L-R): Rosemary Keough, Gayle Palmieri, Ashley Aldefer.
Back Row (L-R): Lori Elwell, Dennis Birchall, Karen L. Eifert and Maura Clifford.

Coram Boy

Photo by Ben Strothmann

Front Row: (L-R): Laura Heisler, Samantha Soule, Dennis Birchall, Maura Clifford, Evangelia Kingsley, Quentin Maré.

Second Row (L-R): Jolly Abraham, Tinashe Kajese, Ivy Vahanian, Cristin Milioti, Kathleen McNenny, Xanthe Elbrick, Jacqueline Antaramian, Chip Prince, Brad Fleischer, Gayle Palmieri, Rose Keough, Jack Anderson.

Third Row (L-R): Martín Solá, Renée Brna, Karron Graves, Charlotte Parry, Angela Lin, John Arbo, Dashiell Eaves, Matthew Melchiorre, Paul Smith.

Fourth Row (L-R): Jay Satterwhite, Judy Sugarman, Nina Negri, Uzo Aduba, Alison Weller, bj Karpen, Tom Riis Farrell, Bill Camp, Katie Geissinger, Daniel Neer, Karen L. Eifert, Kim Vernace, Thom Clay.

Fifth Row (L-R): Anthony Ferrer, Dale Stuckenbruck, Philip Anderson, Charlotte Cohn, Eric William Morris, David Macdonald, Christina Rouner, Gregory Wright, Wally Bullard, Ashley Aldefer, Fred Bockwoldt.

Sixth Row (L-R): Sean Cullen, Wayne Wilcox, Zachary James, Mark Rehnstrom, Sean Attebury and Steven Woods.

Coram Boy

BOX OFFICE
(L-R): Bill Carrick (Treasurer), Jose Gomez, Carlin Blum

CARPENTRY and ELECTRICS
Front Row (L-R): Wally Bullard, Paul Deans, Jack Anderson.
Back Row (L-R): Anthony Ferrer, Jay Satterwhite and Fred Bockwoldt.

Photos by Ben Strothmann

STAFF FOR *CORAM BOY*

GENERAL MANAGEMENT
101 PRODUCTIONS, LTD.
Wendy Orshan Jeffrey M. Wilson
David Auster

COMPANY MANAGER
Thom Clay

GENERAL PRESS REPRESENTATIVE
BONEAU/BRYAN-BROWN
Adrian Bryan-Brown Joe Perrotta
Ian Bjorklund

PRODUCTION MANAGEMENT
DAVID BENKEN
Rose Palombo
JUNIPER STREET PRODUCTIONS
Hillary Blanken Kevin Broomell
Ana Rose Greene Guy Kwan

CASTING
STANCZYK/CHERPAKOV CASTING
Laura Stanczyk, CSA Howie Cherpakov, CSA
Daryl Eisenberg–Casting Assistant

Production Stage Manager ..... Kim Vernace
Stage Manager ..... Paul J. Smith
Assistant Stage Manager ..... Matthew Melchiorre
Assistant to the Director ..... Bruce Perry
Associate Scenic Designers ..... Paul Weimer, Ted LeFevre
Associate Costume Designer ..... Scott Traugott
Costume Assistants ..... Cory Ching, Robert Martin, Brian Russman
U.K. Associate Lighting Designer ..... Nick Simmons
Assistant Lighting Designer ..... Pamela Kupper
Associate Sound Designer ..... Nicholas Borisjuk
Dialect Coach ..... Stephen Gabis
Coram Boy UK Dramaturg ..... Tom Morris
Original Fight Director ..... Alision De Burgh
Fight Captain ..... Eric William Morris

Production Carpenter ..... Jack Anderson
Production Electrician ..... Joe "Fish" Cangelosi
Production Sound Supervisor ..... Brad Gyorgak
Production Properties ..... Steven Wood
Advance Carpenter ..... Patrick Eviston
Advance Electrician ..... Jason Wilkosz
Lighting Programmer ..... Nick Simmons
Wardrobe Supervisor ..... Karen L. Eifert
Assistant Wardrobe Supervisor ..... Sis Obidowski
Dressers ..... Ashley Aldefer, Dennis Birchall, Maura Clifford, Lori Elwell, Dan Foss, Rose Keough
Hair Supervisor ..... David H. Lawrence
Hairdressers ..... Jack Curtin, Jorie Malan, Chelsea Roth, Christal Schanes
Assistant to John Miller ..... Kelly M. Rach
Synthesizer Programmer ..... Karl Mansfield
Music Prep Services ..... Anixter Rice Music Service
Rehearsal Pianists ..... D. Scott Ferguson, Karl Mansfield, Douglas Martin
Production Assistants ..... Elise Hanley, Gregory T. Livoti, Thomas Recktenwald
Music Department Assistant ..... John Bauder

Associate Producer for
Ostar Enterprises ..... Rachel Neuburger
Executive Assistant to Mr. Haber ..... Theresa Pisanelli
Assistant to Mr. Haber ..... Andrew Cleghorn
Assistants to Mr. Boyett ..... Diane Murphy, Alex Libby, Michael Mandell
Strategic Partnerships & Developments ..... Jan Gura
Legal Counsel ..... Lazarus & Harris, LLP/ Scott Lazarus, Esq., Robert C. Harris, Esq.
Accountant ..... Rosenberg, Neuwirth, & Kushner, CPAs,/ Chris Cacace, Jana Jevnikar
Advertising ..... Spot Co., Inc./ Drew Hodges, Jim Edwards, Jim Aquino, Darius Suyama
Marketing ..... HHC Marketing/ Hugh Hysell, Amanda Pekoe, Kerry Minchinton
Banking ..... City National Bank/Anne McSweeney
Insurance ..... DeWitt Stern, Inc./Bethany Weise
Risk Managers ..... Stockbridge Risk Management, Inc./ Neil Goldstein
Theatre Displays ..... King Displays, Inc.
Merchandising ..... Max Merchandising, LLC/ Randi Grossman
Payroll Services ..... Castellana Services, Inc.
Website Design ..... Spot Co.
Opening Night
Coordination ..... Tobak Lawrence Company/ Suzanne Tobak, Michael P. Lawrence
Production Photography ..... Joan Marcus
Artwork Photography ..... Catherine Ashmore, Hans Neleman
Group Sales ..... Telecharge.com Group Sales/ (212) 239-6262

NATIONAL THEATRE, LONDON
Chairman of the Board ..... Sir Hayden Philips
Director ..... Nicholas Hytner
Executive Director ..... Nick Starr

CREDITS
Scenery and scenic automation by Hudson Scenic Studios, Inc. Lighting equipment from Hudson Sound & Light, LLC. Sound equipment from Sound Associates. Special scenic elements by Proof Productions. Costume construction by Euro Co Costumes, Carelli Costumes, David Quinn, Arel Studio, Inc. Millinery by Rodney Gordon Millinery. Custom footwear by Harr Shoes. Natural herb cough drops courtesy of Ricola USA, Inc.

To learn more about the production, please visit
CoramBoyOnBroadway.com

Flying By Foy

CORAM BOY
Rehearsed at New 42nd Street Studios

SPECIAL THANKS
Di Willmott, Kerry McDevitt, Ian Connop, Tamara Albachari, Vicki Liles, Mark d'Inverno

THE SHUBERT ORGANIZATION, INC.
Board of Directors

Gerald Schoenfeld Chairman
Philip J. Smith President

Wyche Fowler, Jr.
John W. Kluge

Lee J. Seidler
Michael I. Sovern

Stuart Subotnick

Robert E. Wankel
Executive Vice President

Peter Entin Vice President Theatre Operations
Elliot Greene Vice President Finance

David Andrews Vice President Shubert Ticketing Services
John Darby Vice President Facilities

D.S. Moynihan
Vice President – Creative Projects

House Manager ..... Joseph Pullara

Coram Boy
Scrapbook

Correspondent: Uzo Aduba, "Toby

Memorable Opening Night Gifts: Jan Maxwell gave us a great opening night gift: a CD of music that could serve as a soundtrack to the various scenes in *Coram Boy*. There's some AC/DC, some Otis Redding and lots of other music. Dashiell Eaves gave us cards that listed historical information from foundling hospitals. We also got really incredible postcards from author Jamila Gavin, from many of the different orphanages and foundling hospitals of the late 1700 and early 1800s. They showed kids marching in lines, getting uniforms, studying in classrooms. She said that doing this show on Broadway was one of the most beautiful experiences of her life and she was so glad it made its voyage to America. She made a different card for each person, and it was so nice that she took the time personally to do that.

Most Exciting Celebrity Visitors: Sigourney Weaver, Taye Diggs and Idina Menzel all came backstage and all said they loved the show.

Actors Who Performed the Most Roles: In this show it's not so much how many roles, but how many times you have to change to play your various roles. The title goes to Jolly Abraham and Cristin Milioti because they have the most changes. Jolly, for instance, goes from Molly, to servant to Coram Girl to Coram Boy to ball guest to Gloucester Boy to a woman. She has nine changes in Act II alone.

Who Has Done the Most Shows in Their Career: That title would be a tossup between Jan Maxwell and Bill Camp.

Special Backstage Rituals: Every day, as a company, we do a 30- or 40-minute yoga warm-up that director Melly gave us. Another small group consisting of Tinashe Kajese, Nina Negri, Charlotte Parry and myself meet stage left at "five minutes" to say a prayer. We love it.

Favorite Moment During Each Performance: Ashbrook Woods, when we're changing the set out of the ball.

Favorite Off-Site Hangouts: The Film Center Café and Luxia.

Favorite Therapy: There's a lot of movement in this show so we use a lot of ice!

Record Number of Cell Phone Rings: Two in one performance.

Memorable Press Encounter: The Vogue shoot where the photographer had hip-hop music playing in the background while we were in period costumes trying to pose for 1700s London.

Memorable Stage Door Fan Encounter: When Jolly Abraham found out we might be closing, she started going over to the TKTS line and barking for the show and we got a lot of people coming over from that. One man waited afterward and told her, "Thanks so much for getting me out of that line. What I was planning to see was nothing compared to what I did see."

Fastest Costume Change: The Coram Girls in Act II. They do the scene where Lord Ashbrook discovers them at the house singing, then they have to literally walk off the stage and walk right back on as Coram Boys. It has to happen just that fast.

Photos by Aubrey Reuben

1. The cast and creative team take bows on opening night.
2. (L-R): Adapter Helen Edmundson, novelist Jamila Gavin and director Melly Still at the opening night party at Tavern on the Green.
3. Actress Uzo Aduba at Tavern on the Green.

Who Wore the Heaviest/Hottest Costumes: Bill Camp and Jan Maxwell are tied there.

Who Wore the Least: Me, in Act II, when Toby's a slave.

Catchphrase Only the Company Would Recognize: "Bonkers, hay!"

Memorable Directorial Note: When director Melly was explaining to Angela Lin how to do the voice of the baby who is being buried alive in the woods. She told her she should distinguish the sound of when she's crying—"Ahh, ahh, ahh" from when she starts to have dirt in her mouth—"Uhh, uhh, uhh." I'm not sure I'll ever forget that.

Company In-Jokes: We have a song, "Surely," in which they sing "Su-ur-ly." When anyone calls Jolly Abraham, they sing it, "Jo-oh-lie."

Company Legend: The day when the noose didn't come all the way down in the hanging scene. Brad Fleischer responded so brilliantly. He could barely see and his hands were tied behind his back so he had no support. But he didn't panic. He walked up those stairs with such bravery and did a wonderfully artistic dropping of his head and struggle. And then it went to black. The audience could see the noose above his head, but he did it so convincingly that the audience thought it was supposed to be that way.

Ghostly Encounter: It only happened once, and never again. The producers announced that the show was closing and everyone was very sad and upset. That night the show was amazing, filled with so much emotion. It was cathartic. At the end of each show we sing the "Hallelujah" chorus. Traditionally people are supposed to stand for that, but most people don't know that. On the day this happened, one by one, everyone in the audience rose to their feet until everyone was standing. It was like somehow they knew. It never happened before and never happened again.

Also: People who actually saw our show were always so blown away by it. We had one group who came and took pictures of us afterward, then returned the following week with the pictures for us to autograph.

Coolest Thing About Being in This Show: We get to work together!

Curtains

First Preview: February 27, 2007. Opened: March 22, 2007.
Still running as of May 31, 2007.

PLAYBILL®

AL HIRSCHFELD THEATRE

A JUJAMCYN THEATRE

ROCCO LANDESMAN
PRESIDENT

PAUL LIBIN
PRODUCING DIRECTOR

JACK VIERTEL
CREATIVE DIRECTOR

JORDAN ROTH
VICE PRESIDENT

ROGER BERLIND ROGER HORCHOW DARYL ROTH
JANE BERGÈRE TED HARTLEY CENTER THEATRE GROUP

present

DAVID HYDE PIERCE *and* DEBRA MONK

in

CURTAINS

Book by
RUPERT HOLMES

Music by
JOHN KANDER

Lyrics by
FRED EBB

Original Book and Concept by
PETER STONE

Additional Lyrics by
JOHN KANDER *and* RUPERT HOLMES

Starring
KAREN ZIEMBA
JASON DANIELEY JILL PAICE
and
EDWARD HIBBERT

Also Starring
JOHN BOLTON MICHAEL X. MARTIN MICHAEL McCORMICK
NOAH RACEY ERNIE SABELLA MEGAN SIKORA

with
ASHLEY AMBER NILI BASSMAN KEVIN BERNARD WARD BILLEISEN PAULA LEGGETT CHASE JENNIFER DUNNE
DAVID EGGERS J. AUSTIN EYER MATT FARNSWORTH PATTY GOBLE MARY ANN LAMB BRITTANY MARCIN
JIM NEWMAN JOE AARON REID DARCIE ROBERTS CHRISTOPHER SPAULDING ALLISON SPRATT JEROME VIVONA

Set Design
ANNA LOUIZOS

Costume Design
WILLIAM IVEY LONG

Lighting Design
PETER KACZOROWSKI

Sound Design
BRIAN RONAN

Hair and Wig Design
PAUL HUNTLEY

Dance Arrangements
DAVID CHASE

Fight Direction
RICK SORDELET

Aerial Effects Design
PAUL RUBIN

Make-Up Design
ANGELINA AVALLONE

Associate Choreographer
JOANN M. HUNTER

Casting
JIM CARNAHAN, CSA

Production Supervisor
BEVERLEY RANDOLPH

Technical Supervisor
PETER FULBRIGHT

Music Coordinator
JOHN MONACO

General Management
101 PRODUCTIONS, LTD.

Marketing Services
TMG-
THE MARKETING GROUP

Press Representative
BONEAU/BRYAN-BROWN

Associate Producers
BARBARA AND PETER FODOR

Orchestrations
WILLIAM DAVID BROHN

Music Director/Vocal Arrangements
DAVID LOUD

Choreography by
ROB ASHFORD

Directed by
SCOTT ELLIS

AMERICAN PREMIERE PRODUCED AT THE AHMANSON THEATRE BY CENTER THEATRE GROUP, LA'S THEATRE COMPANY

3/22/07

CAST

(in order of appearance)

Jessica Cranshaw .... PATTY GOBLE
Randy Dexter .... JIM NEWMAN
Niki Harris .... JILL PAICE
Bambi Bernét .... MEGAN SIKORA
Bobby Pepper .... NOAH RACEY
Johnny Harmon .... MICHAEL X. MARTIN
Georgia Hendricks .... KAREN ZIEMBA
Aaron Fox .... JASON DANIELEY
Carmen Bernstein .... DEBRA MONK
Oscar Shapiro .... MICHAEL McCORMICK
Christopher Belling .... EDWARD HIBBERT
Lieutenant Frank Cioffi .... DAVID HYDE PIERCE
Mona Page .... MARY ANN LAMB
Harv Fremont .... MATT FARNSWORTH
Roberta Wooster .... DARCIE ROBERTS
Sidney Bernstein .... ERNIE SABELLA
Detective O'Farrell .... KEVIN BERNARD
Daryl Grady .... JOHN BOLTON
Sasha Iljinsky .... DAVID LOUD
Marjorie Cook .... PAULA LEGGETT CHASE
Arlene Barruca .... NILI BASSMAN
Roy Stetson .... KEVIN BERNARD
Brick Hawvermale .... WARD BILLEISEN
Jan Setler .... JENNIFER DUNNE
Connie Subbotin .... PATTY GOBLE
Peg Prentice .... BRITTANY MARCIN
Ronnie Driscoll .... JOE AARON REID
Russ Cochran .... CHRISTOPHER SPAULDING

Continued on next page

Photo by Joan Marcus

Debra Monk (center) and company perform "Show People."

Curtains

MUSICAL NUMBERS

ACT I

"Wide Open Spaces"	Randy, Niki, Jessica, Bobby, Ensemble
"What Kind of Man?"	Carmen, Oscar, Aaron, Georgia
"Thinking of Him"	Georgia, Aaron, Bobby
"The Woman's Dead"	Entire Company
"Show People"	Carmen, Cioffi, Entire Company
"Coffee Shop Nights"	Cioffi
"In the Same Boat 1"	Georgia, Niki, Bambi
"I Miss the Music"	Aaron
"Thataway!"	Georgia, Bobby, Ensemble

ACT II

"He Did It"	Entire Company
"In the Same Boat 2"	Bobby, Randy, Harv
"It's a Business"	Carmen, Stagehands
"Kansasland"	Randy, Niki, Harv, Bobby, Bambi, Ensemble
"Thinking of Him"/"I Miss the Music" (Reprise)	Aaron, Georgia
"A Tough Act to Follow"	Cioffi, Niki, Ensemble
"In the Same Boat 3"	Entire Company
"A Tough Act to Follow" (Reprise)	Entire Company

ORCHESTRA

Conductor: DAVID LOUD

Flute, Picc. Clarinet, Alto Sax: STEVE KENYON
Oboe, Eng. Horn, Clarinet, Tenor Sax: AL HUNT
Clarinet, Alto Sax, Soprano Sax:
OWEN KOTLER
Bassoon, Bass Clarinet, Baritone Sax, Flute, Clarinet:
MARK THRASHER
French Horn 1: R.J. KELLEY
French Horn 2: ANGELA CORDELL
Trumpet 1: DON DOWNS
Trumpet 2: MATT PETERSON
Trombone 1, House Contractor:
CHARLES GORDON
Bass Trombone, Tuba: JENNIFER WHARTON
Percussion: GREG LANDES
Drums: BRUCE DOCTOR
Acoustic Guitar, Electric Guitar, Banjo,
Classical Guitar: GREG UTZIG
Acoustic Bass: ROBERT RENINO
Associate Music Director/Piano and Synthesizer:
SAM DAVIS

Musical Coordinator: JOHN MONACO
Music Copying Services: LARRY H. ABEL,
MUSIC PREPARATION INTERNATIONAL

David Hyde Pierce as Lieutenant Frank Cioffi.
Photo by Joan Marcus

Cast Continued

SWINGS

ASHLEY AMBER, DAVID EGGERS,
J. AUSTIN EYER,
ALLISON SPRATT, JEROME VIVONA

UNDERSTUDIES

For Lieutenant Frank Cioffi & Christopher Belling:
KEVIN BERNARD
For Niki Harris:
NILI BASSMAN, ALLISON SPRATT
For Bambi Bernét:
ASHLEY AMBER, JENNIFER DUNNE
For Aaron Fox:
KEVIN BERNARD, MATT FARNSWORTH
For Daryl Grady:
MATT FARNSWORTH, MICHAEL X. MARTIN
For Carmen Bernstein:
PAULA LEGGETT CHASE, PATTY GOBLE
For Oscar Shapiro & Sidney Bernstein:
MICHAEL X. MARTIN, JEROME VIVONA
For Johnny Harmon:
JIM NEWMAN, JEROME VIVONA
For Bobby Pepper:
WARD BILLEISEN, DAVID EGGERS,
JIM NEWMAN
For Georgia Hendricks & Jessica Cranshaw:
PAULA LEGGETT CHASE, DARCIE ROBERTS

Dance Captain:
DAVID EGGERS

SETTING

Act One
The Colonial Theatre in Boston, 1959, during the out-of-town tryout of the new musical, *Robbin' Hood!*

Act Two
The same, much later that night

2006-2007 AWARDS

Tony Award
Best Actor in a Musical
(David Hyde Pierce)

Drama Desk Awards
Outstanding Featured Actress
in a Musical (Debra Monk)
Outstanding Book of a Musical
(Rupert Holmes and Peter Stone)
Special Award to John Kander and Fred Ebb

Outer Critics Circle Award
Outstanding Featured Actress
in a Musical (Karen Ziemba)

David Hyde Pierce
Lieutenant Frank Cioffi

Debra Monk
Carmen Bernstein

Karen Ziemba
Georgia Hendricks

Jason Danieley
Aaron Fox

Jill Paice
Niki Harris

Edward Hibbert
Christopher Belling

John Bolton
Daryl Grady

Michael X. Martin
Johnny Harmon

Michael McCormick
Oscar Shapiro

Noah Racey
Bobby Pepper

Ernie Sabella
Sidney Bernstein

Megan Sikora
Bambi Bernét

Ashley Amber
Swing, Asst. Dance Captain

Nili Bassman
Arlene Barruca

Kevin Bernard
Roy Stetson, Detective O'Farrell

Ward Billeisen
Brick Hawvermale

Paula Leggett Chase
Marjorie Cook

Jennifer Dunne
Jan Setler

David Eggers
Swing, Dance Captain

J. Austin Eyer
Swing

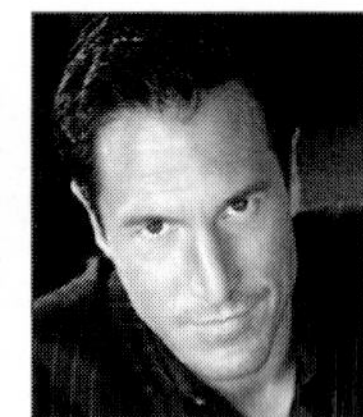
Matt Farnsworth
Harv Fremont

Patty Goble
Jessica Cranshaw

Mary Ann Lamb
Mona Page

Brittany Marcin
Peg Prentice

Jim Newman
Randy Dexter

Joe Aaron Reid
Ronnie Driscoll

Darcie Roberts
Roberta Wooster

Christopher Spaulding
Russ Cochran

Allison Spratt
Swing

Jerome Vivona
Swing

Beverley Randolph
Production Supervisor

John Kander and Fred Ebb
Music, Additional Lyrics; Lyrics

Rupert Holmes
Book, Additional Lyrics

Peter Stone
Original Book & Concept

Curtains

Scott Ellis
Director

Rob Ashford
Choreographer

Anna Louizos
Set Design

William Ivey Long
Costume Design

Peter Kaczorowski
Lighting Design

William David Brohn
Orchestrations

Paul Huntley
Hair and Wig Design

Rick Sordelet
Fight Director

Paul Rubin
Aerial Effects Design

Angelina Avallone
Make-up Design

Joann M. Hunter
Associate Choreographer

Dave Solomon
Assistant Director

Teressa Esposito
Creative Associate to Mr. Holmes

Jim Carnahan, CSA
Casting

Roger Berlind
Producer

Roger Horchow
Producer

Daryl Roth
Producer

Jane Bergère
Producer

Ted Hartley
Producer

Michael Ritchie
Artistic Director, Center Theatre Group

Charles Dillingham
Managing Director, Center Theatre Group

Gordon Davidson
Founding Artistic Director, Center Theatre Group

STAGE MANAGEMENT
(L-R): Kevin Bertolacci (Assistant Stage Manager), Beverley Randolph (Production Supervisor/Production Stage Manager), Jerome Vivona (Assistant Stage Manager), Scott Taylor Rollison (Stage Manager)

ORCHESTRA
Front Row (L-R): Larry Spivak (Percussion), Barry Nudelman (Woodwinds), Owen Kotler (Woodwinds), Bob Renino (Bass), Jen Wharton (Trombone), Don Downs (Trumpet), Charles Gordon (Trombone), Angela Cordell (French Horn), David Loud (Conductor-Musical Director).
Back Row (L-R): Steve Kenyon (Woodwinds), Eric Davis (French Horn), Al Hunt (Woodwinds), Bruce Doctor (Drums) and Greg Utzig (Guitar).

Photos by Ben Strothmann

Curtains

Photos by Ben Strothmann

COMPANY MANAGERS
Bruce Klinger (Company Manager), Beverly Edwards (Associate Company Manager).

SOUND CREW
(L-R): Christopher Sloan (Production Sound), Bonnie Runk (Deck Sound), Andy Funk (Deck Sound).

DOORMAN
Neal Perez

FRONT OF HOUSE
Front Row (L-R): Mary Marzan (Usher), Amelia Tirado (Usher), Lorraine Feeks (Ticket Taker), Janet Polanco (Concessions), Theresa Aceves (Usher).
Second Row (L-R): Jean Marie Eck (Merchandising), Alberta McNamee (Usher), Henry Haywood (Engineer), Carmel Robinson (Manager).
Third Row (L-R): Ruben Rivera (Concessions), Suzanne Perez (Concessions), Henry Menendez (Usher), Kerri Gillen (Usher), Julie Burnham (Usher), Theresa Lopez (Usher).
Fourth Row (L-R): Bary Ryan (Usher) Fernando Colon (Usher).
Back Row (L-R): Hollis Miller (Usher), Tristan Blacer (Ticket Taker), Danielle Devine (Usher), Curt Owens (Usher), Donald Royal (Usher).

CARPENTERS
Front Row (L-R): Bill van DeBogart (House Flyman), Rick Styles (Deck Automation).

Middle Row (L-R): Joe Maher (House Carpenter), Steve Schultz (Deck Carpenter).

Back Row (L-R): Erik Hansen (Fly Automation), Hank Hale (Deck Carpenter), Morgan Chevette (Deck Carpenter), Buck Roberts (Deck Carpenter), Tom Lowery (Deck Carpenter).

ELECTRICS
Front Row (L-R): Tom Burke (Spotlight Operator), Bob Miller (Spotlight Operator), Dermot Lynch (House Electrician).

Back Row (L-R): John Blixt (Spotlight Operator), Cletus Karamon (Head Electrician), Richard Mortell (Production Electrician).

HAIR
Front (L-R): Brendan O'Neal (Hairdresser), Natasha Steinhagen (Assistant Hair Supervisor).

Back (L-R): Gay Boseker (Hairdresser), Larry Boyette (Hair Supervisor).

Photos by Ben Strothmann

WARDROBE
Front Row (Sitting, L-R): Ruth Goya, Pam Kurz.

Second Row (Kneeling, L-R): Cesar Porto, David Mitchell, Derek Moreno (Assistant Wardrobe Supervisor), Frank Scaccia, Growler (Wardrobe Supervisor).

Back Row (L-R): Ken Brown, Jeannie Naughton, Kay Gowenlock, Theresa Distasi, Joe Hickey, Alice Bee, Maggie Horkey, Misty Fernandez.

PROPS CREW
(L-R): Sal Sclafani (House Props), Bob Adams (Head of Props), Justin Sanok (Props), Danny Paulos (Props).

Curtains

Photo by Ben Strothmann

BOX OFFICE
(L-R): Vinnie Siniscalchi and Jeff Nevins.

STAFF FOR *CURTAINS*

GENERAL MANAGEMENT
101 PRODUCTIONS, LTD.
Wendy Orshan Jeffrey M. Wilson
David Auster

COMPANY MANAGER
Bruce Klinger

GENERAL PRESS REPRESENTATIVE
BONEAU/BRYAN-BROWN
Chris Boneau Jim Byk
Juliana Hannett Matt Ross

CASTING
JIM CARNAHAN, CSA

TECHNICAL SUPERVISOR
TECH PRODUCTION SERVICES, INC.
Peter Fulbright Mary Duffe
Colleen Houlehen Jackie Prats

Production Stage Manager .... Beverley Randolph
Stage Manager .... Scott Taylor Rollison
Assistant Stage Manager .... Kevin Bertolacci
Assistant Stage Manager .... Jerome Vivona
Associate Company Manager .... Beverly Edwards
Dance Captain .... David Eggers
Assistant Dance Captain .... Ashley Amber
Creative Associate to Mr. Holmes .... Teressa Esposito
Assistant Director .... Dave Solomon
Assistant to Mr. Ellis .... Kathleen Bond
Associate Scenic Designer .... Michael Carnahan
Assistant to Ms. Louizos .... Zhanna Gurvich
Associate Costume Designer .... Tom Beall
Assistant Costume Designer .... Rachel Attridge
Assistants to Mr. Long .... Cathy Parrott, Brenda Abbandandalo
Associate Lighting Designer .... Hilary Manners
Assistant Lighting Designer .... Joel E. Silver
Assistant to Mr. Kaczorowski .... Lisa Katz
Moving Light Programmer .... Josh Weitzman
Assistant Sound Designer .... Mike Farfalla
Keyboard Programmer .... Stuart Andrews
Production Carpenter .... Paul Wimmer
Fly Automation .... Erik Hansen
Deck Automation .... Rick Styles
Production Electrician .... Richard Mortell
Assistant Electrician .... Cletus Karamon
Production Props Supervisor .... George Wagner
Head Props .... Robert Adams
Production Sound Supervisor .... Christopher Sloan
Wardrobe Supervisor .... Doug Petitjean
Assistant Wardrobe Supervisor .... Michael Growler
Dressers .... Alice Bee, Kenneth Brown, Katherine Gowenlock, Jennifer Griggs-Cennamo, Joseph Hickey, Margaret Horkey, David Mitchell, Derek Moreno, Jeannie Naughton, Melanie Olbrych, Frank Scaccia, Erin Schindler, Mark Trezza
Hair Supervisor .... Larry Boyette
Assistant Hair Supervisor .... Natasha Steinhagen
Hair Dressers .... Brendan O'Neal, Gay Boseker
Rehearsal Pianists .... Paul Ford, Sue Anschutz
Rehearsal Drummer .... Bruce Doctor
Music Department Intern .... Aaron Fischer
Production Assistants .... Lauren Korba, Timothy Eaker, Helen Coney
SSDC Observer .... Andrew Parkhurst
Dialect Coach .... Kate Maré
Assistant to Mr. Berlind .... Jeffrey Hillock
Assistant to Mr. Horchow .... Donna Harper
Assistant to Ms. Roth .... Greg Raby
Assistant to Ms. Bergère .... Amanda Woods
Assistant to Mr. Hartley .... Doris Schwartz
Legal Counsel .... Loeb & Loeb/Seth Gelblum, Esq.
Accountant .... Fried and Kowgios Partners, LLP
Comptroller .... Sarah Galbraith
Advertising .... Serino Coyne/ Scott Johnson, Sandy Block, Jean Leonard
Marketing .... The Marketing Group/ Victoria Cairl, Liz Miller, Sara Rosenzweig, Anne Rippey
Assistant to the General Managers .... John Vennema
101 Productions, Ltd. Staff .... Denys Baker, Ashley Berman, Katharine Croke, Barbara Crompton, Laura Dickinson, Sherra Johnston, Emily Lawson, Heidi Neven, Kyle Pickles, Mary Six Rupert, Evan Storey
101 Productions, Ltd. Intern .... Stewart Miller
Press Intern .... Ann Harris
Banking .... City National Bank/Anne McSweeney
Insurance .... DeWitt Stern, Inc./ Jennifer Brown
Risk Managers .... Stockbridge Risk Management/ Neil Goldstein
Opening Night Coordinator .... Tobak-Lawrence/ Suzanne Tobak, Michael Lawrence
Physical Therapy .... PhysioArts/Jennifer Green
Orthopedist .... Phillip Bauman, M.D.
Theatre Displays .... King Displays, Inc.
Merchandising .... Max Merchandising, LLC
Website Design .... Situation Marketing, LLC/ Damian Bazadona, Lisa Cecchini
Production Photography .... Joan Marcus
Payroll Services .... Castellana Services, Inc.

CREDITS

Scenery and scenic effects by Showmotion, Inc, Norwalk, CT, using the AC2 computerized motion control system. Lighting equipment from PRG Lighting. Sound equipment from PRG Audio. Costumes executed by Barbara Matera Ltd., Carelli Costumes, Euro Co Costumes, JC Theatrical & Custom Footwear, Jennifer Love, Luigi's Quality Tailoring, Scafati, Schneeman Studios, Tricorne Inc., Western Costumes and Timberlake Studio. Shoes by T.O. Dey. Props by The Spoon Group LLC, John Creech Design and Production. Natural herb cough drops courtesy of Ricola USA, Inc. Special thanks to Bra*Tenders for hosiery and undergarments.

Group Sales:
Scott Mallalieu/Stephanie Lee (800) 223-7565

CURTAINS rehearsed at New 42nd Street Studios

SPECIAL THANKS

The director would like to thank Adam Brazier, Aldrin Gonzalez, Alyson Turner, Ann Arvia, Anne L. Nathan, Bernard Dotson, Betsy Wolfe, Boyd Gaines, Burke Moses, Casey Nicholaw, Chip Zien, Dana Lynn Mauro, Daniel Sherman, Danny Burstein, David Andrew McDonald, Deborah Rush, Deven May, Elizabeth Mills, Erin Dilly, Gavin Creel, Gerry Vichi, Gina Lamparella, Gregg Edelman, Hunter Foster, James Clow, James Naughton, Jennifer Laura Thompson, Jessica Lea Patty, Jessica Stone, John Dossett, Kerry O'Malley, Kevin Ligon, Kristine Nielson, Laura Benanti, Lawrence Clayton, Lee Wilkof, Mary Catherine Garrison, Megan Hilty, Mel Johnson Jr., Melina Kanakaredes, Meredith Patterson, Michael Cumpsty, Michael Mendel, Michele Pawk, Paul Michael Valley, Peter Benson, Rachel Coloff, Randy Graff, Ric Stoneback, Robert Walden, Rosena Hill, Ruthie Henshall, Sally Wilfert, Seán Martin Hingston, Stephen Buntrock, Stephen DeRosa, Stephen Lee Anderson, Todd Haimes and the Roundabout Theatre Company, without whom tonight's performance of *Curtains* would not have been possible.

JUJAMCYN THEATERS

ROCCO LANDESMAN
President

PAUL LIBIN Producing Director
JACK VIERTEL Creative Director
JORDAN ROTH Vice President
DANIEL ADAMIAN General Manager
JENNIFER HERSHEY Director of Operations
MEREDITH VILLATORE Chief Financial Officer
JERRY ZAKS Resident Director

Staff for the Al Hirschfeld Theatre

Manager .... Carmel Robinson
Treasurer .... Carmine La Mendola
Carpenter .... Joseph J. Maher, Jr.
Propertyman .... Sal Sclafani
Electrician .... Dermot J. Lynch
Engineer .... Chris Shafer

Curtains

Scrapbook

Photos by Aubrey Reuben

Correspondent: Jill Paice, "Niki Harris"
Memorable Opening Night Note: "Dear Friends, Be as brilliant as you always are...and kill 'em! Love, Your Liza." (note from Liza Minnelli).
Who Got the Gypsy Robe: David Eggers.
Who Has Done the Most Shows in Their Career: Beverley Randolph (20 Broadway shows).
Special Backstage Rituals: Pre-show dances and pratfalls.
Favorite Off-Site Hangout: Any property belonging to DHP.
Favorite Snack Food: Anything from Cletus' Candy Basket and the best birthday cakes on Broadway.
Favorite Therapy: A cocktail of PhysioArts and Tiger Balm.
Who Wore the Least: Megan Sikora as Princess Kickapoo.
Catchphrases Only the Company Would Recognize: "We'll always have Paris!"
Orchestra Members Who Played the Most Instruments: Steve Kenyon: Flute, piccolo, clarinet, and alto sax. Also Al Hunt: Oboe, English horn, clarinet, tenor sax.
Memorable Directorial Note: "Remember! You are being blackmailed!" –Scott Ellis
Company In-Jokes: "SASNAK."
Company Legend: Mary Ann Lamb.
Coolest Thing About Being in This Show: Man on a Horse!

Photo by David Gewirtzman

1. (L-R): Leads Karen Ziemba, David Hyde Pierce, Debra Monk, Jill Paice and Edward Hibbert at Tavern on the Green for the opening night party.
2. Megan Sikora and Noah Racey on opening night.
3. Songwriters John Kander and Rupert Holmes at Tavern on the Green.
4. The cast shares opening night applause with the orchestra.
5. Side entryway to the Al Hirschfeld Theatre in spring 2007.

Deuce

First Preview: April 11, 2007. Opened: May 6, 2007.
Still running as of May 31, 2007.

PLAYBILL

CAST

(in order of appearance)

An Admirer .... MICHAEL MULHEREN
Midge Barker .... MARIAN SELDES
Leona Mullen .... ANGELA LANSBURY
Ryan Becker .... BRIAN HALEY
Kelly Short .... JOANNA P. ADLER

STANDBYS

For Midge:
JENNIFER HARMON
For Leona:
DIANE KAGAN
For Kelly:
LINDA MARIE LARSON
For Ryan/An Admirer:
ROBERT EMMET LUNNEY

THE MUSIC BOX

THE ESTATE OF IRVING BERLIN AND THE SHUBERT ORGANIZATION, OWNERS
239 W. 45th STREET

SCOTT RUDIN STUART THOMPSON MABERRY THEATRICALS
THE SHUBERT ORGANIZATION ROGER BERLIND DEBRA BLACK
BOB BOYETT SUSAN DIETZ DARYL ROTH

present

ANGELA LANSBURY **MARIAN SELDES**

in

by

TERRENCE McNALLY

with

JOANNA P. ADLER BRIAN HALEY MICHAEL MULHEREN

Set Design
PETER J. DAVISON

Costume Design
ANN ROTH

Lighting Design
MARK HENDERSON

Video & Projection Design
SVEN ORTEL

Sound Design
PAUL CHARLIER

Casting
TELSEY + COMPANY

Production Stage Manager
STEVEN BECKLER

Production Management
AURORA PRODUCTIONS

Company Manager
BRIG BERNEY

Press Representative
BONEAU/BRYAN-BROWN

General Management
STP/JAMES TRINER

Directed by

MICHAEL BLAKEMORE

LIVE BROADWAY

The producers wish to express their appreciation to Theatre Development Fund for its support of this production.

5/6/07

2006-2007 AWARDS

OUTER CRITICS CIRCLE AWARDS

Special Achievement Award
(Angela Lansbury)
Special Achievement Award
(Marian Seldes)

(L-R): Marian Seldes and Angela Lansbury acknowledge the crowd's cheers, in character.

Photo by Joan Marcus

Deuce

Angela Lansbury
Leona

Marian Seldes
Midge

Joanna P. Adler
Kelly

Brian Haley
Ryan

Michael Mulheren
An Admirer

Jennifer Harmon
Standby for Midge

Diane Kagan
Standby for Leona

Linda Marie Larson
Standby for Kelly

Robert Emmet Lunney
Standby for Ryan/ An Admirer

Terrence McNally
Playwright

Michael Blakemore
Director

Peter J. Davison
Set Designer

Ann Roth
Costume Design

Mark Henderson
Lighting Designer

Bernard Telsey, Telsey + Company
Casting

Paul Huntley
Wig Designer

James Triner
General Manager

Scott Rudin
Producer

Stuart Thompson
Producer

Gerald Schoenfeld, Chairman, The Shubert Organization
Producer

Roger Berlind
Producer

Debra Black
Producer

Bob Boyett
Producer

Susan Dietz
Producer

Daryl Roth
Producer

FRONT OF HOUSE STAFF
(L-R): Joseph Lopez, Kenneth Kelly, Nic Stavola, Tom Cassano, Joe Amato, Michael Composto, Laura Scanlon, Dennis Scanlon, Jenna Scanlon, Matthew Wickert

BOX OFFICE STAFF
Mike Taustine, Bob Kelly

Photos by Ben Strothmann

Deuce

STAGE CREW
(L-R): Dennis Maher, David Cohen, Brian McGarity, Lee Iwanski, Maeve Fiona Butler, Paul Delcioppo, Kristin Gardner

Photos by Ben Strothmann

STAGE AND COMPANY MANAGEMENT
(L-R): Mary MacLeod, Steve Beckler, Brig Berney

STAFF FOR *DEUCE*

GENERAL MANAGEMENT
STUART THOMPSON PRODUCTIONS
Stuart Thompson Caroline Prugh James Triner

COMPANY MANAGER
Brig Berney

PRODUCTION MANAGEMENT
AURORA PRODUCTIONS INC.
Gene O'Donovan W. Benjamin Heller II
Bethany Weinstein Melissa Mazdra
Meghan VonVett

PRESS REPRESENTATIVE
BONEAU/BRYAN-BROWN
Chris Boneau Jim Byk Danielle Crinnion

CASTING
TELSEY + COMPANY, C.S.A.
Bernie Telsey, Will Cantler, David Vaccari, Bethany Knox, Craig Burns, Tiffany Little Canfield, Rachel Hoffman, Stephanie Yankwitt, Carrie Rosson, Justin Huff, Joe Langworth, Bess Fifer

Production Stage Manager ... Steven Beckler
Stage Manager ... Mary MacLeod
Associate Costume Designer ... Michelle Matland
Associate Lighting Designer ... Daniel Walker
Associate Sound Designers ... Walter Trarbach, Tony Smolenski IV
Makeup Consultant ... Angelina Avallone
Production Electrician ... Brian GF McGarity
Production Sound Operator ... Paul Delcioppo
Projections Operator ... David Cohen
Wardrobe Supervisor ... Kristin Gardner
Miss Lansbury's Dresser ... Maeve Fiona Butler
Hair Supervisor ... Anna Hoffman
Production Assistant ... John Bantay
Assistants to Mr. Rudin ... Mark Rothman, Nathan Kelly
Assistant to Messrs. Kirdahy & Elliott ... Diana Short
Assistant to Mr. Berlind ... Jeffrey Hillock
Assistant to Ms. Black ... Ana Pilar Camacho
Assistant to Ms. Roth ... Greg Raby
Assistant to Mr. Boyett ... Diane Murphy
Assistant to Ms. Dietz ... Angela Sidlow
Assistant to Mr. McNally ... Tessa LaNeve
Assistant Director ... Kim Weild
Tennis Consultant ... Tom Santopietro
General Management Assistant ... Megan Curren
Management Interns ... Aaron Thompson, Diane Alianiello
Banking ... JP Morgan Chase/ Michele Gibbons
Payroll ... Castellana Services, Inc.
Accountant ... Fried & Kowgios CPA's LLP/ Robert Fried, CPA
Controller ... Joseph Kubala
Insurance ... DeWitt Stern Group
Legal Counsel ... Loeb & Loeb Inc./ Seth Gelblum, Esq.
Advertising ... SPOTCO/ Drew Hodges, Jim Edwards, Tom Greenwald, Jim Aquino, Y. Darius Suyama
Marketing ... Leanne Schanzer Promotions, Inc.
Press Associates ... Adrian Bryan-Brown, Jackie Green, Steven Padla, Joe Perrotta, Matt Polk, Susanne Tighe
Production Photographer ... Michal Daniels
Immigration ... Traffic Control Group, Inc./ David King
Theatre Displays ... King Displays, Inc.

Angela Lansbury's appearance by arrangement with Corymore Entertainment, Inc.

Ms. Seldes' wig by Paul Huntley.

CREDITS

Scenery from Hudson Scenic Studio, Inc. Lighting equipment supplied by GSD P roduction Services, Inc., West Hempstead, NY. Sound equipment from Masque Sound. Costumes constructed by Studio Rouge. Video projection system provided by Scharff Weisberg, Inc. *Deuce* rehearsed at the New 42nd Street Studios. Tennis umpire voiced by Rich Kaufman.

STAFF FOR THE MUSIC BOX THEATRE

HOUSE MANAGER ... Jonathan Shulman
Box Office Treasurer ... Robert D. Kelly
Assistant Treasurers ... Michael Taustine, Brendan Berberich, Victoria Radolinski
House Carpenter ... Dennis Maher
House Electrician ... F. Lee Iwanski
House Propertyman ... Kim Garnett
Chief of Staff ... Dennis Scanlon
Accountant ... William C. Grother

Deuce
Scrapbook

Correspondent: Mary MacLeod, Assistant Stage Manager
Opening Night Gifts: Many tennis-related gifts/vintage photos.
Most Exciting Celebrity Visitors: Martina Navratilova and Billie Jean King.
Which Actor Performed the Most Roles in This Show: Michael Mulheren.
Actor Who Has Done the Most Shows in Their Career: Marian Seldes.
Special Backstage Rituals: Joanna P. Adler and Michael Mulheren greet Angela and Marian upstage and downstage left respectively before each performance.
Favorite Moment During Each Performance: Angela and Marian's applause as the lights come up on them at the top of the show.
Favorite In-Theatre Gathering Place: The Stage Managers' room on stage level.
Favorite Snack Food: Michael Blakemore's special nut mix, consisting of dried cherries, dried cranberries, walnuts, and almonds.
Memorable Ad-Lib: Twice Angela has said "If you have anything up your ass, Midge..." instead of "If you have a bug up your ass about anything, Midge...."
Catchphrase Only the Company Would Recognize: "Bounce, bounce, bounce."
Company Legends: Our two leading ladies.
Nicknames: Becky, Mary Mac, Joanna Padler, Michela, "Karen Ziemba," and "Noah Racey."
Coolest Thing About Being in This Show: Watching Angela and Marian get more and more free, comic and profound in their performances.
Also: Steve Beckler, the PSM, draws fabulous doodles pertaining to random lines from the play.

Photos by Aubrey Reuben

1. Marian Seldes and Angela Lansbury take their curtain call on opening night.
2. Opening night guest: tennis star Billie Jean King.
3. Director Michael Blakemore outside the Music Box.
4. (L-R): Playwright Terrence McNally and guest Tom Kirdahy arrive at the Music Box for the premiere.

Dirty Rotten Scoundrels

First Preview: January 31, 2005. Opened: March 3, 2005.
Closed: September 3, 2006 after 36 Previews and 667 Performances.

PLAYBILL

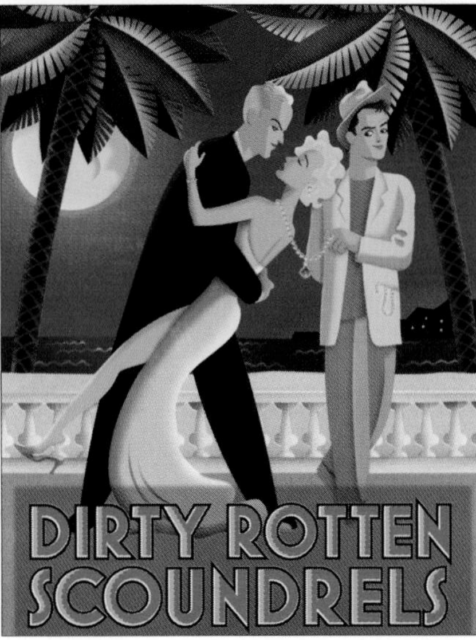

IMPERIAL THEATRE
249 West 45th Street
A Shubert Organization Theatre
Gerald Schoenfeld, *Chairman* **Philip J. Smith,** *President*

Robert E. Wankel, *Executive Vice President*

THE DIRTY ROTTEN PRODUCERS
MARTY BELL DAVID BROWN ALDO SCROFANI ROY FURMAN DEDE HARRIS
AMANDA LIPITZ GREG SMITH RUTH HENDEL CHASE MISHKIN BARRY AND SUSAN TATELMAN
DEBRA BLACK SHARON KARMAZIN JOYCE SCHWEICKERT BERNIE ABRAMS/MICHAEL SPEYER DAVID BELASCO
BARBARA WHITMAN WEISSBERGER THEATER GROUP/JAY HARRIS CHERYL WIESENFELD/JEAN CHEEVER FLORENZ ZIEGFELD
LIVE NATION *and* HARVEY WEINSTEIN
in association with
MGM ON STAGE/DARCIE DENKERT & DEAN STOLBER
and
THE ENTIRE PRUSSIAN ARMY
present

KEITH CARRADINE BRIAN D'ARCY JAMES
SHERIE RENE SCOTT
LUCIE ARNAZ RICHARD KIND
in

DIRTY ROTTEN SCOUNDRELS

Book by JEFFREY LANE
Music and Lyrics by DAVID YAZBEK

BASED ON THE FILM "DIRTY ROTTEN SCOUNDRELS"
WRITTEN BY DALE LAUNER AND STANLEY SHAPIRO & PAUL HENNING

Also Starring
SARA GETTELFINGER

TIMOTHY J. ALEX ROXANE BARLOW JACQUELINE BAYNE STEPHEN CAMPANELLA
JULIE CONNORS JEREMY DAVIS RACHEL DE BENEDET SALLY MAE DUNN WILL ERAT
TOM GALANTICH JASON GILLMAN NINA GOLDMAN GREG GRAHAM AMY HEGGINS
JOAN HESS RACHELLE RAK CHUCK SACULLA TIMOTHY SMITH DENNIS STOWE MATT WALL

Scenic Design DAVID ROCKWELL
Costume Design GREGG BARNES
Lighting Design KENNETH POSNER

Sound Design ACME SOUND PARTNERS
Casting By TELSEY + COMPANY
Associate Choreographer DENIS JONES

Orchestrations HAROLD WHEELER
Vocal Music Arrangements TED SPERLING, DAVID YAZBEK
Dance Music Arrangements ZANE MARK

Conductor FRED LASSEN
Music Coordinator HOWARD JOINES
Technical Supervisor CHRISTOPHER SMITH
Production Stage Manager MICHAEL BRUNNER

Press Representative BARLOW•HARTMAN
Marketing MARGERY SINGER COMPANY
General Management THE CHARLOTTE WILCOX COMPANY

Executive Producer
MARTY BELL / ALDO SCROFANI

Music Direction and Incidental Music Arrangements by
TED SPERLING

Choreographed by
JERRY MITCHELL

Directed by
JACK O'BRIEN

JEWELRY BY QVC

WORLD PREMIERE AT THE OLD GLOBE THEATRE SAN DIEGO, CALIFORNIA.
ARTISTIC DIRECTOR: JACK O'BRIEN / EXECUTIVE DIRECTOR: LOUIS G. SPISTO

9/3/06

CAST

(in order of appearance)

Andre Thibault .... RICHARD KIND
Lawrence Jameson .... KEITH CARRADINE
Lenore .... RACHEL DE BENEDET
Sophia .... JOAN HESS
Muriel Eubanks .... LUCIE ARNAZ
Conductor .... TIMOTHY J. ALEX
Renee .... RACHEL DE BENEDET
Freddy Benson .... BRIAN d'ARCY JAMES
Jolene Oakes .... SARA GETTELFINGER
Hotel Manager .... TOM GALANTICH
Christine Colgate .... SHERIE RENE SCOTT
Sailor #1 .... WILL ERAT
Sailor #2 .... TOM GALANTICH
Nikos .... TOM GALANTICH

THE ENSEMBLE

TIMOTHY J. ALEX, ROXANE BARLOW, JACQUELINE BAYNE, STEPHEN CAMPANELLA, SALLY MAE DUNN, WILL ERAT, TOM GALANTICH, JASON GILLMAN, AMY HEGGINS, JOAN HESS, RACHELLE RAK, CHUCK SACULLA, DENNIS STOWE, MATT WALL

Standby for Lawrence Jameson:
DENNIS PARLATO

SWINGS

JULIE CONNORS, JEREMY DAVIS, NINA GOLDMAN, GREG GRAHAM, TIMOTHY SMITH

Continued on next page

Keith Carradine and Brian d'Arcy James as Lawrence and Freddy.

Photo by Carol Rosegg

Dirty Rotten Scoundrels

MUSICAL NUMBERS

ACT I

Overture	Orchestra, Ensemble
"Give Them What They Want"	Lawrence, Andre, Ensemble
"What Was a Woman To Do?"	Muriel, Women
"Great Big Stuff"	Freddy, Ensemble
"Chimp in a Suit"	Andre
"Oklahoma?"	Jolene, Lawrence, Ensemble
"All About Ruprecht"	Lawrence, Ruprecht, Jolene
"What Was a Woman To Do?" (Reprise)	Muriel
"Here I Am"	Christine, Ensemble
"Nothing Is Too Wonderful To Be True"	Christine, Freddy
"The Miracle" (Act I Finale)	Company

ACT II

Entr'acte	Orchestra, Ensemble
"Rüffhousin' mit Shüffhausen"	Freddy, Christine, Dr. Shüffhausen
"Like Zis/Like Zat"	Andre, Muriel
"The More We Dance"	Lawrence, Christine, Ensemble
"Love Is My Legs"	Freddy, Christine, Ensemble
"Love Sneaks In"	Lawrence
"Son of Great Big Stuff"	Freddy, Christine
"The Reckoning"	Lawrence, Freddy, Andre
"Dirty Rotten Number"	Lawrence, Freddy
Finale	Company

Lucie Arnaz as Muriel.

Richard Kind as Andre.

Photos by Carol Rosegg

Cast Continued

UNDERSTUDIES

For Andre Thibault:
TIMOTHY J. ALEX, DENNIS PARLATO
For Lawrence Jameson:
TOM GALANTICH
For Muriel Eubanks:
RACHEL DE BENEDET, JOAN HESS
For Freddy Benson:
TIMOTHY J. ALEX, JASON GILLMAN
For Jolene Oakes:
JULIE CONNORS, RACHELLE RAK
For Christine Colgate:
JACQUELINE BAYNE, JULIE CONNORS,
JOAN HESS

Dance Captain: GREG GRAHAM

ORCHESTRA

Conductor:
FRED LASSEN
Associate Conductor:
JAN ROSENBERG
Assistant Conductor:
HOWARD JOINES
Concertmaster:
ANTOINE SILVERMAN
Violins:
MICHAEL NICHOLAS, CLAIRE CHAN
Cello:
ANJA WOOD
Woodwinds:
ANDREW STERMAN, DAN WILLIS,
MARK THRASHER
Trumpets:
HOLLIS (BUD) BURRIDGE, JOHN REID
Trombone:
MIKE BOSCHEN
Horn:
RALPH J. KELLEY
Keyboards:
MARCO PAGUIA, JAN ROSENBERG
Guitar:
ERIK DELLAPENNA
Bass:
MIKE DUCLOS
Drums:
DEAN SHARENOW
Percussion:
HOWARD JOINES

Music Coordinator:
HOWARD JOINES
Music Copying:
EMILY GRISHMAN MUSIC PREPARATION/
EMILY GRISHMAN, KATHARINE EDMONDS

Dirty Rotten Scoundrels

Keith Carradine
Lawrence Jameson

Brian d'Arcy James
Freddy Benson

Sherie Rene Scott
Christine Colgate

Lucie Arnaz
Muriel Eubanks

Richard Kind
Andre Thibault

Sara Gettelfinger
Jolene Oakes

Dennis Parlato
Standby for Lawrence Jameson

Timothy J. Alex
Conductor; Ensemble; u/s Andre Thibault

Roxane Barlow
Ensemble; Dance Captain

Jacqueline Bayne
Ensemble

Stephen Campanella
Ensemble

Julie Connors
Swing

Jeremy Davis
Swing

Rachel de Benedet
Ensemble; Lenore; Renee

Sally Mae Dunn
Ensemble

Will Erat
Ensemble; Sailor #1

Tom Galantich
Hotel Manager; Sailor #2; Nikos; Ensemble

Jason Gillman
Ensemble

Nina Goldman
Swing

Greg Graham
Dance Captain; Swing

Amy Heggins
Ensemble

Joan Hess
Sophia; Ensemble

Rachelle Rak
Ensemble

Chuck Saculla
Ensemble

Timothy Smith
Swing

Dennis Stowe
Ensemble

Matt Wall
Ensemble

Jeffrey Lane
Book

David Yazbek
Composter/Lyricist

Jack O'Brien
Director

Jerry Mitchell
Choreographer

Ted Sperling
Music Director, Incidental Music Arranger, Co-Vocal Music Arranger

David Rockwell
Scenic Design

Gregg Barnes
Costume Design

Kenneth Posner
Lighting Design

Dirty Rotten Scoundrels

Tom Clark, Mark Menard and Nevin Steinberg, Acme Sound Partners
Sound Design

Bernard Telsey, Telsey + Company
Casting

Harold Wheeler
Orchestrations

Zane Mark
Dance Music Arranger

Fred Lassen
Conductor

Howard Joines
Music Coordinator

Theatersmith, Inc./ Christopher C. Smith
Production Manager

Jorge Vargas
Makeup Designer

Margery Singer Company
Marketing

Charlotte Wilcox, The Charlotte Wilcox Company
General Manager

Michael Brunner
Production Stage Manager

Daniel S. Rosokoff
Assistant Stage Manager

Dana Williams
Assistant Stage Manager

Marty Bell
Producer/ Executive Producer

David Brown
Producer

Aldo Scrofani
Producer/ Executive Producer

Roy Furman
Producer

Dede Harris
Producer

Amanda Lipitz
Producer

Ruth Hendel
Producer

Chase Mishkin
Producer

Debra Black
Producer

Sharon Karmazin
Producer

Barbara Whitman
Producer

Weissberger Theater Group (WTG)/ Jay Harris
Producer

Harvey Weinstein
Producer

Dirty Rotten Scoundrels

Christine Bokhour
Swing

Norbert Leo Butz
Freddy Benson

Keith Carradine
Lawrence Jameson

Paula Leggett Chase
Swing

Jenifer Foote
Swing

Jason Gillman
Ensemble

Gregory Jbara
Andre Thibault

Jonathan Pryce
Lawrence Jameson

Rachel York
Christine Colgate

Photo by Ben Strothmann

CAST AND CREW

Front Row (L-R): Dina Steinberg (Assistant Company Manager), Bruce Kagel (Company Manager), Therese Costello (Assistant Stage Manager), Michael Brunner (Production Stage Manager), Dan Rosokoff (Assistant Stage Manager), Gregory Jbara (Cast), Greg Graham (Cast), Rhonda Barkow (Physical Therapist).

Second Row (L-R): Tommy Thomson (Propman), Julie Connors (Cast), Jackie Bayne (Cast), Jenifer Foote (Cast), Norbert Leo Butz (Cast), Sally Mae Dunn (Cast), Jeremy Davis (Cast), Fred Lassen (Conductor).

Third Row (L-R): Jack Scott (Dresser), Sonia Rivera (Hair Supervisor), Rachelle Rak (Cast), Laura Marie Duncan (Cast), Dennis Stowe (Cast), Timothy J. Alex (Cast), Rachel York (Cast), Roxane Barlow (Cast), Jan Rosenberg (Associate Conductor), Howard Joines (Percussionist), Kevin Kennedy (Doorman).

Fourth Row (L-R): Kate McAleer (Dresser), Amber Isaac (Dresser), Enrique Vega (Hair), Jonathan Pryce (Cast), Rachel de Benedet (Cast), Jason Gillman (Cast), John Reid (Musician), Mark Thrasher (Musician).

Fifth Row (L-R): Frank Scaccia (Dresser), Jessica Scoblick (Wardrobe Supervisor), Joe Whitmeyer (Hair), Chuck Saculla (Cast), Stephen Campanella (Cast), Will Erat (Cast).

Back Row (L-R): John C. Cooper (Soundman), Pete Donovan (Electrician), Melanie Hansen (Dresser), Lonny McDougal (Electrician), Amy Heggins (Cast), Matt Wall (Cast), Dennis Parlato (Cast), Sara Gettelfinger (Cast) and Tom Galantich (Cast).

Dirty Rotten Scoundrels

Staff for *DIRTY ROTTEN SCOUNDRELS*

WEST EGG ENTERTAINMENT
Creative Director: Marty Bell
Managing Director: Aldo Scrofani
Director, Investor Relations: Tracy Aron
Creative Associate: Justine Lore
Directors: Marty Bell, Roger Lipitz,
Gary McAvay, Tom Owens, Aldo Scrofani

GENERAL MANAGEMENT
THE CHARLOTTE WILCOX COMPANY
Charlotte Wilcox
Matthew W. Krawiec Emily Lawson
Steve Supeck Margaret Wilcox Beth Cochran

GENERAL PRESS RESPRESENTATIVE
BARLOW•HARTMAN
Michael Hartman John Barlow
Wayne Wolfe Andrew Snyder
Gerilyn Shur

MARKETING
Margery Singer Company

COMPANY MANAGER
Bruce Kagel
Associate Company Manager
Dina Steinberg

CASTING
Telsey + Company, C.S.A.:
Bernie Telsey, Will Cantler, David Vaccari,
Bethany Knox, Craig Burns,
Tiffany Little Canfield, Stephanie Yankwitt,
Carrie Rosson, Justin Huff, Joe Langworth

PRODUCTION STAGE MANAGER .... **Michael Brunner**
Stage Manager .... Daniel S. Rosokoff
Assistant Stage Manager .... Dana Williams
Dance Captain .... Greg Graham
Assistant Dance Captain .... Roxane Barlow
Assistant Director .... Benjamin Klein
Associate Scenic Designer .... Richard Jaris
Assistant Scenic Designers Larry Gruber, Todd Ivins, Rachel Short Janocko, Daniel Kuchar
Assistant to the Scenic Designer .... Joanie Schlafer
Associate Costume Designer .... Sky Switser
Assistant Costume Designer at Old Globe .... Charlotte Deveaux
Associate Lighting Designer .... Philip Rosenberg
Assistant Lighting Designer .... Patricia Nichols
Automated Lighting Programmer .... Timothy F. Rogers
Assistant Sound Designer .... Jeffrey Yoshi Lee
Production Electrician .... Jimmy Fedigan
Production Carpenter .... Donald J. Oberpriller
Production Flyman .... Michael Shepp
Production Automation Carpenter .... David M. Cohen
Head Electrician .... Timothy F. Rogers
Assistant Electrician .... Peter Donovan
Production Sound .... Andrew J. Funk
Assistant Sound Operator .... John C. Cooper
Production Properties .... Jerry Marshall
Head Properties .... Steve Wood
Assistant Properties .... Thomas Thomson
Wardrobe Supervisor .... Jessica Scoblick
Assistant Wardrobe Supervisor .... Dolly Williams
Star Dresser to Mr. Carradine .... Patrick Bevilacqua
Dressers .... Janet Anderson, Tom Bertsch, Mel Hansen, Amber Isaac, Kate McAleer, Christel Murdock, Jack Scott, Missy Skop
Hair Supervisor .... Sonia Rivera
Assistant Hair Supervisor .... Joseph Whitmeyer
Hairdresser .... Enrique Vega
Makeup Designer .... Jorge Vargas
Keyboard Programmer .... Zenox Group, Inc.
Synthesizer Programmer .... James Abbott
Drum Music Arranger .... Dean Sharenow
Additional Musical Arrangements .... Dan Lipton
Music Preparation Service .... Emily Grishman Music Preparation
Rehearsal Pianist .... Dan Lipton
Assistant to Mr. Lane .... Ryan Mark Weible
Production Assistants .... Gail Eve Malatesta, Kelly Stillwell
Legal Counsel .... Loeb & Loeb LLP/ Seth Gelblum
Accountants .... Rosenberg, Neuwirth, & Kuchner/ Mark D'Ambrosi, Jana Jevnikar
Advertising .... SpotCo
Drew Hodges, Jim Edwards, Tom Greenwald, Jim Aquino, Y. Darius Suyama
Website Design .... Damian Bazadona
Press Office Manager .... Bethany Larsen
Press Office Associates .... Dennis Crowley, Carol Fineman, Wayne Wolfe, Leslie Baden, Ryan Ratelle, Andrew Snyder
Production Photography .... Carol Rosegg
Theatre Displays .... Interboro Sign and Display Corp.
Banking .... JP Morgan Chase
Stephanie Dalton
Payroll Service .... Castellana Services, Inc.
Physical Therapy .... Performing Arts Physical Therapy
Group Sales .... Group Sales Box Office, Inc.
Education .... Students Live/ Amy Weinstein (Founder/President)
www.studentslive.org
Allyson Morgan, Samuel A. Morris, Petol Weekes
Opening Night Coordinators .. Tobak-Dantchik Events and Promotions
Suzanne Tobak, Joanna B. Koondel
Merchandise ..... Clear Channel Theatrical Merchandising, Karen Davidov
Insurance Consultant .... Stockbridge Risk Management
Information Management Services .. Marion Finkler Taylor
Contracts Consultant .... Elizabeth Schmitt
Travel Services .... Tzell Travel

CREDITS

Scenery and scenic effects built, painted, electrified and automated by Showmotion, Inc., Norwalk, Connecticut. Show control, deck and fly automation effects by Showmotion, Inc., Norwalk, Connecticut, using the AC2 computerized motion control system. Drapery by I. Weiss. Additional scenery construction by the Old Globe Theatre. Costume construction by the Old Globe Theatre, Barbara Matera Limited, Arel Studio and Carelli Costumes. Shoes by LaDuca, J.C. Theatrical & Custom Footwear, T.O. Dey and Capri Shoes. Military accessories by Kaufman's Army and Navy NYC. Lighting equipment from PRG Lighting. Sound equipment by Sound Associates. Wigs by the Old Globe Theatre, Ray Marston wig studio - London, and Bob Kelly Wigs. Properties construction by the Old Globe Theatre. Special thanks to Bra*Tenders for hosiery and undergarments. Ricola natural herb cough drops courtesy of Ricola, USA, Inc. Stock and amateur performance rights are available from Music Theatre International, New York, NY. www.mtishows.com

JEWELRY PROVIDED BY QVC® DESIGNED BY
Kenneth Jay Lane, Nolan Miller and Joan Rivers

Makeup Provided By M·A·C

Drums provided by PEARL.
Pianos provided by BALDWIN PIANO CO.

DIRTY ROTTEN SCOUNDRELS
rehearsed at the New 42nd Street Studios
and 890 Studios.

SPECIAL THANKS
Louis Spisto, Sheryl White, Robert Drake and the entire staff and board of the Old Globe.

THE OLD GLOBE THEATRE STAFF
Artistic Director: Jack O'Brien
Executive Director: Louis G. Spisto
Artistic Director: Craig Noel
General Manager: Michael G. Murphy
Director of Production: Robert Drake
Director of Marketing and Communications: Dave Henson
Director of Development: Todd Schultz
Director of Finance: Mark Somers
Technical Director: Benjamin Thoron
Costume Director: Stacy Sutton
Properties Director: Neil A. Holmes

THE SHUBERT ORGANIZATION, INC.
Board of Directors

Gerald Schoenfeld
Chairman

Philip J. Smith
President

Wyche Fowler, Jr. **John W. Kluge**

Lee J. Seidler **Michael I. Sovern**

Stuart Subotnick

Robert E. Wankel
Executive Vice President

Peter Entin
Vice President
Theatre Operations

Elliot Greene
Vice President
Finance

David Andrews
Vice President
Shubert Ticketing Services

John Darby
Vice President
Facilities

D.S. Moynihan
Vice President – Creative Projects

House Manager .... Joseph Pullara

Dirty Rotten Scoundrels
Scrapbook

Closing a Show—What Does It Feel Like?
Correspondent: Lucie Arnaz, "Muriel Eubanks"

What's it feel like?

Bob Martin said, "We heard the news about your closing backstage at *The Drowsy Chaperone* and there was just silence. Like a death in the family."

Yeah. I remember a sea of microphones being shoved in my face on my way to my car one December dawn while being asked that same answerless question regarding my father's death in 1986. "What's it *feel* like?"

Numbness. Shock. Your eyebrows meet in the middle and freeze for minutes at a time and you say, "*What?*" and "Oh my God!" about five times with five separate inflections and octaves. You sink with sadness for all involved, for those who don't know yet and for all who just found out. You are filled with disappointment. You feel guilt and you're angry, too, damn it, especially when the show seemed to be such a big hit, with audiences screaming with laughter and standing ovations on a daily basis. You feel cheated, caught between political and financial battles over which you have no power. It takes the wind out of you, like a death in the family. Only, this one is like a death *of* the family.

Show People. A theatrical company *is* our family, especially in a long run. It's our home away from home. And no matter how small your individual space (complete with kitchen setup, library, garden, gym and mini office), you live there for a very intense 32-plus hours a week.

My husband and fellow actor Larry Luckinbill said, "It's just so damn sad. I always used to stand in the back of the theatre and say, 'Well, you're dark now. We don't live here anymore.'"

That hit home. Because every time you close a show you are "moving house," which, next to losing a mate, is the most stressful thing any of us will ever do. And you are leaving behind everything that was of that particular experience. In this case (a hit show, a long run), *everyone* who, through the repetition of shared responsibilities for the success of the production, has come to know and love you in every color you've dared to show them, onstage and off. You are saying good-bye to the support, encouragement, unconditional camaraderie created by the sheer challenge of clearing that Herculean hurdle eight times a week together.

Jeanne Lehman, of *Beauty and The Beast*, said, "There is always a sense of loss, of mourning. We actually grieve."

But, for what? The paycheck? Of course. Bill Buell, right now in *History Boys*, told me it was, "A sense of The Abyss. You think, 'God, I can barely make it on a Broadway salary as it is, how the hell am I gonna make it now?' But, somehow you always do."

Photo by Aubrey Reuben

(L-R): Shubert Organization chairman Gerald Schoenfeld with Lucie Arnaz and Jonathan Pryce at the 2006 "Stars in the Alley" event in Shubert Alley.

I think it's more than that. For me, it's the comfort of the routine. A long run in a show (or being in any show, really) is, first of all, knowing you have an answer to that innocent and insufferable question actors are always being tormented with: "So...what are you doing now?"

It's like Cassie sings in *A Chorus Line*, "give me somebody to dance for, give me a place to fit in...let me wake up in the morning to find I have somewhere exciting to go!"

It's *belonging*. "That's my theatre...right there, driver."

It's the immediate recognition as we go through that stage door. Our name on the sign-in sheet, on the dressing rooms. And from our dressers. Those wunderkind mommies and daddies who become our lifelines to survival each day. The dependable laughter. The strangers who become immediate teachers and friends. All the harmless and invigorating gossip. The practical jokes. All the things that come with spending a lot of intense and somewhat stressful times with any large group of hard working professionals. (I imagine it must be much the same for firemen, for doctors in a busy hospital, for airline pilots.)

But theatre people are unique in many respects, with our shared superstitions and individual backstage rituals—traditions created to help us find our comfort zones in this world of make believe that we inhabit. The polite sarcasm that becomes second nature within the crew. God bless the crew, those irascible, irreplaceable guardians who hide in the bowels and black buckets of space within every theatre making certain the magic actually does materialize. The blessed hard-working (sometimes sleeping) crew who, with their relentless capability to lighten up your moods, keep boredom at bay and the balcony set from falling on your head.

Show People: "they smile when they are low." Yes, they do. But, things do change after the dreaded closing announcement settles in. Automatic pilot begins to take over somewhat. Your concentration goes a bit. You make clumsy mistakes. People who were always in the wings during certain numbers to sing along (just because they loved them) now are stone faced and quieter. Announcements at half hour seem half-hearted and sterile. Birthday parties lack the customary enthusiasm...and extra ice cream.

Anything to help raise the morale at this point is appreciated. I hoped my coming back into *Scoundrels*, even when my knee was not entirely healed, just to finish the last performances with everyone, may have done that to some extent. It was the only reason I attempted it. It was going to be hard enough.

And then, there's just the specifics of it. A few days after we all heard the news, Tom Galantich's first thoughts as he stared at the ceiling were "I guess I'll have to get a lot of boxes."

Kate McAleer, my friend of 27 years and my indefatigable dresser, had just given me a huge box full of stationery pads for my birthday imprinted with my name, the logo of the show and the theatre address. I adore them. They're perfect for answering the fan mail that comes to me there. When we shut down, I had only used two pads.

Four days after the announcement, new cases

Dirty Rotten Scoundrels

Scrapbook

of bottled water are still sitting untouched in the girls' hallway.

The printers and copy machines get lower and lower on ink as no one is authorized to purchase extra supplies. Physical therapy scheduled twice a week for the company is eliminated. I guess if you injure yourself in those last days on stage, your next producer pays your Workman's Comp.

And you look around at all of the things that you had taken for granted every day, the things that are just there to get the jobs done more efficiently and you wonder, "Who will get all of the laundry baskets and the organizer drawers from the wardrobe department? Can we take our dance shoes? Can we buy the wig? What about that extra large poster-size photograph of me in the peach satin gown right outside the stage door? Check eBay next week.

But, let's look at the bright side. At least we knew ahead of time.

Michael McCarty, opening soon in *Mary Poppins*, recalled how one show he was in closed while he was on vacation and *no one told him.* He came back to a dark and empty theatre.

Tim Jerome, of Disney's new *Tarzan,* remembered that, after three weeks of previews, he opened *The Mooney Shapiro Songbook* on a Sunday afternoon at the old Morosco Theatre in New York. They attended the opening night party and took the usual Monday off and when they returned on Tuesday, they were told the show had *closed* and to please clear out their dressing rooms as soon as possible.

Some weeks later, as if to add insult to injury, the venerable Morosco Theatre itself was razed to make way for the Marriott marquee. Not the Marriott Marquis Hotel, mind you, but, the marquee of the Marriott Marquis Hotel, which now stands in its place. It was hard to avoid the feeling that the show had been closed so that the Morosco could be torn down. Tim said there was nothing more surreal than seeing vases of opening night flowers on the dressing room tables and all those telegrams still up on the mirrors.

Michael McCarty laughed about the orchestras always being the first to bail. He said during the last weekend of one show that was closing, horrific noises were heard coming out of the pit during the opening number and the cast looked down to see the conductor holding up a sign that read, "17 subs. Don't blame me"!

At least those musicians had the right idea. Go get the next gig! And when all the sniffling stops and the boxes are packed up, that's what we all do: report to unemployment, call the agents, grab a copy of *Back Stage*, or *Theatrical Index* and ask around for what's coming in. Because, we just might be available to move right in and start the whole damn thing all over again. Why? Because that's what we do. We're "Show People." And there's no people like us. We know that even if "you're broken hearted...you go on!" And, when it all does seem too difficult to rise above, just remember what else Mr. Berlin said, "*EVERYTHING* about it is appealing"!!

By the way, I'm available...just for a little while...I hope.

"Carols for a Cure" Carol: "Something Must Be Wrong With My Mistletoe."

Photos by Aubrey Reuben

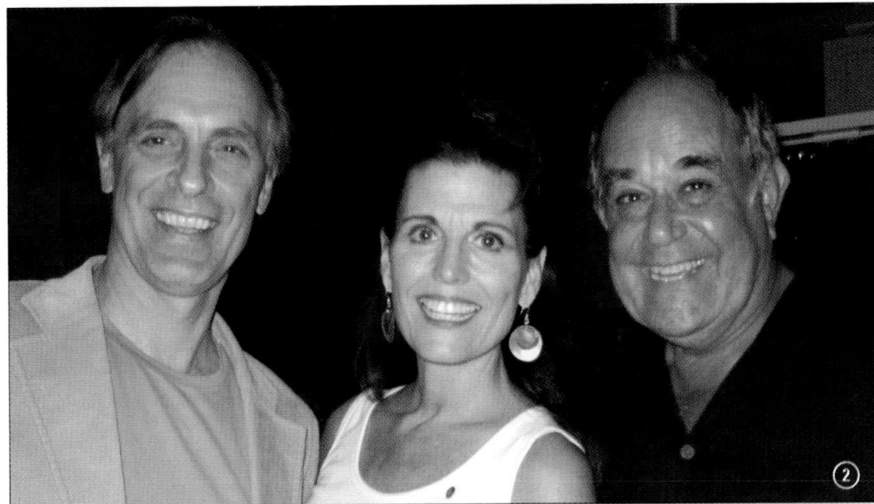

1. Cast members (L-R) Amy Heggins, Sally Mae Dunn, Rachelle Rak and Roxane Barlow at a Trattoria Dopo Teatro party for Norbert Leo Butz and Jonathan Pryce's final performance.
2. (L-R) Keith Carradine, Lucie Arnaz and Laurence Luckinbill at the party.
3. (L-R) Norbert Leo Butz and Jonathan Pryce bid farewell at Trattoria Dopo Teatro.

Dr. Seuss' How the Grinch Stole Christmas!

First Preview: October 25, 2006. Opened: November 8, 2006.
Closed: January 7, 2007 after 10 Previews and 107 Performances.

PLAYBILL

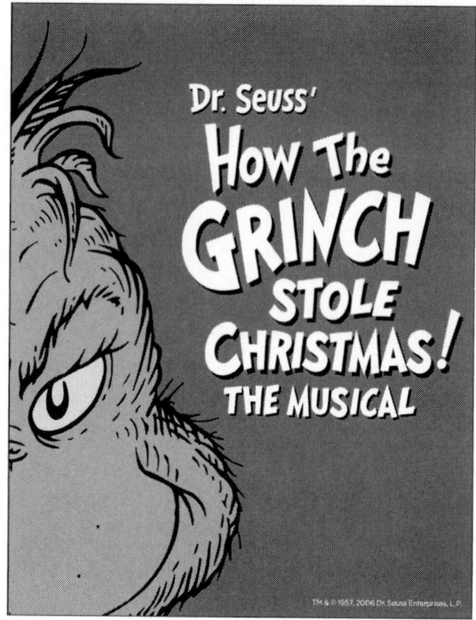

CAST

(in order of appearance)

Old Max .... JOHN CULLUM
Cindy Lou Who
– Red Cast .... NICOLE BOCCHI
– White Cast .... CAROLINE LONDON
JP Who .... PRICE WALDMAN
Mama Who .... KAITLIN HOPKINS
Grandpa Seth Who .... MICHAEL McCORMICK
Grandma Who .... JAN NEUBERGER
Boo Who
– Red Cast .... MALCOLM MORANO
– White Cast .... AARON DWIGHT CONLEY
Annie Who
– Red Cast .... HEATHER TEPE
– White Cast .... CAITLIN BELCIK
Danny Who
– Red Cast .... EAMON FOLEY
– White Cast .... JAMES DU CHATEAU
Betty Who
– Red Cast .... BRYNN WILLIAMS
– White Cast .... LIBBIE JACOBSON
Citizens of Whoville .... JANET DICKINSON, ANDRÉ GARNER, JOSEPHINE ROSE ROBERTS, WILLIAM RYALL, PEARL SUN, JEFF SKOWRON
Little Whos – Red Cast .... ANTONIO D'AMATO, DANIELLE FREID, JESS LEPROTTO, KATIE MICHA, NIKKI ROSE, CORWIN TUGGLES, KELLEY ROCK WIESE

Continued on next page

HILTON THEATRE
A LIVE NATION VENUE

RUNNING SUBWAY
EMI Music Publishing, Michael Speyer & Bernie Abrams
with Allen Spivak, Janet Pailet
Spark Productions/Maximum Entertainment/Jonathan Reinis
Present

Dr. Seuss'
How The GRINCH STOLE CHRISTMAS!
THE MUSICAL

Presented by Target

Based on the book *How the Grinch Stole Christmas* by Dr. Seuss

Book & Lyrics by
Timothy Mason

Music by
Mel Marvin

Additional music and lyrics by Albert Hague and Dr. Seuss

Starring
Patrick Page
with
Rusty Ross

Caitlin Belcik, Nicole Bocchi, Aaron Dwight Conley, James Du Chateau, Eamon Foley, Libbie Jacobson, Kaitlin Hopkins, Caroline London, Michael McCormick, Malcolm Morano, Jan Neuberger, Heather Tepe, Price Waldman, Brynn Williams

Jahaan Amin, Kevin Csolak, Janet Dickinson, Antonio D'Amato, Danielle Freid, André Garner, Brianna Gentilella, Amy Griffin, Sky Jarrett, Kurt Kelly, Jess LeProtto, Daniel Manche, Katie Micha, Jillian Mueller, Josephine Rose Roberts, Nikki Rose, William Ryall, Molly J. Ryan, Jeff Skowron, Pearl Sun, Rafael Luis Tillis, Corwin Tuggles, Kelley Rock Wiese, Lawson Young

and John Cullum as Old Max

Set Designer
John Lee Beatty

Lighting Designer
Pat Collins

Costume Designer
Robert Morgan

Puppet Designer
Michael Curry

Sound Designer
Acme Sound Partners

Wig/Hair Designer
Thomas Augustine

Make-up Designer
Angelina Avallone

Special Effects Designer
Gregory Meeh

Musical Director and Vocal Arranger
Joshua Rosenblum

Orchestrator
Michael Starobin

Dance Music Arranger
David Krane

Music Coordinator
Seymour Red Press

Casting
Telsey + Company

Production Stage Manager
Michael Brunner

Press Representative
Alison Brod Public Relations

Technical Supervisor
Don S. Gilmore

Associate Producer
Audrey Geisel

Associate Producer
Joshua Rosenblum

General Manager
David Waggett

Marketing
Tomm Miller

Choreography Restaged by
Bob Richard

Executive Producer
James Sanna

Original Choreography by
John DeLuca

Directed by
Matt August

Production Created & Supervised by
Jack O'Brien

Based on the production produced at The Old Globe, San Diego, California.
Jack O'Brien, Artistic Director Louis G. Spisto, Executive Director
Originally commissioned by and produced at The Children's Theatre Company, Minneapolis, Minnesota.

Produced by permission of Dr. Seuss Enterprises, L.P.

11/8/06

The Ensemble

Photo by Paul Kolnik

Dr. Seuss' How the Grinch Stole Christmas!

MUSICAL NUMBERS

"Who Likes Christmas?"	Citizens of Whoville
"I Hate Christmas Eve"	The Grinch, Young Max, JP Who, Mama Who, Grandma Who, Grandpa Seth Who, Cindy Lou Who, Betty Who, Annie, Danny, Boo Who
"WhatchamaWho"	The Grinch, Little Whos
"Welcome, Christmas"*	Citizens of Whoville
"I Hate Christmas Eve (Reprise)"	The Grinch
"Once in a Year"	JP Who, Mama Who, Grandma Who, Grandpa Seth Who, Citizens of Whoville, Little Whos
"One of a Kind"	The Grinch
"Now's the Time"	JP Who, Mama Who, Grandma Who, Grandpa Seth Who
"You're a Mean One, Mr. Grinch"*	Old Max, Young Max, The Grinch
"Santa for a Day"	Cindy Lou Who, The Grinch
"You're a Mean One, Mr. Grinch* (Reprise)"	Old Max
"Who Likes Christmas? (Reprise)"	Citizens of Whoville
"One of a Kind (Reprise)"	Young Max, The Grinch, Cindy Lou Who
"Welcome, Christmas* (Reprise)"	Citizens of Whoville
Finale	The Grinch, Cindy Lou Who, Whos Everywhere
"Who Likes Christmas?"	Whos Everywhere, The Grinch

* Music by Albert Hague and Lyrics by Dr. Seuss.
Published by EMI Robbins Catalog Inc.

(L-R): Rusty Ross as Young Max and Patrick Page as The Grinch

ORCHESTRA

Conductor:
JOSHUA ROSENBLUM
Associate Conductor:
SUE ANSCHUTZ
Assistant Conductor:
MARK MITCHELL

Woodwinds:
STEVEN KENYON, ROBERT DeBELLIS, TERRENCE COOK, JOHN WINDER
Trumpets:
CHRISTIAN JAUDES, PHILIP GRANGER, WAYNE Du MAINE
Trombones:
WAYNE GOODMAN, ROBERT FOURNIER

Keyboards:
SUE ANSCHUTZ, MARK MITCHELL
Bass:
LOUIS BRUNO
Drums:
GREGORY LANDES
Percussion:
DAVID ROTH

Music Coordinator:
SEYMOUR RED PRESS
Music Copying:
EMILY GRISHMAN MUSIC PREPARATION/ EMILY GRISHMAN, KATHARINE EDMONDS
Synthesizers Programmed by:
BRUCE SAMUELS

Cast Continued

Little Whos – White Cast	JAHAAN AMIN, KEVIN CSOLAK, BRIANNA GENTILELLA, SKY JARRETT, DANIEL MANCHE, JILLIAN MUELLER, MOLLY J. RYAN
Young Max	RUSTY ROSS
The Grinch	PATRICK PAGE

SWINGS

KURT KELLY, AMY GRIFFIN, RAFAEL LUIS TILLIS, LAWSON YOUNG

UNDERSTUDIES

For Grinch and Old Max:
WILLIAM RYALL
For Young Max:
ANDRÉ GARNER
For JP Who and Grandpa Seth Who:
JEFF SKOWRON
For Mama Who:
PEARL SUN
For Grandma Who:
JANET DICKINSON
For Cindy Lou Who:
KATIE MICHA, MOLLY J. RYAN
For Boo Who:
ANTONIO D'AMATO, DANIEL MANCHE
For Annie Who:
NIKKI ROSE, JILLIAN MUELLER
For Danny Who:
JESS LEPROTTO, KEVIN CSOLAK
For Betty Who:
DANIELLE FREID, JAHAAN AMIN

John Cullum as Old Max

Photos by Paul Kolnik

Dr. Seuss' How the Grinch Stole Christmas!

John Cullum
Old Max

Patrick Page
The Grinch

Rusty Ross
Young Max

Caitlin Belcik
White Cast - Annie Who

Nicole Bocchi
Red Cast - Cindy Lou Who

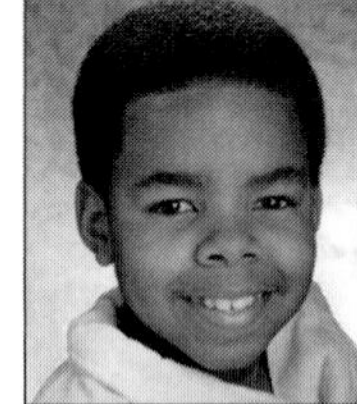
Aaron Dwight Conley
White Cast - Boo Who

James Du Chateau
White Cast - Danny Who

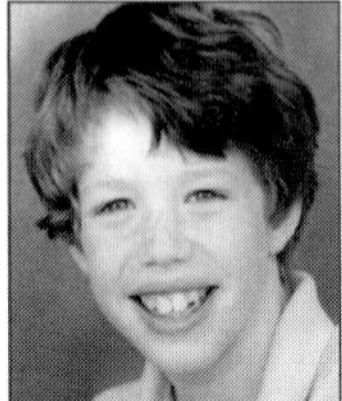
Eamon Foley
Red Cast - Danny Who

Kaitlin Hopkins
Mama Who

Libbie Jacobson
White Cast - Betty Who

Caroline London
White Cast - Cindy Lou Who

Michael McCormick
Grandpa Seth Who

Malcom Morano
Red Cast - Boo Who

Jan Neuberger
Grandma Who

Heather Tepe
Red Cast - Annie Who

Price Waldman
JP Who

Brynn Williams
Red Cast - Betty Who

Jahaan Amin
White Cast - Ensemble

Kevin Csolak
White Cast - Ensemble

Antonio D'Amato
Red Cast - Ensemble

Janet Dickinson
Ensemble

Danielle Freid
Red Cast - Ensemble

André Garner
Ensemble

Brianna Gentilella
White Cast - Ensemble

Amy Griffin
Swing

Sky Jarrett
White Cast - Ensemble

Kurt Kelly
Swing

Jess Leprotto
Red Cast - Ensemble

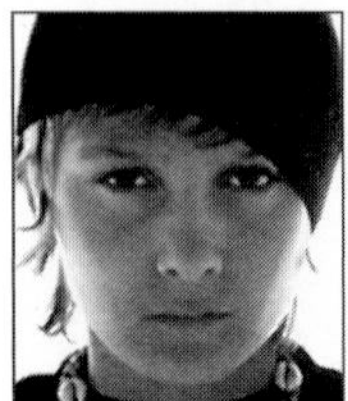
Daniel Manche
White Cast - Ensemble

Katie Micha
Red Cast - Ensemble

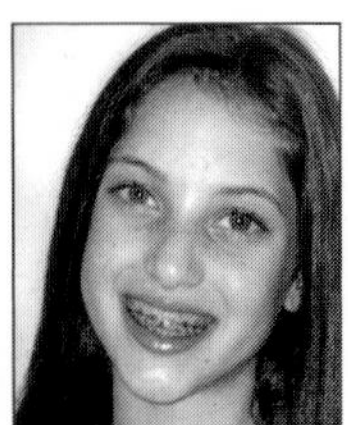
Jillian Mueller
White Cast - Ensemble

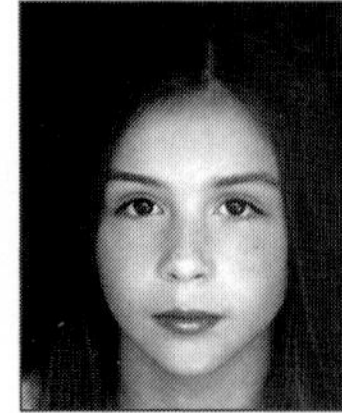
Nikki Rose
Red Cast - Ensemble

Josephine Rose Roberts
Ensemble

William Ryall
Ensemble

Molly J. Ryan
White Cast - Ensemble

Dr. Seuss' How the Grinch Stole Christmas!

Jeff Skowron
Ensemble

Pearl Sun
Ensemble

Rafael Luis Tillis
Swing

Corwin Tuggles
Red Cast - Ensemble

Kelley Rock Wiese
Red Cast - Ensemble

Lawson Young
Swing

Jack O'Brien
Creator/Supervisor

Mel Marvin
Composer

Matt August
Director

John Lee Beatty
Scenic Designer

Pat Collins
Lighting Designer

Tom Clark, Mark Menard and Nevin Steinberg,
Acme Sound Partners
Sound Designer

Michael Curry
Puppet Designer

Angelina Avallone
Makeup Designer

Joshua Rosenblum
Musical Direction, Vocal Arrangements, Incidental Music, Associate Producer

Michael Starobin
Orchestrator

Seymour Red Press
Music Coordinator

Bernard Telsey,
Telsey + Company
Casting

Allen Spivak
Producer

Jonathan Reinis
Producer

Louis G. Spisto
Executive Director, The Old Globe

Jerry Patch
Resident Artistic Director, The Old Globe

Martin Van Treuren
Standby for Old Max

Photo by Ben Strothmann

BOX OFFICE STAFF
(Clockwise, from bottom-left): Michelle Smith, Peter Attanasio Jr. (Box Office Treasurer), Richard Loiacono, Augie Pugliese, Elaine Amplo, Spencer Taustine (Asst. Box Office Treasurer).

Dr. Seuss' How the Grinch Stole Christmas!

Photos by Ben Strothmann

FRONT OF HOUSE
Front Row (L-R): Adam Sarsfield, Denise Williams, Edward Griggs, Emily Fisher, Ilia Smith, Jason McKelvy, Alysha Wright.

Second Row (L-R): Erroll Worthington, Dario Puccini, Charles Catt, Deborah Langenfeld, Lisa Lopez, Delilah Lloyd, Raymond Milan, Tommie Williams, Marlena Young, Jason Bernard.

Third Row (L-R): Paul Fiteli, Nicole Ellingham, Carey Kayser, Mike Chavez, Rita Wozniak, David Prosser, Ken Fuller, Stephanie Wilson, Sharon Hawkins and Fred Mursch.

CREW
Front Row (L-R): Joe Goldman, Sean Jones, John Santagata, Rex Tucker Moss (Assistant Makeup Supervisor), Thomas Smusz (Wig Stylist), Juilet Silva, Angelina Avallone (Makeup Designer and Supervisor), Brannon Gray (Wig Stylist).

Second Row (L-R): Artie Friedlander (Head Electrician), Jim Harris (Head Carpenter), Olivia Booth (Dresser), Holly Nissen (Stitcher/Dresser), Alice Ramos, Carmel Varygas, Talia Krispel.

Third Row (L-R): Carlos Abraham, Emily Ockenfels, Alice Bee, Jeff Wener, Lillian Colon, Robbie Amodeo, Thomas Augustine, Cletus Karamon, Jolie Gabler, DeeAnne Dimmick (Child Wrangler).

Back Row (L-R): Danny Paul (Dresser), Dave Levenberg, Tokuda Moody, Kevin Keene and George Sheer (Dresser).

Dr. Seuss' How the Grinch Stole Christmas!

PRODUCTION STAFF FOR
DR. SEUSS' HOW THE GRINCH STOLE CHRISTMAS!

GENERAL MANAGEMENT
RUNNING SUBWAY

COMPANY MANAGER
Heidi Neven

GENERAL PRESS REPRESENTATIVE
Alison Brod Public Relations
Alison Brod, Robin Edlow, Jodi Simms Hassan

CASTING
TELSEY + COMPANY CSA
Bernie Telsey, Craig Burns,
Justin Huff, Rachel Hoffman

ADVERTISING
MARGEOTES FERTITTA POWELL
Neil Powell, Michael Kantrow, Chris Bradley, Adam Kennedy, Franz Hueber, Brandon Rochon, Mary Williams, Jackie Blum, Marnie Baretz, Mona Rahman, Paul Greenberg, Meredith Volpe

Production Stage Manager .... Michael Brunner
1st Assistant Stage Manager .... Daniel S. Rosokoff
2nd Assistant Stage Manager .... Joel Rosen
2nd Assistant Stage Manager .... Dana Williams
Associate Company Manager .... Jolie Gabler
Assistant Company Manager .... Alyssa Mann
Company Management Intern .... Sarah Hartmann
Assistant Director .... West Hyler
Assistant Choreographer .... Shane Rhoades
Dance Captain .... Kurt Kelly
Associate Scenic Designer .... Eric Renschler
Assistant Scenic Designer .... Yoshinori Tanokura
Associate Lighting Designer .... D.M. Wood
1st Assistant Lighting Designer .... Benjamin Travis
2nd Assistant Lighting Designer .... Keri Thibodeau
Projection Consultant .... Mark Mongold
Associate Costume Designer .... Nancy Palmatier
Assistant Costume Designer .... Chris Meyers
Assistant Sound Designer .... Jeffrey Yoshi Lee
Associate Technical Director .... Bradley Thompson
Production Carpenter .... Michael Kelly
Production Electrician .... Michael S. LoBue
Production Sound .... Dan Robillard
Production Sound Mixer .... Paul Verrity
Production Props Supervisor .... Michael Pilipski
Head Carpenter .... Jimmy Harris
House Fly Man .... Mike Fedigan
Head Electrician/Light Board Operator ... Cletus Karamon
Head Electrician .... Artie Friedlander
Light Board Programmer .... Steve Garner
Head Follow Spot Operator .... John Van Buskirk
Head Props .... Joe Harris
Assistant Props .... Emilio Uriarte
Head Sound .... John Gibson
Wardrobe Supervisor .... Thomas Augustine
Assistant Wardrobe Supervisor .... Robbie Amodeo
Stitcher/Dresser .... Holly Nissen
Dressers .... Alice Bee, Lillian Colon, Danny Paul, Olivia Booth, Emily Ockenfels, George Sheer, Chip White
Associate Wig Designer/Supervisor .... Carmel Varygas
Wig Stylists. .... Brannon Gray, Colleen Liddy, Thomas Smusz, Katie Ward
Makeup Supervisor .... Angelina Avallone
Assistant Makeup Supervisor .... Rex Tucker Moss
Assistant Makeup Artist .... Yanushka Kasabova
Production Assistant .... Christopher Munnell
Child Wranglers .... DeeAnne Dimmick, Talia Krispel
Children's Tutoring .... On Location Education
Tutors .... Kathleen Kenney, Jill Novenstein, Janna Kahr, Nancy Van Ness, Christine Rudakewycz
Legal Counsel .... Frankfurt Kurnit Klein and Selz/ Mark Merriman
Accountant .... Schall and Ashenfarb/Ira Schall
Comptroller .... Anne Stewart Fitzroy
Banking .... JP Morgan Chase/ Michael Friel, Michele Gibbons
Insurance .... AON/Albert G. Ruben Company/ Claudia Kaufman
Physical Therapy .... Performing Arts Physical Therapy
Theatre Displays .... King Displays, Inc.
Concessions .... Spectrum Concessions/ Rosa Hires
Payroll Services .... Axium International/ Martha Palubniak
Sponsorship .... Revolution Marketing/ Andrew Klein
Merchandising .... Max Merchandising/ Randi Grossman, Meridith Maskara

CREDITS

Scenery by Hudson Scenic Studio. Scenery built and painted by F&D Scene Changes LTD., and Great Lakes Scenic Studio. Lighting equipment and special lighting effects by PRG Lighting. Sound equipment from Sound Associates. Props by Spoon Group. Projection equipment from Scharff-Weisberg. Special effects equipment from Jauchem & Meeh, Inc. Costumes executed by Tricorne. Shoes by Capezio, Capri of California, Spears Specialty Clown Shoes, Foot-So-Port. Costume painting by Hochi Asiatico. Fabric dying by Gene Mignola. Grinch finger extensions by Zoe Morsette. Grinch heart by Craig Grigg. Millinery by Rodney Gordon. Knitting by Karen Eifert. Special projects by Material Girl/Arnold Levine. Wigs made by Bob Kelly Wig Creations and Augustine Studios. Ricola natural herb cough drops courtesy of Ricola USA, Inc.

FOR RUNNING SUBWAY

Executive Producer .... James Sanna
Producer .... Joshua Rosenblum
General Manager .... David Waggett
Vice President Marketing .... Tomm Miller
Project Director .... Stacey Lender
Assistant General Manager .... Kathryn Schwarz
Promotions Coordinator .... Megan Skord
Production Coordinator .... Jessica Kingman
Marketing Consultant .... Jennifer Staikos

SPECIAL THANKS

James Claffy Jr., Scott McNulty, Tom Walsh, Frank Gallagher, Ray Polgar, Joel Elrich, Kathryn Haapala, Christopher Brockmeyer, Mary Donovan, Harvey Mars, Lisa Carling, Bra*Tenders for hosiery and undergarments

HILTON THEATRE STAFF

General Manager .... Micah Hollingworth
Assistant General Manager .... Teresa Ryno
Facility Manager .... Jeff Nuzzo
House Manager .... Jeffrey Dobbins
Box Office Treasurer .... Peter Attanasio Jr.
Head Carpenter .... James C. Harris
Head Electrician .... Art J. Friedlander
Head of Properties .... Joseph P. Harris Jr.
Head of Sound .... John R. Gibson
Asst Facility Manager .... Michael Leach
Asst. Box Office Treasurer .... Spencer Taustine
Staff Accountant .... Carmen Martinez
Payroll Administrator .... Tiyana Works
Shipping/Receiving .... Dinara Kratsch
Administrative Assistant .... Jenny Kirlin

Hilton Theatre – A Live Nation Venue

LIVE NATION

President and Chief Executive Officer ..... Michael Rapino

LIVE NATION – VENUES

President and CEO, Venues and Alliances .... Bruce Eskowitz
CFO .... Alan Ridgeway
Vice-President, Finance .... Kathy Porter
Executive Vice President .... Ned Collett
Senior Vice President NY and CT Venues ...... John Huff
Director of Labor Relations .... Chris Brockmeyer

LIVE NATION – THEATRICAL

Chairman, Global Theatre .... David Ian
CEO Theatrical, North America .... Steve Winton
President and COO, North America .. David M. Anderson
CFO, North America .... Paul Dietz
Senior Vice President, Producing .... Jennifer Costello
Executive Vice President/CMO .... Susie Krajsa
Senior Vice President, Operations .... Dan Swartz
Senior Vice President, Business Affairs .... David Lazar
Senior Vice President, Sales and Ticketing .... Courtney Pierce
Vice President, Finance .... Chante Moore
Vice President, Programming .... Alison Spiriti

Live Nation is a leading live content and distribution company focused on creating superior experiences for artists, performers, corporations and audiences. Live Nation owns, operates or has booking rights for 150 venues worldwide and has promoted or produced more than 20,000 events in 2005 and 2006. Current producing credits include *Dr. Seuss' How The Grinch Stole Christmas! The Musical, The Producers, Hairspray* and *Spamalot* on Broadway; an all-new production of Andrew Lloyd Webber's *The Phantom of the Opera* at the Venetian in Las Vegas; and national tours of *Dora the Explorer Live!* and *Barbie Live in Fairytopia.* The theatrical division also presents Broadway Across America, www.BroadwayAcrossAmerica.com, an annual subscription series of top Broadway shows and theatrical entertainment in more than 50 markets across North America. Live Nation is listed on the New York Stock Exchange, trading under the symbol "LYV". More information about Live Nation and its businesses is available at www.LiveNation.com.

Dr. Seuss' How the Grinch Stole Christmas!
SCRAPBOOK

Photo courtesy Nicole Bocchi

Photo by Aubrey Reuben

Photo by Aubrey Reuben

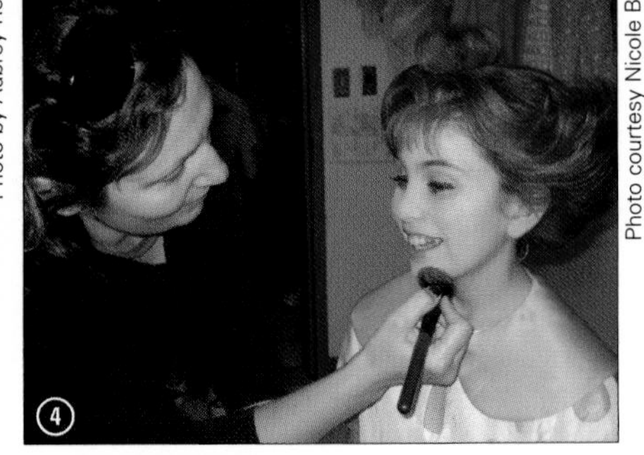
Photo courtesy Nicole Bocchi

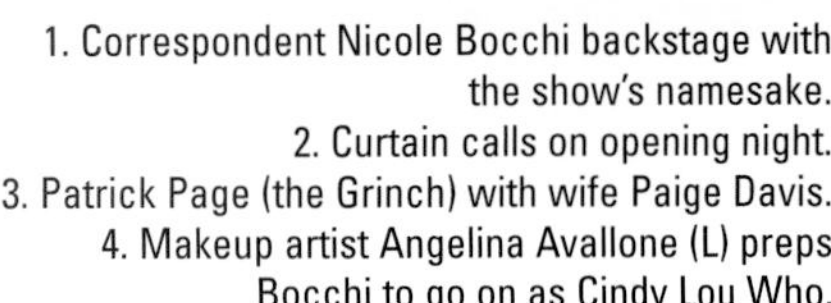
1. Correspondent Nicole Bocchi backstage with the show's namesake.
2. Curtain calls on opening night.
3. Patrick Page (the Grinch) with wife Paige Davis.
4. Makeup artist Angelina Avallone (L) preps Bocchi to go on as Cindy Lou Who.

Correspondent: Nicole Bocchi, "Cindy Lou Who" (Red Cast).

Memorable Opening Night Letter, Fax or Note: I got a nice note from James Sanna and the producers that came with the green iPod nano they gave me. On the note it said: "We are all so proud of you and your performance. Thank you so much for being part of our production. You have a great career ahead of you and we are thrilled we could be a part of it."

Opening Night Gifts: Pink roses from my family, a glass heart ornament from Patrick, a beautiful framed photo of the Grinch billboard from Mel and Tim, a huge green hot air balloon from my agent, Nancy, a sketched drawing of my costume as Cindy Lou, a gold star pin with a red heart on it, an ornament of Grinch going down a chimney, a red scarf and green hat with the Grinch picture on it, Grinch stationery and lots and lots of cards wishing me well.

Exciting Celebrity Visitors: Mrs. Audrey Stone Geisel, Dr. Seuss' wife, was there opening night and she talked to the cast and the audience.
Kelly Ripa came that night before the show began and read to the whole cast and the audience the beginning of the story of Dr. Seuss' "How the Grinch Stole Christmas." She took lots of pictures with everybody.

Gypsy Robe: Bill Ryall got the Gypsy Robe and he put a picture of the Grinch on it. He is so funny!!!!

Most Roles in This Show: The Swings: Amy, Kurt, Lawson and Rafael.

Most Shows in Their Career: I think that John Cullum has done the most shows in his career; second is probably Patrick Page.

Backstage Ritual: Before each show Jeff the stagehand throws me up in the air, and catches me of course!!! We laugh a lot together.

Favorite Moments: Off Stage: getting on my make-up and wig and putting on my costume. On Stage: singing "Santa For a Day" to Patrick (the Grinch) and at the end of the show when the wreath comes down and everybody is singing together.

In-Theatre Gathering Place: The Arts and Crafts room because that's where all the kids create stuff.

Off-Site Hangout: I love to eat at Ciro's, my favorite restaurant near the theatre. The people are so nice and the food is really good!!! Especially the baked clams!!!

Favorite Snack Food: Gouda cheese and fresh strawberries.

Mascot: Bull Dog, the Target dog.

Favorite Therapy: A head and foot massage.

Memorable Ad-Lib: When an audience member, a little boy, heckled at me and Patrick adlibbed "I'll get you later!"

Memorable Stage Door Fan Encounter: One night when I came out the stage door after the show there was a big crowd and they were cheering and clapping and shouting out "Cindy Lou." I never knew it was going to happen.

Who Wore the Heaviest/Hottest Costume: Definitely Patrick.

Catchphrases Only the Company Would Recognize: We have this game we play called "Hit, Snap, Clap!!"

In-House Parody Lyrics: They put an "F" in front of the words in my song "Santa For a Day" (i.e., (f)sometimes (f)when (f)you're (f)all (f)alone....

Memorable Directorial Note: "Remember to always listen, look in the eyes, and speak the meaning not the meter" (rhymes).

Company In-Joke: I like to call Patrick's wife, Paige Davis, Mrs. Grinch.

Nickname: Jellybean.

Sweethearts Within the Company: You'll find out later...

Embarrassing Moment: My shoe almost fell off on stage.

Ghostly Encounters Backstage: One time in 'Whatchama Who,' the scrim almost crashed. I got really scared.

Coolest Thing About Being in This Show: The people in the show because they are all so nice and fun to work with.

Also: The first day of the workshop because it was fun rehearsing my lines for the very first time!!!

Fan Club Info: www.nicolebocchi.com

Doubt

First Preview: March 9, 2005. Opened: March 31, 2005.
Closed: July 2, 2006 after 25 Previews and 525 Performances.

PLAYBILL

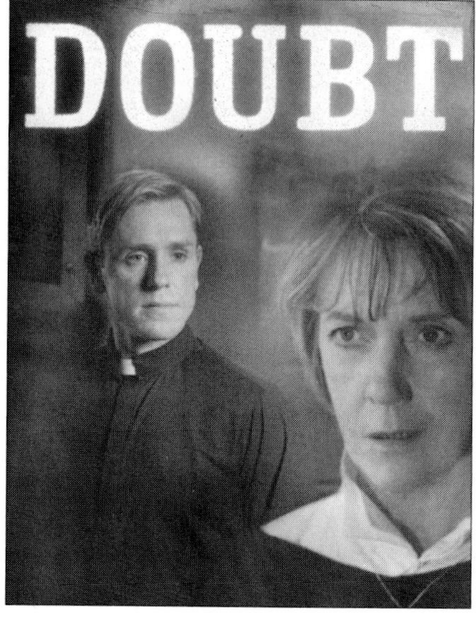

WALTER KERR THEATRE
A JUJAMCYN THEATRE
ROCCO LANDESMAN
PRESIDENT

PAUL LIBIN
PRODUCING DIRECTOR

JACK VIERTEL
CREATIVE DIRECTOR

CAROLE SHORENSTEIN HAYS

MTC PRODUCTIONS, INC.
ARTISTIC DIRECTOR LYNNE MEADOW
EXECUTIVE PRODUCER BARRY GROVE

ROGER BERLIND

SCOTT RUDIN

PRESENT

EILEEN ATKINS RON ELDARD

IN

DOUBT

BY

JOHN PATRICK SHANLEY

WITH

JENA MALONE AND ADRIANE LENOX

SCENIC DESIGN
JOHN LEE BEATTY

COSTUME DESIGN
CATHERINE ZUBER

LIGHTING DESIGN
PAT COLLINS

ORIGINAL MUSIC AND SOUND DESIGN
DAVID VAN TIEGHEM

PRODUCTION STAGE MANAGER
CHARLES MEANS

CASTING
NANCY PICCIONE/DAVID CAPARELLIOTIS

PRODUCTION MANAGEMENT
AURORA PRODUCTIONS

PRESS REPRESENTATIVE
BONEAU/BRYAN-BROWN

MARKETING
TMG–THE MARKETING GROUP

GENERAL MANAGEMENT
STUART THOMPSON PRODUCTIONS/JAMES TRINER

EXECUTIVE PRODUCER
GREG HOLLAND

DIRECTED BY

DOUG HUGHES

ORIGINALLY PRODUCED BY MANHATTAN THEATRE CLUB ON NOVEMBER 23, 2004.
THE PRODUCERS WISH TO EXPRESS THEIR APPRECIATION TO THEATRE DEVELOPMENT FUND FOR ITS SUPPORT OF THIS PRODUCTION.

7/2/06

CAST
(in order of appearance)

Father Flynn ....RON ELDARD
Sister Aloysius ....EILEEN ATKINS
Sister James ....JENA MALONE
Mrs. Muller ....ADRIANE LENOX

Stage Manager: ELIZABETH MOLONEY

TIME:
Autumn, 1964

PLACE:
St. Nicholas Church School in the Bronx

STANDBYS
For Sister James:
NADIA BOWERS

For Father Flynn:
STEVIE RAY DALLIMORE

For Mrs. Muller:
LYNDA GRAVÁTT

(L-R): Jena Malone and Eileen Atkins.
Photo by Joan Marcus

Doubt

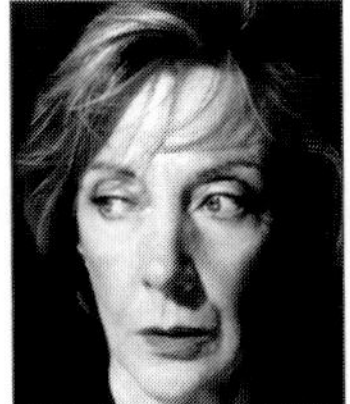
Eileen Atkins
Sister Aloysius

Ron Eldard
Father Flynn

Jena Malone
Sister James

Adriane Lenox
Mrs. Muller

Nadia Bowers
Standby for Sister James

Stevie Ray Dallimore
Standby for Father Flynn

Lynda Gravátt
Standby for Mrs. Muller

John Patrick Shanley
Playwright

Doug Hughes
Director

John Lee Beatty
Set Design

Catherine Zuber
Costume Design

Pat Collins
Lighting Design

Stuart Thompson, Stuart Thompson Productions
General Manager

Carole Shorenstein Hays
Producer

Lynne Meadow
Artistic Director, Manhattan Theatre Club

Barry Grove
Executive Producer, Manhattan Theatre Club

Roger Berlind
Producer

Scott Rudin
Producer

Greg Holland
Executive Producer

STAGE CREW AND MEMBERS OF CAST

Front Row (L-R): Jena Malone (Sister James), Elizabeth Moloney (Stage Manager), Eileen Atkins (Sister Aloysius), Rebecca Heroff (Production Props) and Sister Inflatus (Mascot).

Back Row (L-R): Gina Gornik (Wardrobe), James Gardner (Production Electrician), Ron Eldard (Father Flynn), Eileen Miller (Wardrobe Supervisor), Stevie Ray Dallimore (Standby for Father Flynn), George Fullum (House Carpenter), Tim Bennet (House Props), Charles Means (Production Stage Manager), Caroline Andersen (Production Assistant) and Paul Delcioppo (Production Sound Engineer).

Photo by Ben Strothmann

BOX OFFICE
Stan Shaffer and Gail Yerkovich

FRONT OF HOUSE STAFF
Sitting (L-R): Dayris Fana, Victoria Lauzun, Elizabeth C. Taylor and Tatiana Gomberg.
Standing (L-R): John Barker, Marjorie Glover, Aaron Kendall, Laurie Garcia, Jennifer Artesi, Kishan Redding, Brandon Houghton, Virgilio Estrada, Ralph Santos and Hector Rivera.

STAFF FOR *DOUBT*

GENERAL MANAGEMENT
STUART THOMPSON PRODUCTIONS
Stuart Thompson Caroline Prugh James Triner

COMPANY MANAGER
Bobby Driggers

GENERAL PRESS REPRESENTATIVE
BONEAU/BRYAN-BROWN
Chris Boneau Jim Byk Aaron Meier Heath Schwartz

PRODUCTION MANAGEMENT
AURORA PRODUCTIONS INC.
Gene O'Donovan
W. Benjamin Heller II Bethany Weinstein
Melissa Mazdra Hilary Austin

Production Stage Manager .... **Charles Means**
Stage Manager .... Elizabeth Moloney
Dialect Coach .... Stephen Gabis
Associate Director .... **Mark Schneider**
Associate Set Designer .... Eric Renschler
Assistant Set Designer .... Yoshinori Tanakura
Associate Lighting Designer .... D.M. Wood
Assistant Costume Designers .... T. Michael Hall, Michael Zecker
Assistant Sound Designer .... Walter Trarbach
Production Electrician .... James Gardner
Production Props .... Rebecca Heroff
Production Sound .... Paul Delcioppo
Wardrobe Supervisor .... Eileen Miller
Dresser .... Gina Gornik
Automation .... Danny Braddish
Casting Assistant .... Jennifer McCool
Production Assistants .... Caroline Andersen, Anne Michelson
Assistant to Mrs. Hays .... Kelly Hartgraves
Assistant to Mr. Berlind .... Jeffrey Hillock
Assistant to Mr. Rudin .... Michael Diliberti
General Management Assistant .... Megan Curren
Management Intern .... Zoe Block
Banking .... Chase Manhattan Bank/ Richard L. Callian, Michele Gibbons
Payroll .... Castellana Services, Inc./ Lance Castellana
Accountant .... Robert Fried, CPA
Controller .... Anne Stewart FitzRoy, CPA
Assistant Controller .... Joseph S. Kubala
Insurance .... DeWitt Stern Group, Inc./ Jolyon F. Stern, Peter Shoemaker, Anthony L. Pittari
Legal Counsel .... Paul, Weiss, Rifkind, Wharton & Garrison/ John F. Breglio, Esq., Rachel Hoover, Esq.
Advertising .... SpotCo/Drew Hodges, Jim Edwards, John Lanasa, Lauren Hunter
Marketing Consultants .... The MarketingGroup/ Tanya Grubich, Laura Matalon Trish Santini, Bob Bucci, Amber Glassberg, Liz Miller
Production Photographer .... Joan Marcus
Cover Design by .... SpotCo
Cover Photo Illustration by .... Marc Yankus

CREDITS
Scenery and automation from Hudson Scenic Studio, Inc. Lighting equipment supplied by GSD Productions, Inc., West Hempstead, NY. Sound equipment by Masque Sound. *Doubt* rehearsed at Manhattan Theatre Club's Creative Center. Lozenges by Ricola.

STAFF FOR MANHATTAN THEATRE CLUB

Artistic Director .... Lynne Meadow
Executive Producer .... Barry Grove
General Manager .... Florie Seery
Director of Artistic Production .... Michael Bush
Director of Artistic Development .... Paige Evans
Director of Artistic Operations .... Mandy Greenfield
Artistic Associate/ Assistant to the Artistic Director .... Amy Gilkes Loe
Director of Casting .... Nancy Piccione
Casting Director .... David Caparelliotis
Director of Development .... Jill Turner Lloyd
Director of Marketing .... Debra Waxman
Director of Finance .... Jeffrey Bledsoe
Associate General Manager .... Lindsey T. Brooks
Company Manager/NY City Center .... Lindsey T. Brooks
Assistant to the Executive Producer .... Bonnie Pan
Director of Subscriber Services .... Robert Allenberg
Director of Telesales and Telefunding .... George Tetlow
Director of Education .... David Shookhoff
Production Manager .... Ryan McMahon

JUJAMCYN THEATERS

ROCCO LANDESMAN
President

PAUL LIBIN
Producing Director

JACK VIERTEL
Creative Director

JERRY ZAKS
Resident Director

JORDAN ROTH
Resident Producer

DANIEL ADAMIAN
General Manager

JENNIFER HERSHEY
Director of Operations

MEREDITH VILLATORE
Chief Financial Officer

STAFF FOR THE WALTER KERR THEATRE

Manager .... Susan Elrod
Treasurer .... Stan Shaffer
Carpenter .... George A. Fullum
Propertyman .... Timothy Bennet
Electrician .... Vincent Valvo, Jr.
Engineer .... Ralph Santos

The Drowsy Chaperone

First Preview: April 3, 2006. Opened: May 1, 2006.
Still running as of May 31, 2007.

PLAYBILL

MARQUIS THEATRE

UNDER THE DIRECTION OF JAMES M. NEDERLANDER AND JAMES L. NEDERLANDER

Kevin McCollum Roy Miller Boyett Ostar Productions
Stephanie McClelland Barbara Freitag Jill Furman

present

The DROWSY Chaperone

Music and Lyrics by
Lisa Lambert and Greg Morrison

Book by
Bob Martin and Don McKellar

by Special Arrangement with Paul Mack

Starring
Danny Burstein Georgia Engel Sutton Foster Edward Hibbert Troy Britton Johnson
Eddie Korbich Garth Kravits Jason Kravits Beth Leavel Kecia Lewis-Evans
Bob Martin Jennifer Smith Lenny Wolpe

and
Andrea Chamberlain Jay Douglas Stacia Fernandez Linda Gabler Linda Griffin
Dale Hensley Angela Pupello Joey Sorge Patrick Wetzel

Scenic Design
David Gallo

Costume Design
Gregg Barnes

Lighting Design
Ken Billington
Brian Monahan

Sound Design
Acme Sound Partners

Casting
Telsey + Company

Hair Design
Josh Marquette

Makeup Design
Justen M. Brosnan

Orchestrations by
Larry Blank

Dance and Incidental Music Arrangements by
Glen Kelly

Music Direction and Vocal Arrangements by
Phil Reno

Music Coordinator
John Miller

Production Supervisors
Brian Lynch
Chris Kluth

Production Stage Manager
Karen Moore

Associate Producers
Sonny Everett
Mariano Tolentino, Jr.

Press Representative
Boneau/Bryan-Brown

Marketing
TMG - The Marketing Group

General Management
The Charlotte Wilcox Company

Directed and Choreographed by
Casey Nicholaw

American Premiere produced at the Ahmanson Theatre by Center Theatre Group, LA's Theatre Company
The producers wish to express their appreciation to Theatre Development Fund for its support of this production.

10/2/06

CAST

(in order of appearance)

Man in Chair .... BOB MARTIN
Mrs. Tottendale .... GEORGIA ENGEL
Underling .... EDWARD HIBBERT
Robert Martin .... TROY BRITTON JOHNSON
George .... EDDIE KORBICH
Feldzieg .... LENNY WOLPE
Kitty .... JENNIFER SMITH
Gangster #1 .... JASON KRAVITS
Gangster #2 .... GARTH KRAVITS
Aldolpho .... DANNY BURSTEIN
Janet Van De Graaff .... SUTTON FOSTER
The Drowsy Chaperone .... BETH LEAVEL
Trix .... KECIA LEWIS-EVANS
Super .... JOEY SORGE
Ensemble .... LINDA GRIFFIN, ANGELA PUPELLO, JOEY SORGE, PATRICK WETZEL

SWINGS

ANDREA CHAMBERLAIN,
JAY DOUGLAS,
STACIA FERNANDEZ,
LINDA GABLER,
DALE HENSLEY

DANCE CAPTAIN

ANGELA PUPELLO

Continued on next page

(L-R): Bob Martin and Beth Leavel

Photo by Joan Marcus

The Drowsy Chaperone

MUSICAL NUMBERS

Overture	Orchestra
"Fancy Dress"	Company
"Cold Feets"	Robert, George
"Show Off"	Janet, Company
"As We Stumble Along"	Drowsy Chaperone
"I Am Aldolpho"	Aldolpho, Drowsy Chaperone
"Accident Waiting to Happen"	Robert, Janet
"Toledo Surprise"	Gangsters, Feldzieg, Kitty, Aldolpho, George, Janet, Robert, Underling, Mrs. Tottendale, Drowsy Chaperone and Company
"Message From a Nightingale"	Kitty, Gangsters, Aldolpho, Drowsy Chaperone
"Bride's Lament"	Janet, Company
"Love Is Always Lovely in the End"	Mrs. Tottendale, Underling
"I Do, I Do in the Sky"	Trix and Company
"As We Stumble Along" (Reprise)	Company

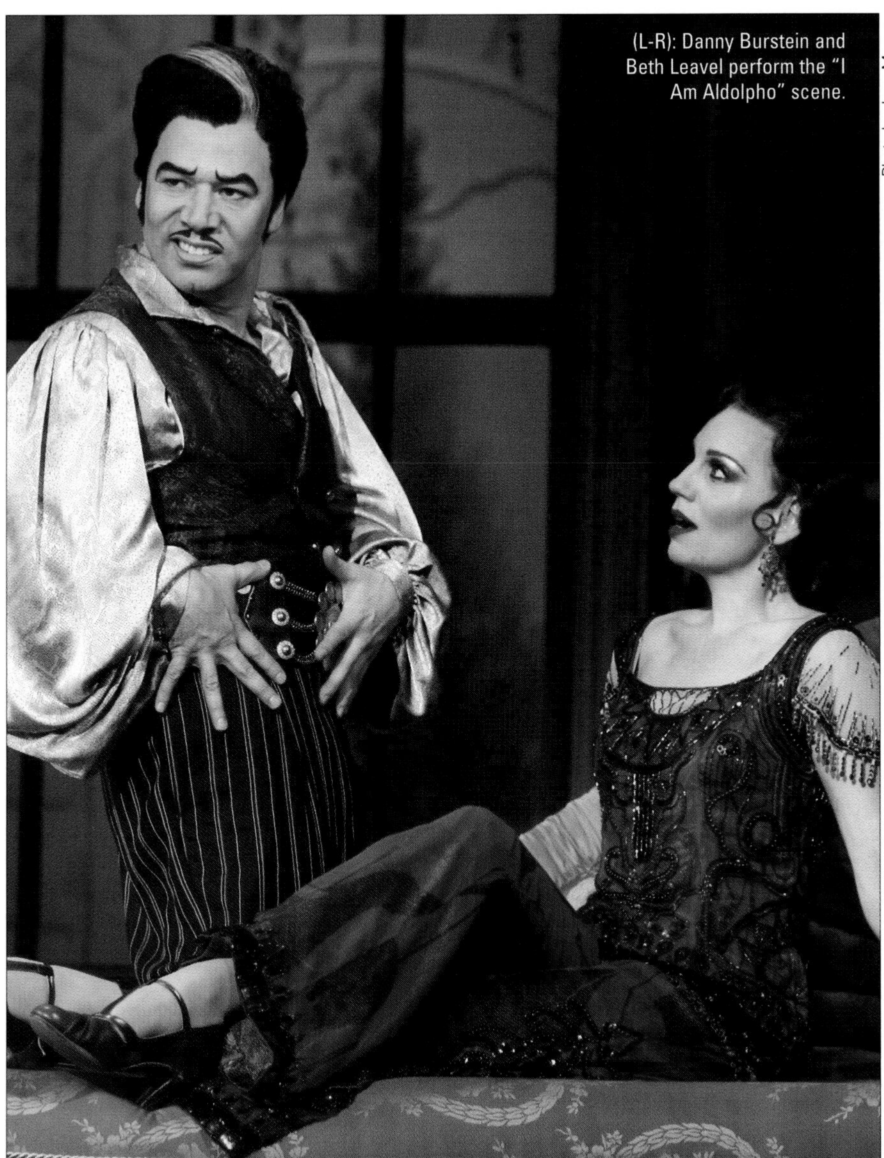

(L-R): Danny Burstein and Beth Leavel perform the "I Am Aldolpho" scene.

Photo by Joan Marcus

Cast Continued

UNDERSTUDIES

For Man in Chair:
JAY DOUGLAS, PATRICK WETZEL
For Janet:
ANDREA CHAMBERLAIN, ANGELA PUPELLO
For Robert:
JAY DOUGLAS, JOEY SORGE
For The Drowsy Chaperone:
STACIA FERNANDEZ, LINDA GRIFFIN
For Mrs. Tottendale:
STACIA FERNANDEZ, LINDA GABLER, LINDA GRIFFIN
For Aldolpho:
JAY DOUGLAS, JOEY SORGE
For Underling:
PATRICK WETZEL, DALE HENSLEY
For Feldzieg:
JAY DOUGLAS, PATRICK WETZEL
For Kitty:
ANDREA CHAMBERLAIN, LINDA GABLER, ANGELA PUPELLO
For George:
PATRICK WETZEL
For Gangsters #1 and #2:
JOEY SORGE, DALE HENSLEY
For Trix:
STACIA FERNANDEZ, LINDA GABLER, LINDA GRIFFIN

ORCHESTRA

Conductor:
PHIL RENO
Associate Conductor:
LAWRENCE GOLDBERG

Reeds:
EDWARD JOFFE, TOM MURRAY, TOM CHRISTENSEN, RON JANNELLI
Trumpets:
DAVE STAHL, GLENN DREWES, JEREMY MILOSZEWICZ
Trombones:
STEVE ARMOUR, JEFF NELSON
Guitar:
ED HAMILTON
Bass:
MICHAEL KUENNEN
Drums:
PERRY CAVARI
Percussion:
BILL HAYES
Keyboards:
MATT PERRI, LAWRENCE GOLDBERG

Music Coordinator:
JOHN MILLER

The Drowsy Chaperone

Danny Burstein
Aldolpho

Georgia Engel
Mrs. Tottendale

Sutton Foster
Janet Van De Graaff

Edward Hibbert
Underling

Troy Britton Johnson
Robert Martin

Eddie Korbich
George

Garth Kravits
Gangster #2

Jason Kravits
Gangster #1

Beth Leavel
The Drowsy Chaperone

Kecia Lewis-Evans
Trix

Bob Martin
Book, Man in Chair

Jennifer Smith
Kitty

Lenny Wolpe
Feldzieg

Andrea Chamberlain
Swing

Jay Douglas
Swing

Stacia Fernandez
Swing

Linda Gabler
Swing

Linda Griffin
Ensemble

Dale Hensley
Swing

Angela Pupello
Ensemble

Joey Sorge
Ensemble, Super

Patrick Wetzel
Ensemble

Lisa Lambert
Music & Lyrics

Greg Morrison
Music & Lyrics

Don McKellar
Book

Casey Nicholaw
Director

David Gallo
Scenic Design

Gregg Barnes
Costume Design

Ken Billington
Co-Lighting Design

Brian Monahan
Co-Lighting Design

Tom Clark, Mark Menard and Nevin Steinberg,
Acme Sound Partners
Sound Design

Bernard Telsey,
Telsey + Company
Casting

Josh Marquette
Hair Design

Justen M. Brosnan
Makeup Design

The Drowsy Chaperone

Larry Blank
Orchestrations

Phil Reno
Music Direction & Vocal Arrangements

John Miller
Music Coordinator

Brian Lynch
Production Supervisor

Casey Hushion
Assistant Director

Josh Rhodes
Assistant Choreographer

Charlie Smith
Associate Scenic Designer

The Charlotte Wilcox Company
General Manager

Kevin McCollum
Producer

Roy Miller
Producer

Bob Boyett
Producer

Bill Haber, OSTAR Enterprises
Producer

Stephanie P. McClelland
Producer

Barbara Heller Freitag
Producer

Jill Furman
Producer

Sonny Everett
Associate Producer

Kilty Reidy
Swing

Noble Shropshire
Underling

Bob Walton
Swing

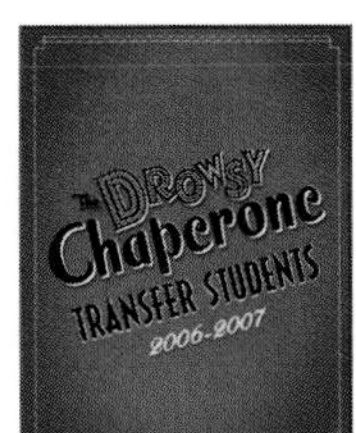

Peter Bartlett
Underling

Jonathan Crombie
Man in Chair

John Glover
Man in Chair

Janine LaManna
Janet Van De Graaff

Kate Loprest
Swing

Brian J. Marcum
Swing

Kilty Reidy
Ensemble, Swing

JoAnne Worley
Mrs. Tottendale

Joanna Young
Ensemble, Swing

The Drowsy Chaperone

WARDROBE DEPARTMENT
Top Row (L-R): Barry Hoff, Joby Horrigan (Assistant Wardrobe Supervisor), Charlie Catanese, Mel Hansen, Julien Havard.

Bottom Row (L-R): Pat Sullivan, John Glover (actor), Lyssa Everett, Margiann Flanagan, Philip R. Rolfe and Terri Purcell (Wardrobe Supervisor).

FRONT OF HOUSE STAFF
Top Row (L-R): (Ushers) Phyllis Weinsaft, Odalis Concepcion, Charlie Spencer, Stanley Seidman, Barbara Corey.

Middle Row (L-R): Lea Lefler, Lulu Caso, David Calhoun (House Manager), Ava Probst (Associate House Manager), Huey Dill.

Bottom Row (L-R): Carol Reilly, John Clark, and Nancy Diaz.

Photos by Ben Strothmann

BOX OFFICE STAFF
(L-R): Larry Waxman, John Giebler, Richie Thigpen and John Rooney.

The Drowsy Chaperone

STAGE AND COMPANY MANAGEMENT
(L-R): Jeffrey Rodriguez (Production Assistant), Karen Moore (Production Stage Manager), Rachel McCutchen (Assistant Stage Manager and Robert Jones (Assistant Company Manager).

HAIR DEPARTMENT
(L-R): Sandy Schlender, Paul Zaya and Carla Muniz.

Photos by Ben Strothmann

ORCHESTRA
Front Row (L-R): Dave Stahl, Tom Murray.

Middle Row (L-R): Bill Hayes, Lawrence Goldberg (Associate Conductor), Matt Perri, Jeff Nelson.

Back Row (L-R): Steve Armour, Perry Cavari, Jeremy Miloszewicz, Ray Kilday, Ed Joffe, Ron Jannelli, Ed Hamilton, Glenn Drewes, Phil Reno (Music Director and Conductor) and Julie Ferrara.

STAGE CREW
Front Row (L-R): John Fullum, Chris Weigel, Augie Mericola, Kenny Sheehan.

Middle Row (L-R): Joe Sardo, Tim Donovan, Tim Shea, Joe Ippolito, Cheyenne Benson, Duke Wilson, Roland Weigel.

Back Row (L-R): Rick Poulin, Brady Jarvis and Keith Buchanan.

The Drowsy Chaperone

STAFF FOR *THE DROWSY CHAPERONE*

GENERAL MANAGEMENT
THE CHARLOTTE WILCOX COMPANY
Charlotte W. Wilcox
Matthew W. Krawiec Emily Lawson
Steve Supeck Margaret Wilcox
Beth Cochran

GENERAL PRESS REPRESENTATION
BONEAU/BRYAN-BROWN
Chris Boneau Joe Perrotta
Heath Schwartz

COMPANY MANAGER
Seth Marquette

ASSISTANT COMPANY MANAGER
Robert E. Jones

CASTING
Telsey + Company, C.S.A.:
Bernie Telsey, Will Cantler, David Vaccari,
Bethany Knox, Craig Burns,
Tiffany Little Canfield, Stephanie Yankwitt,
Carrie Rosson, Justin Huff, Joe Langworth

PRODUCTION STAGE MANAGER .KAREN MOORE
Stage Manager ....Joshua Halperin
Assistant Stage Manager ....Rachel S. McCutchen
Assistant Director ....Casey Hushion
Assistant Choreographer ....Josh Rhodes
Asst. to Mssrs. McCollum & Miller ....David Michael Roth
Assts. to Mr. Boyett ....Diane Murphy, Michael Mandell
Assts. to Mr. Haber ....Theresa Pisanelli, Andrew Cleghorn
Boyett-Ostar Development and Strategic Planning ....Jan Gura
Associate Scenic Designer ....Charlie Smith
Assistant Scenic Designers ....Zhanna Gurvich, Dustin O'Neill, Gaetane Bertol, Bill Beilke, Mary Hamrick
Associate Costume Designer ....Sky Switser
Assistants to Costume Designers ....Cathy Parrott, Sarah Sophia Turner
Costume Intern ....Katharine Sullivan
Associate Lighting Designer ....Stephen N. Boulmetis
Assistant Lighting Designer ....Anthony Pearson
Assistant Sound Designer ....Nick Borisjuk
Production Carpenter ....Chris Kluth
Production Properties ....George Wagner
Moving Lights Programmer ....Hillary Knox
Head Carpenter ....Joe Ippolito
Automation Flyman ....Cheyenne Benson
Production Electrician ....Keith Buchanan
Head Electrician ....Brady Jarvis
Assistant Electrician ....Bruce Liebenow
Production Sound ....Daryl Kral
Head Properties ....Augie Mericola
Wardrobe Supervisor ....Terri Purcell
Assistant Wardrobe Supervisor ....Joby Horrigan
Dressers ....Charles Catanese, Susan Checklick, Lyssa Everett, Margiann Flanagan, Julien Havard, Barry Hoff, Philip R. Rolfe, David Ruble, Pat Sullivan
Hair Supervisor ....Richard Orton
Hairdressers ....Nathaniel Hathaway, Carla Muniz, Sandy Schlender
Assistant to John Miller ....Kelly M. Rach
Synthesizer Programmer ....Jim Abbott
Music Preparation Service ....Hotstave, Ltd.
Music Copyists ....Anixter Rice Music Services
Rehearsal Pianists ....Lawrence Goldberg, Glen Kelly, Matt Perri
Rehearsal Drummer ....Perry Cavari
Production Assistants ....Jeffrey Rodriguez, Rachel Zack
Music Production Assistant ....Colleen Darnall
LA Casting ....Amy Lieberman, C.S.A.
NAMT Presentation Casting ....Cindi Rush Casting
Legal Counsel ....Levine, Plotkin & Menin LLP/ Loren Plotkin, Susan Mindell
Accountants ....Fried & Kowgios LLP/ Robert Fried
Advertising ....SpotCo/ Drew Hodges, Jim Edwards, Pete Milano, Jim McNicholas
Marketing ....TMG – The Marketing Group/ Tanya Grubich, Laura Matalon, Anne Rippey, Nancy Gallagher, Laura Laponte, Meghan Zaneski
Press Assistant ....Erin Hinton
Press Representative Staff ....Adrian Bryan-Brown, Jim Byk, Brandi Cornwell, Jackie Green, Juliana Hannett, Hector Hernandez, Jessica Johnson, Kevin Jones, Amy Kass, Aaron Meier, Linnae Petruzzelli, Matt Polk, Matt Ross, Susanne Tighe
Website Design ....Situation Marketing/ Damian Bazadona, Lisa Cecchini
Banking ....JP Morgan Chase/ Stephanie Dalton
Payroll ....Castellana Services Inc./ Lance Castellana, Norman Seawell, James Castellana
Group Sales ....Group Sales Box Office
Merchandising ....Max Merchandising LLC
Travel Arrangements ....Tzell Travel
Insurance Broker ....D.R. Reiff Associates/ Dennis R. Reiff, Sonny Everett
Computer Consultant ....Marion Taylor
Opening Night Coordinator ....Tobak Lawrence Co./ Joanna B. Koondel, Suzanne Tobak
Production Photographer ....Joan Marcus
Gable and Stein Historian ....David Goldsmith
Theatre Displays ....King Displays

CREDITS

Scenery by Hudson Scenic Studio, Inc Automation by Hudson Scenic Studio, Inc. Costume construction by Barbara Matera Limited, Carelli Costumes and Rodney Gordon. Custom made shoes built by Capri Shoes, J.C. Theatrical and T.O. Dey. Special thanks to Bra*Tenders for hosiery and undergarments. Chinese fan and feathers provided by American Plume and Fancy Feathers, New York, NY. Lights by Production Resource Group. Sound equipment by Sound Associates. Wigs by Ray Marston Wig Studios and Anne Devon Chambless. Natural herb cough drops courtesy of Ricola USA, Inc. Emergen-C super energy booster provided by Alacer Corp. Crash cymbals courtesy of PAISTE America, Brea, CA. Rehearsed at the New 42nd Street Studios.

SPECIAL THANKS
Best Man Productions
Matt Watts
Frederick P. Bimbler, Esq.
Mirvish Productions
Michael Jenkins

Makeup provided by
M•A•C Cosmetics

www.DrowsyChaperone.com

THE DROWSY CHAPERONE was presented

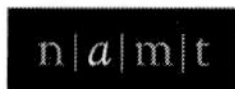

NATIONAL ALLIANCE *for* MUSICAL THEATRE

at the 2004 Festival of New Musicals
Kathy Evans, Executive Director www.namt.org

NEDERLANDER

Chairman ....**James M. Nederlander**
President ....**James L. Nederlander**

Executive Vice President
Nick Scandalios

Vice President
Corporate Development
Charlene S. Nederlander

Senior Vice President
Labor Relations
Herschel Waxman

Vice President
Jim Boese

Chief Financial Officer
Freida Sawyer Belviso

STAFF FOR THE MARQUIS THEATRE
Manager ....David Calhoun
Associate Manager ....Ava Probst
Treasurer ....Rick Waxman
Assistant Treasurer ....John Rooney
Carpenter ....Joseph P. Valentino
Electrician ....James Mayo
Property Man ....Roland Weigel

The Drowsy Chaperone
SCRAPBOOK

Photo by Aubrey Reuben

Photos courtesy Troy Britton Johnson

Correspondent: Troy Britton Johnson, "Robert Martin"

Favorite In-Theatre Gathering Place: We are fortunate to have a greenroom at the Marquis which has been renamed the "Arabian Room" as a nod to the line in the show, "Breakfast will be served in the Arabian room." A design firm came in and truly gave us an Arabian-style room. It's where we all gather all the time. So many of our cast have children and they all visit, so it's very much like a big family reunion often. Personally, I'm also a fan of hanging out in the stage managers' office because they have big Tupperware jugs of M&Ms.

Memorable Opening Night Gift: An organ grinder monkey puppet that was cut after our L.A. run. It was sitting in my dressing room wrapped in a huge box with no card. I'm still not sure who gave it to me but I suspect it was our director, Casey Nicholaw.

Memorable Fan Gifts: Danny Burstein and I both got two sets of salt and pepper shakers from the collection of a fan's grandmother. Danny got a set of skunks and a set of poodles (get it?) and I got a set of monkeys for obvious reasons and a set of Humpty Dumptys because, and I quote, "I'm an egg-cident waiting to happen!"

Best Show Day: We call it Bagel Saturday because Sutton Foster provides bagels and cream cheese every Saturday before the matinee and has done so every week since we opened.

"Gypsy of the Year" Sketch: Our skit this year, "Alternate Ending" by Bob Martin and Casey Hushion, provided an alternate ending to our show culminating in "Man In Chair" and the super having a "moment" together, which is what so many people think is going to happen in the real show anyway.

"Carols for a Cure" Carol: An original Christmas carol called "Rockin' Christmas Angel" composed by our very own Tony Award-winning Lisa Lambert and Greg Morrison.

"Easter Bonnet" Sketch: Untitled by Stacia Fernandez.

Favorite Moment During Each Performance: When I burst through the refrigerator for my first entrance. I love to hear the reaction from the audience. It's an awesome entrance. Thank you, Casey Nicholaw.

1. The cast and producers pose after closing the market at NASDAQ August 25, 2006.
2. Troy Britton Johnson and Bob Martin cut a cake celebrating the show's 100th Broadway performance.
3. Martin and Britton the night Martin won the Tony Award for Best Book of a Musical.
4. Recording the original cast album.
5. Johnson sitting beside a section of the show's block-wide poster in the Marquis Hotel breezeway.

The Drowsy Chaperone
Scrapbook

Catchphrase Only the Cast Would Know: "The popcorn section."
Celebrity Visitors: We've had tons of celebrities see the show, especially when we were doing the show in Los Angeles. Bob Martin and Lisa Lambert used to keep a list. One of my favorites in New York was when Elaine Stritch came backstage after the show and introduced herself. I said, "Hello, I'm Troy." And she said, "Well of course you are. Troy...Troy... Boy, did your mom know how to rob a train!" I'm still not sure what it meant, but I love it.
Special Backstage Rituals: Several people in our cast have backstage rituals. Eddie Korbich spies on the audience from a little cubby hole stage left during the opening monologue. Also during the monologue, a group gathers upstage to connect and gauge the audience response to Bob. Georgia Engel does a mini ballet bar just before "Toledo Surprise." Beth Leavel spits a wad of gum at a target held by stage manager Rachel McCutchen just before "As We Stumble Along." Just before "Accident Waiting to Happen," Sutton Foster and I are hidden upstage and before we enter she fixes my boutonniere and then we turn and pat each other on the butt and out we go. There are tons more.
Biggest Backstage Mystery: Eddie Korbich eats an apple every show immediately following "Cold Feets." One night someone took a bite out of it. All hell broke loose and the culprit has never been revealed—although I know who did it, but will never tell. No, it wasn't me...although, of course, I was the first accused.
Unique for 2007: Our cast recording was turned into a Limited Collectors' Edition LP. Yes, a real vinyl record. It's so amazing to hold that album in your hand and slide the record from its sleeve. Sorry, but CDs don't even compare.
My Own Tradition: We have had two original company members leave the cast as of this writing, Linda Griffin (Ensemble) and Edward Hibbert (Underling). I gave them $40 onstage dares for their last show and they both delivered in spades. I won't tell what the dares were (to protect their good names) but they were awesome and now it's becoming a tradition for final shows. And with our crazy bunch, I fully expect to fork over 40 bucks every time.

Photos by Aubrey Reuben

1. Beth Leavel (R) unveils the show's new neon marquee overlooking Times Square.
2. (L-R): Jennifer Smith and Eddie Korbich at a July 13, 2006 reception at the Hotel Royalton to celebrate the show's success.
3. (L-R): Bob Martin and Sutton Foster at "Stars in the Alley" in Shubert Alley.
4. Members of the cast perform in Times Square to benefit Broadway Cares/Equity Fights AIDS November 9, 2006.

Faith Healer

First Preview: April 18, 2006. Opening: May 4, 2006.
Closed: August 13, 2006 after 19 Previews and 117 Performances.

PLAYBILL

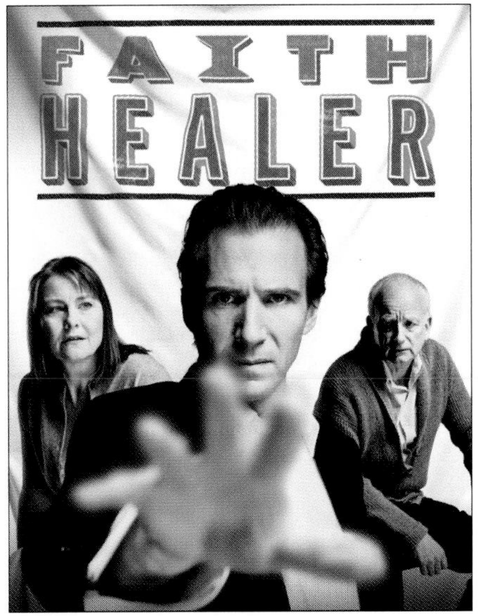

BOOTH THEATRE
222 West 45th Street
A Shubert Organization Theatre
Gerald Schoenfeld, *Chairman* Philip J. Smith, *President*
Robert E. Wankel, *Executive Vice President*

Michael Colgan & Sonia Friedman Productions
The Shubert Organization Robert Bartner Roger Berlind
Scott Rudin Spring Sirkin
present

Ralph Fiennes Cherry Jones Ian McDiarmid

in

the Gate Theatre Dublin production of

FAITH HEALER

by
Brian Friel

Set and Costume Design
Jonathan Fensom

Lighting Design
Mark Henderson

Sound Design
Christopher Cronin

Video Design
Sven Ortel

U.S. Casting
Jim Carnahan, C.S.A.

Production Stage Manager
Jane Grey

Production Management
Aurora Productions

Press Representative
Barlow•Hartman

General Management
Stuart Thompson Productions/
James Triner

Associate Producer
Lauren Doll

Directed by
Jonathan Kent

8/13/06

CAST
(in order of appearance)

Frank Hardy .... RALPH FIENNES
Grace Hardy .... CHERRY JONES
Teddy .... IAN McDIARMID

Part 1: Frank
Part 2: Grace
Part 3: Teddy
Part 4: Frank

STANDBYS
For Frank: PATRICK BOLL
For Teddy: JARLATH CONROY
For Grace: ROBIN MOSELEY

Ian McDiarmid

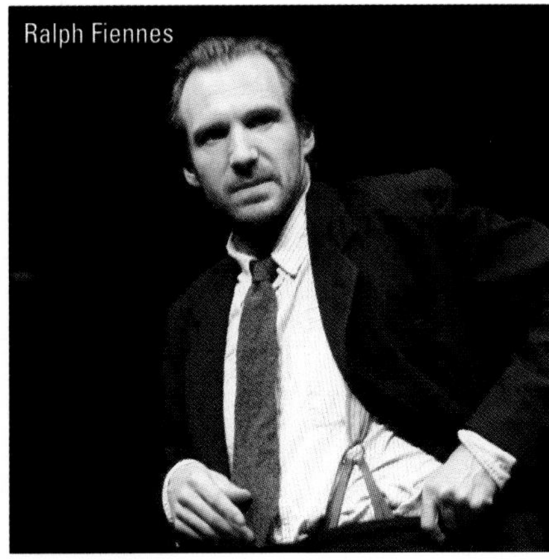
Ralph Fiennes

Cherry Jones

Photos by Joan Marcus

Faith Healer

Ralph Fiennes
Frank Hardy

Cherry Jones
Grace Hardy

Ian McDiarmid
Teddy

Patrick Boll
Standby, Frank Hardy

Jarlath Conroy
Standby, Teddy

Robin Moseley
Standby, Grace Hardy

Brian Friel
Playwright

Jonathan Kent
Director

Jonathan Fensom
Scenic and Costume Design

Mark Henderson
Lighting Design

Christopher Cronin
Sound Design

Jim Carnahan
Casting

Jane Grey
Production Stage Manager

Stuart Thompson Productions
General Manager

Michael Colgan
Producer

Sonia Friedman, Sonia Friedman Productions Ltd
Producer

Gerald Schoenfeld Chairman, The Shubert Organization
Producer

Roger Berlind
Producer

Scott Rudin
Producer

Spring Sirkin
Producer

Lauren Doll
Associate Producer

STAGE CREW
Kneeling (L-R):
Amanda Tramontazzi (Doorman), Jeffrey McGovney (Dresser), Sid King (Stage Manager), Mrs. James Kain (Wife of Production Propman).

Standing (L-R):
James Keane III (House Propman), Ronald Burns, Sr. (House Electrician), Brian McGarity (Production Electrician), Kenneth McDonough (House Carpenter), Jane Grey (Production Stage Manager), Sarah Kain (daughter of Production Propman), James Kain (Production Propman) and Kay Grunder (Wardrobe Mistress).

BOX OFFICE
Rianna Bryceland (Staff)

FRONT OF HOUSE STAFF
(L-R):
John Barbaretti, Bernadette Bokun, Frank Valdinoto, Nirmala Sharma, Teresa Aceves, Laurel Ann Wilson, Katherine Coscia, Jorge Velasquez, Chrissie Collins and, in the center, the bust of Edwin Booth (with Santa hat).

Photos by Ben Strothmann

Faith Healer

Scrapbook

1. Ian McDiarmid at the June 2006 "Stars in the Alley" event in Shubert Alley.

2. Producer Michael Colgan (L) and Ralph Fiennes at the opening night party at Bryant Park Grill.

Photos by Aubrey Reuben

STAFF CREDITS FOR *FAITH HEALER*

GENERAL MANAGEMENT
STUART THOMPSON PRODUCTIONS
Stuart Thompson Caroline Prugh James Triner

COMPANY MANAGER
Shawn M. Fertitta

GENERAL PRESS REPRESENTATIVE
BARLOW•HARTMAN
John Barlow Michael Hartman
Dennis Crowley Ryan Ratelle

PRODUCTION MANAGEMENT
AURORA PRODUCTIONS INC.
Gene O'Donovan W. Benjamin Heller II
Bethany Weinstein Melissa Mazdra

Production Stage Manager ... Jane Grey
Stage Manager ... Sid King
Assistant to the Director ... Will MacAdams
Associate Lighting Designer ... Kristina Kloss
Production Electrician ... Brian GF McGarity
Production Props ... Jim Kane
Production Props ... Donald "Buck" Roberts
Production Props Assistant ... Paul Ashton
House Carpenter ... Kenny McDonough
House Electrician ... Ronnie Burns, Sr.
House Props ... Jim Keane
Wardrobe Supervisor ... Kay Grunder
Dresser ... Jeff McGovney
Hair & Wig Supervisor ... Cynthia Demand
Bob Bartner's Assistant ... Mario Aiello
Assistant to Mr. Berlind ... Jeffrey Hillock
Assistants to Mr. Rudin ... Michael Diliberti, James P. Queen
Assistant to Ms. Sirkin ... Annie Metheany-Pyle
General Management Assistant ... Megan Curran
Management Intern ... Zöe Block
Production Assistant ... Andy Phelan
Press Associates ... Leslie Baden, Jon Dimond, Carol Fineman, Bethany Larsen, Rick Miramontez, Gerilyn Shur, Andrew Snyder, Wayne Wolfe
Banking ... JP Morgan Chase/Michele Gibbons
Payroll ... Castellana Services, Inc.
Accountant ... Fried & Kowgios CPA's LLP/ Robert Fried, CPA
Controller ... Joseph S. Kubala
Insurance ... DeWitt Stern Group
Legal Counsel ... Lazarus & Harris LLP/ Scott Lazarus, Esq., Robert C. Harris, Esq.
Opening Night Coordination ... Tobak Lawrence Company/ Joanna B. Koondel, Suzanne Tobak
Advertising ... SPOTCO/Drew Hodges, Jim Edwards, Jim Aquino, Y. Darius Suyama
Production Photographer ... Joan Marcus
Travel ... Tzell Travel/Andi Henig
Immigration ... Traffic Control Group, Inc.
Theatre Displays ... King Displays, Inc.

Dialect Coach for Ms. Jones
Stephen Gabis

CREDITS

Scenery and scenic effects built and painted by Showmotion, Inc., Norwalk, CT. Scenic by Scenic Arts Studio, Inc. Fly automation, show control and finale effects by Showmotion, Inc., Norwalk, CT, using the AC2 computerized motion control system. Lighting equipment supplied by GSD Productions, Inc., West Hempstead, NY. Sound equipment by Masque Sound and Recording Corporation.

SPECIAL THANKS

The Brewer's Apprentice; Ricola natural herb cough drops courtesy of Ricola USA, Inc. Emer'gen-C super energy booster provided by Alacer Corp.

THE GATE THEATRE DUBLIN

Michael Colgan ... Director
Marie Rooney ... Deputy Director
Teerth Chungh ... Head of Production
Padraig Heneghan ... Financial Controller

SONIA FRIEDMAN PRODUCTIONS

Sonia Friedman ... Producer
Diane Benjamin ... General Manager
Matthew Gordon ... Associate Producer
Emily Merko ... Production Assistant
Howard Panter, Rosemary Squire, Helen Enright ... Board

THE SHUBERT ORGANIZATION, INC.
Board of Directors

Gerald Schoenfeld
Chairman

Philip J. Smith
President

Wyche Fowler, Jr. **John W. Kluge**

Lee J. Seidler **Michael I. Sovern**

Stuart Subotnick

Robert E. Wankel
Executive Vice President

Peter Entin
Vice President
Theatre Operations

Elliot Greene
Vice President
Finance

David Andrews
Vice President
Shubert Ticketing Services

John Darby
Vice President
Facilities

D.S. Moynihan
Vice President – Creative Projects

House Manager ... Laurel Ann Wilson

Frost/Nixon

First Preview: March 31, 2007. Opened: April 22, 2007.
Still running as of May 31, 2007.

PLAYBILL

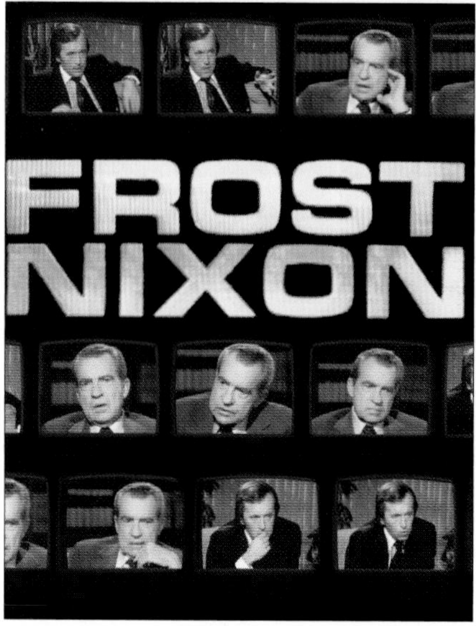

CAST

(in order of speaking)

Richard Nixon .... FRANK LANGELLA
Jim Reston .... STEPHEN KUNKEN
David Frost .... MICHAEL SHEEN
Jack Brennan .... COREY JOHNSON
Evonne Goolagong .... SHIRA GREGORY
John Birt .... REMY AUBERJONOIS
Manolo Sanchez .... TRINEY SANDOVAL
Swifty Lazar/Mike Wallace .... STEPHEN ROWE
Caroline Cushing .... SONYA WALGER
Bob Zelnick .... ARMAND SCHULTZ
Ensemble .... DENNIS COCKRUM, ANTONY HAGOPIAN, ROXANNA HOPE

All other parts played by members of the company.

UNDERSTUDIES

For Richard Nixon: BOB ARI
For David Frost: REMY AUBERJONOIS
For Swifty Lazar, Bob Zelnick: DENNIS COCKRUM
For John Birt, Jack Brennan: ANTONY HAGOPIAN
For Evonne Goolagong, Caroline Cushing: ROXANNA HOPE
For Jim Reston: TRINEY SANDOVAL

Michael Sheen is appearing with the permission of Actors' Equity Association pursuant to an exchange program between American Equity and UK Equity.

BERNARD B. JACOBS THEATRE

242 West 45th Street
A Shubert Organization Theatre
Gerald Schoenfeld, *Chairman* **Philip J. Smith,** *President*

Robert E. Wankel, *Executive Vice President*

ARIELLE TEPPER MADOVER MATTHEW BYAM SHAW ROBERT FOX ACT PRODUCTIONS
DAVID BINDER DEBRA BLACK ANNETTE NIEMTZOW/HARLENE FREEZER THE WEINSTEIN COMPANY

Present

THE DONMAR WAREHOUSE PRODUCTION

FRANK LANGELLA MICHAEL SHEEN

FROST NIXON

A New Play By

PETER MORGAN

With

REMY AUBERJONOIS SHIRA GREGORY COREY JOHNSON STEPHEN KUNKEN
STEPHEN ROWE TRINEY SANDOVAL ARMAND SCHULTZ SONYA WALGER
BOB ARI DENNIS COCKRUM ANTONY HAGOPIAN ROXANNA HOPE

Set and Costume Designer
CHRISTOPHER ORAM

Lighting Designer
NEIL AUSTIN

Composer and Sound Designer
ADAM CORK

Video Designer
JON DRISCOLL

Hair and Wig Designer
RICHARD MAWBEY

Casting
DANIEL SWEE

UK Casting
ANNE McNULTY

Press Representative
BONEAU/BRYAN-BROWN

Marketing
ERIC SCHNALL

General Management
101 PRODUCTIONS, LTD.

Production Stage Manager
RICK STEIGER

US Technical Supervisor
AURORA PRODUCTIONS

UK Technical Supervisor
PATRICK MOLONY

Directed by

MICHAEL GRANDAGE

LIVE BROADWAY

Frost/Nixon originally opened at The Donmar Warehouse on August 15, 2006.
Matthew Byam Shaw, Arielle Tepper Madover, Robert Fox, Act Productions transferred
The Donmar Warehouse Production to the Gielgud Theatre, Opening Night November 16, 2006.

Original Production Sponsor
BARCLAYS CAPITAL

The producers wish to express their appreciation to Theatre Development Fund for its support of this production.

4/22/07

(L-R): Michael Sheen and Frank Langella

Photo by Johan Persson

Frost/Nixon

Frank Langella
Richard Nixon

Michael Sheen
David Frost

Remy Auberjonois
John Birt

Shira Gregory
Evonne Goolagong

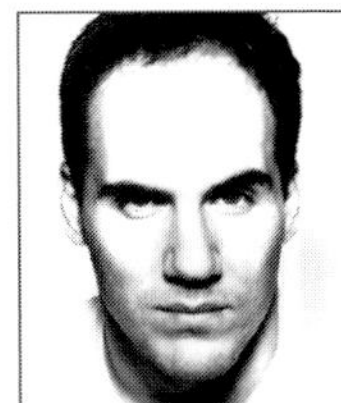
Corey Johnson
Jack Brennan

Stephen Kunken
Jim Reston

Stephen Rowe
Swifty Lazar/ Mike Wallace

Triney Sandoval
Manolo Sanchez

Armand Schultz
Bob Zelnick

Sonya Walger
Caroline Cushing

Bob Ari
Understudy for Richard Nixon

Dennis Cockrum
Ensemble

Antony Hagopian
Ensemble

Roxanna Hope
Ensemble

Peter Morgan
Playwright

Michael Grandage
Director

Jon Driscoll
Video Designer

Arielle Tepper Madover
Producer

Robert Fox
Producer

Debra Black
Co-Producer

Annette Niemtzow
Co-Producer

Harlene Freezer
Co-Producer

Bob Weinstein, The Weinstein Company
Co-Producer

Harvey Weinstein, The Weinstein Company
Co-Producer

Seth Sklar-Heyn
Assistant to the Director

2006-2007 AWARDS

Tony Award
Best Leading Actor in a Play
(Frank Langella)

Drama Desk Award
Outstanding Actor in a Play
(Frank Langella)

Outer Critics Circle Award
Outstanding Actor in a Play
(Frank Langella)

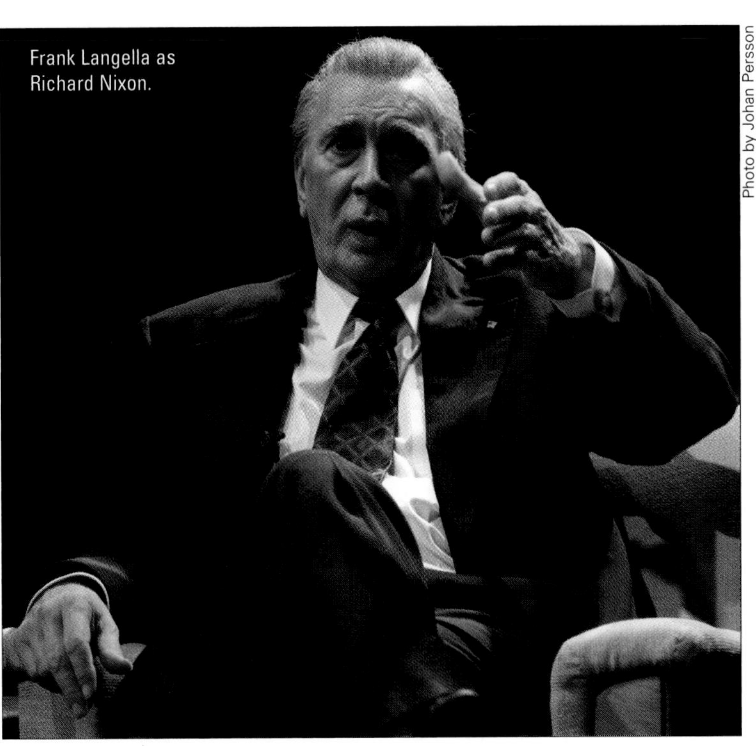
Frank Langella as Richard Nixon.

Photo by Johan Persson

Frost/Nixon

STAGE CREW
Front Row (L-R): Joel Mendenhall (Hair Supervisor), Dave Fulton (Production Props), Alfred Ricci (House Props), Michael Van Praagh (House Carpenter), Edward Ruggiero (Flyman).

Back Row (L-R): Daniel Carpio (Props), John Alban (Props), Lyle Jones (Dresser), Kelly Saxon (Wardrobe Supervisor), Christopher Kurtz (Production Video), Philip Heckman (Dresser), Wayne Smith (Production Sound) and Herbert Messing (House Electrician).

DOORMAN
Jerry Klein

FRONT OF HOUSE STAFF
Seated (L-R):
Rosa Pesante, Sean Cutler, Eva Laskow, Kathleen Wehmeyer.

Standing (L-R):
Al Luongo, Billy Mitchell, Patanne McEvoy, John Minore, Al Nazario and Roxanne Gayol.

Frost/Nixon

BOX OFFICE
Jose Hernandez and Karen Coscia.

Photos by Ben Strothmann

STAGE MANAGEMENT
(L-R): Rick Steiger (Production Stage Manager), Lisa Buxbaum (Stage Manager) and Timothy Eaker (Production Assistant).

STAFF FOR *FROST/NIXON*

GENERAL MANAGEMENT
101 PRODUCTIONS, LTD.
Wendy Orshan Jeffrey M. Wilson
David Auster

COMPANY MANAGER
Alexandra Gushin

GENERAL PRESS REPRESENTATIVE
BONEAU/BRYAN-BROWN
Adrian Bryan-Brown Steven Padla
Heath Schwartz

U.S TECHNICAL SUPERVISOR
AURORA PRODUCTIONS
Gene O'Donovan W. Benjamin Heller II
Bethany Weinstein Meghan Von Vett
Melissa Mazdra

Production Stage Manager .... Rick Steiger
Stage Manager .... Lisa Buxbaum
UK Technical Supervisor .... Patrick Molony
Assistant to the Director .... Seth Sklar-Heyn
Associate Costume Designer .... Scott Traugott
Assistant Costume Designer .... Brian Russman
Costume Design Assistants ....Cory Ching, Robert Martin
Associate Lighting Designer .... Daniel Walker
Associate Lighting Designer/
Moving Lights Programmer .... Victoria Smerdon
Associate Sound Designer .... Chris Cronin
Screen Technician .... Colin Barnes
Casting Associate .... Camille Hickman

Production Carpenter .... Michael Van Praagh
Production Flyman .... Edward Ruggiero
Production Electrician .... Jon Lawson
House Electrician .... Herbert Messing
Assistant Electrician (Video) .... Christopher Kurtz
Production Props Supervisor .... Dave Fulton
House Properties .... Fred Ricci
Wardrobe Supervisor .... Kelly A. Saxon
Mr. Langella's Dresser .... Patrick Bevilacqua
Mr. Sheen's Dresser .... Lyle Jones
Dresser .... Philip Heckman
Hair Supervisor .... Joel Mendenhall
Make-Up Designer .... Angelina Avallone
Production Assistants .... Timothy Eaker, Brian Maschka
Assistant to Ms. Tepper Madover .... Holly Ferguson

Legal Counsel .... Lazarus & Harris, LLP/ Scott R. Lazarus, Esq., Robert C. Harris, Esq.
Accountant .... Fried & Kowgios
Controller .... Galbraith & Co Inc./ Sarah Galbraith, Tabitha Falcone
Advertising .... SPOTCO/ Drew Hodges, Jim Edwards, Tom McCann, Stephen Sosnowski
Assistant to the General Managers .... John Vennema
101 Productions, Ltd. Staff .... Denys Baker, Ashley Berman, Katharine Croke, Barbara Crompton, Laura Dickinson, Sherra Johnston, Emily Lawson, Heidi Neven, Kyle Pickles, Mary Six Rupert, Evan Storey
101 Productions, Ltd. Intern .... Stewart Miller
Press Representative Staff .... Chris Boneau, Brandi Cornwell, Linnae Petruzzelli, Jim Byk, Adriana Douzos, Jackie Green, Joe Perrotta, Matt Polk, Susanne Tighe, Juliana Hannett, Jessica Johnson, Aaron Meier, Hector Hernandez, Allison Houseworth, Kevin Jones, Ian Bjorklund, Danielle Crinnion, Amy Kass, Christine Olver, Matt Ross
Banking .... City National Bank/Anne McSweeney
Insurance .... Tanenbaum Harber Insurance Group/ Carol Bressi
Theatre Displays .... King Displays, Inc.
Payroll Services .... Castellana Services, Inc.
Production Photographers .... Joan Marcus, Johan Persson (UK)
Website Design .... Situation Marketing
Opening Night Coordinator ...Tobak Lawrence Company/ Suzanne Tobak, Michael P. Lawrence

DONMAR WAREHOUSE

Artistic Director .... Michael Grandage
Executive Producer .... Lucy Davies
General Manager .... James Bierman
Creative & Casting Associate .... Anne McNulty
Marketing Manager .... Ruth Waters
Literary Manager &
Production Administrator .... Sarah Nicholson
Executive Coordinator .... Simon Woolley
General Assistant .... Eleanor Lang
Development Director .... Kate Mitchell
Development Manager .... Tania Hutt
Development Officer .... Aimée Barnett
Development Administrator .... Nicola Stockley
Resident Assistant Director .... Alex Sims
Deputy Production Manager .... Lucy McEwan
Deputy Production Manager
(Maternity Cover) .... Lorna Cobbold
Press Representative .... Kate Morley for Blueprint PR

CREDITS

London scenery by Rocket Scenery. Lighting by PRG. Sound equipment from Sound Associates. Video equipment by XL Video. Costumes executed by Leonard Logsdail Custom Tailor, Arel Studio, David Quinn, Allmeier Custom Shirts, Carlo Manzi, Keith Watson and Angels. Wigs made by Wig Specialities Ltd. Ricola products used. Video footage licensed by Huntley Film Archives. "Frost Over Australia" footage courtesy of Seven Network. Photo of Santa Pacifica courtesy of Getty Images. Special thanks to Bra-Tenders for hosiery and undergarments.

FROST/NIXON rehearsed at New 42nd Street Studios.

SPECIAL THANKS
Sarah Waling

www.frostnixononbroadway.com

THE SHUBERT ORGANIZATION, INC.
Board of Directors

Gerald Schoenfeld
Chairman

Philip J. Smith
President

Wyche Fowler, Jr.

John W. Kluge

Lee J. Seidler

Michael I. Sovern

Stuart Subotnick

Robert E. Wankel
Executive Vice President

Peter Entin
Vice President –
Theatre Operations

Elliot Greene
Vice President –
Finance

David Andrews
Vice President –
Shubert Ticketing Services

John Darby
Vice President –
Facilities

D.S. Moynihan
Vice President – Creative Projects

House Manager .... William Mitchell

Frost/Nixon
Scrapbook

Photos by Aubrey Reuben

1. Frank Langella arrives with daughter Sara at the premiere party at Tavern on the Green.
2. Michael Sheen poses on opening night with the real-life David Frost.

Correspondent: Stephen Kunken, "Jim Reston"
Memorable Opening Night Letter: For me, it was a congratulations letter from Jim Reston. It was both thrilling and daunting knowing that the character you were playing would be sitting in the audience watching the show.
Opening Night Gifts: *Frost/Nixon* comic book from Stephen Kunken, gift certificates to Becco from Michael Grandage, airplane pillows from Sonya Walger, books from Michael Sheen, flowers galore, martini sets engraved with *Frost/Nixon* logo from producers, *F/N* beer steins from wardrobe, and finger puppets from Frank.
Most Exciting Celebrity Visitors: While just about anybody who is anybody seems to have made their way backstage at the Jacobs, the most exciting group was surely on opening night when the "real" David Frost, Jim Reston, and Bob Zelnick, arrived with several Watergate prosecutors and the civil rights advocate Julian Bond. Queen Noor of Jordan made an appearance, as did our own King and Queen Paul Newman and Joanne Woodward. I personally found the evening with Susan Lucci, Allison Janney, Lauren Bacall, Natasha Richardson and Swoosie Kurtz to be the most densely damerriffic.
"Easter Bonnet" Sketch: We didn't open in time for the Easter Bonnet Sketch to be fully realized. If it had I'm sure that Michael Sheen would have graced us all with his stirring rendition of "Bring Him Home" from *Les Misérables*, as sung by Tony Blair.
Actor Who Performed the Most Roles in This Show: Shira Gregory, who played Evonne Goolagong, Sasha the stewardess, Rhonda room service, and Cameron the camera girl.
Actor Who Has Done the Most Shows in Their Career: Frank Langella has done 12,243 shows in his career. Not performances...shows. Since his arrival in NYC at the age of 2 in the short-lived *Infant Dracula* he has not stopped working. After leaving Nixon behind he will make his return to Broadway in show 12,244 with *Dracula and His Pension*.
Special Backstage Rituals: The rubbing of ASM Tim's Ear. Corey Johnson and his famous walking into tables routine. Remy stealing Dave's peanuts (Oops. Sorry, Remy). Michael Sheen's backstage kissing booth. And the group waiting to see if the audience would clap after the Nixon/Frost midnight love meeting.
Favorite Moment During Each Performance (On Stage or Off): It's a tie between Stephen Rowe's multi-octave "*FIVE*-FOUR-THREE" or Corey Johnson's voice crackling "a *sickening* moment."
Favorite In-Theatre Gathering Places: Frank's "Hall of mirrors." The hall of testosterone with Michael Sheen, Stephen Kunken, Armand Schultz, Corey Johnson, and don't forget the baddest of them all...Kelly Saxon.
Favorite Off-Site Hangouts: Monday night...home. Tuesday night...Angus. Wednesday between shows...Sardi's. Wednesday post show...Joe Allen's. Thursday and Friday...a toss up between Joe Allen's, Angus, Orzo, and Bar Centrale. Saturday between shows...Vinyl. Sunday...the basement for brunch and Schultz waffles.
Favorite Snack Food: Nerd's Rope. Club sandwiches and lemonade.
Mascot: Olivia.
Favorite Therapies: Vinyl chicken wings. Pinot Noir at Angus, and chicken curry at Sardi's.
Most Memorable Ad-Libs: Stephen Kunken going up in the first monologue. Real line: "Rather than suffer the humiliation of a trial with all of the damage that could do the president, Nixon offered his resignation." Ad-lib: "Rather...um...Nixon. Instead of covering it up...Nixon offered his resignation." (Note the sheer historical mangle.)
Armand Schultz in the television scene. Real line: "When he trails off like that at the end of a sentence then, Bam, you should jump in with another sentence." Ad-lib: "When he stops like that...Bam...you should get him."
Michael Sheen skipping two-thirds of the play by starting the first interview with the line that begins the third interview and then catching himself. Real line: "There is one question above all others that we are dying to know." Ad lib: "Looking back over...I mean...well...no...let's start with...There is one question...."
Record Number of Cell Phone Rings During a Performance: Not as bad as one might think. Maybe two or three.
Memorable Stage Door Fan Encounter: Ah yes. After walking through the stage door alley which we share with *Avenue Q* and *Phantom* a couple proceeded to fawn over the show and my performance. I was thrilled and walked down the street with them. After spending five minutes in their presence they let it slip that they loved *Avenue Q* and wanted to know if I had done the show in Vegas. Oops. Of course I didn't have the heart to tell them that I indeed did not have my hand up a puppet's ass, but perhaps their heads were.
Latest Audience Arrival: Richard Nixon. We are still waiting.
Catchphrases Only the Company Would Recognize: "Abuse the Power."
Memorable Directorial Note: "Just make sure that as your work expands and grows that it doesn't declare liberation from the rest of the proceedings."
Nicknames: Michael Sheen on the pitching mound known as "MA-CHINE" (or "MA-SHEEN"). Corey Johnson, a.k.a. "John" "The Cyborg," or "Rock."
Sweethearts Within the Company: Michael Sheen and Frank Langella. Michael Sheen and softball.

Grey Gardens

First Preview: October 3, 2006. Opened: November 2, 2006.
Still running as of May 31, 2007.

PLAYBILL

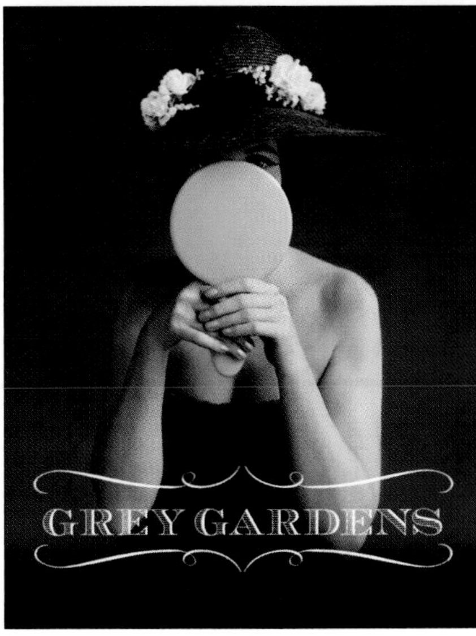

WALTER KERR THEATRE
A JUJAMCYN THEATRE
ROCCO LANDESMAN
PRESIDENT

PAUL LIBIN
PRODUCING DIRECTOR

JACK VIERTEL
CREATIVE DIRECTOR

EAST OF DOHENY
STAUNCH ENTERTAINMENT   RANDALL L. WREGHITT / MORT SWINSKY
MICHAEL ALDEN   EDWIN W. SCHLOSS

in association with
PLAYWRIGHTS HORIZONS

present

CHRISTINE EBERSOLE

in

Book by
DOUG WRIGHT

Music by
SCOTT FRANKEL

Lyrics by
MICHAEL KORIE

Based on the film "Grey Gardens" by David Maysles, Albert Maysles, Ellen Hovde, Muffie Meyer & Susan Froemke

Starring
MARY LOUISE WILSON

Featuring
MATT CAVENAUGH
SARAH HYLAND
ERIN DAVIE
MICHAEL POTTS
KELSEY FOWLER
BOB STILLMAN

and
JOHN McMARTIN

Scenic Design
ALLEN MOYER

Costume Design
WILLIAM IVEY LONG

Lighting Design
PETER KACZOROWSKI

Sound Design
BRIAN RONAN

Projection Design
WENDALL K. HARRINGTON

Hair and Wig Design
PAUL HUNTLEY

Orchestrations
BRUCE COUGHLIN

Music Director
LAWRENCE YURMAN

Music Coordinator
JOHN MILLER

Executive Producer
BETH WILLIAMS

General Management
ALAN WASSER -
ALLAN WILLIAMS

Production Stage Manager
JUDITH SCHOENFELD

Production Management
JUNIPER STREET
PRODUCTIONS

Press Representative
THE PUBLICITY OFFICE

Marketing
TMG -
THE MARKETING GROUP

Musical Staging by
JEFF CALHOUN

Directed by
MICHAEL GREIF

Grey Gardens was developed with the assistance of the Sundance Institute.

11/2/06

CAST

(in order of appearance)

PROLOGUE (1973)

Edith Bouvier Beale ...... MARY LOUISE WILSON
"Little" Edie Beale .... CHRISTINE EBERSOLE

ACT ONE (1941)

Edith Bouvier Beale .... CHRISTINE EBERSOLE
Young "Little" Edie Beale .... ERIN DAVIE
George Gould Strong .... BOB STILLMAN
Brooks, Sr. .... MICHAEL POTTS
Jacqueline "Jackie" Bouvier .... SARAH HYLAND
Lee Bouvier .... KELSEY FOWLER
Joseph Patrick Kennedy, Jr. .. MATT CAVENAUGH
J.V. "Major" Bouvier .... JOHN McMARTIN

ACT TWO (1973)

Edith Bouvier Beale ...... MARY LOUISE WILSON
"Little" Edie Beale .... CHRISTINE EBERSOLE
Brooks, Jr. .... MICHAEL POTTS
Jerry .... MATT CAVENAUGH
Norman Vincent Peale .... JOHN McMARTIN

Continued on next page

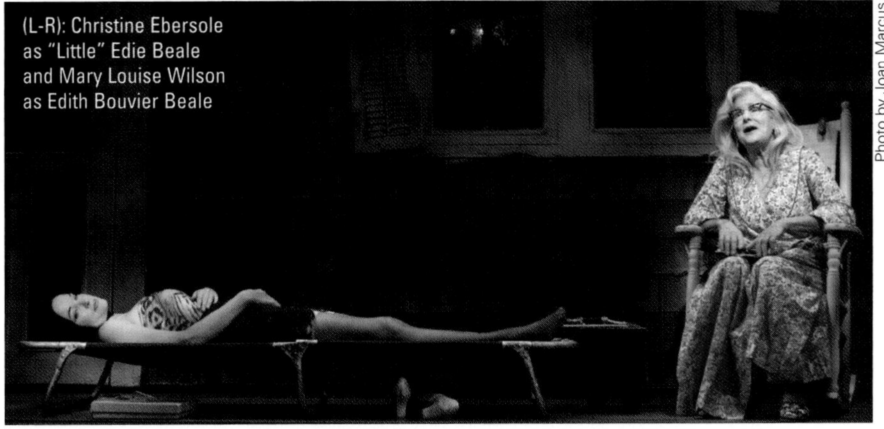

(L-R): Christine Ebersole as "Little" Edie Beale and Mary Louise Wilson as Edith Bouvier Beale

Photo by Joan Marcus

Grey Gardens

SONGS

PROLOGUE (1973)

"The Girl Who Has Everything"... Edith

ACT ONE (1941)

"The Girl Who Has Everything" Edith
"The Five-Fifteen"... Edith, Gould, Jackie, Lee, Brooks
"Mother, Darling" Edie, Edith, Gould
"Goin' Places" Joe & Edie
"Marry Well" Major Bouvier, Brooks, Jackie, Lee, Edie
"Hominy Grits" Edith, Gould, Jackie, Lee
"Peas in a Pod" Edie & Edith
"Drift Away" Gould & Edith
"The Five-Fifteen" (Reprise) Edith
"Daddy's Girl" Edie
"The Telegram" Edie
"Will You?" Edith

ACT TWO (1973)

"The Revolutionary Costume for Today" Edie
"The Cake I Had" Edith
"Entering Grey Gardens" Company
"The House We Live In" Edie & Company
"Jerry Likes My Corn" Edith & Edie
"Around the World" Edie
"Will You?" (Reprise) Edith & Edie
"Choose to Be Happy" Norman Vincent Peale & Company
"Around the World" (Reprise) Edie
"Another Winter in a Summer Town" Edie & Edith
"The Girl Who Has Everything" (Reprise) Edith & Edie

THE STORY OF THE EDIES

As a young society debutante in the early 1940s, "Little" Edie Bouvier Beale (1917-2002) was one of the brightest names in the social register. Known as "Body Beautiful Beale," she was the "It Girl" of her generation, even eclipsing her young cousin, Jacqueline Bouvier. In the years following World War II, however, life at Grey Gardens, their 28-room mansion, took an unexpected turn. While Jackie and her sister Lee Radziwill played out their lives on the world stage, Edie and her mother, Edith Bouvier Beale (1896-1977), became East Hampton's most notorious recluses. Filled with stray cats and in disrepair, the house was condemned by the Suffolk County Board of Health in 1972. Their squalid living conditions were plastered across the tabloids, and a public scandal erupted, forcing their famous relatives to step in and assist with the clean-up. In the end, the Edies proved to be indomitable, and their fierce individualism and nonconformist spirit has made them enduring icons.

In 1974, filmmakers Albert and David Maysles chronicled six weeks in the lives of the Beales at the Grey Gardens estate. The brothers would ultimately revolutionize documentary filmmaking with their series of landmark films, and *Grey Gardens* would become one of the most controversial examples of the emerging nonfiction style known as "cinema verite." The film is in the International Documentary Association's "Top Ten of All Time" list.

The musical *Grey Gardens*, which premiered Off-Broadway at Playwrights Horizons in March 2006, helped usher in a new resurgence in the *Grey Gardens* phenomenon. It was followed by the Maysles Brothers' own companion movie, *The Beales of Grey Gardens*, featuring previously unseen outtakes from the original documentary. The musical and the new film will be followed by several upcoming books on the Beales (including a collection of Edie's own poetry), the DVD release of the new documentary and a future Hollywood feature based on the original film.

Cast Continued

STANDBYS

Standby for Christine Ebersole:
MAUREEN MOORE
For Mary Louise Wilson:
DALE SOULES
For Jacqueline Bouvier and Lee Bouvier:
ABIGAIL FERENCZY
For J.V. "Major" Bouvier/Norman Vincent Peale:
DONALD GRODY
For Brooks, Sr./Brooks, Jr.:
MICHAEL W. HOWELL
For Young "Little" Edie Beale:
MEGAN LEWIS
For Joseph Patrick Kennedy, Jr./Jerry and Gould:
ASA SOMERS

SETTING

Act One takes place in July, 1941, Grey Gardens, East Hampton, Long Island, NY

Act Two takes place in 1973, Grey Gardens, East Hampton, Long Island, NY

The events of the play are based on both fact and fiction.

MUSICIANS

Conductor:
LAWRENCE YURMAN
Associate Conductor/Keyboards:
PAUL STAROBA

Violin:
ERIC DeGIOIA
Cello:
ANIK OULIANINE
Reeds:
KEN HITCHCOCK, TODD GROVES
Trumpet/Flugelhorn:
DANIEL URNESS
French Horn:
PATRICK PRIDEMORE
Acoustic Bass:
BRIAN CASSIER
Percussion/Drums:
TIM McLAFFERTY

Music Copying:
EMILY GRISHMAN MUSIC PREPARATION/
EMILY GRISHMAN, KATHARINE EDMONDS

Christine Ebersole
"Little" Edie Beale/ Edith Bouvier Beale

Mary Louise Wilson
Edith Bouvier Beale

Grey Gardens

John McMartin
J.V. "Major" Bouvier/ Norman Vincent Peale

Matt Cavenaugh
Joseph Patrick Kennedy, Jr./Jerry

Erin Davie
Young "Little" Edie Beale

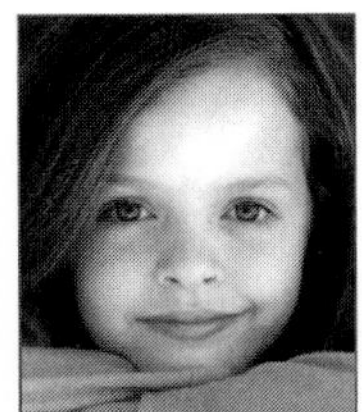
Kelsey Fowler
Lee Bouvier

Sarah Hyland
Jacqueline Bouvier

Michael Potts
Brooks, Sr./ Brooks, Jr.

Bob Stillman
George Gould Strong

Maureen Moore
Standby for Christine Ebersole

Dale Soules
Standby for Mary Louise Wilson

Donald Grody
Standby for J.V. "Major" Bouvier/ Norman Vincent Peale

Abigail Ferenczy
Standby for Jacqueline Bouvier & Lee Bouvier

Michael W. Howell
Standby for Brooks, Sr./ Brooks, Jr.

Megan Lewis
Standby for Young "Little" Edie Beale/ Dance Captain

Asa Somers
Standby for Joseph Patrick Kennedy, Jr./ Jerry & Gould

Doug Wright
Book

Scott Frankel
Music

Michael Korie
Lyrics

Michael Greif
Director

Jeff Calhoun
Musical Staging

Allen Moyer
Scenic Designer

William Ivey Long
Costume Designer

Peter Kaczorowski
Lighting Designer

Brian Ronan
Sound Designer

Wendall K. Harrington
Projections

Paul Huntley
Hair and Wig Design

Bruce Coughlin
Orchestrations

John Miller
Music Coordinator

Alan Wasser Associates
General Manager

Guy Kwan, John Paull III, Hillary Blanken, Kevin Broomell, Ana Rose Greene, Juniper Street Productions
Production Manager

Bernard Telsey, Telsey + Company
Casting

Randall L. Wreghitt
Producer

Mort Swinsky
Producer

Michael Alden
Producer

Edwin W. Schloss
Producer

Grey Gardens

ORCHESTRA

Front Row Sitting (L-R): Anik Oulianine (Cello), Patrick Pridemore (Horn).

Back Row Standing (L-R): John Meyers (Percussion Sub), Todd Groves (Reed 1), Lawrence Yurman (Conductor), Paul Staroba (Keyboard), Michael Blanco (Bass Sub), Eric DeGioia (Violin) and Dan Urness (Trumpet).

Not Pictured: Brian Cassier (Bass), Tim McLafferty (Percussion), Ken Hitchcock (Reed 2).

STAGE MANAGERS

(L-R): Judith Schoenfeld, Vanessa Brown, Bryan Landrine, Colleen Danaher.

Photos by Ben Strothmann

BOX OFFICE

(L-R): Stan Shaffer (Treasurer) and Gail Yerkovich (Ticket Seller).

Grey Gardens

Photos by Ben Strothmann

USHERS

(L-R): Michelle Fleury, TJ D'Angelo, Kelvin Loh, Victoria Lauzun, Alison Traynor and Henry Leo Linton.

MERCHANDISING

(L-R): Rodrigo Bolanos, Greg Watson, Molly Lehmann and Tammy Fowler.

WARDROBE

(L-R): Lisa Tucci (Wardrobe Supervisor), Vangeli Kaseluris (Dresser), Jill Frese (Dresser), Jane Rottenbach (Dresser) and Hilda Garcia-Suli (Dresser).

Grey Gardens

STAGE CREW

(L-R): P.J. Stasuk (Head Sound Engineer), Patrick McCormack (Stagehand), Jack Cennamo (Carpenter), Drayton Allison (Electrician), Angelo Torre (Production Props), Tim Bennet (Propman), George Fullum (Carpenter), Amber Adams (Assistant Sound Engineer), Lonny MacDougall (Electrician) and Matt Lynch (Automation).

HAIR

(L-R): Jodi Jackson (Hair Swing) and Erin Kennedy Lunsford (Hair Supervisor).

Photos by Ben Strothmann

DOORMAN
John Raymond Barker

USHER
Aaron Kendall

Grey Gardens

2006-2007 AWARDS

TONY AWARDS
Best Leading Actress in a Musical
(Christine Ebersole)
Best Featured Actress in a Musical
(Mary Louise Wilson)
Best Costume Design of a Musical
(William Ivey Long)

ACTORS' EQUITY RICHARD SEFF AWARD
Best Performance in a Supporting Role by a Character Actress Age 50 or Older
(Mary Louise Wilson)

DRAMATISTS GUILD AWARD
Frederick Loewe Award for Dramatic Composition (Scott Frankel)

THEATRE WORLD AWARD
Outstanding Broadway Debut
(Erin Davie)

STAFF FOR *GREY GARDENS*

EAST OF DOHENY
President
Kelly S. Gonda
Chief Operating Officer
Harvey Gettleson
Chief Financial Officer
Tara Cornwell
Vice President of Development
Anastasia Barzee
Executive Assistants to Kelly Gonda
Marcia Johnson EJ Steier Will Willoughby
Assistants in NYC Office
Rachel Murch Alena Kastin

EAST OF DOHENY
321 West 44th Street, Suite 603, NY, NY 10036
Tel: 212-957-5510
www.eastofdoheny.com

GENERAL MANAGEMENT
ALAN WASSER ASSOCIATES
Alan Wasser Allan Williams
Mark Shacket

GENERAL PRESS REPRESENTATION
THE PUBLICITY OFFICE
Marc Thibodeau Bob Fennell
Michael S. Borowski Candi Adams

CASTING BY
TELSEY + COMPANY, C.S.A.:
Bernie Telsey, Will Cantler, David Vaccari,
Bethany Knox, Craig Burns
Tiffany Little Canfield, Rachel Hoffman
Stephanie Yankwitt, Carrie Rosson
Justin Huff, Joe Langworth, Bess Fifer

ORIGINAL CASTING BY
Alan Filderman C.S.A., Alaine Alldaffer C.S.A.,
James Calleri C.S.A.

PRODUCTION MANAGEMENT
JUNIPER STREET PRODUCTIONS
Hillary Blanken Guy Kwan

MERCHANDISING
QUASIWORLD MERCH!

COMPANY MANAGER ....MARK SHACKET
PRODUCTION
STAGE MANAGER ....JUDITH SCHOENFELD
Stage Manager ....J. Philip Bassett
Assistant Stage Manager ....Stephen R. Gruse
Associate Director ....Johanna McKeon
Assistant Company Manager ....Carrie Sherriff
Associate Choreographer ....Jodi Moccia
Dance Captain ....Megan Lewis
Dialect Coach ....Deborah Hecht
Associate Scenic Designer ....Warren Karp
Assistant Lighting Designers ....Joel E. Silver, John Viesta III
Associate Projections Designer ....Zachary Borovay
Assistant Sound Designer ....David Stollings
Associate Costume Designers ....Scott Traugott, Donald Sanders
Assistant Costume Designer ....Robert Martin
Production Carpenter ....Anthony Menditto
Production Electrician ....Dan Coey
Production Properties Supervisor ......Christopher Pantuso
Production Sound ....Michael Farfalla
Head Carpenter ....Geoffrey Vaughn
Advance Carpenter (Flyman) ....Mark Hallisey
Head Electrician ....Drayton Allison
Automated Lights Programmer ....Josh Weitzman
Projections Programmer ....Zachary Borovay
Head Sound Engineer ..............P.J. Stasuk
Production Wardrobe Supervisor ....Lisa Tucci
Ms. Ebersole's Dresser ....Jill Frese
Dressers ....Vangeli Kaseluris, Timothy Greer, Hilda Garcia Suli
Hair Supervisor ....Cindy Demand
Child Wrangler ....Vanessa Brown
Tutoring ....On Location Education
Synthesizer Programmer ....Randy Cohen
Production Management Associates ....Kevin Broomell, Ana Rose Greene, Elena Soderblom
Assistant to John Miller ....Charles Butler
Press Assistant ....Matthew Fasano
Production Assistants ....Ron Amato, Colleen Danaher, Casey Schmal, Amber Wilkerson
Legal Counsel ....Levine, Plotkin & Menin LLP/ Loren Plotkin, Susan Mindell, Conrad Rippy, Cris Criswell
Insurance ....USI Entertainment Insurance Svcs/ Shel Bachrach
Banking ....Commerce Bank/Ellen S. Baker
Accounting ....Rosenberg Neuwirth & Kuchner/ Chris Cacace, Mark D'Ambrosi
Payroll Service ....Castellana Services Inc./ Lance Castellana
Advertising ....Serino Coyne/Nancy Coyne Victoria Cairl, Greg Corradetti, Neal Leibowitz, Hunter Robertson
Art Development ....@Radical Media
Marketing ....The Marketing Group/ Laura Matalon, Tanya Grubich, Anne Rippey, Bob Bucci, Daya Wolterstorff, Elizabeth Miller, Sara Rosenzweig
General Management Associates ....Thom Mitchell, Lane Marsh, Aaron Lustbader, Connie Yung
General Management Office ....Jennifer Mudge, Chris Betz, Jake Hirzel, Jason Hewitt
Web Designer ....Bay Bridge Productions Inc.
Theatre Displays ....King Displays
Production Photographer ....Joan Marcus

CREDITS
Scenery and scenic effects built and electrified by PRG Scenic Technologies, New Windsor, NY. Scenery painted by Scenic Arts Studios, Cornwall NY. Show control and scenic motion control featuring Stage Command Systems by PRG Scenic Technologies. Costumes by Douglas Earl, Euroco, Jennifer Love, Lynne Bacchus, Tohma Couture, Tricorne Inc. Fabric painting by Jeff Fender. Millinery by Rodney Gordon. Shoes by LaDuca Shoes. Lighting equipment provided by PRG Lighting, North Bergen, NJ. Sound equipment provided by Masque Sound, East Rutherford, NJ. Video equipment provided by Scharff Weisberg Inc., Long Island City, NY. "Little" Edie afghan custom knit by Susan Butler. Portrait of Mr. Beale by Eric March. Makeup provided by M•A•C. Piano furnished by Beethoven Pianos.

SPECIAL THANKS
The MacDowell Colony, McCarter Theatre Center, Jason Baruch, Jocelyn Clark, Siobhan Engle, Ethan Geto, Jung Griffin, Patrick Herold, Philip Himberg, Sarah Jane Leigh, Janice Paran, Sally Quinn and Benjamin Bradlee, Nathan Riley, Judy and Robert Rubin, Larry Tatelbaum, Garrick Utley.

PLAYWRIGHTS HORIZONS
Artistic Director ....Tim Sanford
Managing Director ....Leslie Marcus
General Manager ....William Russo
Director of Musical Theater ....Christie Evangelisto

Visit the official *GREY GARDENS* website
www.greygardensthemusical.com

JUJAMCYN THEATERS

ROCCO LANDESMAN
President

PAUL LIBIN
Producing Director
JACK VIERTEL
Creative Director
JERRY ZAKS
Resident Director
JORDAN ROTH
Resident Producer
DANIEL ADAMIAN
General Manager
JENNIFER HERSHEY
Director of Operations
MEREDITH VILLATORE
Chief Financial Officer

STAFF FOR THE WALTER KERR THEATRE
Manager ....Susan Elrod
Treasurer ....Stan Shaffer
Carpenter ....George A. Fullum
Propertyman ....Timothy Bennet
Electrician ....Vincent Valvo, Jr.
Engineer ....Ralph Santos

Grey Gardens
Scrapbook

Drawing by Michael J. DiMotta

Photo by Aubrey Reuben

1. Caricature of cast, drawn by Michael J. DiMotta.
2. (L-R): Mary Louise Wilson and Christine Ebersole embrace as they arrive at the Central Park Boathouse for the opening night party.

Correspondent: Matt Cavenaugh, Joe Kennedy Jr./Jerry.

Memorable Letter: Edie Beale sent a letter to Scott Frankel, the composer, before she passed, and he shared it with us. Albert Maysles had told Edie that someone was turning the film into a musical, and she wrote to say that she was just thrilled, and (I'm paraphrasing here) "The one thing I always wanted to see more of in the film was more singing and dancing." So Scott and all of us feel she gave her blessing to the musical.

Opening Night Gifts: Randall Wreghitt gave us a great rendering of all the characters from the show. It was done by Michael J. DiMotta, a worthy heir to Al Hirschfeld. Very cool! Another collector's item given by East of Doheney was a six-by-four-foot hand-sewn throw of the show's logo. So we now all have Christine peering at us from our couch or bed.

Exciting Celebrity Visitors: We have had a lot of really cool people come back. Meryl Streep caught us at our last performance at Playwrights Horizons. Jerry Torre, whom I play in the second act, visits quite often. Angela Lansbury, Tom Brokaw, and, of course, Rosie. Elaine Stritch saw us at Playwrights. Her advice: "Get the first act down to 30 minutes and you got a hit!"

Favorite Therapies: There's always a big jar of Ricolas. Though I may be only 28, my knees sometimes feel much older. I use a lot of Icy Hot balm and the cast knows when I have it on.

Actor Who Has Done the Most Shows in His/Her Career: John McMartin.

Actor Who Performed the Most Roles: Almost everyone in the show plays two or more roles, so you'd have to say the person with the most roles is Asa Somers, who covers myself and Bob Stillman.

Special Backstage Rituals: Mary Louise Wilson plays Boggle with her dresser, Vangeli Kaseluris, to keep her mind fresh. Erin Davie and I dance around a bit before our first entrance.

Favorite Moments During Each Performance: I love sharing the "Jerry Likes My Corn" scene with Mary Louise. I also love the moment when I'm in the choir and John McMartin is singing "Choose To Be Happy." John McMartin can raise a smile from anyone. Any moment with Mary Louise or John McMartin is golden.

Favorite In-Theatre Gathering Place: The Walter Kerr is a rather small space for a musical, there's no a greenroom or common room. People gather in the stage manager's office to watch YouTube marathons, or gather in the office of Vincent Valvo Jr. (house electrician) to watch the Mets. We're all big Mets fans here at *Grey Gardens*. Especially in fall 2006 when the Mets were in the playoffs.

Favorite Off-Site Hangout: Hurley's, right across the street, is a great pub restaurant. They certainly all know the Walter Kerr regulars, the house guys who have been going there for years. And they get to know the actors in the new shows. The bartenders are really great. They always find us a place to sit even when they're busy. It's the best.

Favorite Snack Food: A perk of working for East of Doheny is that they cater. From the auditions to every day at rehearsals, and now every two-show day, there's catering that comes in.

Mascot: There was this miniature horse that Lisa Tucci, our wardrobe supervisor, had. Everyone took a candid Polaroid with the horse, and now they decorate the wardrobe room. But Christine might have that topped. She has a dog named Spot Bouvier Beale. He is our ambassador-at-large.

Memorable Ad-Libs: Most of the gems come from Mary Louise or John McMartin. Sometimes they don't even know it. While singing "Jerry Likes My Corn," Mary Louise got stuck on the lyric about the Superbowl. The real lyric is "Mountain Dew, Super Bowl, sex and drugs and rock 'n' roll," but she sang, "Superbowl, Superbowl, Super-duper-duper-bowl!" It happens. What's great is that both Mary Louise and John are able to laugh at it, so that gives us license to laugh. Also, John being the old pro that he is, has been known to play like the character is drunk whenever he goes up. It's really quite brilliant.

Memorable Fan Encounters: One of our first previews at Playwrights Horizons, we had a whole gaggle of women from Seattle come dressed in Edie garb. They had a grand time at that performance. We also have two women from Carolina, both named Carolyn, who are huge fans of the documentary and our show. They've probably seen the show upwards of 50 times. They send us letters and pictures. I've even seen footage of their personal trips to Grey Gardens mansion. They are definitely our number-one fans.

Who Wore the Heaviest/Hottest Costume: Christine, with the mink.

Grey Gardens
Scrapbook

Who Wore the Least: As Joe, I used to make my first entrance in swim trunks. Thankfully, that only lasted for a dress rehearsal.
Catchphrase Only the Company Would Recognize: "Yeah, yeah…yeah, yeah."
Orchestra Story: The orchestra just loves when Mary Louise calls for the kitties during her first entrance. The line as written is "Here, kitty," but slowly it morphed to "Here, puss." They get the biggest kick out of it.
Best In-House Parody Lyrics: Stephen, our ASM, has a favorite. The real lyric is, "and Edie sat." But he likes to sing, "And Edie shat." Another fave is "Time rushes by, mammaries fade," instead of "...memories fade."
Memorable Directorial Note: "Get off stage faster!"
Company In-Joke: My hair. I realize that the reason I have a career is because I have great hair. and that takes a lot of work. The cast like to poke fun at how much time goes into that effort.
Company Legend: John McMartin. He is a walking legend.
Nickname: "Douchebag."
Sweethearts Within the Company: We're all in love with Mary Louise Wilson. Who isn't?
Embarrassing Moment: The turntable stopped at Playwrights Horizons one night. That's always kind of embarrassing. The real issue was that it happened to be the night Ben Brantley was there. Also, during our gypsy run-through at the Kerr, Christine made her entrance for "The House We Live In" and her dress had ripped all down the side. She was having to hold it up. Well, that is also when publicity photos were being taken. Christine, with her ever-present wit, broke character and shouted out to the photographers, "Oh, honey, you don't want any of these!" The audience loved it.
Coolest Thing About Working on This Show: We have the most generous producers in town. They shower us with gifts. And, of course, there is the catering! It's a luxury we all appreciate very much.

Photos by Aubrey Reuben

1. Celebrating the show's 100th performance with a cake on the stage of the Walter Kerr Theatre.
2. Sarah Hyland arrives at the opening night party.
3. Ebersole smiles for the paparazzi on opening night.
4. Composer Scott Frankel at the cast party.
5. Director Doug Hughes.

Hairspray

First Preview: July 18, 2002. Opened: August 15, 2002.
Still running as of May 31, 2007.

PLAYBILL

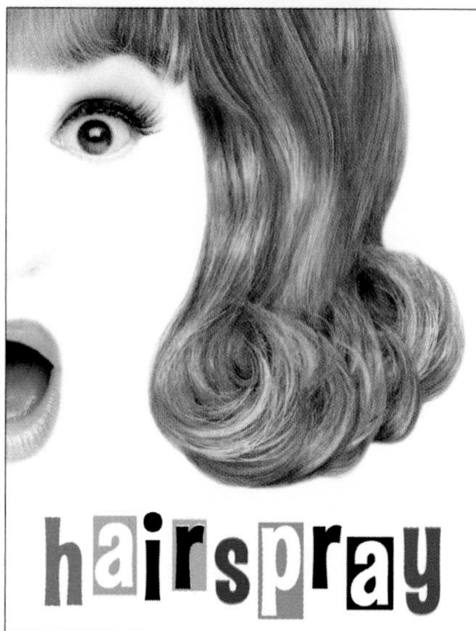

CAST

(in order of appearance)

Tracy Turnblad .... SHANNON DURIG
Corny Collins .... JONATHAN DOKUCHITZ
Amber Von Tussle .... HAYLIE DUFF
Brad .... MICHAEL CUNIO
Tammy .... LINDSAY NICOLE CHAMBERS
Fender .... DANIEL ROBINSON
Brenda .... LESLIE GODDARD
Sketch .... BRYAN WEST
Shelley .... LORI EVE MARINACCI
IQ .... TODD MICHEL SMITH
Lou Ann .... LESLIE McDONEL
Link Larkin .... AARON TVEIT
Prudy Pingleton .... LISA JOLLEY
Edna Turnblad .... BLAKE HAMMOND
Penny Pingleton .... DIANA DeGARMO
Velma Von Tussle .... ISABEL KEATING
Harriman F. Spritzer .... KEVIN MEANEY
Wilbur Turnblad .... STEPHEN DeROSA
Principal .... KEVIN MEANEY
Seaweed J. Stubbs .... TEVIN CAMPBELL
Duane .... TYRICK WILTEZ JONES
Gilbert .... ARBENDER J. ROBINSON
Lorraine .... TERITA R. REDD
Thad .... TOMMAR WILSON
The Dynamites .... CARLA J. HARGROVE,
JUDINE SOMERVILLE,
CANDICE MARIE WOODS
Mr. Pinky .... KEVIN MEANEY
Gym Teacher .... LISA JOLLEY
Inez .... NATURI NAUGHTON

Continued on next page

NEIL SIMON THEATRE

UNDER THE DIRECTION OF JAMES M. NEDERLANDER AND JAMES L. NEDERLANDER

Margo Lion Adam Epstein The Baruch · Viertel · Routh · Frankel Group
James D. Stern/Douglas L. Meyer Rick Steiner/Frederic H. Mayerson
SEL & GFO New Line Cinema
In Association With
Live Nation A. Gordon/E. McAllister
D. Harris/M. Swinsky J. & B. Osher
Present

HAIRSPRAY

Book By
Mark O'Donnell
Thomas Meehan

Music By
Marc Shaiman

Lyrics By
Scott Wittman
Marc Shaiman

Based upon the New Line Cinema film written and directed by John Waters

Starring
Shannon Durig **Blake Hammond**

With
Diana DeGarmo **Haylie Duff**

Also Starring
Tevin Campbell Scott Davidson Jonathan Dokuchitz Lisa Jolley
Isabel Keating Kevin Meaney Naturi Naughton Aaron Tveit
with Stephen DeRosa and Darlene Love

With
Joe Abraham Gretchen Bieber Lindsay Nicole Chambers Michael Cunio Michelle Dowdy
Leslie Goddard Carla J. Hargrove Tyrick Wiltez Jones Lauren Kling Abdul Latif Lori Eve Marinacci Leslie McDonel
Rusty Mowery CJay Hardy Philip Nicole Powell Terita R. Redd Arbender J. Robinson Daniel Robinson Todd Michel Smith
Jason Snow Judine Somerville Bryan West Tommar Wilson Candice Marie Woods

Scenery Designed by
David Rockwell

Costumes Designed by
William Ivey Long

Lighting Designed by
Kenneth Posner

Sound Designed by
Steve C. Kennedy

Casting by
Bernard Telsey Casting

Wigs & Hair Designed by
Paul Huntley

Production Stage Manager
Lois Griffing

Associate Director
Matt Lenz

Associate Choreographer
Michele Lynch

Orchestrations by
Harold Wheeler

Music Direction by
Lon Hoyt

Arrangements by
Marc Shaiman

Music Coordinator
John Miller

General Management
Richard Frankel Productions
Laura Green

Technical Supervisor
Tech Production
Services, Inc.

Press Representative
Richard Kornberg
Don Summa

Associate Producers
Rhoda Mayerson
The Aspen Group
Daniel C. Staton

Choreography by
Jerry Mitchell

Direction by
Jack O'Brien

The world premiere of "HAIRSPRAY" was produced with the 5th Avenue Theatre in Seattle, Washington David Armstrong, Producing Artistic Director; Marilynn Sheldon, Managing Director

The producers wish to express their appreciation to Theatre Development Fund for its support of this production.

ORIGINAL BROADWAY CAST RECORDING ON SONY CLASSICAL

LIVE BROADWAY

10/2/06

(L-R): Diana DeGarmo and Tevin Campbell

(L-R): Haylie Duff and Isabel Keating

Photos by Paul Kolnik

Hairspray

SCENES & MUSICAL NUMBERS

Baltimore, 1962

Act One

Prologue: "Good Morning Baltimore" .... Tracy & Company
Scene 1: **TV Station WZZT & Turnblad Home**
"The Nicest Kids in Town" .... Corny Collins & Council Members
Scene 2: **At the Vanities**
"Mama, I'm a Big Girl Now" .... Edna & Tracy, Velma & Amber, Penny & Prudy
Scene 3: **TV Station WZZT**
"I Can Hear the Bells" .... Tracy
"(The Legend of) Miss Baltimore Crabs" .... Velma & Council Members
Scene 4: **Detention**
Scene 5: **Patterson Park High School Gymnasium**
"The Madison" .... Corny & Company
Scene 6: **WZZT & Turnblad Home**
"The Nicest Kids in Town" (Reprise) .... Corny & Council Members
"It Takes Two" .... Link & Tracy
Scene 7: **Turnblad Home and Streets of Baltimore**
"Welcome to the '60s" .... Tracy, Edna, The Dynamites & Company
Scene 8: **Patterson Park Playground**
"Run and Tell That" .... Seaweed
Scene 9: **Motormouth Maybelle's Record Shop**
"Run and Tell That" .... Seaweed, Little Inez & Company
"Big, Blonde & Beautiful" .... Motormouth, Little Inez, Tracy, Edna, Wilbur

Act Two

Scene 1: **Baltimore Women's House of Detention**
"The Big Dollhouse" .... Women
"Good Morning Baltimore" (Reprise) .... Tracy
Scene 2: **The Har-De-Har Hut**
"Timeless to Me" .... Wilbur & Edna
Scene 3: **Tracy's Jail Cell & Penny's Bedroom**
"Without Love" .... Link, Tracy, Seaweed, Penny
Scene 4: **Motormouth Maybelle's Record Shop**
"I Know Where I've Been" .... Motormouth & Company
Scene 5: **The Baltimore Eventorium**
"Hairspray" .... Corny & Council Members
"Cooties" .... Amber & Council Members
"You Can't Stop the Beat" .... Tracy, Link, Penny, Seaweed, Edna, Wilbur, Motormouth & Company

ORCHESTRA

Conductor: Lon Hoyt
Associate Conductor: Keith Cotton
Assistant Conductor: Seth Farber
Guitars: David Spinozza, Peter Calo; Keyboards: Lon Hoyt, Keith Cotton, Seth Farber; Electric Bass: Francisco Centeno; Drums: Clint de Ganon; Percussion: Walter "Wally" Usiatynski; Reeds: David Mann, Dave Riekenberg; Trumpet: Bob Milliken; Trombone: Birch Johnson; Violins: Rob Shaw, Carol Pool; Cello: Sarah Hewitt Roth
Music Coordinator: John Miller

ONSTAGE MUSICIANS

Guitar: Aaron Tveit
Keyboards: Isabel Keating
Glockenspiel: Kevin Meaney
Harmonica: Diana DeGarmo

Music Copying: Emily Grishman Music Preparation/Emily Grishman, Katharine Edmonds

Cast Continued

Motormouth Maybelle .... DARLENE LOVE
Matron .... LISA JOLLEY
Guard .... KEVIN MEANEY
Denizens of Baltimore .... LINDSAY NICOLE CHAMBERS, MICHAEL CUNIO, LESLIE GODDARD, CARLA J. HARGROVE, LISA JOLLEY, TYRICK WILTEZ JONES, LORI EVE MARINACCI, LESLIE McDONEL, KEVIN MEANEY, TERITA R. REDD, ARBENDER J. ROBINSON, DANIEL ROBINSON, TODD MICHEL SMITH, JUDINE SOMERVILLE, BRYAN WEST, TOMMAR WILSON, CANDICE MARIE WOODS

Dance Captain .... RUSTY MOWERY

SWINGS

JOE ABRAHAM, GRETCHEN BIEBER, LAUREN KLING, ABDUL LATIF, RUSTY MOWERY, CJAY HARDY PHILIP, NICOLE POWELL, JASON SNOW

UNDERSTUDIES

Understudy for Tracy Turnblad — MICHELLE DOWDY, LORI EVE MARINACCI; for Edna Turnblad — SCOTT DAVIDSON, KEVIN MEANEY; for Wilbur Turnblad — SCOTT DAVIDSON, KEVIN MEANEY; for Velma Von Tussle — GRETCHEN BIEBER; LISA JOLLEY, LORI EVE MARINACCI, LESLIE McDONEL; for Amber Von Tussle — GRETCHEN BIEBER, LESLIE McDONEL; for Motormouth Maybelle — CARLA J. HARGROVE, TERITA R. REDD; for Seaweed — ARBENDER J. ROBINSON, TOMMAR WILSON; for Link Larkin — DANIEL ROBINSON, BRYAN WEST; for Corny Collins — MICHAEL CUNIO, RUSTY MOWERY, DANIEL ROBINSON, BRYAN WEST; for Penny Pingleton — LINDSAY NICOLE CHAMBERS, LESLIE GODDARD, LAUREN KLING; for Inez — CARLA J. HARGROVE, CANDICE MARIE WOODS; for Spritzer/Principal/Mr. Pinky/Guard — MICHAEL CUNIO, SCOTT DAVIDSON; for Prudy, Gym Teacher, Matron — GRETCHEN BIEBER, LINDSAY NICOLE CHAMBERS, LORI EVE MARINACCI, LESLIE McDONEL; for Dynamites — NICOLE POWELL, TERITA R. REDD, TOMMAR WILSON.

Hairspray

Shannon Durig
Tracy Turnblad

Blake Hammond
Edna Turnblad

Diana DeGarmo
Penny Pingleton

Haylie Duff
Amber Von Tussle

Stephen DeRosa
Wilbur Turnblad

Darlene Love
Motormouth Maybelle

Tevin Campbell
Seaweed J. Stubbs

Scott Davidson
u/s Edna Turnblad, Wilbur Turnblad, Harriman F. Spritzer, Principal, Mr. Pinky, Guard

Jonathan Dokuchitz
Corny Collins

Lisa Jolley
Prudy Pingleton, Gym Teacher, Matron

Isabel Keating
Velma Von Tussle

Kevin Meaney
Harriman F. Spritzer, Principal, Mr. Pinky, Guard

Naturi Naughton
Inez

Aaron Tveit
Link

Joe Abraham
Swing

Gretchen Bieber
Swing

Lindsay Nicole Chambers
Tammy

Michael Cunio
Brad

Michelle Dowdy
u/s Tracy Turnblad

Leslie Goddard
Brenda

Carla J. Hargrove
Dynamite

Tyrick Wiltez Jones
Duane

Lauren Kling
Swing

Abdul Latif
Swing

Lori Eve Marinacci
Shelley

Leslie McDonel
Lou Ann

Rusty Mowery
Dance Captain/ Swing

CJay Hardy Philip
Swing

Nicole Powell
Swing

Terita R. Redd
Lorraine

Arbender J. Robinson
Gilbert

Daniel Robinson
Fender

Jason Snow
Swing

Judine Somerville
Dynamite

Todd Michel Smith
IQ

Hairspray

Bryan West
Sketch

Tommar Wilson
Thad

Candice Marie Woods
Dynamite

Mark O'Donnell
Book

Thomas Meehan
Book

Marc Shaiman
Music & Lyrics/ Arrangements

Scott Wittman
Lyrics

Jack O'Brien
Director

Jerry Mitchell
Choreographer

David Rockwell
Scenic Designer

William Ivey Long
Costume Designer

Kenneth Posner
Lighting Designer

Steve Canyon Kennedy
Sound Designer

Paul Huntley
Wig & Hair Design

John Waters
Consultant

Bernard Telsey, Telsey + Company
Casting

Richard Kornberg & Associates
Press Representative

Harold Wheeler
Orchestrations

Lon Hoyt
Music Director

John Miller
Music Coordinator

Laura Green, Richard Frankel Productions
General Management

Michele Lynch
Associate Choreographer

Margo Lion
Producer

Adam Epstein
Producer

Steven Baruch, The Baruch•Viertel• Routh•Frankel Group
Producer

Thomas Viertel, The Baruch•Viertel• Routh•Frankel Group
Producer

Marc Routh, The Baruch•Viertel• Routh•Frankel Group
Producer

Richard Frankel, The Baruch•Viertel• Routh•Frankel Group
Producer

Douglas L. Meyer
Producer

Rick Steiner
Producer

Frederic H. Mayerson
Producer

Allan S. Gordon
Producer

Elan V. McAllister
Producer

Dede Harris
Producer

Morton Swinsky, Kardana Swinsky Productions
Producer

Hairspray

John and Bonnie Osher
Producer

Daniel C. Staton
Associate Producer

Rhoda Mayerson
Associate Producer

David Armstrong, 5th Avenue Theatre
Presented World Premiere of Hairspray

Marilynn Sheldon, 5th Avenue Theatre
Presented World Premiere of Hairspray

Cameron Adams
Swing

Katrina Rose Dideriksen
Standby for Tracy Turnblad

Becky Gulsvig
Amber Von Tussle

Julie Halston
Prudy Pingleton, Gym Teacher, Matron, Denizen of Baltimore

Tyler Hanes
Fender, Denizen of Baltimore

Leah Hocking
Velma Von Tussle

Michelle Kittrell
Swing, Dance Captain

Caissie Levy
Penny Pingleton

Rashad Naylor
Thad, Denizen of Baltimore

Andrew Rannells
Link Larkin

Donna Vivino
Shelley, Denizen of Baltimore

Willis White
Duane, Gilbert, Denizen of Baltimore, Swing

Cameron Adams
Lou Ann, Denizen of Baltimore, Swing

Ashley Parker Angel
Link Larkin

Jere Burns
Wilbur Turnblad

Ryan Christopher Chotto
Swing

Brooke Leigh Engen
Swing, Dance Captain

Jesse L. Johnson
IQ, Denizen of Baltimore

Tara Macri
Amber Von Tussle

Susan Mosher
Prudy Pingleton, Gym Teacher, Matron, Denizen of Baltimore

Brynn O'Malley
Amber Von Tussle

Hayley Podschun
Tammy, Denizen of Baltimore

Andrew Rannells
Fender, Denizen of Baltimore

Robbie Roby
Swing, Dance Captain

Lindsay Thomas
Swing, Dance Captain

Alexa Vega
Penny Pingleton

Paul C. Vogt
Edna Turnblad

Willis White
Swing

Hairspray

Photos by Melissa Merlo

HAIR DEPARTMENT
(L-R): Isabelle Decauwert (Hairdresser), Richard Fabris (Swing), John Roberson (Hairdresser), Alex Bartlett (Hairdresser), and Stephanie Barnes (Assistant Supervisor).

ORCHESTRA
Front Row Seated (L-R):
John Benthal (Guitar), Maru Phaneuf (Reeds), Robert Milliken (Trumpet), Sarah Hewitt-Roth (Cello), Conrad Harris (Violin).

Back Row Standing (L-R):
Clint De Ganon (Drums), Carol Pool (Violin), Scott Burroughs (Trombone), Cherisse Rogers (Bass), Seth Farber (Keyboard/Assistant Conductor), Jim Morgan (Keyboard), Ed Alstrom (Keyboard), Peter Calo (Guitar), and David Richards (Reeds).

BOX OFFICE
(L-R): Billy Dorso (Assistant Treasurer), Erich Von Stollberger (Assistant Treasurer), and Marc Needleman (Assistant Treasurer).

Hairspray

STAGE CREW
Front Row (L-R):
Mark Hannan (Follow Spot Operator), Arthur Lutz (Sound), Pat Amari (Props),
Steve Vessa (Follow Spot Operator),
Lorena Sullivan (Props),
Richard J. Kirby,
James Travers, Sr. (House Electrician),
Brent Oakley (Head Electrician).

Back Row (L-R):
Mike Bennet (Carpenter), Jessica Morton (Assistant Electrician), Greg Reiff (Sound), John Kelly (Deck Electrician), Michael Pilipski (Head Props), Scott Mecionis (House Props), Istvan Tamas (Carpenter),
Tommy Green (Head Carpenter)
and Ben Horrigan (Carpenter).

STAGE MANAGEMENT
(L-R): Thom Gates (Assistant Stage Manager),
Marisha Ploski (Stage Manager),
and Lois Griffing (Production Stage Manager).

Photos by Melissa Merlo

WARDROBE
Front Row (L-R):
Mindy Eng (Dresser), Alessandro Fedrico (Swing/Day Worker).

Second Row (L-R):
Laura Horner (Dresser), Susie Ghebresillassie (Swing/Stitcher), Liz Goodrum (Dresser).

Third Row (L-R):
Kate McAleer (Dresser), Meghan Carsella (Assistant Supervisor), Tanya Blue (Dresser).

Back Row (L-R):
Anthony Hoffman (Dresser), Joe Armon (Dresser), Sara Foster (Swing/Day Worker)
and Eugene Nicks (Dresser).

Hairspray

FRONT OF HOUSE
Front Row (L-R):
Maureen Santos (Ticket Taker), Cecelia Luna (Directress), Jessica Mroz (Usher).

Back Row (L-R):
Evelyn Olivero (Usher), Chris Langdon (Ticket Taker), Adrienne Watson (Usher), Michelle Smith (Usher), Steven Ouellette (House Manager), and Mariea Crainicuic (Usher).

USHERS
(L-R):
Jose Lopez (Porter), Michelle Vargas (Ticket Taker), Christina Vargas (Usher), Mary Ellen Palermo (Directress), Dolores Banyai (Usher), Christine Bentley (Usher), and Marisol Olavarrio (Usher).

Photos by Ben Strothmann

BOX OFFICE ASSISTANT
Dylan Carusona

PORTERS
(L-R): James Mosaphir (Stage Doorman), Errolyn Rosa (Swing/Elevator Operator)

Hairspray

STAFF FOR HAIRSPRAY

GENERAL MANAGEMENT
RICHARD FRANKEL PRODUCTIONS
Richard Frankel Marc Routh Laura Green
Rod Kaats Jo Porter Joe Watson

COMPANY MANAGER
Aliza Wassner
Assistant Company Manager .... Tracy Geltman

GENERAL PRESS REPRESENTATIVE
RICHARD KORNBERG & ASSOCIATES
Richard Kornberg Don Summa
Tom D'Ambrosio Carrie Friedman

CASTING
Telsey + Company, C.S.A.:
Bernie Telsey, Will Cantler, David Vaccari, Bethany Knox, Craig Burns, Tiffany Little Canfield, Stephanie Yankwitt, Carrie Rosson, Justin Huff, Joe Langworth

PRODUCTION STAGE MANAGER .... **Lois L. Griffing**
Stage Manager .... Jason Brouillard
Assistant Stage Manager .... Kim Vernace
Associate Director .... Matt Lenz
Associate Choreographer .... Michele Lynch
Production Dance Supervisor .... Rusty Mowery
Technical Supervision ...... Tech Production Services, Inc./ Peter Fulbright, Elliot Bertoni, Mary Duffe, Colleen Houlehen, Jarid Sumner, Michael Altbaum
Associate Set Designer .... Richard Jaris
Assistant Set Designers .... Emily Beck, Robert Bissinger, Ted LeFevre
Associate to David Rockwell .... Barry Richards
Assistants to David Rockwell .... Michael Dereskewicz, Joanie Schlafer
Associate Costume Designer .... Martha Bromelmeier
Assistant Costume Designer .... Laura Oppenheimer
Assistants to William Ivey Long .... Melissa-Anne Blizzard, Donald Sanders
Automated Light Programmer .... Paul J. Sonnleitner
Associate Lighting Designer .... Philip Rosenberg
Assistant Lighting Designer .... Paul Miller
Associate Sound Designer .... John Shivers
Associate Wig and Hair Designer .... Amy Solomon

Make-Up Design by .... Randy Houston Mercer

Supervising Production Carpenter .... Ken Fieldhouse
Head Carpenter .... Brian Munroe
Assistant Carpenters .... Bryan Davis, Ben Horrigan
Supervising Production Electrician .... Michael Lo Bue
Head Electrician .... Brent Oakley
Assistant Electrician .... Jessica Morton
Head Sound Engineer .... Andrew Keister
Assistant Sound Engineer .... Michael Bogden
Deck Sound .... Art Lutz
Head Property Master .... Michael Pilipski
Assistant Property Master .... Lorena Sullivan
Wardrobe Supervisor .... Michael Sancineto
Assistant Wardrobe Supervisor .... Meghan Carsella
Star Dressers .... Del Miskie, Joseph Phillip Armon
Dressers .... Alex Bartlett, Mindy Eng, Larry Foster, Laura Horner, Liz Goodrum, Tanya Blue, Vangeli Kaseluris, Jean Stinlein
Hair and Makeup Supervisor .... Jon Jordan
Assistant Hair Supervisor .... Adenike Wright
Hair Assistants .... Stephanie Barnes, Isabelle Decauwert, Mark Manalanasan
Music Coordinator .... John Miller
Associate Conductor .... Keith Cotton
Drummer .... Clint DeGanon
Assistant Music Coordinator .... Matthew Ettinger, Chuck Butler
Electronic Music System Design and Programming .... Music Arts Technologies, Jim Harp, Brett Sommer
Rehearsal Pianist .... Edward Rabin
Producing Assoc. to Ms. Lion .... Lily Hung
Asst. to Mr. Baruch .... Sonja Soper
Asst. to Mr. Viertel .... Tania Senewiratne
Associate Producer/ Adam Epstein Productions .... Lynn Shaw
Asst. to Mr. Steiner .... Kathy Wall
Asst. to Mr. Stern .... Leah Callaghan, Shira Sergant
Management Assistant .... Tracy Geltman
Orthopedic Consultant .... Phillip Bauman, MD
Physical Therapy .... Performing Arts Physical Therapy
Production Assistants .... Sharon DelPilar, Daniel Kelly, Travis Milliken, Adam M. Muller, Noah Pollock
Press Intern .... Alyssa Hart
Advertising .... Serino Coyne, Inc./ Nancy Coyne, Greg Coradetti, Joaquin Esteva, Hunter Robertson
Promotions/Marketing ..... TMG - The Marketing Group/ Tanya Grubich, Laura Matalon, Trish Santini, Bob Bucci, Amber Glassberg, Liz Miller
Photographer .... Paul Kolnik
Web Designer .... Simma Park
Theatre Displays .... King Displays
Insurance .... DeWitt Stern Group
Legal Counsel .... Patricia Crown, Coblence & Warner
Banking .... Chase Manhattan Bank/ Richard Callian, Michael Friel
Payroll Service .... Castellana Services, Inc.
Accounting .... Fried and Kowgios Partners LLP
Travel Agency .... JMC Travel
Concessions .... Rick Steiner Productions
New York Rehearsals .... The New 42nd Street Studios
New York Opening Night Coordinator .... Tobak-Dantchik Events and Promotions, Suzanne Tobak, Jennifer Falik
New York Group Sales .... Show Tix (212) 302-7000

EXCLUSIVE TOUR DIRECTION:
On the Road

LIVE NATION, THEATRICAL DIVISION
David Ian, Steve Winton, David Anderson, Wendy Connor, Jennifer Costello, Jennifer DeLange, Paul Dietz, Susie Krajsa, David Lazar, Courtney Pierce, Alison Spiriti, Dan Swartz

RICHARD FRANKEL PRODUCTIONS STAFF
Finance Director .... **Michael Naumann**
Assistant to Mr. Frankel .... Jeff Romley
Assistant to Mr. Routh .... Seth Soloway
Assistant to Ms. Green .... Joshua A. Saletnik
Assistant Finance Director .... John DiMeglio
Information Technology Manager .... Roddy Pimentel
Management Assistant .... Heidi Schading
Accounting Assistants .... Heather Le Blanc, Nicole O'Bleanis
National Sales and Marketing Director .. **Ronni Mandell**
Marketing Manager .... Melissa Marano
Director of Business Affairs .... **Michael Sinder**
Office Manager .... **Lori Steiger-Perry**
Assistant Office Manager .... Stephanie Adamczyk
Receptionist .... Kathleen Kiernan, Matt Posner
Interns .... Kristi Bergman, Ashley Berman, Kevin Condardo, Yie Foong, Annie Grappone, Julie Griffith, Christina Macchia, Anthony Nunziata, Will Nunziata, Kimberly Jade Tompkins

CREDITS AND ACKNOWLEDGEMENTS

Scenery and scenic effects built, painted, electrified and automated by Showmotion, Inc., Norwalk, CT. Scenery automation by Showmotion, Inc., using the Autocue Computerized Motion Control System. Lighting equipment from Fourth Phase, New Jersey. Sound equipment by Sound Associates, Inc. Specialty props by Prism Production Services, Rahway, NJ. Costumes built by Euro Co Costumes Inc., Jennifer Love Costumes, Scafati Incorporated, Schneeman Studios, Tricorne New York City and Timberlake Studios, Inc. Custom shoes by LaDuca Shoes NYC. Champagne provided by Veuve Clicquot. Lite Brite Wall engineered, constructed and electrified by Showmotion, Inc. Soft goods by Rosebrand Textiles, Inc. Scenic painting by Scenic Art Studios. Hair Curtain Main Drape by I. Weiss and Sons, Inc. Rusk hair products. Herbal cough drops supplied by Ricola.

NEDERLANDER

Chairman .... **James M. Nederlander**
President .... **James L. Nederlander**

Executive Vice President
Nick Scandalios

Vice President Corporate Development
Charlene S. Nederlander

Senior Vice President Labor Relations
Herschel Waxman

Vice President
Jim Boese

Chief Financial Officer
Freida Sawyer Belviso

STAFF FOR THE NEIL SIMON THEATRE
Theatre Manager .... Steve Ouellette
Treasurer .... Richard Aubrey
Associate Treasurer .... Eddie Waxman
House Carpenter .... Thomas Green
Flyman .... Douglas McNeill
House Electrician .... James Travers, Sr.
House Propman .... Scott Mecionis
House Engineer .... John Astras

Hairspray

Scrapbook

Correspondent: Naturi Naughton, "Inez."

Most Exciting Celebrity Visitor: Laurence Fishburne was really exciting. He came with his daughter to see the show and they came backstage afterwards to meet the cast. He said that he loved the show and how much energy we have. That was such a great moment.

"Gypsy of the Year" Sketch: It was basically a spoof of the "I Can Hear the Bells" song mixed with a spoof of the Dodgeball scene in the show, written by Tommar Wilson and Bryan West. It was hilarious. When Tracy Turnblad gets hit in the head with the dodgeball and falls out, instead of Link running to her to help her, he runs to Fender and asks him if he is OK. Tracy is dumbfounded, because Link is all into Fender! Then, when Link and Fender sing, "I Can Hear the Bells," Tracy is, like, "Wait a minute...that's my song!" But everyone's focus is Link and Fender. Lots of the cast was in it…Bryan West, Andrew Rannells, Michelle Dowdy, Aaron Tveit, Diana DeGarmo, Candice Woods, Tyrick Jones and so many more.

"Carols for a Cure" Carol: "Gospel Hallelujah."

"Easter Bonnet" Sketch: "Small House of Edna Turnblad" by Tommar Wilson.

Actor Who Performed the Most Roles in This Show: Gretchen Bieber has played a lot of different roles in our show: Amber Von Tussle, Velma Von Tussle, Lou Ann and Brenda. The list might be longer than that. But she is one of our swings and she definitely plays a lot of roles.

Special Backstage Rituals: Some of the cast members get together on stage once they've called places and pray together. We gather in a circle before every single show and just pray that God gets us through the week and keeps us safe on stage and that the audience is touched by the messages in our show.

Favorite Moment During Each Performance: The Finale, when Darlene Love (Motormouth Maybelle) comes out in "You Can't Stop the Beat." She is dressed up like a police guard but she pulls off the pants and takes off the shirt and underneath she has this amazing gold dress on. And that moment is just so much fun because the entire cast is surrounding her and we are all just singing and dancing and really enjoying that moment. It's definitely a highlight and it's a lot of fun!

Favorite In-Theatre Gathering Place: The fourth floor hallway. I'm on that floor along with Susan Mosher (Female Authority Figure), Ashley Parker Angel (Link Larkin), Tevin Campbell (Seaweed J. Stubbs) and Darlene Love (Motormouth Maybelle). We have a blast. We talk in the hallway about the business, our days, what's going on in the news, and sometimes we just act silly! I have so much fun with the people on my floor and they are all good people to be around.

Photos by Aubrey Reuben

Photo by Robert S. Cross/Tulsa World

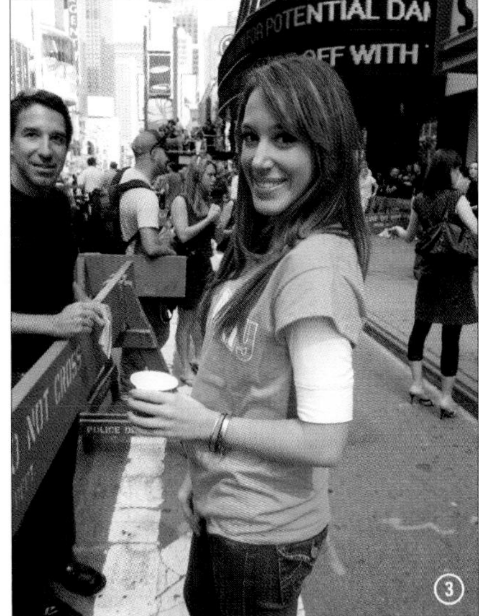

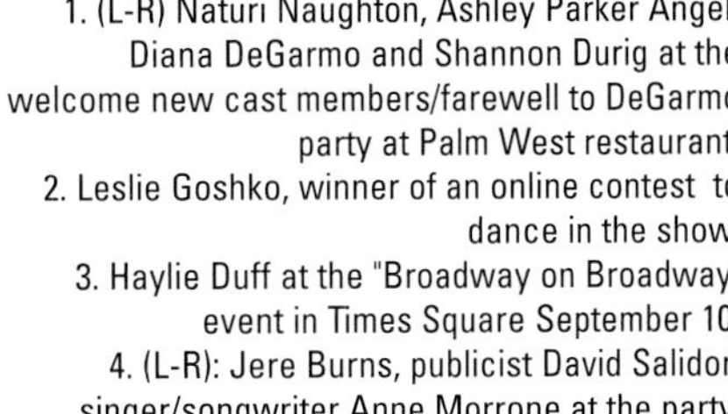

1. (L-R) Naturi Naughton, Ashley Parker Angel, Diana DeGarmo and Shannon Durig at the welcome new cast members/farewell to DeGarmo party at Palm West restaurant.
2. Leslie Goshko, winner of an online contest to dance in the show.
3. Haylie Duff at the "Broadway on Broadway" event in Times Square September 10.
4. (L-R): Jere Burns, publicist David Salidor, singer/songwriter Anne Morrone at the party.

Hairspray
Scrapbook

Photo by Greg Kalafatis

Photos by Aubrey Reuben

1. Cast bows at the finale of Alexa Vega's opening night.
2. (L-R): Tevin Campbell hugs Diana DeGarmo at her farewell party at the Palm West restaurant.
3. (L-R): Hayley Podschun, Keith Cotton, Brooke Engen at Vega's welcoming party.
4. (L-R): Paul C. Vogt and Shannon Durig at the Palm West restaurant party.

Favorite Off-Site Hangout: Sosa Borella, which is right around the corner from our theatre. They have really great food and good service. Cute spot.
Favorite Snack Foods: OHHH, I love snacks! I buy lots of goodies sometimes for my dressing room and I share them with the cast. I love popcorn and I love mini Snickers!
Favorite Therapies: Wellness Tea is great and Throat-Coat. I love physical therapy in between shows, too.
Memorable Ad-Lib: In the Motormouth scene right before Motormouth is about to sing "I Know Where I've Been," Darlene Love forgot her line and said, "We gon' get through this and just do what we have to do!" It was funny! It definitely wasn't the line but she always ad-libs in such a way where it still makes sense. She makes her ad-libbing fit the scene!
Record Number of Cell Phone Rings During a Performance: One time I remember someone's cell phone went off in the middle of a scene...it was really loud too! I only remember that happening once though.
Memorable Stage Door Fan Encounter: My opening night, which was April 4, 2006. I will never forget how shocked and overwhelmed I was when I walked out the stage door and the fans all started screaming and cheering for me. I felt so honored and extremely blessed to be a part of something so big and so special where people are truly affected by what we do.
Latest Audience Arrival: Someone came into the show right before "Big Dollhouse" which is the beginning of Act II. I couldn't believe it...they missed a lot of the show.
Fastest Costume Change: After "Welcome to the '60s" the ensemble runs off and has to change in about one minute into their clothes for Dodgeball which is the scene immediately after. So that is one of the fastest costume changes I've seen.
Who Wore the Heaviest/Hottest Costume: Paul Vogt, who plays Edna Turnblad. He definitely has a lot to wear: Fat suit, lots of makeup, big wigs, and the costume.
Who Wore the Least: I think I do. I play a little girl "Inez" and I have very little makeup and my costumes are very light and simple.
Memorable Directorial Note: Jack O'Brien said to us all at a note session, "You're not funny...*it* is!" I keep that in mind because it just reminds me that we don't have to overdo it. The script is excellent and funny all by itself.
Nicknames: People call me "Naturis." Don't really know why but it's just my name, with an "S." Tommar Wilson ("Thad") started it and it spread like wildfire!
Embarrassing Moments: When I fell in the Finale. It was a big noticeable fall and I actually sprained my ankle. Not only was that moment embarrassing, it really hurt!!!
Coolest Thing About Being in This Show: That we get to do something that we love to do and that the audience loves to see! Also, we get to meet so many great people and other celebrities in our field. It's really cool to be on Broadway but it's twice as cool to be on Broadway and be in *Hairspray*! Great cast, amazing crew, the music is awesome and it's a great story.

Heartbreak House

First Preview: September 15, 2006. Opened: October 11, 2006.
Closed: December 17, 2006 after 30 Previews and 79 Performances.

PLAYBILL®

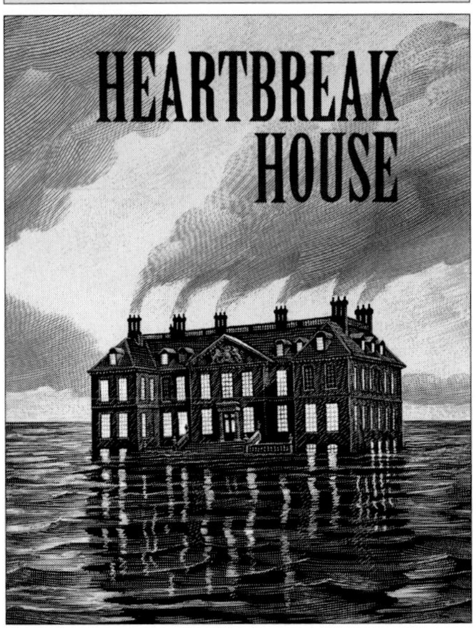

CAST

(in order of appearance)

Ellie Dunn .... LILY RABE
Nurse Guinness .... JENNY STERLIN
Captain Shotover .... PHILIP BOSCO
Ariadne Utterword .... LAILA ROBINS
Hesione Hushabye .... SWOOSIE KURTZ
Mazzini Dunn .... JOHN CHRISTOPHER JONES
Hector Hushabye .... BYRON JENNINGS
Boss Mangan .... BILL CAMP
Randall Utterword .... GARETH SAXE

TIME AND PLACE

Sussex; A fine evening at the end of September

UNDERSTUDIES

For Hector/Mangan/Randall:
TONY CARLIN
For Captain/Mazzini:
DOUG STENDER
For Ellie/Ariadne:
ANGELA PIERCE
For Hesione/Nurse Guinness:
ROBIN MOSELEY

Production Stage Manager:
LESLIE C. LYTER
Stage Manager:
JONATHAN DONAHUE

AMERICAN AIRLINES THEATRE

ROUNDABOUTTHEATRECOMPANY

TODD HAIMES, Artistic Director
HAROLD WOLPERT, Managing Director
JULIA C. LEVY, Executive Director

Presents

Philip Bosco Swoosie Kurtz
Byron Jennings Lily Rabe Laila Robins

in

HEARTBREAK HOUSE

by

George Bernard Shaw

Bill Camp John Christopher Jones Gareth Saxe Jenny Sterlin

Set Design John Lee Beatty
Costume Design Jane Greenwood
Lighting Design Peter Kaczorowski
Original Music & Sound Design John Gromada

Hair & Wig Design Tom Watson
Dialect Coach Stephen Gabis
Production Stage Manager Leslie C. Lyter

Casting Jim Carnahan, C.S.A. Mele Nagler, C.S.A.
Technical Supervisor Steve Beers
General Manager Sydney Beers

Press Representative Boneau/Bryan-Brown
Director of Marketing David B. Steffen
Founding Director Gene Feist
Associate Artistic Director Scott Ellis

Directed by
Robin Lefevre

This program is supported, in part, by public funds from the New York City Department of Cultural Affairs.

Roundabout Theatre Company is a member of the League of Resident Theatres.
www.roundabouttheatre.org

10/11/06

Photo by Joan Marcus

(L-R): Swoosie Kurtz, Lily Rabe and Byron Jennings.

Heartbreak House

Philip Bosco
Captain Shotover

Swoosie Kurtz
Hesione Hushabye

Byron Jennings
Hector Hushabye

Lily Rabe
Ellie Dunn

Laila Robins
Ariadne Utterword

Bill Camp
Boss Mangan

John Christopher Jones
Mazzini Dunn

Gareth Saxe
Randall Utterword

Jenny Sterlin
Nurse Guinness

Tony Carlin
Understudy Hector, Mangan, Randall

Robin Moseley
Understudy Hesione, Nurse Guinness

Angela Pierce
Understudy Ellie Dunn/ Ariadne

Doug Stender
Understudy Captain Shotover, Mazzini Dunn

George Bernard Shaw
Playwright

Robin Lefevre
Director

John Lee Beatty
Scenic Designer

Jane Greenwood
Costume Designer

Peter Kaczorowski
Lighting Designer

John Gromada
Original Music and Sound

Tom Watson
Hair and Wig Design

Stephen Gabis
Dialect Coach

Todd Lundquist
Associate Director

Jim Carnahan
Casting

Gene Feist
Founding Director, Roundabout Theatre Company

Todd Haimes
Artistic Director, Roundabout Theatre Company

Photo by Joan Marcus

(L-R): Philip Bosco as Captain Shotover and Lily Rabe as Ellie Dunn.

Heartbreak House

Photos by Ben Strothmann

STAGE CREW
Front Row (L-R): Glenn Merwede (Production Carpenter), Susan Fallon (Wardrobe Supervisor), Brian Maiuri (Production Electrician), Jonathan Donahue (Stage Manager).

Back Row (L-R): Andrew Forste (Production Properties), Melissa Crawford (Day Worker), Victoria Grecki (Dresser), Julie Hilimire (Dresser), Jill Anania (Local One IATSE Apprentice), Leslie C. Lyter (Production Stage Manager), Dann Wojnar (Sound Engineer), and Chris Mattingly (Flyman).

BOX OFFICE STAFF
(L-R): Robert Morgan (Assistant Box Office Manager), Mead Margulies (Ticket Services) and Ted Osborne (Box Office Manager).

FRONT OF HOUSE STAFF
Front Row (L-R): Ilia Diaz (House Staff), Adam Wier (House Staff), Cari Chrisostomou (Bar Staff), Jacklyn Rivera (House Staff).

Back Row (L-R): Bernice Diaz (House Staff), Zipporah Aguasvivas (Associate House Manager), Eddie Camacho (Head Usher) and Michael Jackson (House Staff).

ROUNDABOUT THEATRE COMPANY STAFF
ARTISTIC DIRECTOR ....TODD HAIMES
MANAGING DIRECTOR ....HAROLD WOLPERT
EXECUTIVE DIRECTOR ....JULIA C. LEVY
ASSOCIATE ARTISTIC DIRECTOR ...SCOTT ELLIS

ARTISTIC STAFF
DIRECTOR OF ARTISTIC DEVELOPMENT/
DIRECTOR OF CASTING ....Jim Carnahan
Artistic Consultant ....Robyn Goodman
Associate Artists ....Scott Elliott, Doug Hughes, Bill Irwin, Joe Mantello, Mark Brokaw, Kathleen Marshall
Consulting Dramaturg ....Jerry Patch
Artistic Associate ....Jill Rafson
Casting Director ....Mele Nagler
Casting Associate ....Carrie Gardner
Casting Assistant ....Kate Schwabe
Casting Assistant ....Stephen Kopel
Artistic Interns ....Nicholas Stimler, Jill Valentine

EDUCATION STAFF
EDUCATION DIRECTOR ...Margie Salvante-McCann
Director of Instruction and
Curriculum Development ....Renee Flemings
Education Associate ....Jennifer DeBruin
Education Program Manager ....David Miller
Administrative Assistant for Education .....Allison Baucom
Education Interns ....George Keveson, Christina Neubrand
Education Dramaturg ....Ted Sod
Teaching Artists ....Phil Alexander, Tony Angelini, Cynthia Babak, Victor Barbella,

Heartbreak House

Brigitte Barnett-Loftis, Caitlin Barton, Joe Basile, LaTonya Borsay, Bonnie Brady, Lori Brown-Niang, Michael Carnahan, Stella Cartaino, Joe Clancy, Melissa Denton, Joe Doran, Katie Down, Tony Freeman, Aaron Gass, Katie Gorum, Sheri Graubert, Adam Gwon, Susan Hamburger, Karla Hendrick, Lisa Renee Jordan, Alvin Keith, Rebecca Lord, Robin Mates, Erin McCready, Jordana Oberman, Andrew Ondrecjak, Laura Poe, Nicole Press, Jennifer Rathbone, Chris Rummel, Drew Sachs, Anna Saggese, Robert Signom, David Sinkus, Derek Straat, Vickie Tanner, Olivia Tsang, Jennifer Varbalow, Leese Walker, Eric Wallach, Diana Whitten, Gail Winar

---

ADMINISTRATIVE STAFF

GENERAL MANAGER ..... **Sydney Beers**
Associate Managing Director ..... Greg Backstrom
General Manager, Steinberg Center ..... Rebecca Habel
General Counsel ..... Nancy Hirschmann
Human Resources Manager ..... Stephen Deutsch
MIS Director ..... Jeff Goodman
Facilities Manager ..... Abraham David
Manager of Corporate and Party Rentals ..... Jetaun Dobbs
Office Manager ..... Scott Kelly
Assistant to the General Manager ..... Maggie Cantrick
Management Associate ..... Tania Camargo
MIS Assistant ..... Micah Kraybill
Receptionists ..... Dena Beider, Elisa Papa, Allison Patrick, Monica Sidorchuk
Messenger ..... Robert Weisser
Management Intern ..... Jen McArdle

FINANCE STAFF

CONTROLLER ..... **Susan Neiman**
Assistant Controller ..... John LaBarbera
Accounts Payable Administrator ..... Frank Surdi
Business Office Associate ..... David Solomon
Financial Associate ..... Yonit Kafka
Business Intern ..... Li Shen

DEVELOPMENT STAFF

DIRECTOR OF DEVELOPMENT ..... **Jeffory Lawson**
Director, Institutional Giving ..... Julie K. D'Andrea
Director, Individual Giving ..... Julia Lazarus
Director, Special Events ..... Steve Schaeffer
Manager, Donor Information Systems ..... Tina Mae Bishko
Capital Campaign Manager ..... Mark Truscinski
Manager, Friends of Roundabout ..... Jeff Collins
Corporate Relations Manager ..... Sara Bensman
External Affairs Associate ..... Robert Weinstein
Institutional Giving Associate ..... Sarah Krasnow
Special Events Associate ..... Ginger Vallen
Patrons Services Assistant ..... John Haynes
Development Assistants ..... Jillian Brewster, Christopher Taggart
Individual Giving Intern ..... Arielle Kahaner
Special Events Intern ..... Erica Rotstein
Development Intern ..... Christopher DeRocha

MARKETING STAFF

DIRECTOR OF MARKETING ..... **David B. Steffen**
Marketing/Publications Manager ..... Margaret Casagrande
Assistant Director of Marketing ..... Sunil Ayyagari
Marketing Assistant ..... Stefanie Schussel
Website Consultant ..... Keith Powell Beyland

DIRECTOR OF TELESALES SPECIAL PROMOTIONS ..... **Daniel Weiss**
Telesales Manager ..... Anton Borissov
Telesales Office Coordinator ..... J.W. Griffin
Marketing Intern ..... Darra Messing

TICKET SERVICES STAFF

DIRECTOR OF SALES OPERATIONS ..... **Jim Seggelink**
Ticket Services Manager ..... Ellen Holt
Subscription Manager ..... Charlie Garbowski, Jr.
Box Office Managers ..... Edward P. Osborne, Jaime Perlman, Jessica Bowser
Group Sales Manager ..... Jeff Monteith
Assistant Box Office Managers ..... Andrew Clements, Steve Howe, Robert Morgan
Assistant Ticket Services Managers ..... Robert Kane, Ethan Ubell, Carlos Morris
Customer Services Coordinator ..... Trina Cox
Ticket Services ..... Rachel Bauder, Solangel Bido, Jessie Blum, Jacob Burstein-Stern, William Campbell, Lauren Cartelli, David Carson, Tom Dahl, Nisha Dhruna, Adam Elsberry, Lindsay Ericson, John Finning, Catherine Fitzpatrick, Tova Heller, Dottie Kenul, Bill Klemm, Krystin MacRitchie, Elisa Mala, Mead Margulies, Chuck Migliaccio, Nicole Nicholson, Adam Owens, Thomas Protulipac, Jackie Rocha, Heather Siebert, Lillian Soto, Pam Unger, Tiffany Wakely
Ticket Services Intern ..... Heather Forman

SERVICES

Counsel ..... Paul, Weiss, Rifkind, Wharton and Garrison LLP, John Breglio, Deborah Hartnett
Counsel ..... Rosenberg & Estis
Counsel ..... Andrew Lance, Gibson, Dunn, & Crutcher, LLP
Counsel ..... Harry H. Weintraub, Glick and Weintraub, P.C.
Immigration Counsel ..... Mark D. Koestler and Theodore Ruthizer
House Physicians ..... Dr. Theodore Tyberg, Dr. Lawrence Katz
House Dentist ..... Neil Kanner, D.M.D.
Insurance ..... DeWitt Stern Group, Inc.
Accountant ..... Lutz & Carr CPAs, LLP
Sponsorship ..... The Marketing Group, Tanya Grubich, Laura Matalon, Anne Rippey, Erik Gensler
Advertising ..... Eliran Murphy Group/ Denise Ganjou, Kara Eldridge
Events Photography ..... Anita and Steve Shevett
Production Photographer ..... Joan Marcus
Theatre Displays ..... King Displays, Wayne Sapper

MANAGING DIRECTOR EMERITUS ..... ELLEN RICHARD

Roundabout Theatre Company
231 West 39th Street, New York, NY 10018
(212) 719-9393.

GENERAL PRESS REPRESENTATIVES
BONEAU/BRYAN-BROWN
Adrian Bryan-Brown Matt Polk
Jessica Johnson Amy Kass

CREDITS FOR *HEARTBREAK HOUSE*

GENERAL MANAGER ..... Sydney Beers
Company Manager ..... Nichole Larson
Production Stage Manager ..... Leslie C. Lyter
Stage Manager ..... Jonathan Donahue
Associate Director ..... Todd Lundquist
Assistant Set Designer ..... Tim Mackabee
Assistant Costume Designer ..... Jennifer Moeller
Costume Intern ..... Anya Klepikov
Assistant Lighting Designer ..... Scott Davis
Assistant Sound Designer ..... Ryan Rumery
Assistant Technical Supervisor ..... Elisa Kuhar
Production Carpenter ..... Glenn Merwede
Production Electrician ..... Brian Maiuri
Production Properties ..... Andrew Forste
Assistant Production Properties ..... Sean Haines
Wardrobe Supervisor ..... Susan J. Fallon
Hair and Wig Supervisor ..... Manuela LaPorte
Sound Engineer ..... Dann Wojnar
Day Worker ..... Melissa Crawford
Dressers ..... Julie Hilimire, Vickie Grecki
Production Assistants ..... Sarah Izzo, Katie McKee
Local One IATSE Apprentice ..... Jill Anania
Scenery Constructed by ..... Great Lakes Scenic Studios
Deck Construction and Automation of Scenery ..... Showman Fabricators, Inc.
Lighting Equipment provided by ..... PRG Lighting
Sound Equipment provided by ..... Sound Associates
Flyman ..... Chris Mattingly
Costumes constructed by ..... Tricorne, Inc. and Angels, The Costumiers
Millinery provided by ..... Rodney Gordon, Inc.
Women's Shoes built by ..... Pompei 2000 S.R.L.
Boots built by ..... Montana Leatherworks
Additional Set and Hand Props courtesy of ..... George Fenmore, Inc.
China Tea Service courtesy of ..... Mikasa

Special thanks to Hudson Scenic Studio, Inc. and New York City Center.

AMERICAN AIRLINES THEATRE STAFF

General Manager ..... Sydney Beers
House Carpenter ..... Glenn Merwede
House Electrician ..... Brian Maiuri
Wardrobe Supervisor ..... Susan J. Fallon
Box Office Manager ..... Ted Osborne
House Manager ..... Steve Ryan
Associate House Managers ..... Zipporah Aguasvivas, LaConya Robinson
Head Usher ..... Edwin Camacho
House Staff ..... Peter Breaden, Ilia Diaz, Anne Ezell, Elsie Jamin-Maguire, Rich McNanna, Jacklyn Rivera, Tiesha Rivera, Adam Wier
Security ..... Julious Russell
Additional Security Provided by ..... Gotham Security
Maintenance ..... Jerry Hobbs, Daniel Pellew, Willie Philips
Lobby Refreshments ..... Sweet Concessions
Merchandising ..... George Fenmore/ More Merchandising International

Heartbreak House
Scrapbook

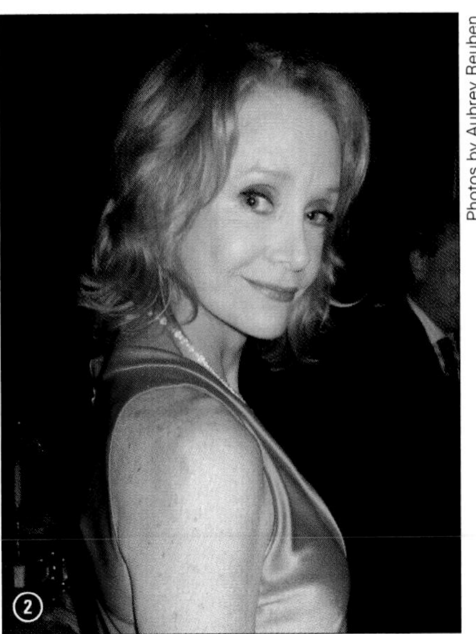

Photos by Aubrey Reuben

1. Curtain call on opening night (L-R:) Gareth Saxe, John Christopher Jones, Byron Jennings, Swoosie Kurtz, Philip Bosco, Lily Rabe, Laila Robins, Bill Camp and Jenny Sterlin.
2. Swoosie Kurtz at the opening night party at the Marriott Marquis Hotel.
3. Byron Jennings and guest Carolyn McCormick at the cast party.
4. Laila Robins at the Marquis.

Correspondent: Laila Robin, "Ariadne Utterword"
Memorable Opening Night Letter: Swoosie Kurtz received a letter from Bryony Lavery, the author of *Frozen*, wishing us the best, since we had both been in her play.
Opening Night Gifts: Philip Bosco gave all of us a little silver chest that had the show's title and opening date engraved on it. Really lovely. Knowing that I play a character who has come home to escape influenza, Swoosie gave me a photo Avedon had done of me screaming for *Frozen*, but she put it in a frame she found at an influenza event that said "Faces of Influenza."
Most Exciting Celebrity Visitor: One Wednesday matinee we had a mixed crowd: about 200 students from the Bronx and a lot of subscribers who are mostly elderly. You might say the show was a little loosey-goosey that day. So who came to visit that performance? Meryl Streep. I got to meet my idol, finally. She came backstage and said she thought the audience enhanced everything. But I didn't hear anything else she said because I was bowing at her feet. We've also had John Guare, Marsha Mason, Brian Cox and Victoria Tennant.
Who Has Done the Most Shows in Their Career: That would be Mr. Bosco.
Special Backstage Rituals: Wardobe Supervisor Susan J. Fallon hosts a brunch every weekend, and that is our favorite ritual.
Favorite Moment During Each Performance: John Christopher Jones says his favorite moment is when his character says, "I hope so." It speaks to the actor as well.
Favorite In-Theatre Gathering Place: Swoosie's dressing room, which is right across the hall from mine. That's where I go for sound advice.
Favorite Off-Site Hangout: Orzo and the West Bank Café. And if we're not at either of those, who can blame us? After three hours of Shaw we have no time for such frivolities. We're all living like nuns.
Favorite Snack Food: Swoosie Kurtz got us started on kettle-baked potato chips, and they're delicious. A lot of us have long stretches of time offstage, and we tend to eat something. Those chips are the ones.
Mascot: Philip Bosco's beard.
Favorite Therapy: Grether's blackcurrant pastilles are the ones we love.
Memorable Ad-Lib: "Aaaargh!" when Mr. Bosco can't remember something he goes "Arggh," and then we know it's our turn to talk.
Memorable Press Encounter: John Christopher Jones said one press person on opening night said, "I love your choice to play him like you didn't know what comes next."
Memorable Stage Door Fan Encounter: People have asked us to sign unusual items, from a DVD case to a fishbowl.
Latest Audience Arrival: One couple didn't arrive until the post-show discussion.
Fastest Costume Change: Billy Camp taking his clothes off in Act II.
Who Wore the Least: Bill Camp, for the same scene.
Catchphrases Only the Company Would Recognize: "Gently, gently." "Tickle it. Tickle it."
Memorable Directorial Notes: "Stand still!" "Plant your feet and say it!" "Get out of the way of the play!"
Company In-Joke: On opening night Swoosie received some glasses with thick Coke-bottle lenses. We found that when we work on lines in her dressing room, we wear those glasses and they help us find laughs in lines that are getting no laughs. They're so good, we're tempted to hide them in Shotover's desk onstage!
Coolest Thing About Being in This Show: All the cool people.

High Fidelity

First Preview: November 20, 2006. Opened: December 7, 2006.
Closed December 17, 2006 after 19 Previews and 13 Performances.

PLAYBILL

IMPERIAL THEATRE
249 West 45th Street
A Shubert Organization Theatre
Gerald Schoenfeld, *Chairman* Philip J. Smith, *President*

Robert E. Wankel, *Executive Vice President*

Jeffrey Seller Kevin McCollum Robyn Goodman
Live Nation Roy Miller Dan Markley Ruth Hendel/Danzansky Partners Jam Theatricals

present

HIGH FIDELITY

Music by **Tom Kitt** Lyrics By **Amanda Green** Book By **David Lindsay-Abaire**

Based on the novel "High Fidelity" by Nick Hornby and the Touchstone Pictures Film

Starring
Will Chase
Jenn Colella
Christian Anderson Jay Klaitz
Jeb Brown Rachel Stern
Emily Swallow Jon Patrick Walker Kirsten Wyatt
Justin Brill Andrew C. Call Matt Caplan Caren Lyn Manuel Anne Warren
Paul Castree George Merrick Betsy Morgan Tom Plotkin J.B. Wing

Set Design Anna Louizos
Costume Design Theresa Squire
Lighting Design Ken Billington
Sound Design Acme Sound Partners

Music Director Adam Ben-David
Orchestrations Tom Kitt & Alex Lacamoire
Vocal Arrangements Stephen Oremus
Music Coordinator Michael Keller
Music Supervision Alex Lacamoire

Casting Telsey + Company
Technical Supervisor Brian Lynch
Press Representative Sam Rudy Media Relations
Marketing Scott A. Moore

General Manager John S. Corker
Production Supervisor Steven Beckler
Company Manager Brig Berney
Associate Director Marc Bruni
Associate Producers Sonny Everett, Mariano Tolentino, Jr.

Choreographer
Christopher Gattelli

Directed by
Walter Bobbie

The producers wish to express their appreciation to Theatre Development Fund for its support of this production.

topfivebreakups.com

LIVE BROADWAY

12/7/06

CAST

(in order of appearance)

Rob .... WILL CHASE
Hipster/Roadie .... ANDREW C. CALL
Futon Guy .... JUSTIN BRILL
Guy with Mohawk .... MATT CAPLAN
Dick .... CHRISTIAN ANDERSON
Barry .... JAY KLAITZ
Laura .... JENN COLELLA
Anna/Alison .... KIRSTEN WYATT
Penny/Back-up Singer .... ANNE WARREN
Charlie/Marie LaSalle .... EMILY SWALLOW
Sarah .... CAREN LYN MANUEL
Liz/Jackie .... RACHEL STERN
T.M.P.M.I.T.W./Bruce .... JON PATRICK WALKER
Ian/Middle-Aged Guy .... JEB BROWN

PLACE

A remote neighborhood in Brooklyn

TIME

The recent present

Continued on next page

(L-R): Andrew C. Call, Justin Brill, Matt Caplan, Will Chase, Jay Klaitz and Christian Anderson.

Photo by Joan Marcus

High Fidelity

Cast Continued

UNDERSTUDIES

For Rob:
MATT CAPLAN, JON PATRICK WALKER
For Laura:
CAREN LYN MANUEL, BETSY MORGAN, EMILY SWALLOW, ANNE WARREN
For Dick:
JUSTIN BRILL, PAUL CASTREE
For Barry:
ANDREW C. CALL, MATT CAPLAN
For Ian/Middle-Aged Guy:
GEORGE MERRICK, TOM PLOTKIN
For Liz/Jackie:
CAREN LYN MANUEL, BETSY MORGAN, J.B. WING
For Charlie/Marie:
CAREN LYN MANUEL, BETSY MORGAN, J.B. WING
For Anna/Alison:
BETSY MORGAN, J.B. WING
For T.M.P.M.I.T.W./Bruce:
ANDREW C. CALL, TOM PLOTKIN

SWINGS

PAUL CASTREE (Dance Captain), GEORGE MERRICK, BETSY MORGAN, TOM PLOTKIN, J.B. WING

BAND

Conductor/Piano/Harmonica:
ADAM BEN-DAVID
Associate Conductor/Organ/Keyboard:
MATT GALLAGHER
Guitars:
KENNY BRESCIA
Guitars/Sitar/Banjo/Mandolin:
MICHAEL AARONS
Bass:
RANDY LANDAU
Drums/Percussion:
DAMIEN BASSMAN
Reeds:
DAN WILLIS
Trumpet:
BUD BURRIDGE
Violin:
ANTOINE SILVERMAN
Cello:
PETER SACHON

Will Chase
Rob

Jenn Colella
Laura

Christian Anderson
Dick

Jay Klaitz
Barry

Jeb Brown
Ian/Middle-Aged Guy

Rachel Stern
Liz/Jackie

Emily Swallow
Charlie/Marie

Jon Patrick Walker
T.M.P.M.I.T.W./Bruce

Kirsten Wyatt
Anna/Alison

Justin Brill
Futon Guy

Andrew C. Call
Hipster/Roadie

Matt Caplan
Guy with Mohawk

Caren Lyn Manuel
Sarah

Anne Warren
Penny/ Back-up Singer

Paul Castree
Male Swing

George Merrick
Male Swing

Betsy Morgan
Female Swing

Tom Plotkin
Male Swing

J.B. Wing
Female Swing

Tom Kitt
Composer/ Orchestrations

High Fidelity

Amanda Green
Lyrics

David Lindsay-Abaire
Book

Walter Bobbie
Director

Anna Louizos
Set Design

Theresa Squire
Costume Design

Ken Billington
Lighting Design

Adam Ben-David
Music Director/ Conductor

Alex Lacamoire
Music Supervision/ Orchestrations

Tom Clark, Mark Menard and Nevin Steinberg/ Acme Sound Partners
Sound Design

Stephen Oremus
Vocal Arrangements

Michael Keller
Music Coordinator

Steven Beckler
Production Supervisor

Marc Bruni
Associate Director

Bernard Telsey, Telsey + Company
Casting

Brig Berney
Company Manager

Thomas J. Gates
Stage Manager

Brian Lynch, Theatretech, Inc.
Technical Supervisor

John S. Corker
General Manager

Jeffrey Seller
Producer

Kevin McCollum
Producer

Robyn Goodman
Producer

Roy Miller
Producer

Ruth Hendel
Producer

Sonny Everett
Associate Producer

Photo by Joan Marcus

(L-R): Will Chase as Rob and Jenn Colella as Laura.

High Fidelity

Photos by Ben Strothmann

MUSICIANS
Bottom Row (L-R): Kenny Brescia, Adam Ben-David (conductor), Rachel Stern (actress), Matt Gallagher, Michael Aarons, Bud Burridge.
Top Row (L-R): Damien Bassman, Peter Sachon, Antoine Silverman; Dan Willis and Randy Landau.

ELECTRICS CREW
(L-R):
Chris Kurtz, Jennifer Lerner, Paul Dean, Jr., Keith Buchanan, Pete Donovan and Billy Rowland, Jr.

WARDROBE CREW
(L-R): Fran Curry, Marisa Tchornobai and Jessica Scoblick.

PROPS CREW
(L-R): Jay Satterwhite, Freddie Buchtwalt and Ron Groomes.

STAGE DOORMAN
Azim Gadsden.

High Fidelity

CARPENTRY CREW
(L-R): Scott Dixon, Kevin Clifford, unknown, Chris Kluth, Wally Bullard, Terry McGarty, Bob Griffin and McBrien Dunbar.

USHERS/FRONT OF HOUSE STAFF
Front Row (L-R): Unknown, Francis Barbaretti, Michael Knowles. Middle Row: Yenny Fernandez, Dennis Norwood, Ed Phillips, Tim Young. Back Row: Azim Gadsden, Jerry Bell, Doug Massell and Christopher Caoili.

Understudy Betsy Morgan (with closing notice).

STAGE AND COMPANY MANAGERS
Bottom: (L-R): Tim Semon, Thom Gates. Top: Brig Berney and Steve Beckler.

HAIR DEPARTMENT
(L-R): Sakie Onozawa-Snow and Heather Wright.

Photos by Ben Strothmann

High Fidelity

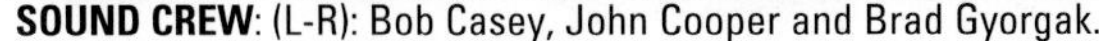
SOUND CREW: (L-R): Bob Casey, John Cooper and Brad Gyorgak.

Photos by Ben Strothmann

BOX OFFICE STAFF: (L-R): Jose Gomez, Bill Carrick and Paul Blaver.

Staff for *HIGH FIDELITY*

General Manager John S. Corker

General Press Representatives
SAM RUDY MEDIA RELATIONS
Dale R. Heller Robert Lasko

Director of Marketing Scott A. Moore

Casting
TELSEY + COMPANY, CSA
Bernie Telsey, Will Cantler, David Vaccari,
Bethany Berg Knox, Craig Burns, Tiffany Little Canfield,
Stephanie Yankwitt, Justin Huff, Carrie Rosson,
Joe Langworth, Rachel Hoffman

COMPANY MANAGER .... Brig Berney

PRODUCTION STAGE MANAGER ...... Steven Beckler

Associate General Manager .... R. Erin Craig
Technical Supervision .... Brian Lynch/ Theatre Tech, Inc.
Wig Designer .... Charles LaPointe
Stage Manager .... Thomas J. Gates
Assistant Stage Manager .... Timothy R. Semon
Assistant Choreographer .... Shanna Van Derwerker
Assistant to the Director .... Robert Ross Parker
Associate Scenic Designers .... Donyale Werle, Todd Potter
Associate Costume Designer .... Heather Dunbar
Associate Lighting Designer .... John Demous
Assistant Sound Designer .... Sten Severson
Assistant Scenic Designers .... Eric Lewis Beauzay, Court Watson
Assistant Costume Designers .... Amanda Bujak, Amelia Dombrowski, Chris Rumery, Lisa Zinni
Assistant Lighting Designer .... Anthony Pearson
Assistant Wig Designer .... Leah Loukas
Music Copying .... Emily Grishman Music Preparation/ Emily Grishman, Katharine Edmonds
Additional Drum Arrangements .... Damien Bassman
Moving Light Programmer .... David Arch
Production Carpenter/
Associate Technical Supervisor .... Christopher Kluth
Production Electrician .... Keith Buchanan
Properties Coordinator .... Kathy Fabian/Propstar
Propmaster .... Ronald Groomes
Flyman .... Robert Griffin
Deck Automation .... McBrien Dunbar
Deck Electrician/
Moving Light Operator .... Christopher Kurtz
Fly Automation .... Scott Dixon
Follow Spot Operator .... Jennifer Lerner
Production Sound .... Robert Biassetti
Sound Engineer .... Brad Gyorgak
Wardrobe Supervisor .... Edmund Harrison
Hair Supervisor .... Heather Wright
Hair Dresser .... Sakie Onozawa
Haircuts & Coloring .... Lois Stoeffhaas
Dressers .... Jessica Scoblick, Frances Curry, Jennifer Griggs-Cennamo, Marisa Tchornobai
Synthesizer Programmer .... Jim Abbott
Associate Synthesizer Programmer .... Randy Cohen
Propstar Associates .... Carrie Hash, Carrie Mossman, Eliza Brown, Mary Wilson, Alise Ninivaggi, Michael Kennedy
SSDC Foundation Observer .... Jordan Young
Production Assistants .... Alexander Libby, Caroline Andersen
Executive Assistant to
Messrs. Seller & McCollum .... Ryan Hill
Assistant to Messrs. McCollum & Miller .... David Roth
Assistant to Ms. Goodman .... Jessica White
Assistant to Mr. Corker .... Kim Vasquez
Legal Counsel .... Levine Plotkin Menin, LLP/ Loren Plotkin, Susan Mindell
Advertising .... Spotco/Drew Hodges, Jim Edwards, Peter Milano, Lauren Hunter
Accountant .... FK Partners/Robert Fried
Controller .... Sarah Galbraith
Insurance .... D. R. Reiff & Associates/ Sonny Everett, Dennis Reiff
Banking .... Signature Bank
Payroll .... Castellana Services
Website .... Situation Marketing
Pre-production Photographer .... Stewart Ferebee
Production Photographer .... Joan Marcus

THE PRODUCING OFFICE
Kevin McCollum Jeffrey Seller
John S. Corker Debra Nir Ryan Hill

AGED IN WOOD
Robyn Goodman Stephen Kocis
Josh Fiedler Jessica White

SPECIAL THANKS

Academy Records; John Ninivaggi; Richard Caplan; East Coast Punk; Jessica Liebman; Sarah Cubbage; Alan Schuster; Baryshnikov Dance Foundation; Melinda Ball; Ralph Larmann, Chris Brucato, Guitars, Guitar amps and Slingerland Drums provided by Gibson USA, Ziljian Cymbal Company (Jimmy McGathey and AnnMarie Sanfilippo), Toca Percussion (Victor Filonovich).

CREDITS

Scenery constructed by Hudson Scenic Studio, Inc. Certain scenery and scenic effects built, painted, electrified and automated by Show Motion, Inc. Show control and scenery automation by Show Motion, Inc. using the AC2 Computer Motion Control System. Additional scenery constructed by Cigar Box Studios, Inc. Lighting equipment from PRG Lighting. Sound equipment from Sound Associates. Specialty prop construction – Plum Square, Tom Carroll Scenery, John Ninivaggi and Jonathan Boggs. Custom soft goods – Ann Guay, Julie Sattman. Sculpted effects and custom lamps – SPS Effects, Melissa Martin, Costume Armour Inc. Foliage – American Foliage. Chain motors from Show Motion, Inc. Trucking by Clark Transfer, Inc. Special electronics equipment by Perfection Electricks. Natural herb cough drops courtesy of Ricola USA, Inc. Emergen-C super energy booster supplied by Alacer Corp. Onstage guitars provided by First Act Guitar Studio.

High Fidelity rehearsed at 37 Arts.

THE SHUBERT ORGANIZATION, INC.
Board of Directors

Gerald Schoenfeld, Chairman
Philip J. Smith, President
Wyche Fowler, Jr.
John W. Kluge
Lee J. Seidler
Michael I. Sovern
Stuart Subotnick

Robert E. Wankel
Executive Vice President

Peter Entin, Vice President – Theatre Operations
Elliot Greene, Vice President – Finance
David Andrews, Vice President – Shubert Ticketing Services
John Darby, Vice President – Facilities

D.S. Moynihan
Vice President – Creative Projects

House Manager .... Joseph Pullara

High Fidelity
Scrapbook

Correspondent: Steven Beckler, Production Stage Manager

View From Back Stage: *High Fidelity* lasted just four months for me, from when I got involved out of town, to closing night. Walter Bobbie, the director of *High Fidelity*, was in the original production of *Grease*, which was my first Broadway job, back in 1974. I came onto that show as assistant stage manager and what struck me about that show is how loving and physical and unexpurgated they were. Not since *Grease* have I ever seen anything like that kind of freedom and openness—until *High Fidelity*.

The cast was led by Will Chase, a brilliantly talented guy who set a very high bar for everyone else. Other than when new pages were thrown at him, I never remember him holding a script. He's one of the most letter-perfect actors I've ever worked with.

But the cast was talented right down the line. There wasn't a weak link. Every actor brought something unique and special to the stage with them. Every night the company gathered in the stage-left wing and wished each other good luck. They hugged each other and patted each other and goosed each other—it was that kind of team spirit. On opening night the entire cast gathered on the stage to hear Jenn Colella read a letter she had gotten at one time. It was about the importance of acting and the importance of listening and the importance of respecting one another. At the end she said, "Now let's go out there and be great because I need this job!"

And then those reviews appeared the next morning!

Everyone who came to see the show loved it. Garrison Keillor wrote a letter to *The New York Times* talking about the cruelty of critic Ben Brantley, though they never published it. In it, he said that clearly what Mr. Brantley saw was not what he and the rest of the audience saw when they rose to cheer for this show.

Nickname: The character of Dick was played by Christian Anderson, who was one of the greatest sources of energy backstage. He was loved by everyone. Everyone would talk about "that asshole" but meant it sarcastically. It became a loving term of endearment.

Hidden Talent: Jenn Colella had an alter-ego name Marcy who was a great gospel rock singer. The composer wrote three or four different opening numbers for her character, and they all went in and out of the show at different times. Finally it was reduced to just a scene. When Jenn was onstage for final tech, she began to sing all her cut numbers in a black gospel style, it was very funny.

Backstage Rituals: We started a tradition during the Boston tryout. At the end of Act I, when Will Chase was getting ready to go into the song "Nine Percent," he would have to look offstage left. A group of actors or crew would do a montage in the wing in various poses, like the "Grecian Urn" scene in *The Music Man*, but sometimes in various states of undress. It was hilarious, but Will is so unflappable, he never let

Photos by Aubrey Reuben

1. (L-R): Cast members Andrew Call and Justin Brill arrive on opening night.
2. (L-R): Leads Jenn Colella and Will Chase.
3. (L-R): Jay Klaitz and Christian Anderson take curtain calls in character.
4. (L-R): Composer Tom Kitt and Rita Pietropinto-Kitt.

it show. It became a nightly ritual. This was the atmosphere backstage.

The only time I ever saw Will Chase really react was at one of the final performances when the montage consisted of three of our carpenters mooning him. All he did was put his hand over his mouth, but that was probably his biggest reaction. Afterwards he went backstage and told them, "Guys, you have got to start exfoliating!"

Other Backstage Fun: The cast all through rehearsals, when they weren't onstage, would sit and play board games: Candyland, Uno, like that.

Opening Night Gift: For opening night gifts, the producers gave us all a *High Fidelity* fleece. I wear it all the time.

Understudy Anecdote: During the final week, Will Chase got sick. He tried to come back, but just couldn't make it through the show and the understudy, Jon Patrick Walker, had to take over in the middle of the performance. He gave an absolutely amazing two and half performances. And Tom Plotkin had to jump into his roles for him. Then, the wife of Jeb Brown, the fellow who played Ian, had a baby the same day the closing notice went up, and George Merrick went on for him. We had an incredible group of understudies.

Regarding the Producers: I just want to write a love letter to our producers, who were one of a kind. They were incredibly generous despite the fact that ticket sales were awful. Our opening night party was at Roseland and we had a great deejay, fantastic food and thousands of people whose connection to the show I had no idea of.

The producers also threw a closing night party with food and an open bar.

Another classy thing they did was, the day after reviews came out, instead of giving one of those "We're gonna fight!" speeches, they came in and thanked everyone for their wonderful work.

They helped keep the morale up when the actors would go out and play to these excruciatingly small houses. What was it about this show that was so uncommercial? I worked on *Caine Mutiny Court-Martial* last season and it was the same thing: A great show, but for some reason, nobody came. We ran all of two weeks.

In spite of all that, the producers went on to record a cast album of *High Fidelity.* They felt it was important for the score and lyrics to be preserved. The recording session, which came about a month after the closing, was an incredible reunion. After all the money they lost on the show, it was a real act of generosity.

The History Boys

First Preview: April 14, 2006. Opened: April 23, 2006.
Closed: October 1, 2006 after 10 Previews and 185 Performances.

PLAYBILL®

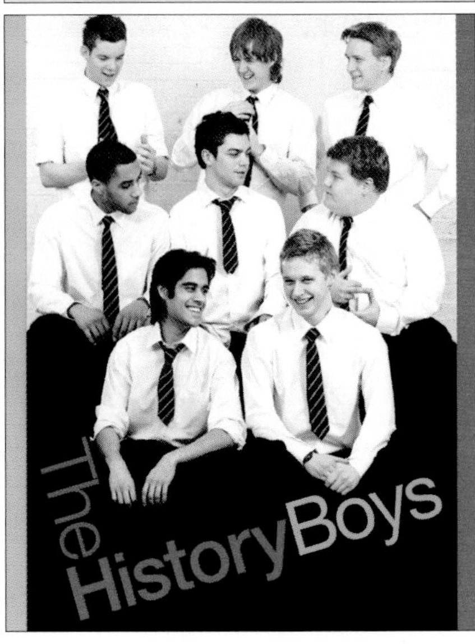

BROADHURST THEATRE

235 West 44th Street
A Shubert Organization Theatre

Gerald Schoenfeld, *Chairman* **Philip J. Smith,** *President*

Robert E. Wankel, *Executive Vice President*

Boyett Ostar Productions
Roger Berlind Debra Black Eric Falkenstein Roy Furman
Jam Theatricals Stephanie P. McClelland Judith Resnick
Scott Rudin Jon Avnet/Ralph Guild Dede Harris/Mort Swinsky

Present
NT The National Theatre of Great Britain's
production of

A New Play By
Alan Bennett

with
Samuel Anderson Samuel Barnett Dominic Cooper
James Corden Frances de la Tour Sacha Dhawan
Richard Griffiths Andrew Knott Clive Merrison
Stephen Campbell Moore Jamie Parker Russell Tovey

Bill Buell LeRoy McClain Pippa Pearthree
Alex Tonetta Jeffrey Withers

Designer
Bob Crowley

Lighting Designer
Mark Henderson

Music
Richard Sisson

Video Director
Ben Taylor

Sound Designer
Colin Pink

Press Representative
Boneau/Bryan Brown

Marketing
HHC Marketing

General Management
101 Productions, Ltd.

Production Stage Manager
Bonnie L. Becker

Technical Supervisor
David Benken

Directed by
Nicholas Hytner

LIVE BROADWAY

10/1/06

CAST

The Boys
Akthar .... SACHA DHAWAN
Crowther .... SAMUEL ANDERSON
Dakin .... DOMINIC COOPER
Lockwood .... ANDREW KNOTT
Posner .... SAMUEL BARNETT
Rudge .... RUSSELL TOVEY
Scripps .... JAMIE PARKER
Timms .... JAMES CORDEN

The Teachers
Headmaster .... CLIVE MERRISON
Mrs. Lintott .... FRANCES de la TOUR
Hector .... RICHARD GRIFFITHS
Irwin .... STEPHEN CAMPBELL MOORE

TV Director .... BILL BUELL
Make-up Lady .... PIPPA PEARTHREE
Other Boys .... LeROY McCLAIN, ALEX TONETTA, JEFFREY WITHERS

UNDERSTUDIES

For Hector, Headmaster:
BILL BUELL
For Dakin, Rudge, Akthar:
LeROY McCLAIN
For Mrs. Lintott:
PIPPA PEARTHREE
For Posner, Scripps, Timms, TV Director:
ALEX TONETTA
For Irwin, Crowther, Lockwood:
JEFFREY WITHERS
For Other Boys, TV Director:
SETH SKLAR-HEYN

Photo by Joan Marcus

The Teachers: Hector (Richard Griffiths), Mrs. Lintott (Frances de la Tour) and Irwin (Stephen Campbell Moore).

The History Boys

Samuel Anderson
Crowther

Samuel Barnett
Posner

Dominic Cooper
Dakin

James Corden
Timms

Frances de la Tour
Mrs. Lintott

Sacha Dhawan
Akthar

Richard Griffiths
Hector

Andrew Knott
Lockwood

Clive Merrison
Headmaster

Stephen Campbell Moore
Irwin

Jamie Parker
Scripps

Russell Tovey
Rudge

Bill Buell
TV Director

LeRoy McClain
Company

Pippa Pearthree
Make-up Lady

Alex Tonetta
Company

Jeffrey Withers
Company

Bonnie L. Becker
Production Stage Manager

Alan Bennett
Playwright

Nicholas Hytner
Director

Bob Crowley
Scenic and Costume Design

Mark Henderson
Lighting Design

Hugh Hysell, HHC Marketing
Marketing

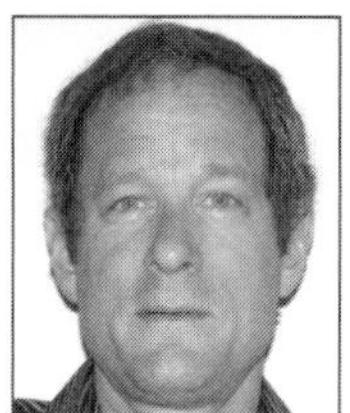
David Benken
Technical Supervisor

Bob Boyett
Producer

Bill Haber, OSTAR Enterprises
Producer

Roger Berlind
Producer

Debra Black
Producer

Eric Falkenstein
Producer

Roy Furman
Producer

Stephanie P. McClelland
Producer

Scott Rudin
Producer

Jon Avnet
Producer

Dede Harris
Producer

Mort Swinsky
Producer

The History Boys

Desmond Barrit
Hector

Malcolm Sinclair
Headmaster

Maggie Steed
Mrs. Lintott

COMPANY MANAGER
Gregg Arst

BOX OFFICE
(L-R): Michael Lynch and Gerard O'Brien.

Photos by Ben Strothmann

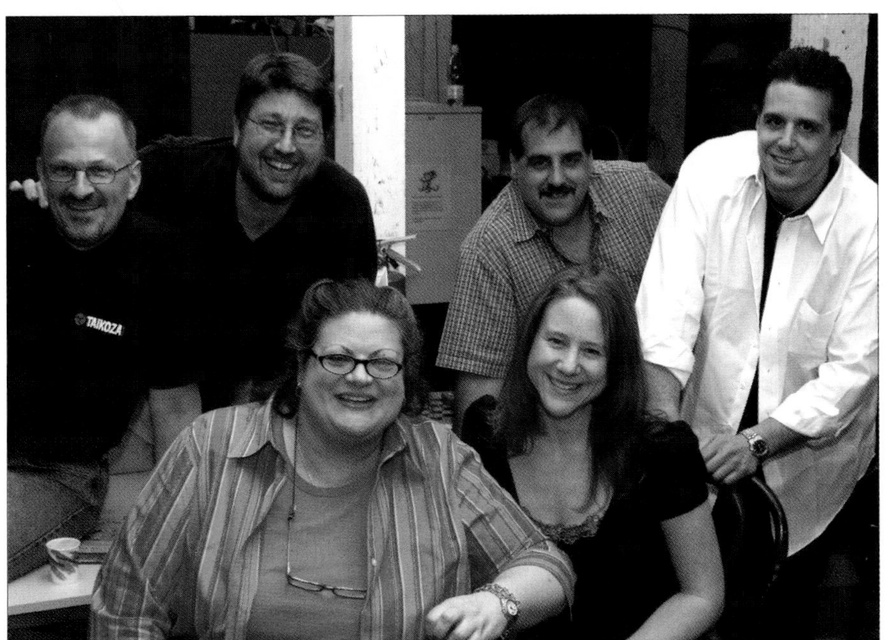

STAGE CREW
Front Row (L-R):
Helen Toth (Wardrobe Supervisor)
and Maya Hardin (Dresser).

Back Row (L-R):
Geoffrey Polischuck (Dresser),
Kevin Keene (Production Sound Supervisor),
Ron Vitteli Jr. (House Properties)
and Craig Laicata (Propman).

The History Boys
Scrapbook

Photo by Aubrey Reuben

Richard Griffiths at the Celebrity Table at the 20th Annual Broadway Flea Market and Grand Auction in Shubert Alley.

FRONT OF HOUSE STAFF
Front Row (L-R):
Karen Diaz (Usher), Henry Bethea (Ticket Taker), Hugh Barnett (Theatre Manager) and Le'Shone Cleveland (Directress).

Middle Row (L-R):
Jennifer Veja (Usher), Hugh Lynch (Usher), Juliette Cipriatti (Usher) and Janet Kay (Usher).

Back Row (L-R):
Juan "Tony" Lopez (Usher), Alfredo Rosario (Usher) and Matt Blank (Usher).

Photos by Ben Strothmann

STAGE MANAGEMENT
(L-R):
Charlie Underhill (Stage Manager), Seth Sklar-Heyn (Stage Manager) and Michael Passaro (Stage Manager).

The History Boys

STAFF FOR *THE HISTORY BOYS*

GENERAL MANAGEMENT
101 PRODUCTIONS, LTD.
Wendy Orshan Jeffrey M. Wilson
David Auster

COMPANY MANAGER
Gregg Arst

GENERAL PRESS REPRESENTATIVE
BONEAU/BRYAN-BROWN
Adrian Bryan-Brown Jim Byk
Juliana Hannett

CASTING
U.K. Casting ....Toby Whale
U.K. Casting Assistant ....Alastair Coomer
U.S. Casting ....Tara Rubin Casting/Laura Schutzel

Production Stage Manager ....Bonnie L. Becker
Stage Managers ....Michael J. Passaro, Charles Underhill, Seth Sklar-Heyn, David M. Beris
U.K. Musical Director ....Tom Attwood
U.S. Musical Director ....Alex Tonetta
Associate Lighting Designer ....Daniel Walker
U.K. Associate Production Manager ....Andy Ward
Assistant Technical Supervisor ....Rosemarie Palombo
Movement Director ....Jack Murphy

Production Carpenter ....Brian McGarty
Production Electrician ....Jon Lawson
Head Electrician ....Tom Lawrey
Production Props Supervisor ....Robert Adams
Production Sound Supervisor ....Kevin Keene
Moving Light Programmer ....Bobby Harrell
Wardrobe Supervisor ....Helen Toth
Dressers ....Geoffrey Polischuck, Maya Hardin
Production Assistant ....Seth Sklar-Heyn
Technical Production Assistant ....Will O'Hare

Boyett Ostar Senior Vice President, Strategic Partnerships & Development ....Jan Gura

Assistants to Mr. Boyett ....Diane Murphy, Ingrid Kloss, Michael Mandell
Assistants to Mr. Haber ....Theresa Pisanelli, Andrew Cleghorn
Legal Counsel ....Lazarus & Harris, LLP/ Scott R. Lazarus, Esq., Robert C. Harris, Esq.
Accountant ....Rosenberg, Neuwirth & Kushner, CPAs/ Chris Cacace
Comptroller ....Patricia Pedersen
Advertising ....Spotco/ Drew Hodges, Jim Edwards, Jim Aquino, Y. Darius Suyama
Marketing ....HHC Marketing/ Hugh Hysell, Michael Redman
Housing Coordinator ....Megan Trice
101 Productions, Ltd. Staff ....Katharine Croke, Laura Dickinson, Scott Falkowski, Heidi Neven, Jason Paradine, Kyle Pickles, David Renwanz, Mary Six Rupert, John Vennema
Press Assistant ....Matt Ross
Press Interns ....Megan Gentry, Cait Ruegger
Banking ....City National Bank/ Anne McSweeney
Insurance ....DeWitt Stern, Inc./ Jennifer Brown
Immigration ....Traffic Control Group, Inc./ David King
Theatre Displays ....King Displays, Inc.
Music Rights ....BZ Rights and Permissions, Inc./ Barbara Zimmerman
Merchandising ....Max Merchandising, LLC
Payroll Services ....Castellana Services, Inc.
Production Photographer ....Joan Marcus
Website Design ....Situation Marketing/ Damian Bazadona, Lisa Cecchini, Tom Lorenzo
Opening Night Coordinators ....Tobak Lawrence Company/ Suzanne Tobak, Michael P. Lawrence

NATIONAL THEATRE, LONDON
Chairman of the Board ....Sir Hayden Phillips
Director ....Nicholas Hytner
Executive Director ....Nick Starr
Assistant Producer ....Tim Levy

CREDITS
Lighting equipment from Hudson Sound and Light LLC. Sound equipment from Sound Associates. Video equipment from Scharff Weisberg, Inc. U.K. scenery properties and costumes constructed by the National Theatre of Great Britain. Additional scenery by Hudson Scenic Studio, Inc. Ricola natural herb cough drops courtesy of Ricola USA, Inc.

MUSIC CREDITS
"Baggy Trousers," written by Graham McPherson, Michael Barson, Mark Bedford, Lee Thompson, Chris Foreman, Daniel Woodgate and Carl Smyth. Published by EMI Blackwood Music Inc. **"Bewitched, Bothered and Bewildered,"** music by Richard Rodgers, lyrics by Lorenz Hart. This selection is used by special arrangement with the Rodgers and Hammerstein Organization, 1065 Ave. of the Americas, Suite 2400, New York NY 10018. ©1941 (renewed), Chappell & Co. and Williamson Music Inc. All rights reserved. Used by permission. **"Brief Encounter,"** Cyril Ornadel; Sony/ATV Songs LLC (BMI), o/b/o Sony/ATV Music Publishing UK Ltd. (PRS) 100%. **"Bye Bye Blackbird,"** written by Mort Dixon and Ray Henderson. Published by Ray Henderson Music Co., Inc. and Olde Clover Leaf Music (ASCAP). Administered by Bug Music. Used by permission. **"Just Can't Get Enough,"** by Vince Clark (PRS), Sony/ATV Songs LLC (BMI) obo Sony/ATV Music Publishing UK Ltd., Musical Moments Ltd. (PRS). **"La Vie en Rose"** (Louiguy, Edith Piaf, Mack Davis); ©1947 (renewed). Editions Paul Beuscher SA (SACEM) and WB Music Corp. (ASCAP). All rights admin. by WB Music Corp. All rights reserved. Used by permission. **"L'Accordeoniste,"** written by Michael Elmer. Used by permission of Southern Music Publishing Co., Inc. **"Money for Nothing,"** written by Sting and Mark Knopfler. Published by EMI Blackwood Music Inc. and by Chariscourt Ltd. and Rondor Music (London) Ltd. Administered by Almo Music Corp. **"Now, Voyager"** (Max Steiner); WB Music Corp. (ASCAP). All rights reserved. Used by permission. **"Rio,"** by Duran Duran. Used by arrangement with Gloucester Place Music. **"Sing As We Go,"** written by Harry Parr-Davies. Published by Colgems-EMI Music Inc. **"Weak in the Presence of Beauty,"** by Robert Clarke and Michael Ward. **"Will You,"** written by Wesley Magoogan and Hazel O'Connor. Used with permission of Complete Music USA, Inc. (ASCAP) and Lipservices Music Publishing, Brooklyn NY. Published by EMI April Music Inc. and Complete Music USA Inc. All rights reserved. **"Wish Me Luck (As You Wave Me Goodbye)"** (Harry Parr-Davies, Phil Park); ©1939 Chappell Music Ltd. UK. All rights reserved. Used by permission.

Music Clearance: BZ/Rights & Permissions, Inc.

SPECIAL THANKS
The National Theatre wishes to thank Fiona Bardsley, Andrew Speed, Charles Evans, Bella Rodrigues, Mary Parker.

To learn more about upcoming National Theatre productions, please visit our website at www.NTNY.org

THE SHUBERT ORGANIZATION, INC.
Board of Directors

Gerald Schoenfeld Chairman

Philip J. Smith President

Wyche Fowler, Jr.

John W. Kluge

Lee J. Seidler

Michael I. Sovern

Stuart Subotnick

Robert E. Wankel
Executive Vice President

Peter Entin Vice President Theatre Operations

Elliot Greene Vice President Finance

David Andrews Vice President Shubert Ticketing Services

John Darby Vice President Facilities

D.S. Moynihan
Vice President – Creative Projects

House Manager ....Hugh Barnett

Hot Feet

First Preview: April 20, 2006. Opened: April 30, 2006.
Closed: July 23, 2006 after 12 Previews and 97 Performances.

PLAYBILL®

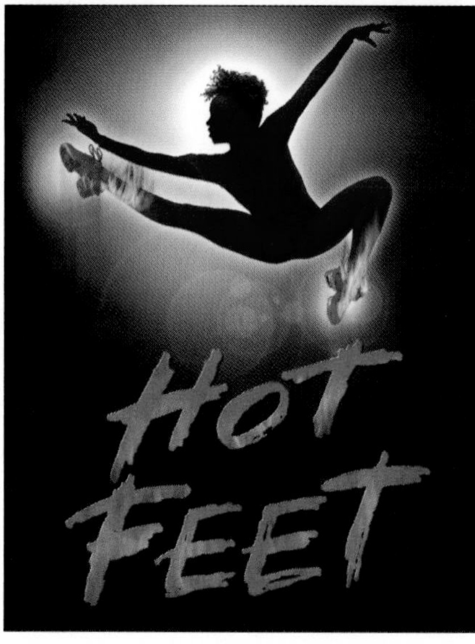

CAST

(in order of appearance)

Louie .... ALLEN HIDALGO
Emma .... SAMANTHA POLLINO
(Tues., Wed., Thurs., Fri. & Sat. Eves.; Sun. Mat.)
SARAH LIVINGSTON
(Wed. & Sat. Mats.)
Kalimba .... VIVIAN NIXON
Mom .... ANN DUQUESNAY
Anthony .... MICHAEL BALDERRAMA
Victor .... MEL JOHNSON, JR.
Naomi .... WYNONNA SMITH
Rahim .... DARYL SPIERS
Ensemble .... KEVIN AUBIN,
GERRARD CARTER,
DIONNE FIGGINS,
RAMÓN FLOWERS,
KARLA PUNO GARCIA,
NAKIA HENRY,
DUANE LEE HOLLAND*,
IQUAIL S. JOHNSON,
DOMINIQUE KELLEY,
STEVE KONOPELSKI,
SUMIE MAEDA,
JON-PAUL MATEO,
VASTHY MOMPOINT,
TERA-LEE POLLIN,
MONIQUE SMITH,
DARYL SPIERS,
FELICITY STIVERSON,
HOLLIE E. WRIGHT

Continued on next page

HILTON THEATRE
A LIVE NATION VENUE

TRANSAMERICA

PRESENTS
A NEW DANCE MUSICAL PRODUCED BY
RUDY DURAND
IN ASSOCIATION WITH
KALIMBA ENTERTAINMENT, INC.
Meir A & Eli C, LLC Polymer Global Holdings Godley Morris Group, LLC

HOT FEET

CONCEIVED BY
MAURICE HINES

BOOK BY
HERU PTAH

MUSIC & LYRICS BY*
MAURICE WHITE

NEW SONGS ADDITIONAL MUSIC & LYRICS BY
CAT GRAY, BRETT LAURENCE, BILL MEYERS, HERU PTAH, and ALLEE WILLIS

starring
MEL JOHNSON, JR. ANN DUQUESNAY
ALLEN HIDALGO WYNONNA SMITH
MICHAEL BALDERRAMA SAMANTHA POLLINO
and
VIVIAN NIXON
with
KEVIN AUBIN BRENT CARTER GERRARD CARTER DIONNE FIGGINS RAMÓN FLOWERS
KEITH ANTHONY FLUITT KARLA PUNO GARCIA NAKIA HENRY DUANE LEE HOLLAND
IQUAIL S. JOHNSON DOMINIQUE KELLEY STEVE KONOPELSKI SARAH LIVINGSTON
SUMIE MAEDA JON-PAUL MATEO VASTHY MOMPOINT TERA-LEE POLLIN MONIQUE SMITH
DARYL SPIERS FELICITY STIVERSON THERESA THOMASON HOLLIE E. WRIGHT

SET DESIGN
JAMES NOONE

COSTUME DESIGN
PAUL TAZEWELL

LIGHTING DESIGN
CLIFTON TAYLOR

SOUND DESIGN
ACME SOUND PARTNERS

HAIR DESIGN
QODI ARMSTRONG

MUSIC DIRECTOR & CONDUCTOR
JEFFREY KLITZ

ARRANGEMENTS & ORCHESTRATIONS
BILL MEYERS

MUSIC COORDINATOR
JOHN MILLER

PRODUCTION MANAGER
ARTHUR SICCARDI

CASTING
STUART HOWARD,
AMY SCHECTER
& PAUL HARDT

ASSISTANT DIRECTOR
RICARDO KHAN

PRODUCTION STAGE MANAGER
MICHAEL E. HARROD

MARKETING
HHC MARKETING

PRESS REPRESENTATIVE
SPRINGER ASSOCIATES PR
JOE TRENTACOSTA

GENERAL MANAGEMENT
LEONARD SOLOWAY
STEVEN M. LEVY

DIRECTED & CHOREOGRAPHED BY
MAURICE HINES

*ADDITIONAL MUSIC & LYRICS : Philip Bailey, Reginald Burke, Valerie Carter, William B. Champlin, Peter Cor, Eddie Del Barrio, Larry Dunn, David Foster, Garry Glenn, Jay Graydon, James N. Howard, Jonathan G. Lind, Al McKay, Skip Scarbrough, Skylark, Charles Stepney, Beloyd Taylor, Wayne Vaughn, Wanda Vaughn, Verdine White, Allee Willis

7/23/06

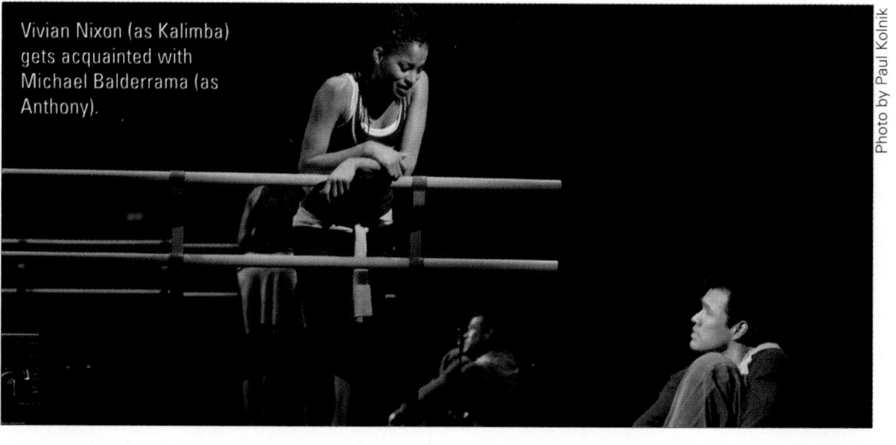

Vivian Nixon (as Kalimba) gets acquainted with Michael Balderrama (as Anthony).

Photo by Paul Kolnik

Hot Feet

MUSICAL NUMBERS

ACT I

Overture ....The Band
"In the Stone" ....The Band
"Rock That/Boogie Wonderland" ....The Band; Lead Vocals Brent Carter
"When I Dance" ....The Band; Lead Vocals Theresa Thomason
"Dearest Heart" ....Mom, Kalimba
"September" ....The Band; Lead Vocals Brent Carter
"Turn It Into Something Good" ....The Band; Lead Vocals Brent Carter
"Ponta de Areia" ....The Band
"Thinking of You" ....The Band; Lead Vocals Brent Carter
"Mighty Mighty" ....The Band; Lead Vocals Brent Carter
"Serpentine Fire" ....The Band; Lead Vocals Brent Carter
"Fantasy" ....The Band; Lead Vocals Keith Anthony Fluitt, Theresa Thomason

ACT II

"Louie's Welcome" ....Louie
"Getaway" ....The Band; Lead Vocals Brent Carter
"Dirty" ....The Band; Lead Vocals Brent Carter
"After the Love Has Gone" ....The Band; Lead Vocals Brent Carter
"Can't Hide Love" ....Victor
"You Don't Know" ....Mom, Victor

Hot Feet Ballet

Ballet Intro ....The Band
"Hot Feet" ....Louie
"Let Your Feelings Show" ....The Band; Lead Vocals Brent Carter, Keith Anthony Fluitt
"System of Survival" ....The Band; Lead Vocals Brent Carter, Keith Anthony Fluitt
"Saturday Night" ....The Band; Lead Vocals Brent Carter
"Africano" ....The Band
"Star" ....The Band
"Faces" ....The Band

ORCHESTRA

Conductor: JEFFREY KLITZ
Associate Conductor: ANDY EZRIN

Guitar:
KEITH ROBINSON, BERND SCHOENHART
Electric Bass/Bass Synthesizer:
ARTIE C. REYNOLDS, III
Drums:
BRIAN DUNNE
Percussion:
ERROL CRUSHER BENNETT
Synthesizer:
JEFFREY KLITZ, ANDY EZRIN, DAVE KEYES
Saxophone:
SCOTT KREITZER
Trumpets:
DON DOWNS, DAVID TRIGG
Trombone:
KEITH O'QUINN

Music Coordinator: JOHN MILLER

Wynonna Smith as Naomi.
Photo by Paul Kolnik

Cast Continued

PLACE: New York City
TIME: Present

SWINGS

JESSICA HOPE COHEN,
DANA MARIE INGRAHAM,
TERACE JONES,
MATTHEW WARNER KIERNAN,
DANITA SALAMIDA

BAND VOCALISTS

BRENT CARTER,
KEITH ANTHONY FLUITT,
THERESA THOMASON

BAND VOCALIST SWINGS

MARVEL J. ALLEN,
JOHN A. JAMES

UNDERSTUDIES/STANDBYS/ALTERNATES

Standby for Victor:
ADRIAN BAILEY
For Mom:
SANDRA REAVES-PHILLIPS
For Louie:
CAESAR SAMAYOA
Alternate/Standby for Emma:
SARAH LIVINGSTON

Understudy for Kalimba:
DIONNE FIGGINS,
HOLLIE E. WRIGHT,
TERA-LEE POLLIN
For Anthony:
DARYL SPIERS,
MATTHEW WARNER KIERNAN
For Naomi:
NAKIA HENRY
For Rahim:
JON-PAUL MATEO

*Lead dancer, "Getaway"

Dance Captain: DANITA SALAMIDA

Hot Feet

Vivian Nixon
Kalimba

Mel Johnson, Jr.
Victor

Ann Duquesnay
Mom

Allen Hidalgo
Louie

Wynonna Smith
Naomi

Michael Balderrama
Anthony

Samantha Pollino
Emma

Sarah Livingston
Alternate/Standby Emma

Marvel J. Allen
Band Vocalist

Kevin Aubin
Ensemble

Adrian Bailey
Standby Victor

Brent Carter
Band Vocalist

Gerrard Carter
Ensemble

Jessica Hope Cohen
Swing

Dionne Figgins
Ensemble

Ramón Flowers
Ensemble

Keith Anthony Fluitt
Band Vocalist

Karla Puno Garcia
Ensemble

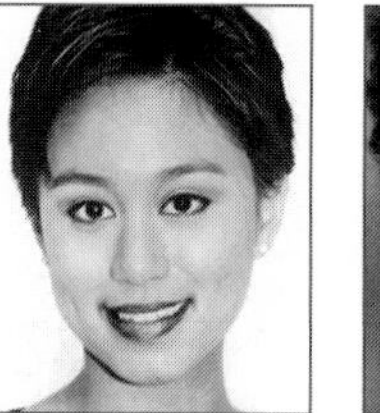
Nakia Henry
Ensemble

Duane Lee Holland
Ensemble, Assistant Dance Captain, Assistant Choreographer

Dana Marie Ingraham
Swing

John A. James
Band Vocalist Swing

Iquail S. Johnson
Ensemble

Terace Jones
Swing

Dominique Kelley
Ensemble

Matthew Warner Kiernan
Swing

Steve Konopelski
Ensemble

Sumie Maeda
Ensemble

Jon-Paul Mateo
Ensemble

Vasthy Mompoint
Ensemble

Tera-Lee Pollin
Ensemble

Sandra Reaves-Phillips
Standby Mom

Danita Salamida
Swing, Dance Captain, Assistant Choreographer

Caesar Samayoa
Standby Louie

Monique Smith
Ensemble

Hot Feet

Daryl Spiers
Ensemble

Felicity Stiverson
Ensemble

Theresa Thomason
Band Vocalist

Hollie E. Wright
Ensemble

Maurice Hines
Creator, Director and Choreographer

Maurice White
Music and Lyrics

Heru Ptah
Book

James Noone
Scenic Design

Paul Tazewell
Costume Design

Clifton Taylor
Lighting Design

Tom Clark, Mark Menard and Nevin Steinberg, Acme Sound Partners
Sound Design

Qodi Armstrong
Hair Design

Arthur Siccardi
Production Manager

Michael E. Harrod
Production Stage Manager

John Miller
Music Coordinator

Jeffrey Klitz
Musical Director and Conductor

Bill Meyers
Arrangements and Orchestrations

Leonard Soloway
General Manager

Steven M. Levy
General Manager

Ricardo Khan
Assistant Director

Lon Olejniczak, Transamerica
Producer

Rudy Durand
Producer

Art Macnow, Kalimba Entertainment
Associate Producer

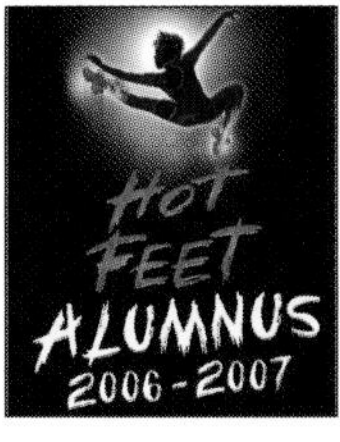

Mel Johnson, Jr.
Victor

Photo courtesy of John Miller

ORCHESTRA
Front Row (L-R): Artie C. Reynolds (Bass/Bass Synth), Theresa Thomason (Singer), Marvel Allen (Singer), Donald Downs (Trumpet).
Middle Row (L-R): John Miller (Music Coordinator), Errol "C" Bennett (Congas & Miscellaneous Percussion), Andy Ezrin (Synthesizer), Keith O'Quinn (Trombone), Keith Robinson (Guitar #1).
Back Row (L-R): Jeffrey Klitz (Conductor/Synthesizer), Bernd Schoenhart (Guitar), Brian Dunne (Drums), Dave Keyes (Synthesizer), Scott Kreitzer (Saxophone/Flute), Brent Carter (Singer), Keith Fluitt (Singer), John James (Singer), and Dave Trigg (Trumpet).

Hot Feet

WARDROBE DEPARTMENT
Front Row (L-R):
Joelyn Wilkosz (Dresser), Andrea Gonzalez (Dresser), Christina Foster (Dresser), Ginene Licata (Dresser), Gerbie Connolly (Wardrobe Supervisor)

Middle Row (L-R):
Marc Borders (Stitcher), Teri Pruitt (Dresser), Mary Miles (Master Stitcher), Bob Kwiatkowski (Dresser), Donna Hulland (Dresser), Marisa Tchornobai (Dresser), Timothy Hanlon (Dresser) and Michael P. Murphy (Assistant Wardrobe Supervisor).

Back Row:
Paul Riner (Dresser).

Photos by Ben Strothmann

STAGE CREW
Front Row (L-R):
Mike Kondrat (Laser Tech), Sean Jones (Carpenter), Joe Goldman (Carpenter), John Warburton (Props).

Second Row (L-R):
John Santagata (Carpenter), Richard Fedeli (Carpenter).

Back Row (L-R):
Jim Harris (Head Carpenter), Bill Garvey (Road Carpenter), Rob Presley (Road Props), Art Friedlander (House Electrician), Jeff Wever (Frontlight) and Jim Stapleton (Carpenter).

Bill Blackstock
Doorman

Gabriel Maysonette
Doorman

Hot Feet

FRONT OF HOUSE STAFF
First Row (L-R):
Jeffrey Dobbins (House Manager), Delilah Lloyd (Assistant House Manager), Edward Griggs (Usher), Alysha Wright (Usher), Charles Catt (Usher), Jason McKelvy (Usher), Nicole March (Usher), Ryan Tschetter (Usher).

Second Row (L-R):
John Wescott (Assistant House Manager), Deborah Langenfeld (Usher), Juana Rivas (Usher), Lisa Lopez (Usher), Cristin Whitley (Usher), Anna Robillard (Usher).

Third Row (L-R):
Billy Pena (Usher), Robert Phelps (Usher), Lydia Soto (Usher), Mike Chavez (Usher), Vicki Herschman (Usher), Tommie Williams (Usher), Danielle Fazio (Usher).

Fourth Row (L-R):
Kirssy Toribio (Usher), Erroll Worthington (Usher), Alan Toribio (Usher), Shoanna Charles (Usher), Sharon Hawkins (Usher), Ken Fuller (Usher), Dario Puccini (Usher) and Christina Gutierrez (Usher).

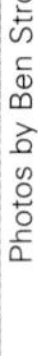

Photos by Ben Strothmann

HAIR DEPARTMENT
(L-R):
Laverne Long (Assistant to Hair Designer), Leslie (Goddess) Zeigler (Hair Assistant), Qodi Armstrong (Hair Designer), Carol (C.C.) Campbell (Hair Stylist)

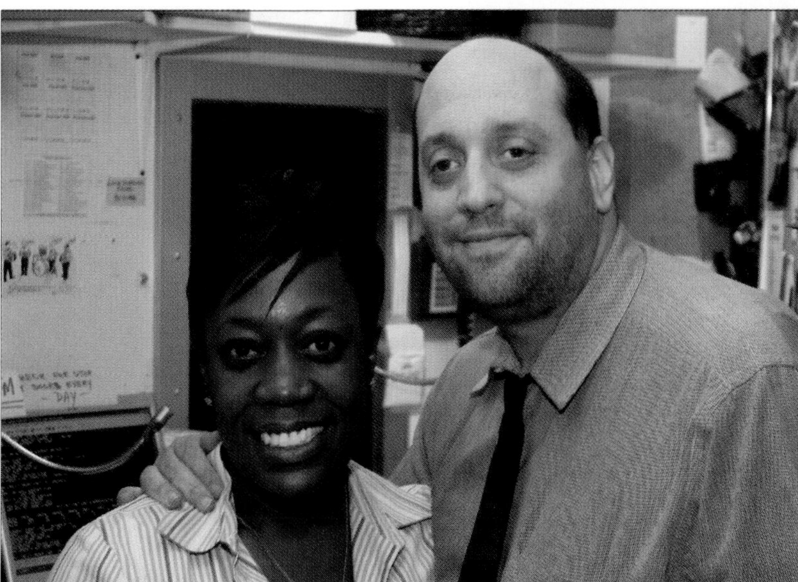

BOX OFFICE
(L-R): Michelle Smith (Treasurer) and Spencer Taustine (Treasurer)

Hot Feet

STAGE MANAGEMENT
(L-R): Dan Shaheen (Stage Manager), Michael E. Harrod (Production Stage Manager), Frances W. Falcone (Assistant Stage Manager) and Michael Krug (Production Assistant)

PRODUCTION STAFF FOR *HOT FEET*

GENERAL MANAGEMENT
Leonard Soloway Steven M. Levy

COMPANY MANAGER
Alexandra Gushin

PRESS REPRESENTATION
SPRINGER ASSOCIATES PR
Gary Springer/Joe Trentacosta
D'Arcy Drollinger

CASTING
Stuart Howard Amy Schecter Paul Hardt

Production Stage Manager .... Michael E. Harrod
Stage Managers .... Dan Shaheen, Lisa Dawn Cave
Assistant Stage Manager .... Frances W. Falcone
Assistant Director .... Ricardo Khan
Assistant Choreographer .... Danita Salamida
Assistant Choreographer .... Duane Lee Holland
Production Manager .... Arthur Siccardi
Assistant Company Manager .... Sara Jane Baldwin
Assistant Set Designer .... Jon Savage
Assistants to James Noone .... Kenichi Takahashi, Eric Allgeier
Associate Costume Designer .... Dennis Ballard
Assistant Costume Designers .... Stacey Galloway, Michael McAleer
Costume Assistant .... Caitlin Kanapka Hunt
Associate Lighting Designer .... Ed McCarthy
Assistant Lighting Designer .... Greg Guarnaccia
Automated Lighting Programmer .... Paul J. Sonnleitner
Assistant Sound Designer .... Michael A. Creason
Production Carpenter .... Bill Van DeBogart
Deck Automation .... Stephen Burns
Automation Flyman .... Gabe Harris
Production Electrician .... Drayton L. Allison
Head Electrician .... Joe "Fish" Cangelosi
Deck Electrician .... Craig Aves
Follow Spot Operator .... Jennifer Lerner
Production Sound Engineer .... Scott Sanders
Advance Production Sound .... John Dory
Monitor Mixer .... Dan Robillard
Synthesizer Programmer .... Kenny Seymour
Production Property Master .... Mike Pilipski
Wardrobe Supervisor .... Gerbie Connoly
Wardrobe Assistant .... Michael Murphy
Dressers .... Christina Foster, Andrea Gonzalez, Joe Godwin, Timothy Hanlon, Donna Holland, Robert K. Kwiatkowski, Ginene Licata, Teri Pruitt, Paul Riner, Marisa Tchornobai, Joelyn Wilkosz
Wardrobe Day Workers .... Greg Holtz, Ruth Goya, Marc Borders
Tailor .... Mary Miles
Wynonna Smith Hair Design .... Lillie Frierson King
Hair Supervisor .... Qodi Armstrong
Hairstylist .... Caroline (C.C.) Campbell
Assistant to Hair Designer .... Laverne Long
New Vocal Arrangements .... Cat Gray, Brett Laurence, Bill Meyers, Maurice White
Additional Orchestrations .... Ray Brown, Michael Rubino
Associate Conductor .... Andy Ezrin
Assistant to John Miller .... Kelly M. Rach
Digital Music Editor .... Jimi Randolph
Music Copyist .... Robert Nowak and Associates, Inc.
Production Assistant .... Michael Krug
Advertising .... Eliran Murphy Group LTD/ Barbara Eliran, Ann Murphy, Steve Knight, Betsy Gershaw
Artwork .... Frank Fraver Verlizzo
Artwork Concept .... Rudy Durand
Artwork Photography .... Lois Greenfield
Media and Publicity Consultant for Mr. White and Mr. Hines .... Mark Young/ The Fame Factory
Marketing .... HHC Marketing/ Hugh Hysell, Amanda Pekoe, Jennifer Scherer, Jessica Hinds, Mandi Messina, Matt Sicoli, Caitlin Strype, Michael Redman, Keita Williams
Marketing ...... Marketing On Demand/Davett Singletary
Multicultural Marketing .... Gwendolyn Quinn, Sandie M. Smith
Viral Marketing .... TheatreMAMA/Michelin Hall, Timothy Wooster
Merchandising .... LTS Enterprises, LLC/ Larry Turk, Randi Grossman
Production Photographer .... Paul Kolnik
Rehearsal Photographer .... Alexandra Seegers
General Management Staff .... Errolyn Rosa
Kalimba Entertainment Staff .... Robert Weissman
Theatre Displays .... King Displays
Opening Night Coordination .... Tobak Lawrence
Insurance Services .... Tanenbaum Harber Insurance Group Carol A. Bressi-Cilona
Legal Counsel .... Cowan, DeBaets, Abrahams & Sheppard LLP/ Frederick P. Bimbler, Esq.
Payroll .... Castellana Services, Inc.
Production Accountant .... Annemarie Aguanno, CPA
Accounting .... Rosenberg, Neuwirth & Kuchner CPAs/ Chris Cacace, CPA
Travel Agent .... Express Travel/Michael Dietz
Hotel Booking .... Road Rebel
Massage Therapist .... Ryan Blanchard
Web Design .... Carrie Schoenfeld
Child Wrangler .... Vanessa Brown
Tutoring .... On Location Education

EXCLUSIVE BOOKING DIRECTION
WILLIAM MORRIS AGENCY, INC.
Susan Weaving
1325 Avenue of the Americas
New York, NY 10019
Phone: (212) 903-1170
Fax: (212) 903-1446

CREDITS AND ACKNOWLEDGEMENTS

Scenery constructed by Hudson Scenic Studios. Costumes executed by John Kristiansen New York Inc.; Parsons-Meares, Ltd.; Eric Winterling, Inc., New York, New York; Donna Langman; Barbara Matera Ltd; C.C. Wei. Electronic costumes by Janet Hansen. Hosiery and undergarments provided by Bra*Tenders. Shoes by Capezio; custom shoes by LaDuca Shoes NYC.; T.O. Dey. Hats by Arnold Levine. Lighting equipment from PRG Lighting. Laser equipment provided by Nth Degree Creative. Soft goods, digitally printed drops and fiberoptics hangers by I. Weiss. Sound equipment by Sound Associates, Inc. Production properties by Spoon Group.

Hot Feet

SPECIAL THANKS

Ricola natural herb cough drops courtesy of Ricola USA. Thanks to Stanley Kaye, Sherrie Maricle. Special thanks to Beverley Randolph.

MUSIC & PUBLISHER CREDITS

"**Africano**," music by Lorenzo Dunn and Maurice White. Published by EMI. "**After the Love Is Gone**," music by William B. Champlin, David Foster, and Jay Graydon. Published by EMI Blackwood Music, Inc., Foster Frees Music, Garden Rake Music, Inc., Music Sales Corp. and Noted for the Record. "**Boogie Wonderland**," music by Jonathan G. Lind and Allee Willis. Published by Big Mystique Music and EMI Blackwood Music, Inc. "**Can't Hide Love**," music by Skip Scarborough. Published by Alexscarmusic and UniChappell Music. "**Dearest Heart**," music by William Keith Meyers, Maurice White and Allee Willis. Published by Electric Bill Music, Maurice White Music and Tonepet Music. "**Dirty**," music by Maurice White. Published by Maurice White Music and Sony/ATV Tunes LLC. "**Faces**," music by Philip Bailey, Lorenzo Dunn, Maurice White and Verdine White. Published by Cherubim Music, EMI April Music, Inc., Sir & Trini Music and Verdine White Songs. "**Fantasy**," music by Eduardo Del Barrio, Maurice White and Verdine White. Published by Criga Music and EMI April Music, Inc. "**Getaway**," music by Peter Cor and Bernard Taylor. Published by EMI April Music, Inc. "**Gratitude**," music by Lorenzo Dunn, Maurice White and Verdine White. Published by EMI April Music. "**Hot Feet**," music by Brett Laurence, William Keith Meyers and Maurice White. Published by Digable Tunes, Electric Bill Music and Maurice White Music. "**In the Stone**," music by David Foster, Maurice White, Allee Willis. Published by EMI April Music, EMI Blackwood Music, Foster Frees Music, Irving Music. "**Kali**," music by Brett Laurence, William Keith Meyers and Maurice White. Published by Digable Tunes, Electric Bill Music and Maurice White Music. "**Let Your Feelings Show**," music by David Foster, Maurice White and Allee Willis. Published by EMI April Music, Inc.; EMI Blackwood Music, Inc.; Foster Frees Music; and Irving Music, Inc. "**Let's Groove**," music by Wayne Vaughn and Maurice White. Published by EMI April Music Inc. and Music Sales Corp. "**Louie's Welcome**," music by Cat Gray and Heru Ptah. Published by Heru Ptah Music and Pretty Little Kitty Music. "**Mighty Mighty**," music by Maurice White and Verdine White. Published by EMI April Music, Inc. "**Ponta De Areia**," music by Fernando Brant and Milton Nascimento. Published by EMI April Music and BMG Songs. "**Reasons**," music by Philip James Bailey, Charles Stepney and Maurice White. Published by EMI April Music, Inc.; Eibur Music; Embassy Music; and Music Sales Corporation. "**Rock That**," music by David Foster and Maurice White. Published by EMI April Music, Foster Frees Music and Irving Music, Inc. "**Saturday Night**," music by Philip J. Bailey, Albert Phillip McKay and Maurice White. Published by EMI April Music, Inc. "**September**," music by Albert Philip McKay, Maurice White and Allee Willis. Published by EMI April Music, Inc., EMI Blackwood Music, Inc., Irving Music, Inc. and Steel Chest Music. "**Serpentine Fire**," music by Reginald Burke, Maurice White and Verdine White. Published by EMI April Music, Inc. "**Shining Star**," music by Philip J. Bailey, Lorenzo Dunn, Maurice White. Published by EMI April Music. "**Star**," music by Eduardo Del Barrio, Maurice White and Allee Willis. Published by Criga Music, EMI April Music, Inc., EMI Blackwood Music, Inc. and Irving Music."**System of Survival**," music by Skylark. Published by EMI April Music, Inc. and Sputnik Adventure Music. "**That's the Way of the World**," music by Charles Stepney, Maurice White and Verdine White. Published by Eibur Music, EMI April Music, Inc. and Embassy Music Corp. "**Thinking of You**," music by Wanda Vaughn, Wayne Vaughn and Maurice White. Published by EMI April Music and Music Sales Corp. "**Turn It Into Something Good**," music by Valerie Carter, James Howard and Maurice White. Published by Careers BMG Music Publishing, EMI April Music, Inc., Newton House Music and River Honey Music. "**When I Dance**," music by William Keith Meyers, Maurice White and Allee Willis. Published by Electric Bill Music, Maurice White Music and Tonepet Music. "**You Don't Know**," music by William Keith Meyers, Maurice White and Heru Ptah. Published by Electric Bill Music, Heru Ptah Music and Maurice White Music.

HILTON THEATRE STAFF

General Manager ....Micah Hollingworth
Assistant General Manager ....Teresa Ryno
House Manager ....Jeffrey Dobbins
Facility Manager ....Jeff Nuzzo
Box Office Treasurer ....Peter Attanasio Jr.
Head Carpenter ....James C. Harris
Head Electrician ....Art J. Friedlander
Head of Properties ....Joseph P. Harris Jr.
Head of Sound ....John R. Gibson
Asst. Box Office Treasurer ....Spencer Taustine
Payroll Administrator ....Tiyana Works
Shipping/Receiving ....Dinara Ferreira
Administrative Assistant ....Jenny Kirlin

LIVE NATION

President and Chief Executive Officer ......Michael Rapino

Live Nation - Venues

President ....Bruce Eskowitz
CFO ....Alan Ridgeway
Vice President, Finance ....Kathy Porter
Executive Vice President ....Ned Collette
Senior Vice President, NY and CT Venues ....John Huff
Director of Labor Relations ....Chris Brockmeyer

Live Nation - Theatrical

Chairman, Global Theatre ....David Ian
CEO Theatrical, North America ....Steve Winton
President and COO, North America ...David M. Anderson
CFO, North America ....Paul Dietz
Senior Vice President, Producing ....Jennifer Costello
Executive Vice President/CMO ....Susie Krajsa
Senior Vice President, Operations ....Dan Swartz
Senior Vice President, Business Affairs ....David Lazar
Senior Vice President, Sales & Ticketing ...Courtney Pierce
Vice President, Marketing ....Jennifer DeLange
Vice President, Finance ....Chante Moore
Vice President, Programming ....Alison Spiriti

The Ensemble performs "Rock That."

Photo by Paul Kolnik

Inherit the Wind

First Preview: March 19, 2007. Opened: April 12, 2007.
Still running as of May 31, 2007.

PLAYBILL

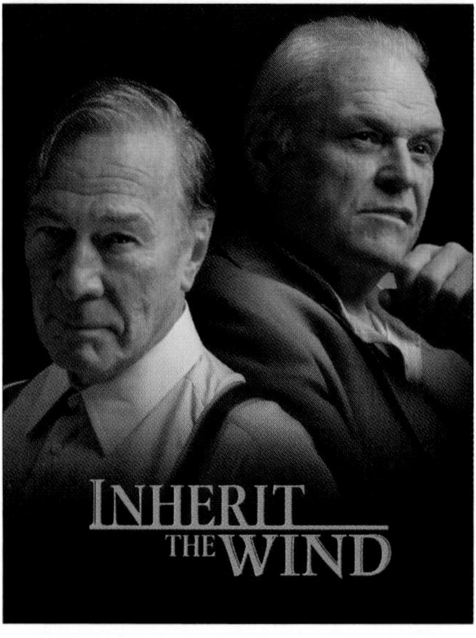

LYCEUM THEATRE
149 West 45th Street
A Shubert Organization Theatre
Gerald Schoenfeld, *Chairman* **Philip J. Smith,** *President*
Robert E. Wankel, *Executive Vice President*

Boyett Ostar Productions The Shubert Organization Lawrence Horowitz
Jon Avnet/Ralph Guild Roy Furman Debra Black/Daryl Roth
Bill Rollnick/Nancy Ellison Rollnick Stephanie McClelland

present

Christopher Plummer Brian Dennehy

in

By

Jerome Lawrence and Robert E. Lee

Also Starring
Byron Jennings

Terry Beaver Anne Bowles Steve Brady Bill Buell Bill Christ
Carson Church Conor Donovan Lanny Flaherty Kit Flanagan Beth Fowler
Sherman Howard Katie Klaus Maggie Lacey Jordan Lage Mary Kate Law
Philip LeStrange Kevin C. Loomis David M. Lutken Charlotte Maier Matthew Nardozzi
Randall Newsome Jay Patterson Pippa Pearthree Scott Sowers Amanda Sprecher
Erik Steele Jeff Steitzer Henry Stram Benjamin Walker Andrew Weems

and

Denis O'Hare

Set & Costume Design
Santo Loquasto

Lighting Design
Brian MacDevitt

Original Music and Sound Design
David Van Tieghem

Hair & Wig Design
Paul Huntley

Casting
Jay Binder/Jack Bowdan

Production Stage Manager
Michael Brunner

Technical Supervisor
Peter Fulbright

Press Representative
Boneau/Bryan Brown

Marketing
HHC Marketing

General Management
101 Productions, Ltd.

Associate Producer
Judith Resnick

Directed by
Doug Hughes

4/12/07

CAST

(in order of appearance)

Howard .... CONOR DONOVAN
Melinda .... AMANDA SPRECHER
Rachel .... MAGGIE LACEY
Mr. Meeker .... SCOTT SOWERS
Bert Cates .... BENJAMIN WALKER
Mr. Goodfellow .... HENRY STRAM
Mrs. Krebs .... CHARLOTTE MAIER
Reverend Jeremiah Brown .... BYRON JENNINGS
Sillers .... ANDREW WEEMS
Dunlap .... JAY PATTERSON
Bannister .... BILL BUELL
Mrs. Loomis .... ANNE BOWLES
Mrs. Blair .... PIPPA PEARTHREE
Vendor .... BILL CHRIST
Elijah .... LANNY FLAHERTY
Timmy .... MATTHEW NARDOZZI
E.K. Hornbeck .... DENIS O'HARE
Monkey Man .... KEVIN C. LOOMIS
Matthew Harrison Brady .... BRIAN DENNEHY
Mrs. Brady .... BETH FOWLER
Mayor .... JEFF STEITZER
Judge .... TERRY BEAVER
Tom Davenport .... JORDAN LAGE
Photographer .... RANDALL NEWSOME
Henry Drummond .... CHRISTOPHER PLUMMER
Reuters Reporter .... ERIK STEELE
Esterbrook .... ERIK STEELE
Gospel Quartet .... CARSON CHURCH, KATIE KLAUS, MARY KATE LAW, DAVID M. LUTKEN

Continued on next page

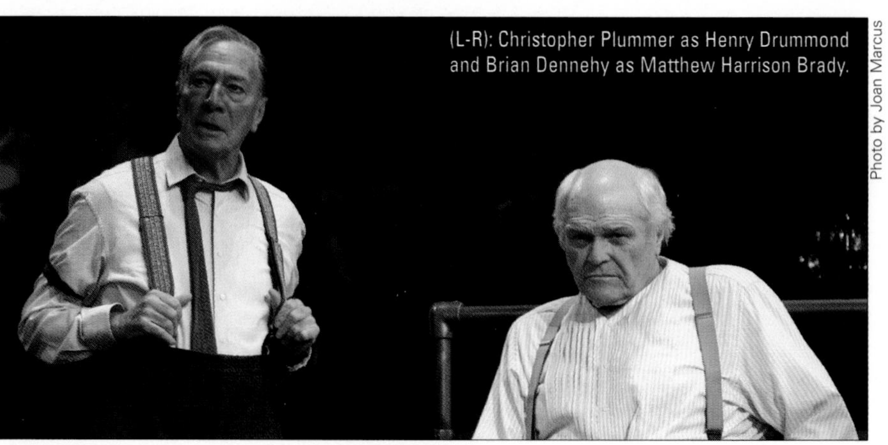

(L-R): Christopher Plummer as Henry Drummond and Brian Dennehy as Matthew Harrison Brady.

Photo by Joan Marcus

Inherit the Wind

Cast Continued

Townspeople ....ANNE BOWLES,
STEVE BRADY,
BILL CHRIST,
KIT FLANAGAN,
SHERMAN HOWARD,
PHILIP LeSTRANGE,
KEVIN C. LOOMIS,
CHARLOTTE MAIER,
MATTHEW NARDOZZI,
RANDALL NEWSOME,
JAY PATTERSON,
PIPPA PEARTHREE,
ERIK STEELE,
ANDREW WEEMS

PLACE

A small town.

TIME

Summer. Not too long ago.

UNDERSTUDIES

Henry Drummond, Monkey Man:
SHERMAN HOWARD
Matthew Harrison Brady:
JEFF STEITZER
E.K. Hornbeck:
JORDAN LAGE
Rachel Brown:
ANNE BOWLES
Mr. Meeker, Reuters Reporter:
KEVIN C. LOOMIS
Bert Cates, Photographer:
ERIK STEELE
Mr. Goodfellow, Reverend Jeremiah Brown:
BILL CHRIST
Mrs. Krebs, Mrs. Blair, Mrs. Brady:
KIT FLANAGAN
Sillers, Dunlap, Elijah:
STEVE BRADY
Bannister, Mayor, Judge:
PHILIP LeSTRANGE
Howard, Melinda:
MATTHEW NARDOZZI

Christopher Plummer
Henry Drummond

Brian Dennehy
Matthew Harrison Brady

Denis O'Hare
E.K. Hornbeck

Byron Jennings
Reverend Jeremiah Brown

Terry Beaver
Judge

Beth Fowler
Mrs. Brady

Anne Bowles
Mrs. Loomis/ Townsperson

Steve Brady
Townsperson

Bill Buell
Bannister

Bill Christ
Vendor/Townsperson

Carson Church
Gospel Quartet

Conor Donovan
Howard

Lanny Flaherty
Elijah

Kit Flanagan
Townsperson

Sherman Howard
Townsperson

Katie Klaus
Gospel Quartet

Maggie Lacey
Rachel Brown

Jordan Lage
Tom Davenport

Mary Kate Law
Gospel Quartet

Philip LeStrange
Townsperson

Inherit the Wind

Kevin C. Loomis
Monkey Man/ Townsperson

David M. Lutken
Music Supervisor/ Gospel Quartet

Charlotte Maier
Mrs. Krebs/ Townsperson

Matthew Nardozzi
Timmy

Randall Newsome
Photographer/ Townsperson

Jay Patterson
Dunlap/Townsperson

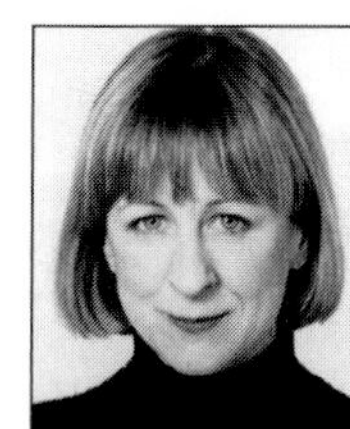
Pippa Pearthree
Mrs. Blair/ Townsperson

Scott Sowers
Mr. Meeker

Amanda Sprecher
Melinda

Erik Steele
Esterbrook/ Reuters Reporter/ Townsperson

Jeff Steitzer
Mayor

Henry Stram
Mr. Goodfellow

Benjamin Walker
Bert Cates

Andrew Weems
Sillers/Townsperson

Doug Hughes
Director

Santo Loquasto
Set & Costume Design

Brian MacDevitt
Lighting Design

Paul Huntley
Hair and Wig Designer

Jay Binder C.S.A.
Casting

Jack Bowdan C.S.A.
Casting

Bill Haber, OSTAR Enterprises
Producer

Bob Boyett
Producer

Gerald Schoenfeld, Chairman, The Shubert Organization
Producer

Lawrence Horowitz, M.D.
Producer

Jon Avnet
Producer

Roy Furman
Producer

Debra Black
Producer

Daryl Roth
Producer

Stephanie P. McClelland
Producer

Raynor Scheine
Elijah

Inherit the Wind

CAST
Front Row (L-R): Christopher Plummer, Brian Dennehy.

Second Row (L-R): Michael Brunner (Production Stage Manager), Benjamin Walker, Jordan Lage, Kevin C. Loomis, Jeff Spritzer, Byron Jennings, Philip LeStrange.

Third Row (L-R): Matthew Nardozzi, Carson Church, Raynor Scheine, Conor Donovan, Mary Kate Law, Denis O'Hare, Charlotte Maier, Terry Beaver.

Fourth Row (L-R): Beth Fowler, Jay Patterson, Maggie Lacey, Erik Steele, Kit Flanagan, Amanda Sprecher, Barclay Stiff (Stage Manager).

Fifth Row (L-R): Henry Stram, Randall Newsome, Andrew Weems, Steve Brady, Pippa Pearthree, Bill Buell, David Lutken, Bill Christ.

Back Row (L-R): Anne Bowles, Katie Klaus, Scott Sowers, Sherman Howard.

BOX OFFICE
Tara Giebler and Mike Cadunz.

Photos by Ben Strothmann

THEATRE STAFF
Front Row (L-R): Joann Swanson (House Manager), Susan Houghton (Ticket Taker), Carmen Sanchez (Assistant Porter).
Middle Row (L-R): Lorriane Aponte (Usher), Miriam Rincon (Cleaner), Laura Garanda (Cleaner).
Back Row: Neville Hinds (Doorman).

STAGE CREW
Front Row (L-R):
Charley P. Mann (Production Carpenter), Talia Krispel (Child Wrangler), Kimberly Prentice (Dresser), Jennifer Barnes (Dresser), Jennifer Molloy (Dresser), Andrea Gonzalez (Dresser).

Back Row (L-R):
Robin Day (Hair Supervisor), John Paul III (Head Props), William Rowland II (Head Electrician), Corina Frerotte (Spot Operator), Paul Riner (Dresser), Dave Rogers (Wardrobe Supervisor), Brien Brannigan (Production Sound Supervisor).

Inherit the Wind

STAFF FOR *INHERIT THE WIND*

GENERAL MANAGEMENT
101 PRODUCTIONS, LTD.
Wendy Orshan Jeffrey M. Wilson
David Auster

COMPANY MANAGER
Gregg Arst

GENERAL PRESS REPRESENTATIVE
BONEAU/BRYAN-BROWN
Adrian Bryan-Brown Jackie Green
Danielle Crinnion

PRODUCTION MANAGEMENT
TECH PRODUCTION SERVICES, INC.
Peter Fulbright, Mary Duffe,
Colleen Houlehen, Jackie Prats

CASTING
BINDER CASTING
Jay Binder, CSA
Jack Bowdan, CSA, Mark Brandon, Megen Larche
Assistants: Nikole Vallins, Allison Estrin

Production Stage Manager .... Michael Brunner
Stage Manager .... Barclay Stiff
Associate Director .... Mark Schneider
Music Supervisor .... David M. Lutken
Associate Scenic Designer .... Jenny B. Sawyers
Scenic Assistants .... Tobin Ost, Kanae Heike
Associate Costume Designer .... Matthew Pachtman
Costume Assistant .... Sarah Sophia Turner
Associate Lighting Designer .... Michael O'Connor
Associate Sound Designer .... Jill BC DuBoff

Production Carpenter .... Charley P. Mann
Production Props Supervisor .... Abraham Morrison
Production Electrician .... Brian GF McGarity
Production Sound Supervisor .... Brien Brannigan
Head Properties .... John Paull III
Head Electrician .... William Rowland II
Lighting Programmer .... Marc Polimeni
Wardrobe Supervisor .... Dave Olin Rogers
Mr. Plummer's Dresser .... Andrea Gonzalez
Mr. Dennehy's Dresser .... Kimberly Prentice
Dressers .... Jennifer Barnes, Jennifer Molloy, Paul Riner
Hair Supervisor .... Robin Maginsky Day
Production Assistant .... Chris Munnell

Associate Producer for Ostar Enterprises .... Rachel Neuburger
Executive Assistant to Mr. Haber .... Theresa Pisanelli
Assistant to Mr. Haber .... Andrew Cleghorn
Assistants to Mr. Boyett .... Diane Murphy, Alex Libby, Michael Mandell
SVP, Strategic Partnerships & Developments ...... Jan Gura
Legal Counsel .... Lazarus & Harris, LLP/ Scott Lazarus, Esq., Robert C. Harris, Esq.
Accountant ...... Rosenberg, Neuwirth, & Kushner, CPAs/ Chris Cacace, Patricia Pedersen, Alla Loyfman
Advertising .... Serino Coyne, Inc./ Greg Corradetti, Tom Callahan, Steve Knight, Natalie Serota
Marketing .... HHC Marketing/ Hugh Hysell, Amanda Pekoe, Kerry Minchinton
Children's Tutoring .... On Location Education/ Alan Simon, Jodi Green, Anna Smith, Abigail Dyer, Irene Karasik
Child Guardian .... Talia Krispel
Assistant to the General Managers .... John Vennema
101 Productions, Ltd. Staff .... Denys Baker, Ashley Berman, Katharine Croke, Barbara Crompton, Laura Dickinson, Sherra Johnston, Emily Lawson, Heidi Neven, Kyle Pickles, Mary Six Rupert, Evan Storey
101 Productions, Ltd. Intern .... Stewart Miller
Press Associates .... Chris Boneau, Ian Bjorklund, Jim Byk, Brandi Cornwell, Juliana Hannett, Allison Houseworth, Hector Hernandez, Jessica Johnson, Kevin Jones, Amy Kass, Aaron Meier, Christine Olver, Steven Padla, Joe Perrotta, Linnae Petruzzelli, Matt Polk, Matt Ross, Heath Schwartz, Susanne Tighe
Banking .... City National Bank/Anne McSweeney
Insurance .... DeWitt Stern, Inc./Peter Shoemaker
Risk Managers .... Stockbridge Risk Management, Inc./ Neil Goldstein
Theatre Displays .... King Displays, Inc.
Merchandising .... Max Merchandising, LLC/ Randi Grossman
Payroll Services .... Castellana Services, Inc.
Website Design .... Situation Marketing/ Damian Bazadona, Lisa Cecchini, Lisa Donnelly
Opening Night Coordination .... Tobak Lawrence Company/ Suzanne Tobak, Michael P. Lawrence
Artwork Photography .... Timothy White
SSDC Observer .... Kel Haney

CREDITS

Scenery by Showmotion, Inc. Scenery automation and show control by Showmotion, Inc., Norwalk, CT, using the AC2 computerized motion control system. Lighting equipment from PRG Lighting. Sound equipment from Masque Sound. Costume construction by Euro Co Costumes, Werner Russold, Seamless Costumes, Felsen, Luigi Custom Tailors, Lynne Baccus and Arel Studios. Millinery by Leslie Norgate. Custom dyeing by Dye-Namix, Inc. Properties provided by Bergen Office Furniture, Waves Radio, Spoon Group Production. Tables by Golden Oldies Furniture. Audience chairs by Demolition Depot. Sconces by City Knickerbocker. Prop construction by Craig Grigg. Paper props by Pete Sarafin. Natural herb cough drops courtesy of Ricola USA, Inc. Emergen-C super energy booster provided by Alacer Corp. Special thanks to Bra*Tenders for hosiery and undergarments.

MUSIC CREDITS

"I Shall Not Be Moved," words by John Benson, Jr., music by Mrs. James A. Pate; "When the Roll Is Called Up Yonder" by James M. Black; "Faith of Our Fathers" by H.F. Hemy and J.G. Walton; "Not Made With Hands" by Ulysses Phillips; "Do Lord," words by Julia Ward Howe, arranged by Lewis G. Scharpf, Jr.; "Dwelling in Beulah Land" by C. Austin Miles; "Shall We Gather at the River?" by Robert Lowry; "The Old Rugged Cross" by George Bennard; "This World Is Not My Home" by Albert E. Brumley; "You Can't Make a Monkey of Me" by Billy Rose; "Gospel Ship" by A.P. Carter; "Down by the Riverside"; "Farther Along" by J.R. Baxter and W.B. Stevens; "The Unclouded Day" by J.K. Alwood; "Love Lifted Me" by Howard E. Smith; "There's a Great Day Coming" by W.L. Thompson.

To learn more about the production, please visit
InheritTheWindOnBroadway.com

Inherit the Wind rehearsed at New 42nd Street Studios.

SPECIAL THANKS
The producers wish to thank
Eddie Marks and Western Costumes.

ACKNOWLEDGEMENTS

Online study guide provided courtesy of Novelguide.com. The producers also wish to thank Alan Dershowitz, the American Civil Liberties Union (ACLU), Kevin Anderson, AntiEssays.com, Berea College, Bryan College, Matthew Chapman, Scott Fowler, Edward Larson, Jennifer Leeson (Commemorative Collection Curator), Merriam-Webster Online Dictionary, Doug Sharp, Doug Stone, Robert Schneider, The Baltimore Sun, Jeffrey P. Moran

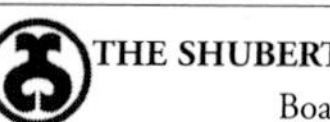

THE SHUBERT ORGANIZATION, INC.
Board of Directors

Gerald Schoenfeld
Chairman

Philip J. Smith
President

Wyche Fowler, Jr.

John W. Kluge

Lee J. Seidler

Michael I. Sovern

Stuart Subotnick

Robert E. Wankel
Executive Vice President

Peter Entin
Vice President – Theatre Operations

Elliot Greene
Vice President – Finance

David Andrews
Vice President – Shubert Ticketing Services

John Darby
Vice President – Facilities

D.S. Moynihan
Vice President – Creative Projects

House Manager .... Joann Swanson

Inherit the Wind
SCRAPBOOK

Correspondents: Various Cast Members
Memorable Opening Night Letter, Fax or Note: We received the traditional opening night greetings via fax machine from many Broadway shows. It was such a nice gesture that greeted the cast when they arrived at the theatre on opening night. All the faxes covered the hallway leading to the callboard. It was a great way to start the evening.
Opening Night Gift: The most unusual opening night gift we received was a small metal statue of a monkey sitting on a stack of books. Stephanie McClelland, one of our kind producers, gave every member of the company one. It was interesting to see how cast members incorporated the monkey statue into their dressing rooms. Some of the cast even gave their monkey a name.
Favorite In-Theatre Gathering Place: We had to fit a cast of 34 into the Lyceum Theatre. This theatre is traditionally home to one-person shows and small-cast dramas. After we squeezed into the tiny dressing rooms, the crew created something of a greenroom in the basement. Our greenroom consisted of leftover furniture from the ladies of *Steel Magnolias* and some beautiful furniture that Whoopi Goldberg left at the theatre after her solo show closed a few years ago. This small area slowly turned into the place that we would gather before and during the show. Over time this area became home to where we would celebrate birthdays and have many Sunday brunches.
Favorite Snack Food: Anything with sugar was very popular. Kevin Loomis, who played the Monkey Man, would make incredible apple pies and bring them to the theatre. They never lasted very long.
Special Backstage Rituals: Benjamin Walker had to do at least ten pull-ups on the back of the set right before the show started every night. Often some of the cast joined in with Ben. Some were more successful than others.
Favorite Therapy: Ricola. Thank you Ricola USA!
Mascot: Early in the run Philip LeStrange received a large package at the theatre. It turns out it was a birthday gift of a life-sized stuffed golden retriever. Philip named him Bob and he became our official *Inherit the Wind* mascot. We were also very fond of the stuffed monkeys they sold in the theatre lobby.
Who Wore the Heaviest/Hottest Costume: Kevin Loomis played the Monkey Man. His costume was a full body gorilla suit. It was heavy and hot, but Kevin never complained. We often dared him to go to the fruit stand on the corner and buy a banana wearing the full suit.
Record Number of Cell Phone Rings: Not too many episodes of annoying cell phones. We had only one or two phone rings a week. Sixty-three audience members sat onstage right in the middle of the action. We made those kind patrons lock up their personal belongings in lockers offstage before the show started.
Company In-Jokes: "Where's the banner?" "Whooooo are you?" "Jose, you forgot your…." "Broom, give him a broom." "Is your mother gay?"
Busiest Day at the Box Office: The day after opening night. Business was brisk
Funny Directorial Note: "Eehhhmmm…."
Coolest Thing About Being in This Show: Working on play with a cast of 34. A play of this size produced today on Broadway happens so rarely. It was a great show with a fantastic company.

Photo by Aubrey Reuben

Photo courtesy the *Inherit the Wind* cast.

1. The cast takes a curtain call at the premiere.
2. Director Doug Hughes shares a joke with Kate Jennings Grant at the opening night party at Bryant Park Grill.
3. Opening night gift from producer Stephanie McClelland.
4. Cast member Conor Donovan at the opening night party.
5. Cast member Maggie Lacey at Bryant Park Grill.

Jay Johnson: The Two and Only!

First Preview: September 9, 2006. Opened: September 28, 2006.
Closed: November 26, 2006 after 10 Previews and 70 Performances.

PLAYBILL

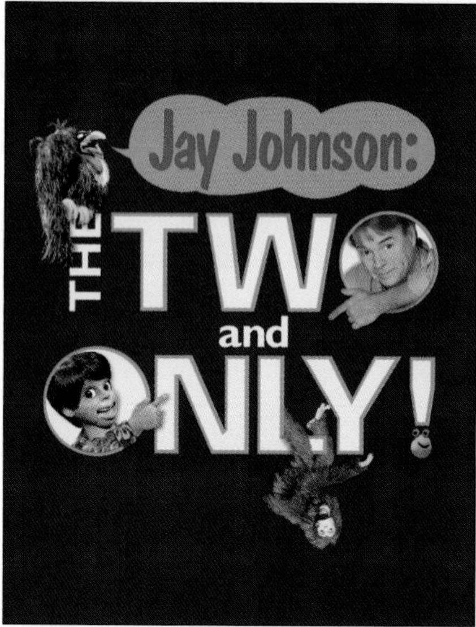

Jay Johnson (R) with Bob.

Photo by Carol Rosegg

THE HELEN HAYES THEATRE

MARTIN MARKINSON DONALD TICK

ROGER ALAN GINDI STEWART F. LANE & BONNIE COMLEY DAN WHITTEN
HERBERT GOLDSMITH PRODUCTIONS KEN GROSSMAN BOB & RHONDA SILVER
MICHAEL A. JENKINS/DALLAS SUMMER MUSICALS, INC. WETROCK ENTERTAINMENT

present

Jay Johnson:
THE TWO and ONLY!

written and performed by
JAY JOHNSON

conceived by
JAY JOHNSON MURPHY CROSS PAUL KREPPEL

scenery by BEOWULF BORITT
lighting by CLIFTON TAYLOR
sound by DAVID GOTWALD
original music by MICHAEL ANDREAS

production management ROBERT G. MAHON III JEFF WILD
production stage manager LORI ANN ZEPP

marketing HHC MARKETING
press representatives O&M ORIGLIO/MIRAMONTEZ Co.
associate producer JAMIE deROY

directed by
MURPHY CROSS & PAUL KREPPEL

World Premiere Presented at Atlantic Theater Company, New York City, 2004
Presented by Colony Theatre, Burbank, and American Repertory Theatre, Cambridge, 2006

The producers wish to express their appreciation to Theatre Development Fund for its support of this production.

9/28/06

Jay Johnson

Murphy Cross
Director/Producer

Paul Kreppel
Director/Producer

Beowulf Boritt
Set Designer

Jay Johnson: The Two and Only!

Clifton Taylor
Lighting Designer

David Gotwald
Sound Design

Roger Alan Gindi
Producer/
General Manager

Stewart F. Lane and Bonnie Comley
Producer

Dan Whitten
Producer

Michael Jenkins
Producer

Jamie deRoy
Associate Producer

CAST & FRONT OF HOUSE STAFF
Front Row (L-R):
Unidentified (Usher), C. J. Gelfand (Usher).

Middle Row (L-R):
Carol Channing (Hello Dolly!), Alan Markinson (House Manager), Natasha Thomas (Usher), Jay Johnson (Cast), Linda Maley (Ticket-Taker).

Back Row (L-R):
Harry Joshi (Usher), Melanie Willford (Usher), Abigail Hardin (Merchandising), John Biancamano (Head Usher), Berd Vaval (Ticket-Taker).

Photos by Melissa Merlo

2006-2007 AWARD

TONY AWARD
Best Special Theatrical Event

CAST & CREW
(L-R): A. Scott Falk (Company Manager), Roger Keller (Production Propmaster), Doug Purcell (Production Carpenter), Joe Beck (Electrician), Lori Ann Zepp (Production Stage Manager), Bob Etter (Sound Engineer), Jay Johnson (Ventriloquist and Star).

CAST & MANAGEMENT
(L-R): Jay Johnson (Cast), Lori Ann Zepp (Production Stage Manager), A. Scott Falk (Company Manager).

Jay Johnson: The Two and Only!
Scrapbook

Photo by Alan Markinson

Photo by Aubrey Reuben

1. (L-R): Roger Alan Gindi (producer/general manager), Herbert Goldsmith (producer), Stewart F. Lane (producer), "Bob," Jay Johnson, Paul Kreppel (producer/director), Murphy Cross (producer/director) and Dan Whitten (producer).
2. Jay Johnson and columnist Liz Smith prepare Johnson's caricature for hanging on the wall of Sardi's restaurant.

STAFF FOR *JAY JOHNSON: THE TWO AND ONLY!*

GENERAL MANAGEMENT
GINDI THEATRICAL MANAGEMENT
ROGER ALAN GINDI

GENERAL PRESS REPRESENTATIVE
O&M
Origlio/Miramontez Co.
Rick Miramontez Richard Hillman

COMPANY MANAGER
A. Scott Falk

Production Stage Manager .... Lori Ann Zepp
Associate Set Designer .... Jo Winiarski
Assistant Set Designer .... Jessie Moore
Assistant Lighting Designer .... Nicholas Phillips
Assistant Lighting Designer .... Steve O'Shea
Head Carpenter .... Doug Purcell
Head Property Man .... Roger Keller
Head Electrician .... Joseph Beck
Sound Technician .... Robert Etter
Assistant to Ms. Cross and Mr. Kreppel ...... Ryan J. Davis
Assistant to Mr. Gindi .... David M. Brenner
Assistants to Mr. Lane ...... Jeanine Holiday, Diana Prince
Assistants to Mr. Whitten .... Fiona Landers, Olivia D'Ambrosio
Assistants to Mr. Jenkins .... Wanda Beth, Jenny Cagle
Advertising .... Serino Coyne Inc. Roger Micone, Neal Leibowitz, Christin Seidel, Morgan Schreiber
Marketing .... HHC Marketing Hugh Hysell, Amanda Pekoe, Jessica Hinds, Kristen Donnelly
Press Associates .... Tony Origlio, Kip Vanderbilt, Philip Carrubba, Jon Dimond, Yufen Kung, Sarah Talisman, Molly Barnett
Photography .... Ed Krieger, Carol Rosegg
Legal Counsel .... Richard Garmise, Esq. Loeb & Loeb, LLP
Insurance .... DeWitt Stern Group/Peter Shoemaker
Banking .... JP Morgan Chase & Co./Michele Gibbons
Accounting .... Barry Thomashow, CPA
Payroll Services .... Axium/Martha Palubniak
Audience Development and Promotions .... Match-Tix Jeff Duchen, Joe Aiello
Website Design .... Vonderland Studios, Inc.
Opening Night Coordination .. Tobak Lawrence Company Joanna B. Koondel, Michael P. Lawrence

CREDITS

Scenery built by Downtime Productions and Blackwalnut. Lighting and sound equipment provided by Production Resource Group.

Jay Johnson's wardrobe provided by Nick Graham from his nick(it) collection.

SPECIAL THANKS

Faye Armon, Jo Ann Veneziano, Sam Ellis, Felicity Huffman and Bill Macy, Arlene and Joe Mantegna, Nanci Hammond and Joe Malone, Eleanor Albano, Jules Fisher, Susan Grushkin, Rob Krausz, Eileen and Allan Pepper, Linda and Jay Sandrich, Abby and Liz Tetenbaum, Dan Hirsch, The Secret Rose, Neil Kreppel, Laurel and Jim Cross, Flo Cross, Bill Brunelle and Maurice LaMarche

MUSIC CREDITS

"I AIN'T GOT NOBODY"
Written by Roger Graham and Spencer Williams
Public domain.

"JUST A GIGOLO"
Written by Julius Brammer, Irving Caesar and Leonello Casucci

"MY WAY"
Written by Paul Anka, Jacques Revaux, Claude Francois and Gilles Thibault
© 1967 by Chrysalis Standards, Inc. (BMI)
All rights on behalf of itself administered by Chrysalis Standards, Inc.
Used by permission. All rights reserved.

"SEND IN THE CLOWNS"
Written by Stephen Sondheim

"TEDDY BEAR TWO-STEP"
Written by John W. Bratton
Public domain.

THE HELEN HAYES THEATRE
owned and operated by
MARTIN MARKINSON and DONALD TICK

General Manager .... SUSAN S. MYERBERG
Associate General Manager .... Sharon Fallon

STAFF FOR THE HELEN HAYES THEATRE

HOUSE MANAGER .... ALAN R. MARKINSON
Treasurer .... David Heveran
Assistant Treasurers .... Chuck Stuis, Andrew Chen
Engineer .... Hector Angulo
Head Usher .... John Biancamano
Stage Door .... Robert Seymour, Jon Angulo
Accountant .... Chen-Win Hsu, CPA., P.C.

Jersey Boys

First Preview: October 4, 2005. Opened: November 6, 2005.
Still running as of May 31, 2007.

PLAYBILL

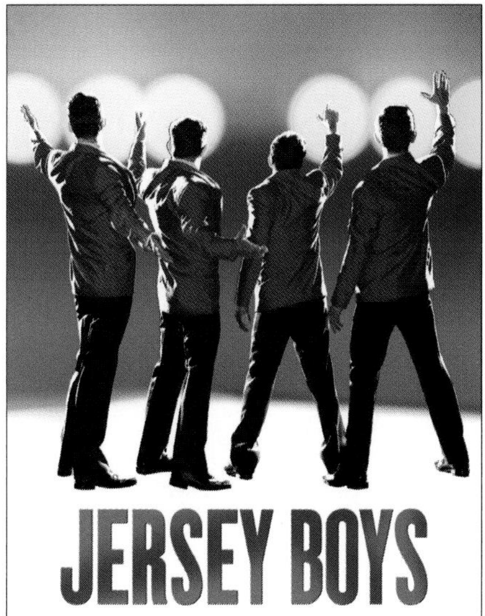

AUGUST WILSON THEATRE
A JUJAMCYN THEATRE
ROCCO LANDESMAN
PRESIDENT

PAUL LIBIN
PRODUCING DIRECTOR

JACK VIERTEL
CREATIVE DIRECTOR

Dodger Theatricals Joseph J. Grano Pelican Group Tamara and Kevin Kinsella
in association with Latitude Link Rick Steiner/Osher/Staton/Bell/Mayerson Group

present

JERSEY BOYS

The Story of Frankie Valli & The Four Seasons

Book by
Marshall Brickman & Rick Elice

Music by
Bob Gaudio

Lyrics by
Bob Crewe

with

Christian Hoff Daniel Reichard J. Robert Spencer and John Lloyd Young

Kris Coleman Ken Dow Heather Ferguson Steve Gouveia Donnie Kehr
John Leone Michael Longoria Jennifer Naimo Dominic Nolfi Joe Payne
Erica Piccininni Sara Schmidt Matthew Scott with Peter Gregus and Mark Lotito

Scenic Design
Klara Zieglerova

Costume Design
Jess Goldstein

Lighting Design
Howell Binkley

Sound Design
Steve Canyon Kennedy

Projection Design
Michael Clark

Wig and Hair Design
Charles LaPointe

Fight Director
Steve Rankin

Production Stage Manager
Richard Hester

Orchestrations
Steve Orich

Music Coordinator
John Miller

Technical Supervisor
Peter Fulbright

East Coast Casting
Tara Rubin Casting

West Coast Casting
Sharon Bialy C.S.A.
Sherry Thomas C.S.A.

Company Manager
Sandra Carlson

Associate Producers
Lauren Mitchell
Rhoda Mayerson
Stage Entertainment

Executive Producer
Sally Campbell Morse

Promotions
HHC Marketing

Press Representative
Boneau/Bryan-Brown

Music Direction, Vocal Arrangements & Incidental Music
Ron Melrose

Choreography
Sergio Trujillo

Directed by
Des McAnuff

World Premiere Produced by La Jolla Playhouse, La Jolla, CA
Des McAnuff, Artistic Director & Steven B. Libman, Managing Director

The producers wish to thank Theatre Development Fund for its support of this production.

LIVE BROADWAY

10/2/06

CAST

(in alphabetical order)

French Rap Star, Detective One, Hal Miller, Barry Belson, Police Officer, Davis (and others) .... KRIS COLEMAN
Stanley, Hank Majewski, Crewe's PA, Joe Long (and others) .... STEVE GOUVEIA
Bob Crewe (and others) .... PETER GREGUS
Tommy DeVito .... CHRISTIAN HOFF
Nick DeVito, Stosh, Billy Dixon, Norman Waxman, Charlie Calello (and others) .... DONNIE KEHR
Joey, Recording Studio Engineer (and others) .... MICHAEL LONGORIA
Gyp DeCarlo (and others) .... MARK LOTITO
Mary Delgado, Angel (and others) .... JENNIFER NAIMO
Church Lady, Miss Frankie Nolan, Bob's Party Girl, Angel, Lorraine (and others) .... ERICA PICCININNI
Bob Gaudio .... DANIEL REICHARD
Frankie's Mother, Nick's Date, Angel, Francine (and others) ... SARA SCHMIDT
Nick Massi .... J. ROBERT SPENCER
Frankie Valli .... JOHN LLOYD YOUNG

Thugs .... KEN DOW, JOE PAYNE

Continued on next page

(L-R): John Lloyd Young, Daniel Reichard, Christian Hoff and J. Robert Spencer as The Four Seasons.

Photo by Joan Marcus

MUSICAL NUMBERS

ACT ONE

"Ces Soirées-La (Oh What a Night)" – Paris, 2000 .... French Rap Star, Backup Group
"Silhouettes" .... Tommy DeVito, Nick Massi, Nick DeVito, Frankie Castelluccio
"You're the Apple of My Eye" .... Tommy DeVito, Nick Massi, Nick DeVito
"I Can't Give You Anything But Love" .... Frankie Castelluccio
"Earth Angel" .... Tommy DeVito, Full Company
"Sunday Kind of Love" .... Frankie Valli, Tommy DeVito, Nick Massi, Nick's Date
"My Mother's Eyes" .... Frankie Valli
"I Go Ape" .... The Four Lovers
"(Who Wears) Short Shorts" .... The Royal Teens
"I'm in the Mood for Love/Moody's Mood for Love" .... Frankie Valli
"Cry for Me" .... Bob Gaudio, Frankie Valli, Tommy DeVito, Nick Massi
"An Angel Cried" .... Hal Miller and The Rays
"I Still Care" .... Miss Frankie Nolan and The Romans
"Trance" .... Billy Dixon and The Topix
"Sherry" .... The Four Seasons
"Big Girls Don't Cry" .... The Four Seasons
"Walk Like a Man" .... The Four Seasons
"December, 1963 (Oh What a Night)" .... Bob Gaudio, Full Company
"My Boyfriend's Back" .... The Angels
"My Eyes Adored You" .... Frankie Valli, Mary Delgado, The Four Seasons
"Dawn (Go Away)" .... The Four Seasons
"Walk Like a Man" (reprise) .... Full Company

ACT TWO

"Big Man in Town" .... The Four Seasons
"Beggin'" .... The Four Seasons
"Stay" .... Bob Gaudio, Frankie Valli, Nick Massi
"Let's Hang On (To What We've Got)" .... Bob Gaudio, Frankie Valli
"Opus 17 (Don't You Worry 'Bout Me)" .... Bob Gaudio, Frankie Valli and The New Seasons
"Bye Bye Baby" .... Frankie Valli and The Four Seasons
"C'mon Marianne" .... Frankie Valli and The Four Seasons
"Can't Take My Eyes Off You" .... Frankie Valli
"Working My Way Back to You" .... Frankie Valli and The Four Seasons
"Fallen Angel" .... Frankie Valli
"Rag Doll" .... The Four Seasons
"Who Loves You" .... The Four Seasons, Full Company

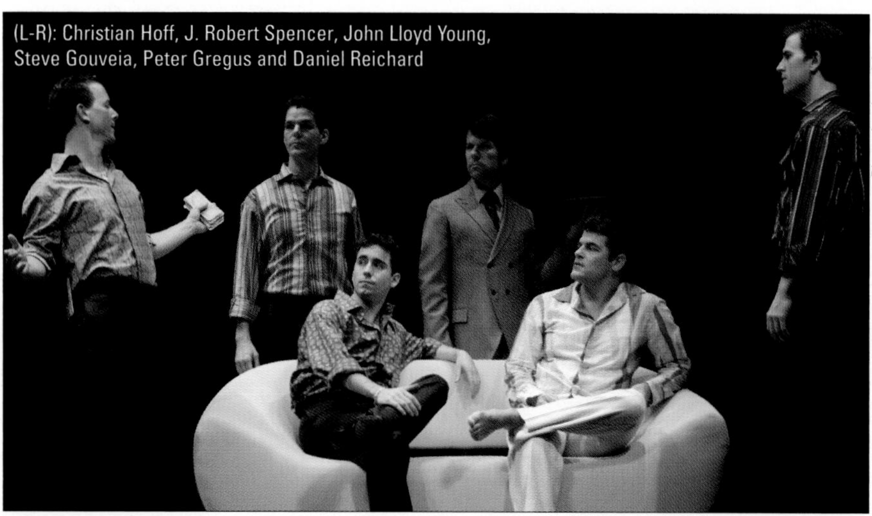
(L-R): Christian Hoff, J. Robert Spencer, John Lloyd Young, Steve Gouveia, Peter Gregus and Daniel Reichard

Photo by Joan Marcus

Cast Continued

UNDERSTUDIES

For Tommy DeVito:
DONNIE KEHR, JOHN LEONE, DOMINIC NOLFI, MATTHEW SCOTT
For Nick Massi:
STEVE GOUVEIA, JOHN LEONE
For Frankie Valli:
MICHAEL LONGORIA, DOMINIC NOLFI, MATTHEW SCOTT
For Bob Gaudio:
STEVE GOUVEIA, DOMINIC NOLFI, MATTHEW SCOTT
For Gyp DeCarlo:
DONNIE KEHR, JOHN LEONE
For Bob Crewe:
DONNIE KEHR, JOHN LEONE

SWINGS

HEATHER FERGUSON, JOHN LEONE, DOMINIC NOLFI, MATTHEW SCOTT

Dance Captain: PETER GREGUS
Assistant Dance Captain: DOMINIC NOLFI

ORCHESTRA

Conductor:
RON MELROSE
Associate Conductor:
DEBORAH N. HURWITZ

Keyboards:
DEBORAH N. HURWITZ, RON MELROSE, STEPHEN "HOOPS" SNYDER
Guitars:
JOE PAYNE
Bass:
KEN DOW
Drums:
KEVIN DOW
Reeds:
MATT HONG, BEN KONO
Trumpet:
DAVID SPIER

Music Coordinator:
JOHN MILLER

Jersey Boys

Christian Hoff
Tommy DeVito

Daniel Reichard
Bob Gaudio

J. Robert Spencer
Nick Massi

John Lloyd Young
Frankie Valli

Peter Gregus
Bob Crewe and others

Mark Lotito
Gyp DeCarlo and others

Kris Coleman
Hal Miller and others

Ken Dow
Thug, Bass

Heather Ferguson
Swing

Steve Gouveia
Hank Majewski and others

Donnie Kehr
Norm Waxman and others

John Leone
Swing

Michael Longoria
Joey and others

Jennifer Naimo
Mary Delgado and others

Dominic Nolfi
Swing

Joe Payne
Thug, Guitars

Erica Piccininni
Lorraine and others

Sara Schmidt
Francine and others

Matthew Scott
Swing

Marshall Brickman
Book

Rick Elice
Book

Bob Gaudio
Composer

Bob Crewe
Lyricist

Des McAnuff
Director

Sergio Trujillo
Choreographer

Ron Melrose
Music Direction, Vocal Arrangements and Incidental Music

Klara Zieglerova
Set Design

Jess Goldstein
Costume Design

Howell Binkley
Lighting Designer

Steve Canyon Kennedy
Sound Design

Steve Rankin
Fight Director

Steve Orich
Orchestrations

John Miller
Music Coordinator

Sharon Bialy and Sherry Thomas
West Coast Casting

Jersey Boys

Tara Rubin,
Tara Rubin Casting
East Coast Casting

Stephen Gabis
Dialect Coach

Michael David,
Dodger Theatricals
Producer

Edward Strong,
Dodger Theatricals
Producer

Rocco Landesman,
Dodger Theatricals
Producer

Ivor Royston,
The Pelican Group
Producer

Ralph Bryan,
Latitude Link
Producer

Tamara and Kevin Kinsella
Producer

Rick Steiner
Producer

John and Bonnie Osher
Producers

Dan Staton
Producer

Marc Bell
Producer

Frederic H. Mayerson
Producer

Lauren Mitchell
Associate Producer

Rhoda Mayerson
Associate Producer

Joop van den Ende,
Stage Entertainment
Associate Producer

Tituss Burgess
French Rap Star, Detective One, Hal Miller, Barry Belson, Police Officer, Davis (and others)

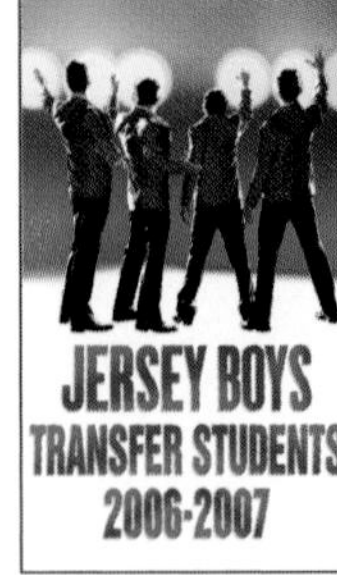

Travis Cloer
Understudy for Frankie Vallie, Joey, Recording Engineer

Colin Donnell
Stanley, Hank Majewski, Crewe's PA, Joe Long (and others)

SOUND ENGINEER
Julie Randolph

DOORMAN
Gustavo Catuy

Photos by Ben Strothmann

HAIR DEPARTMENT
(L-R): John Janas, Hazel Higgins

Jersey Boys

CARPENTRY DEPARTMENT
(L-R): Ronald Fucarino, Bruce Thiel, Peter Wright, Richard Anderson, Daniel Dour and Greg Burton.

Photos by Ben Strothmann

WARDROBE DEPTARTMENT
(Clockwise from lower right): Lee Austin, Nancy Ronan, Kelly Kinsella, Shaun Ozminski, Soomi Marano, Nicholas Staub, Ricky J. Yates and Michelle Sesco.

SOUND & ELECTRIC DEPARTMENT
First Row (L-R): Robert Fehribach, Michael Lyons, Paul Phillips, Jennifer Fagant.

Second Row (L-R): Patrick Ainge, Michael Bogden, Sean Fedigan, Donald Terpstra and David Shepherd.

Jersey Boys

FRONT OF HOUSE
Front Row (L-R): Sally Lettieri, Winny Sekulo, Susie Spillane, Gail Worthman.

Back Row (L-R): Robert Fowler, Russell Saylor, Barbara Kagan, Rose Balsamo, Barbara Hill and Amy Marquez.

PROPS DEPARTMENT
(L-R): Ken Harris, Jr., John Thomson, Emiliano Pares and Scott Mulrain.

Photos by Ben Strothmann

STAGE MANAGEMENT
(L-R): Rachel Wolff, Michelle Bosch and Michael Clarkston.

STAFF FOR *JERSEY BOYS*

GENERAL PRESS REPRESENTATION
BONEAU/BRYAN-BROWN
Adrian Bryan-Brown Susanne Tighe
Heath Schwartz

COMPANY MANAGER
Sandra Carlson

PRODUCTION
STAGE MANAGER ....RICHARD HESTER
Stage Manager ....Michelle Bosch
Assistant Stage Manager ....Michael T. Clarkston
Associate General Manager ....Jennifer F. Vaughan
Technical Supervision ....Tech Production Services/ Peter Fulbright, Mary Duffe, Colleen Houlehen, Lauren A. Duffy
Music Technical Design ....Deborah N. Hurwitz
Assistant Director ....Holly-Anne Ruggiero
Second Assistant Director ....Alex Timbers
Assistant Choreographer ....Kelly Devine
Dialect Coach ....Stephen Gabis
Assistant Company Manager ....Tim Sulka
Fight Captain ....Peter Gregus
Associate Scenic Designers ....Nancy Thun, Todd Ivins
Assistant Scenic Designers ....Sonoka Gozelski, Matthew Myhrum
Associate Costume Designer ....Alejo Vietti
Assistant Costume Designers ....China Lee, Elizabeth Flauto
Associate Lighting Designer ....Patricia Nichols
Assistant Lighting Designer ....Sarah E. C. Maines
Associate Sound Designer ....Andrew Keister
Assistant Projection Designers ....Jason Thompson, Chris Kateff
Story Board Artist ....Don Hudson
Casting Associates ....Dunja Vitolic, Eric Woodall, Laura Schutzel
Casting Assistants Mona Slomsky, Rebecca Carfagna
Automated Lighting Programmer ....Hillary Knox
Projection Programming ....Paul Vershbow
Set Model Builder ....Anne Goelz
Costume Intern ....Jessica Reed
Production Carpenter ....Michael W. Kelly
Deck Automation ....Greg Burton
Fly Automation ....Ron Fucarino
Flyman ....Peter Wright
Production Electrician ....James Fedigan
Head Electrician ....Brian Aman
Assistant Electrician ....Patrick Ainge
Follow Spot Operator ....Sean Fedigan
Production Sound Engineer ....Andrew Keister
Head Sound Engineer ....Julie M. Randolph
Production Props ....Emiliano Pares
Assistant Props ....Kenneth Harris Jr.
Wardrobe Supervisor ....Lee J. Austin
Assistant Wardrobe Supervisor ....Nancy Ronan
Wardrobe Department ....Davis Duffield, Kelly Kinsella, Shaun Ozminski, Nicholas Staub, Jessica Worsnop, Ricky Yates
Hair Supervisor ....Amy Neswald
Hair Assistant ....Craig Kilander
Hair Department ....Frederick G. Waggoner
Assistant to John Miller ....Charles Butler
Synthesizer Programming ....Deborah N. Hurwitz, Steve Orich
Music Copying ....Anixter Rice Music Service
Music Production Assistant ....Alexandra Melrose
Production Assistants ...Kerry McGrath, Michelle Reupert, Bryan Rountree, Deborah Wolfson

Jersey Boys

Dramaturg ....Allison Horsley
Associates to Messrs. Michael David
and Ed Strong.................Pamela Lloyd, James Love
Advertising ....Serino Coyne, Inc./
Scott Johnson, Sandy Block,
Ben Downing, Jean Leonard
Marketing ....Dodger Marketing/
Gordon Kelly, Jessica Ludwig
Promotions ....HHC Marketing/
Hugh Hysell, Michael Redman,
Jim Glaub, Jay Johnson, Amanda Pekoe,
Matt Sicoli, Caitlin Strype
Press Representative Staff..........Chris Boneau, Jim Byk,
Brandi Cornwell, Jackie Green,
Juliana Hannett, Hector Hernandez,
Erin Hinton, Jessica Johnson, Amy Kass,
Kevin Jones, Aaron Meier,
Joe Perrotta, Linnae Petruzzelli,
Matt Polk, Matt Ross
Sponsorship/
Partnership Marketing ....Kobin Enterprises. Ltd.
Banking ....Commerce Bank/Barbara von Borstel
Payroll ....Castellana Services Inc./
Lance Castellana, Norman Seawell,
James Castellana
Accountants ....Schall and Ashenfarb, C.P.A.
Finance Director...........................Paula Maldonado
Insurance ....AON/
Albert G. Rubin Insurance Services, Inc./
George Walden, Claudia Kaufman
Counsel ....Nan Bases, Esq.
Special Events ....John L. Haber
Travel Arrangements ....The "A" Team at Tzell Travel/
Andi Henig
MIS Services ....Rivera Technics: Sam Rivera
Web Design/Maintenance ......Curious Minds Media, Inc.
www.curiousm.com
Production Photographer.......................Joan Marcus
Theatre Displays ....King Displays

DODGERS

Dodger Theatricals

Sandra Carlson, Michael David, John L. Haber, Gordon Kelly, Pamela Lloyd, James Elliot Love, Jessica Ludwig, Paula Maldonado, Lauren Mitchell, Sally Campbell Morse, Samuel Rivera, Maureen Rooney, Bill Schaeffer, Edward Strong, Tim Sulka, Jennifer F. Vaughan

LA JOLLA PLAYHOUSE

Artistic Director ....Des McAnuff
Managing Director.......................Steven B. Libman
Associate Artistic Director ....Shirley Fishman
Literary Manager ....Allison Horsley
General Manager ....Debby Buchholz
Director of Communications................Lendre Kearns
Marketing Manager ....Gigi Cantin
Public Relations Manager ....Jill McIntyre
Director of Finance ....Elizabeth Doran
Director of Operations ....Ellery Brown
Director of Institutional Advancement ....James Forbes
Individual Gifts Officer ....Jill Smayo
Manager, Special Events..........................Mary Reitz
Production Manager ....Peter J. Davis
Company Manager ....Jenny Case
Technical Director............................Chad Woerner
Corporate/Legal Counsel ....Robert C. Wright,
Wright & L'Estrange
Theatre/Legal Counsel ....F. Richard Pappas, Esq.

Dodger Group Sales 1-877-5DODGER
Exclusive Tour Direction ....Dodger Touring, Ltd.

CREDITS

Scenery, show control and automation by ShowMotion, Inc., Norwalk, CT. Lighting equipment from PRG Lighting. Sound equipment by Masque Sound. Projection equipment by Sound Associates. Selected men's clothing custom made by Saint Laurie Merchant Tailors, New York City. Costumes executed by Carelli Costumes, Studio Rouge, Carmen Gee, John Kristiansen New York, Inc. Selected menswear by Carlos Campos. Props provided by The Spoon Group, Downtime Productions, Tessa Dunning. Laundry services provided by Ernest Winzer Theatrical Cleaners. Additional set and hand props courtesy of George Fenmore, Inc. Rosebud matches by Diamond Brands, Inc., Zippo lighters used. Rehearsed at the New 42nd Street Studios. Natural herb cough drops courtesy of Ricola USA, Inc. Emergen-C by Alacer Corporation. PLAYBILL® cover photo by Chris Callis.

www.JerseyBoysBroadway.com

Scenic drops adapted from *George Tice: Urban Landscapes*/W.W. Norton. Other photographs featured are from *George Tice: Selected Photographs 1953–1999*/David R. Godine. (Photographs courtesy of the Peter Fetterman Gallery/Santa Monica.)

SONG CREDITS

"Ces Soirees-La ("Oh What a Night")" (Bob Gaudio, Judy Parker, Yannick Zolo, Edmond David Bacri). Jobete Music Company Inc., Seasons Music Company (ASCAP). **"Silhouettes"** (Bob Crewe, Frank Slay, Jr.), Regent Music Corporation (BMI). **"You're the Apple of My Eye"** (Otis Blackwell), EMI Unart Catalog Inc. (BMI). **"I Can't Give You Anything But Love"** (Dorothy Fields, Jimmy McHugh), EMI April Music Inc., Aldi Music Company, Cotton Club Publishing (ASCAP). **"Earth Angel"** (Jesse Belvin, Curtis Williams, Gaynel Hodge), Embassy Music Corporation (BMI). **"Sunday Kind of Love"** (Barbara Belle, Anita Leanord Nye, Stan Rhodes, Louis Prima), LGL Music Inc./Larry Spier, Inc. (ASCAP). **"My Mother's Eyes"** (Abel Baer, L. Wolfe Gilbert), Abel Baer Music Company, EMI Feist Catalog Inc. (ASCAP). **"I Go Ape"** (Bob Crewe, Frank Slay, Jr.), MPL Music Publishing Inc. (ASCAP). **"(Who Wears) Short Shorts"** (Bob Gaudio, Bill Crandall, Tom Austin, Bill Dalton), EMI Longitude Music, Admiration Music Inc., Third Story Music Inc., and New Seasons Music (BMI). **"I'm in the Mood for Love"** (Dorothy Fields, Jimmy McHugh), Famous Music Corporation (ASCAP). **"Moody's Mood for Love"** (James Moody, Dorothy Fields, Jimmy McHugh), Famous Music Corporation (ASCAP). **"Cry for Me"** (Bob Gaudio), EMI Longitude Music, Seasons Four Music (BMI). **"An Angel Cried"** (Bob Gaudio), EMI Longitude Music (BMI). **"I Still Care"** (Bob Gaudio), Hearts Delight Music, Seasons Four Music (BMI). **"Trance"** (Bob Gaudio), Hearts Delight Music, Seasons Four Music (BMI). **"Sherry"** (Bob Gaudio), MPL Music Publishing Inc. (ASCAP). **"Big Girls Don't Cry"** (Bob Gaudio, Bob Crewe), MPL Music Publishing Inc. (ASCAP). **"Walk Like a Man"** (Bob Crewe, Bob Gaudio), Gavadima Music, MPL Communications Inc. (ASCAP). **"December, 1963 (Oh What a Night)"** (Bob Gaudio, Judy Parker), Jobete Music Company Inc, Seasons Music Company (ASCAP). **"My Boyfriend's Back"** (Robert Feldman, Gerald Goldstein, Richard Gottehrer), EMI Blackwood Music Inc. (BMI). **"My Eyes Adored You"** (Bob Crewe, Kenny Nolan), Jobete Music Company Inc, Kenny Nolan Publishing (ASCAP), Stone Diamond Music Corporation, Tannyboy Music (BMI). **"Dawn, Go Away"** (Bob Gaudio, Sandy Linzer), EMI Full Keel Music, Gavadima Music, Stebojen Music Company (ASCAP). **"Big Man in Town"** (Bob Gaudio), EMI Longitude Music (BMI), Gavadima Music (ASCAP). **"Beggin'"** (Bob Gaudio, Peggy Farina), EMI Longitude Music, Seasons Four Music (BMI). **"Stay"** (Maurice Williams), Cherio Corporation (BMI). **"Let's Hang On (To What We've Got)"** (Bob Crewe, Denny Randell, Sandy Linzer), EMI Longitude Music, Screen Gems-EMI Music Inc., Seasons Four Music (BMI). **"Opus 17 (Don't You Worry 'Bout Me)"** (Denny Randell, Sandy Linzer) Screen Gems-EMI Music Inc, Seasons Four Music (BMI). **"Everybody Knows My Name"** (Bob Gaudio, Bob Crewe), EMI Longitude Music, Seasons Four Music (BMI). **"Bye Bye Baby"** (Bob Crewe, Bob Gaudio), EMI Longitude Music, Seasons Four Music (BMI). **"C'mon Marianne"** (L. Russell Brown, Ray Bloodworth), EMI Longitude Music and Seasons Four Music (BMI). **"Can't Take My Eyes Off You"** (Bob Gaudio, Bob Crewe), EMI Longitude Music, Seasons Four Music (BMI). **"Working My Way Back to You"** (Denny Randell, Sandy Linzer), Screen Gems–EMI Music Inc, Seasons Four Music (BMI). **"Fallen Angel"** (Guy Fletcher, Doug Flett), Chrysalis Music (ASCAP). **"Rag Doll"** (Bob Crewe, Bob Gaudio), EMI Longitude Music (BMI), Gavadima Music (ASCAP). **"Who Loves You?"** (Bob Gaudio, Judy Parker), Jobete Music Company Inc, Seasons Music Company (ASCAP).

SPECIAL THANKS

Peter Bennett, Elliot Groffman, Karen Pals, Janine Smalls, Chad Woerner of La Jolla Playhouse, Alma Malabanan-McGrath and Edward Stallsworth of the New 42nd Street Studios, David Solomon of the Roundabout Theatre Company, Dan Whitten. The authors, director, cast and company of *Jersey Boys* would like to express their love and thanks to Jordan Ressler.

Original cast album now available on Rhino Records.

JUJAMCYN THEATERS

President

PAUL LIBIN Producing Director	**JACK VIERTEL** Creative Director
JERRY ZAKS Resident Director	**JORDAN ROTH** Resident Producer
DANIEL ADAMIAN General Manager	**JENNIFER HERSHEY** Director of Operations

MEREDITH VILLATORE
Chief Financial Officer

STAFF FOR THE AUGUST WILSON THEATRE

Manager ....Matt Fox
Treasurer...Nick Russo
Assistant Manager ....Albert T. Kim
Carpenter...Dan Dour
Propertyman ....Scott Mulrain
Electrician ....Robert Fehribach
Engineer ....Arthur VanSalisbury

Jersey Boys
Scrapbook

Photos by Aubrey Reuben

Correspondent: Daniel Reichard, "Bob Gaudio"
Memorable Guests: We had a great, wild party on the night of the Tony Awards at the Hard Rock Café, which was attended by Frankie Valli, Bob Gaudio and Joe Pesci. We've had backstage visits from Alan Cumming, Cyndi Lauper and Harry Connick Jr.
Favorite Remedies: Pau D'Arco Tea, herbal gargle (myrrh, licorice root and goldenseal) and Simply Saline nasal spray.
Anniversary Party: We had a party at Gallaghers and Rick Elice read a poem about our show. I did a parody of the Circle Game: "The Season Goes Round and Round." Supposedly KFed was there—wow!
"Carols for a Cure" Carol: "O Holy Night."
Special Backstage Rituals: Every Saturday night at five minutes till, we have a screamfest to *Hairspray* across the street. We do a "Hello Broadway" chant and they return it. In the boys' dressing room they do a kickline to "New York, New York."
Favorite Moment During Each Performance: The final number, "Who Loves You," because it's the one time in the show when the whole family of actors is onstage having a great time together.
Favorite Off-Site Hangout: Sunday nights we get together at the Russian Samovar. Our other favorite: Arriba Arriba (predictable).
Cell Phone Issues: We hear beeps and rings all the time. The occasional ring can be amusing, but when you hear the voicemail signal a few minutes later, you get a little peeved. We still have people photographing the show and videotaping the show.
Memorable Stage Door Fan Encounters: Some fans make T-shirts with our pictures on them. Every day at the stage door they let us know how many times they've seen the show. They'll say, "This was number seven for me" or number ten, or number fifteen!
Understudy Anecdotes: Dominic Nolfi and Matthew Scott have both played three of the Four Seasons as well as other roles.Travis Cloer made his Frankie Valli debut on April 25.
Catchphrases Only the Company Would Recognize: "How dare You!" "Mamma's busted." "It's so dry!"
Coolest Thing About Being in This Show: We all believe in it so much. The theme of hard work and persistence keeps every actor inspired to do their very best every single show.
Fan Club: There are various unofficial MySpace sites like www.myspace.com/jerseyboysfans, but no official fan site.

1. (L-R): Michael Longoria, Christian Hoff and J. Robert Spencer at the June 2006 "Broadway under the Stars" event in Central Park.
2. Des McAnuff at the ceremony to have his caricature hung at Sardi's Restaurant.
3. Girlfriend Alison Franck and John Lloyd Young celebrate Young's birthday with the cast at Zanzibar restaurant, July 6, 2006.
4. Young at the 20th Annual Broadway Flea Market & Grand Auction in Shubert Alley September 24, 2006.

Journey's End

First Preview: February 8, 2007. Opened: February 22, 2007.
Still running as of May 31, 2007.

PLAYBILL

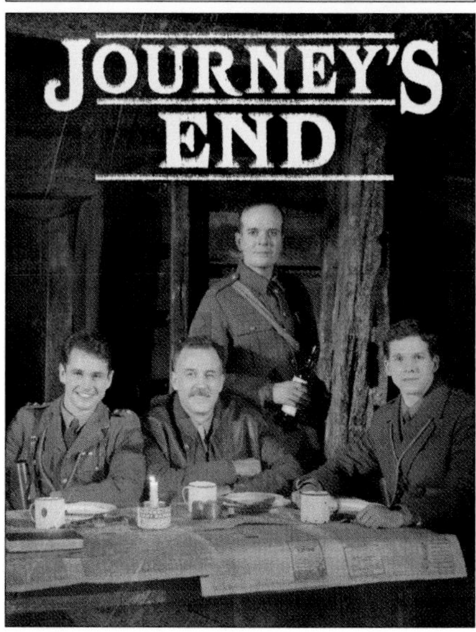

BELASCO THEATRE
111 West 44th Street
A Shubert Organization Theatre
Gerald Schoenfeld, *Chairman* **Philip J. Smith,** *President*
Robert E. Wankel, *Executive Vice President*

BOYETT OSTAR PRODUCTIONS

STEPHANIE P. McCLELLAND **BILL ROLLNICK** **JAMES D'ORTA** **PHILIP GEIER**

present

HUGH DANCY **BOYD GAINES** **JEFFERSON MAYS**

in

JOURNEY'S END

By **R.C. SHERRIFF**

Featuring

JOHN AHLIN **NICK BERG BARNES** **JOHN BEHLMANN**

JUSTIN BLANCHARD **KIERAN CAMPION** **JOHN CURLESS** **RICHARD POE**

and **STARK SANDS** as Raleigh

Casting by **JAY BINDER JACK BOWDAN**
Production Stage Manager **ARTHUR GAFFIN**
Technical Supervisor **LARRY MORLEY**

Marketing **HHC MARKETING**
Press Representation **THE PETE SANDERS GROUP**
General Management **ALAN WASSER ALLAN WILLIAMS**

Scenic & Costume Design **JONATHAN FENSOM**
Lighting Design **JASON TAYLOR**
Sound Design **GREGORY CLARKE**

Directed by
DAVID GRINDLEY

Originally produced in London by Background Productions
The producers wish to express their appreciation to Theatre Development Fund for its support of this production.

2/22/07

CAST

(in order of appearance)

Captain Hardy .... JOHN CURLESS
Lieutenant Osborne .... BOYD GAINES
Private Mason .... JEFFERSON MAYS
2nd Lieutenant Raleigh .... STARK SANDS
Captain Stanhope .... HUGH DANCY
2nd Lieutenant Trotter .... JOHN AHLIN
Private Albert Brown .... JOHN BEHLMANN
2nd Lieutenant Hibbert .... JUSTIN BLANCHARD
Sergeant Major .... JOHN CURLESS
Colonel .... RICHARD POE
German Soldier.................. KIERAN CAMPION
Lance Corporal Broughton .. NICK BERG BARNES

THE SCENE

A dugout in the British trenches near St. Quentin, France

ACT I

Evening on Monday, March 18, 1918

ACT II

Scene 1: Tuesday morning
Scene 2: Tuesday afternoon

ACT III

Scene 1: Wednesday afternoon
Scene 2: Wednesday night
Scene 3: Thursday, towards dawn

Continued on next page

Hugh Dancy as Captain Stanhope and Stark Sands as 2nd Lieutenant Raleigh.

Photo by Paul Kolnik

Journey's End

NOTES FROM THE DIRECTOR

It is remarkable that *Journey's End* was ever produced. In 1928 an insurance agent from the suburbs, R.C. Sherriff, sent out his manuscript to as many producers as he could; none of them wanted to take up the project. The First World War had ended only ten years previously, and everyone knew somebody who had either been killed or wounded in the conflict that had claimed 770,000 British lives and injured three million others. The total losses suffered by the participating countries numbered 10 million. Not surprisingly, the subject was considered too painful to address in the theatre.

Against the odds, the Incorporated Stage Society was prepared to give the play two staged readings in November at the Apollo Theatre in London's West End, directed by the novice James Whale. In this first outing, an unknown Laurence Olivier played the lead role of Stanhope. Despite the tremendous reaction by press and public alike, the commercial producers would still not risk mounting the play. They said that having an all male cast, recreating an underground dugout as the set and using the war as the story's backdrop posed too many problems.

It took a maverick like Maurice Browne to make it happen. Returning to England in penury after failing to set Chicago alight with his classical productions, Browne was determined to make his mark. Fortunately he made the acquaintance of the Elmhirsts, a couple who were renowned arts lovers and philanthropists. They agreed to fund a production of any play that Browne wanted, irrespective of its commercial appeal. It did not matter to them if they lost their investment; in retrospect Sherriff thought the Elmhirsts wanted to show that the public's taste was more sophisticated than it was given credit for. Despite his reservations about Browne, Sherriff agreed to his offer of a production as long as the originating cast members were invited to appear in the fully-fledged production. Only Olivier was unable to return, since he had signed up for a production of *Beau Geste*, so Colin Clive replaced him.

The omens were not good for the opening night at the Savoy Theatre on January 21, 1929. Regretfully, the box office manager informed Sherriff that with no advance sales the production's chances were slim. Even when the first reviews appeared, ticket sales remained slow. It was only after word of mouth started spreading that *Journey's End* became popular: within days every performance was sold out. By the end of the year there were 14 productions in English, including one on Broadway, and 17 in translation around Europe. The play proved a cathartic experience for a generation. Sherriff's audiences recognized the authenticity of his characters, inspired by the men who had served beside him in the 9th East Surrey Regiment.

The production transformed the lives of those who created it. Sherriff became a full-time writer, penning British cinema classics like *Goodbye, Mr. Chips*; *The Four Feathers*; and *The Dam Busters*. James Whale and Colin Clive came to Hollywood as director and star of *Frankenstein*. Always following his heart, Maurice Browne never managed to repeat the success of *Journey's End*, enduring a string of failures and ending his life in poverty once more. Reflecting the experience of the original, this production was only meant to play the West End for eight weeks, but ended up staying 18 months. After a gap of more than 70 years, I'm delighted that *Journey's End* is returning to Broadway at the Belasco Theatre.

— David Grindley

Cast Continued

UNDERSTUDIES

For Stanhope, German Soldier, Broughton:
JOHN BEHLMANN
For Osborne:
RICHARD POE
For Mason, Colonel:
JOHN CURLESS
For Raleigh, Hibbert, Albert, Broughton:
KIERAN CAMPION
For Hardy, Sergeant Major, Trotter:
NICK BERG BARNES

Hugh Dancy is appearing with the permission of Actors' Equity Association pursuant to an exchange program between American Equity and UK Equity.

An alternate cover used during previews.

Hugh Dancy
Captain Stanhope

Boyd Gaines
Lieutenant Osborne

Jefferson Mays
Private Mason

Stark Sands
2nd Lieutenant Raleigh

John Ahlin
2nd Lieutenant Trotter

Nick Berg Barnes
Lance Corporal Broughton

John Behlmann
Private Albert Brown

Justin Blanchard
Hibbert

Kieran Campion
German Soldier

John Curless
Captain Hardy, Sergeant Major

Journey's End

Richard Poe
Colonel

David Grindley
Director

Jonathan Fensom
Set and Costume Designer

Jay Binder C.S.A.
Casting

Jack Bowdan C.S.A.
Casting

Alan Wasser Associates
General Manager

The Pete Sanders Group
Press Representative

Hugh Hysell, HHC Marketing
Marketing

Bill Haber/ OSTAR Enterprises
Producer

Bob Boyett
Producer

Stephanie P. McClelland
Producer

2006-2007 AWARDS

Tony Award
Best Revival of a Play

NY Drama Critics' Circle Award
Special Citation (The Ensemble)

Outer Critics Circle Awards
Outstanding Revival of a Play
Outstanding Featured Actor in a Play (Boyd Gaines)

Drama League Award
Distinguished Revival of a Play

Drama Desk Awards
Outstanding Revival of a Play
Outstanding Featured Actor in a Play (Boyd Gaines)
Outstanding Sound Design (Gregory Clarke)

Theatre World Award
Outstanding Broadway Debut (Stark Sands)

Photos by Ben Strothmann

STAGE MANAGERS & COMPANY MANAGER
(L-R): David Sugarman (Stage Manager), Penelope Daulton (Company Manager), Arthur Gaffin (Production Stage Manager)

STAGE CREW
Front Row (L-R): Penelope Daulton (Company Manager), Arthur Gaffin (Production Stage Manager).

Second Row (L-R): Joe Moritz (House Flyman), Kay Grunder (Wardrobe Supervisor), David Sugarman (Stage Manager).

Third Row (L-R): Susan Goulet (House Electrician), Jeff McGovney (Dresser), Eric Castaldo (Production Props).

Back Row (L-R): Tucker Howard (Production Sound), Heidi Brown (House Props) and George Dummitt (House Carpenter).

Journey's End

WARDROBE
(L-R): Jeff McGovney (Dresser) and Kay Grunder (Wardrobe Supervisor).

Photos by Ben Strothmann

FRONT OF HOUSE STAFF
Front Row (L-R): Dexter Luke, unknown, Elisabel Ascensio
Back Row (L-R): Eugenia Raines, Meaghan McElroy, Marissa Gioffre, Gwen Coley, Eileen Kinberg and Kathy Dunn.

STAFF FOR *JOURNEY'S END*

GENERAL MANAGEMENT
ALAN WASSER ASSOCIATES
Alan Wasser Allan Williams
Aaron Lustbader Connie Chong

GENERAL PRESS REPRESENTATIVE
THE PETE SANDERS GROUP
Pete Sanders Glenna Freedman

CASTING
JAY BINDER CASTING
Jay Binder CSA
Jack Bowdan CSA, Mark Brandon, Megan Larche
Assistants: Nikole Vallins, Allison Estrin

COMPANY MANAGER
PENELOPE DAULTON

PRODUCTION STAGE MANAGER
ARTHUR GAFFIN

U.S. TECHNICAL SUPERVISOR
LARRY MORLEY

UK TECHNICAL SUPERVISOR
THE PRODUCTION DESK, LTD.
Paul Hennessy

Stage Manager .....David Sugarman
Dialect Coach .....Majella Hurley
Fight Director .....Thomas Schall
Fight Captain .....John Behlmann
Scenic Artist .....James Rowse at Decorative Arts Project, Ltd.
Scenic Drop Artwork .....Alasdair Oliver
House Carpenter .....George Dummitt
House Flyman .....Joe Moritz
House Electrician .....Susan Goulet
Electrician .....Neil McShane
House Props .....Heidi Brown
Production Props .....Eric J. Castaldo
UK Props Supervisor .....Fahmida Bakht
Production Sound .....Tucker Howard
Sound .....Brien Brannigan
UK Wardrobe Consultant .....Charlotte Bird
US Wardrobe Consultant .....Patrick Bevilacqua
Wardrobe Supervisor .....Kay Grunder
Dresser .....Jeff McGovney

Production Photographer .....Paul Kolnik
Logo & Artwork Design .....Frank "Fraver" Verlizzo
Advertising .....Eliran Murphy Group Ltd./ Jon Bierman, Frank Verlizzo
Marketing .....HHC Communications Hugh Hysell, Michael Redman
Website Design .....Carrie Schoenfeld
Legal Counsel .....Lazarus & Harris LLP/ Scott Lazarus, Esq., Robert C. Harris, Esq.
Accounting .....Rosenberg, Neuwirth & Kuchner/ Chris Cacace, Pat Pedersen
Assistants to Mr. Haber .....Theresa Pisanelli, Andrew Cleghorn
Associate Producer for Ostar Enterprises .....Rachel Neuburger
Assistant to Mr. Boyett .....Diane Murphy
General Management Office .....Christopher Betz, Jason Hewitt, Jake Hirzel, Patty Montesi, Jennifer Mudge
Press Assistant .....Katie Kirby
Production Assistant .....Mary Kathryn Flynt
Insurance .....Ventura Insurance Brokerage/ Janice Brown
Banking .....City National Bank/ Anne McSweeney
Payroll .....Castellana Services, Inc.
Merchandising .....Max Merchandising/ Randi Grossman
Travel Services .....Road Rebel Entertainment Touring
Housing Services .....Premier Relocation Services/ Christine Sodikoff
Opening Night Coordination .....Tobak Lawrence Company/ Suzanne Tobak, Michael P. Lawrence
Group Sales .....Telecharge.com Group Sales (212) 239-6262

www.journeysendonbroadway.com

CREDITS AND ACKNOWLEDGEMENTS

Set built by Set-up Scenery Ltd. Automation by Hudson Scenic Studios. Lighting equipment provided by PRG Lighting. Sound equipment provided by PRG Audio. Period uniforms and hand props by Khaki Devil Ltd. and Western Costume Company. Yarn supplied by Andrea at Seaport Yarn, NYC and Portland, ME. Knitting by Margiann Flanagan, Phillip Rolfe, Penny Daulton and Susan Lyons. Moustaches by Ryan P. McWilliams. Select military accessories provided by Kaufman's Army & Navy. Weaponry provided by Weapons Specialist. Natural herb cough drops courtesy of Ricola USA, Inc. Emergen-C super energy booster provided by Alacer Corp.

Special thanks to Max Arthur,
Author of "Forgotten Voices of the Great War."

House Manager .....Carol Flemming

Journey's End

SCRAPBOOK

Photo by Aubrey Reuben

Artwork by John Behlmann

Left: Curtain call on opening night.
Right: Parody poster of *Journey's End: The Musical* designed by John Behlmann.

Correspondent: Justin Blanchard, "2nd Lieutenant Hibbert"

Opening Night Gifts: Two great posters of musical parodies of *Journey's End* from John Behlmann (*Journey's End: The Musical*) and Nick Berg Barnes (*Hullo, Stanhope: A Whizzbang Musical Romance*). Also, a do-it-yourself survival kit containing a compass (Boyd Gaines), Zippo (Nick Berg Barnes), and Swiss Army Knife (Stark Sands).

Most Exciting Celebrity Visitor: Claire Danes. Rumor has it she's been seen around town canoodling with someone in the cast!

Special Backstage Rituals: John Curless' "Alright, chaps, see you on the Green" before every show. Listening to the cast do the vocal warm-up that our dialect coach, Majella Hurley, left for us to do. Thank goodness hunting season is over.

Jeff placing mud on everyone's boots followed by a good spraying down with a Hudson.

Favorite Off-Site Hangout: St. Andrew's Scotch Bar or Café Un Deux Trois.

Favorite In-Theatre Gathering Place: The greenroom. Who knows what kind of candy or cookies lurk inside the war chest?

Favorite Snack Food: Any food left in the greenroom is usually devoured by the end of the show.

Memorable Ad-Libs: "Shanks are legs!" "Trotter, I mean Mason." "Dennis, I mean Jimmy." "Stanhope, I mean Hibbert."

Cell Phone Issues: One really long set of rings at one of the quietest moments of the play (when Stanhope is collecting the items left behind by the recently killed Osborne). An audience member finally told the patron to "Turn the damn thing off!"

Ghostly Encounter: John Ahlin, Justin Blanchard, Nick Berg Barnes and other members of the company saw the ghost of David Belasco walk across the balcony during the curtain call.

Latest Audience Arrival: The show looks as if it's lit by candlelight. A latecomer decided to use her own flashlight to help her find the first row seat and shone her flashlight all over the stage.

Busiest Day at the Box Office: We're still waiting for it.

Best Onstage Aroma: The smell of Boyd Gaines' cherry pipe tobacco.

Worst Onstage Aroma: The smell of cigars (just ask Heidi).

Embarrassing Moment: Before we started rehearsing, our producer, Bill Haber, invited the company to a wonderful dinner at Trattoria Dell'Arte. Someone, who shall remain nameless, asked to be introduced to the playwright, R.C. Sherriff. Mr. Sherriff died on November 13, 1975 and was therefore unable to attend the dinner.

Coolest Thing About Being in This Show: To see the effect of the lack of a traditional curtain call on an audience.

Favorite Moment During Each Performance: When the audience decides to clap when the curtain rises on our final tableau.

An Amazing Fan Letter: In a letter addressed to the cast, the fans recount trying to summon the strength to give a standing ovation. The note is a relentless apology for their "shell-shock" and not knowing if it was OK to stand. However, their "hearts [did] stand up."

Memorable Directorial Notes/Company In-Jokes:
"The Little Show That Could." "OK, gents, let's just give it a trotty trot from the toppy top." "Softly, Softly Catch the Monkey." "Grace note."
"Notette." "I've given you a bit of a bum steer." "Questions? Queries?" "Are you all right?"

Easter Bonnet Skit: "*Journey's End, The Musical*," conceived, written, and designed by: John Ahlin, Nick Berg Barnes, John Behlmann and Kay Gruder. The Journey Boys were Nick Berg Barnes, John Behlmann, Justin Blanchard, Kieran Campion, and Stark Sands. Richard Poe played General Patton and John Ahlin wore the Bonnet. Winner "best bonnet presentation."

Nicknames: Starky!, Dirty Dancy, Little Ricky Poe, Ahly, Gutterballs, Grindley, RT, Shugs, and The Wonder Pony.

Highest Score on the *Journey's End* "The Play's the Thing" Quiz: George Dummitt.

Lowest Score on the *Journey's End* "The Play's the Thing" Quiz: Jeff McGovney. (His dog ate it.)

Amount of Money Tucker (Sound) Charges for a Nude Portrait: He'll pay you.

Why an Audience Should See *Journey's End* Multiple Times: To hear John Ahlin's variations on the theme of "There's a Long, Long Trail A-Windin'."

Favorite *Journey's End* Moments: "Early in rehearsals—a Grindley oral essay with pictures on Minnies and Trench Mortars. Pictures included a smiling Grindley. All was serious and workmanlike till Dancy asked, 'Who's the prat?' thus establishing his irreverent *bona fides* and giving us our first (of many) belly laughs." —Richard Poe

"One night I inhaled an unusually large dose of puddle water, jarring something loose deep inside my brain. I performed the rest of the scene with three inches of snot dangling from my nose." —Kieran Campion

"During rehearsal when General Grindley, while searching for a response to one of Hugh's challenges, set the world record for consecutive 'Ers' in a sentence." —Stark Sands

"When the producer called everyone to a post-show meeting and told us 'We won't get through May'—and then we realized it was April Fool's Day!!" —Artie Gaffin

Another Coolest Thing About Being in This Show: Camaraderie.

Kiki & Herb: Alive on Broadway

First Preview: August 11, 2006. Opened: August 15, 2006.
Closed: September 10, 2006 after 5 Previews and 27 Performances.

PLAYBILL

THE HELEN HAYES THEATRE
MARTIN MARKINSON DONALD TICK

David J. Foster Jared Geller Ruth Hendel Jonathan Reinis, Inc. Billy Zavelson Jamie Cesa Anne Strickland Squadron Jennifer Manocherian
in association with
Gary Allen Melvin Honowitz

present

KIKI & HERB
ALIVE ON BROADWAY

created and executed by
Justin Bond and Kenny Mellman

Scenic Design Scott Pask
Lighting Design Jeff Croiter
Costume Design Marc Happel
Sound Design Brett Jarvis

Publicity/Marketing The Karpel Group
Company Manager Josh Lowenthal

General Management Foster Entertainment
Production Management Aurora Productions
Production Stage Manager Peter Hanson

8/15/06

CAST
(in alphabetical order)

Kiki .... JUSTIN BOND
Herb .... KENNY MELLMAN

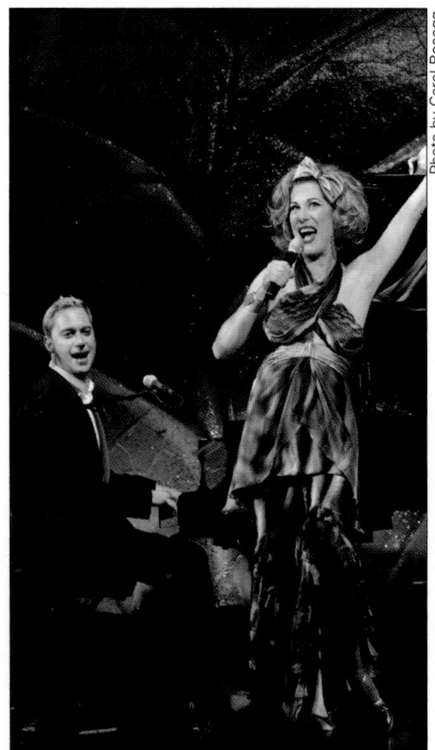
Photo by Carol Rosegg

(L-R): Kenny Mellman and Justin Bond

Justin Bond
Kiki

Kenny Mellman
Herb

Scott Pask
Set Design

Jeff Croiter
Lighting Designer

Kiki & Herb: Alive on Broadway

Bridget Klapinski, The Karpel Group
Publicity & Marketing

Ruth Hendel
Producer

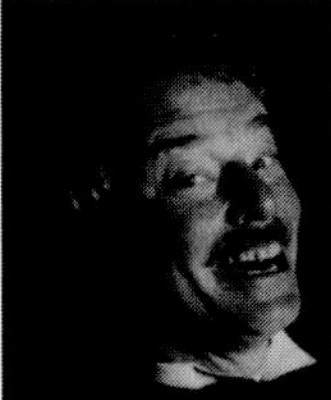
Jonathan Reinis, Inc.
Producer

Billy Zavelson
Producer

Jennifer Manocherian
Producer

Gary Allen
Associate Producer

Melvin D. Honowitz
Associate Producer

BOX OFFICE
(L-R):
Andrew Chen (Assistant Box Office Treasurer) and Chuck Stuis (Assistant Box Office Treasurer)

Not Pictured:
David Heveran (Box Office Treasurer)

Photos by Ben Strothmann

FRONT OF HOUSE STAFF
Front Row (L-R): Harry Joshi (Usher), Alan Markinson (House Manager) holding Daisy, C.J. Gelfand (Usher), Rita Sussman (Usher), Linda Maley (Ticket-Taker), Berd Vaval (Ticket-Taker).
Back Row (L-R): Chuck Stuis (Assistant Box Office Treasurer), John Biancamano (Head Usher), Yuri Ivanov (Usher), Ron Johnson (Usher), Robert LoBiondo (Usher), Natasha Thomas (Usher).

Kiki & Herb: Alive on Broadway

Photo by Ben Strothmann

CAST & CREW
Sitting (L-R):
Gary Allen (Producer), Kenny Mellman (Herb), Justin Bond (Kiki DuRane), Robert Etter (Sound), Peter Hanson (Production Stage Manager)

Standing (L-R):
Jamie Cesa (Producer), Marc Happel (Costume Designer), Jennifer Malloy (Wardrobe), Josh Lowenthal (Company Manager), Dan Novi (Spotlight), Joseph Beck (Head Electrician), Bridget Klapinski (Press)

Perched on top of Piano: Daisy (Immortal Cow)

STAFF FOR ***KIKI & HERB: ALIVE ON BROADWAY***

GENERAL MANAGEMENT
Foster Entertainment

COMPANY MANAGER
Josh Lowenthal

GENERAL PRESS REPRESENTATIVE
THE KARPEL GROUP
Bridget Klapinski/Billy Zavelson

PRODUCTION MANAGEMENT
AURORA PRODUCTIONS, INC
Gene O'Donovan, W. Benjamin Heller II, Bethany Weinstein, Tuesday Curran, Melissa Mazdra

Production Stage Manager ....Peter Hanson
Wardrobe Coordinator ....Jennifer Malloy
Assistant Scenic Designer ....Jeffrey Hinchee
Assistant Lighting Designer ....Joel Silver
Assistant to Mr. Croiter ....Grant W.S. Yeager
Head Property Man ....Roger Keller
Head Carpenter ....Doug Purcell
Head Electrician ....Joseph Beck
Sound Technician ....Robert Etter
Follow Spot Operator ....Dan Novi
Lighting equipment provided by ....GSD Productions
Sound equipment provided by ....One Dream Sound
Props provided by ....Scenic Art Studios and Cigar Box Studio

Banking ....Citibank
Accountant ....Sarah P. Galbraith
Payroll ....Lance Castellana/ Castellana Services, Inc.
Insurance ......C&S International Insurance Brokers, Inc./ Debra Kozec, Iris Lugo
Advertising ....Eliran Murphy Group/ Barbara Eliran, Steve Knight, Betsy Gershaw
Marketing ....The Karpel Group/ Craig Karpel, Marc Mannino, Vinny Moschetta, Kurt Bauccio
Publicity Assistant ....Randy Rainbow
Video Production ....Sniper Films/ Chris Gallagher, Matt Gallagher
Photography ....Joe Oppedisano
Production Photographer ....Carol Rosegg
Poster Art ....Billy Mitchell
Additional Marketing ....dlist.com
Web Design ....kitmetro.com

Makeup provided by M•A•C Cosmetics.

FOSTER ENTERTAINMENT

Director ....David J. Foster
Executive Producer ....Jared Geller
General Manager ....Sally Gibson
Project Manager ....Robyn Sunderland
Development ....Kim Miner
Accounts ....David Reynolds
Associate ....Jay Riedl
Associate ....Lucy Foster
Office Manager ....Emerald Brooke

SPECIAL THANKS

Madame Tussauds, Drew Elliott, Meryl Scheinman, Gary Rausenberger, David Herriman, MCT Bold, Barry Taylor, Paula Quijano, Sniper Films, Chris Gallagher, Matt Gallagher, Michaline Babich, Wilma Theater, Rufus Wainwright, Brent Peek Productions, The Phoenix, Daniel Nardicio, Cowgirl Hall of Fame, Snowshow, Spiegelworld, The Shubert Organization, Victoria Leacock, Stephen Hendel, The Knitting Factory, Carnegie Hall

THE HELEN HAYES THEATRE
owned and operated by
MARTIN MARKINSON and DONALD TICK

General Manager ....SUSAN S. MYERBERG
Associate General Manager ....Sharon Fallon
General Management Intern ....Abigail Hardin

STAFF FOR THE HELEN HAYES THEATRE
HOUSE MANAGER ....ALAN R. MARKINSON
Treasurer ....David Heveran
Assistant Treasurers ....Chuck Stuis, Andrew Chen
Engineer ....Hector Angulo
Head Usher ....John Biancamano
Stage Door ....Robert Seymour, Jon Angulo
Accountant ....Chen-Win Hsu, CPA., P.C.

Kiki & Herb: Alive on Broadway

Scrapbook

Photos by Aubrey Reuben

Correspondent: Kenny Mellman, "Herb"
Memorable Opening Night Note: A congratulations from Valerie Cherish (Lisa Kudrow's character from "The Comeback").
Opening Night Gifts: Lots and lots of champagne!
Most Exciting Celebrity Visitors: Anne Meara and Jerry Stiller. Both amazing. No words can say....
"Carols for a Cure" Carol: "Like a Snowman" by Stephin Merritt.
Special Backstage Ritual: Watching the Bea Arthur special on a projector between the matinee and evening performances.
Favorite In-Theatre Gathering Place: The greenroom.
Favorite Off-Site Hangout: Angus McIndoe.
Favorite Snack Food: Dark chocolate.
Mascot: Daisy the Cow.
Record Number of Cell Phone Rings, Cell Phone Photos or Texting Incidents During a Performance: 6.
Coolest Thing About Being in This Show: We actually played Broadway!

1. Justin Bond (L) and Kenny Mellman at the opening night party at the Time Hotel.
2. Bond and Mellman take a curtain call on opening night.
3. Guest Deborah Harry mugs for the camera at the Time Hotel.
4. (L-R): Guests The World Famous Bob and Murray Hill arrive at the Helen Hayes Theatre on opening night.
5. Deborah Harry (third from left) and friends arrive for the opening.

Legally Blonde

First Preview: April 3, 2007. Opened: April 29, 2007.
Still running as of May 31, 2007.

PLAYBILL

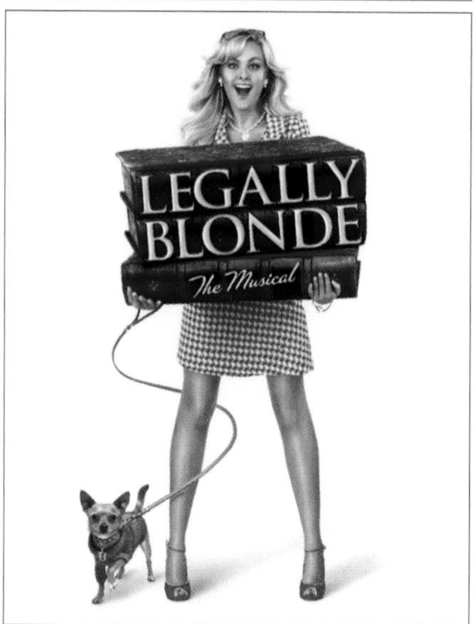

~N~ PALACE THEATRE

UNDER THE DIRECTION OF
STEWART F. LANE, JAMES M. NEDERLANDER AND JAMES L. NEDERLANDER

Hal Luftig Fox Theatricals Dori Berinstein

James L. Nederlander Independent Presenters Network Roy Furman Amanda Lipitz
Broadway Asia Barbara Whitman FWPM Group Hendel/Wiesenfeld
Goldberg/Binder Stern/Meyer Lane/Comley Bartner-Jenkins/Nocciolino
and Warren Trepp

In Association with MGM ON STAGE  Darcie Denkert and Dean Stolber

Present

LEGALLY BLONDE *The Musical*

Music and Lyrics by
LAURENCE O'KEEFE and NELL BENJAMIN

Book by
HEATHER HACH

BASED UPON THE NOVEL BY AMANDA BROWN
and THE METRO-GOLDWYN-MAYER MOTION PICTURE

Starring
LAURA BELL BUNDY
CHRISTIAN BORLE ORFEH
RICHARD H. BLAKE KATE SHINDLE NIKKI SNELSON
and MICHAEL RUPERT

With
ANNALEIGH ASHFORD APRIL BERRY PAUL CANAAN LINDSAY NICOLE CHAMBERS BETH CURRY
TRACY JAI EDWARDS AMBER EFÉ GAELEN GILLILAND JASON GILLMAN BECKY GULSVIG
ROD HARRELSON MANUEL HERRERA NATALIE JOY JOHNSON ANDY KARL NICK KENKEL
MICHELLE KITTRELL LESLIE KRITZER DeQUINA MOORE RUSTY MOWERY KEVIN PARISEAU
MATTHEW RISCH JASON PATRICK SANDS NOAH WEISBERG KATE WETHERHEAD

Produced for Fox Theatricals by
KRISTIN CASKEY and MIKE ISAACSON

Scenic Design
DAVID ROCKWELL

Costume Design
GREGG BARNES

Lighting Design
KEN POSNER & PAUL MILLER

Sound Design
ACME SOUND PARTNERS

Casting
TELSEY + COMPANY

Hair Design
DAVID BRIAN BROWN

Associate Director
MARC BRUNI

Associate Choreographer
DENIS JONES

Technical Supervisor
SMITTY/THEATERSMITH, INC.

Animal Trainer
WILLIAM BERLONI

Production Stage Manager
BONNIE L. BECKER

General Management
NLA/MAGGIE BROHN

Press Representative
BARLOW•HARTMAN

Marketing
TMG-THE MARKETING GROUP

Associate Producers
PMC PRODUCTIONS
YASUHIRO KAWANA
ANDREW ASNES/ADAM ZOTOVICH

Music Director/Conductor
JAMES SAMPLINER

Orchestrations
CHRISTOPHER JAHNKE

Arrangements
LAURENCE O'KEEFE & JAMES SAMPLINER

Music Contractor
MICHAEL KELLER

Directed and Choreographed by
JERRY MITCHELL

4/29/07

CAST

Elle Woods .... LAURA BELL BUNDY
Warner Huntington III .... RICHARD H. BLAKE
Vivienne Kensington .... KATE SHINDLE
Emmett Forrest .... CHRISTIAN BORLE
Professor Callahan .... MICHAEL RUPERT
Paulette .... ORFEH
Serena .... LESLIE KRITZER
Margot .... ANNALEIGH ASHFORD
Pilar .... DeQUINA MOORE
Shandi/Brooke Wyndham .... NIKKI SNELSON
Kate/Chutney .... KATE WETHERHEAD
Leilani .... BECKY GULSVIG
Cece .... MICHELLE KITTRELL
Kristine .... APRIL BERRY
Gabby .... BETH CURRY
Veronica/Enid .... NATALIE JOY JOHNSON
Judge .... AMBER EFÉ
Mom/Whitney .... GAELEN GILLILAND
Grandmaster Chad/Dewey/Kyle .... ANDY KARL
Dad/Winthrop .... KEVIN PARISEAU
Carlos .... MATTHEW RISCH
Padamadan/Nikos .... MANUEL HERRERA
Aaron/Guard .... NOAH WEISBERG
Bruiser .... CHICO
Rufus .... CHLOE
Harvard Students, Marching Band, Cheerleaders, Inmates, Salespeople .... APRIL BERRY, PAUL CANAAN, BETH CURRY, AMBER EFÉ, GAELEN GILLILAND, JASON GILLMAN, BECKY GULSVIG, MANUEL HERRERA,

Continued on next page

Photo by Paul Kolnik

(L-R): Kate Shindle, Richard H. Blake, Laura Bell Bundy and Michael Rupert.

Legally Blonde

SCENES AND MUSICAL NUMBERS

ACT I

Scene 1: UCLA Delta Nu Sorority House/Mall/Elle's Door
"Omigod You Guys" .... Margot, Serena, Pilar, Delta Nu's, Elle, Shopgirl, Manager
Scene 2: Restaurant
"Serious" .... Warner, Elle
Scene 3: Delta Nu Sorority House/Golf Course/Harvard Law School Admissions Office
"Daughter of Delta Nu" .... Margot, Serena, Pilar, Kate, Delta Nu's
"What You Want" .... Elle, Margot, Serena, Pilar, Kate, Mom, Dad, Grandmaster Chad, Winthrop, Pforzheimer, Lowell, Delta Nu's and Company
Scene 4: Harvard Yard
"The Harvard Variations" .... Emmett, Aaron, Enid, Padamadan and Harvard Students
Scene 5: Callahan's Classroom
"Blood in the Water" .... Callahan and Company
Scene 6: Harvard Yard
"Positive" .... Elle, Margot, Serena, Pilar, Greek Chorus
Scene 7: The Hair Affair
"Ireland" .... Paulette
"Ireland" (Reprise) .... Paulette
Scene 8: Harvard Party
"Serious" (Reprise) .... Elle, Warner
Scene 9: Harvard Yard/Elle's Room/Callahan's Classroom
"Chip on My Shoulder" .... Emmett, Elle, Greek Chorus, Company
Scene 10: Dewey's Trailer
Scene 11: Harvard Hallway
"So Much Better" .... Elle, Greek Chorus and Company

ACT II

Scene 1: Conference Room of Hearne, Fox, Zyskowski & Callahan/Women's Prison
"Whipped Into Shape" .... Brooke, Callahan and Company
Scene 2: Hansen-Harkness Department Store
"Take It Like a Man" .... Elle, Emmett, Salespersons
Scene 3: The Hair Affair
"Bend and Snap" .... Elle, Paulette, Serena, Margot, Pilar, Salonfolk
Scene 4: Courtroom
"There! Right There!" .... Elle, Callahan, Emmett, Brooke, Vivienne, Warner, Enid, Judge, Nikos, Carlos and Company
Scene 5: Callahan's Office/Elle's Door
"Legally Blonde" .... Elle, Emmett
Scene 6: The Hair Affair
"Legally Blonde Remix" .... Vivienne, Enid, Elle, Company
Scene 7: Courtroom/Bathroom of the Wyndham Mansion
"Omigod You Guys" (Reprise) .... Elle and Company
Scene 8: Harvard Law Graduation
"Find My Way/Finale" .... Elle, Paulette and Company

Cast Continued

NATALIE JOY JOHNSON,
ANDY KARL, NICK KENKEL,
MICHELLE KITTRELL,
KEVIN PARISEAU, MATTHEW RISCH,
JASON PATRICK SANDS,
NOAH WEISBERG, KATE WETHERHEAD

UNDERSTUDIES

For Elle Woods:
ANNALEIGH ASHFORD, BECKY GULSVIG
For Emmett Forrest:
ANDY KARL, NOAH WEISBERG
For Professor Callahan:
ANDY KARL, KEVIN PARISEAU
For Paulette:
AMBER EFÉ, GAELEN GILLILAND
For Warner Huntington III:
JASON GILLMAN, MATTHEW RISCH
For Vivienne Kensington:
TRACY JAI EDWARDS, GAELEN GILLILAND
For Brooke Wyndham/Shandi:
BETH CURRY, MICHELLE KITTRELL

SWINGS

LINDSAY NICOLE CHAMBERS,
TRACY JAI EDWARDS,
RUSTY MOWERY, ROD HARRELSON

DANCE CAPTAINS

RUSTY MOWERY, MICHELLE KITTRELL

SETTING

In and around the Delta Nu house,
Southern California.
In and around the Harvard Law campus,
Cambridge, Massachusetts.

Bruiser
Photo by Paul Kolnik

LEGALLY BLONDE ORCHESTRA

Conductor: JAMES SAMPLINER
Associate Conductor: JASON DeBORD
Concertmaster: ANTOINE SILVERMAN
Viola: JONATHAN DINKLAGE
Cello: PETER SACHON
Lead Trumpet: DAVE TRIGG
Trumpet: BUD BURRIDGE
Trombone: KEITH O'QUINN
Reed 1: VINCENT DELLAROCCA
Reed 2: DAN WILLIS
Reed 3: CHAD SMITH
French Horn: ROGER WENDT
Drums: GREG JOSEPH
Bass: MARK VANDERPOEL
Keyboard 1: JAMES SAMPLINER
Keyboards: JASON DeBORD,
MATT GALLAGHER
Guitars: JOHN PUTNAM, KENNY BRESCIA
Percussion: PABLO RIEPPI
Music Coordinator: MICHAEL KELLER

Copyist: EMILY GRISHMAN
MUSIC PREPARATION
Synthesizer Programming: LELAND MUSIC CO.

Legally Blonde

Laura Bell Bundy
Elle

Christian Borle
Emmett

Orfeh
Paulette

Michael Rupert
Callahan

Richard H. Blake
Warner Huntington III

Kate Shindle
Vivienne

Nikki Snelson
Brooke Wyndham

Annaleigh Ashford
Margot

April Berry
Ensemble

Paul Canaan
Ensemble

Lindsay Nicole Chambers
Swing

Beth Curry
Ensemble

Tracy Jai Edwards
Swing

Amber Efé
Judge/Ensemble

Gaelen Gilliland
Ensemble

Jason Gillman
Pforzhiemer

Becky Gulsvig
Ensemble

Rod Harrelson
Swing

Manuel Herrera
Nikos/Padamadan

Natalie Joy Johnson
Enid

Andy Karl
Ensemble

Nick Kenkel
Ensemble/Assistant Choreographer

Michelle Kittrell
DA Joyce Riley, Ensemble/ Co-Dance Captain

Leslie Kritzer
Serena

DeQuina Moore
Pilar

Rusty Mowery
Dance Captain/ Swing

Kevin Pariseau
Ensemble

Matthew Risch
Carlos/Lowell

Jason Patrick Sands
Ensemble

Noah Weisberg
Aaron, Ensemble

Kate Wetherhead
Kate/Chutney

Heather Hach
Book Writer

Laurence O'Keefe and Nell Benjamin
Music and Lyrics

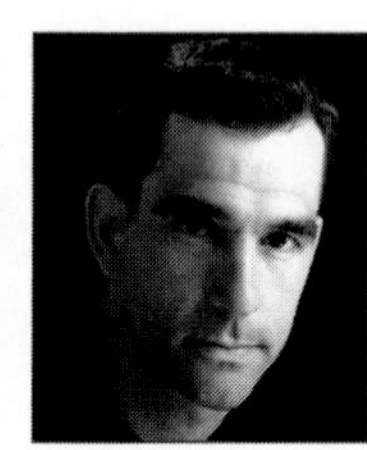
Jerry Mitchell
Director/ Choreographer

Legally Blonde

David Rockwell
Scenic Designer

Gregg Barnes
Costume Design

Kenneth Posner
Lighting Designer

Paul Miller
Lighting Designer

Tom Clark, Mark Menard and Nevin Steinberg
Acme Sound Partners
Sound Design

David Brian Brown
Wig/Hair Design

Justen M. Brosnan
Makeup Design

Bernard Telsey,
Telsey + Company
Casting

James Sampliner
Music Director/
Conductor/
Co-Arranger

Christopher Jahnke
Orchestrations

Michael Keller
Music Coordinator

Smitty/
Theatersmith, Inc/
Christopher C. Smith
Technical Supervisor

William Berloni
Animal Trainer

Marc Bruni
Associate Director

Denis Jones
Associate
Choreographer

Hal Luftig
Producer

Dori Berinstein
Producer

James L.
Nederlander
Producer

Roy Furman
Producer

Amanda Lipitz
Producer

Simone Genatt-Haft,
Broadway Asia
Producer

Marc Routh,
Broadway Asia
Producer

Barbara Whitman
Producer

Barbara Freitag,
FWPM Group
Producer

Jennifer Maloney,
FWPM Group
Producer

Ruth Hendel,
Hendel/Wiesenfeld
Producer

Hal Goldberg,
Goldberg/Binder
Producer

Douglas L. Meyer,
Stern/Meyer
Producer

Stewart F. Lane and
Bonnie Comley
Producers

Michael A. Jenkins,
Bartner-Jenkins/
Nocciolino
Producer

Adam Zotovich
Associate Producer

Andrew Asnes
Associate Producer

2006-2007 AWARD

ACTORS' EQUITY
DERWENT AWARD
Most Promising Female Performer
on the New York Metropolitan
Scene
(Leslie Kritzer)

Legally Blonde

FRONT OF HOUSE STAFF

Front Row (L-R):
Rachel Brentley (Usher), Distiny Rivera (Usher), Jennifer Butt (Usher), Verne Shayne (Usher), Distiny Bivona (Usher), Scott Muso (Usher).

Middle Row (L-R):
Shirley Riorden (Usher), Frank Tupper (Usher), Fran McKiernan, Lorraine O'Sullivan (Usher), Sandy Darbasie (Usher), Kelly Collins (Usher), Fran Lacorte (Usher).

Back Row (L-R):
Robert Collins (Usher), Gloria Hill (Head Usher), Patricia Marsh (Usher), Dixon Rosario (House Manager), Gary Cabana (Usher) and William Mullen (Usher).

SECURITY

(L-R): Manny Cruz (Security), Alfredo Quinones (Doorman), Richardare Henkin

Photos by Ben Strothmann

STAGE CREW

Front Row (L-R): Marcia McIntosh, Dolly Williams.
Second Row (L-R): Pamela Sorensen, Jessica Scoblick, Tasha Cowd, Jeff Johnson, Robert N. Valli.
Third Row (L-R): Robert W. Kelly, Gina Gornik, Veneda Truesdale, Larry Callahan, Carole Morales.
Back Row (L-R): Robert J. Keller, Jr., Timothy Kovalenko, Bobby Terrell, Donald J. Oberpriller, Paul Baker, Fred Castner, Christel Murdock, Brian Penney, Joel Hawkins, Seth Sklar-Heyn, Eddie Webber, Joe Whitmeyer, Scott Rowen, Laura Ellington and Ken Keneally.

Legally Blonde

STAFF FOR *LEGALLY BLONDE*

GENERAL MANAGER
NINA LANNAN ASSOCIATES
Maggie Brohn

Company Manager
Kimberly Kelley
Associate Company Manager .... Nathan Gehan

GENERAL PRESS REPRESENTATIVE
Barlow•Hartman
Michael Hartman John Barlow
Carol Fineman Kevin Robak

CASTING
TESLEY + COMPANY
Bernie Telsey, Will Cantler, David Vaccari, Bethany Knox, Craig Burns, Tiffany Little Canfield, Rachel Hoffman, Stephanie Yankwitt, Carrie Rosson, Justin Huff, Joe Langworth, Bess Fifer

Associate Director .... Marc Bruni
Associate Choreographer .... Denis Jones
Assistant Choreographer .... Nick Kenkel
PRODUCTION STAGE MANAGER .. Bonnie L. Becker
Stage Manager .... Kimberly Russell
Assistant Stage Manager .... Scott Rowen
Dance Captains .... Rusty Mowery, Michelle Kittrell
Assistant to David Rockwell .... Barry Richards
Associate Designer .... Richard Jaris
Assistant Designers .... Todd Ivins, Gaetane Bertol, Brian Drucker, Rob Bissinger, Larry Brown, Corrine Merrill
Modelmakers .... Joanie Schlafer, Rachael Short-Janocko, Morgan Moore, Tomo Tanaka
Set Design Graphics .... Alexi Logothetis, Charles Rush, Jerry Sabatini, Matthew Goodrich
Associate Costume Designer .... Sky Switser
Assistant Costume Designer .... Matthew R Pachtman
Costume Assistants .... Sarah Sophia Turner, Jeriana Hochberg
Costume Interns .... Nina Damato, Sydney Gallas
Assistant Lighting Designer .... Jonathan Spencer
Advance Sound .... Dan Robillard
Assistant Sound Designer .... Jeffrey Yoshi Lee
Automated Lighting Programmer .... Timothy F. Rogers
Dialect Coach .... Stephen Gabis
Fight Director .... Thomas Schall

MAKEUP DESIGN .... JUSTEN M. BROSNAN

Production Carpenter .... Donald J. Oberpriller
Fly Automation Carpenter .... Robert M. Hentze
Carpenters .... Jeff Lunsford, Ian Michaud
Production Electricians ... James J. Fedigan, Randall Zaibek
Head Electrician .... Dan Coey
Assistant Electricians .... Michael Cornell, Ron Martin
Production Sound .... Robert Biasetti
Production Properties .... Timothy M. Abel
Head Properties .... Robert N. Valli
Assistant Properties .... Ken Keneally
Wardrobe Supervisors ...... Jessica Scoblick, Dolly Williams
Star Dresser .... Laura Ellington
Dressers .... Larry Callahan. Fred Castner, Tasha Cowd, Shana Dunbar, Gina Gornik, Michael Harrell, James Hodun, Jeff Johnson, Melanie McClintock, Marcia McIntosh, Jack Scott, Pamela Sorensen, Veneda Truesdale
Hair Supervisor .... Carole Morales
Hair Assistant .... Joseph Whitmeyer
Hair Dressers .... Tom Augustine, Joel Hawkins
Additional Arrangements .... Alex Lacamoire
Rehearsal Musicians .... Jason DeBord, Greg Joseph
Production Assistants .... Caroline Andersen, Christopher Munnell
Dog Handler .... William Berloni
Dog Handler .... Rob Cox
Assistant Trainer .... Dorothy Berloni
Company Physical Therapist .... Sean Gallagher, PAPT

Advertising .... Serino Coyne, Inc./ Sandy Block, Albert Lin, Roger Micone, Christin Seidel
Website Design/
Online Marketing Strategy ... Situation Marketing LLC/ Damian Bazadona, Chris Powers, Ian Bennett, Jimmy Lee
Comptroller .... Sarah Galbraith/ Sarah Galbraith Company
Accountants .... Robert Fried CPA, Fried & Kowgios CPAs LLP
General Management Associates ...... Katherine McNamee, Roseanna Sharrow
General Management Intern .... Jessica Morris
Press Associates .... Leslie Baden, Dennis Crowley, Tom D'Ambrosio, Tommy Prudenti, Ryan Ratelle, Wayne Wolfe
Press Office Manager .... Bethany Larsen
Production Photographer .... Paul Kolnik
Insurance .... Albert G. Ruben Company Inc./ Claudia Kaufman
Banking .... City National Bank, Gregg Santos
Payroll .... Castellana Services, Inc.
Merchandising .... Max Merchandising, Randi Grossman
Travel Agent .... Tzell Travel/The "A" Team, Andi Henig
Legal
Counsel ..... Franklin, Weinrib, Rudell & Vassallo, P.C./ Elliot H. Brown, Daniel M. Wasser, Matthew C. Lefferts
Associate to Mr. Luftig .... Shannon Morrison
Assistant to Ms. Caskey .... Christopher Tulysewski
Assistant to Mr. Isaacson .... Holly Gitlin
SSDC Observer .... Christine O'Grady
Music Intern .... Evan Jay Newman

GROUP SALES
Theatre Direct/Showtix
1-800-BROADWAY

www.legallyblondethemusical.com

ACKNOWLEDGEMENTS

The producers wish to thank the following partners for their generous support: VISA, TIFFANY & CO., MATRIX and ELLE MAGAZINE.
Other products graciously provided by the following partners: Puma, Juicy Couture, UPS, Manhattan Portage and Nanette Lepore. Mobile phones provided by Verizon Wireless; iPods and Elle Woods' computer provided by Apple; "Peanut" remote and sound effects by Tivo, Inc.; and Elle's dorm room furnished by Pottery Barn Teen.

CREDITS

Scenery constructed and automation equipment provided by Showmotion Inc. Scenic drops painted by Scenic Arts Studio. Costumes constructed by Barbara Matera Ltd., Carelli Costumes, Donna Langman, John David Ridge, Tricorne and D.D. Dolan. Custom millinery by Lynne Mackey Studio, Killer. Custom shoes by Capri Shoes, J.C. Theatrical, LaDuca Productions and T.O. Dey. Custom painting by Jeff Fender, screenprinting by Steven Gillespie and knitting by C.C. Wei. Undergarments provided by Bra*Tenders. Lighting Equipment by PRG Lighting. Sound equipment supplied by Sound Associates. Props provided by Spoon Group, Beyond Imagination, Jennie Marino/Moonboots. Special assistant with hand prop construction Meghan Abel. Receptors provided by Muse Research. Guitar amps by Mega Boogie. Pianos provided by Yamaha Musical Theatre Corp. Dogs adopted from Associated Humane Society of New Jersey, Four Paws Rescue of New Jersey, the Connecticut Humane Society and Bulldog Rescue of Connecticut. Rehearsed at the New 42nd Street Studios. Natural herb cough drops supplied by Ricola USA Inc. Emergen-C super energy booster provided by Alacer Corp. Makeup provided by M•A•C Cosmetics.

SPECIAL THANKS

Michael Harrell, Rosemary Phelps, Cory Ching, Dr. Wayne Goldberg, Rachel Pachtman, Tom LaMere, Stephanie Steele, Stewart Adelson, Joe Ortmeyer, Marc Platt, Karen McCullah, Kirsten Smith, Gail Cannold, Sue Spiegel, Ken Marsolais, Mitchell Cannold, Bairbre Finn. San Francisco Business Agent FX Crowley. Our production team would like to thank the San Francisco crew for their terrific work.

N
NEDERLANDER

Chairman .... **James M. Nederlander**
President .... **James L. Nederlander**

Executive Vice President
Nick Scandalios

Vice President
Corporate Development
Charlene S. Nederlander

Senior Vice President
Labor Relations
Herschel Waxman

Vice President
Jim Boese

Chief Financial Officer
Freida Sawyer Belviso

STAFF FOR THE PALACE THEATRE
Theatre Manager .... Dixon Rosario
Treasurer .... Cissy Caspare
Assistant Treasurer .... Anne T. Wilson
Carpenter .... Thomas K. Phillips
Flyman .... Robert W. Kelly
Electrician .... Eddie Webber
Propertymaster .... Steve Camus
Chief Usher .... Gloria Hill

Legally Blonde
Scrapbook

Correspondent: Christian Borle, "Emmett Forrest."
Memorable Opening Night Gift: Larry O'Keefe, Nell Benjamin, Paul Canaan and Gaelen Gilliland collaborated on a CD titled "The 'Bonecake' Remix," a song splicing together years' worth of cut dialogue and inside jokes, all set to what the kids call a "phat beat."
Most Exciting Celebrity Visitor and What They Said: Bette Midler offered Laura Bell Bundy this sage advice—"Turn out."
Who Got the Gypsy Robe and What They Put On It: Michelle Kittrell was the honored recipient. The robe is as yet unadorned, but I'm guessing *Legally Blonde*'s addition will be pink. Just a shot in the dark.
Actor Who Performed the Most Roles in the Show: A competitive category, with Paul Canaan winning by a nose with nine roles. Extra points because one of his characters wears a poncho. An actual poncho.
Who Has Done the Most Shows in Their Career: While no official tally was made, gotta go with Michael Rupert on this one, right? The man is royalty.
Backstage Rituals: Chico the Chihuahua makes the rounds; a breathing circle ending in a dog show kickline; Tequila Wednesday; Paycheck Thursday; Dollar Friday; Saturday Night Disco Party; Fondue Sunday.
Favorite In-Theater Gathering Place: It's a toss-up between "the quad," a luxurious stretch of carpet by the callboard, and the men's ensemble room, which probably takes the title by sheer number of tighty-whities.
Favorite Off-Site Hangout: (San Francisco Edition) Rye Bar.
Favorite Snack Food: Red Bull, protein bars, birthday cake, Chico's treats...sadly not just for Chico.
Mascot: Jason Gillman, obviously.
Favorite Therapy: Throat Coat tea and foam rollers, in that order.
Most Memorable Ad-Lib: "And if you learn to suck up like Emmett here, you... will... be... in... heaven." —Michael Rupert, 2007.
Who Wore the Heaviest/Hottest Costume: Tie: Laura Bell Bundy's spangled band uniform (20 pounds)/Paul Canaan's aforementioned poncho (Hot on both fronts.)
Who Wore the Least: April Berry's entire costume plot.
Catchphrase Only the Company Would Recognize: "Let me be you."
Best In-House Parody Lyrics: (To the tune of "I am so much better than before...") "I am so much fatter than last week..."
Company In-Jokes: "Hey-oh," "So Jammy," "You do the math." Hilarious, no?
Company Legends: Beth Curry's special skill. Much as I'd love to divulge details, I had to sign a confidentiality agreement during tech rehearsals. I *can* say it's really quite a thing to see. And hear. I've said too much.
Nicknames: Chancho (Manny Herrera), JPS (Jason Patrick Sands), The PMS Girls (Pilar, Margot and Serena of the Delta Nu clan).
Most Memorable Moment in Tech Rehearsal: Chris the Stripping Policeman paying a visit on Jerry Mitchell's birthday. Footage available on YouTube.
An Incomplete List of Cut Songs: "Bad Idea," "Here Boy," "To Hell With Them," "Beacon of Positivity," "Love and War," "Off to Harvard Law," and "You're a Rockstar Lawyer Girl."

Photos by Aubrey Reuben

1. (L-R): Composer/lyricists Nell Benjamin and Laurence O'Keefe, librettist Heather Hach and director/choreographer Jerry Mitchell arrive at the Palace Theatre for the premiere.
2. Christian Borle, Laura Bell Bundy and Chico take curtain call at the Palace Theatre on opening night.
3. Laura Bell Bundy on opening night.
4. Five cast members arrive at Cipriani for the opening night cast party.
5. Orfeh and Andy Karl at Cipriani.

Les Misérables

First Preview: October 24, 2006. Opened: November 9, 2006.
Still running as of May 31, 2007.

PLAYBILL

CAST

(in order of appearance)

Jean Valjean .... ALEXANDER GEMIGNANI
Javert .... NORM LEWIS
Farmer .... DOUG KREEGER
Innkeeper .... DREW SARICH
Innkeeper's Wife .... KAREN ELLIOTT
Laborer .... JD GOLDBLATT
The Bishop of Digne ..... JAMES CHIP LEONARD
Constables .... NEHAL JOSHI, JEFF KREADY
Factory Foreman .... ROBERT HUNT
Fantine .... DAPHNE RUBIN-VEGA
Factory Girl .... HAVILAND STILLWELL
Factory Workers .... BECCA AYERS, DANIEL BOGART, JUSTIN BOHON, KATE CHAPMAN, NIKKI RENÉE DANIELS, KAREN ELLIOTT, MARYA GRANDY, BLAKE GINTHER, JD GOLDBLATT, VICTOR HAWKS, NEHAL JOSHI, JEFF KREADY, DOUG KREEGER, JAMES CHIP LEONARD, MEGAN MCGINNIS, DREW SARICH, IDARA VICTOR
Sailors .... JUSTIN BOHON, VICTOR HAWKS, NEHAL JOSHI
Pimp .... JD GOLDBLATT
Madame .... KATE CHAPMAN
Whores .... BECCA AYERS, NIKKI RENÉE DANIELS, ALI EWOLDT, CELIA KEENAN-BOLGER, MEGAN McGINNIS, HAVILAND STILLWELL, IDARA VICTOR

Continued on next page

BROADHURST THEATRE
235 West 44th Street
A Shubert Organization Theatre
Gerald Schoenfeld, *Chairman* **Philip J. Smith,** *President*
Robert E. Wankel, *Executive Vice President*

CAMERON MACKINTOSH
presents

Les Misérables

By ALAIN BOUBLIL and CLAUDE-MICHEL SCHÖNBERG
Based on the novel by VICTOR HUGO

Music by CLAUDE-MICHEL SCHÖNBERG
Lyrics by HERBERT KRETZMER

Original French text by ALAIN BOUBLIL and JEAN-MARC NATEL
Additional material by JAMES FENTON

New Orchestrations by CHRISTOPHER JAHNKE
Co-Orchestrator STEPHEN METCALFE
Original Orchestrations by JOHN CAMERON
Orchestral Adaptation and Musical Supervision STEPHEN BROOKER
Music Director KEVIN STITES
Sound Design by JON WESTON

Associate Lighting Designer TED MATHER
Executive Producers NICHOLAS ALLOTT, MATTHEW DALCO and FRED HANSON
Casting by TARA RUBIN CASTING, C.S.A.
General Management ALAN WASSER ASSOCIATES

Designed by JOHN NAPIER
Lighting by DAVID HERSEY
Original Sound Design by ANDREW BRUCE
Costumes by ANDREANE NEOFITOU

Associate Director SHAUN KERRISON
Directed and Adapted by JOHN CAIRD & TREVOR NUNN

Is there not in every human soul, and was there not in the soul of Jean Valjean, an essential spark, an element of the divine; indestructible in this world and immortal in the next, which goodness can preserve, nourish and fan into glorious flame, and which evil can never quite extinguish?

VICTOR HUGO

Original London production by
CAMERON MACKINTOSH and THE ROYAL SHAKESPEARE COMPANY

11/9/06

Ali Ewoldt and Alexander Gemignani (front) lead the cast in singing "One Day More."

Photo by Joan Marcus

Les Misérables

MUSICAL NUMBERS

PROLOGUE: 1815, DIGNE

Prologue	The Company
"Soliloquy"	Valjean
PROLOGUE: 1823, MONTREUIL-SUR-MER	
"At the End of the Day"	Unemployed and factory workers
"I Dreamed a Dream"	Fantine
"Lovely Ladies"	Ladies and clients
"Who Am I?"	Valjean
"Come to Me"	Fantine and Valjean
"Castle on a Cloud"	Young Cosette
1823, MONTFERMEIL	
"Master of the House"	Thénardier, Mme Thénardier and customers
"Thénardier Waltz"	M. and Mme. Thénardier and Valjean
1832, PARIS	
"Look Down"	Gavroche and the beggars
"Stars"	Javert
"Red and Black"	Enjolras, Marius and the students
"Do You Hear the People Sing?"	Enjolras, the students and the citizens
"In My Life"	Cosette, Valjean, Marius and Eponine
"A Heart Full of Love"	Cosette, Marius and Eponine
"One Day More"	The Company
"On My Own"	Eponine
"A Little Fall of Rain"	Eponine and Marius
"Drink With Me to Days Gone By"	Grantaire, students and women
"Bring Him Home"	Valjean
"Dog Eats Dog"	Thénardier
"Soliloquy"	Javert
"Empty Chairs at Empty Tables"	Marius
"Wedding Chorale"	Guests
"Beggars at the Feast"	M. And Mme. Thénardier
Finale	The Company

UNDERSTUDIES

For Jean Valjean:
VICTOR HAWKS, JEFF KREADY
For Javert:
ROBERT HUNT
For Thénardier:
JAMES CHIP LEONARD
For Madame Thénardier:
KAREN ELLIOTT
For Fantine:
NIKKI RENÉE DANIELS,
HAVILAND STILLWELL
For Cosette:
IDARA VICTOR
For Marius:
DANIEL BOGART
For Eponine:
MEGAN McGINNIS, MARISSA McGOWAN
For Enjolras:
DREW SARICH

ORCHESTRA

Conductor: KEVIN STITES
Associate Conductor: PAUL RAIMAN
Assistant Conductor: ANNBRITT duCHATEAU
Flute/Piccolo/Alto Flute/Alto Recorder:
BOB BUSH
Oboe/English Horn: LAURA WALLIS
Clarinet/Bass Clarinet/Tenor Recorder:
JONATHAN LEVINE
Trumpet/Flugel: TIM SCHADT
Bass Trombone/Tuba: CHRIS OLNESS
French Horns:
BRAD GEMEINHARDT, SARA CYRUS
Violin: MARTIN AGEE
Viola: DEBRA SHUFELT-DINE
Cello: CLAY RUEDE
Bass: DAVE PHILLIPS
Mallets/Timpani/Percussion:
CHARLES DESCARFINO
Keyboards:
PAUL RAIMAN, ANNBRITT duCHATEAU
Music Coordinator: JOHN MILLER

Cast Continued

Old Woman .... KAREN ELLIOTT
Crone .... MARYA GRANDY
Bamatabois .... DANIEL BOGART
Fauchelevant .... JEFF KREADY
Champmathieu .... ROBERT HUNT
Young Cosette .... TESS ADAMS,
or KYLIE LIYA GOLDSTEIN,
or CARLY ROSE SONENCLAR
Thénardier .... GARY BEACH
Madame Thénardier .... JENNY GALLOWAY
Young Eponine .... TESS ADAMS,
or KYLIE LIYA GOLDSTEIN,
or CARLY ROSE SONENCLAR
Old Beggar Woman .... KAREN ELLIOTT
Madeleine .... NIKKI RENÉE DANIELS
Gavroche .... BRIAN D'ADDARIO,
or JACOB LEVINE,
or AUSTYN MYERS
Eponine .... CELIA KEENAN-BOLGER
Cosette .... ALI EWOLDT
Major Domo .... JUSTIN BOHON

THÉNARDIER'S GANG

Montparnasse .... JD GOLDBLATT
Babet .... JEFF KREADY
Brujon .... VICTOR HAWKS
Claquesous .... JAMES CHIP LEONARD

STUDENTS

Enjolras .... AARON LAZAR
Marius .... ADAM JACOBS
Combeferre .... DANIEL BOGART
Feuilly .... BLAKE GINTHER
Courfeyrac .... ROBERT HUNT
Joly .... JUSTIN BOHON
Grantaire .... DREW SARICH
Lesgles .... NEHAL JOSHI
Jean Prouvaire .... DOUG KREEGER

Swings .... MATT CLEMENS,
MARISSA McGOWAN,
Q. SMITH, STEPHEN TRAFTON

Dance Captain .... MATT CLEMENS

Chain Gang, The Poor, Factory Workers, Sailors, Whores, Pimps and Wedding Guests will be played by members of the Ensemble.

Movement Consultant .... Kate Flatt

Jenny Galloway is appearing with the permission of Actors' Equity Association pursuant to an exchange program between American Equity and UK Equity.

Les Misérables

Tess Adams
Young Cosette/ Young Eponine

Becca Ayers
Ensemble

Gary Beach
Thénardier

Daniel Bogart
Combeferre

Justin Bohon
Joly

Kate Chapman
Ensemble

Matt Clemens
Swing

Brian D'Addario
Gavroche

Nikki Renée Daniels
Ensemble

Karen Elliott
Ensemble

Ali Ewoldt
Cosette

Jenny Galloway
Madame Thénardier

Alexander Gemignani
Jean Valjean

Blake Ginther
Feuilly

JD Goldblatt
Montparnasse

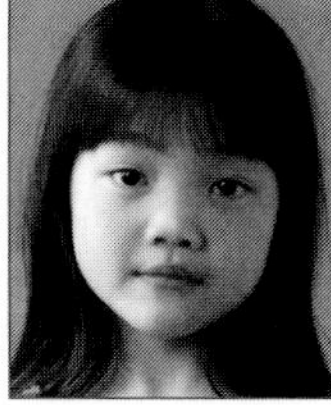
Kylie Liya Goldstein
Young Cosette/ Young Eponine

Marya Grandy
Ensemble

Victor Hawks
Brujon

Robert Hunt
Courfeyrac

Adam Jacobs
Marius

Nehal Joshi
Lesgles

Celia Keenan-Bolger
Eponine

Jeff Kready
Babet

Doug Kreeger
Jean Prouvaire

Aaron Lazar
Enjolras

James Chip Leonard
Bishop of Digne/ Claquesous

Jacob Levine
Gavroche

Norm Lewis
Javert

Megan McGinnis
Ensemble

Marissa McGowan
Swing

Austyn Myers
Gavroche

Daphne Rubin-Vega
Fantine

Drew Sarich
Grantaire

Q. Smith
Swing

Carly Rose Sonenclar
Young Cosette/ Young Eponine

Les Misérables

Haviland Stillwell
Ensemble

Stephen Trafton
Swing

Idara Victor
Ensemble

Alain Boublil
Conception, Book and Original French Lyrics

Claude-Michel Schönberg
Composer

Herbert Kretzmer
Lyricist

Cameron Mackintosh
Producer

John Caird
Direction and Adaptation

Trevor Nunn
Direction and Adaptation

John Napier
Production Designer

David Hersey
Lighting Designer

Andreane Neofitou
Costumes

Andrew Bruce
Sound

Christopher Jahnke
New Orchestrations

Stephen Brooker
Orchestral Adaptation and Musical Supervision

Stephen Metcalfe
Co-Orchestrator

John Cameron
Original Orchestrations

Shaun Kerrison
Associate Director

Kate Flatt
Movement Consultant

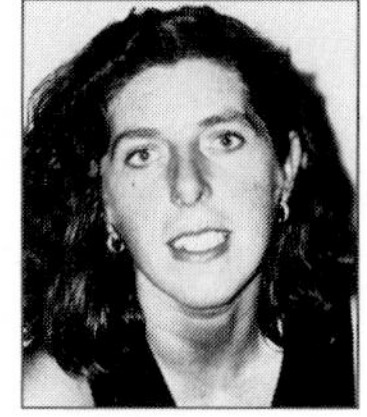
Sue Jenkinson DiAmico
Associate Set Designer

Tom Watson
Hair Designer

Tara Rubin Casting
Casting

John Miller
Music Coordinator

Nick Allott
Executive Producer

Alan Wasser Associates
General Manager

Justin Bohon
Joly

Mandy Bruno
Eponine, Whore

Ben Crawford
Champmathieu, Courfeyrac, Factory Foreman

Anderson Davis
Factory Worker, Joly, Laborer, Major Domo, Montparnasse, Pimp, Sailor

Ben Davis
Javert

Christy Faber
Factory Worker, Madeleine, Whore

Ann Harada
Madame Thénardier

Zach Rand
Gavroche

Kristine Reese
Crone, Factory Worker

Les Misérables

Sara-Joye Ross
Factory Worker, Innkeeper's Wife, Old Beggar Woman, Old Woman

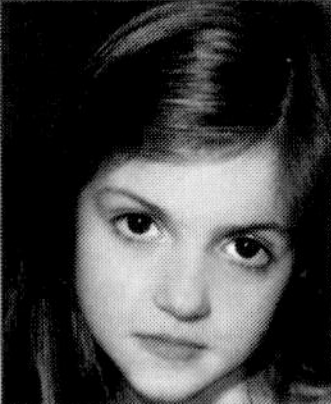
Kaylie Rubinaccio
Young Cosette, Young Eponine

Lea Salonga
Fantine

Kevin David Thomas
Factory Worker, Joly, Major Domo, Sailor

Max von Essen
Enjolras

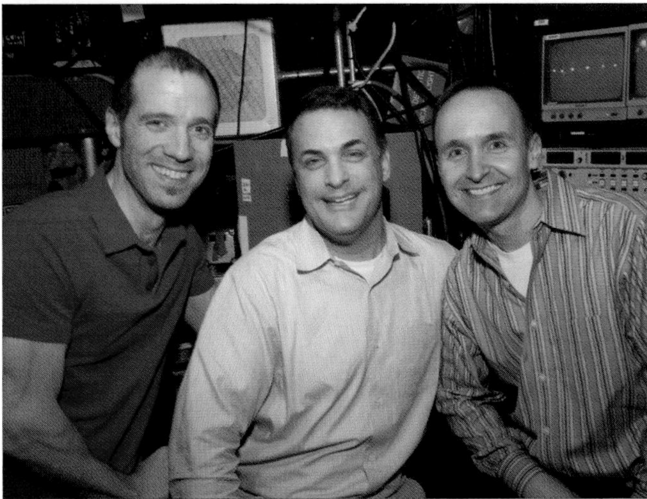
STAGE MANAGEMENT
(L-R): Jim Athens (Stage Manager), Michael Passaro (Production Stage Manager) and Charles Underhill (Stage Manager).

COMPANY MANAGEMENT
(L-R): Steve Greer (Associate Company Manager) and Abra Stanley Leonard (Company Manager).

Photos by Ben Strothmann

STAGEHANDS
Back Row (L-R): Charlie DeVerna, Patrick Pummill, Dan Novi, Jeremy Wahlers, Jonathan Cohen, William Rowland, Spencer Bell, Todd Frank, Brian "Boomer" Bullard, Chris Martin, William Garvey.
Middle Row (L-R): Dave Karlson, Brian McGarty.
Front Row (L-R): Joanna Staub, Steve "Woof" Callahan, Sandra Paradise, Steve Abbott, Rob Brenner and Ron Vitelli.

BOX OFFICE
(L-R): Clifford Cobb, Noreen Morgan and Mike Lynch.

Not Pictured: Al Crivelli, Gerard O'Brien

Les Misérables

Photos by Ben Strothmann

FRONT OF HOUSE
Front Row (L-R): Rose Ann Cipriano, Yenny Fernandez, Karen Diaz and Christian Leguia.

Back Row (L-R): Juan Lopez, Josh Rosier and Hugh Lynch.

ORCHESTRA
Front Row (L-R): Sara Cyrus (French Horn), Kevin Stites (Conductor).

Second Row (L-R): Annbritt duChateau (Keyboard/Assistant Conductor), Laura Bontrager (Cello), Jonathan Levine (Clarinet/Recorder).

Third Row (L-R): Junah Chung (Viola), Charles Descarfino (Percussion), Laura Wallis (Oboe).

Fourth Row (L-R): Chris Olness (Trombone), Martin Agee (Violin).

Back Row (L-R): Bob Bush (Flute), Ray Kilday (Bass) and Tim Schadt (Trumpet).

Not Pictured: Michael Atkinson (French Horn), Debra Shufelt-Dine (Viola), Dave Phillips (Bass), Paul Raiman (Keyboard/Associate Conductor).

WARDROBE
Front Row (Floor): Christina M. Ainge.

Second Row: Sarah Schaub (Asst. Wardrobe Supervisor), Kimberly Baird, Jason Heisey.

Third Row: Mary Ann Lewis-Oberpriller, Julienne Schubert Blechman, Hiro Hosomizu.

Back Row: Bob Kwiatkowski and Alan Berkoski.

WARDROBE
Front Row (L-R): Stacia Williams, Mark Caine.

Back Row (L-R): Marisa Lerette and Francine Buryiak.

Not Pictured: Barry Ernst (Hair/Make-Up Supervisor), Jackie Weiss (Asst. Hair/Make-Up Supervisor), Gary Biangone, Christel Murdock and Leslie Thompson.

WARDROBE SUPERVISOR/ ASSOCIATE COSTUME DESIGNER
Rick Kelly

Les Misérables

STAFF FOR *LES MISÉRABLES*

GENERAL MANAGEMENT
ALAN WASSER ASSOCIATES
Alan Wasser Allan Williams Robert Nolan

GENERAL PRESS REPRESENTATIVE
THE PUBLICITY OFFICE
Marc Thibodeau Bob Fennell Michael Borowski
Candi Adams

TECHNICAL PRODUCTION MANAGER
Jake Bell

COMPANY MANAGER
Abra Stanley Leonard

PRODUCTION STAGE MANAGER
Michael J. Passaro

Stage Managers ....Charles Underhill, Jim Athens
Associate Company Manager ....Steve Greer
Dance Captain ....Matt Clemens

ASSOCIATE SCENIC DESIGNERS (UK) ...SUE JENKINSON DiAMICO, MATT KINLEY
ASSOCIATE COSTUME DESIGNER (UK) ....ELISE NAPIER
ASSOCIATE COSTUME DESIGNER .....RICK KELLY
HAIR DESIGNER ....TOM WATSON
Moving Lights Programmers ....Alan Boyd, Rob Halliday
Assistant Scenic Designer ....Josh Zangen
Assistant Lighting Designer ....Mark Simpson
Assistant Sound Designer ....Jason Strangfeld
Synthesizer Programmer ....Stuart Andrews
Assistant to the Lighting Designer ...Amith Chandrashaker

Production Carpenter ....Todd Frank
Production Electrician ....Robert Fehribach
Production Propertyman ....Timothy Abel
Head Carpenter ....Todd Frank
Head Electrician ....Michael Pitzer
Head Propertyman ....Steven Callahan
Head Sound Operator ....Patrick Pummill
Automation Operator ....Henry Baker
Assistant Electrician ....Paul Ker
Assistant Propertyman ....Spencer Bell
Assistant Sound Operator ....Mary McFadden
Wardrobe Supervisor ....Rick Kelly
Assistant Wardrobe Supervisor ....Sarah Schaub
Hair/Make-Up Supervisor ....Barry Ernst
Assistant Hair/Make-Up Supervisor ....Kevin Phillips
Dressers ....Christina Ainge, Kim Baird, Alan Berkoski, Gary Biangone, Julienne Schubert Blechman, Francine Buryiak, Mark Caine, Misty Fernandez, Jason Heisy, Hiro Hosomizu, Bob Kwiatkowski, Mary Ann Lewis-Oberpriller, Christel Murdock, Stacia Williams

Music Coordinator ....JOHN MILLER
Assistant to John Miller ....Kelly M. Rach
Associate Conductor/Rehearsal Pianist ....Paul Raiman
Assistant Conductor/ Rehearsal Pianist ....Annbritt duChateau
Rehearsal Pianist ....Andy Grobengieser
Music Copyists (US) ....Emily Grishman Music Prep
Music Copyists (UK) ....Dakota Music Service
Music Publisher ....Alain Boublil Music Ltd./ Steve Tenenbaum

Legal Counsel ....F. Richard Pappas, Esquire
Accounting ....Rosenberg, Neuwirth & Kuchner/ Christopher Cacace, Mark D'Ambrosi
Logo Design and Graphics ....Dewynters PLC London
Merchandising and Licensing ....Dewynters Advertising, Inc.
Advertising (New York) ....Serino Coyne/ Greg Corradetti, Joaquin Esteva, Natalie Serota
Press Assistant ....Matthew Fasano
Production Photographers ....Michael Le Poer Trench, Joan Marcus
General Management Staff...............Christopher Betz, Chris D'Angelo, Jason Hewitt, Jake Hirzel, Thom Mitchell, Patty Montesi, Jennifer Mudge, Connie Yung
Associate Casting Director ....Dunja Vitolic
Casting Associates ....Eric Woodall, Laura Schutzel, Merri Sugarman
Casting Assistants ....Rebecca Carfagna, Jeff Siebert
Insurance (US) ....DeWitt Stern Group/ Peter Shoemaker
Insurance (UK) ....Walton & Parkinson/ Richard Walton
Banking ....Commerce Bank/ Barbara von Borstel, Ashley Elezi
Immigration Attorney ....Shannon K. Such
Customs Brokers ....Network Brokers Int'l.
Payroll ....Castellana Services, Inc.
Travel Services ....Road Rebel Entertainment Touring
Chaperone ....Amanda Whitford Grundy
Tutor ....On Location Education, Beverly Brennan
Production Assistants ....Timothy Eaker, Alison M. Roberts, Alyssa Stone
Opening Night Coordination ....McNabb Roick & Associates/ Jim McNabb; Tobak Lawrence Company/ Michael P. Lawrence
Group Sales ....Broadway Inbound 212-302-0995/866-302-0995

Visit the official ***Les Misérables*** website at www.lesmis.com

STOCK AND AMATEUR RIGHTS exclusively represented by Music Theatre International, 421 West 54 Street, New York, NY 10019; Tel: 212-541-4684; Fax: 212-397-4684

CREDITS AND ACKNOWLEDGEMENTS

Scenery built and electrified by PRG Scenic Technologies and Terry Murphy Scenery Limited. Automation equipment provided by PRG Scenic Technologies. Lighting equipment provided by PRG Lighting and DHA. Sound equipment provided by Masque Sound & Recording Corporation. Costumes by the Costume Workshop and Tricorne. Properties by the Spoon Group. Custom created hand and set properties – Jennie Marino, Moonboots Prod. Inc., NY. Emergen-C super energy booster provided by Alacer Corp. Special thanks to Suzanne Strout, Nic Harris, Jerry Donaldson and Tracy Stiles. Rehearsed at the Lawrence A. Wien Center for Dance and Theater.

CAMERON MACKINTOSH, INC.

Joint Managing Directors ....Nicholas Allott, Matthew Dalco
Executive Producer ....Fred Hanson
Production Associate ....Shidan Majidi
Production Assistant ....Ed Greenall

THE SHUBERT ORGANIZATION, INC.
Board of Directors

Gerald Schoenfeld
Chairman

Philip J. Smith
President

Wyche Fowler, Jr.

John W. Kluge

Lee J. Seidler

Michael I. Sovern

Stuart Subotnick

Robert E. Wankel
Executive Vice President

Peter Entin
Vice President
Theatre Operations

Elliot Greene
Vice President
Finance

David Andrews
Vice President
Shubert Ticketing Services

John Darby
Vice President
Facilities

D.S. Moynihan
Vice President – Creative Projects

House Manager ....Hugh Barnett

Les Misérables
Scrapbook

Correspondent: Ali Ewoldt, "Cosette"
Memorable Opening Night Note: Original co-director Trevor Nunn sent us a lovely note apologizing for his absence.
Opening Night Gifts: Celia found an antique copy of the novel "Les Misérables" broken up into its chapters (Fantine, Cosette, Javert, Marius, Valjean…) and gave each of us our chapter with a lovely photo and inscription.
Most Exciting Celebrity Visitor: The young Cosettes/Eponines (Carly, Kylie and Tess) were most excited about Kelly Clarkson.
Who Got the Gypsy Robe: Nikki Renee Daniels.
"Easter Bonnet" Sketch: "Anything You Can Do" with Anne Runolfsson and Tess Adams.
Actor Who Performed the Most Roles in This Show: The male swings, Matt Clemens and Stephen Trafton each cover eleven tracks and each track plays about ten roles.
Who Has Done the Most Shows in Their Career: Cast guesses include Gary Beach and Jenny Galloway.
Special Backstage Rituals: There's always a rousing game of hacky-sack onstage before the shows. They've actually gotten quite good at it!
Favorite Moment During Each Performance: "Heart Full of Love" brings out the young, awkward, excited girl in me, which is always fun. The ensemble loves to lie back onstage and listen to "Bring Him Home."
Favorite In-Theatre Gathering Place: The dressing room I share with Celia is popular because of our array of candy. During the show people also congregate at the orchestra table and in Norm's room.
Favorite Off-Site Hangout: Irish Rogue and Angus.
Favorite Snack Food: The sugar in our dressing room: jelly beans, Gummi worms, candied ginger, Swedish fish….
Mascot: "Tumor" the Paris baby.
Favorite Therapy: Zicam nose swabs.
Memorable Ad-Libs: The runaway cart makes for fun ad-libs, among them "He's just a butcher!" (Justin Bohon) and "You're no longer a man!" (JD Goldblatt).
Cell Phone Rings: They always seem to come at the most inopportune moments, i.e. "and rain will make the flowers grow" ring ring! And "to love another person is to see the face of God" ring ring!
Memorable Press Encounters: The amazing Marc Thibodeau has sent me on many fun interviews. I talked to a Japanese camera crew wishing their production a happy twentieth(?) birthday. The next week, a crew of French camera people followed me all over the theatre and were excited to see the "exact place I stand before I go on stage."
Fastest Costume Change: I think Fantine's behind-the-barricade change from long hair to short hair and then lady to prostitute holds the record.

1
Photo courtesy Ali Ewoldt

2
Photo by David Gewirtzman

3
Photo by Aubrey Reuben

4
Photo courtesy Ali Ewoldt

5
Photo courtesy Ali Ewoldt

6
Photo courtesy Ali Ewoldt

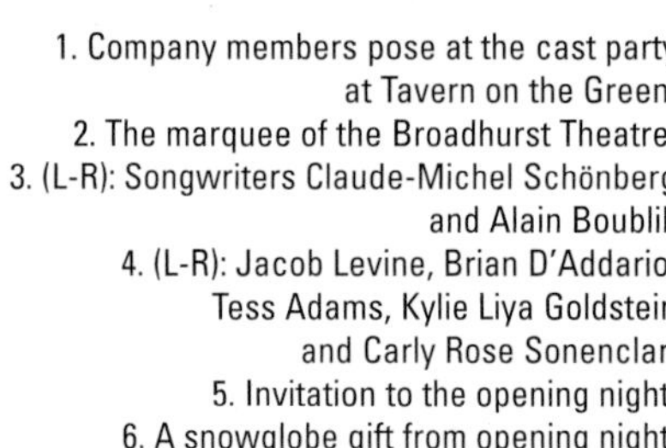
1. Company members pose at the cast party at Tavern on the Green.
2. The marquee of the Broadhurst Theatre.
3. (L-R): Songwriters Claude-Michel Schönberg and Alain Boublil.
4. (L-R): Jacob Levine, Brian D'Addario, Tess Adams, Kylie Liya Goldstein and Carly Rose Sonenclar.
5. Invitation to the opening night.
6. A snowglobe gift from opening night.

Les Misérables
Scrapbook

1. (L-R): Gary Beach, Alexander Gemignani and Jeff Barnett at the opening night party at Tavern on the Green.
2. (L-R): Ali Ewoldt and director John Caird on opening night.
3. (L-R): Daphne Rubin-Vega and Celia Keenan-Bolger.
4. (L-R): Norm Lewis and Ali Ewoldt.

Who Wore the Heaviest/Hottest Costume: I think my wedding dress is the heaviest. It's certainly the largest. Norm's probably the hottest in his heavy coats and big hats.
Who Wore the Least: Adam, Aaron and JD have "pants-less Fridays."
Memorable Stage Door Fan Encounter: Christine Jimenez is an amazing fan of ours who draws our portraits. It's always nice to see her before the show and see what fun picture she's created.
Latest Audience Arrival: Latecomers have to wait until "At the End of the Day" to be seated. I'm sure there's nothing semi-embarrassed theatregoers enjoy more than having an entire cast scream and run at them as they try to take their seats.
Catchphrases Only the Company Would Recognize: "Settle, I have asked."—John Caird. "Finished!"—Celia.
Orchestra Member Who Played the Most Instruments: Charlie Descarfino is our percussionist and plays 42 instruments during the show.
Orchestra Member Who Played the Most Consecutive Performances Without A Sub: Annbritt DuChateau, keyboards.
Best In-House Parody Lyrics: There's the Bread Song: "Rye and raisin, pumpernickel, whole wheat scones and seven grain…."
The post wedding song: "See you all in hell…."
And whatever slightly obscene things Daphne would shout during "At the End of the Day."
Memorable Creative-Team Note: Claude-Michel Schönberg told us we needed "more vitamins."
Company In-Jokes: Victor Hawks is notorious for not wearing "dirt." One day the boys ambushed him and covered him in it.
Understudy Anecdote: In our first week of previews Alex (Valjean) got sick and had to miss the entire weekend. Victor Hawks, one of his understudies, had to go on with virtually no rehearsal. The first day he had our assistant director coaching him between scenes in the dressing room, and a stage manager leading him around. (I occasionally had to lead him around onstage as well.) Luckily he was a quick learner and pulled it off quite nicely!
Nicknames: Jeff Kready: "Dupes." Justin Bohon: "Boon." Nehal Joshi: "Neji."
Sweethearts Within the Company: No one. However, Justin has some fancy moves in "Lovely Ladies."
Embarrassing Moments: I was talking to some of the women and we couldn't think of a single embarrassing moment. Later that night, the Rue Plumet gate unhooked, almost sending itself and Adam Jacobs flying into the audience. The rest of the act was about the gates and the two men standing onstage trying to hold them together. Not quite embarrassing, but certainly memorable.
Coolest Thing About Being in This Show: I love being a part of perhaps the most inspiring musical of my childhood. I think it was the first show I was fully obsessed with and memorized completely. Getting to do it every night with such amazing performers is pretty cool too.

The Lieutenant of Inishmore

First Preview: April 18, 2006. Opened: May 3, 2006.
Closed: September 3, 2006 after 16 Previews and 142 Performances.

PLAYBILL

LYCEUM THEATRE
149 West 45th Street
A Shubert Organization Theatre
Gerald Schoenfeld, *Chairman* Philip J. Smith, *President*
Robert E. Wankel, *Executive Vice President*

RANDALL L. WREGHITT DEDE HARRIS ATLANTIC THEATER COMPANY
DAVID LEHRER HARRIET NEWMAN LEVE & RON NICYNSKI
ZAVELSON MEYRELLES GREINER GROUP
MORT SWINSKY & REDFERN GOLDMAN PRODUCTIONS
RUTH HENDEL
present

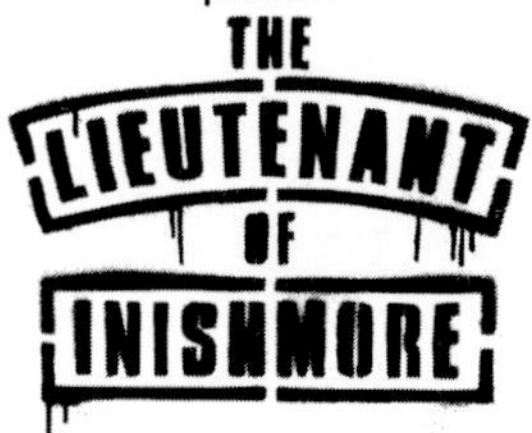

by
MARTIN McDONAGH

with
DAVID WILSON BARNES JORDAN BRIDGES
ANDREW CONNOLLY CHRISTOPHER DENHAM
DASHIELL EAVES PETER GERETY
JERZY GWIAZDOWSKI ALISON PILL

set design SCOTT PASK
costume design THERESA SQUIRE
lighting design MICHAEL CHYBOWSKI

sound design OBADIAH EAVES
music MATT McKENZIE
arrangements ANDREW RANKEN

casting PAT McCORKLE, CSA
fight director J. DAVID BRIMMER
dialect coach STEPHEN GABIS

production stage manager JAMES HARKER
production management AURORA PRODUCTIONS
general management RICHARDS/CLIMAN, INC.

associate producer BRAUN-McFARLANE PRODUCTIONS
marketing HHC MARKETING
press representative BONEAU/BRYAN-BROWN

directed by
WILSON MILAM

Originally produced by Atlantic Theater Company on February 27th, 2006
by special arrangement with Randall L. Wreghitt & Dede Harris.

The producers wish to express their appreciation to the
Theatre Development Fund for its support of this production.

9/3/06

CAST

(in order of speaking)

Davey .... JERZY GWIAZDOWSKI
Donny .... PETER GERETY
Padraic .... CHRISTOPHER DENHAM
James .... JORDAN BRIDGES
Mairead .... ALISON PILL
Christy .... ANDREW CONNOLLY
Joey .... DASHIELL EAVES
Brendan .... DAVID WILSON BARNES

TIME/PLACE

The play is set in 1993
on the island of Inishmore, County Galway.

UNDERSTUDIES

For Donny & Christy:
JOHN AHLIN
For Davey, Padraic, James, Christy & Joey:
BRIAN AVERS
For James:
DAVID WILSON BARNES
For Mairead:
CRISTIN MILIOTI
For Brendan:
JORDAN BRIDGES

(L-R): Domhnall Gleeson and Peter Gerety

Photo by Monique Carboni

The Lieutenant of Inishmore

David Wilson Barnes
Brendan

Jordan Bridges
James

Andrew Connolly
Christy

Christopher Denham
Padraic

Dashiell Eaves
Joey

Peter Gerety
Donny

Jerzy Gwiazdowski
Davey

Alison Pill
Mairead

John Ahlin
Understudy for Donny & Christy

Brian Avers
Understudy for Padraic, Joey, Davey, James & Christy

Cristin Milioti
Understudy for Mairead

Martin McDonagh
Playwright

Wilson Milam
Director

Scott Pask
Set Designer

Theresa Squire
Costume Designer

Michael Chybowski
Lighting Designer

Obadiah Eaves
Sound Designer

Matt McKenzie
Music

Andrew Ranken
Arrangements

Pat McCorkle, C.S.A.
Casting

J. David Brimmer
Fight Director

Stephen Gabis
Dialect Coach

Thom Clay
Company Manager

David Richards and Tamar Climan, Richards/Climan, Inc.
General Manager

Randall L. Wreghitt
Producer

Dede Harris
Producer

Neil Pepe
Artistic Director Atlantic Theater Company

Andrew D. Hamingson
Managing Director, Atlantic Theater Company

David Lehrer
Producer

Harriet Newman Leve
Producer

Ron Nicynski
Producer

Billy Zavelson, Zavelson Meyrelles Greiner Group
Producer

Chip Meyrelles, Zavelson Meyrelles Greiner Group
Producer

Kenneth Greiner, Zavelson Meyrelles Greiner Group
Producer

Mort Swinsky
Producer

The Lieutenant of Inishmore

Eric Goldman, Redfern Goldman Productions *Producer*

Katrin Redfern, Redfern Goldman Productions *Producer*

Ruth Hendel *Producer*

Laurence Braun, Braun-McFarlane Productions *Associate Producer*

R.J. McFarlane, Braun-McFarlane Productions *Associate Producer*

Jeff Binder *James*

Domhnall Gleeson *Davey*

Brian D'Arcy James *Brendan*

David Wilmot *Padraic*

Photos by Ben Strothmann

STAGE CREW
(L-R): Jim Harker (Production Stage Manager), Leah Nelson (House Props), Jenny Montgomery (Production Sound), Anmaree Rodibaugh (Production Props), Adam Braunstein (House Carpenter), Heather Richmond Wright (Hair & Makeup), Freda Farrell (Stage Manager), Laura Koch (House Props), Cathy Prager (House Props), Bill Rowland (House Electrician)

BOX OFFICE
(L-R):
Sidney J. Burgoyne (Assistant Treasurer) and Tim Moran (Assistant Treasurer)

FRONT OF HOUSE STAFF
Front Row (L-R): Joann Swanson (House Manager), Merida Cohen (Chief Usher), Elsie Grosvenor (Directress), Lorraine Bellaflores (Usherette)

Middle Row (L-R): Susan Houghton (Ticket Taker), Rosie Rodriguez (Head Porter), Gerry Belitsis (Usher), Tim Moran (Assistant Treasurer), Sonia Moreno (Usherette)

Back Row (L-R): Judy Pinouz (Usher), Ramona (Usherette), Jack Kearns (Security), John Donovan (Night Doorman), Robert Dejesus (Usher)

The Lieutenant of Inishmore

SCRAPBOOK
David Wilmot and Alison Pill take part in the 2006 "Stars in the Alley" event in Shubert Alley.

Photos by Aubrey Reuben

Brian d'Arcy James gets ready to perform at the 2006 "Broadway under the Stars" concert in Central Park

STAFF FOR *THE LIEUTENANT OF INISHMORE*

GENERAL MANAGEMENT
RICHARDS/CLIMAN, INC.
David R. Richards Tamar Haimes
Laura Janik Cronin

COMPANY MANAGER
Thom Clay

PRODUCTION MANAGEMENT
AURORA PRODUCTIONS, INC.
Gene O'Donovan, W. Benjamin Heller II,
Bethany Weinstein, Hilary Austin, Melissa Mazdra

GENERAL PRESS REPRESENTATIVE
BONEAU/BRYAN-BROWN
Chris Boneau Susanne Tighe
Heath Schwartz

PRODUCTION STAGE MANAGER JAMES HARKER
Stage Manager ... Freda Farrell
Assistant to the Director ... Nick Leavens
Wig Designer ... Charles LaPointe
Associate Set Designer ... Nancy Thun
Assistant Set Designer ... Lauren Alvarez
Assistant Costume Designer ... Renee Mariotti
Assistant Lighting Designer ... Dale Knoth
Assistant Sound Designer ... Ryan Powers
Production Management ... Aurora Productions/ Gene O'Donovan, W. Benjamin Heller II, Bethany Weinstein, Hilary Austin, Melissa Mazdra
Head Carpenter ... Adam Braunstein
Advance Carpenter ... Paul Wimmer
Head Electrician ... William Rowland
Production Electrician ... James Gardner
Production Sound ... Jenny Montgomery
Production Properties Supervisor ... Anmaree Rodibaugh
Head Props ... Leah Nelson
Wardrobe Supervisor ... Nancy Schaefer
Hair Supervisor ... Heather Richmond Wright
Fight Captain ... Dashiell Eaves
Properties Crew ... Laura Koch, Cathy Prager
Dresser ... Edmund Harrison
Prop Shopper ... Peter Sarafin
Casting Associate ... Kelly Gillespie
Casting Assistant ... Joe Lopick
Production Assistant ... Kirsten Lake
Press Associates ... Adrian Bryan-Brown, Jim Byk, Brandi Cornwell, Jackie Green, Juliana Hannett, Hector Hernandez, Erin Hinton, Jessica Johnson, Kevin Jones, Amy Kass, Eric Louie, Aaron Meier, Joe Perrotta, Linnae Petruzzelli, Matt Polk, Matt Ross
Banking ... Commerce Bank/ Ashley Elezi, Barbara Von Borstel
Payroll ... Castellana Services, Inc./Lance Castellana
Accountant ... FK Partners/ Robert Fried, Elliott Aronstam
Insurance ... DeWitt Stern Group, Inc./ Anthony Pittari
Legal ... Cowan DeBaets Abrahams & Sheppard LLP/ Frederick P. Bimbler
Advertising ... Spot Co/ Drew Hodges, Jim Edwards, Amelia Heape, Jen McClelland
Marketing ... HHC Marketing/ Hugh Hysell, Amanda Pekoe, Jennifer Scherer
Group Sales ... Shubert Group Sales
Merchandising ... Cardinal Theatrical
Website ... Late August Design
Production Photographer ... Monique Carboni
Opening Night Coordination ... Tobak Lawrence Company

ATLANTIC THEATER COMPANY STAFF
Artistic Director ... Neil Pepe
Managing Director ... Andrew D. Hamingson
School Executive Director ... Mary McCann
General Manager ... Melinda Berk
Associate Artistic Director ... Christian Parker
Development Director ... Erika Mallin
Development Associate ... Rose Yndigoyen
Production Manager ... Lester Grant
Marketing Director ... Jodi Sheeler
Membership Coordinator ... Sara Montgomery
Operations Manager ... Brian Isaacs
Company Manager ... Nick Leavens
Assistant to the Artistic and Managing Directors ... Laura Savia
School Associate Director ... Kate Blumberg
School Associate Director ... Steven Hawley
Business Manager ... Diana Ascher
Education Director ... Frances Tarr
School Production Director ... Geoff Berman
School Production Manager ... Eric Southern
School Admissions ... Brandon Thompson
Resident Director ... William H. Macy
Resident Lighting Designer ... Howard Werner
Resident Fight Director ... Rick Sordelet
Box Office Treasurer ... Frances Tarr
House Managers ... Josh Cole, Sarah Heartley, Nick Leavens, David Toomey

CREDITS
Scenery constructed and painted by Showmotion, Inc. Original scenery constructed by Tom Carroll Scenery. Scenic charge for the cottage by Brian D. Cote. Lighting and sound equipment by GSD Productions. Costumes constructed by Lee Purdy, Kyra Svetlovsky, Piort Candelario. Aerographic services by Flying by Foy. Special effects by Waldo Warshaw. Mannequins by Peter Sarafin, Craig Grigg. Firearms provided by IAR, Inc.

SPECIAL THANKS
Bill Berloni and Mr. Ed, Lester Grant, Camryn Duff, Erin Lorek, Griffith Maloney, Anton Nadler, Stephanie Parsons, Austin Tidwell, Barbara Milam, Mary McDonagh and the use of her music library

www.InishmoreOnBroadway.com

THE SHUBERT ORGANIZATION, INC.
Board of Directors

Gerald Schoenfeld
Chairman

Philip J. Smith
President

Wyche Fowler, Jr.

John W. Kluge

Lee J. Seidler

Michael I. Sovern

Stuart Subotnick

Robert E. Wankel
Executive Vice President

Peter Entin
Vice President
Theatre Operations

Elliot Greene
Vice President
Finance

David Andrews
Vice President
Shubert Ticketing Services

John Darby
Vice President
Facilities

D.S. Moynihan
Vice President – Creative Projects

House Manager ... Joann Swanson

The Light in the Piazza

First Preview: March 17, 2005. Opened: April 18, 2005.
Closed: July 2, 2006 after 36 Previews and 504 Performances.

PLAYBILL

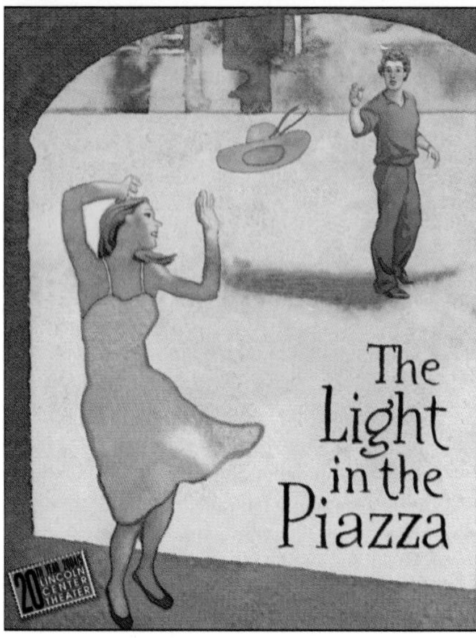

LINCOLN CENTER THEATER
AT THE VIVIAN BEAUMONT

under the direction of
André Bishop and Bernard Gersten
presents

The Light in the Piazza

book
Craig Lucas

music and lyrics
Adam Guettel

based on the novel by Elizabeth Spencer

with (in alphabetical order)

Michael Berresse Sarah Uriarte Berry David Bonanno David Burnham
Victoria Clark Katie Clarke Patti Cohenour Beau Gravitte Laura Griffith
Prudence Wright Holmes Jennifer Hughes Felicity LaFortune
Catherine LaValle Aaron Lazar Michel Moinot Adam Overett
Peter Samuel Chris Sarandon Joseph Siravo Diane Sutherland

sets Michael Yeargan
costumes Catherine Zuber
lighting Christopher Akerlind
sound ACME Sound Partners

orchestrations Ted Sperling and Adam Guettel
additional orchestrations Bruce Coughlin
conductor Kimberly Grigsby

casting Janet Foster, C.S.A.
production stage manager Peter Wolf
general press agent Philip Rinaldi
musical theater associate producer Ira Weitzman

general manager Adam Siegel
production manager Jeff Hamlin
director of development Hattie K. Jutagir
director of marketing Linda Mason Ross

music direction
Ted Sperling

musical staging
Jonathan Butterell

direction
Bartlett Sher

This production of "The Light in the Piazza" is dedicated to the memory of Andrew Heiskell, who, during his lifetime, gave off a lovely light of his own.

LCT thanks the Blanchette Hooker Rockefeller Fund for its outstanding support.
Major support is provided by The Shen Family Foundation and generous support by The New York Community Trust–Mary P. Oenslager Foundation Fund and the Henry Nias Foundation.
LCT gratefully acknowledges an extraordinary gift from the Estate of Edith K. Ehrman.
Special thanks to The Harold and Mimi Steinberg Charitable Trust for supporting new American plays at LCT.

American Airlines is the official airline of Lincoln Center Theater.
Merrill Lynch is a 2006 LCT Season Sponsor.

LCT wishes to express its appreciation to Theatre Development Fund for its support of this production.

The World Premiere of THE LIGHT IN THE PIAZZA was produced by the Intiman Theatre, Seattle, Washington; Bartlett Sher, Artistic Director, Laura Penn, Managing Director; and the Goodman Theatre, Chicago, Illinois, Robert Falls, Artistic Director, Roche Schulfer, Executive Director.
Developed with the Assistance of the Sundance Institute Theatre Laboratory.
Produced by arrangement with Turner Entertainment Co, Owner of the original motion picture "Light in the Piazza."

7/2/06

CAST

(in order of appearance)

Margaret Johnson .... VICTORIA CLARK
Clara Johnson, her daughter .... KATIE CLARKE
Fabrizio Naccarelli .... AARON LAZAR
Signor Naccarelli,
Fabrizio's father .... CHRIS SARANDON
Giuseppe Naccarelli,
Fabrizio's brother .... MICHAEL BERRESSE
Franca Naccarelli,
Giuseppe's wife .... SARAH URIARTE BERRY
Signora Naccarelli,
Fabrizio's mother .... PATTI COHENOUR
Roy Johnson,
Margaret's husband .... BEAU GRAVITTE
Tour Guide .... FELICITY LaFORTUNE
Priest .... JOSEPH SIRAVO
Ensemble .... DAVID BONANNO,
DAVID BURNHAM, LAURA GRIFFITH,
PRUDENCE WRIGHT HOLMES,
JENNIFER HUGHES,
FELICITY LaFORTUNE,
MICHEL MOINOT, JOSEPH SIRAVO

At Tuesday and Wednesday evening performances:

Margaret Johnson .... PATTI COHENOUR
Signora Naccarelli,
Fabrizio's mother .... DIANE SUTHERLAND

Continued on next page

(L-R): Victoria Clark and Katie Clarke as Margaret and Clara Johnson

Photo by Joan Marcus

The Light in the Piazza

ACT ONE

Overture
Statues and Stories .... Margaret and Clara
The Beauty Is .... Clara
Il Mondo Era Vuoto .... Fabrizio
Passeggiata .... Fabrizio and Clara
The Joy You Feel .... Franca
Dividing Day .... Margaret
Hysteria .... Clara and Margaret
Say It Somehow .... Clara and Fabrizio

ACT TWO

Aiutami .... The Naccarelli Family
The Light in the Piazza .... Clara
Octet .... Company
Tirade .... Clara
Octet (Reprise) .... Company
The Beauty Is (Reprise) .... Margaret
Let's Walk .... Signor Naccarelli and Margaret
Love to Me .... Fabrizio
Fable .... Margaret

ORCHESTRA

Conductor:
KIMBERLY GRIGSBY
Associate Conductor, Piano, Celesta:
MARK MITCHELL

Violins:
SYLVIA D'AVANZO (Concertmaster), MATTHEW LEHMANN, JAMES TSAO, LISA MATRICARDI, KATHERINE LIVOLSI-STERN, KARL KAWAHARA
Celli:
ROGER SHELL, ROBERT BURKHART
Harp:
VICTORIA DRAKE
Bass:
BRIAN CASSIER
Clarinet/English Horn/Oboe:
DENNIS ANDERSON
Bassoon/Contrabassoon:
GILI SHARETT
Percussion:
MATTHEW GOLD
Guitar/Mandolin/Cymbal:
ANDREW SCHWARTZ

Music Coordinator:
SEYMOUR RED PRESS

(L-R): Chris Sarandon as Signor Naccarelli and Patti Cohenour as Margaret.

TIME AND PLACE

The Light in the Piazza takes place in Florence and Rome in the summer of 1953, with occasional side trips to America.

Assistant Stage Managers .... CLAUDIA LYNCH, MATTHEW MELCHIORRE
Swings .... CATHERINE LaVALLE, ADAM OVERETT, PETER SAMUEL

UNDERSTUDIES

For Margaret:
DIANE SUTHERLAND
For Clara:
LAURA GRIFFITH, JENNIFER HUGHES
For Fabrizio:
DAVID BURNHAM, ADAM OVERETT
For Signor Naccarelli and Roy Johnson:
PETER SAMUEL, JOSEPH SIRAVO
For Signora Naccarelli:
FELICITY LaFORTUNE, DIANE SUTHERLAND
For Giuseppe:
DAVID BONANNO, ADAM OVERETT
For Franca:
LAURA GRIFFITH, CATHERINE LaVALLE
For Tour Guide:
CATHERINE LaVALLE, DIANE SUTHERLAND
For Priest:
ADAM OVERETT, PETER SAMUEL

Photos by Joan Marcus

(L-R): Katie Clarke and Aaron Lazar as Clara and Fabrizio.

The Light in the Piazza

Michael Berresse
Giuseppe Naccarelli

Sarah Uriarte Berry
Franca Naccarelli

David Bonnano
Ensemble

David Burnham
Ensemble

Victoria Clark
Margaret Johnson

Katie Clarke
Clara Johnson

Patti Cohenour
Signora Naccarelli, Margaret at certain performances

Beau Gravitte
Roy Johnson

Laura Griffith
Ensemble

Prudence Wright Holmes
Ensemble

Jennifer Hughes
Ensemble

Felicity LaFortune
Tour Guide, Ensemble

Catherine LaValle
Swing

Aaron Lazar
Fabrizio Naccarelli

Michel Moinot
Ensemble

Adam Overett
Swing

Peter Samuel
Swing

Chris Sarandon
Signor Naccarelli

Joseph Siravo
Priest, Ensemble

Diane Sutherland
Signora Naccarelli at certain perform-ances

Craig Lucas
Book

Adam Guettel
Music and Lyrics, Orchestrations

Bartlett Sher
Director

Ted Sperling
Orchestrations, Musical Direction

Michael Yeargan
Sets

Catherine Zuber
Costumes

Christopher Akerlind
Lighting

Bruce Coughlin
Additional Orchestrations

Tom Clark, Mark Menard and Nevin Steinberg, Acme Sound Partners
Sound

Kimberly Grigsby
Conductor

Janet Foster, C.S.A.
Casting

Seymour Red Press
Music Coordinator

André Bishop and Bernard Gersten, Lincoln Center Theater
Producers

The Light in the Piazza

HAIR DEPARTMENT
(L-R): Alice Ramos (Hair Assistant), Mary Micari (Hair Assistant) and Lazaro Arencibia (Hair Supervisor).

WARDROBE DEPARTMENT
(L-R): Sarah Rochford (Dresser), Jerome Parker (Dresser), Cathy Cline (Dresser), Lynn Bowling (Wardrobe Supervisor), Liam O'Brien (Dresser), Tony Hoffman (Dresser) and Amanda Scott (Dresser).

Photos by Ben Strothmann

ORCHESTRA
Front Row:
Kimberly Grigsby (Music Director).

Second Row:
Katherine Livolsi-Stern (Violin).

Third Row (L-R):
Andrew Schwartz (Guitar) and Victoria Drake (Harp).

Fourth Row (L-R):
Sylvia D'Avanzo (Concertmaster), Dennis Anderson (Reeds), Karl Kawahara (Violin), James Tsao (Violin).

Fifth Row (L-R):
Matthew Gold (Percussion), Mark Mitchell (Piano/Associate Conductor), Gili Sharett (Bassoon/Contrabassoon), Matthew Lehmann (Violin), David Calhoun (Cello, sub).

Back Row (L-R):
Lisa Matricardi (Violin), Robert Burkhart (Cello), David Phillips (Bass, sub).

Not Pictured:
Brian Cassier (Bass) and Roger Shell (Cello).

The Light in the Piazza

STAGE CREW
Front Row (L-R):
Nick Irons (Electrician/Follow Spot Operator), Walter Murphy (Production Carpenter), John Ross (Props), Karl Rausenberger (Production Props), Rudy Wood (Props), Will Coholan (Props), Ray Skillin (Carpenter).

Back Row (L-R):
Frank Linn (Electrician/Automated Tech), Bruce Rubin (Electrician/Board Operator), Marc Salzberg (Production Soundman), Gary Simon (Deck Sound), Juan Bustamante (Automation Carpenter), Pat Merryman (Production Electrician), Linda Heard (Electrician), Jeff Ward (Electrician/Follow Spot Operator), Kristina Clark (Electrician), John Howie (Carpenter), Mat Altman (Electrician/Follow Spot Operator), Scott Jackson (Props), Kevin McNeill (Automation Carpenter) and Andrew Belits (Carpenter).

Not Pictured:
Mark Dignam (Props), Bill Nagle (Production Flyman), Joe Pizzuto (Electrician/Follow Spot).

Photos by Ben Strothmann

STAGE MANAGEMENT
(L-R): Jen Nelson (Production Assistant), Matthew Melchiorre (Assistant Stage Manager), Peter Wolf (Production Stage Manager) and Claudia Lynch (Assistant Stage Manager).

BOX OFFICE
(L-R): Bob Belkin, Marc Friedenreich and Fred Bonis.

FRONT OF HOUSE STAFF
Front Row (L-R):
Miriam Miller, Jodi Gigliobianco, Susan Lehman, Barbara Hart.

Middle Row (L-R):
Larry Hincher, Alexandra Zavilowicz, Justin McCulla.

Back Row (L-R):
Nick Andors, Manny Billingslea, Mim Pollock, Margareta Shakridge-Cottington, Judith Fanelli and Steve Spear.

Not Pictured:
Rheba Flegelman (House Manager)

The Light in the Piazza

LINCOLN CENTER THEATER
ANDRÉ BISHOP **BERNARD GERSTEN**
ARTISTIC DIRECTOR **EXECUTIVE PRODUCER**

ADMINISTRATIVE STAFF

GENERAL MANAGER .... ADAM SIEGEL
Associate General Manager .... Melanie Weinraub
General Management Assistant .... Beth Dembrow
Facilities Manager .... Alex Mustelier
Assistant Facilities Manager .... Michael Assalone
GENERAL PRESS AGENT .... PHILIP RINALDI
Press Associate .... Barbara Carroll
PRODUCTION MANAGER .... JEFF HAMLIN
Associate Production Manager .... Paul Smithyman
DIRECTOR OF DEVELOPMENT .... HATTIE K. JUTAGIR
Associate Director of Development .... Rachel Norton
Manager of Special Events and Young Patron Program .... Karin Schall
Grants Writer .... Neal Brilliant
Coordinator, Patron Program .... Sheilaja Rao
Development Associate .... Chris Chrzanowski
Assistant to the Director of Development .... Marsha Martinez
Development Assistant/ Special Events .... Nicole Lindenbaum
DIRECTOR OF FINANCE .... DAVID S. BROWN
Controller .... Susan Knox
Systems Manager .... Stacy Thomas
Finance Assistant .... Kellie Kroyer
DIRECTOR OF MARKETING .... Linda Mason Ross
Marketing Associate .... Denis Guerin
Marketing Assistant .... Elizabeth Kandel
DIRECTOR OF EDUCATION .... KATI KOERNER
Associate Director of Education .... Dionne O'Dell
Assistant to the Executive Producer ... Barbara Hourigan
Office Assistant .... Kenneth Collins
Messenger .... Esau Burgess
Reception .... Andrew Elsesser, Daryl Watson

ARTISTIC STAFF

ASSOCIATE DIRECTORS ...... GRACIELA DANIELE, NICHOLAS HYTNER, SUSAN STROMAN, DANIEL SULLIVAN
DRAMATURG and DIRECTOR, LCT DIRECTORS LAB .... ANNE CATTANEO
CASTING DIRECTOR .... DANIEL SWEE, CSA
MUSICAL THEATER ASSOCIATE PRODUCER .... IRA WEITZMAN
Artistic Administrator .... Julia Judge
Casting Associate .... Camille Hickman

In Loving Memory of
GERALD GUTIERREZ
Associate Director 1991-2003

HOUSE STAFF

HOUSE MANAGER .... RHEBA FLEGELMAN
Production Carpenter .... Walter Murphy
Production Electrician .... Patrick Merryman
Production Propertyman .... Karl Rausenberger
Production Flyman .... William Nagle
House Technician .... Bill Burke
Chief Usher .... M.L. Pollock
Box Office Treasurer .... Fred Bonis
Assistant Treasurer .... Robert A. Belkin

SPECIAL SERVICES

Advertising .... Serino-Coyne/ Jim Russek, Christin Seidel
Principal Poster Artist .... James McMullan
Poster Art for *The Light in the Piazza* .... James McMullan
Counsel .... Peter L. Felcher, Esq.; Charles H. Googe, Esq.; and Rachel Hoover, Esq. of Paul, Weiss, Rifkind, Wharton & Garrison
Immigration Counsel .... Theodore Ruthizer, Esq.; Mark D. Koestler, Esq. of Kramer, Levin, Naftalis & Frankel LLP
Auditor .... Douglas Burack, C.P.A. Lutz & Carr, L.L.P.
Insurance .... Jennifer Brown of DeWitt Stern Group
Photographer .... Joan Marcus
Travel .... Tygon Tours
Web Design and Development .... Four Eyes Productions
Consulting Architect .... Hugh Hardy, Hardy Holzman Pfeiffer Associates
Construction Manager .... Yorke Construction
Payroll Service .... Castellana Services, Inc.

STAFF FOR *THE LIGHT IN THE PIAZZA*

COMPANY MANAGER .... JOSH LOWENTHAL
Assistant Company Manager .... Jessica Perlmeter Cochrane
Assistant Director .... Sarna Lapine
Assistant to Mr. Lucas .... Troy Miller
Dance Captain .... Laura Griffith
Assistant Set Designer .... Mikiko Suzuki
Assistant Costume Designers .... David Newell, Michael Zecker
Assistant Lighting Designer .... Michael J. Spadaro
Assistant Sound Designer .... Jeffrey Yoshi Lee
Associate Orchestrator .... Bruce Coughlin
Rehearsal Pianist .... Adam Ben-David
Music Copyist .... Emily Grishman Music Preparation/ Emily Grishman, Katharine Edmonds
Dialect Coach .... Ralph Zito
Props .... Christopher Schneider
Production Soundman .... Marc Salzberg
Light Board Operator .... Bruce Rubin
Moving Light Programmer .... Victor Seastone
Wardrobe Supervisor .... Lynn Bowling
Dressers .... Cathy Cline, Virginia Neininger, Liam O'Brien, Jerome Parker, Sarah Rochford, Jane Rottenbach
Hair and Wig Designer .... Jerry Altenburg
Make-up Designer .... Angelina Avallone
Hair Supervisor .... Lazaro Arencibia
Hair Assistants .... Mary Micari, Alice Ramos
Production Assistants .... Andrew Einhorn, Melanie T. Morgan, Jen Nelson

Italian translation for "Il Mondo Era Vuoto"
by Judith Blazer.

L.A. Casting Consultant .... Julia Flores

CREDITS

Show control and scenic motion control featuring stage command systems by Scenic Technologies, a division of Production Resource Group, LLC, New Windsor, NY. Scenery fabrication by PRG Scenic Technologies, a division of Production Resource Group, LLC, New Windsor, NY. Men's costumes executed by Tim McKelvey, Angels the Costumier and Vos Savant, Inc. Women's costumes by Parson-Meares, Ltd. and Euro Co. Costumes. Millinery by Hugh Hanson for Carelli Costumes Inc. Shoes by LaDuca Shoes NYC. Special thanks to Bra*Tenders for hosiery and undergarments. Lighting equipment from PRG Lighting. Sound equipment by Sound Associates. Piano by Steinway & Sons. Natural herb cough drops courtesy of Ricola USA, Inc. Emer'gen-C vitamin C drink mix provided by Alacer Corp.

Stock and amateur performance rights to *The Light in the Piazza* are licensed by R&H Theatricals: rnhtheatricals.com

Mr. Guettel would like to thank the following people: Loy Arcenas, Judith Blazer, Ted Chapin, Mary Cleere Haran, Alison Cochrill, Stephanie Coen, Eric Ebbenga, Michael Feinstein, Peter Franklin, Father John Fraser, Pat Graney, Michael Greif, John Guare, Robert Hurwitz, Celia Keenan-Bolger, Tina Landau, Arthur Laurents, Marcella Lorca, John McDermott, Steven Pasquale, Stephen Sondheim, Alfred Uhry, and Wayne Wilcox.

Lobby refreshments by Sweet Concessions

For groups of 20 or more:
Caryl Goldsmith Group Sales
(212) 889-4300

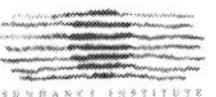
Developed with the assistance of the Sundance Institute Theatre Laboratory.

Light in the Piazza
Scrapbook

Correspondent: Victoria Clark.

Closing Night Curtain Speech: The closest thing I can compare this performance to is natural childbirth. We knew it was coming, we faced it with equal parts dread and excitement, the head was down, we knew this baby was coming. And then it hurt like hell, it is a relief to have it over, and look what a beautiful baby we have.

I hope nobody has a roast in the oven, because today we leave the piazza, and there are a number of folks we want to acknowledge and thank. First of all, we are all storytellers up here, and we are no good without a great story. We were given that story by Elizabeth Spencer, a wonderful, Mississippi-born writer who wrote the novella of *The Light in the Piazza*. She is alive and well in Durham, North Carolina, and could not be with us today, but sends her love.

Next, we were fortunate and blessed enough to have this source material fall into the genius talented hands of Adam Guettel and Craig Lucas, whose work stands alone separately as a play, without any music, and as an opera, of sorts, without any scenes. And you put them together and you have, two! Two! Two shows in one, and this complexity and strength in the individual components is what gives *Piazza* its depth and texture.

Next, you have to have a director who knows what to do with this material, and Bartlett Sher made us all better than we ever knew we were.

I thank Jonathan Butterell, the magic unseen hand of the *Piazza*, who gave us our beautiful subtle body language, gave the piece its fluid movement of staging and transitions, and kept us all firmly grounded and rooted in our bodies.

I thank our designers Michael Yeargan (sets), Catherine Zuber (costumes) and Christopher Ackerlind (lights) along with Nevin Steinberg (sound) who could not be here.

I thank the Intiman Theater in Seattle, the Goodman Theater in Chicago and its Artistic Director Robert Falls, and especially our Broadway producers, Lincoln Center Theater, Bernard Gersten and André Bishop for their courage and dedication, and for giving us the perfect theatre, the Vivian Beaumont Theater, to bring this piece to life.

I thank our marvelous conductor Kimberly Grigsby and the orchestra (who have to stay in the pit to play the exit music!) And I thank our orchestrators Adam Guettel, Ted Sperling, and Bruce Coughlin. I thank our unbelievable cast; I could write a book about each and every one of them.

Those beautiful men and women you saw pushing the scenery around, and riding the bicycle, and serving the coffee, and bringing the props on and off the stage, are each understudying one of the principal roles in the show. And they are all superstars, and each and every one of them has had to step in and fill their roles on a moment's notice, and they have so brilliantly with great style and leadership.

Photo by Jeff Meshel

Victoria Clark delivering her heartfelt curtain speech from the stage of the Beaumont Theater after the final performance.

And I have to personally thank Patti Cohenour, who, besides myself, is the only remaining cast member who has performed all three productions of *Piazza*. In addition to doing Signora every night, for the past four months she has been the Margaret alternate, going back and forth between doing six shows a week of Signora (and yes, that's a high C she is singing), and also Margaret twice a week, and she has done this all with tremendous grace and leadership, and I guarantee you she is the only woman on the planet who could have done that!

And to prove to you that it truly takes a village to put on a show, I would like to introduce you to our crew. Our props, sound, lights, set, automation, wardrobe, and hair crew who all work so hard to make the show work.

And lastly, I want to thank you, the audience for being here today, and for giving us so much energy. I will just speak for myself, and say that there were many days when I wasn't sure I had the strength required to tell the emotional story of *Piazza*, the strength to climb that mountain. And those were the days when we could literally feel your support coming out at us, almost as though you were somehow building a road between your hearts and the stage. And we could feel it. It was palpable and strong, so strong we could stand on it. And that's what we did, and you gave us that strength and that love and that support.

It has been a magnificent ride.

P.S. I didn't get to say this at the final performance: There was so much talk about what a rainy, dark winter and spring we had here in New York, but I will tell you something. The sun was always shining at the Vivian Beaumont. The light in the piazza came from all of us, from the cast, crew, musicians, the writers, the audience, and we were all able to grow and bask in it and become better people, better lovers of life, better citizens of the planet.

So, as the Naccarellis would say, "Alla bellezza della vita"—"To the beauty of life."

May we all see each other again soon.

Photo by Jeff Meshel

The cast and crew take their final curtain call on closing night.

The Lion King

First Preview: October 15, 1997. Opened: November 13, 1997.
Still running as of May 31, 2007.

PLAYBILL

CAST

(in order of appearance)

RAFIKI ..... Tshidi Manye
MUFASA ..... Alton Fitzgerald White
SARABI ..... Jean Michelle Grier
ZAZU ..... Tony Freeman
SCAR ..... Derek Smith
YOUNG SIMBA ..... Justin Martin
(Wed. Mat., Thurs., Sat. Eve., Sun. Mat.)
YOUNG SIMBA ..... Jarrell J. Singleton
(Wed. Eve., Fri., Sat. Mat., Sun. Eve.)
YOUNG NALA ..... Ashley Renee Jordan
(Wed. Mat., Thurs., Sat. Mat., Sun. Eve.)
YOUNG NALA ..... Alex de Castro
(Wed. Eve., Fri., Sat. Eve., Sun. Mat.)
SHENZI ..... Bonita J. Hamilton
BANZAI ..... Benjamin Sterling Cannon
ED ..... Enrique Segura
TIMON ..... Danny Rutigliano
PUMBAA ..... Tom Alan Robbins
SIMBA ..... Josh Tower
NALA ..... Kissy Simmons
ENSEMBLE SINGERS ..... Alvin Crawford, Lindiwe Dlamini, Bongi Duma, Andrea Frierson, Jean Michelle Grier, Michael Alexander Henry, Joel Karie, Ron Kunene, Sheryl McCallum, S'bu Ngema, Mpume Sikakane, Rema Webb, Kenny Redell Williams

Continued on next page

MINSKOFF THEATRE

UNDER THE DIRECTION OF
JAMES M. NEDERLANDER, JAMES L. NEDERLANDER,
SARA MINSKOFF ALLAN AND THE MINSKOFF FAMILY

Music & Lyrics by
ELTON JOHN & TIM RICE

Additional Music & Lyrics by
LEBO M, MARK MANCINA, JAY RIFKIN, JULIE TAYMOR, HANS ZIMMER

Book by
ROGER ALLERS & IRENE MECCHI

Starring
DEREK SMITH ALTON FITZGERALD WHITE TSHIDI MANYE
TONY FREEMAN TOM ALAN ROBBINS DANNY RUTIGLIANO
JOSH TOWER KISSY SIMMONS
BENJAMIN STERLING CANNON BONITA J. HAMILTON ENRIQUE SEGURA
ALEX DE CASTRO ASHLEY RENEE JORDAN JUSTIN MARTIN JARRELL J. SINGLETON

KRISTINA MICHELLE BETHEL JOHN E. BRADY KYLIN BRADY CAMILLE M. BROWN
MICHELLE AGUILAR CAMAYA ALVIN CRAWFORD GABRIEL A. CROOM
GARLAND DAYS LINDIWE DLAMINI BONGI DUMA ANGELICA EDWARDS ALICIA FISHER ANDREA FRIERSON
IAN YURI GARDNER JEAN MICHELLE GRIER MICHAEL ALEXANDER HENRY TONY JAMES DENNIS JOHNSTON
CORNELIUS JONES, JR. JOEL KARIE GREGORY A. KING JACK KOENIG RON KUNENE LISA LEWIS
SHERYL McCALLUM RAY MERCER JENNIFER HARRISON NEWMAN S'BU NGEMA
BRANDON CHRISTOPHER O'NEAL DAWN NOEL PIGNUOLA MPUME SIKAKANE SOPHIA N. STEPHENS
RYAN BROOKE TAYLOR STEVEN EVAN WASHINGTON REMA WEBB KENNY REDELL WILLIAMS

Adapted from the screenplay by
IRENE MECCHI & JONATHAN ROBERTS & LINDA WOOLVERTON

Produced by
PETER SCHNEIDER & THOMAS SCHUMACHER

Scenic Design RICHARD HUDSON
Costume Design JULIE TAYMOR
Lighting Design DONALD HOLDER
Mask & Puppet Design JULIE TAYMOR & MICHAEL CURRY

Sound Design STEVE CANYON KENNEDY
Hair & Makeup Design MICHAEL WARD
Associate Director JOHN STEFANIUK
Production Dance Supervisor MAREY GRIFFITH

Associate Producers TODD LACY, AUBREY LYNCH II
Technical Director DAVID BENKEN
Production Stage Manager THERESA BAILEY
Production Supervisor DOC ZORTHIAN

Music Director KARL JURMAN
Associate Music Producer ROBERT ELHAI
Music Coordinator MICHAEL KELLER
Orchestrators ROBERT ELHAI, DAVID METZGER, BRUCE FOWLER

Music Produced for the Stage & Additional Score by MARK MANCINA
Additional Vocal Score, Vocal Arrangements & Choral Director LEBO M
Casting BINDER CASTING/ MARK BRANDON
Press Representative BONEAU/ BRYAN-BROWN

Choreography by
GARTH FAGAN

Directed by
JULIE TAYMOR

10/2/06

Josh Tower (center) as Simba, with chorus.

Photo by Joan Marcus

The Lion King

SCENES AND MUSICAL NUMBERS

ACT ONE

Scene 1	Pride Rock	
	"Circle of Life" with "Nants' Ingonyama"	Rafiki, Ensemble
Scene 2	Scar's Cave	
Scene 3	Rafiki's Tree	
Scene 4	The Pridelands	
	"The Morning Report"	Zazu, Young Simba, Mufasa
Scene 5	Scar's Cave	
Scene 6	The Pridelands	
	"I Just Can't Wait to Be King"	Young Simba, Young Nala, Zazu, Ensemble
Scene 7	Elephant Graveyard	
	"Chow Down"	Shenzi, Banzai, Ed
Scene 8	Under the Stars	
	"They Live in You"	Mufasa, Ensemble
Scene 9	Elephant Graveyard	
	"Be Prepared"	Scar, Shenzi, Banzai, Ed, Ensemble
Scene 10	The Gorge	
Scene 11	Pride Rock	
	"Be Prepared" (Reprise)	Scar, Ensemble
Scene 12	Rafiki's Tree	
Scene 13	The Desert/The Jungle	
	"Hakuna Matata"	Timon, Pumbaa, Young Simba, Simba, Ensemble

ACT TWO

Entr'acte	"One by One"	Ensemble
Scene 1	Scar's Cave	
	"The Madness of King Scar"	Scar, Zazu, Banzai, Shenzi, Ed, Nala
Scene 2	The Pridelands	
	"Shadowland"	Nala, Rafiki, Ensemble
Scene 3	The Jungle	
Scene 4	Under the Stars	
	"Endless Night"	Simba, Ensemble
Scene 5	Rafiki's Tree	
Scene 6	The Jungle	
	"Can You Feel the Love Tonight"	Timon, Pumbaa, Simba, Nala, Ensemble
	"He Lives in You" (Reprise)	Rafiki, Simba, Ensemble
Scene 7	Pride Rock	
	"King of Pride Rock"/"Circle of Life" (Reprise)	Ensemble

SONG CREDITS

All songs by Elton John (music) and Tim Rice (lyrics) except as follows:

"Circle of Life" by Elton John (music) and Tim Rice (lyrics)
with **"Nants' Ingonyama"** by Hans Zimmer and Lebo M
"He Lives in You" ("They Live in You"): Music and lyrics by Mark Mancina, Jay Rifkin, and Lebo M
"One by One": Music and lyrics by Lebo M
"Shadowland": Music by Lebo M and Hans Zimmer, lyrics by Mark Mancina and Lebo M
"Endless Night": Music by Lebo M, Hans Zimmer, and Jay Rifkin, lyrics by Julie Taymor
"King of Pride Rock": Music by Hans Zimmer, lyrics by Lebo M

ADDITIONAL SCORE

Grasslands chant and Lioness chant by Lebo M; Rafiki's chants by Tsidii Le Loka.

Cast Continued

ENSEMBLE DANCERS ..Kristina Michelle Bethel, Kylin Brady, Camille M. Brown, Michelle Aguilar Camaya, Gabriel A. Croom, Alicia Fisher, Gregory A. King, Lisa Lewis, Ray Mercer, Brandon Christopher O'Neal, Ryan Brooke Taylor, Steven Evan Washington

SWINGS AND UNDERSTUDIES

RAFIKI: Angelica Edwards, Sheryl McCallum, Mpume Sikakane, Rema Webb
MUFASA: Alvin Crawford, Michael Alexander Henry
SARABI: Camille M. Brown, Sheryl McCallum
ZAZU: John E. Brady, Enrique Segura
SCAR: Tony Freeman, Jack Koenig
SHENZI: Angelica Edwards, Alicia Fisher, Sophia N. Stephens, Rema Webb
BANZAI: Garland Days, Ian Yuri Gardner, Cornelius Jones, Jr., Kenny Redell Williams
ED: Ian Yuri Gardner, Dennis Johnston, Cornelius Jones Jr.
TIMON: John E. Brady, Enrique Segura
PUMBAA: John E. Brady, Jack Koenig
SIMBA: Dennis Johnston, Cornelius Jones, Jr., Joel Karie
NALA: Kylin Brady, Sophia N. Stephens, Rema Webb

SWINGS: Garland Days, Angelica Edwards, Ian Yuri Gardner, Tony James, Dennis Johnston, Cornelius Jones, Jr., Jennifer Harrison Newman, Dawn Noel Pignuola, Sophia N. Stephens

DANCE CAPTAINS

Garland Days, Jennifer Harrison Newman

SPECIALTIES

CIRCLE OF LIFE VOCALS: Bongi Duma, S'bu Ngema
MOUSE SHADOW PUPPET: Joel Karie
ANT HILL LADY: Kristina Michelle Bethel
GUINEA FOWL: Ryan Brooke Taylor
BUZZARD POLE: Gregory A. King
GAZELLE WHEEL: Michelle Aguilar Camaya
BUTTERFLIES: Michelle Aguilar Camaya
GAZELLE: Brandon Christopher O'Neal
LIONESS CHANT VOCAL: S'bu Ngema
ACROBATIC TRICKSTER: Ray Mercer
STILT GIRAFFE CROSS: Gabriel A. Croom
GIRAFFE SHADOW PUPPETS: Kenny Redell Williams, Brandon Christopher O'Neal
CHEETAH: Lisa Lewis
SCAR SHADOW PUPPETS: Kenny Redell Williams, Brandon Christopher O'Neal, Ryan Brooke Taylor

The Lion King

Cast Continued

SIMBA SHADOW PUPPETS: Gregory A. King, Steven Evan Washington, Ray Mercer
ONE BY ONE VOCAL: Bongi Duma, Andrea Frierson
ONE BY ONE DANCE: Bongi Duma, Ron Kunene, S'bu Ngema
FIREFLIES: Camille M. Brown
PUMBAA POLE PUPPET: Kenny Redell Williams
NALA POLE PUPPET: Lisa Lewis
FLOOR DANCERS: Kristina Michelle Bethel, Ryan Brooke Taylor
FLYING DANCERS: Michelle Aguilar Camaya, Gabriel A. Croom, Lisa Lewis, Brandon Christopher O'Neal
LIONESS/HYENA SHADOW PUPPETS: Lindiwe Dlamini, Andrea Frierson, Ron Kunene, Sheryl McCallum, Mpume Sikakane, Rema Webb

Bongi Duma, S'bu Ngema, and Mpume Sikakane are appearing with the permission of Actors' Equity Association.

ORCHESTRA
CONDUCTOR: Karl Jurman

KEYBOARD SYNTHESIZER/ ASSOCIATE CONDUCTOR: Cherie Rosen
SYNTHESIZERS: Ted Baker, Paul Ascenzo
WOOD FLUTE SOLOIST/FLUTE/PICCOLO: David Weiss
CONCERTMASTER: Francisca Mendoza
VIOLINS: Krystof Witek, Avril Brown
VIOLIN/VIOLA: Ralph Farris
CELLOS: Eliana Mendoza, Bruce Wang
FLUTE/CLARINET/BASS CLARINET: Bob Keller
FRENCH HORNS: Alexandra Cook, Katie Dennis, Greg Smith
TROMBONE: Rock Ciccarone
BASS TROMBONE/TUBA: George Flynn
UPRIGHT AND ELECTRIC BASSES: Tom Barney
DRUMS/ASSISTANT CONDUCTOR: Tommy Igoe
GUITAR: Kevin Kuhn
PERCUSSION/ASSISTANT CONDUCTOR: Rolando Morales-Matos
MALLETS/PERCUSSION: Valerie Dee Naranjo, Tom Brett
PERCUSSION: Junior "Gabu" Wedderburn

MUSIC COORDINATOR: Michael Keller

Derek Smith
Scar

Alton Fitzgerald White
Mufasa

Tshidi Manye
Rafiki

Tony Freeman
Zazu

Tom Alan Robbins
Pumbaa

Danny Rutigliano
Timon

Josh Tower
Simba

Kissy Simmons
Nala

Benjamin Sterling Cannon
Banzai

Bonita J. Hamilton
Shenzi

Enrique Segura
Ed

Alex de Castro
Young Nala

Ashley Renee Jordan
Young Nala

Justin Martin
Young Simba

Jarrell J. Singleton
Young Simba

Kristina Michelle Bethel
Ensemble

John E. Brady
Standby Timon, Pumbaa, Zazu

Kylin Brady
Ensemble

Camille M. Brown
Ensemble

Michelle Aguilar Camaya
Ensemble

The Lion King

Alvin Crawford
Ensemble

Gabriel A. Croom
Ensemble

Garland Days
Swing, Dance Captain

Lindiwe Dlamini
Ensemble

Bongi Duma
Ensemble

Angelica Edwards
Swing

Alicia Fisher
Ensemble

Andrea Frierson
Ensemble

Ian Yuri Gardner
Swing

Jean Michelle Grier
Sarabi/Ensemble

Michael Alexander Henry
Ensemble

Tony James
Swing

Dennis Johnston
Swing

Cornelius Jones, Jr.
Swing

Joel Karie
Ensemble

Gregory A. King
Ensemble

Jack Koenig
Standby for Scar and Pumbaa

Ron Kunene
Ensemble

Lisa Lewis
Ensemble

Sheryl McCallum
Ensemble

Ray Mercer
Ensemble

Jennifer Harrison Newman
Swing, Dance Captain

S'bu Ngema
Ensemble

Brandon Christopher O'Neal
Ensemble

Dawn Noel Pignuola
Swing

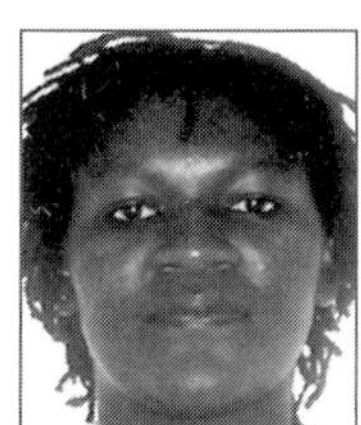
Mpume Sikakane
Ensemble

Sophia N. Stephens
Swing

Ryan Brooke Taylor
Ensemble

Steven Evan Washington
Ensemble, Fight Captain

Rema Webb
Ensemble

Kenny Redell Williams
Ensemble

Sir Elton John
Music

Tim Rice
Lyrics

Roger Allers
Book

Irene Mecchi
Book

The Lion King

Julie Taymor
Director, Costume Design, Mask/Puppet Co-Design, Additional Lyrics

Garth Fagan
Choreographer

Lebo M
Additional Music & Lyrics, Additional Vocal Score, Vocal Arrangements, Choral Director

Mark Mancina
Additional Music & Lyrics, Music Produced for the Stage, Additional Score

Hans Zimmer
Additional Music & Lyrics

Jay Rifkin
Additional Music & Lyrics

Richard Hudson
Scenic Design

Donald Holder
Lighting Design

Michael Curry
Mask & Puppet Design

Steve Canyon Kennedy
Sound Design

Mark Brandon, Binder Casting
Casting

David Benken
Technical Director

John Stefaniuk
Associate Director

Karl Jurman
Music Director/ Conductor

Brian Hill
Resident Director

Ruthlyn Salomons
Resident Dance Supervisor

Robert Elhai
Associate Music Producer, Orchestrator

Michael Keller
Music Coordinator

Thomas Schumacher, Disney Theatrical Productions

Bob Amaral
Pumbaa

Vincent Cuny
Ensemble Dancer, Simba Shadow Puppet

Keswa
Ensemble Singer, Lioness/Hyena Shadow Puppet, One by One Vocal

Patrick Page
Scar

Ensemble Singer, Lioness/Hyena Shadow Puppet

Torya
Dance Captain, Swing

Kyle Wrentz
Ensemble Singer

The Lion King

Kyle R. Banks
Ensemble Singer, Lioness/Hyena Shadow Puppet, One by One Dance

Jeff Binder
Zazu

Christopher Freeman
Ensemble Dancer, Floor Dancer, Guinea Fowl, Scar Shadow Puppet

India
Young Nala

Julian Ivey
Young Simba

André Jackson
Circle of Life Vocals, Ensemble Singer, Lioness Chant Vocal, One by One Dance, One by One Vocal

Meena T. Jahi
Ensemble Singer, Sarabi

Dennis Lue
Ensemble Dancer, Simba Shadow Puppet

Shavar McIntosh
Young Simba

Selloane A. Nkhela
Ensemble Singer, Lioness/Hyena Shadow Puppet, One by One Vocal

Patrick Page
Scar

Natalie Ridley
Cheetah, Ensemble Dancer, Flying Dancer, Nala Pole Puppet

Angelo Rivera
Ensemble Dancer, Flying Dancer, Stilt Giraffe Cross

Halle Vargas Sullivan
Young Nala

Torya
Dance Captain, Swing

Phillip W. Turner
Ensemble Dancer, Flying Dancer, Gazelle, Giraffe Shadow Puppet, Scar Shadow Puppet

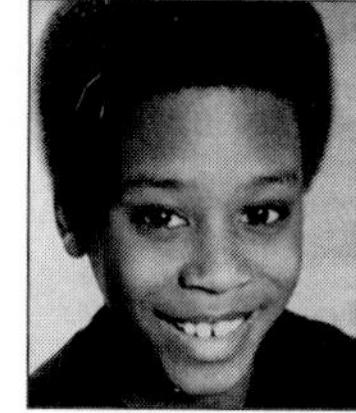

Christian A. Phenix Warner
Young Simba

Patrick Page as Scar.

Alton Fitzgerald White as Mufasa.

Photos by Joan Marcus

The Lion King

CREW

Front Row (L-R): Alain Van Achte (Head Sound), Douglas Hamilton (Dresser), Adenike Wright, Elaine Healey, Judy Pirouz, Niki White (Child Wrangler).

Second Row (L-R): Brendan Nolan, Doug Graf (Key Spot Operator), Elizabeth Cohen (Production Makeup Supervisor), Bill Mullen, Cheryl Budd, Walter Weiner (Dresser), Dave Tisue (Dresser), Mark Houston (Dresser).

Third Row (L-R): Avril Brown (Violin), Karl Jurman (Musical Director/Conductor), Flo Coulter, Chris Cuartana, Florence Compton, Marion Mooney.

Fourth Row (L-R): Milagros Medina-Cerdeira (Assistant Makeup Supervisor), Marian Torre (Makeup Artist), Paul Ascenzo (Synthesizer), Rolando Morales-Matos (Percussion/Assistant Conductor), Irina Karlin, Cherie Rosen (Keyboard Synthesizer/Associate Conductor), Paul Riner (Dresser), Tom Daniel (Dresser).

Back Row (L-R): Brendan Lynch (Assistant Electricians), Matthew Lavaia (Props), Billy Brennan, Don McKennan (Sound Assistants), Victor Irving (House Manager), Carmen I. Abrazado (Assistant Stage Manager), Michael Height (Assistant Company Manager) and Thomas Schlenk (Company Manager).

Staff for *THE LION KING* Worldwide

Associate Producer ....Todd Lacy
Associate Producer ....Aubrey Lynch II
Associate Director ....John Stefaniuk
Production Dance Supervisor ....Marey Griffith
Senior Production Manager ....Anne Quart
Production Supervisor ....Doc Zorthian
Dance Supervisor ....Celise Hicks
Associate Scenic Designer ....Peter Eastman
Associate Costume Designer ....Mary Nemecek Peterson
Associate Mask & Puppet Designer ....Louis Troisi
Associate Sound Designer ....John Shivers
Associate Hair & Makeup Designer ....Carole Hancock
Associate Lighting Designer ....Jeanne Koenig
Assistant Lighting Designer ....Marty Vreeland
Automated Lighting Programmer ....Aland Henderson
Global Casting Associate ....Egil Kipste
Management Assistants ....Suyin Chan, Tara Engler

GENERAL PRESS REPRESENTATIVES
BONEAU/BRYAN-BROWN
Chris Boneau Jackie Green Matt Polk Aaron Meier

Staff for *THE LION KING* New York

Company Manager ....THOMAS SCHLENK
Assistant Company Manager ....Michael Height

Production Stage Manager ....Theresa Bailey
Resident Director ....Brian Hill
Resident Dance Supervisor ....Ruthlyn Salomons
Musical Director/Conductor ....Karl Jurman

Stage Managers ....Carmen I. Abrazado, Victoria Epstein, Antonia Gianino, Ron Vodicka
Fight Captain ....Steven Evan Washington
Assistant Choreographers ....Norwood J. Pennewell, Natalie Rogers
Fight Consultant ....Rick Sordelet
South African Dialect Coach ....Ron Kunene
Casting Associates ....Jack Bowdan, C.S.A.; Mark Brandon; Megan Larche
Casting Assistants ...Rachel Shapiro-Cooper, Nikole Vallins
Corporate Counsel ....Michael Rosenfeld
Physical Therapy ....Neuro Tour Physical Therapy/ Kristin Walthers
Consulting Orthopedist ....Phillip A. Bauman, M.D.
Child Wrangler ....Niki White
Executive Travel ....Robert Arnao, Patt McRory
Production Travel ....Jill Citron
Web Design Consultant ....Joshua Noah
Advertising ....Serino/Coyne Inc.

Production Carpenter ....Drew Siccardi
Head Carpenter ....Michael Trotto
House Carpenter ....Patrick Sullivan
Assistant Carpenters ....Kirk Bender, Michael Phillips
Automation Carpenters ....Aldo "Butch" Servilio, George Zegarsky
Carpenters ....Jerry Griffin, Gabe Harris, Brian Hutchinson, Duane Mirro
Production Flymen ....Kraig Bender, Dylan Trotto
House Flyman ....Richard McQuail
Production Electrician ....James Maloney
House Electrician ....Michael Lynch
Board Operator ....Edward Greenberg
House Assistant Electrician ....Stephen Speer
Automated Lighting Technician ....Sean Strohmeyer
Key Spot Operator ....Doug Graf
Assistant Electricians ....David Holliman, Robert Keller Jr., Brendan Lynch, Thomas Richards
Production Propman ....Victor Amerling
House Propman ....Frank Lavaia
Props ....Matthew Lavaia, Michael Lavaia, Robert McCauley
Head Sound ....Alain Van Achte
Sound Assistants ....Donald McKennan, Scott Scheidt
Production Wardrobe Supervisor ....Kjeld Andersen
Assistant Wardrobe Supervisor ....Cynthia Boardman
Puppet Supervisor ....Anne Salt
Puppet Dayworkers ....Islah Abdul-Rahiim, Sue McLaughlin, Ilya Vett

The Lion King

Mask/Puppet Studio .... Jeff Curry
Dressers .... Meredith Chase-Boyd, Andy Cook, Tom Daniel, Donna Doiron, April Fernandez-Taylor, Michelle Gore, Douglas Hamilton, Mark Houston, Sara Jablon, Kathy Karadza, Mark Lauer, Michelle Palladino, Paul Riner, Sarah Stith, Sheila Little Terrell, Dave Tisue, Walter Weiner
Stitcher .... Janeth Iverson
Production Hair Supervisor .... Monica Costea
Assistant Hair Supervisor .... Alison Wadsworth
Production Makeup Supervisor .... Elizabeth Cohen
Assistant Makeup Supervisor .... Milagros Medina-Cerdeira
Makeup Artist .... Marian Torre

Music Development .... Nick Glennie-Smith
Music Preparation .... Donald Oliver and Evan Morris/ Chelsea Music Service, Inc.
Synthesizer Programmer .... Ted Baker
Orchestral Synthesizer Programmer ...... Christopher Ward
Electronic Drum Programmer .... Tommy Igoe
Addt'l Percussion Arrangements .... Valerie Dee Naranjo
Music Assistant .... Elizabeth J. Falcone
Personal Assistant to Elton John .... Bob Halley
Assistant to Tim Rice .... Eileen Heinink
Assistant to Mark Mancina .... Chuck Choi

Associate Scenic Designer .... Jonathan Fensom
Assistant Scenic Designer .... Michael Fagin
Lighting Design Assistant .... Karen Spahn
Automated Lighting Tracker .... Lara Bohon
Projection Designer .... Geoff Puckett
Projection Art .... Caterina Bertolotto
Assistant Sound Designer .... Kai Harada
Assistant Costume Designer .... Tracy Dorman
Stunt Consultant .... Peter Moore
Children's Tutoring .... On Location Education
Production Photography .... Joan Marcus, Marc Bryan-Brown
Associate Producer 1996–1998 .... Donald Frantz
Project Manager 1996–1998 .... Nina Essman
Associate Producer 1998–2002 .... Ken Denison
Associate Producer 2000-2003 .... Pam Young
Original Music Director .... Joseph Church

Disney's *The Lion King* is a registered trademark owned by The Walt Disney Company and used under special license by Disney Theatrical Productions, Ltd.

HOUSE STAFF FOR THE MINSKOFF THEATRE

House Manager .... Victor Irving
Treasurer .... Nicholas Loiacono
Assistant Treasurer .... Cheryl Loiacono

---

CREDITS

Scenery built and mechanized by Hudson Scenic Studio, Inc. Additional scenery by Chicago Scenic Studios, Inc.; Edge & Co., Inc.; Michael Hagen, Inc.; Piper Productions, Inc.; Scenic Technologies, Inc.; I. Weiss & Sons, Inc. Lighting by Westsun, vari*lite® automated lighting provided by Vari-Lite, Inc. Props by John Creech Design & Production. Sound equipment by Pro-Mix, Inc. Additional sound equipment by Walt Disney Imagineering. Rehearsal Scenery by Brooklyn Scenic & Theatrical. Costumes executed by Barbara Matera Ltd., Parsons-Meares Ltd., Donna Langman, Eric Winterling, Danielle Gisiger, Suzie Elder. Millinery by Rodney Gordon, Janet Linville, Arnold Levine. Ricola provided by Ricola, Inc. Shibori dyeing by Joan Morris. Custom dyeing and painting by Joni Johns, Mary Macy, Parsons-Meares Ltd., Gene Mignola. Additional Painting by J. Michelle Hill. Knitwear by Maria Ficalora. Footwear by Sharlot Battin, Robert W. Jones, Capezio, Vasilli Shoes. Costume Development by Constance Hoffman. Special Projects by Angela M. Kahler. Custom fabrics developed by Gary Graham and Helen Quinn. Puppet Construction by Michael Curry Design, Inc. and Vee Corporation. Shadow puppetry by Steven Kaplan. Pumbaa Puppet Construction by Andrew Benepe and Flying by Foy. Trucking by Clark Transfer. Wigs created by Wig Workshop of London. Marimbas by De Morrow Instruments, Ltd. Latin Percussion by LP Music Group. Drumset by DrumWorkshop. Cymbals by Zildjian. Bass equipment by Eden Electronics.

Song excerpts (used by permission): "It's a Small World" written by Richard M. Sherman and Robert B. Sherman; "Five Foot Two, Eyes of Blue" written by Sam Lewis, Joe Young, and Ray Henderson; "The Lion Sleeps Tonight" written by Hugo Peretti, George David Weiss, and Luigi Creatore.

N
NEDERLANDER

Chairman .... **James M. Nederlander**
President .... **James L. Nederlander**

Executive Vice President
Nick Scandalios

Vice President• Corporate Development **Charlene S. Nederlander**	Senior Vice President• Labor Relations **Herschel Waxman**
Vice President **Jim Boese**	Chief Financial Officer **Freida Sawyer Belviso**

DISNEY THEATRICAL PRODUCTIONS

President .... Thomas Schumacher
SVP & General Manager .... Alan Levey
SVP, Managing Director & CFO .... David Schrader

Senior Vice President, Creative Affairs .... Michele Steckler
Senior Vice President, International .... Ron Kollen
Vice President, International Marketing .... Fiona Thomas
Vice President, Operations .... Dana Amendola
Vice President, Labor Relations .... Allan Frost
Vice President, Domestic Touring .... Jack Eldon
Director, Domestic Touring .... Michael Buchanan
Vice President, Theatrical Licensing .... Steve Fickinger
Director, Human Resources .... June Heindel
Manager, Labor Relations .... Stephanie Cheek
Manager, Human Resources .... Cynthia Young
Manager, Information Systems .... Scott Benedict
Senior Computer Support Analyst .... Kevin A. McGuire

Production

Executive Music Producer .... Chris Montan
Vice President, Creative Affairs .... Greg Gunter
Vice President, Physical Production .... John Tiggeloven
Senior Manager, Safety .... Canara Price
Manager, Physical Production .... Karl Chmielewski
Purchasing Manager .... Joseph Doughney
Staff Associate Designer .... Dennis W. Moyes
Staff Associate Dramaturg .... Ken Cerniglia

Marketing

Vice President, Broadway .... Andrew Flatt
Manager, Broadway .... Michele Groner
Manager, Broadway .... Leslie Barrett
Website Manager .... Eric W. Kratzer
Assistant Manager, Communications .... Dana Torres

Sales

Vice President, Ticketing .... Jerome Kane
Manager, Group Sales .... Jacob Lloyd Kimbro
Assistant Manager, Group Sales .... Juil Kim
Group Sales Representative .... Jarrid Crespo

Business and Legal Affairs

Senior Vice President .... Jonathan Olson
Vice President .... Robbin Kelley
Director .... Harry S. Gold
Attorney .... Seth Stuhl
Paralegal/Contract Administration .... Colleen Lober

Finance

Director .... Joe McClafferty
Senior Manager, Finance .... Dana James
Manager, Finance .... Justin Gee
Manager, Finance .... John Fajardo
Production Accountants .... Joy Brown, Nick Judge, Barbara Toben, Jodi Yaeger
Assistant Production Accountant .... Darrell Goode
Senior Financial Analyst .... Tatiana Bautista
Analyst .... Liz Jurist

Controllership

Director, Accounting .... Leena Mathew
Manager, Accounting .... Erica McShane
Senior Analysts .... Stephanie Badie, Mila Danilevich, Adrineh Ghoukassian
Analysts .... Bilda Donado, Ken Herrell

Administrative Staff

Dusty Bennett, Jane Buchanan, Craig Buckley, Lauren Daghini, Jessica Doina, Cristi Finn, Cristina Fornaris, Dayle Gruet, Gregory Hanoian, Jonathan Hanson, Jay Hollenback, Connie Jasper, Kerry McGrath, Lisa Mitchell, Ryan Pears, Flora Rhim, Roberta Risafi, Bridget Ruane, Kisha Santiago, David Scott, Andy Singh

---

BUENA VISTA THEATRICAL MERCHANDISE, L.L.C.

Vice President .... Steven Downing
Merchandise Manager .... John F. Agati
Operations Manager .... Shawn Baker
Assistant Manager, Inventory .... Suzanne Jakel
Associate Buyer .... Violeta Burlaza
Retail Supervisor .... Mark Nathman
On-Site Retail Manager .... Keith Guralchuk
On-Site Assistant Retail Manager .... Justin Hall

Disney Theatrical Productions • 1450 Broadway
New York, NY 10018

guestmail@disneytheatrical.com

The Lion King
Scrapbook

Correspondent: Tom Alan Robbins, "Pumbaa"
Most Exciting Celebrity Visitor: EVERYONE has come to the show, and many have come backstage. They're always asked to autograph the set, and when we moved from the New Amsterdam in summer 2006 the crew cut out the parts of the set with the signatures and fastened them up on the new set at the Minskoff. You'll find almost anybody there: Bill Clinton, Muhammad Ali, Coretta Scott King, Steven Spielberg, Robin Williams, Elizabeth Taylor, you name it.
"Gypsy of the Year" Sketch: This year's piece, "Red," was created by Ray Mercer, and was performed by Ray, Rema Webb, Cornelius Jones Jr., Kristina Michelle Bethel and Brandon O'Neal. It was a light, fun dance piece about youthful flirtation.
"Carols for a Cure" Carol: "Go Tell It on the Mountain."
"Easter Bonnet" Sketch: "The End Starts Here," directed and choreographed by Gregory A. King.
Who Has Done the Most Shows: Camille Brown, one of our dancers. She's been with the show from the beginning and never misses. She's done well over 3600 performances.
Favorite Moment: I don't get to enjoy my favorite moment anymore. In Minneapolis the camera aimed at the conductor also caught the first few rows of the audience. Every night I'd come to the stage and watch their faces on the monitor when the show started. The moment the sun rose and the Giraffes came onstage someone always burst into tears because the moment was so beautiful. I miss seeing that.
Favorite In-Theater Gathering Place: The hair and make-up room. There's no green room at the Minskoff.
Favorite Off-Site Hangout: Jack's.
Favorite Snack Food: Any of the variations on Reese's Cups.
Mascot: Stiffy.
Favorite Therapy: Our resident Physical Therapist, Kristin, keeps us all ticking with ultra-sound, e-stim, hydroculator pads and borderline sadistic "massage" therapy.
Memorable Ad-Lib: One night when the actor playing Timon got stuck with a broken elevator and wasn't able to re-emerge from the river into which he had fallen, a heartbroken Pumbaa turned to the audience and said, "Poor Timon. We were going to go to Paris."
Memorable Stage Door Encounter: One of our cast members had just given a backstage tour to some friends. Saying goodbye at the stage door, one of them said, "I have a friend coming next month. How can I get her a backstage tour?" The cast member replied, "Just call me." A stranger standing nearby piped up sadly, "But I don't have your number."
Earliest Audience Arrival: An entire busload of patrons showed up a year early. No one thought to check the tickets. They spent the first act on folding chairs in the lobby waiting for their bus to come back!

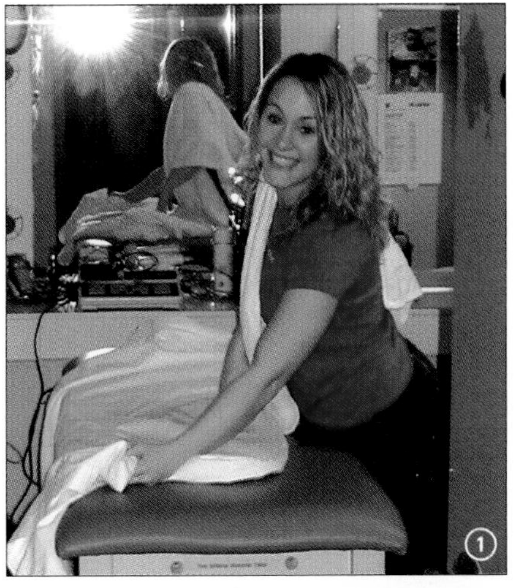

Photos courtesy Tom Alan Robbins

1. Kristin Walthers, the physical therapist, is ready for another "customer."
2. Inside the stage managers' office.
3. Getting into make-up.
4. Dressing room for Timon and Pumbaa.

Heaviest Costume: The heaviest costume worn by one person is probably Pumbaa. He weighs about 47 pounds.
Who Wore the Least: Ryan Brooke Taylor's ballet costume leaves nothing to the imagination.
Catchphrase Only the Company Would Recognize: "Pink pajamas, penguins on the bottom."
Sweethearts Within the Company: We've had too many to count. By now we're counting wedding and babies. Some of the babies born to company members are almost old enough to play Young Simba and Nala.
Ghostly Encounter: The Minskoff is too new to be haunted, but the New Amsterdam had Olive, a former Ziegfeld girl. One of the security guards swore she walked by him in a long period dress on the stage late one night.
Embarrassing Moment: One night at the New Am, Patrick Page, who plays Scar, found he was locked in his dressing room at the beginning of Act II. Everyone was down on the stage, including the stage managers, so there was no one he could call. He hammered on the door and yelled while the opening number went on and finally a passing dresser heard him and let him out, but we still had to stop the show until he could make it to the stage.
Second Embarrassing Moment: Early in his run, Josh Tower, who plays grown-up Simba, was in the make-up chair shortly before his first entrance in "Hakuna Matata." The make-up artist was taking extra care because she hadn't done Josh's makeup before. He became more and more nervous as he heard his cue approaching. Finally he bolted from the chair and raced for the stage, but too late. He started singing on cue and his microphone sent his voice booming out into the house, but Timon and Pumbaa were left onstage alone looking around for the source of this invisible newcomer until he finally made it to the jungle.
Who Plays the Most Instruments: It's hard to say. The percussionists play an unbelievable number of small, strange instruments, but Dave Weiss plays 13 different flutes, including some traditional African woodwinds.
Understudy Anecdote: It's hard to beat the time Rema Webb went on as Nala eight months pregnant. Thank goodness for those beaded corsets.

The Little Dog Laughed

First Preview: October 26, 2006. Opened: November 13, 2006.
Closed February 18, 2007 after 22 Previews and 112 Performances.

PLAYBILL

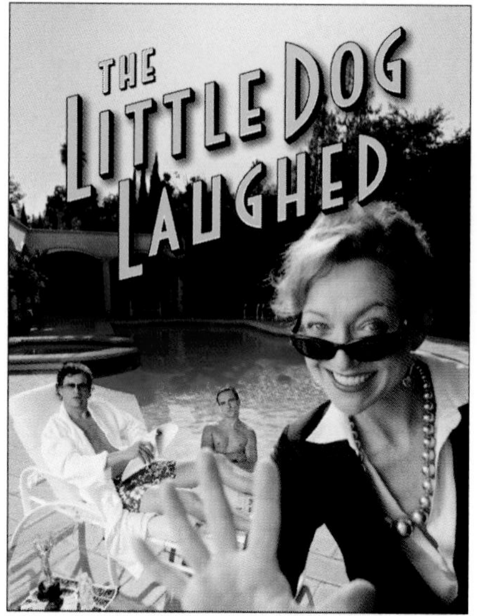

CORT THEATRE
138 West 48th Street
A Shubert Organization Theatre
Gerald Schoenfeld, *Chairman* **Philip J. Smith,** *President*

Robert E. Wankel, *Executive Vice President*

ROY GABAY SUSAN DIETZ
MORRIS BERCHARD STEVE BOZEMAN TED SNOWDON
JERRY FRANKEL / DOUG NEVIN JENNIFER MANOCHERIAN / INA MEIBACH

SECOND STAGE THEATRE
CAROLE ROTHMAN, *Artistic Director* ELLEN RICHARD, *Executive Director*

present

TOM EVERETT SCOTT
JULIE WHITE

in

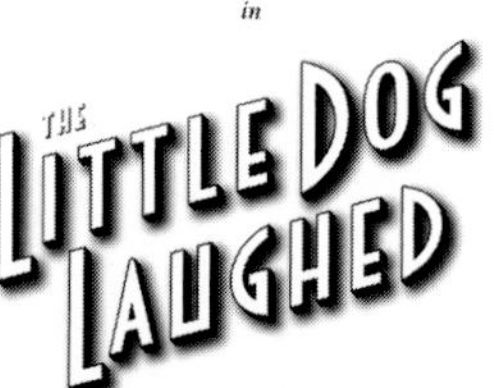

A New Play by
DOUGLAS CARTER BEANE

with
ARI GRAYNOR

also starring
JOHNNY GALECKI

Set Design ALLEN MOYER
Costume Design JEFF MAHSHIE
Lighting Design DONALD HOLDER
Original Music LEWIS FLINN

Casting MELE NAGLER, C.S.A.
Production Stage Manager LINDA MARVEL
Press Representative RICHARD KORNBERG & ASSOCIATES/ TOM D'AMBROSIO

Production Management ROBERT G. MAHON III JEFF WILD
General Manager ROY GABAY PRODUCTIONS
Company Manager BRUCE KLINGER

Directed by
SCOTT ELLIS

World Premiere produced by Second Stage Theatre, New York, December 13th, 2005 Carole Rothman, Artistic Director
The producers wish to express their appreciation to Theatre Development Fund for its support of this production.

11/13/06

CAST

(in order of appearance)

Diane .... JULIE WHITE
Mitchell .... TOM EVERETT SCOTT
Alex .... JOHNNY GALECKI
Ellen .... ARI GRAYNOR

UNDERSTUDIES

For Mitchell/Alex:
BRIAN HENDERSON

For Diane/Ellen:
DANA SLAMP

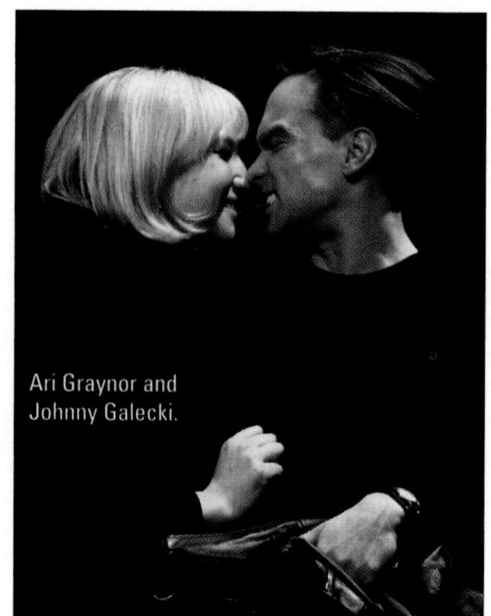
Ari Graynor and Johnny Galecki.

(L-R): Tom Everett Scott, Julie White and Johnny Galecki.

Photos by Carol Rosegg

The Little Dog Laughed

Tom Everett Scott
Mitchell

Julie White
Diane

Johnny Galecki
Alex

Ari Graynor
Ellen

Brian Henderson
Understudy for Mitchell/Alex

Dana Slamp
Understudy for Diane/Ellen

Douglas Carter Beane
Playwright

Scott Ellis
Director

Allen Moyer
Set Design

Donald Holder
Lighting Design

Richard Kornberg & Associates
Press Representative

Roy Gabay
Producer/ General Manager

Susan Dietz
Producer

Morris Berchard
Producer

Ted Snowdon
Producer

Jerry Frankel
Producer

Jennifer Manocherian
Producer

Carole Rothman, Second Stage Theatre
Producer

Zoe Lister-Jones
Ellen

2006-2007 AWARDS

TONY AWARD
Best Leading Actress in a Play (Julie White)

THEATRE WORLD AWARD
Outstanding Broadway Debut (Johnny Galecki)

Julie White as Diane.

Photo by Carol Rosegg

The Little Dog Laughed

STAGE CREW
Front Row (L-R):
Alex Volckhausen (Stage Manager),
Linda Marvel (Production Stage Manager),
Kevin Diaz (Automation Carpenter).

Back Row (L-R):
Ed Diaz (Head Carpenter),
Scott DeVerna (Head Electrician) and
Lonnie Gaddy (Head Props).

BOX OFFICE
(L-R):
Diane Heatherington and Chuck Loesche.

Photos by Melissa Merlo

FRONT OF HOUSE STAFF
Front Row (L-R):
John Mallon, Lauren Amick, Darien Jones, Jessica Hidalgo.

Middle Row (L-R):
Robert Evans, William Denson, Nicole McIntyre, Lea Hekler.

Back Row (L-R):
Robert DeJesus, Unknown and Daryl Smith.

The Little Dog Laughed

ASSOCIATE TO SUSAN DIETZ
Jayson Raitt

Photo by Carol Rosegg

(L-R): Julie White and Tom Everett Scott

STAFF FOR *THE LITTLE DOG LAUGHED*

GENERAL MANAGEMENT
ROY GABAY THEATRICAL PRODUCTION & MANAGEMENT
Chris Aniello Hilary Austin
Clayton Boyd Daniel Kuney

COMPANY MANAGER
BRUCE KLINGER

GENERAL PRESS REPRESENTATIVE
RICHARD KORNBERG & ASSOCIATES
TOM D'AMBROSIO DON SUMMA

PRODUCTION MANAGEMENT
ROBERT G. MAHON III JEFF WILD

PRODUCTION STAGE MANAGER .LINDA MARVEL
Assistant Stage Manager ....Alex Lyu Volckhausen
Assistant Director ....Vijay Mathew
Associate Set Designer..........................Warren Karp
Production Properties Coordinator ....Susan Barras
Assistant to Mr. Mahshie.......................Kyle LaColla
Associate Lighting Designer ....Hilary Manners
Assistant to Mr. Holder ....Catherine Tate
Associate to Mr. Flinn..........................Mark Huang
Assistant to Ms. Nagler ....Stephen Kopel
Associates to Ms. Dietz ....Tom Kirdahy, Jayson Raitt, Devlin Elliot
Assistant to Ms. Dietz ....Angela Sidlow
Assistant to Mr. Snowdon ....Ted Seifman
Production Assistant ....Heather Prince
Press Assistants ....Carrie Friedman, Alyssa Hart, Laura Kaplow-Goldman
Production Carpenter ....Ed Diaz
Production Electrician ....Scott DeVerna
Production Properties.........................Lonnie Gaddy
Assistant Props.................................John Lofgren
Automation Carpenter ....Kevin Diaz
Wardrobe Supervisor ....Kay Grunder
Dresser ....Kyle LaColla
Legal Counsel ....Donald C. Farber
Banking ....JP Morgan Chase
Accountant ....Rosenberg, Neuwith & Kuchner, CPAs/ Mark A. D'Ambrosi/Jana Jevnikar
Insurance ....DeWitt Stern Group/ Peter Shoemaker, Stan Levine
Advertising...SpotCo/ Drew Hodges, Jim Edwards, Dale Edwards
Production Photographer ....Carol Rosegg
Website ....Pygmalion Designs/David Risley
Payroll Services ....Castellana Services Inc.
Opening Night Coordination ..Tobak/Lawrence Company
Merchandising ....Andrew Rasmussen/ Cardinal Theatricals

CREDITS
Scenery and scenic effects built, painted, electrified and automated by Showmotion, Inc., Norwalk, CT. Lighting equipment by PRG Lighting, Inc. Sound equipment by One Dream Sound. Jewelry provided by Alexis Bittar. Ricola natural herb cough drops courtesy of Ricola USA, Inc. Bedding courtesy of Eileen Fisher Home by Garnet Hill.

Original Second Stage casting by
Tara Rubin, CSA, and Laura Schutzel

SPECIAL THANKS
The production would like to thank Halston, Jessica Weinstein, Lenny Beer, John Barrett Salon, Judith Leiber, Neal Huff and Zoe Lister-Jones.

SECOND STAGE THEATRE STAFF
ARTISTIC DIRECTOR ....CAROLE ROTHMAN
EXECUTIVE DIRECTOR ....ELLEN RICHARD

ADMINISTRATIVE
Director of Finance ....Janice B. Cwill
Director of Management ....Don-Scott Cooper
Administrative Manager.....................John Mackessy
Director of Development ....Sarah Bordy
Manager of Special Events ....Lisa Golden
Manager of Institutional Giving..........Kristen Bolibruch
Director of Marketing ....Hector Coris
Marketing Associate ....Ryan Meisheid
Marketing Assistant ....Nathan Leslie
Ticket Services Manager ....Greg Turner
Box Office Treasurer ....JJ Shebesta

ARTISTIC
Associate Artistic Director ....Christopher Burney
Literary Manager ....Sarah Bagley
Artistic Associates ....Jo Bonney, Moisés Kaufman

PRODUCTION
Production Manager ....Jeff Wild
Technical Director ....Robert G. Mahon, III
Facilities Manager ....Jason Walters
House Manager ....Joshua Schleifer

CORT THEATRE
House Manager ....Joseph Traina

The Little Dog Laughed

SCRAPBOOK

Photos by Aubrey Reuben

Photo by David Gewirtzman

Correspondent: Linda Marvel, Production Stage Manager

Opening Night Gifts: Tiffany's jewelry, dildoes, gay porn and art.

Most Exciting Celebrity Visitors and What They Did/Said: Phil Collins, Elaine Stritch, Jane Fonda, and Bill Murray, who told Julie to leave a joke on his answering machine.

Special Backstage Ritual: Johnny singing The Doors' "Backdoor Man" on the fire escape.

Favorite In-Theatre Gathering Place: The dark third-floor fire escape, a.k.a. The Smoking Lounge.

Favorite Off-Site Hangout: Bar Centrale.

Mascot: Lulu the Pomeranian dog owned by Julie.

Favorite Therapy: Jungian.

Most Memorable Ad-Lib: Instead of "Calm, resigned and, whatever, depleted," Ari came out with "I'm sad, upset and OK."

Latest Arrival: After a misunderstanding about when the first matinee started, Julie arrived thirty minutes late for a 2 PM show.

Who Wore the Least: The boys wore nothing but jewelry for about thirty seconds.

Catchphrases Only the Company Would Recognize: "Fuck you."

Nicknames: Tom is "Bean Salad" (for his unfortunate choice of first day snack). Stage manager Alex is "Cato" to Julie.

"Gypsy of the Year" Sketch: "Untitled" by Douglas Carter Beane.

1. Cast members (L-R): Johnny Galecki, Ari Graynor, Julie White, Tom Everett Scott at the opening night party at Planet Hollywood.
2. Marquee of the Cort Theatre.
3. Julie White arrives at Planet Hollywood.
4. Playwright Douglas Carter Beane and Cady Huffman at the cast party.
5. Curtain call on the stage of the Cort Theatre on opening night.

Losing Louie

First Preview: September 21, 2006. Opened: October 12, 2006.
Closed: November 26, 2006 after 24 Previews and 53 Performances.

PLAYBILL

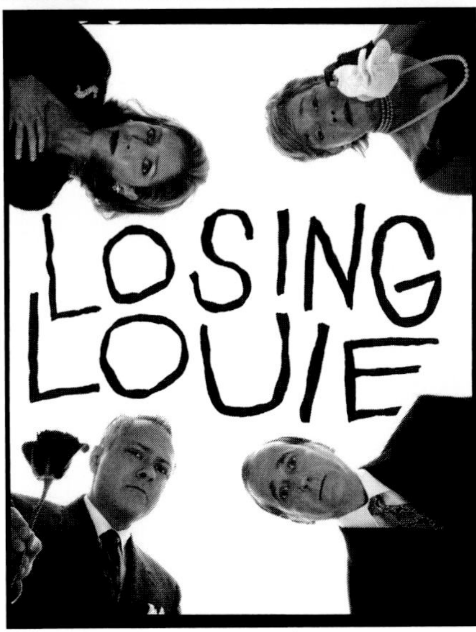

CAST

(in order of appearance)

Bella Holland .... JAMA WILLIAMSON
Louie Ellis .... SCOTT COHEN
Tony Ellis .... MARK LINN-BAKER
Sheila Ellis .... MICHELE PAWK
Bobbie Ellis .... REBECCA CRESKOFF
Elizabeth Ellis .... PATRICIA KALEMBER
Reggie Ellis .... MATTHEW ARKIN

TIME:
Early '60s and the present

PLACE:
Pound Ridge, NY

Stage Manager .... DAVID H. LURIE

UNDERSTUDIES

For Louie Ellis, Tony Ellis, Reggie Ellis:
JOHN BOLGER
For Bella Holland, Bobbie Ellis:
JULIE LAUREN
For Sheila Ellis, Elizabeth Ellis:
CHARLOTTE MAIER

BILTMORE THEATRE

MANHATTAN THEATRE CLUB

Artistic Director **LYNNE MEADOW** Executive Producer **BARRY GROVE**

Presents

LOSING LOUIE

by

SIMON MENDES DA COSTA

with

MATTHEW ARKIN SCOTT COHEN REBECCA CRESKOFF
PATRICIA KALEMBER MARK LINN-BAKER
MICHELE PAWK JAMA WILLIAMSON

Scenic Design **JOHN LEE BEATTY** Costume Design **WILLIAM IVEY LONG** Lighting Design **PAUL GALLO**

Sound Design **DAN MOSES SCHREIER** Production Stage Manager **BARCLAY STIFF**

Casting **NANCY PICCIONE/ DAVID CAPARELLIOTIS** Director of Artistic Operations **MANDY GREENFIELD** Production Manager **RYAN McMAHON**

Director of Development **JILL TURNER LLOYD** Director of Marketing **DEBRA A. WAXMAN** Press Representative **BONEAU/ BRYAN-BROWN**

General Manager **FLORIE SEERY** Director of Artistic Development **PAIGE EVANS**

By Special Arrangement with James L. Nederlander and Michael Codron

Directed by

JERRY ZAKS

First presented at Hampstead Theatre in association with Michael Codron, directed by Robin Lefévre, subsequently transferring to London's West End produced by Michael Codron.

Manhattan Theatre Club wishes to express its appreciation to Theatre Development Fund for its support of this production.

10/12/06

Photo by Joan Marcus

(L-R): Mark Linn-Baker, Matthew Arkin, Patricia Kalember and Michele Pawk.

Losing Louie

Matthew Arkin
Reggie Ellis

Scott Cohen
Louie Ellis

Rebecca Creskoff
Bobbie Ellis

Patricia Kalember
Elizabeth Ellis

Mark Linn-Baker
Tony Ellis

Michele Pawk
Sheila Ellis

Jama Williamson
Bella Holland

John Bolger
Understudy

Julie Lauren
Understudy

Charlotte Maier
Understudy

Simon Mendes da Costa
Playwright

Jerry Zaks
Director

John Lee Beatty
Scenic Design

William Ivey Long
Costume Designer

Paul Gallo
Lighting Designer

Dan Moses Schreier
Sound Design

Lynne Meadow
Artistic Director, Manhattan Theatre Club, Inc.

Barry Grove
Executive Producer, Manhattan Theatre Club, Inc.

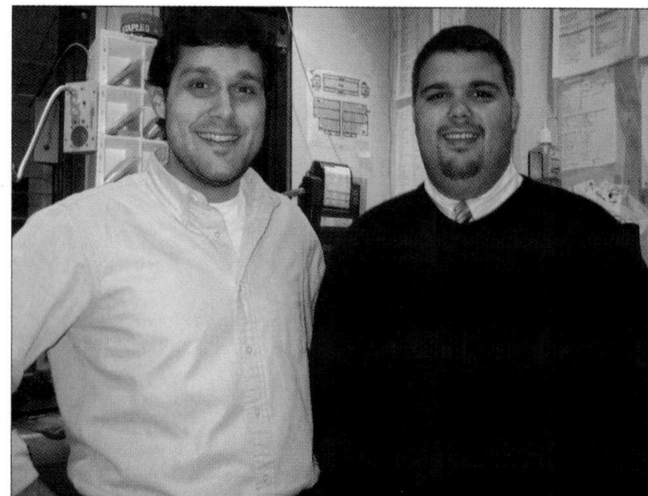
BOX OFFICE STAFF
(L-R): Tevy Bradley (Asst. Treasurer) and Jonathan Pate (Asst. Treasurer)
Not Pictured: David Dillon (Head Treasurer).

MANAGEMENT
(L-R): Barclay Stiff (Production Stage Manager),
David Lurie (Stage Manager), Denise Cooper (Company Manager).

Photos by Melissa Merlo

Losing Louie

Photos by Melissa Merlo

STAGE CREW
Front Row (L-R): Natasha Steinhagen (Hair and Makeup Supervisor), Angela Simpson (Wardrobe Supervisor), Sue Poulin.
Back Row (L-R): Louis Shapiro (Sound Engineer), Tim Hanlon (Dresser), Timothy Walters (Head Propertyman), Marc Grimshaw (Apprentice) and Andrew Sliwinski (Apprentice).
Not Pictured: Jeff Dodson (Master Electrician) and Chris Wiggins (Head Carpenter).

FRONT OF HOUSE STAFF
Front Row (L-R): Pamela Gittlitz, Miranda Scopel, Mayuha Kunisue.
Second Row (L-R): Dinah Glorioso, Catherine Burke, Beren Willwerth, Bruce Dye and Ed Brashear.
Back Row (L-R): Patricia Polhill, Jackson Ero and Russ Ramsey.

Losing Louie

MANHATTAN THEATRE CLUB STAFF

Artistic Director ..... **Lynne Meadow**
Executive Producer ..... **Barry Grove**
General Manager ..... **Florie Seery**
Director of Artistic Development ..... **Paige Evans**
Director of Artistic Operations ..... **Mandy Greenfield**
Director of Artistic Administration/ Assistant to the Artistic Director ..... **Amy Gilkes Loe**
Associate Director of Artistic Operations ..... Lisa McNulty
Artistic Assistant ..... Kacy O'Brien
Artistic Administrative Assistant ..... Maureen Donohue
Director of Casting ..... **Nancy Piccione**
Casting Director ..... **David Caparelliotis**
Casting Assistant ..... Kristin Svenningsen
Literary Manager ..... **Emily Shooltz**
Play Development Associate/ Sloan Project Manager ..... Aaron Leichter
Play Development Assistant ..... Annie MacRae
Director of Musical Development ..... **Clifford Lee Johnson III**
Director of Development ..... **Jill Turner Lloyd**
Director, Special Events ..... Allison Gutstein
Director, Foundation & Government Relations ..... Josh Jacobson
Director, Corporate Relations ..... Karen Zornow Leiding
Director, Individual Giving ..... Jon W. Haddorff
Senior Development Associate, Individual Giving ..... Antonello Di Benedetto
Development Associate/Foundation & Government Relations ..... Andrea Gorzell
Development Associate/ Planning & Projects ..... Liz Halakan
Development Associate/ Corporate Relations ..... Jessica Sadowski
Development Database Coordinator ..... Rey Pamatmat
Patrons' Liaison ..... Sage Young
Director of Marketing ..... **Debra A. Waxman**
Marketing and Website Manager ..... Ryan Klink
Marketing Associate ..... Tom O'Connor
Director of Finance ..... **Jeffrey Bledsoe**
Business Manager ..... Holly Kinney
HR/Payroll Manager ..... Darren Robertson
Senior Business Associate & HR Coordinator ..... Denise L. Thomas
Business Assistant ..... Adam Cook
Manager of Systems Operations ..... Avishai Cohen
Systems Analyst ..... Andrew Dumawal
Associate General Manager ..... **Lindsey Brooks Sag**
Company Manager/NY City Center ..... Erin Moeller
Assistant to the Executive Producer ..... Bonnie Pan
Director of Subscriber Services ..... **Robert Allenberg**
Associate Subscriber Services Manager ..... Andrew Taylor
Subscriber Services Representatives ..... Mark Bowers, Rebekah Dewald, Matthew Praet, Rosanna Consalva Sarto
Director of Telesales and Telefunding ..... **George Tetlow**
Assistant Manager ..... Terrence Burnett
Director of Education ..... **David Shookhoff**
Asst. Director of Education/ Coordinator, Paul A. Kaplan Theatre Management Program ..... Amy Harris
Education Assistants ..... Kayla Cagan, Sarah Ryndak
MTC Teaching Artists ..... Stephanie Alston, David Auburn, Michael Bernard, Carl Capotorto, Chris Ceraso, Charlotte Colavin, Dominic Colon, Gilbert Girion, Andy Goldberg, Elise Hernandez, Jeffrey Joseph, Julie Leedes, Kate Long, Louis D. Moreno, Melissa Murray, Angela Pietropinto, Alfonso Ramirez, Carmen Rivera, Judy Tate, Candido Tirado, Joe White
Theatre Management Interns ..... Monica Ammirati, Nicky Barton, Chanda Calentine, Li Cornfeld, Jocelyn Florence, L. Jared Franzman, Meghan Goria, Charles Graytok, Patricia Jordan, Mayuha Kunisue, Elizabeth McGorty, Laura Roumanos, Hannah Shafran, Marielle Solan, Rachel Swan

---

The Paul A. Kaplan Theatre Management Program, MTC's internship program, is designed to train the next generation of theatre leaders.

Randy Carrig Casting Intern ..... Shira Sandler
Reception/Studio Manager ..... Lauren Butler
Production Manager ..... **Ryan McMahon**
Associate Production Manager ..... Bridget Markov
Lights and Sound Supervisor ..... **Matthew T. Gross**
Properties Supervisor ..... **Scott Laule**
Assistant Properties Supervisor ..... Julia Sandy
Props Carpenter ..... Peter Grimes
Costume Supervisor ..... **Erin Hennessy Dean**
Assistant Costume Supervisor ..... Michelle Sesco

GENERAL PRESS REPRESENTATION
BONEAU/BRYAN-BROWN
Chris Boneau Jim Byk
Aaron Meier Heath Schwartz

Script Readers ..... Erin Detrick, Liz Jones, Michelle Tattenbaum, Kathryn Walat, Ethan Youngerman
Musical Theatre Reader ..... Emily King

SERVICES

Accountants ..... ERE, LLP
Advertising ..... SpotCo/ Drew Hodges, Jim Edwards, Tom McCann, Laura Price
Web Design ..... Pilla Marketing Communications
Legal Counsel ..... John Breglio, Deborah Hartnett/ Paul, Weiss, Rifkind, Wharton and Garrison LLP
Real Estate Counsel ..... Marcus Attorneys
Labor Counsel ..... Harry H. Weintraub/ Glick and Weintraub, P.C.
Immigration Counsel ..... Theodore Ruthizer/ Framer, Levin, Naftalis & Frankel, LLP
Special Projects ..... Elaine H. Hirsch
Insurance ..... Dewitt Stern Group, Inc./Anthony Pittari
Maintenance ..... Reliable Cleaning
Production Photographer ..... Joan Marcus
Cover Photo ..... Henry Leutwyler
Cover Design ..... SpotCo
Theatre Displays ..... King Display

For more information visit
www.ManhattanTheatreClub.com

PRODUCTION STAFF FOR *LOSING LOUIE*

Company Manager ..... **Denise Cooper**
Production Stage Manager ..... **Barclay Stiff**
Stage Manager ..... David H. Lurie
Dramaturg ..... Aaron Leichter
Assistant Director ..... Michael Goldfried
Assistant Scenic Designer ..... Yoshinori Tanokura
Associate Costume Designer ..... Jennifer Robin Arnold
Associate Lighting Designer ..... John Viesta
Assistant Sound Designer ..... Ryan Rumery
Hair and Makeup Supervisor ..... Natasha Steinhagen
Lighting Programmer ..... Marc Polimeni
Dresser ..... Tim Hanlon
Production Assistant ..... Brandon Kahn

CREDITS

Scenery by Great Lakes Scenic Studios; Lighting equipment provided by PRG Lighting; Sound equipment provided by t/c. Natural herbal cough drops courtesy of Ricola USA.

MUSIC CREDITS

"Happy Birthday to You" (Mildred J. Hill, Patty S. Hill), ©1935 (renewed); Summy-Birchard Company (ASCAP), all rights reserved. Used by permission.

SPECIAL THANKS

ABC Carpet, Paul Huntley

MANHATTAN THEATRE CLUB/ BILTMORE THEATRE STAFF

Theatre Manager ..... **Valerie D. Simmons**
Assistant House Managers ..... Johannah-Joy Magyawe, Miranda Scopel
Box Office Treasurer ..... **David Dillon**
Assistant Box Office Treasurers ..... Tevy Bradley, Jonathan Pate
Head Carpenter ..... Chris Wiggins
Head Propertyman ..... Timothy Walters
Sound Engineer ..... Louis Shapiro
Master Electrician ..... Jeff Dodson
Wardrobe Supervisor ..... Angela Simpson
Apprentices ..... Marc Grimshaw, Andrew Sliwinski
Engineers ..... Robert Allen, Richardo Deosarran, Byron Johnson
Security ..... Initial Security
Lobby Refreshments ..... Sweet Concessions

Losing Louie
Scrapbook

Correspondent: Barclay Stiff, PSM.
Favorite Moment During Each Performance (On Stage or Off): The top of Act II was always a fun time for the entire company. Mark Linn-Baker, Michele Pawk, Patricia Kalember and Matthew Arkin walk onstage covered from head to toe with a Latex-based mud. Ten minutes into the intermission we would do our nightly ritual called "WET-DOWN!" This involved Mark, Michele, Patricia and Matthew standing in a large sink and being sprayed down with water and then smothered in mud. Lots of fun!
Favorite In-Theatre Gathering Place: The Biltmore stage managers' office seemed to be the place where the company gathered the most.
Favorite Snack Food: CHOCOLATE! CHOCOLATE! CHOCOLATE!, Ricola, Altoids, and more CHOCOLATE.
Funny Onstage Moments: Rebecca Creskoff usually says "best friends forever" to her fellow actor Jama Williamson. One night she accidentally said "breast friends forever." It was a brilliant moment that the audience never picked up on, but it provided many laughs for the entire company backstage. Rebecca was not the only one that had line goofs throughout the run. Every single cast member had their own VERY unique moment. It was always a wild ride every night!
Who Wore the Least: Patricia Kalember had the lovely task of turning upstage nightly and opening up her robe to reveal her nude body to Matthew Arkin. In addition to that she then had to discreetly show Matthew a unique piercing that she had done in an intimate spot. A great moment for the American Theatre!

Photo by Aubrey Reuben

Photo by David Gewirtzman

Photo by Aubrey Reuben

Photo by Aubrey Reuben

1. (L-R): Playwright Simon Mendes Da Costa, director Jerry Zaks, Scott Cohen, Jama Williamson, Patricia Kalember, Rebecca Creskoff, Mark Linn-Baker, Michele Pawk and Matthew Arkin at the opening night party at the Boathouse in Central Park.
2. Marquee of the Biltmore Theatre.
3. (L-R): Matthew Arkin and Mark Linn-Baker.
4. The cast takes a curtain call on opening night.

LoveMusik

First Preview: April 12, 2007. Opened: May 3, 2007.
Still running as of May 31, 2007.

PLAYBILL

BILTMORE THEATRE

MANHATTAN THEATRE CLUB

Artistic Director
LYNNE MEADOW

Executive Producer
BARRY GROVE

by special arrangement with
MARTY BELL ALDO SCROFANI BOYETT OSTAR PRODUCTIONS
TRACY ARON ROGER BERLIND/DEBRA BLACK CHASE MISHKIN TED SNOWDON

Presents

LOVEMUSIK

book by
ALFRED UHRY

music by
KURT WEILL

Suggested by the letters of Kurt Weill and Lotte Lenya

Lyrics by
MAXWELL ANDERSON BERTOLT BRECHT HOWARD DIETZ ROGER FERNAY IRA GERSHWIN OSCAR HAMMERSTEIN II
LANGSTON HUGHES ALAN JAY LERNER MAURICE MAGRE OGDEN NASH ELMER RICE KURT WEILL

with
MICHAEL CERVERIS DONNA MURPHY DAVID PITTU JOHN SCHERER
JUDITH BLAZER EDWIN CAHILL HERNDON LACKEY ERIK LIBERMAN ANN MORRISON
GRAHAM ROWAT RACHEL ULANET JESSICA WRIGHT

Scenic Design
BEOWULF BORITT

Costume Design
JUDITH DOLAN

Lighting Design
HOWELL BINKLEY

Sound Design
DUNCAN ROBERT EDWARDS

Wig Design
PAUL HUNTLEY

Make-Up Design
ANGELINA AVALLONE

Production Stage Manager
JOSHUA HALPERIN

Casting
MARK SIMON

Orchestrations
JONATHAN TUNICK

Musical Supervisor
KRISTEN BLODGETTE

Music Coordinator
SEYMOUR RED PRESS

Additional Vocal Arrangements
MILTON GRANGER

Conductor
NICHOLAS ARCHER

Musical Staging by
PATRICIA BIRCH

Directed by
HAROLD PRINCE

Director of Artistic Operations
MANDY GREENFIELD

Production Manager
RYAN McMAHON

Director of Development
JILL TURNER LLOYD

Director of Marketing
DEBRA A. WAXMAN

Press Representative
BONEAU/BRYAN-BROWN

General Manager
FLORIE SEERY

Director of Artistic Development
PAIGE EVANS

Special funding thanks to the Harold and Mimi Steinberg Charitable Trust for supporting new American plays and musicals at Manhattan Theatre Club.
Manhattan Theatre Club wishes to express its appreciation to Theatre Development Fund for its support of this production.

5/3/07

CAST

(in order of appearance)

Kurt Weill .... MICHAEL CERVERIS
Lotte Lenya .... DONNA MURPHY
Bertolt Brecht .... DAVID PITTU
George Davis .... JOHN SCHERER
Woman on Stairs .... JUDITH BLAZER
Magistrate/Judge .... HERNDON LACKEY
Court Secretary .... RACHEL ULANET
Brecht's Women .... JUDITH BLAZER, ANN MORRISON, RACHEL ULANET
Auditioners .... HERNDON LACKEY, RACHEL ULANET
Interviewer .... ERIK LIBERMAN
Otto .... GRAHAM ROWAT
Photographer .... ANN MORRISON
Allen Lake .... GRAHAM ROWAT
Handyman .... ERIK LIBERMAN

Stage Manager .... JASON BROUILLARD

UNDERSTUDIES

For Bertolt Brecht, Kurt Weill:
EDWIN CAHILL
For Bertolt Brecht:
ERIK LIBERMAN
For Lotte Lenya:
ANN MORRISON
For George Davis:
GRAHAM ROWAT

Continued on next page

(L-R): Michael Cerveris and Donna Murphy, as Weill and Lenya, have a torrid meeting in a rowboat.

Photo by Carol Rosegg

MUSICAL NUMBERS

ACT I — EUROPE

Speak Low (lyrics by Ogden Nash)	Weill, Lenya
Nanna's Lied (lyrics by Bertolt Brecht)	Woman on Stairs
Kiddush	Weill's Family
Song of the Rhineland (lyrics by Ira Gershwin)	Lenya's Family
Klops Lied (Meatball Song)	Weill
Berlin Im Licht (lyrics by Kurt Weill)	Lenya
Wooden Wedding (lyrics by Ogden Nash)	Weill, Lenya, Magistrate, Court Secretary
Tango Ballad (lyrics by Bertolt Brecht)	Brecht, Brecht's Women
Alabama Song (lyrics by Bertolt Brecht)	Auditioners, Lenya
Girl of the Moment (lyrics by Ira Gershwin)	Ensemble
Moritat (lyrics by Bertolt Brecht)	Brecht, Lenya, Otto, Ensemble
Schickelgruber (lyrics by Howard Dietz)	Weill, Brecht
Come to Paris (lyrics by Ira Gershwin)	Ensemble
I Don't Love You (lyrics by Maurice Magre)	Weill, Lenya
Wouldn't You Like to Be on Broadway? (lyrics by Langston Hughes & Elmer Rice)	Weill, Lenya
Alabama Song, Reprise (lyrics by Bertolt Brecht)	Lenya, Weill, Brecht, Ensemble

ACT II — AMERICA

How Can You Tell an American? (lyrics by Maxwell Anderson)	Ensemble
Very, Very, Very (lyrics by Ogden Nash)	Weill
It's Never Too Late to Mendelssohn (lyrics by Ira Gershwin)	Weill, Lenya, Stenographer, Judge
Surabaya Johnny (lyrics by Bertolt Brecht)	Lenya
Youkali (lyrics by Roger Fernay)	Brecht, Brecht's Women
Buddy on the Night Shift (lyrics by Oscar Hammerstein II)	Allen
That's Him (lyrics by Ogden Nash)	Weill
Hosannah Rockefeller (lyrics by Bertolt Brecht)	Brecht, Brecht's Women
I Don't Love You, Reprise (lyrics by Maurice Magre)	Lenya, Weill
The Illusion Wedding Show (lyrics by Alan Jay Lerner)	Davis, Ensemble
It Never Was You (lyrics by Maxwell Anderson)	Weill
A Bird of Passage (lyrics by Maxwell Anderson)	Ensemble
September Song (lyrics by Maxwell Anderson)	Lenya, Davis

Cast Continued

SWINGS
EDWIN CAHILL, JESSICA WRIGHT

Dance Captain: ANN MORRISON

ORCHESTRA
Conductor/Piano:
NICHOLAS ARCHER
Violins:
KATHERINE LIVOLSI-LANDAU,
SUZY PERELMAN
Viola:
DAVID BLINN
Cello:
MAIRI DORMAN
Woodwinds:
JAMES ERCOLE, JOHN WINDER
Trumpet:
CHRISTIAN JAUDES
Bass:
JEFFREY COOPER
Drums/Percussion:
BILLY MILLER
Associate Conductor:
STAN TUCKER

Music copying:
EMILY GRISHMAN MUSIC PREPARATION—
KATHARINE EDMONDS/EMILY GRISHMAN

Michael Cerveris
Kurt Weill

Donna Murphy
Lotte Lenya

David Pittu
Bertold Brecht

John Scherer
George Davis

Judith Blazer
Woman on Stairs, Brecht's Woman

Edwin Cahill
Swing

Herndon Lackey
Magistrate/Judge, Auditioner

Erik Liberman
Interviewer, Handyman

Ann Morrison
Brecht's Woman, Photographer

Graham Rowat
Otto, Allen Lake

LoveMusik

Rachel Ulanet
Court Secretary, Brecht's Woman, Auditioner

Jessica Wright
Swing

Alfred Uhry
Book

Harold Prince
Director

Patricia Birch
Musical Staging

Beowulf Boritt
Scenic Design

Howell Binkley
Lighting Design

Paul Huntley
Wig Design

Angelina Avallone
Make-up Design

Jonathan Tunick
Orchestrations

Kristen Blodgette
Musical Supervisor

Seymour Red Press
Musical Coordinator

Lynne Meadow
Artistic Director, Manhattan Theatre Club

Barry Grove
Executive Producer, Manhattan Theatre Club

Marty Bell
Producer

Aldo Scrofani
Producer

Bob Boyett, Boyett OSTAR Productions
Producer

Bill Haber, Boyett OSTAR Productions
Producer

Tracy Aron
Producer

Roger Berlind
Producer

Debra Black
Producer

Chase Mishkin
Producer

Ted Snowdon
Producer

2006-2007 AWARDS

Drama Desk Awards
Outstanding Actress in a Musical
(Donna Murphy)
Outstanding Orchestrations
(Jonathan Tunick)

Outer Critics Circle Awards
Outstanding Actress in a Musical
(Donna Murphy)
Outstanding Featured Actor in a Musical
(David Pittu)

Obie Award
Sustained Excellence in Set Design
(Beowulf Boritt)

Photo by Ben Strothmann

STAGE CREW
Back Row (L-R): Gerard Fortunato, Taurance Williams, Josh Halperin, Andrew Sliwinski Lou Shapiro, Marc Grimshaw, Brandon Maloney, Matt Maloney, Jeff Dodson.
Middle Row (L-R): Jessica Deromody, Suzanne Williams, Tracey Boone, Sue Poulin, Rich Wichrowksi, Seth Shepsle.
Front Row (L-R): Angie Simpson, Ryan Rossetto (with unicorn), Rachel Miller and Megan Schneid.

LoveMusik

ORCHESTRA
Front Row (L-R): David Blinn (Viola), Nicholas Archer (Conductor), Katherine Livolsi-Landau (Concertmaster), Jeffrey Cooper (Bass).

Back Row (L-R): Stan Tucker (Associate Conductor), James Ercole (Reeds), Mairi Dorman (Cello), Billy Miller (Percussion) and John Winder (Reeds).

FRONT OF HOUSE STAFF
Front Row (L-R): Wendy Wright (Head Usher), Ed Brashear (Ticket Taker), Miranda Scopel (Assistant House Manager).

Middle Row (L-R): Jonathan Pate (Treasurer), Alana Samuels (Biltmore Intern), Taylor Holt (Usher), Quanda Johnson (Usher), Bru Dye (Usher), David Dillon (Head Treasurer).

Back Row (L-R): Russ Ramsey (Theatre Manager) and Jackson Ero (Usher).

Photos by Ben Strothmann

MANHATTAN THEATRE CLUB STAFF

Artistic Director .... **Lynne Meadow**
Executive Producer .... **Barry Grove**
General Manager .... **Florie Seery**
Director of Artistic Development .... **Paige Evans**
Director of Artistic Operations .... **Mandy Greenfield**
Artistic Consultant .... **Daniel Sullivan**
Director of Artistic Administration/ Assistant to the Artistic Director .... **Amy Gilkes Loe**
Associate Director of Artistic Operations ..... Lisa McNulty
Artistic Assistant .... Kacy O'Brien
Administrative Assistant .... Rebecca Stang
Director of Casting .... **Nancy Piccione**
Casting Director .... **David Caparelliotis**
Casting Assistants .... Rebecca Atwood, Kristin Svenningsen
Literary Manager .... **Emily Shooltz**
Play Development Associate/ Sloan Project Manager .... Annie MacRae
Director of Musical Development .... **Clifford Lee Johnson III**
Director of Development .... **Jill Turner Lloyd**
Director, Special Events .... Allison Gutstein
Director, Foundation & Government Relations .... Josh Jacobson
Director, Corporate Relations .... Karen Zornow Leiding
Director, Individual Giving .... Jon W. Haddorff
Manager, Individual Giving .... Antonello Di Benedetto
Development Associate/ Foundation & Government Relations .. Andrea Gorzell
Development Associate/ Planning & Projects .... Liz Halakan
Development Associate/ Corporate Relations .... Jessica Sadowski
Development Database Coordinator .... Ann Mundorff
Patrons' Liaison .... Sage Young
Director of Marketing .... **Debra A. Waxman**
Marketing Associate .... Tom O'Connor
Marketing Associate .... Andrea D. Paul
Director of Finance .... **Jeffrey Bledsoe**
Business Manager .... Holly Kinney
Human Resources Manager .... Darren Robertson
Business & HR Associate .... Adam Cook
Business Assistant .... Charles Graytok
Manager of Systems Operations .... Avishai Cohen
Systems Analyst .... Alexis M. Allen
Associate General Manager .... **Lindsey Brooks Sag**
Company Manager/NY City Center .... Erin Moeller
General Management Assistant .... Laura Roumanos
Assistant to the Executive Producer .... Ashley Dunn
Director of Subscriber Services .... **Robert Allenberg**
Associate Subscriber Services Manager .... Andrew Taylor
Subscriber Services Representatives .... Mark Bowers, Eric Gerdts, Matthew Praet, Rosanna Consalva Sarto
Director of Telesales and Telefunding ..... **George Tetlow**
Assistant Manager, Telesales and Telefunding .... Terrence Burnett
Director of Education .... **David Shookhoff**
Asst. Director of Education/ Coordinator, Paul A. Kaplan Theatre Management Program .... Amy Harris
Education Assistants .... Kayla Cagan, Sarah Ryndak
MTC Teaching Artists .... Stephanie Alston, David Auburn, Michael Bernard, Carl Capotorto, Chris Ceraso, Charlotte Colavin, Dominic Colon, Gilbert Girion, Andy Goldberg, Elise Hernandez, Jeffrey Joseph, Julie Leedes, Kate Long, Louis D. Moreno, Andres Munar, Melissa Murray, Angela Pietropinto, Alfonso Ramirez, Carmen Rivera, Judy Tate, Candido Tirado, Joe White

Theatre Management Interns ....Nicky Barton, Stephanie Cowan, Marie Darden, Ian Darrah, Jocelyn Florence, Jennifer Gibson, Diana Glazer, Cia Jordan, Kara McGann, Katie Murray, Alana Samuels, Hannah Shafran, Marielle Solan, Rachel Swan

The Paul A. Kaplan Theatre Management Program, MTC's internship program, is designed to train the next generation of theatre leaders.

Randy Carrig Casting Intern ....Shira Sandler
Reception/Studio Manager ....Lauren Butler
Production Manager ....Ryan McMahon
Associate Production Manager ....Bridget Markov
Assistant Production Manager ....Stephanie Madonna
Lights and Sound Supervisor ....Matthew T. Gross
Properties Supervisor ....Scott Laule
Assistant Properties Supervisor ....Julia Sandy
Props Carpenter ....Peter Grimes
Costume Supervisor ....Erin Hennessy Dean

GENERAL PRESS REPRESENTATION
BONEAU/BRYAN-BROWN
Chris Boneau Jim Byk
Aaron Meier Heath Schwartz Christine Olver

Script Readers ....Erin Detrick, Liz Jones, Asher Richelli, Michelle Tattenbaum, Kathryn Walat, Ethan Youngerman
Musical Theatre Reader ....Emily King

SERVICES

Accountants ....ERE, LLP
Advertising ....SpotCo/ Drew Hodges, Jim Edwards, Ben Downing, Laura Price
Web Design ....Pilla Marketing Communications
Legal Counsel ....John Breglio, Deborah Hartnett/ Paul, Weiss, Rifkind, Wharton and Garrison LLP
Real Estate Counsel ....Marcus Attorneys
Labor Counsel ....Harry H. Weintraub/ Glick and Weintraub, P.C.
Immigration Counsel ....Theodore Ruthizer/ Kramer, Levin, Naftalis & Frankel, LLP
Special Projects ....Elaine H. Hirsch
Insurance ....Dewitt Stern Group, Inc./Anthony Pittari
Maintenance ....Reliable Cleaning
Production Photographer ....Carol Rosegg
Cover Photo ....Henry Leutwyler
Cover Design ....SpotCo
Theatre Displays ....King Display

PRODUCTION STAFF FOR *LOVEMUSIK*

Company Manager ....Seth Shepsle
Production Manager ....Bridget Markov
Production Stage Manager ....Joshua Halperin
Stage Manager ....Jason Brouillard
Assistant to Mr. Prince ....Daniel Kutner
Assistant Choreographer ....Deanna Dys
Rehearsal Pianist ....Stan Tucker
Associate Scenic Designer ....Jo Winiarski
Assistant Scenic Designer ....Camille Connolly
Assistant Scenic Designer ....Jessie T. Moore
Assistant Scenic Designer ....Jason Lajka
Assistant Costume Designer ....Rebecca Lustig
Associate Lighting Designer ....Ryan O'Gara
Assistant Lighting Designer ....Brad King
Assistant Sound Designer ....Nathaniel Hare
Assistant to Paul Huntley ....Darlene Dannenfelser
Assistant Costume Supervisor ....Michelle Sesco
Dialect Consultant ....Stephen Gabis
Automation Operator ....Patrick Murray
Flymen ....John Fullum, Leomar Susana, Rich Wichrowski
Assistant Carpenter ....Gerard Fortunato
Assistant Propertyman ....Sue Poulin
Moving Light Programmer ....Hillary Knox
Conventional Light Programmer ....J. Day
Frontlight Operators ....Timothy Coffey, Matt Maloney
Light Board Operator ....Suzanne Williams
Dressers ....Janet Anderson, Tracey Boone, Dolores Jones, Ryan Rossetto
Hair Supervisor ....Alice Ramos
Assistant Hair Supervisor ....Taurance Williams
Production Sound Engineer ....Jens Muehlhausen
Production Assistant ....Rachel Miller
Directing Intern ....Josh Halloway
Costume Intern ....Maggie Whitaker
SDCF Observer ....Andy Sandberg
Music Fellow ....Brian Scott Taylor

MARK SIMON CASTING
Casting Assistant: Selby Brown

LoveMusik is suggested by *Speak Low (When You Speak Love)*, edited and translated by Lys Symonette and Kim H. Kowalke (U. of California Press, 1996). Professor Kowalke has served as historical and musical consultant for this production.

MUSIC CREDITS

Use of the musical compositions in the play is by permission of European American Music Corporation.

Lyrics: "Speak Low" (from *One Touch of Venus*) used by permission from Curtis Brown, Ltd. Copyright ©1944; all rights reserved. "Nanna's Lied," translation by Michael Feingold, used by arrangement with European American Music Corporation. "Kiddush" used by arrangement with European American Music Corporation. "Klops Lied (Meatball Song)," translation by Milton Granger, used by arrangement with European American Music Corporation. "Berlin Im Licht," translation by Milton Granger, used by arrangement with European American Music Corporation. "Wooden Wedding" (from *One Touch of Venus*) by permission from Curtis Brown, Ltd. Copyright ©1944; all rights reserved. "Tango Ballad" (from *The Threepenny Opera*), translation by Marc Blitzstein, used by arrangement with European American Music Corporation. "Alabama Song" (from *Rise and Fall of the City of Mahagonny*) used by arrangement with European American Music Corporation. "Girl of the Moment" (from *Lady in the Dark*) used with permission. "Moritat" (from *The Threepenny Opera*), translation by Marc Blitzstein, used by arrangement with European American Music Corporation. "Schickelgruber," adapted by Alfred Uhry, used by arrangement with European American Music Corporation. "Come to Paris" (from *The Firebrand of Florence*) used with permission. "I Don't Love You," translation by Michael Feingold, used by arrangement with European American Music Coporation on behalf of Heugel S. A. "Wouldn't You Like to Be on Broadway?" (from *Street Scene*), book by Elmer Rice; lyrics by Langston Hughes. "How Can You Tell an American?" (from *Knickerbocker Holiday*) used with permission. "Very, Very, Very" (from *One Touch of Venus*) used by permission from Curtis Brown, Ltd. Copyright ©1944; all rights reserved. "Surabaya Johnny" (from *Happy End*), translation by Michael Feingold, used by arrangement with European American Music Corporation. "Youkali" used by arrangement with European American Music Corporation on behalf of Heugel S.A. "That's Him" (from *One Touch of Venus*) used by permission from Curtis Brown, Ltd. Copyright ©1944; all rights reserved. "Hosannah Rockefeller" (from *Happy End*), translation by Michael Feingold, used by arrangement with European American Music Corporation. "The Illusion Wedding Show" (from *Love Life*) used with permission of the Alan Jay Lerner Testamentary Trust. "It Never Was You" (from *Knickerbocker Holiday*) used with permission. "A Bird of Passage" (from *Lost in the Stars*) used with permission. "September Song" (from *Knickerbocker Holiday*) used with permission.

CREDITS

Show control and scenic motion control featuring Stage Command Systems® by PRG-Scenic Technologies, a division of Production Resource Group, LLC, New Windsor, NY. Scenery fabrication by PRG-Scenic Technologies and Great Lakes Scenic Studios. Additional hanging and deck scenery provided by Global Scenic Services. Lighting equipment by PRG Lighting. Projected imagery by Adam Larsen. Sound equipment by Masque Sound. Costume construction by Barbara Matera Limited, Carelli Costumes, Paul Chang and Tricorne, Inc. Millinery by Rodney Gordon, Inc. Piano provided by Steinway & Sons. Natural herbal cough drops courtesy of Ricola USA. MTC wishes to thank the TDF Costume Collection for its assistance in this production.

SPECIAL THANKS
Irish Repertory Theatre

For more information visit
www.ManhattanTheatreClub.com

MANHATTAN THEATRE CLUB/
BILTMORE THEATRE STAFF

Theatre Manager ....Russ Ramsey
Assistant House Manager ....Miranda Scopel
Box Office Treasurer ....David Dillon
Assistant Box Office Treasurers ....Tevy Bradley, Jonathan Pate
Head Carpenter ....Chris Wiggins
Head Propertyman ....Timothy Walters
Sound Engineer ....Louis Shapiro
Master Electrician ....Jeff Dodson
Wardrobe Supervisor ....Angela Simpson
Apprentices ....Marc Grimshaw, Andrew Sliwinski
Engineers ....Robert Allen, Richardo Deosarran, Byron Johnson
Security ....Initial Security
Lobby Refreshments ....Sweet Concessions

LoveMusik
Scrapbook

1. Donna Murphy and Michael Cerveris at the opening night party at the Supper Club.
2. David Pittu at the cast party.
3. Curtain call on opening night at the Biltmore Theatre.
4. Director Harold Prince on opening night.
5. John Scherer at the Supper Club.

Correspondent: John Scherer, "George Davis."
Opening Night Gifts: A cactus from Donna Murphy, an original Playbill from *One Touch of Venus* from Michael Cerveris.
Most Exciting Celebrity Visitor: Stephen Sondheim.
Actor Who Performs the Most Roles: I think it's Herndon Lackey...and he plays my favorite character, a guy auditioning for Brecht and Weill, named Erik Giebel.
Most Shows in Their Career: Our director, Hal Prince.
Backstage Ritual: Watching Michael's dresser, Ryan Rossetto, doing an improvised dance during the Entr'acte.
Favorite Moment: Singing "September Song" with Donna.
Favorite In-Theater Gathering Place: The Ladies Dressing Room (they have candy).
Favorite Off-Site Gathering Place: Joe Allen.
Favorite Snack Food: Chocolate.
Mascot: Tammy, a fox head that was on Donna's coat.
Favorite Therapy: Sudoku during the first act (I'm only in Act II).
Record Number of Cell Phone Rings: Four during the nightclub scene with Michael, then at the same performance, another right after my speech to Donna at the end...amazing timing on their part.
Memorable Press Encounter: Harry Haun with that tape recorder...does he sleep with that thing under his pillow???
Memorable Stage Door Encounter: My mom.
Fastest Costume Change: Into my silver tux for "The Illusion Wedding Show"...with Rachel Ulanet always hoping that I' m wearing smiley face underwear, which I don't.
Catchphrase Only the Company Would Recognize: "Sunshine, Rainbows and Corn."
Memorable Director's Note: "It sounds like this...'DING'." That's Hal telling our musical director Kristen Blodgette what a bell from a punch-in clock should sound like.
Company In-Jokes: Again, Sunshine, Rainbows and Corn.
Company Legend: Hal Prince.
Understudy Anecdote: Jessica Wright going on for Ann Morrison AND Judy Blazer at the same performance!
Nickname: Ryan (Michael's dresser) calls me "Skimbleshanks."
Sweethearts: Unless I'm missing something, none.
Coolest Thing About Being in This Show: Among many others things (working with Hal, Alfred Uhry and this amazing company), I have a late call and I live one block from the theater.

Mamma Mia!

First Preview: October 5, 2001. Opened: October 18, 2001.
Still running as of May 31, 2007.

PLAYBILL

CADILLAC WINTER GARDEN THEATRE

1634 Broadway
A Shubert Organization Theatre
Gerald Schoenfeld, *Chairman* **Philip J. Smith**, *President*

Robert E. Wankel, *Executive Vice President*

JUDY CRAYMER, RICHARD EAST AND BJÖRN ULVAEUS
FOR LITTLESTAR IN ASSOCIATION WITH UNIVERSAL

PRESENT

MAMMA MIA!

MUSIC AND LYRICS BY
BENNY ANDERSSON
BJÖRN ULVAEUS
AND SOME SONGS WITH STIG ANDERSON

BOOK BY CATHERINE JOHNSON

PRODUCTION DESIGNED BY
MARK THOMPSON

LIGHTING DESIGNED BY
HOWARD HARRISON

SOUND DESIGNED BY
ANDREW BRUCE &
BOBBY AITKEN

MUSICAL SUPERVISOR, ADDITIONAL MATERIAL
& ARRANGEMENTS
MARTIN KOCH

CHOREOGRAPHY
ANTHONY VAN LAAST

DIRECTED BY
PHYLLIDA LLOYD

LIVE BROADWAY

10/2/06

CAST

(in order of speaking)

Sophie Sheridan .... CAREY ANDERSON
Ali .... VERONICA J. KUEHN
Lisa .... SAMANTHA EGGERS
Tanya .... JUDY McLANE
Rosie .... OLGA MEREDIZ
Donna Sheridan .... CAROLEE CARMELLO
Sky .... ANDY KELSO
Pepper .... BEN GETTINGER
Eddie .... RAYMOND J. LEE
Harry Bright .... DAVID BEACH
Bill Austin .... MARK L. MONTGOMERY
Sam Carmichael .... DAVID McDONALD
Father Alexandrios .... BRYAN SCOTT JOHNSON

THE ENSEMBLE

MEREDITH AKINS, BRENT BLACK,
ANGELA ARA BROWN, ISAAC CALPITO,
CHRISTOPHER CARL,
MEGHANN DREYFUSS, SHAKIEM EVANS,
LORI HALEY FOX, BRYAN SCOTT JOHNSON,
CORINNE MELANÇON,
STEVE MORGAN, JOI DANIELLE PRICE,
SANDY ROSENBERG,
GERARD SALVADOR, BRITT SHUBOW,
LEAH ZEPEL

Continued on next page

(L-R): Judy McLane, Carolee Carmello and Olga Merediz

Photo by Joan Marcus

Mamma Mia!

MUSICAL NUMBERS

(in alphabetical order)

CHIQUITITA
DANCING QUEEN
DOES YOUR MOTHER KNOW
GIMME! GIMME! GIMME!
HONEY, HONEY
I DO, I DO, I DO, I DO, I DO
I HAVE A DREAM
KNOWING ME, KNOWING YOU
LAY ALL YOUR LOVE ON ME
MAMMA MIA
MONEY, MONEY, MONEY
ONE OF US
OUR LAST SUMMER
SLIPPING THROUGH MY FINGERS
S.O.S.
SUPER TROUPER
TAKE A CHANCE ON ME
THANK YOU FOR THE MUSIC
THE NAME OF THE GAME
THE WINNER TAKES IT ALL
UNDER ATTACK
VOULEZ-VOUS

THE BAND

Music Director/Conductor/Keyboard 1:
WENDY BOBBITT CAVETT
Associate Music Director/Keyboard 3:
ROB PREUSS
Keyboard 2:
STEVE MARZULLO
Keyboard 4:
MYLES CHASE
Guitar 1:
DOUG QUINN
Guitar 2:
JEFF CAMPBELL
Bass:
PAUL ADAMY
Drums:
RAY MARCHICA
Percussion:
DAVID NYBERG
Music Coordinator:
MICHAEL KELLER
Synthesizer Programmer:
NICHOLAS GILPIN

Photos by Joan Marcus

(L-R): Carey Anderson and Carolee Carmello as Sophie and Donna Sheridan.

Carolee Carmello performs the finale.

Cast Continued

UNDERSTUDIES

For Sophie Sheridan:
MEGHANN DREYFUSS,
SAMANTHA EGGERS, BRITT SHUBOW
For Ali:
ANGELA ARA BROWN, JOI DANIELLE PRICE,
LEAH ZEPEL
For Lisa:
MEREDITH AKINS, BRITT SHUBOW
For Tanya:
LORI HALEY FOX, CORINNE MELANÇON
For Rosie:
LORI HALEY FOX, SANDY ROSENBERG
For Donna Sheridan:
LORI HALEY FOX, CORINNE MELANÇON
For Sky:
STEVE MORGAN, RYAN SANDER
For Pepper:
ISAAC CALPITO, GERARD SALVADOR
For Eddie:
SHAKIEM EVANS, MATTHEW FARVER,
RYAN SANDER
For Harry Bright:
CHRISTOPHER CARL,
BRYAN SCOTT JOHNSON
For Bill Austin:
BRENT BLACK, CHRISTOPHER CARL,
BRYAN SCOTT JOHNSON
For Sam Carmichael:
BRENT BLACK, CHRISTOPHER CARL
For Father Alexandrios:
BRENT BLACK, CHRISTOPHER CARL,
MATTHEW FARVER

SWINGS

LANENE CHARTERS, MATTHEW FARVER,
RYAN SANDER, COLLETTE SIMMONS

DANCE CAPTAIN

JANET ROTHERMEL

On a Greek Island, a wedding is about to take place...

PROLOGUE

Three months before the wedding

ACT ONE

The day before the wedding

ACT TWO

The day of the wedding

Mamma Mia!

Carolee Carmello
Donna Sheridan

Carey Anderson
Sophie Sheridan

Judy McLane
Tanya

Olga Merediz
Rosie

David McDonald
Sam Carmichael

David Beach
Harry Bright

Mark L. Montgomery
Bill Austin

Andy Kelso
Sky

Samantha Eggers
Lisa

Veronica J. Kuehn
Ali

Ben Gettinger
Pepper

Raymond J. Lee
Eddie

Meredith Akins
Ensemble

Brent Black
Ensemble

Angela Ara Brown
Ensemble

Isaac Calpito
Ensemble

Christopher Carl
Ensemble

Lanene Charters
Swing

Meghann Dreyfuss
Ensemble

Shakiem Evans
Ensemble

Matthew Farver
Swing

Lori Haley Fox
Ensemble

Bryan Scott Johnson
Father Alexandrios, Ensemble

Corinne Melançon
Ensemble

Steve Morgan
Ensemble

Joi Danielle Price
Ensemble

Sandy Rosenberg
Ensemble

Janet Rothermel
Dance Captain

Gerard Salvador
Ensemble

Ryan Sander
Swing

Britt Shubow
Ensemble

Collette Simmons
Swing

Leah Zepel
Ensemble

Björn Ulvaeus
Music & Lyrics

Benny Andersson
Music & Lyrics

Mamma Mia!

Phyllida Lloyd
Director

Anthony Van Laast
Choreographer

Howard Harrison
Lighting Designer

Andrew Bruce
Sound Designer

Bobby Aitken
Sound Designer

Martin Koch
Musical Supervisor; Additional Material; Arrangements Musical Supervisor

Nichola Treherne
Associate Choreographer

Martha Banta
Resident Director

Tara Rubin Casting
Casting

David Grindrod
Casting Consultant

Arthur Siccardi Theatrical Services, Inc.
Production Manager

Judy Craymer
Producer

Richard East
Producer

Timothy Booth
Father Alexandrios, Ensemble

Jen Burleigh-Bentz
Ensemble

John Dossett
Sam Carmichael

Jon-Erik Goldberg
Ensemble

Leah Hocking
Donna Sheridan

Erica Mansfield
Ensemble, Swing

Megan Osterhaus
Ensemble

Michael James Scott
Eddie

Timothy Booth
Ensemble

Pearce Bunting
Bill Austin

Jen Burleigh-Bentz
Tanya, Ensemble

Allyson Carr
Ensemble

Gina Ferrall
Rosie

Jon-Erik Goldberg
Ensemble, Swing

Joelle Graham
Ensemble

Frankie James Grande
Ensemble

Lori Hammel
Ensemble

Monica Kapoor
Ensemble

Michael Mastro
Harry Bright

Mamma Mia!

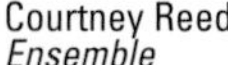

Courtney Reed
Ensemble

Amina Robinson
Ensemble

Laurie Wells
Ensemble

2006-2007 AWARD

"Mr. Broadway" Award
Frankie James Grande

Photo by Ben Strothmann

CAST & MANAGEMENT

Front Row: Samantha Eggers (Lisa), Courtney Reed (Ensemble), Corinne Melançon (Ensemble), Gina Ferrall (Rosie), Pearce Bunting (Bill Austin), Collette Simmons (Swing), Carolee Carmello (Donna Sheridan), Carey Anderson (Sophie Sheridan).

Middle Row: Raymond J. Lee (Eddie), Steve Morgan (Ensemble), Joi Danielle Price (Ensemble), Jen Burleigh-Bentz (Tanya), Leah Zepel (Ensemble), Ryan Sander (Swing), Matthew Farver (Swing), Monica Kapoor (Ensemble), Lanene Charters (Swing), Ben Gettinger (Pepper), Allyson Carr (Ensemble), Sandy Rosenberg (Ensemble), Meghann Dreyfuss (Ensemble).

Back Row: Erica Mansfield (Ensemble), Sherry Cohen (Stage Manager), Andy Kelso (Sky), Dean R. Greer (Stage Manager), Bryan Scott Johnson (Father Alexandrios/Ensemble), Rina Saltzman (Company Manager), Gerard Salvador (Ensemble), Isaac Calpito (Ensemble), Michael Mastro (Harry Bright), David McDonald (Sam Carmichael), Andy Fenton (Production Stage Manager).

Mamma Mia!

Photos by Ben Strothmann

CREW
Front Row (L-R): Reginald Carter (House Crew), Christine Richmond (Dresser), Douglas Couture, I Wang (Dresser), Irene L. Bunis (Wardrobe Supervisor), Carey Bertini (Dresser), Elvia Pineda (Dresser), Josh Marquette (Associate Hair Designer/Hair Supervisor), Vickey Walker (Assistant Hair Supervisor).

Back Row (L-R): Eric Anthony Pregent (Dresser), Art Soyk, Glenn Russo (House Crew), Meredith Kievit (House Crew), Mai-Linh Lofgren DeVirgilio (House Crew), Andy Sather (Assistant Electrician), Stephen Burns (Assistant Carpenter), and Don Lawrence (Head Electrician).

FRONT OF HOUSE
Front Row (L-R): Laurie Dank, Dennis Marion, Ken Costigan, John Mitchell, Nicole McIntyre, Sherry McIntyre.

Back Row (L-R): Michael Bosch, Malcolm Perry, Sabiel Almonte , Manuel Levine (House Manager), Kevin Kelly and Tucker Gray.

BAND
David Nyberg (Percussion), Wendy Bobbitt Cavett (Music Director/Conductor/Keyboard 1) and Paul Adamy (Bass).

LITTLESTAR SERVICES LIMITED

Directors .... Judy Craymer, Richard East, Benny Andersson, Björn Ulvaeus
International Executive Producer .... Andrew Treagus
Business & Finance Director .... Ashley Grisdale
Administrator .... Peter Austin
PA to Judy Craymer .... Mel Bartram
Marketing & Communications Manager .... Claire Teare
Marketing & Communications Coordinator .Liz McGinity
Head of Accounts .... Jo Reedman
Accountant .... Sheila Egbujie
Accountant .... Kerri Jordan
Accounts Assistant .... Eleanor Booth
Administrative Assistant .... Matthew Willis
Receptionist .... Amy Smith
Legal Services .... Barry Shaw
Howard Jones at Sheridans
Production Insurance Services .... Walton & Parkinson Ltd.
Business Manager for
Benny Andersson and
Björn Ulvaeus & Scandinavian Press ...... Görel Hanser

Mamma Mia!

NINA LANNAN ASSOCIATES

GENERAL MANAGERS .... DEVIN M. KEUDELL, AMY JACOBS
ASSOCIATE GENERAL MANAGER/ COMPANY MANAGER .... RINA L. SALTZMAN
Assistant Company Manager .... Liza Garcia
Management Associate .... Katherine McNamee

ANDREW TREAGUS ASSOCIATES LIMITED

General Manager .... Julian Stoneman
Production Coordinator .... Daniel Sparrow
PA to Andrew Treagus .... Jacki Harding
PA to Julian Stoneman .... Stella Warshaw
Production Assistant .... Maria Persson

PRODUCTION TEAM

ASSOCIATE CHOREOGRAPHER .... NICHOLA TREHERNE
DANCE SUPERVISOR .... JANET ROTHERMEL
RESIDENT DIRECTOR .... MARTHA BANTA
ASSOCIATE MUSIC SUPERVISOR ...... DAVID HOLCENBERG
ASSOCIATE SCENIC DESIGNER (US) .... NANCY THUN
ASSOCIATE SCENIC DESIGNER (UK) ..... JONATHAN ALLEN
ASSOCIATE COSTUME DESIGNERS .... LUCY GAIGER, SCOTT TRAUGOTT
ASSOCIATE HAIR DESIGNER .. JOSH MARQUETTE
ASSOCIATE LIGHTING DESIGNERS .... DAVID HOLMES, ED MCCARTHY, ANDREW VOLLER
ASSOCIATE SOUND DESIGNERS .. BRIAN BEASLEY, DAVID PATRIDGE
MUSICAL TRANSCRIPTION ...... ANDERS NEGLIN
CASTING CONSULTANT .... DAVID GRINDROD

CASTING

TARA RUBIN CASTING (U.S.)

PRESS REPRESENTATIVE

BONEAU/BRYAN-BROWN
Adrian Bryan-Brown Joe Perrotta
Erin Hinton

MARKETING U.S.

TMG – THE MARKETING GROUP
TANYA GRUBICH LAURA MATALON
Anne Rippey Bob Bucci

MUSIC PUBLISHED BY EMI GROVE PARK MUSIC, INC. AND EMI WATERFORD MUSIC, INC.

STAFF FOR *MAMMA MIA!*

PRODUCTION STAGE MANAGER .... ANDREW FENTON
Stage Managers .... Sherry Cohen, Charlene Speyerer
Assistant Dance Captain .... Meredith Akins

PRODUCTION MANAGER ...... ARTHUR SICCARDI

Head Carpenter .... Chris Nass
Assistant Carpenters .... McBrien Dunbar, Clark Middleton
Production Electrician .... Rick Baxter
Head Electrician .... Don Lawrence
Assistant Electrician .... Andy Sather
Vari*Lite Programmer .... Andrew Voller
Production Sound .... David Patridge
Head Sound .... Craig Cassidy
Assistant Sound .... George Huckins
Production Properties .... Simon E.R. Evans
Head Properties .... Gregory Martin
Wardrobe Supervisor .... Irene L. Bunis
Assistant Wardrobe .... Ron Glow
Dressers .... Carey Bertini, Jessica Boyd, Jim Collum, Lauren Kievit, Elvia Pineda, Eric Pregent, Christine Richmond, I Wang
Hair Supervisor .... Josh Marquette
Assistant Hair Supervisor .... Vickey Walker
Assistant Lighting Designer .... Jeffrey Lowney
Assistant Costume Designer .... Angela Kahler
House Crew .... Richard Carney, Reginald Carter, Gregory Chabay, Gary DeVirgilio, Meredith Kievit, Aarne Lofgren, Francis Lofgren, John Maloney, Glenn Russo, Dennis Wiener
Box Office .... Mary Cleary, Lee Cobb, Steve Cobb, James Drury, Sue Giebler, Bob McCaffrey, Ron Schroeder
Casting Directors .... Tara Rubin CSA, Eric Woodall
Casting Associates .... Dunja Vitolic, Laura Schutzel
Casting Assistants .... Mona Slomsky, Rebecca Carfagna
Canadian Casting .... Stephanie Gorin Casting, C.D.C.
Associate to Casting Consultant .... Stephen Crockett
London Casting Assistant .... James Orange
Legal Counsel (U.S.) .... Lazarus & Harris LLP/ Scott Lazarus, Esq., Robert Harris, Esq.
Immigration Counsel .... Mark Koestier
Accounting .... Rosenberg, Neuwirth and Kuchner/ Chris Cacace, In Woo
Advertising .... Serino Coyne, Inc./ Nancy Coyne, Greg Corradetti, Ryan Greer, Caroline Lenher, Ruth Rosenberg
Press Office Staff .... Chris Boneau, Jim Byk, Brandi Cornwell, Jackie Green, Juliana Hannett, Hector Hernandez, Jessica Johnson, Kevin Jones, Eric Louie, Aaron Meier, Linnae Petruzzelli, Matthew Polk, Matt Ross, Heath Schwartz, Susanne Tighe
Production Photographer .... Joan Marcus
Merchandising .... Max Merchandise, LLC/ Randi Grossman, Victor Romero
Theater Displays .... King Display
Insurance .... Dewitt, Stern/ Walton & Parkinson Ltd.
Banking .... JP Morgan Trust
Travel Agent .... Tzell Travel
Original Logo Design .... © Littlestar Services Limited

CREDITS AND ACKNOWLEDGMENTS

Scenery constructed and painted by Hudson Scenic Studio, Inc. and Hamilton Scenic Specialty. Computer motion control and automation by Feller Precision, Inc. SHOWTRAK computer motion control for scenery and rigging. Sound equipment supplied by Masque Sound. Lighting equipment supplied by Fourth Phase and Vari*Lite, Inc. Soft goods by I. Weiss and Sons. Costumes by Barbara Matera, Ltd., Tricorne New York City and Carelli Costumes, Inc. Additional costume work by Allan Alberts Productions. Millinery by Lynne Mackey. Wet suits by Aquatic Fabricators of South Florida. Custom men's shirts by Cego. Custom knitting by C.C. Wei. Custom fabric printing and dyeing by Dye-namix and Gene Mignola. Shoes by Native Leather, Rilleau Leather and T. O. Dey. Gloves by Cornelia James - London. Hair color by Redken. Properties by Paragon Theme and Prop Fabrication. Cough drops provided by Ricola U.S.A. Physical therapy provided by Sean Gallagher.

Mamma Mia! was originally produced in London by LITTLESTAR SERVICES LIMITED on April 6, 1999.

Experience ***Mamma Mia!*** in these cities:
London/Prince of Wales Theatre/mamma-mia.com
Broadway/Winter Garden Theatre/telecharge.com
Las Vegas/Mandalay Bay Theatre/mandalaybay.com
North American Tour/ticketmaster.com
International Tour/mamma-mia.com

For more information on the above and our other productions in Hamburg, Stuttgart, Madrid, Osaka, Stockholm and Moscow, visit and book at: www.mamma-mia.com

Mamma Mia! How Can I Resist You? The Inside Story of Mamma Mia! and the songs of ABBA available October 17, 2006. Pre-order now at www.amazon.com.

For more information and tour schedules visit: www.mamma-mia.com

House Manager .... Manuel Levine

Mamma Mia!

Scrapbook

Correspondent: Carey Anderson, "Sophie"
Memorable First-Night Letter: I got a card attached to some gorgeous flowers from Benny and Bjorn of ABBA and the producer, Judy Craymer, saying, "Thanks for being our Rock Chic Supremo." It was really cool to receive a gift from them on my Broadway debut!
First-Night Gifts: My parents gave me a framed picture of myself in front of the Winter Garden from my first trip to New York in 1996 after I graduated from high school and wrote on the back, "This is always where you knew you should be." It was so special, and still up in my dressing room.
Most Exciting Celebrity Visitors: We heard that Faith Hill and Tim McGraw were in the audience in disguise, but they slipped out right after the show was over.
"Gypsy of the Year" Sketch: Sandy Rosen-berg, Britt Shubow and Leah Zepel put on "Calling in Sick," a parody of "The Telephone Hour" from *Bye Bye Birdie*, with Sally Williams, Jimmy Smagula, Jessica Radetsky, Carly Blake Sebouhian, Harriet Clark, Kara Klein, Dianna Warren, Gianna Loungway, Tregoney Shepherd, Justin Peck, Gregory Emanuel Rahming, Shaun Colledge and George Lee Andrews.
"Carols for a Cure" Carol: "O Come, O Come Emmanuel."
"Easter Bonnet" Sketch: "Optimism" by Matthew Farver, music by Sean Altman and Billy Straus.
Special Backstage Rituals:
1. Judy McLane goes around to every dressing room before each show and has a little bag of "angel cards" in which each actor pulls out a card, and it sort of makes you think about that particular word, i.e. forgiveness, happiness, sisterhood/brotherhood, etc.
2. There is also a group of us who have to be onstage at the top of the show and there is a certain place in the overture where we do a group clap. It gets us pumped to start the show!

Favorite Moment During Each Performance: It would have to be the beginning and end of each show. With the role of "Sophie" I get to open and close the show with the same song. It's a different journey every show in between those two moments but those moments stay the same. It is a really special thing that I get to do.
Favorite In-Theatre Gathering Place: It's probably the greenroom. We do birthday celebrations in there before shows and "Happy Trails" when someone is leaving the show. There are two comfy couches and a microwave, refrigerator and decent sized table to eat on.
Favorite Off-Site Hangout: This would definitely have to be The Harmony View on 50th Street and Broadway, right next to Duane Reade. Some group from our cast is almost always there on a Sunday night after the show.
Favorite Snack Food: I know they are not supposed to be snacks, but I love my Grether's Pastilles! I'm addicted to them.
Favorite Therapy: *Mamma Mia!* is set on a pretty severely raked stage. So, needless to say, we have lots of sore knees and quads and calves. The best thing to help relieve those muscles is a roller.
Memorable Ad-Lib: When Jen Burleigh-Bentz was on for one of her first performances in the role of Donna and during the wedding scene, instead of saying "Don't go getting all self-righteous..." she said "Don't go getting all self-disrespecting on me..."
Record Number of Cell Phones, Cameras, etc.: Without fail, there are always at least two cameras or video cameras being used at our show. I don't even want to think about cell phone pics being taken.
Memorable Press Encounter: I sang the national anthem at the 2006 Image Awards and it was so much fun. My husband went with me and we got to dress up in black tie and walk the red carpet. We sat at the head table with all of the star guests and got treated like VIPs with a huge gift bag and everything. It was awesome!
Memorable Stage Door Fan Encounter: There was this particular young girl one evening who was so excited to meet Sophie that she started screaming. It got to the point where I could literally see her tonsils coming out of her mouth! She was the sweetest thing and made me feel like I had really made her evening something so special and inspired her.

Photos by Aubrey Reuben

1. Cast members Andy Kelso and Carey Anderson at the fifth anniversary party at Bar American.
2. ABBA's Björn Ulvaeus toasts the cast.
3. Leading lady Carolee Carmello, with cast member David Beach, flashes her pass to get into the party.
4. The 2006 "Gypsy of the Year" sketch.

Latest Audience Arrival: We have an odd schedule that we perform both a 2 PM and a 7 PM show on Sundays. Inevitably, someone always assumes that the show starts at 8 PM not 7 PM and comes in very late. We had someone come once right at the end of Act I!!!
Fastest Costume Change: That would have to go to the role of Donna. She changes dresses in the wedding in less than thirty seconds.
Who Wore the Heaviest Costumes: I'd have to say all of the Dynamos and the Dads, who wear the Spandex jumpsuits.
Who Wore the Least: That has to go to Andy Kelso who plays "Sky," who at one point is only wearing a Speedo.
Catchphrase Only the Company Would Recognize: Calling the show "The Mia."
Memorable Directorial Note: "Keep the stakes high!"
Understudy Anecdote: Samantha Eggers who understudies "Sophie" was on in the role and realized that the journal was not preset so she had to tell her friends Ali and Lisa she had memorized her mother's journal and this is what it said.
Coolest Thing About Being in This Show: Getting able to feel like a real Rock Star during certain songs like "Name of the Game" and especially in the concert at the end of the show. It's such a high!

Martin Short: Fame Becomes Me

First Preview: July 29, 2006. Opened: August 17, 2006.
Closed: January 7, 2007 after 22 Previews and 165 Performances.

PLAYBILL®

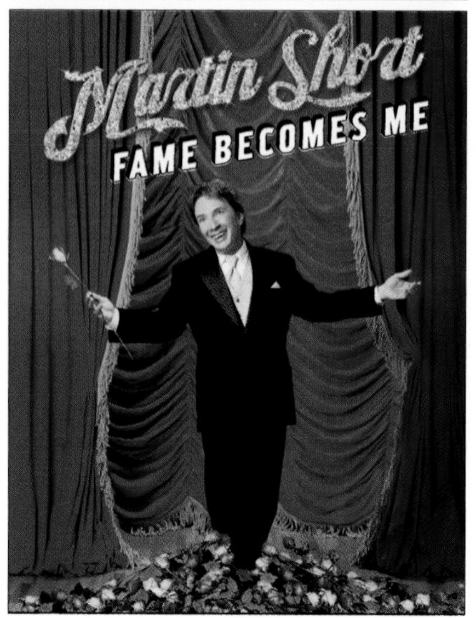

CAST
MARTIN SHORT

THE COMEDY ALL STARS
(in order of appearance)
BROOKS ASHMANSKAS
MARY BIRDSONG
NICOLE PARKER
MARC SHAIMAN
CAPATHIA JENKINS

UNDERSTUDIES
JILL ABRAMOVITZ
CHARLIE ALTERMAN
AISHA DEHAAS
EDWARD STAUDENMAYER

BERNARD B. JACOBS THEATRE
242 West 45th Street
A Shubert Organization Theatre
Gerald Schoenfeld, *Chairman* Philip J. Smith, *President*
Robert E. Wankel, *Executive Vice President*

BASE ENTERTAINMENT
HARBOR ENTERTAINMENT ROY FURMAN JEFFREY A. SINE
in association with LISA LAPAN and TERRY E. SCHNUCK
Present

Book by
MARTIN SHORT
DANIEL GOLDFARB

Music and Arrangements by
MARC SHAIMAN

Lyrics by
SCOTT WITTMAN
MARC SHAIMAN

Conceived by
MARTIN SHORT and SCOTT WITTMAN

Additional Material by ALAN ZWEIBEL

Featuring
BROOKS ASHMANSKAS MARY BIRDSONG CAPATHIA JENKINS NICOLE PARKER MARC SHAIMAN

Scenic Design by
SCOTT PASK

Costume Design by
JESS GOLDSTEIN

Lighting Design by
CHRIS LEE

Sound Design by
PETER HYLENSKI

Orchestrations by
LARRY BLANK

Musical Direction by
CHARLIE ALTERMAN

Music Co-ordinator
JOHN MILLER

Casting by
TELSEY + COMPANY

Wig Design by
CHARLES LAPOINTE

Production Stage Manager
BESS MARIE GLORIOSO

Production Management by
JUNIPER STREET PRODUCTIONS

Press Representative
BARLOW • HARTMAN

Marketing Services
TMG - THE MARKETING GROUP

Executive Producer
JOANNA HAGAN
BERNIE BRILLSTEIN

General Management
ALAN WASSER • ALLAN WILLIAMS

Associate Producer
BROWN-PINTO PRODUCTIONS

Choreographed by
CHRISTOPHER GATTELLI

Directed by
SCOTT WITTMAN

LIVE BROADWAY

8/17/06

Capathia Jenkins and Marc Shaiman sing "Heaven, Heaven."

Mary Birdsong and Martin Short perform "Sittin' on the Fence."

Photos by Paul Kolnik

Martin Short: Fame Becomes Me

MUSICAL NUMBERS

"Another Curtain Goes Up"	NICOLE, BROOKS, MARY, CAPATHIA & MARC
"All I Ask"	MARTIN
"Three Gorgeous Kids"	MARTIN
"Babies"	NICOLE, MARTIN, BROOKS, MARY
"The Farmer's Daughter"	MARY
"Sittin' on the Fence"	MARTIN & MARY
"Don't Wanna Be Me"	MARTIN
"Ba-Ba-Ba-Bu-Duh Broadway!"	MARY, NICOLE & BROOKS
"Hello Boy!"	MARTIN
"Step Brother de Jesus"	MARTIN, MARY, NICOLE & BROOKS
"Married to Marty"	NICOLE
"The Triangle Song"	MARTIN
"Sniff, Sniff"	MARTIN, MARY, NICOLE & BROOKS
"Twelve Step Pappy"	MARTIN
"Would Ya Like to Star in Our Show?"	BROOKS, NICOLE, MARY
"I Came Just As Soon As I Heard"	MARTIN
"The Lights Have Dimmed on Broadway"	NICOLE & MARY
"Michael's Song"	BROOKS
"Heaven, Heaven"	MARY, NICOLE, BROOKS & MARC
"Stop the Show"	CAPATHIA, MARY, NICOLE, BROOKS & MARTIN
"All I Ask" (Reprise)	MARTIN
"Another Curtain Comes Down"	NICOLE, MARY, BROOKS, CAPATHIA, MARC & MARTIN
"Glass Half Full"	MARTIN

Martin Short as Jiminy Glick.

Photo by Paul Kolnik

ORCHESTRA

Conductor:
CHARLIE ALTERMAN
Associate Conductor:
CRAIG BALDWIN

Trumpet/Piccolo Trumpet/Flugelhorn:
DAVE TRIGG
Tenor Sax/Alto Sax/Clarinet/Flute:
EDDIE SALKIN
Trombone/Bass Trombone:
MIKE CHRISTIANSON
Piano:
MARC SHAIMAN
Keyboards:
CHARLIE ALTERMAN, CRAIG BALDWIN
Drums:
RICH MERCURIO
Bass/Electric Bass:
DICK SARPOLA
Percussion:
ED SHEA

Music Coordinator: JOHN MILLER

Martin Short
Concept, Book and Himself

Marc Shaiman
Music & Lyrics and Comedy All-Star

Brooks Ashmanskas
Comedy All-Star

Mary Birdsong
Comedy All-Star

Capathia Jenkins
Comedy All-Star

Nicole Parker
Comedy All-Star

Jill Abramovitz
Understudy

Charlie Alterman
Musical Director, Standby for Mr. Shaiman

Aisha deHaas
Understudy

Edward Staudenmayer
Understudy

Martin Short: Fame Becomes Me

Scott Wittman
Concept, Director, Lyrics

Alan Zweibel
Additional Material

Scott Pask
Scenic Design

Jess Goldstein
Costume Designer

Peter Hylenski
Sound Design

2006-2007 AWARD

THEATRE WORLD AWARD
Outstanding Broadway Debut
(Mary Birdsong)

Larry Blank
Orchestrations

John Miller
Music Coordinator

Guy Kwan, John Paull III, Hillary Blanken, Kevin Broomell, Ana Rose Greene, Juniper Street Productions
Production Manager

Bernard Telsey
Telsey + Company
Casting

Alan Wasser
Associates
General Manager

Roy Furman
Producer

David Broser and Aaron Harnick, Harbor Entertainment
Producer

Terry E. Schnuck
Associate Producer

Donna Vivino
Comedy All-Star

Photo by Ben Strothmann

FRONT OF HOUSE STAFF
Seated (L-R): Rosa Pesante, Al Peay, Al Nazario, Eva Frances.

Standing (L-R): Carrie Hart, Gwen Coley, Michaela Martos, William Mitchell, Roxanne Gayol, Patanne McEvoy, Sean Cutter, Elsie Grosvenor.

Not Pictured: John Minore, Martha Rodriguez, and Greg Marlow.

Martin Short: Fame Becomes Me

Photo by Ben Strothmann

STAGE & COMPANY MANAGEMENT
Front Row (L-R): Jerry Klein (Stage Doorman), Robert Valli (Production Property), Fred Ricci (House Property), Ana M. García (Stage Manager), Melanie Morgan (Production Assistant), Bess Marie Glorioso (Production Stage Manager), Growler (Wardrobe Supervisor).

Second Row (L-R): Stephen Long (Assistant Electrician), Bonnie Runk (Assistant Sound), Brian Dawson (Head Electrician), Mike Van Praagh (House Carpenter), Daniel E. Carpio (Assistant House Property), Derek Moreno (Dresser for Mr. Short), Jill Johnson (Assistant Property), Susan Corrado (Hair & Make-Up Supervisor), Lisa Acevedo (Hair & Make-Up Assistant), Tucker Howard (Head Sound).

Third Row (L-R): Eddie Ruggiero (House Flyman), John Paull (Head Carpenter/ZFX Operator), Amanda Scott (Dresser), Brent Peterson (Stage Manager).

Back Row (L-R): Chris Latsch (Assistant Carpenter/ZFX Operator), Maura Clifford (Dresser), Joe Hickey (Dresser), and Andrea Gonzalez (Dresser).

Photo by Ben Strothmann

BOX OFFICE
(L-R): Michael Kohlbrenner and José Hernandez

Photo by Melissa Merlo

DOORMAN
Terence O'Connor

Martin Short: Fame Becomes Me

STAFF FOR *MARTIN SHORT: FAME BECOMES ME*

GENERAL MANAGEMENT
ALAN WASSER ASSOCIATES
Alan Wasser Allan Williams
Lane Marsh

GENERAL PRESS REPRESENTATIVE
BARLOW•HARTMAN
Michael Hartman John Barlow
Dennis Crowley Ryan Ratelle

CASTING BY
TELSEY + COMPANY, C.S.A.
Bernie Telsey, Will Cantler, David Vaccari, Bethany Knox, Craig Burns, Tiffany Little Canfield, Stephanie Yankwitt, Joe Langworth, Carrie Rosson, Justin Huff

COMPANY MANAGER
Penelope Daulton

PRODUCTION MANAGEMENT
JUNIPER STREET PRODUCTIONS
Hillary Blanken Guy Kwan

Production Stage Manager ....Bess Marie Glorioso
Stage Manager ....Ana M. Garcia
Assistant Stage Manager ....Brent Peterson
General Management Associates ....Connie Yung, Thom Mitchell, Robert Nolan, Aaron Lustbader, Jake Hirzel
Associate Director ....Paul Dobie
Assistant Choreographer ....Bethany Pettigrew
Associate Scenic Designer ....Orit Jacoby Carroll
Assistant Scenic Designer ....Lauren Alvarez
Associate Costume Designer ....China Lee
Makeup Designer ....Angelina Avallone
Prosthetics ....Kevin Haney
Assistant Lighting Designer ....Joel Shier
Associate Lighting Designer ....Jason Jeunnette
Associate Sound Designer ....TJ McEvoy
Production Carpenter/ ZFX Operator ....David "Pfish" Terry
Assistant Carpenter/ ZFX Operator ....Chris Latsch
Advance Carpenter ....Ken St. Peter
Production Electrician ....Dan D. Coey
Head Electrician ....Brian Dawson
Assistant Electrician ....Stephen Long
Automated Light Programmer ....Rich Tyndall
Production Property ....Robert N. Valli
Assistant Property ....Jill Johnson
Production Sound ....TJ McEvoy
Head Sound ....Tucker Howard
Assistant Sound ....Bonnie Runk
Wardrobe Supervisor ....Michael Growler
Dresser For Mr. Short ....Derek Moreno
Hair & Makeup Supervisor ....Susan Corrado
Assistant Hair & Makeup Supervisor ....Janelle Leone
Additional Orchestrations ....Peter Myers
Music Coordinator ....John Miller
Music Preparation ....Paul Holderbaum/ Chelsea Music Service
Electronic Music System Design and Programming ....Jim Harp/ Music Arts Technologies Inc.
Assistant to John Miller ....Charles Butler
Production Management Associates ....Ana Rose Greene, Kevin Broomell, Elena Soderblom
Press Associates ....Leslie Baden, Carol Fineman, Bethany Larsen, Gerilyn Shur, Andrew Snyder, Wayne Wolfe
Production Assistants ....Julia D'Angelo, Leslie Grisdale, Maya Klauser, Melanie T. Morgan, Hilary Schweitzer, Joel Shier, Connor "Mac" Smith, Lindsay Zweibel
Asst. to Messrs. Shaiman and Wittman ....Richard Read
Music Associate ....Lucian Piane
Legal ....Franklin Weinrib Rudell & Vassallo/ Elliot Brown, Jonathan Lonner
Accounting ....Rosenberg, Neuwirth & Kuchner/ Chris Cacace
Insurance ....DeWitt Stern Group, Inc./ Peter Shoemaker
Banking ....JPMorgan Chase/Michele Gibbons
Payroll ....Castellana Services, Inc./ Lance Castellana
Travel ....Navigant, Inc./Janice Kessler
Housing ....Road Rebel Entertainment/ Lindsay Olson
Marketing ....TMG - The Marketing Group/ Tanya Grubich, Laura Matalon, Bob Bucci, Amber Glassberg, Liz Miller, Anne Rippey
Advertising ....SpotCo/Drew Hodges, Jim Edwards, Tom Greenwald, Tom McCann, Laura Price
Production Photographer ....Paul Kolnik
Theatre Displays ....King Displays
Website Design ....Situation Marketing/ Damian Bazadona, Ian Bennett, Lisa Cecchini, Tom Lorenzo
Group Sales TDI/800.BROADWAY
Opening Night Coordination ....Tobak Lawrence Company/ Michael Lawrence, Suzanne Tobak

FOR BASE ENTERTAINMENT
Brian Becker, Faith Clairy, Jennie Connery, Elin Eggertsdottir, Joanna Hagan, Howard Karp, Denise Perry, Lauren Reid, Scott Zeiger

CREDITS
Scenery and scenic effects built and electrified by PRG Scenic Technologies, New Windsor, NY; Showman Fabricators, Inc., Long Island City, NY; and Cigar Box Studios, Inc., Newburgh, NY. Scenery painted by Scenic Art Studios, Cornwall, NY. Show control and scenic motion control featuring Stage Command Systems® by PRG Scenic Technologies, New Windsor, NY. Flying effects provided by ZFX, Inc. Softgoods built by I. Weiss and Sons, Inc., Long Island City, NY. Lighting equipment provided by PRG Lighting, North Bergen, NJ. Sound equipment provided by PRG Audio, Mt. Vernon, NY. Furniture and props executed by John Creech Design and Production, Brooklyn, NY. Additional set and hand props courtesy of the Spoon Group, Rahway, NJ. Costumes executed by Martin Izquierdo Studio and Studio Rouge. Custom wigs executed by Watson Associates. Interstate hauling by Clark Transfer, Inc. Throat lozenges provided by Ricola. Thank you to Alacer Corp. for Emer'gen-C. Thank you to Yogi Tea. Thank you to See's Candies. Thank you Krispy Kreme Doughnuts.

Souvenir Merchandise designed and created by
Araca Merch, LLC
www.aracamerch.com

SPECIAL THANKS
Dick Blasucci, Andy Breckman, David Feldman, Paul Flaherty, Warren Leight, Matt Roberts, Michael Short, Jennifer DeLange, Hailey Ferber, Elyce Henken

www.martinshortthemusical.com

THE SHUBERT ORGANIZATION, INC.
Board of Directors

Gerald Schoenfeld Chairman	**Philip J. Smith** President
Wyche Fowler, Jr.	**John W. Kluge**
Lee J. Seidler	**Michael I. Sovern**

Stuart Subotnick

Robert E. Wankel
Executive Vice President

Peter Entin Vice President Theatre Operations	**Elliot Greene** Vice President Finance
David Andrews Vice President Shubert Ticketing Services	**John Darby** Vice President Facilities

D.S. Moynihan
Vice President – Creative Projects

House Manager ....William Mitchell

Photo by Paul Kolnik

(L-R): Nicole Parker, Martin Short and Mary Birdsong pay tribute to Bob Fosse.

Martin Short: Fame Becomes Me

Scrapbook

1. (L-R): Martin Short, Nicole Parker, Mary Birdsong, Capathia Jenkins at the opening night party at Tavern on the Green.
2. Brooks Ashmanskas at the opening night party.
3. Capathia Jenkins.
4. Marc Shaiman and friend at the opening.
5. Martin Short eats "The Martin Short Stack," a dish named for him, at the Stage Deli.

Photos by Aubrey Reuben

Correspondent: Mary Birdsong, "Comedy All-Star"

Memorable Opening Night Note: A note from an 87-year-old Austrian actress I know who is a Holocaust survivor, which said "Toi toi toi, the best is yet to come!"

Also, it wasn't on opening night, but a friend who had just been asked for a divorce by her husband sent me flowers with a note that said "Fame becomes you. Divorce becomes me."

Opening Night Gift: All of my family and friends and my boyfriend being there to share the night was really the best gift.

Most Exciting Celebrity Visitor: Roseanne Barr, because she had no problem saying who were the biggest bitches she'd ever worked with.

"Gypsy of the Year" Sketch: "And Now a Word from Marc" by Marc Shaiman. Martin Short was one of the hosts.

Actor Who Performed the Most Roles in This Show: Probably Nicole Parker.

Who Has Done the Most Shows in Their Career: I would assume Martin Short.

Special Backstage Ritual: Wonderfully off-color, un-p.c. jabs at each other right before curtain at stage left.

Favorite Moment During Each Performance: Marc Shaiman's shameless and balletic display of his buttocks.

Favorite In-Theatre Gathering Place: Stage left, right next to the stage manager's station.

Favorite Snack Food: Chocolate mint Zone protein bars.

Favorite Therapy. Qui gong/tui na massage.

Memorable Stage Door Fan Encounter: A drunk homeless guy in San Francisco, when we were on tour and playing the Curran Theatre before our Broadway opening. This guy wandered through the stage door and ran into Marty and hugged him and picked him up in the air before Marty could even realize he didn't know the guy.

Fastest Costume Change: Brooks Ashmanskas, getting into his Tommy Tune costume, complete with stilts.

Who Wore the Heaviest/Hottest Costume: Marty Short as Jiminy Glick (a fat suit).

Who Wore the Least: Marc Shaiman (just an open hospital gown and a dance belt).

Catchphrases Only the Company Would Recognize: "There's an emptiness...."

Memorable Directorial Note: "Yeah yeah yeah no no no."

Nickname: Capathia Jenkins is sometimes referred to as "Scoopy Jenkins."

Superstitions That Turned Out to Be True: Marty's wonderful wife Nancy being present always threw the show off.

Coolest Thing About Being in This Show: Meeting so many celebrity guests, and just getting to play with our amazing cast night after night.

Mary Poppins

First Preview: October 14, 2006. Opened: November 16, 2006.
Still running as of May 31, 2007.

SHOWBILL

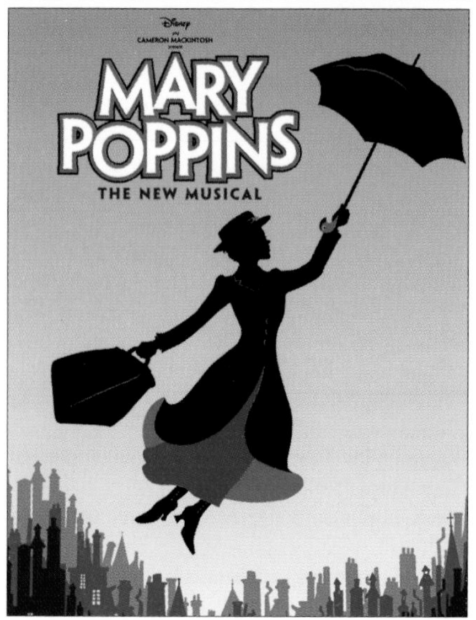

CAST OF CHARACTERS

(in order of appearance)

Bert .... GAVIN LEE
George Banks .... DANIEL JENKINS
Winifred Banks .... REBECCA LUKER
Jane Banks ... KATHERINE LEIGH DOHERTY or KATHRYN FAUGHNAN or DELANEY MORO
Michael Banks .... MATTHEW GUMLEY or HENRY HODGES or ALEXANDER SCHEITINGER
Katie Nanna .... MEGAN OSTERHAUS
Policeman .... JAMES HINDMAN
Miss Lark .... ANN ARVIA
Admiral Boom .... MICHAEL McCARTY
Mrs. Brill .... JANE CARR
Robertson Ay .... MARK PRICE
Mary Poppins .... ASHLEY BROWN
Park Keeper .... NICK CORLEY
Neleus .... BRIAN LETENDRE
Queen Victoria .... RUTH GOTTSCHALL
Bank Chairman .... MICHAEL McCARTY
Miss Smythe .... RUTH GOTTSCHALL
Von Hussler .... SEAN McCOURT
Northbrook .... MATT LOEHR
Bird Woman .... CASS MORGAN
Mrs. Corry .... JANELLE ANNE ROBINSON
Fannie .... VASTHY E. MOMPOINT
Annie .... MEGAN OSTERHAUS
Valentine .... TYLER MAYNARD
William .... ERIC B. ANTHONY
Mr. Punch .... JAMES HINDMAN

Continued on next page

NEW AMSTERDAM THEATRE

and

CAMERON MACKINTOSH

present

MARY POPPINS

A MUSICAL BASED ON THE STORIES OF P.L. TRAVERS AND THE WALT DISNEY FILM

with

ASHLEY BROWN GAVIN LEE
DANIEL JENKINS REBECCA LUKER
CASS MORGAN MARK PRICE RUTH GOTTSCHALL MICHAEL McCARTY
and
JANE CARR

KATHERINE LEIGH DOHERTY KATHRYN FAUGHNAN MATTHEW GUMLEY HENRY HODGES DELANEY MORO ALEXANDER SCHEITINGER
ANN ARVIA NICK CORLEY JAMES HINDMAN BRIAN LETENDRE MATT LOEHR SEAN McCOURT JANELLE ANNE ROBINSON

ERIC B. ANTHONY PAM BRADLEY KRISTIN CARBONE BRIAN COLLIER CASE DILLARD NICOLAS DROMARD
SUZANNE HYLENSKI STEPHANIE KURTZUBA MICHELLE LOOKADOO TONY MANSKER
TYLER MAYNARD VASTHY E. MOMPOINT JESSE NAGER KATHLEEN NANNI MEGAN OSTERHAUS
DOMINIC ROBERTS ROMMY SANDHU SHEKITRA STARKE CATHERINE WALKER KEVIN SAMUAL YEE

Original Music and Lyrics by
RICHARD M. SHERMAN and ROBERT B. SHERMAN

Book by
JULIAN FELLOWES

New Songs and Additional Music and Lyrics by
GEORGE STILES and ANTHONY DREWE

Co-created by
CAMERON MACKINTOSH

Produced for Disney Theatrical Productions by
THOMAS SCHUMACHER

Music Supervisor
DAVID CADDICK

Music Director
BRAD HAAK

Orchestrations by
WILLIAM DAVID BROHN

Broadway Sound Design
STEVE CANYON KENNEDY

Dance and Vocal Arrangements
GEORGE STILES

Associate Choreographer
GEOFFREY GARRATT

Associate Director
ANTHONY LYN

Associate Producer
JAMES THANE

Makeup Design
NAOMI DONNE

Casting
TARA RUBIN CASTING

Technical Director
DAVID BENKEN

Production Stage Manager
TOM CAPPS

Resident Choreographer
TOM KOSIS

Press Representative
BONEAU/BRYAN-BROWN

Co-choreographer
STEPHEN MEAR

Lighting Design
HOWARD HARRISON

Scenic and Costume Design
BOB CROWLEY

Co-direction and Choreography
MATTHEW BOURNE

Directed by
RICHARD EYRE

11/16/06

Photo by Joan Marcus

(L-R): Ashley Brown, Katherine Leigh Doherty, Alexander Scheitinger and Gavin Lee

Mary Poppins

MUSICAL NUMBERS

Mary Poppins takes place in and around the Banks' household somewhere in London at the turn of the last century.

ACT I

"Chim Chim Cher-ee" † .... Bert
"Cherry Tree Lane" (Part 1)* .... George and Winifred Banks, Jane and Michael, Mrs. Brill, and Robertson Ay
"The Perfect Nanny" .... Jane and Michael
"Cherry Tree Lane" (Part 2) .... George and Winifred Banks, Jane, and Michael, Mrs. Brill, and Robertson Ay
"Practically Perfect"* .... Mary Poppins, Jane, and Michael
"Jolly Holiday" † .... Bert, Mary Poppins, Jane, Michael, Neleus, and the Statues
"Cherry Tree Lane" (Reprise),
"Being Mrs. Banks,"*
"Jolly Holiday" (Reprise) .... George, Winifred, Jane, and Michael
"A Spoonful of Sugar" .... Mary Poppins, Jane, Michael, Robertson Ay, and Winifred
"Precision and Order"* .... Bank Chairman and the Bank Clerks
"A Man Has Dreams" † .... George Banks
"Feed the Birds" .... Bird Woman and Mary Poppins
"Supercalifragilisticexpialidocious" † .... Mary Poppins, Mrs. Corry, Bert, Jane, Michael, Fannie, Annie, and Customers
"Temper, Temper"* .... Valentine, William, Mr. Punch, the Glamorous Doll, and other Toys
"Chim Chim Cher-ee" (Reprise) .... Bert and Mary Poppins

ACT II

"Cherry Tree Lane" (Reprise) .... Mrs. Brill, Michael, Jane, Winifred, Robertson Ay, and George
"Brimstone and Treacle" (Part 1)* .... Miss Andrew
"Let's Go Fly a Kite" .... Bert, Park Keeper, Jane, and Michael
"Cherry Tree Lane" (Reprise),
"Being Mrs. Banks" (Reprise) .... George and Winifred
"Brimstone and Treacle" (Part 2) .... Mary Poppins and Miss Andrew
"Practically Perfect" (Reprise) .... Jane, Michael, and Mary Poppins
"Chim Chim Cher-ee" (Reprise) .... Bert
"Step in Time" † .... Bert, Mary Poppins, Jane, Michael, and the Sweeps
"A Man Has Dreams,"
"A Spoonful of Sugar" (Reprise) .... George and Bert
"Anything Can Happen"* .... Jane, Michael, Mary Poppins, and the Company
"A Spoonful of Sugar" (Reprise) .... Mary Poppins
"A Shooting Star" † .... Orchestra

* New Songs † Adapted Songs

ORCHESTRA

Conductor: BRAD HAAK
Associate Conductor/2nd Keyboard: KRISTEN BLODGETTE

Piano: MILTON GRANGER
Bass: PETER DONOVAN
Drums: DAVE RATAJCZAK
Percussion: DANIEL HASKINS
Guitar/Banjo/E-Bow: NATE BROWN
Horns: RUSSELL RIZNER, LAWRENCE DIBELLO
Trumpets: JOHN SHEPPARD, LOUIS HANZLIK
Trombone/Euphonium: MARC DONATELLE
Bass Trombone/Tuba: RANDY ANDOS
Clarinet: PAUL GARMENT
Oboe/English Horn: ALEXANDRA KNOLL
Flutes: BRIAN MILLER
Cello: STEPHANIE CUMMINS

Music Contractor: DAVID LAI

Cast Continued

Glamorous Doll .... CATHERINE WALKER
Miss Andrew .... RUTH GOTTSCHALL

ENSEMBLE

ERIC B. ANTHONY, ANN ARVIA, KRISTIN CARBONE, NICK CORLEY, CASE DILLARD, RUTH GOTTSCHALL, JAMES HINDMAN, BRIAN LETENDRE, MATT LOEHR, MICHELLE LOOKADOO, TONY MANSKER, TYLER MAYNARD, MICHAEL McCARTY, SEAN McCOURT, VASTHY E. MOMPOINT, JESSE NAGER, KATHLEEN NANNI, MEGAN OSTERHAUS, DOMINIC ROBERTS, JANELLE ANNE ROBINSON, SHEKITRA STARKE, CATHERINE WALKER, KEVIN SAMUAL YEE

SWINGS

PAM BRADLEY, BRIAN COLLIER, NICOLAS DROMARD, SUZANNE HYLENSKI, STEPHANIE KURTZUBA, ROMMY SANDHU

Statues, bank clerks, customers, toys, chimney sweeps, lamp lighters and inhabitants of Cherry Tree Lane played by members of the company.

UNDERSTUDIES

Mary Poppins:
KRISTIN CARBONE, CATHERINE WALKER
Bert:
ERIC B. ANTHONY, MATT LOEHR
George Banks:
JAMES HINDMAN, SEAN McCOURT
Mrs. Banks:
KRISTIN CARBONE, MEGAN OSTERHAUS
Mrs. Brill:
ANN ARVIA
Robertson Ay:
TYLER MAYNARD, DOMINIC ROBERTS
Mrs. Corry:
MEGAN OSTERHAUS
Von Hussler:
NICOLAS DROMARD
Northbrook:
NICOLAS DROMARD

DANCE CAPTAIN

ROMMY SANDHU

Mary Poppins

Ashley Brown
Mary Poppins

Gavin Lee
Bert

Daniel Jenkins
George Banks

Rebecca Luker
Winifred Banks

Jane Carr
Mrs. Brill

Cass Morgan
Bird Woman

Mark Price
Robertson Ay

Ruth Gottschall
Miss Andrew, Queen Victoria, Miss Smythe, Ensemble

Michael McCarty
Admiral Boom, Bank Chairman, Ensemble

Katherine Leigh Doherty
Jane Banks at certain performances

Kathryn Faughnan
Jane Banks at certain performances

Matthew Gumley
Michael Banks at certain performances

Henry Hodges
Michael Banks at certain performances

Delaney Moro
Jane Banks at certain performances

Alexander Scheitinger
Michael Banks at certain performances

Ann Arvia
Miss Lark, Ensemble

Nick Corley
Park Keeper, Ensemble

James Hindman
Policeman, Mr. Punch, Ensemble

Brian Letendre
Neleus, Ensemble

Matt Loehr
Northbrook, Ensemble

Sean McCourt
Von Hussler, Ensemble

Janelle Anne Robinson
Mrs. Corry, Ensemble

Eric B. Anthony
William, Ensemble

Pam Bradley
Swing

Kristin Carbone
Ensemble

Brian Collier
Swing

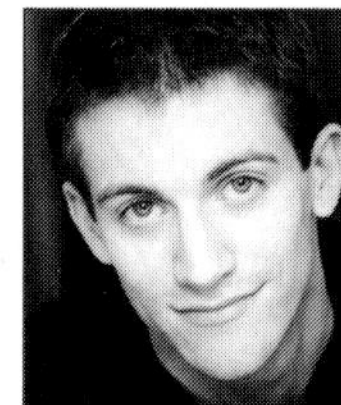
Case Dillard
Ensemble

Nicolas Dromard
Swing

Suzanne Hylenski
Swing

Stephanie Kurtzuba
Swing

Michelle Lookadoo
Ensemble

Tony Mansker
Ensemble

Tyler Maynard
Valentine, Ensemble

Vasthy E. Mompoint
Fannie, Ensemble

Jesse Nager
Ensemble

Mary Poppins

Kathleen Nanni
Ensemble

Megan Osterhaus
Katie Nanna, Annie, Ensemble

Dominic Roberts
Ensemble

Rommy Sandhu
Swing, Dance Captain

Shekitra Starke
Ensemble

Catherine Walker
Glamorous Doll, Ensemble

Kevin Samual Yee
Ensemble

P.L. Travers
Author of the Mary Poppins stories

Cameron Mackintosh
Producer & Co-Creator

Thomas Schumacher
Producer

Robert B. Sherman and Richard M. Sherman
Original Music & Lyrics

Julian Fellowes
Book

George Stiles
New Songs, Additional Music, Dance & Vocal Arrangements

Anthony Drewe
New Songs & Additional Lyrics

Richard Eyre
Director

Matthew Bourne
Co-Director & Choreographer

Bob Crowley
Scenic & Costume Design

Stephen Mear
Co-Choreographer

Howard Harrison
Lighting Designer

Steve Canyon Kennedy
Broadway Sound Designer

William David Brohn
Orchestrations

David Caddick
Music Supervisor

Brad Haak
Music Director

Naomi Donne
Makeup Designer

Angela Cobbin
Wig Creator

Geoffrey Garratt
Associate Choreographer

Anthony Lyn
Associate Director

Tom Kosis
Resident Choreographer

David Benken
Technical Director

Tara Rubin Casting
Casting

Nicole Bocchi
Jane Banks

Regan Kays
Swing

Mary Poppins

Jacob Levine
Michael Banks

Jeff Metzler
Swing

Devynn Pedell
Jane Banks

2006-2007 AWARDS

TONY AWARD
Best Set Design of a Musical
(Bob Crowley)

THEATRE WORLD AWARD
Outstanding Broadway Debut
(Gavin Lee)

DRAMA DESK AWARDS
Outstanding Featured Actor in a Musical
(Gavin Lee)
Outstanding Set Design of a Musical (Bob Crowley)

Photo by Ben Strothmann

STAGE CREW
Front Row (L-R): Joe Garvey (Electrics), Jodi Zanetti (Wardrobe), Drew Siccardi (Head Carpenter).
Second Row (L-R): Ed Ackerman (Carpenter), Gail Luna (Stage Manager), Alexis R.Prussack (Stage Manager), Jason Trubitt (Stage Manager), Valerie Lau Kee Lai (Stage Manager), Carla Dawson (Usher).
Third Row (L-R): Gary Matarazzo (Carpenter), Bill Romanello (Sound), Marie Renee Foucher (Sound), Brett Daley (Carpenter), Ray King (Carpenter), Debbie Vogel (Usher).
Fourth Row (L-R): Gary Wilner (Props), Karen Zabinski (Sound), Carlos Martinez (Electrics), Kevin Strohmeyer (Electrics), Al Manganaro (Electrics), Mike Corbett (Carpenter).
Fifth Row (L-R): Tim Abel (Props), Steve Stackle (Automation), Andy Catron (Electrics), Kurt Fischer (Sound), Dave Helck (Carpenter), Tony Goncalves (Carpenter), Jimmy Maloney (Head Electrician).
Sixth Row (L-R): Victor Amerling (Head Props), John Taccone (Props), John Saye (Props), Joe Bivone (Props), Kevin Barry (Electrics), and Angela Johnson (Make-up Supervisor).

STAFF FOR *MARY POPPINS*

COMPANY MANAGER .... DAVE EHLE
Production Associate .... Jeff Parvin
Assistant Company Manager .... Laura Eichholz
Show Accountant .... Barbara Toben
Production Stage Manager .... Tom Capps
Stage Manager .... Mark Dobrow
Assistant Stage Managers .... Valerie Lau-Kee Lai, Jason Trubitt
Dance Captain .... Rommy Sandhu
Production Assistants .... Sarah Bierenbaum, Will O'Hare, Alexis Prussack, Thomas Recktenwald, Verity Van Tassel

GENERAL PRESS REPRESENTATIVE
BONEAU/BRYAN-BROWN
Chris Boneau Jackie Green Aaron Meier
Matt Polk Matt Ross

Associate Scenic Designer .... Bryan Johnson
Scenic Design Associate .... Rosalind Coombes
US Scenic Assistants .... Dan Kuchar, Rachel Short Janocko, Frank McCullough
UK Scenic Assistants .... Al Turner, Charles Quiggin, Adam Wiltshire
Associate Costume Designer .... Christine Rowland
Associate Costume Designer .... Mitchell Bloom
Assistant Costume Designer .... Patrick Wiley
Assistant Costume Designer .... Rick Kelly
Associate Lighting Designer .... Daniel Walker
Assistant Lighting Designer .... Kristina Kloss
Lighting Programmer .... Robert Halliday
Associate Sound Designer .... John Shivers
Wig Creator .... Angela Cobbin
Illusions Designer .... Jim Steinmeyer
Technical Director .... David Benken
Scenic Production Supervisor .... Patrick Eviston
Assistant Technical Supervisor .... Rosemarie Palombo
Production Carpenter .... Drew Siccardi
Production Flyman .... Michael Corbett
Foy Flying Operator .... Raymond King
Automation .... Steve Stackle, David Helck
Carpenters .... Edward Ackerman, Frank Adler, Fudie Carriocia, Tony Goncalves, Raymond Ranellone, Brett Daley
Production Electrician .... James Maloney
Key Spot Operator .... Joseph P. Garvey
Lighting Console Operator .... Kevin Barry
Pyro Operator .... Kevin Strohmeyer
Automated Lighting Technician .... Andy Catron
Assistant Electricians .... Gregory Dunkin, Joseph Jay Lynch, Carlos Martinez, Al Manganaro
Production Propman .... Victor Amerling
Assistant Propman .... Tim Abel
Props .... Joe Bivone, John Saye

Mary Poppins

Production Sound Engineer .... Andrew Keister
Sound Engineer .... Kurt Fischer
Sound Engineer .... Marie Renee Foucher
Sound Assistant .... Bill Romanello
Production Wardrobe Supervisor .... Helen Toth
Assistant Wardrobe Supervisor .... Abbey Rayburn
Dressers ....Elizabeth Cline, Russell Easley, Ron Fleming, Maya Hardin, Ginny Hounsel, Jeff McGovney, Eileen Miller, Janet Netzke, Geoffrey Polischuk, Kelly Saxon, Jean Steinline, Mark Trezza, Pat White
Production Hair Supervisor .... Gary Martori
Hair Dept Assistants .... Chris Calabrese, Wanda Gregory, Kelly Reed
Production Makeup Supervisor .... Angela Johnson
UK Prop Coordinators .... Kathy Anders, Lisa Buckley
UK Wig Shop Assistant .... Beatrix Archer

Music Copyist ....Emily Grishman Music Preparation – Emily Grishman/ Katharine Edmonds
Keyboard Programming ....Stuart Andrews

DIALECT & VOCAL COACH ....DEBORAH HECHT

Associate General Manager .... Alan Wasser
Production Co-Counsel .... F. Richard Pappas
Casting .... Tara Rubin Casting, CSA/ Tara Rubin, Eric Woodall
Child Guardians ....Christina Huschle, Rick Plaugher
Children's Tutoring .... On Location Education
Press Associates ....Adrian Bryan-Brown, Susanne Tighe, Jim Byk, Brandi Cornwell, Linnae Petruzzelli, Joe Perrotta, Juliana Hannett, Jessica Johnson, Heath Schwartz, Hector Hernandez, Kevin Jones, Amy Kass, Erin Hinton
Advertising .... Serino Coyne, Inc
Web Design Consultant .... Joshua Noah
Production Photography .... Joan Marcus
Production Travel .... Jill L. Citron
Payroll Managers .... Cathy Guerra, Johnson West
Corporate Counsel .... Michael Rosenfeld

CREDITS

Scenery by Hudson Scenic, Inc.; Adirondack Studios, Inc.; Proof Productions, Inc.; Scenic Technologies, a division of Production Resource Group, LLC, New Windsor NY. Drops by Scenic Arts. Automation by Hudson Scenic, Inc. Lighting equipment by Hudson Sound & Light, LLC. Sound Equipment by Masque Sound. Projection equipment by Sound Associates Inc. Magic props by William Kennedy of Magic Effects. Props by The Spoon Group, LLC; Moonboots Productions Inc.; Russell Beck Studio Ltd. Costumes by Barbara Matera Ltd.; Parsons-Meares, Ltd.; Eric Winterling; Werner Russold; Studio Rouge; Seamless Costumes. Millinery by Rodney Gordon, Arnold Levine, Lynne Mackey Studio. Shoes by T.O. Dey. Shirts by Cego. Puppets by Puppet Heap. Flying by Foy. Ricola cough drops courtesy of Ricola USA, Inc. Emergen-C super energy booster provided by Alcer Corp. Makeup provided by M•A•C.

THE ORIGINAL FILM SCREENPLAY FOR WALT DISNEY'S *MARY POPPINS* BY BILL WALSH * DON DA GRADI.
DESIGN CONSULTANT TONY WALTON

MARY POPPINS rehearsed at the New 42nd Street Studios.

THANKS

Thanks to Marcus Hall Props, Claire Sanderson, James Ince and Sons, Great British Lighting, Bed Bazaar, The Wakefield Brush Company, Heron and Driver, Ivo and Kay Covney, Mike and Rosi Compton, Bebe Barrett, Charles Quiggin, Nicola Kileen Textiles, Carl Roberts Shaw, David Scotcher Interiors, Original Club Fenders Ltd., Lauren Pattison, Robert Tatad.

FOR CAMERON MACKINTOSH LIMITED

Directors ....Nicholas Allott, Matthew Dalco
Associate Producer and Casting Director ....Trevor Jackson
Technical Director ....Nicolas Harris
Financial Controller ....Richard Knibb
General Manager ....Robert Noble
Production Administrator ....Darinka Nenadovic
Head of Marketing and Press ....Kendra Reid
Head of Musical Development ....Stephen Metcalfe
Production Associate ....Shidan Majidi
New York Production Assistant ....Ed Greenall

DISNEY THEATRICAL PRODUCTIONS

President ....Thomas Schumacher
SVP & General Manager ....Alan Levey
SVP, Managing Director & CFO ....David Schrader

Senior Vice President, Creative Affairs .....Michele Steckler
Senior Vice President, International ....Ron Kollen
Vice President, International Marketing .....Fiona Thomas
Vice President, Operations ....Dana Amendola
Vice President, Labor Relations ....Allan Frost
Vice President, Domestic Touring ....Jack Eldon
Director, Domestic Touring ....Michael Buchanan
Vice President, Theatrical Licensing ....Steve Fickinger
Director, Human Resources ....June Heindel
Manager, Labor Relations ....Stephanie Cheek
Manager, Human Resources ....Cynthia Young
Manager, Information Systems ....Scott Benedict
Senior Computer Support Analyst ....Kevin A. McGuire

Production

Executive Music Producer ....Chris Montan
Vice President, Physical Production ....John Tiggeloven
Senior Manager, Safety ....Canara Price
Manager, Physical Production ....Karl Chmielewski
Purchasing Manager ....Joseph Doughney
Staff Associate Designer ....Dennis W. Moyes
Dramaturg & Literary Manager ....Ken Cerniglia

Marketing

Vice President, Broadway ....Andrew Flatt
Senior Manager, Broadway ....Michele Groner
Website Manager ....Eric W. Kratzer
Assistant Manager, Communications ....Dana Torres

Sales

Vice President, Ticketing ....Jerome Kane
Manager, Group Sales ....Jacob Lloyd Kimbro
Assistant Manager, Group Sales ....Juil Kim
Group Sales Representative ....Jarrid Crespo

Business and Legal Affairs

Senior Vice President ....Jonathan Olson
Vice President ....Robbin Kelley
Director ....Harry S. Gold
Attorney ....Seth Stuhl
Paralegal/Contract Administration ....Colleen Lober

Finance

Director ....Joe McClafferty
Senior Manager, Finance ....Dana James
Manager, Finance ....Justin Gee
Manager, Finance ....John Fajardo
Production Accountants ....Joy Brown, Nick Judge, Barbara Toben, Jodi Yaeger
Assistant Production Accountant ....Isander Rojas
Senior Financial Analyst ....Tatiana Bautista
Analyst ....Liz Jurist

Controllership

Director, Accounting ....Leena Mathew
Senior Analysts ....Stephanie Badie, Mila Danilevich, Adrineh Ghoukassian
Analysts ....Bilda Donado, Ken Herrell

Administrative Staff

Dusty Bennett, Craig Buckley, Stephanie Carnright, Lauren Daghini, Jessica Doina, Cristi Finn, Cristina Fornaris, Dayle Gruet, Lance Gutterman, Gregory Hanoian, Jonathan Hanson, Jay Hollenback, Connie Jasper, Tom Kingsley, Kerry McGrath, Lisa Mitchell, Ryan Pears, Flora Rhim, Roberta Risafi, Bridget Ruane, Kisha Santiago, David Scott, Andy Singh

BUENA VISTA THEATRICAL MERCHANDISE, L.L.C.

Vice President ....Steven Downing
Merchandise Manager ....John F. Agati
Operations Manager ....Shawn Baker
Assistant Manager, Inventory ....Suzanne Jakel
Associate Buyer ....Violeta Burlaza
Retail Supervisor ....Mark Nathman
On-site Retail Manager ....Jeff Knizner
On-site Assistant Retail Manager ....Jonathan LaCombe

Disney Theatrical Productions • 1450 Broadway
New York, NY 10018

guestmail@disneytheatrical.com

STAFF FOR THE NEW AMSTERDAM THEATRE

Theatre Manager .... John Loiacono
Guest Services Manager .... Ryan Gregoli
Box Office Treasurer .... Helen Cullen
Assistant Treasurer .... Harry Jaffie
Chief Engineer .... Frank Gibbons
Engineer .... Dan Milan
Security Supervisor ....Richard Gonzalez
Security Manager ....Carmine Lebo
Head Usher .... Susan Linder
Lobby Refreshments .... Sweet Concessions
Special thanks ....Lynn Beckemeyer, Amy Bawden, Nancy Holland

Mary Poppins
Scrapbook

Photo by Aubrey Reuben

Photo by Aubrey Reuben

Photo courtesy Cass Morgan

1. Curtain call on opening night.
2. The creative team at the New Amsterdam Theatre on opening night (L-R): George Stiles, Richard M. Sherman, Robert B. Sherman, Julian Fellowes and Anthony Drewe.
3. Ensemble member Sean McCourt gets into makeup.

Correspondent: Cass Morgan, "Bird Woman"

Memorable Opening Night Letters: "It's always the one from my husband Danny and stepsons Alex and Zach"—Rebecca Luker.

"The entire London cast of *Mary Poppins* sent an opening night fax to the company. Every individual character in the show wrote to their American counterpart. Jane Banks wrote to Jane Banks, etc..."—Mark Dobrow

Opening Night Gifts: "From Matthew Bourne: A kite, from Richard Eyre: A purple velvet scarf"—Nic Dromard

"The kids from London sent us a handmade card. We each got tons of things but the one I remember the most was a signed Mary Poppins book."—Kat Doherty

"My agent sent me a huge tub of popcorn; and when I say huge I mean HUMONGOUS! I don't really eat popcorn so I gave it to the other guys in the male ensemble dressing room. Even they couldn't finish it."—Kevin Yee

"I loved the real tuppence! Two one-pence coins you could hold in your hand and feel, from the composer and lyricist of our new tunes. Very cool. Also, my wife and boys made me a kite with sweet messages on each bow of the tail. Can't beat that!"—Dan Jenkins

Most Exciting Celebrity Visitors: "Well, we just opened, but I got to meet a hero of mine, James Taylor, and I did the stupid gushing thing. I did get to tell him he changed my life and that was worth a great deal to me."—Dan Jenkins

"Rebecca Luker...she gave me a high-five backstage by the water cooler."—Kevin Yee

"James Taylor and he said he loved the show."—Kat Doherty

Who Got the Gypsy Robe: "Rommy Sandhu was the recipient, and he put the *Mary Poppins* London skyline with all the names of the cast."—Nic Dromard

"Carols for a Cure" Carol: "This Little Light of Mine."

Actor Who Performed the Most Roles in This Show: Sean McCourt and Jim Hindman are tied. Between them they have performed: The Policeman, The Park Keeper, Mr. Punch, The Surprise Witness, Von Hussler, Admiral Boom and Mr. Northrup.

Who Has Done the Most Shows in Their Career: It has to be Michael McCarty, with over 200 productions under his belt!

Special Backstage Rituals: "The hide and seek in the Banks house at intermission is a real joy to witness...!"—Dan Jenkins

"Playing hide and seek with the kids on the house set during the intermission."—Mark Price

"Kissing Willoughby the dog before every show."—Kat Doherty

Favorite Moment During Each Performance: "When Bert taps across the proscenium."—Nic Dromard

"I love watching the amazing ensemble perform

Mary Poppins
Scrapbook

Photos courtesy Cass Morgan

1. Ensemble members Katty Nanni, Shekitra Starke and Michelle Lookadoo get into makeup.
2. The "extended" Banks family including all three sets of children who play Jane and Michael at various performances: (L-R): Delaney Moro, Rebecca Luker, Alexander Scheitinger, Kathryn Faughnan, Henry Hodges, Katherine Leigh Doherty, Daniel Jenkins and Matthew Gumley.

'Supercal.' A real testament to discipline, joy and magic."—Dan Jenkins
"'Step in Time.'"—Kat Doherty
Favorite In-Theatre Gathering Place: "The water cooler on stage right seems to be a real 'water cooler' work gathering place. Lots of good silliness there...."—Dan Jenkins
"The ethnic quick-change pod."—Kevin Yee
"The girls' dressing room."—Kat Doherty
"After the Sunday night matinee, the boys ensemble dressing room is a nice hangout."—Nic Dromard
"Teatime in Cass and Ruth's dressing room."—Mark Price
Favorite Off-Site Hangout: "The Hilton bar."—Rebecca Luker and Nic Dromard
"Vynl."—Kevin Yee
"Paxx and the park."—Kat Doherty
Favorite Snack Food: "The boys in the 'ethnic' quick-change pod are addicted to Skittles. Ever since someone (me) got a Halloween candy dispenser filled with Skittles for Elizabeth, the Australian dresser, as her 'Boo.' Some of the guys like to eat them one by one and savour them... I like to shove a handful of them in my mouth before I go on stage, although I find the sugar makes me spit extra when I sing."—Kevin Yee
"M&M's, Hershey Kisses, the candies in the stage right and stage left candy bags, Dominic Roberts' aunt's cookies."—Nic Dromard
"Clementines/chocolate."—Mark Price
"Any of the candy in the carpenters' stage right candy bag."—Mark Dobrow
Mascot: "Thomas Schumacher."—Kevin Yee
"Willoughby."—Nic Dromard
Favorite Therapy: Ricola, Emergen-C, all kinds of tea, Instant Ice Packs.
Memorable Ad-Libs: "Children who leaaarrnnnnnnnnnn...."—Jim Hindman
"Don't you dare lock that dollhouse!"—Delaney Moro
"Sorry mum, you'll have to take the back exit. This one's stuck."—Ashley Brown
"Yes, Bacon!"—Eric B. Anthony
Memorable Press Encounter: "This is the first year I've actually kissed a photographer. Nothing romantic, it was just a goofy kissing opening night."—Dan Jenkins
"'The Today Show' and 'The View.'"—Kat Doherty
Memorable Stage Door Fan Encounters:
Fan: "Were you Mary Poppins?"
Me: "No, I was Mrs. Banks. I look nothing like Mary Poppins. She's very young."
Fan: "You look nothing like Mrs. Banks either. She's very old."—Rebecca Luker
"A little girl who hugged me."—Kat Doherty
Latest Audience Arrival: 3:55 p.m., for a 2 p.m. matinee.
Fastest Costume Change: Bert and Mary's head to toe quick-change after "Jolly Holiday," in 35 seconds. Also, the messenger change during "Step in Time" features a new hat and coat and a make up soot wipe in about 30 seconds.
Heaviest/Hottest Costume: Hands down it is Dominic Roberts and Brian Letendre as a bear and a rabbit in "Temper, Temper." Ann Arvia's Miss Lark outfit and Cass' Bird Woman layers would be second and third.
Who Wore the Least: Brian Letendre as Neleus.
Catchphrases Only the Company Would Recognize: "Cleverclogs." "Janet/Ginny, I'll meet you in the nursery." "Anything can happen if you're FIERCE."
Which Orchestra Member Played the Most Consecutive Performances Without A Sub: Actually, it was a Sub: Brian Miller on Flutes! Go figure.
Best In-House Parody Lyric: "Being Mrs. Banks is sort of fierce I guess."
Memorable Directorial Note: "Richard Eyre at every other rehearsal: 'I have another idea for your door routine with Jane.'"—Mark Price
"Once Richard said, 'Your performance last night was rather...strange.'"—Rebecca Luker
Understudy Anecdote: Most of the swings have been on all the time, including Nic and Brian going on for Catherine Walker. Brian was bummed he didn't get to be the Glamour Doll, though. Stephanie, who had never swung before, did all six tracks in a matter of weeks.
Nickname: "Carrot" (Kevin Yee).
Embarrassing Moments: "My fly was open during 'Jolly Holiday'... but I wasn't really embarrassed...just hungry."—Kevin Yee
"Actually went on stage with my fly undone and sat on a bench revealing my nice white undies while singing, 'Illusions may shatter....'"—Dan Jenkins
"Audience members caught fornicating in the mezzanine during 'Supercal'!"—Mark Price
(Eeeew! What happened to our family show!?!)
Ghostly Encounters Backstage: Olive Thomas! Olive Thomas! Olive Thomas! She is making her displeasure at not being cast in *Mary Poppins* known regularly.
"Halloween night. Olive was being particularly rambunctious. The evening started with having to hold the curtain to replace a microphone on Michael Banks. After 'Jolly Holiday' we stopped the show due to a power outage on the light board and sound console. Then Michael Banks lost his voice and had to be replaced during the show. Then the Kitchen Unit door got stuck and the actors couldn't exit properly. Then the remote 'Step in Time' chimney stopped working. Lastly, one of the fog machines in a chimney on the rooftop unit overheated and caught fire."—Mark Dobrow
"Halloween. I ended up speaking to our resident ghost, Olive, telling her to cool it after many ghostly-inspired incidents. Don't know if she heard me, but I was earnest in my request for her to stop messing around before someone got hurt!"—Dan Jenkins
"Still waiting for an Olive Thomas appearance."—Rebecca Luker
Coolest Things About Being in This Show: "The people I get to work with."—Dan Jenkins
"It's *Mary Poppins*, y'all"—Mark Price
"Getting to be on Broadway!"—Kat Doherty
"#1: It's *Mary Poppins*! #2: More magic and effects than I've ever seen in my career."—Mark Dobrow

Monty Python's Spamalot

First Preview: February 14, 2005. Opened: March 17, 2005.
Still running as of May 31, 2007.

PLAYBILL

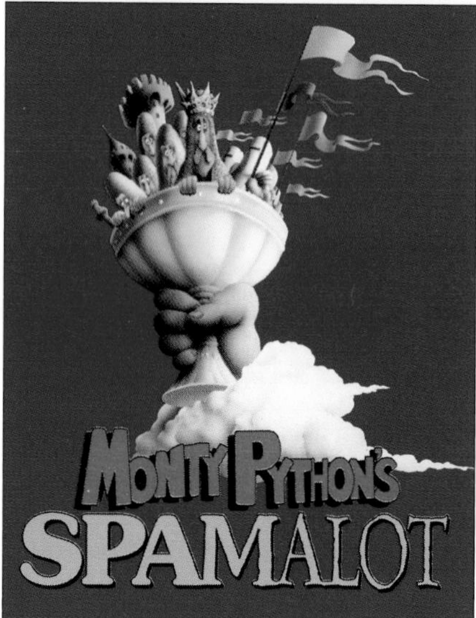

CAST OF CHARACTERS

(in order of appearance)

Historian, Not Dead Fred, French Guard, Minstrel, Prince Herbert .... CHRISTIAN BORLE
Mayor, Patsy, Guard 2 .... MICHAEL McGRATH
King Arthur .... HARRY GROENER
Sir Robin, Guard 1, Brother Maynard .... MARTIN MORAN
Sir Lancelot, The French Taunter, Knight of Ni, Tim the Enchanter .... CHRIS HOCH
Sir Dennis Galahad, The Black Knight, Prince Herbert's Father .... LEWIS CLEALE
Dennis's Mother, Sir Bedevere, Concorde .... STEVE ROSEN
The Lady of the Lake .... LAUREN KENNEDY
Sir Not Appearing .... KEVIN COVERT
Monk .... KEVIN COVERT
Nun .... BRIAN SHEPARD
God .... JOHN CLEESE
French Guards .... THOMAS CANNIZZARO, GREG REUTER
Minstrels .... BRAD BRADLEY, ASMERET GHEBREMICHAEL, GREG REUTER
Sir Bors .... BRAD BRADLEY

Continued on next page

SAM S. SHUBERT THEATRE

225 West 44th Street
A Shubert Organization Theatre
Gerald Schoenfeld, *Chairman* **Philip J. Smith,** *President*

Robert E. Wankel, *Executive Vice President*

Boyett Ostar Productions The Shubert Organization
Arielle Tepper Stephanie McClelland/Lawrence Horowitz Elan V. McAllister/Allan S. Gordon
Independent Presenters Network Roy Furman GRS Associates
Jam Theatricals TGA Entertainment Live Nation

present

Monty Python's
SPAMALOT

Book & Lyrics by
Eric Idle

Music by
John Du Prez & Eric Idle

A new musical lovingly *ripped off from the motion picture "Monty Python and the Holy Grail"*

starring
Harry Groener Lauren Kennedy

also starring
Steve Rosen Christian Borle Martin Moran Lewis Cleale Chris Hoch

with
Brad Bradley Thomas Cannizzaro Kevin Covert Jennifer Frankel
Asmeret Ghebremichael Amy Heggins Rosena M. Hill Anthony Holds Beth Johnson
Kristie Kerwin Lindsay Lopez James Ludwig Pamela Remler Greg Reuter
Brian Shepard Vanessa Sonon Rick Spaans Billy Sprague, Jr. Lee A. Wilkins

and
Michael McGrath

Set & Costume Design by Tim Hatley
Lighting Design by Hugh Vanstone

Sound Design by Acme Sound Partners
Hair & Wig Design by David Brian Brown
Special Effects Design by Gregory Meeh
Projection Design by Elaine J. McCarthy

Music Director/Vocal Arrangements Todd Ellison
Orchestrations by Larry Hochman
Music Arrangements by Glen Kelly
Music Coordinator Michael Keller

Casting by Tara Rubin Casting
Associate Director Peter Lawrence
Associate Choreographer Darlene Wilson
Production Management Gene O'Donovan

General Management 101 Productions, Ltd.
Press Representative Boneau/Bryan-Brown
Marketing HHC Marketing
Associate Producers Randi Grossman, Tisch/Avnet Financial

Choreography by
Casey Nicholaw

Directed by
Mike Nichols

ORIGINAL CAST ALBUM
AVAILABLE ON DECCA BROADWAY

LIVE BROADWAY

10/2/06

Michael McGrath and Jonathan Hadary sing "Always Look on the Bright Side of Life."

Photo by Joan Marcus

Monty Python's Spamalot

SCENES & MUSICAL NUMBERS

ACT I

Overture

Scene 1: The Mighty Portcullis

Scene 2: Moose Village

"Fisch Schlapping Song" .... Historian, Mayor, Villagers

Scene 3: Mud Castle

"King Arthur's Song" .... King Arthur, Patsy

Scene 4: Plague Village

"I Am Not Dead Yet" .... Not Dead Fred, Lance, Robin and Bodies

Scene 5: Mud Village

Scene 6: The Lady of the Lake and The Laker Girls

"Come With Me" .... King Arthur, Lady of the Lake and Laker Girls

"The Song That Goes Like This" .... Sir Galahad and Lady of the Lake

Scene 7: The Knights

"All for One" .... King Arthur, Patsy, Sir Robin, Sir Lancelot, Sir Galahad and Sir Bedevere

Scene 8: Camelot

"Knights of the Round Table" .... Lady of the Lake, King Arthur, Patsy, Sir Robin, Sir Lancelot, Sir Galahad, Sir Bedevere and The Camelot Dancers

"The Song That Goes Like This (Reprise)" .... Lady of the Lake

Scene 9: The Feet of God

Scene 10: Find Your Grail

"Find Your Grail" .... Lady of the Lake, King Arthur, Patsy, Sir Robin, Sir Lancelot, Sir Galahad, Sir Bedevere, Knights and Grail Girls

Scene 11: The French Castle

"Run Away" .... French Taunters, King Arthur, Patsy, Sir Robin, Sir Lancelot, Sir Galahad, Sir Bedevere, French Guards and French Citizens

ACT II

Scene 1: The Mighty Portcullis

Scene 2: A Very Expensive Forest

"Always Look on the Bright Side of Life" .... Patsy, King Arthur, Knights and The Knights of Ni

Scene 3: Sir Robin and His Minstrels

"Brave Sir Robin" .... Sir Robin and Minstrels

Scene 4: The Black Knight

Scene 5: Another Part of the Very Expensive Forest

"You Won't Succeed on Broadway" .... Sir Robin and Ensemble

Scene 6: A Hole in the Universe

"The Diva's Lament" .... Lady of the Lake

Scene 7: Prince Herbert's Chamber

"Where Are You?" .... Prince Herbert

"Here Are You" .... Prince Herbert

"His Name Is Lancelot" .... Sir Lancelot, Prince Herbert and Ensemble

Scene 8: Yet Another Part of the Very Expensive Forest

"I'm All Alone" .... King Arthur, Patsy and Knights

"The Song That Goes Like This (Reprise)" .... Lady of the Lake and King Arthur

Scene 9: The Killer Rabbit

"The Holy Grail" .... King Arthur, Patsy, Sir Robin, Sir Lancelot, Sir Galahad, Sir Bedevere and Knights

Finale

"Find Your Grail Finale - Medley" .... The Company

Cast Continued

ENSEMBLE

BRAD BRADLEY, THOMAS CANNIZZARO, KEVIN COVERT, JENNIFER FRANKEL, ASMERET GHEBREMICHAEL;, AMY HEGGINS, KRISTIE KERWIN, LINDSAY LOPEZ, GREG REUTER, BRIAN SHEPARD, VANESSA SONON, BILLY SPRAGUE, JR.

STANDBYS

ROSENA M. HILL, ANTHONY HOLDS, JAMES LUDWIG

UNDERSTUDIES

BRAD BRADLEY, THOMAS CANNIZZARO, ASMERET GHEBREMICHAEL, GREG REUTER, BRIAN SHEPARD

SWINGS

BETH JOHNSON, PAMELA REMLER, RICK SPAANS, LEE A. WILKINS

DANCE CAPTAIN

PAMELA REMLER

ORCHESTRA

Conductor: TODD ELLISON
Associate Conductor: ETHYL WILL
Assistant Conductor: ANTONY GERALIS
Concertmaster: ANN LABIN
Violins: MAURA GIANNINI, MING YEH
Viola: RICHARD BRICE
Cello: DIANE BARERE
Reeds: KEN DYBISZ, ALDEN BANTA
Lead Trumpet: CRAIG JOHNSON
Trumpet: ANTHONY GORRUSO
Trombone: MARK PATTERSON
French Horn: ZOHAR SCHONDORF
Keyboard 1: ETHYL WILL
Keyboard 2 and Accordion: ANTONY GERALIS
Guitars: SCOTT KUNEY
Bass: DAVE KUHN
Drums: SEAN McDANIEL
Percussion: DAVE MANCUSO

Music Coordinator:
MICHAEL KELLER
Music Copying:
EMILY GRISHMAN MUSIC PREPARATION/
EMILY GRISHMAN, KATHARINE EDMONDS

Monty Python's Spamalot

Harry Groener
King Arthur

Lauren Kennedy
The Lady of the Lake

Michael McGrath
Mayor, Patsy, Guard 2

Steve Rosen
Dennis's Mother, Sir Bedevere, Concorde

Christian Borle
Historian, Not Dead Fred, French Guard, Minstrel, Prince Herbert

Martin Moran
Sir Robin, Guard 1, Brother Maynard

Lewis Cleale
Sir Dennis Galahad, The Black Knight, Prince Herbert's Father

Chris Hoch
Sir Lancelot, The French Taunter, Knight of Ni, Tim the Enchanter

Brad Bradley
Minstrel, Sir Bors, Ensemble

Thomas Cannizzaro
French Guard, Ensemble

John Cleese
God

Kevin Covert
Sir Not Appearing, Monk, Ensemble

Jennifer Frankel
Ensemble

Asmeret Ghebremichael
Minstrel, Ensemble

Amy Heggins
Ensemble

Rosena M. Hill
Standby for Lady of the Lake

Anthony Holds
Standby for Arthur, Lancelot, Galahad, Robin, Bedevere

Beth Johnson
Swing

Kristie Kerwin
Ensemble

Lindsay Lopez
Ensemble

James Ludwig
Standby for Robin, Bedevere, Patsy, Historian, Not Dead Fred, Prince Herbert, Lancelot

Pamela Remler
Swing, Dance Captain

Greg Reuter
French Guard, Minstrel, Fight Captain

Brian Shepard
Nun, Ensemble

Vanessa Sonon
Ensemble

Rick Spaans
Swing

Billy Sprague, Jr.
Ensemble

Lee A. Wilkins
Swing

Mahlon Kruse
Production Stage Manager

Jim Woolley
Stage Manager

Eric Idle and John Du Prez
Book, Lyrics and Music; Composer

Mike Nichols
Director

Casey Nicholaw
Choreographer

Tim Hatley
Set & Costume Design

Monty Python's Spamalot

Hugh Vanstone
Lighting Design

Tom Clark, Mark Menard and Nevin Steinberg,
Acme Sound Partners
Sound Design

David Brian Brown
Wig & Hair Design

Gregory Meeh
Special Effects Design

Todd Ellison
Musical Director/ Vocal Arranger

Larry Hochman
Orchestrations

Michael Keller
Music Coordinator

Peter Lawrence
Associate Director

Tara Rubin Casting
Casting

Bill Haber,
OSTAR Enterprises
Producer

Bob Boyett
Producer

Gerald Schoenfeld,
Chairman,
The Shubert Organization
Producer

Philip J. Smith,
President,
The Shubert Organization
Producer

Arielle Tepper
Producer

Stephanie P. McClelland
Producer

Lawrence Horowitz, M.D.
Producer

Elan V. McAllister
Producer

Allan S. Gordon
Producer

Roy Furman
Producer

Morton Swinsky,
GRS Associates
Producer

Steve Tisch,
Tisch-Avnet Financial
Associate Producer

Jon Avnet
Tisch-Avnet Financial
Associate Producer

Steve Kazee
Sir Lancelot, The French Taunter, Knight of Ni, Tim the Enchanter

Drew McVety
Standby

Abbey O'Brien
Ensemble

Ariel Reid
Ensemble

Christopher Sieber
Sir Dennis Galahad, The Black Knight, Prince Herbert's Father

Scott Taylor
Ensemble, Dance Captain

Monty Python's Spamalot

Matthew Crowle
Ensemble, Nun

Jeff Dattilo
Dennis's Mother, Sir Bedevere, Concorde

Tom Deckman
Historian, Not Dead Fred, French Guard, Minstrel, Prince Herbert

Napiera Groves
Standby

Jonathan Hadary
King Arthur

David Hibbard
Mayor, Patsy, Guard 2

Jenny Hill
Ensemble

Rick Holmes
Sir Lancelot, The French Taunter, Knight of Ni, Tim the Enchanter

Emily Hsu
Minstrel, Ensemble

Jeffrey Kuhn
Dennis's Mother, Sir Bedevere, Concorde

Brian J. Marcum
Ensemble

Marin Mazzie
The Lady of the Lake

Ariel Reid
Ensemble

Christopher Sieber
Sir Dennis Galahad, The Black Knight, Prince Herbert's Father

Scott Taylor
Ensemble, Dance Captain

Brandi Wooten
Ensemble

Photo by Randy Morrison

ORCHESTRA
Seated (L-R): Todd Ellison, Ming Yeh, Sean McDaniel, Diane Barere, Zohar Schondorf, Antony Geralis, Alden Banta, Craig Johnson.

Standing (L-R): Dave Kuhn, Dave Mancuso, Ken Dybisz, Maura Giannini, Richard Brice, Scott Kuney, Anthony Gorruso, Mark Patterson, Ethyl Will and Ann Labin.

Monty Python's Spamalot

Photos by Ben Strothmann

STAGE CREW
Front Row (Sitting, L-R): James Roy, Mitch Ely, Jameson Eaton, Rose Alaio, Sheri Turner, Meredith Benson, Sonya Wysocki.
Second Row (Kneeling, L-R): Bones Malone, Roy Franks, Rodd Sovar, Susan Corrado, Ron Mack, Tim Altman, Jim Woolley, Chaz Peek, Chad Lewis.
Back Row (Standing, L-R): Andrea Roberts, Tom Manoy, TJ Manoy, Cavin Jones, Mike Martinez, Adam Bair, Amelia Haywood, James Spradling, Brian Gaynair, Dave Karlson, John Dory, Shannon January, Gary Fernandez, Greg Cushna, Mahlon Kruse, John Kenny and Linda Lee.

USHERS
Front Row (L-R): Stephen Ivelja, Maura Gaynor, Delia Pozo, Giovanni LaDuke.
Second Row (L-R): Joe Lupo, Erin O'Donnell, Tomas Ortiz, Elvis Caban, Aspacia Savas.
Third Row (L-R): Alex Cooper, Kimberley Deandrade, Luis Rodriguez, Paul Rodriguez, Katherine Benoit.
Fourth Row (L-R): Stephanie Layton, Robert Rokicki, Brian Gallagher, Brian Gaynair, Susan Maxwell.

STAFF FOR *SPAMALOT*

GENERAL MANAGEMENT
101 PRODUCTIONS, LTD.
Wendy Orshan Jeffrey M. Wilson
David Auster

COMPANY MANAGER
Elie Landau

GENERAL PRESS REPRESENTATIVE
BONEAU/BRYAN-BROWN
Adrian Bryan-Brown Jackie Green
Aaron Meier

CASTING
TARA RUBIN CASTING
Tara Rubin
Dunja Vitolic Eric Woodall Laura Schutzel
Mona Slomsky Rebecca Carfagna

Monty Python's Spamalot

PRODUCTION MANAGEMENT
AURORA PRODUCTIONS, INC.
Gene O'Donovan
W. Benjamin Heller II   Bethany Weinstein
Melissa Mazdra   Hilary Austin

Fight Director .... **David DeBesse**

Make-Up Designer .... **Joseph A. Campayno**

Production Stage Manager .... Mahlon Kruse
Stage Manager .... Jim Woolley
Stage Managers .... Sheri K. Turner, Chad Lewis
Associate Company Manager .... Nathan Gehan
Dance Captains .... Pamela Remler
Fight Captain .... Greg Reuter
Assistant to Mike Nichols .... Colleen O'Donnell
Associate Scenic Designer .... Paul Weimer
Assistant Scenic Designers ... Raul Abrego, Derek Stenborg
UK Assistant Designer .... Andy Edwards
Associate Costume Designer .... Scott Traugott
Costume Associate .... Ilona Somogyi
Assistant Costume Designers .... Cory Ching, Robert J. Martin
Costume Assistant .... Jessica Wegener
Magic Consultant .... Marshall Magoon
Puppetry Consultant .... Michael Curry
Associate Lighting Designer .... Philip S. Rosenberg
Assistant Lighting Designer .... John Viesta
Moving Light Programmer .... Laura Frank
Assistant Sound Designer .... Sten Severson
Associate Special Effects Designer .... Vivien Leone
Associate Projection Designer .... Gareth Smith
Assistant Projection Designers .... Ariel Sachter-Zeltzer, Jake Pinholster
Projection Programmers ...... Randy Briggs, Paul Vershbow
Projection Illustrator .... Juliann E. Kroboth
Production Carpenter .... Michael Martinez
Assistant Carpenters .... Bill Partello, Jason Volpe
Production Electrician .... Michael S. LoBue
Head Electrician .... Michael Hyman
Assistant Electricians .... Roy Frank, Karen Zitnick
Production Props Supervisor .... Will Sweeney
Assistant Props .... James Cariot
Props Shopper .... Maggie Kuypers
Production Sound Supervisor .... Bones Malone
Assistant Sound .... Mike Wojchik
Wardrobe Supervisor .... Linda Lee
Assistant Wardrobe Supervisor .... Sonya Wysocki
Dressers .... Meredith Benson, Robert Condon, Lori Elwell, Amelia Haywood, Jeffrey Johnson, Shannon McDowell, Jean Marie Naughton, Andrea Roberts, Jack Scott, Keith Shaw
Hair Supervisor .... Larry Boyette
Assistant Hair Supervisor .... Lair Paulsen
Hairdresser .... Stephen R. Keough
Hair and Make-Up Stylist .... Brandon-Scott Claflin
Vocal Coach .... Kate Wilson
Rehearsal Pianists .. Glen Kelly, Ethyl Will, Antony Geralis
Rehearsal Drummer .... Sean McDaniel
Electronic Music Programming .... James Abbott
Production Associate .... Lisa Gilbar
Production Assistants .... Chad Lewis, Mary Kathryn Flynt
Strategic Partnerships & Development .... Jan Gura
Assistant to Mr. Haber .... Theresa Pisanelli
Assistant to Mr. Boyett .... Diane Murphy
Assistant to Messrs. Granat & Traxler .... Katrine Heintz
Legal Counsel .... Lazarus & Harris LLP/ Scott Lazarus, Esq., Robert C. Harris, Esq.
Accountant ...... Rosenberg, Neuwirth, & Kuchner, CPAs/ Christopher Cacace
Comptroller .... Jana Jevnikar
Advertising .... Serino Coyne/ Thomas Mygatt, Victoria Cairl
Marketing .... HHC Marketing/ Hugh Hysell, Matt Sicoli, Michael Redman, Chris Hall, Amanda Pekoe, Caitlin Strype
Marketing Interns .... Mandy Messina, Alyssa Provenzano, Jennifer Scherer
101 Productions, Ltd. Staff .... Katharine Croke, Scott Falkowski, Heidi Neven, Mary-Six Rupert, John Vennema
101 Productions, Ltd. Intern .... Laura Dickinson
Press Associates .... Chris Boneau, Jim Byk, Brandi Cornwell, Jackie Green, Matt Polk, Susanne Tighe
Press Assistants .... Juliana Hannett, Hector Hernandez, Jessica Johnson, Kevin Jones, Amy Kass, Eric Louie, Joe Perrotta, Linnae Petruzzelli, Matt Ross, Heath Schwartz
Banking .... City National Bank/Anne McSweeney
Insurance .... DeWitt Stern, Inc./Jennifer Brown
Travel .... Altour International, Inc./Melissa Casal
Housing .... Road Rebel Entertainment Touring/ Alison Muffitt
Opening Night Coordinator .... Tobak-Dantchik/ Suzanne Tobak, Michael Lawrence
Physical Therapy .... PhysioArts/Jennifer Green
Orthopedist .... David S. Weiss, M.D.
Immigration .... Traffic Control Group, Inc./ David King
Theatre Displays .... King Displays, Inc.
Merchandising .... Max Merchandising, LLC/ Shopalot, LLC
Merchandise Manager .... David Eck
Production Photographer .... Joan Marcus
Payroll Services .... Castellana Services, Inc.

Finnish program by Michael Palin.

www.MontyPythonsSpamalot.com

CREDITS

Scenery and scenic automation by Hudson Scenic Studio, Inc. Additional scenery by Scenic Art Studios, Inc., Chicago Scenic Studios, Hawkeye Scenic Studios. Lighting equipment from Fourth Phase. Sound equipment from PRG Audio. Costumes executed by Barbara Matera Ltd.; Carelli Costumes; Euro Co Costumes; Parsons-Meares, Ltd.; Tricorne, Inc. Additional costumes by Costume Armour, Inc., John Kristiansen; Western Costumes. Shoes by T.O. Dey; LaDuca Shoes NYC; Capri Shoes; Capezio. Millinery by Lynne Mackey Studio, Rodney Gordon. Hair by Ray Marston Wig Studio Ltd., Bob Kelly Wig Creations. Selected make-up furnished by M•A•C. Props by The Spoon Group LLC; The Rabbit's Choice; Cigar Box Studios, Inc.; Costume Armour, Inc.; Jerard Studio; Gilbert Center; Margaret Cusack; Elizabeth Debbout; Erin Edmister; George Fenmore. Some specialty props and costumes furnished by Museum Replicas Inc. Piano from Ortigara's Musicville, Inc. Spamahorn created and provided by Dominic Derasse. Video projection system provided by Scharff-Weisberg, Inc. Video projection services by Vermillion Border Productions. Flying by Foy. Black Knight illusion executed by Entertainment Design & Fabrication. Spam cam and film furnished by Polaroid. Lozenges by Ricola.

SPAM® is a registered trademark of Hormel Foods LLC.

Air travel consideration furnished by Orbitz®.

Housing consideration in NYC furnished by Millennium Broadway, 145 W. 44th St., NYC. Diarmaid O'Sullivan, Bernadette D'Arcy

SPAMALOT
rehearsed at New 42nd Street Studios

SPECIAL THANKS
Bill Link, Devin Burgess, Veronica DeMartini, John Malakoff

THE SHUBERT ORGANIZATION, INC.
Board of Directors

Gerald Schoenfeld
Chairman

Philip J. Smith
President

Wyche Fowler, Jr.

John W. Kluge

Lee J. Seidler

Michael I. Sovern

Stuart Subotnick

Robert E. Wankel
Executive Vice President

Peter Entin
Vice President – Theatre Operations

Elliot Greene
Vice President – Finance

David Andrews
Vice President – Shubert Ticketing Services

John Darby
Vice President – Facilities

D.S. Moynihan
Vice President – Creative Projects

House Manager .... Brian Gaynair

Monty Python's Spamalot
SCRAPBOOK

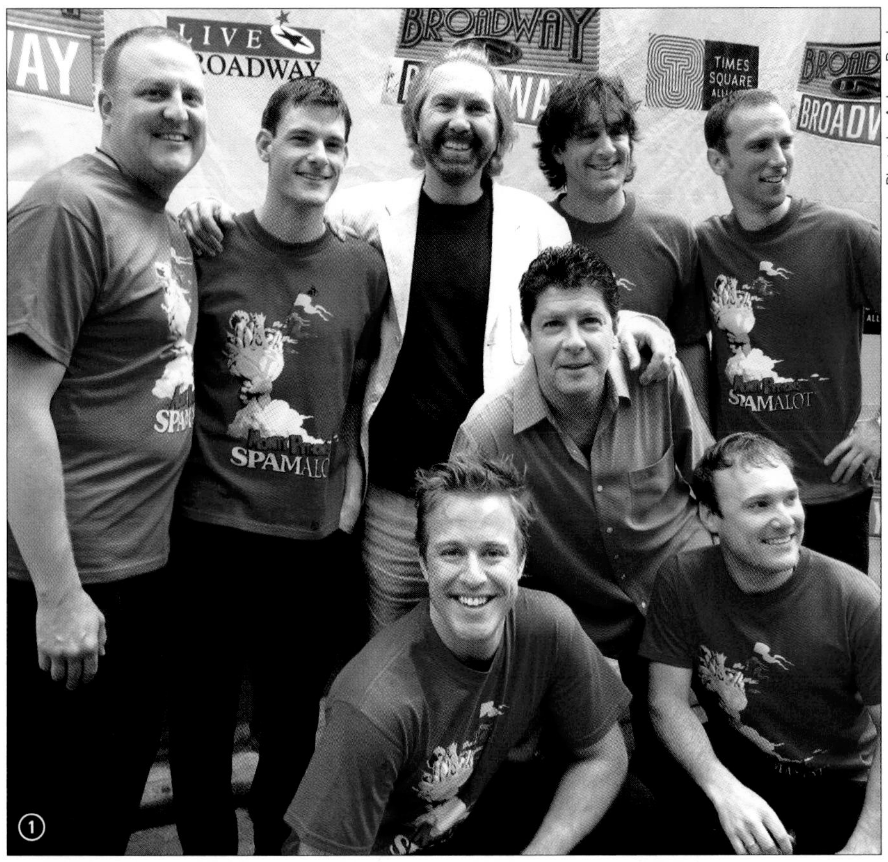

Photo by Aubrey Reuben

Photo courtesy Greg Reuter

Photo courtesy Greg Reuter

1. All for One at the September 2006 "Broadway on Broadway" event. Top Row (L-R): Kevin Covert, Brian Shepard, Harry Groener, Thomas Cannizzaro, Billy Sprague.
Bottom Row (L-R:) Greg Reuter, Michael McGrath and Lee Wilkins.
2. Christian Borle in the Prince Herbert scene, photographed from backstage.
3. Minstrels, photographed from stage left wing.

Correspondent: Greg Reuter, "Minstrel"
Producers' Gift: *Spamalot* watch for Christmas.
Most Exciting Celebrity Visitors: John Kerry, Sacha Baron Cohen.
"Gypsy of the Year" Sketch: "Broadway News Update," a "Weekend Update" style news segment spoofing several Broadway news items. Written by Greg Reuter and Steve Rosen, and performed by Reuter and Jennifer Frankel.
"Carols for a Cure" Carol: "Oh Little Town of Bethlehem."
"Easter Bonnet" Sketch: "Burn Her" by Eric Idle and John Du Prez.
Who Has Done the Most Shows: Jonathan Hadary.
Special Backstage Rituals: Everyone meets on stage at "places" to hang out and socialize. Once the show starts, we never have a spare moment!
Favorite Moment During Each Performance: We have an infrared camera backstage that is pointed at the audience. We like to zoom in and out and watch audience members watch the show. It's really great when we catch a celebrity picking their nose (yes, it has happened more than once).
Favorite In-Theatre Gathering Place: The Bungalow (male dressing room and garden).
Memorable Press Encounter: Having (getting?) to perform with the Naked Cowboy at a luncheon.
Favorite Snack Foods: Dust (gotta stay thin).
Favorite Therapy: Airborne.
Memorable Ad-Libs: "I told you guys not to cook liver in the dressing room." "Have a drink now for free/We'll be back for Act III…." "It's your turn to shoot, Mr. Vice President…."
Record Number of Cell Phone Rings, Cell Phone Photos or Texting Incidents During a Performance: Unlimited here at Shubert, although there is a sign on the door that leads to the orchestra pit forbidding cell phone use…hmmm….
Fastest Costume Changes: 1) Michael McGrath (Patsy) transforming from the Mayor in "Finland" to a mud-covered Patsy. 2) Brad Bradley and Greg Reuter in Act II, full chain-mail and facial hair to velvet and wool clothed minstrel in thirty seconds.
Busiest Week at the Box Office: The week between Christmas and New Year's Eve.
Who Wore the Heaviest/Hottest Costume: Chris Sieber/Lewis Cleale win both the heaviest and hottest costumes in the show. **Heaviest:** The Black Knight. **Hottest:** Prince Herbert's Father.
Who Wore the Least: Ariel Reid, when her top popped off on stage!
Sweethearts Within the Company: Strictly forbidden at our theatre! Whenever a cast romance is brewing, we hold a quick full-company meeting (two to two-and-a-half hours) to defuse it.
Catchphrases Only the Company Would Recognize: "That's your Guy…." "Bear Down…."
Orchestra Member Who Played the Most Instruments: Sean McDaniel, our drummer. He must have at least 14 drums and shiny metal things at his spot. Impressive!
Orchestra Member Who Played the Most Consecutive Performances Without A Sub: Dave Kuhn (bass). I am told it's because his calluses are freakishly thick.
Best In-House Parody Lyrics: "If you trust, opera soul."
Company In-Jokes: "Luke, I am your father."
Company Legends: Rick Spaans really likes Cher. Maybe a little too much.
Tale From the Put-In: Someone missed an entrance at their own put-in! The cast promptly stoned her and hid the body.
Nicknames: C3PO, Shooters, Frank, Tommy, Shady, Evil, DHP, Bones, Ice Queen, and Oxygen Thief.
Embarrassing Moments: Nothing is embarrassing in the world of Monty Python.
Superstitions That Turned Out to Be True: If you hit a midget over the head, he/she turns into forty gold coins! Who knew?
Coolest Thing About Being in This Show: The unbelievably cold wind that whips through Shubert Alley.

A Moon for the Misbegotten

First Preview: March 29, 2007. Opened: April 9, 2007.
Still running as of May 31, 2007.

PLAYBILL

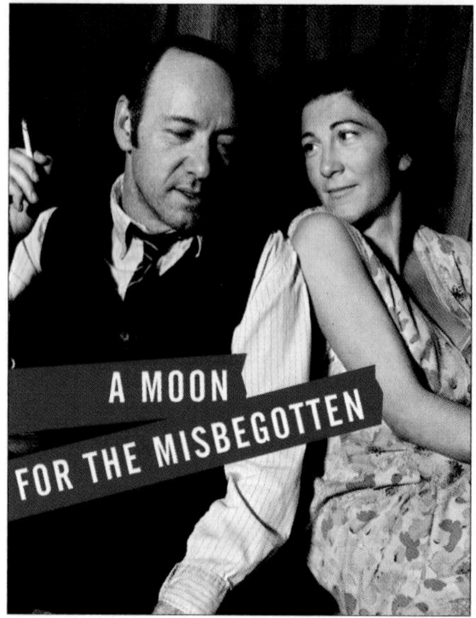

BROOKS ATKINSON THEATRE

UNDER THE DIRECTION OF JAMES M. NEDERLANDER AND JAMES L. NEDERLANDER

Elliot Martin, Nica Burns, Spring Sirkin, Ian Osborne, Max Cooper, Max Weitzenhoffer, Wendy Federman, Thomas Steven Perakos, Ben Sprecher, The Old Vic, Louise Forlenza, James L. Nederlander

present

Eve Best Kevin Spacey

in

The Old Vic Theatre Company

production of

A MOON FOR THE MISBEGOTTEN

by

Eugene O'Neill

also starring

Colm Meaney

with

Billy Carter and Eugene O'Hare

Costume Design: Lynette Mauro
Lighting Design: Mark Henderson
Sound Design: Christopher Shutt
Sound System Design: T. Richard Fitzgerald & Carl Casella
Original Music: Dominic Muldowney
Casting: Maggie Lunn
American Casting: Stuart Howard Associates
Production Manager: Brian Lynch
Production Stage Manager: Bruce A. Hoover
Press Representative: Barlow Hartman
General Manager: Peter Bogyo
Set Design: Bob Crowley

Directed by

Howard Davies

This production first performed at the Old Vic London on September 15, 2006, produced by The Old Vic, Elliot Martin, Nica Burns, Max Weitzenhoffer

4/9/07

CAST

(in order of appearance)

Josie Hogan .... EVE BEST
Mike Hogan .... EUGENE O'HARE
Phil Hogan .... COLM MEANEY
Jim Tyrone .... KEVIN SPACEY
T Stedman Harder .... BILLY CARTER

The action takes place in Connecticut, September 1923.

UNDERSTUDIES

For Josie:
KATI BRAZDA

For Phil Hogan:
BILLY CARTER

For Mike, T Stedman Harder:
NICK WESTRATE

Eve Best, Billy Carter and Eugene O'Hare are appearing with the permission of Actors' Equity Association pursuant to an exchange program between American Equity and UK Equity.

Kevin Spacey and Eve Best

Eve Best and Colm Meaney

Photos by Simon Annand

A Moon for the Misbegotten

Eve Best
Josie Hogan

Kevin Spacey
Jim Tyrone/ Artistic Director, The Old Vic

Colm Meaney
Phil Hogan

Billy Carter
T Stedman Harder

Eugene O'Hare
Mike Hogan

Kati Brazda
u/s Josie

Nick Westrate
u/s Mike, Harder

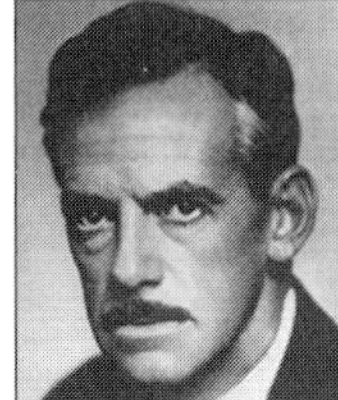
Eugene O'Neill
Playwright

Bob Crowley
Scenic Design

Mark Henderson
Lighting Design

Carl Casella
Sound System Design

Brian Lynch/ Theatretech, Inc.
Technical Management

Peter Bogyo
General Manager

Ben Sprecher
Producer

Spring Sirkin
Producer

James L. Nederlander
Producer

2006-2007 AWARDS

DRAMA DESK AWARD
Outstanding Actress in a Play (Eve Best)

OUTER CRITICS CIRCLE AWARD
Outstanding Actress in a Play (Eve Best)

THEATRE WORLD AWARD
Outstanding Broadway Debut (Eve Best)

CREW
Front Row (L-R):
Cyrille Blackburn (Production Assistant), Bernita Robinson (Stage Manager).

Second Row (L-R):
Manuel Becker (Production Electrician), Joseph DePaulo (Production Properties), Yvonne Jensen (Dresser), Joseph Maher (Production Flyman) Kathleen Gallagher (Wardrobe Supervisor) and Wallace Flores (Production Sound).

Photo by Ben Strothmann

A Moon for the Misbegotten

USHERS
Standing in the back row of the theatre (L-R): Diana Vidaic (Matron), Khadija Dib (Usher), Alexandra Kinter (Usher).
Next theatre row (Seated, L-R): Marie Gonzalez (Usher), Michelle Gonzalez (usher), Barbara Hart (Usher), Arlene Reilly (Usher).
Front theatre row (L-R): Barbara Carrellas (Theatre Manager) and Kimberlee Imperato (Usher).

Photos by Ben Strothmann

BOX OFFICE STAFF
(L-R): William O'Brien and Elaine Amplo.

STAFF LISTING FOR
A MOON FOR THE MISBEGOTTEN

GENERAL MANAGER
Peter Bogyo

GENERAL PRESS REPRESENTATIVE
BARLOW•HARTMAN, INC.
John Barlow Michael Hartman
Dennis Crowley Michelle Bergmann

COMPANY MANAGER
Mary Miller

PRODUCTION MANAGER
THEATRETECH, INC.
Brian Lynch

ORIGINAL LONDON LIGHTING DESIGN
Paule Constable

PRODUCTION STAGE MANAGER ... Bruce A. Hoover
Stage Manager ... Bernita Robinson
Production Assistant ... Cyrille Blackburn
Assistant Director ... Nathan Curry
Production Assistant to Elliot Martin ... Kristin Scafuri
Assistant to Ben Sprecher ... Michael Moss
Associate UK Set Designers ... Paul Atkinson, Alistair Turner
Associate U.S. Set Designer ... Bryan Johnson
Assistant Lighting Designer ... Daniel Walker
Associate Sound Designer ... Colin Pink
Production Carpenter ... Thomas A. Lavaia
Production Electrician ... Manuel Becker
Production Properties ... Joseph DePaulo
Production Sound ... Wallace Flores
Wardrobe Supervisor ... Kathleen Gallagher
Dresser ... Yvonne Jensen
Production Legal Counsel ... Robinson, Brog, Leinwand et al./ Richard Ticktin, Esq.
Insurance ... DeWitt Stern/Peter Shoemaker
Accountant ... Fried & Kowgios CPA's LLP/ Robert Fried, CPA
Controller ... Galbraith & Company, Inc./ Sarah Galbraith
Casting Consultant ... Marjorie Martin
Advertising ... SpotCo/ Drew Hodges, Jim Edwards, Dale Edwards, Peter Duffy
Production Photography ... Lorenzo Agius
Press Office Associates ... Leslie Baden, Tom D'Ambrosio, Steve Dow, Carol Fineman, Bethany Larsen, Ryan Ratelle, Wayne Wolfe, Kevin Robak, Tom Prudenti
Theatre Displays ... BAM Signs, Inc./Adam Miller
Opening Night Coordination ... Broadway Parties/ Wendy Federman, Lisa Rice
Banking ... JP Morgan Chase/Michele Gibbons
Payroll Service ... CSI, Castellana Services Inc.
Car Service ... Broadway Trans, Inc./Ralph Taliercio
Rehearsal Space ... Manhattan Theatre Club

CREDITS

Scenery built and painted b y Hudson Scenic Studios, Inc. Lighting equipment supplied by GSD Production Services, Inc., West Hempstead, NY. Sound equipment from Sound Associates, Inc. Costumes rented from Cosprop. Special thanks to Bra*Tenders for hosiery and undergarments.

THE OLD VIC

Chief Executive ... Sally Greene
Artistic Director ... Kevin Spacey
Assistant Producer ... Simon Fliegner
Production Manager ... Dominic Fraser
Production Assistant ... Hamish Jenkinson
Finance Director ... Helen O'Donnell
Producer ... Kate Pakenham
Marketing Director ... Fiona Richards
Producer ... John Richardson
Managing Director ... Ann Samuel
New Voices Manager ... Rachael Stevens
Events Manager ... Tina Temple-Morris
Development Director ... Vivien Wallace
General Manager ... Dagmar Walz
Education Manager ... Steve Winter
Associates ... Edward Hall, David Liddiment, Anthony Page, Matthew Warchus

For Old Vic Productions plc
Administrator ... Becky Barber
Associate Producer ... Ros Povey
Producer ... Joseph Smith

For Nica Burns and Max Weitzenhoffer
Commercial Director ... Laurence Miller
Production Assistants ... Stephanie Creed, Jennie Jacques
U.S. Legal Counsel ... Nan Bases

Thanks to The Old Vic production team: Louise Askins, Annabel Bolton, Tracey Clarke, Stuart Crane, Alex Fox, PJ Holloway, Tom Humphrey, Olivia Kerslake, Fiona Lehmann, Claire Murphy, Jane Semark

N
NEDERLANDER

Chairman ... **James M. Nederlander**
President ... **James L. Nederlander**

Executive Vice President
Nick Scandalios

Vice President
Corporate Development
Charlene S. Nederlander

Senior Vice President
Labor Relations
Herschel Waxman

Vice President
Jim Boese

Chief Financial Officer
Freida Sawyer Belviso

A Moon for the Misbegotten
Scrapbook

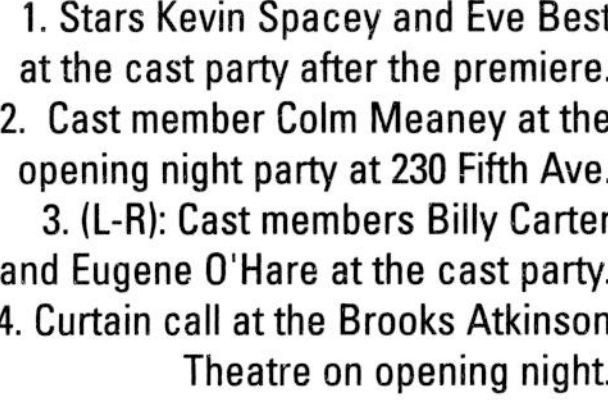
1. Stars Kevin Spacey and Eve Best at the cast party after the premiere.
2. Cast member Colm Meaney at the opening night party at 230 Fifth Ave.
3. (L-R): Cast members Billy Carter and Eugene O'Hare at the cast party.
4. Curtain call at the Brooks Atkinson Theatre on opening night.

Photos by Aubrey Reuben

Correspondent: Billy Carter, "T Stedman Harder"

Opening Night Gifts: Paperweight with the cast names and show logo on it, two bottles of whiskey, three bottles of bubbly and a huge basket of candy...all consumed within the first week!!

Most Exciting Backstage Visitors: Bill Clinton, Alec Baldwin and the one and only Sean Penn—all on one night! What great company!!

Favorite Off-Site Hangout: Start at Bar Centrale above Joe Allen's (very civilized) then Colm, Eugene and myself have an Irish boys night out ending up at Malachy's on 72nd (where all hell breaks loose).

Mascot: Dutch Maisie (Eve's teddy bear).

Memorable Ad-lib: A phone went off just after Kevin's entrance. He turned to the audience and told them to tell them he was busy. It brought the house down. On another evening some old dear had a ten-minute coughing fit and, to finish, her cell went off. God, the audience hated her. Bless her.

Memorable Directorial Note: "Don't be crap."

Company In-Jokes: No in-jokes as we're British and very uptight.

Nicknames: The cast called me Peggy, as I got the Dame Peggy Ashcroft dressing room at The Old Vic and the bloody name stuck with me. They even wrote "Peggy" on my dressing-room door at the Brooks.

Coolest Thing About Being in This Show: Being an actor from London, to take the curtain call on Broadway with the audience on their feet every night is a great buzz.

The Odd Couple

First Preview: October 4, 2005. Opened: October 27, 2005.
Closed June 4, 2006 after 28 Previews and 249 Performances.

PLAYBILL

CAST

(in order of appearance)

Speed .... ROB BARTLETT
Murray .... MIKE STARR
Roy .... PETER FRECHETTE
Vinnie .... LEE WILKOF
Oscar Madison .... NATHAN LANE
Felix Ungar .... MATTHEW BRODERICK
Gwendolyn Pigeon .... OLIVIA d'ABO
Cecily Pigeon .... JESSICA STONE

TIME: 1965
PLACE: Oscar Madison's Riverside Drive apartment

ACT I

Scene 1: A hot summer night
Scene 2: Two weeks later, about 11 PM

ACT II

Scene 1: A few days later, about 8 PM
Scene 2: The next evening, about 7:30 PM

UNDERSTUDIES

For Oscar Madison:
ROB BARTLETT
For Oscar Madison, Murray, Speed, Roy, Vinnie:
GENE GABRIEL
For Felix Ungar, Murray, Speed, Roy, Vinnie:
MARC GRAPEY
For Gwendolyn Pigeon, Cecily Pigeon:
CHRISTY PUSZ

⇛N⇚ BROOKS ATKINSON THEATRE
UNDER THE DIRECTION OF JAMES M. NEDERLANDER AND JAMES L. NEDERLANDER

Ira Pittelman Jeffrey Sine Ben Sprecher Max Cooper Scott E. Nederlander and Emanuel Azenberg
Present

NATHAN LANE MATTHEW BRODERICK
IN
NEIL SIMON'S

With
Rob Bartlett Olivia d'Abo Peter Frechette
Mike Starr Jessica Stone Lee Wilkof

Scenic Design
John Lee Beatty

Costume Design
Ann Roth

Lighting Design
Kenneth Posner

Sound Design
Peter Fitzgerald

Original Music
Marc Shaiman

Casting
Bernard Telsey Casting

Hair Design
David Brian Brown

Production Stage Manager
Jill Cordle

Technical Supervision
Brian Lynch

Associate Producers
Roy Furman & Jay Binder

Press Representative
Bill Evans & Associates

General Manager
Abbie M. Strassler

Directed by
JOE MANTELLO

6/4/06

Photo by Carol Rosegg

(L-R): Nathan Lane, Lee Wilkof, Rob Bartlett, Matthew Broderick, Brad Garrett and Peter Frechette.

The Odd Couple

Nathan Lane
Oscar Madison

Matthew Broderick
Felix Unger

Rob Bartlett
Speed

Olivia d'Abo
Gwendolyn Pigeon

Peter Frechette
Roy

Mike Starr
Murray

Jessica Stone
Cecily Pigeon

Lee Wilkof
Vinnie

Gene Gabriel
Understudy for Oscar Madison, Murray, Speed, Roy, Vinnie

Marc Grapey
Understudy for Felix Ungar, Murray, Speed, Roy, Vinnie

Christy Pusz
Understudy for Gwendolyn Pigeon, Cecily Pigeon

Neil Simon
Playwright

Joe Mantello
Director

John Lee Beatty
Scenic Design

Ann Roth
Costume Design

Kenneth Posner
Lighting Design

Marc Shaiman
Original Music

Bernard Telsey, Bernard Telsey Casting, C.S.A
Casting

David Brian Brown
Hair Design

Jill Cordle
Production Stage Manager

Brian Lynch/ Theatretech, Inc.
Technical Supervision

Roy Furman
Associate Producer

Jay Binder
Associate Producer

Ira Pittelman
Producer

Ben Sprecher
Producer

Emanuel Azenberg
Producer

Photo by Ben Strothmann

FRONT OF HOUSE STAFF
Front Row (L-R): Kimberlee Imperato, Brenda Brauer (Head Usher), Barbara Carrellas (Theatre Manager), Khadija Dib.
Middle Row (L-R): Marie Gonzalez, Judith Pirouz, Michele Gonzalez, Stephen Flaherty.
Back Row (L-R): James Holley, Timothy Newsome, Arlene Reilly and Robert Prensa.

The Odd Couple

STAGE CREW

Seated (L-R): Augie Mericola (Head Props), William "Billy" Joseph Barnes (Production Supervisor), Jill Cordle (Stage Manager), Michael Attianese, Joseph DePaulo (House Properties).
Standing (L-R): Manuel Becker (Production Electrician), Carmel Vargyas, Richard Costabile (Stage Manager), Ken Brown (Star Dresser), Wallace Flores (Production Sound Engineer), Douglas Petitjean (Wardrobe Supervisor), Kelly Smith (Dresser), Mark Trezza (Star Dresser), Maura Clifford (Dresser), Danny Paulos (Props), Thomas A. Lavaia (House Carpenter).

Photo by Ben Strothmann

STAFF FOR *THE ODD COUPLE*

GENERAL MANAGEMENT
ABBIE M. STRASSLER

COMPANY MANAGER
JOHN E. GENDRON

GENERAL PRESS REPRESENTATIVE
BILL EVANS & ASSOCIATES
JIM RANDOLPH

CASTING
Bernard Telsey Casting, C.S.A.:
Bernie Telsey, Will Cantler, David Vaccari, Bethany Knox, Craig Burns, Tiffany Little Canfield, Stephanie Yankwitt, Betsy Sherwood

ASSISTANT DIRECTOR
Lisa Leguillou

Production Supervisor .... William Joseph Barnes
Production Stage Manager .... Jill Cordle
Stage Manager .... Richard Costabile
Associate Scenic Designer .... Eric Renschler
Assistant Scenic Designer .... Yoshi Tanokura
Assistant Costume Designer .... John Glaser
Associate Lighting Designer .... Philip Rosenberg
Associate Sound Designer .... Jill B.C. DuBoff
Technical Supervision .... Brian Lynch, Neil A. Mazzella
Production Electrician .... Manuel Becker
Production Sound Engineer .... Wallace Flores
Production Properties .... George Wagner
Head Props .... Chuck Dague
Wardrobe Supervisor .... Douglas C. Petitjean
Dresser to Mr. Lane .... Ken Brown
Dresser to Mr. Broderick .... Mark Trezza
Dressers .... Maura Clifford, Cesar Porto, Kelly Smith
Hair Supervisor .... Carmel Vargyas
Make-Up Design .... Angelina Avallone
Production Assistants .... Annette Verga-Lagier, Maura Farver
Management Assistant .... Michael Salonia
Assistant to Ms. Roth .... Melissa Haley
Asst. to Mr. Lane .... Andrea Wolfson
Asst. to Mr. Broderick .... Melanie Hansen
Accountants .... Fried & Kowgios CPAs LLP/ Robert Fried, CPA, Elliott Aronstam
Advertising .... Serino Coyne Inc./Angelo Desimini
Insurance .... Tanenbaum Harber of Florida/ Carol Bressi-Cilona
Legal Counsel .... Brooks & Distler/ Marsha S. Brooks, Thomas R. Distler
Merchandising .... Max Merchandising
Production Photographer .... Carol Rosegg
Makeup Design .... Angelina Avallone
Banking .... JPMorgan Chase/Richard Callian
Payroll Service .... Castellana Services Inc./ Lance Castellana
Rehearsals .... The New 42nd Street Studios
Displays .... King Displays
Opening Night
Coordination .... Tobak Lawrence Company/ Suzanne Tobak, Michael P. Lawrence

CREDITS AND ACKNOWLEDGEMENTS
Scenery by Hudson Scenic Studio, Inc. Lighting equipment from Hudson Sound and Light LLC. Sound equipment by Sound Associates, Inc. Costumes constructed by Studio Rouge, Inc. and Werner Russold. Makeup provided by M•A•C. Custom upholstery and draperies provided by Martin-Albert Interiors, Manhattan, NY. Graphic props provided by Proper Decorum, Inc., Kinnelon, NJ. Playing cards courtesy of US Playing cards, Cincinnati, OH. Utz potato chip bags provided by Utz Quality Foods, Inc., Hanover, PA. Period furniture provided by Chatsworth Auction Rooms, Mamaroneck, NY. Natural herb cough drops courtesy of Ricola USA, Inc. Emer'gen-C super energy booster provided by Alacer Corp.

STAFF FOR THE BROOKS ATKINSON THEATRE
House Manager .... Barbara Carrellas
Treasurer .... Keshave Sattaur
Assistant Treasurers .... William Dorso, William O'Brien, Mohammed Sattaur
House Carpenter .... Thomas A. Lavaia
House Flyman .... Joseph J. Maher
House Properties .... Joseph P. DePaulo
House Electrician .... Manuel Becker
Engineer .... Kevin Mac

N
NEDERLANDER

Chairman .... **James M. Nederlander**
President .... **James L. Nederlander**

Executive Vice President
Nick Scandalios

Vice President
Corporate Development
Charlene S. Nederlander

Senior Vice President
Labor Relations
Herschel Waxman

Vice President
Jim Boese

Chief Financial Officer
Freida Sawyer Belviso

110 in the Shade

First Preview: April 13, 2007. Opened: May 9, 2007.
Still running as of May 31, 2007.

PLAYBILL

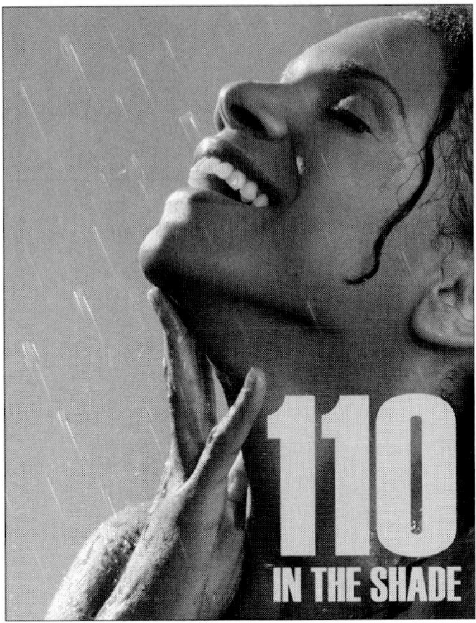

STUDIO 54

ROUNDABOUT THEATRE COMPANY

Todd Haimes, Artistic Director
Harold Wolpert, Managing Director
Julia C. Levy, Executive Director

Present

Audra McDonald

John Cullum *in* Steve Kazee

110
IN THE SHADE

Book by N. Richard Nash

Music by Harvey Schmidt

Lyrics by Tom Jones

Based on a play by N. Richard Nash

Chris Butler Carla Duren Christopher Innvar Bobby Steggert
Elisa Van Duyne Colleen Fitzpatrick Valisia Lekae Little
Darius Nichols Mamie Parris Devin Richards
Michael Scott Will Swenson Matt Wall Betsy Wolfe

Set & Costume Design Santo Loquasto

Lighting Design Christopher Akerlind

Sound Design Dan Moses Schreier

Hair and Wig Design Tom Watson

Dance Music Arranged by David Krane

Dialect Coach Stephen Gabis

Production Stage Manager Peter Hanson

Fight Director Rick Sordelet

Casting Jim Carnahan, C.S.A.

Technical Supervisor Steve Beers

General Manager Sydney Beers

Press Representative Boneau/Bryan-Brown

Director of Marketing & Sales Promotion David B. Steffen

Director of Development Jeffory Lawson

Founding Director Gene Feist

Associate Artistic Director Scott Ellis

Orchestrations by Jonathan Tunick
Music Direction by Paul Gemignani
Choreographed by Dan Knechtges

Directed by Lonny Price

Lead support provided by Roundabout's Musical Theatre Fund partners:
Perry and Marty Granoff, The Kaplen Foundation, John and Gilda McGarry, Tom and Diane Tuft
Major support provided by JPMorgan Chase and The Blanche and Irving Laurie Foundation
Additional support provided by the National Endowment for the Arts

Roundabout Theatre Company is a member of the League of Resident Theatres. www.roundabouttheatre.org

5/9/07

CAST

(in order of appearance)

File .... CHRISTOPHER INNVAR
H.C. Curry .... JOHN CULLUM
Noah Curry .... CHRIS BUTLER
Jimmy Curry .... BOBBY STEGGERT
Lizzie Curry .... AUDRA McDONALD
Snookie .... CARLA DUREN
Starbuck .... STEVE KAZEE
Little Girl .... VALISIA LEKAE LITTLE
Clarence .... DARIUS NICHOLS
Townspeople
Odetta Clark .... COLLEEN FITZPATRICK
Vivian Lorraine Taylor .... VALISIA LEKAE LITTLE
Clarence J. Taylor .... DARIUS NICHOLS
Curjith (Curt) McGlaughlin .... DEVIN RICHARDS
Reverend Clark .... MICHAEL SCOTT
Cody Bridger .... WILL SWENSON
Lily Ann Beasley .... ELISA VAN DUYNE
Katheryn Brawner .... BETSY WOLFE

Continued on next page

Photo by Joan Marcus

(L-R): John Cullum (background in denim), Christopher Innvar, Audra McDonald and Company revel in a downpour in the finale.

110 in the Shade

MUSICAL NUMBERS

Time: July 4, 1936
Place: Texas Panhandle

ACT I

Scene 1: Outside on the Prairie
"Another Hot Day" .... File and Townspeople
Scene 2: The Curry Ranch
"Lizzie's Comin' Home" .... H.C., Noah, Jimmy
"Love, Don't Turn Away" .... Lizzie
Scene 3: File's Office
"Poker Polka" .... File, H.C., Noah, Jimmy
Scene 4: The Picnic Grounds
"The Hungry Men" .... Lizzie and Townspeople
"The Rain Song" .... Starbuck and Townspeople
"You're Not Fooling Me" .... Starbuck and Lizzie
"Cinderella" .... Little Girl
"Raunchy" .... Lizzie
"A Man and a Woman" .... File and Lizzie
"Old Maid" .... Lizzie

ACT II

Scene 1: Outside, twilight
"Evenin' Star" .... Starbuck
Scene 2: Picnic Area
"Everything Beautiful" .... Lizzie and Townspeople
Scene 3: Near Starbuck's Wagon
"Melisande" .... Starbuck
"Simple Little Things" .... Lizzie
Scene 4: Picnic Area
"Little Red Hat" .... Jimmy and Snookie
Scene 5: Starbuck's Lean-to
"Is It Really Me?" .... Lizzie
Scene 6: Picnic Area
"Wonderful Music" .... Starbuck, File and Lizzie
"The Rain Song (Reprise)" .... Townspeople

ORCHESTRA

Conductor:
PAUL GEMIGNANI
Associate Conductor:
MARK MITCHELL
Violins:
SYLVIA D'AVANZO, SEAN CARNEY
Viola:
JOSEPH GOTTESMAN
Cello:
ROGER SHELL
Flute/Piccolo:
SUSAN ROTHOLZ
Woodwinds:
RICK HECKMAN, ERIC WEIDMAN, DON McGEEN
Trumpets:
DOMINIC DERASSE, MIKE PONELLA

Trombone:
BRUCE EIDEM
Harp:
JENNIFER HOULT
Keyboard:
MARK MITCHELL
Bass:
JOHN BEAL
Drums/Percussion:
PAUL PIZZUTI

Music Associate:
PAUL FORD
Music Copying:
EMILY GRISHMAN MUSIC PREPARATION/KATHARINE EDMONDS, EMILY GRISHMAN

Cast Continued

UNDERSTUDIES

For Lizzie:
COLLEEN FITZPATRICK
For Starbuck:
WILL SWENSON
For H.C. and File:
MICHAEL SCOTT
For Noah:
DEVIN RICHARDS
For Jimmy:
DARIUS NICHOLS
For Snookie:
VALISIA LEKAE LITTLE

Swings:
MATT WALL, MAMIE PARRIS
Dance Captain:
MATT WALL

Production Stage Manager:
PETER HANSON
Assistant Stage Manager:
DAN DA SILVA

(L-R): Audra McDonald and Christopher Innvar
Photo by Joan Marcus

110 in the Shade

Audra McDonald
Lizzie Curry

John Cullum
H.C. Curry

Steve Kazee
Starbuck

Chris Butler
Noah Curry

Carla Duren
Snookie

Christopher Innvar
File

Bobby Steggert
Jimmy Curry

Elisa Van Duyne
Lily Ann Beasley

Colleen Fitzpatrick
Odetta Clark

Valisia Lekae Little
Vivian Lorraine Taylor

Darius Nichols
Clarence J. Taylor

Mamie Parris
Female Swing

Devin Richards
Curjith McGlaughlin

Michael Scott
Reverend Clark

Will Swenson
Cody Bridger

Matt Wall
Male Swing

Betsy Wolfe
Katheryn Brawner

Tom Jones
Lyrics

Harvey Schmidt
Music

Lonny Price
Director

Dan Knechtges
Choreographer

Paul Gemignani
Musical Director

Jonathan Tunick
Orchestration

Santo Loquasto
Set and Costume Design

Christopher Akerlind
Lighting Design

Dan Moses Schreier
Sound Design

Tom Watson
Hair and Wig Design

Stephen Gabis
Dialect Coach

Rick Sordelet
Fight Director

Jim Carnahan
Casting

Gene Feist
Founding Director, Roundabout Theatre Company

Todd Haimes
Artistic Director, Roundabout Theatre Company

2006-2007 AWARD

Drama Desk Award
Outstanding Actress in a Musical
(Audra McDonald)

Irene Sharaff Award
Robert L.B. Tobin Award for Lifetime Achievement in Design
(Santo Loquasto)

110 in the Shade

Photos by Ben Strothmann

COMPANY AND STAGE MANAGEMENT

(L-R): Dan da Silva, Nancy Mulliner and Peter Hanson

WARDROBE

(L-R): Yleana Nunez, Steven R. Cozzi, Joe Godwin and Nadine Hettel.

ORCHESTRA

(L-R): Susan Rotholz, Dominic Derasse, Dennis Anderson, Don McGeen, Jennifer Hoult and John Beal.

BOX OFFICE

(L-R): David Carson (Ticket Services), Adam Owens (Ticket Services), Krystin MacRitchie (Ticket Services), Scott Falkowski and Jaime Perlman (Box Office Manager).

110 in the Shade

STAGE CREW

Back Row (L-R): John Wooding, Dan Schultheis, Dan Mendeloff, David Gotwald, Larry White, Dan Hoffman.

Middle Row: Josh Weitzman, Rob Manesman, Steve Jones, Bill Lombardi.

Front Row (L-R): Dorian Fuchs, Rachel Bauder, Larry Jennino and Erin Delaney.

FRONT OF HOUSE STAFF

Front Row (L-R): Stella Varriale, LaConya Robinson (House Manager), Jonathan Martinez (House Staff), Nicholas Wheatley (House Staff).

Back Row (L-R): Elicia Edwards (House Staff), Franco Roman (House Staff), Jose Cuello, Katherine Longosky (House Staff) and Ana Bak-Kvapil.

Photos by Ben Strothmann

ROUNDABOUT THEATRE COMPANY STAFF

ARTISTIC DIRECTOR .... **TODD HAIMES**
MANAGING DIRECTOR .... **HAROLD WOLPERT**
EXECUTIVE DIRECTOR .... **JULIA C. LEVY**
ASSOCIATE ARTISTIC DIRECTOR .... **SCOTT ELLIS**

ARTISTIC STAFF

DIRECTOR OF ARTISTIC DEVELOPMENT/ DIRECTOR OF CASTING .... **Jim Carnahan**
Artistic Consultant .... Robyn Goodman
Associate Artists .... Scott Elliott, Doug Hughes, Bill Irwin, Joe Mantello, Mark Brokaw, Kathleen Marshall
Consulting Dramaturg .... Jerry Patch
Artistic Associate .... Jill Rafson
Casting Director .... Mele Nagler
Senior Casting Associate .... Carrie Gardner
Casting Associate .... Kate Schwabe
Casting Associate .... Stephen Kopel
Artistic Intern .... Michelle Lehrman

EDUCATION STAFF

EDUCATION DIRECTOR .... Margie Salvante-McCann
Director of Instruction and Curriculum Development .... Reneé Flemings
Education Program Manager .... David A. Miller
Education Associate .... Jennifer DeBruin
Education Assistant .... Allison Baucom
Education Dramaturg .... Ted Sod
Teaching Artists .... Phil Alexander, Cynthia Babak, Victor Barbella, LaTonya Borsay, Rob Bronstein, Lori Brown-Niang, Miss Stella, Hamilton Clancy, Joe Doran, Katie Down, Amy Fortoul, Tony Freeman, Sheri Graubert, Matthew Gregory, Adam Gwon, Karla Hendrick, Jim Jack, Lisa Renee Jordan, Alvin Keith, Jonathan Lang, Rebecca Lord, Tami Mansfield, Erin McCready, Jordana Oberman, Evan O'Brient, Deirdre O'Connor, Andrew Ondrecjak, Laura Poe, Alexa Polmer-Spencer, Nicole Press, Jennifer Rathbone, Leah Reddy, Amanda Rehbein, Taylor Ruckel, Chris Rummel, Cassy Rush, Drew Sachs, Nick Simone, Derek Straat, Daniel Robert Sullivan, Vickie Tanner, Olivia Tsang, Cristina Vaccaro, Jennifer Varbalow, Leese Walker, Eric Wallach, Gail Winar
Education Interns .... Anna Jamie Scanlon, Morgan Tylar Waite

ADMINISTRATIVE STAFF

GENERAL MANAGER .... **Sydney Beers**
Associate Managing Director .... Greg Backstrom
General Manager, Steinberg Center .... Rebecca Habel
General Counsel .... Nancy Hirschmann
Human Resources Manager .... Stephen Deutsch
MIS Director .... Jeff Goodman
Facilities Manager .... Abraham David
Manager of Corporate and Party Rentals ..... Jetaun Dobbs
Office Manager .... Scott Kelly
Database Manager .... Dollye Evans
Assistant General Manager .... Maggie Cantrick
Management Associate .... Tania Camargo

MIS Assistant .... Micah Kraybill
Receptionists .... Dena Beider, Raquel Castillo, Elisa Papa, Allison Patrick, Monica Sidorchuk
Messenger .... Darnell Franklin
Management Intern .... Alanna Degner

FINANCE STAFF

DIRECTOR OF FINANCE .... Susan Neiman
Assistant Controller .... John LaBarbera
Accounts Payable Administrator .... Frank Surdi
Financial Associate .... Yonit Kafka
Business Office Assistant .... Joshua Cohen
Business Interns .... Li Shen, Richard Patterson

DEVELOPMENT STAFF

DIRECTOR OF DEVELOPMENT .... Jeffory Lawson
Director, Institutional Giving .... Julie K. D'Andrea
Director, Individual Giving .... Julia Lazarus
Director, Special Events .... Steve Schaeffer
Manager, Donor Information Systems .... Tina Mae Bishko
Corporate Relations Manager .... Sara Bensman
Manager, Individual Giving .... Kara Kandel
Telefundraising Manager .... Douglas Sutcliffe
External Affairs Associate .... Robert Weinstein
Special Events Associate .... Ginger Vallen
Institutional Giving Associate .... Sarah Krasnow
Individual Giving Associate .... Kate Bartoldus
Patrons Services Assistant .... John Haynes
Development Assistants .... Jillian Brewster, Christopher Taggart
Individual Giving Intern .... Ashley Turner
Special Events Intern .... Erica Rotstein

MARKETING STAFF

DIRECTOR OF MARKETING AND SALES PROMOTION .... David B. Steffen
Marketing/Publications Manager .... Margaret Casagrande
Assistant Director of Marketing .... Sunil Ayyagari
Marketing Assistant .... Stefanie Schussel
Website Consultant .... Keith Powell Beyland
DIRECTOR OF TELESALES SPECIAL PROMOTIONS .... Daniel Weiss
Telesales Manager .... Anton Borissov
Telesales Office Coordinator .... J.W. Griffin
Marketing Intern .... Trina McCarron

TICKET SERVICES STAFF

DIRECTOR OF SALES OPERATIONS .... Jim Seggelink
Ticket Services Manager .... Ellen Holt
Subscription Manager .... Charlie Garbowski, Jr.
Box Office Managers .... Edward P. Osborne, Jessica Bowser
Group Sales Manager .... Jeff Monteith
Assistant Box Office Managers .... Andrew Clements, Krystin MacRitchie, Robert Morgan
Assistant Ticket Services Managers .... Robert Kane, Ethan Ubell, Carlos Morris
Customer Services Coordinator .... Trina Cox
Ticket Services .... Rachel Bauder, Solangel Bido, Jessie Blum, Jacob Burstein-Stern, William Campbell, Lauren Cartelli, David Carson, Nisha Dhruna, Adam Elsberry, Lindsay Ericson, Scott Falkowski, John Finning, Catherine Fitzpatrick, Daniel Gabriel, James Graham, Tova Heller, Bill Klemm, Elisa Mala, Mead Margulies, Chuck Migliaccio, Nicole Nicholson, Bekah Nutt, Adam Owens, Ethan Paulini, David Pittman, Thomas Protulipac, Kate Regan, Jackie Rocha, Heather Siebert, Lillian Soto, DJ Thacker, Farra Ungar, Pam Unger, Thomas Walsh
Ticket Services Intern .... Heather Forman

SERVICES

Counsel .... Paul, Weiss, Rifkind, Wharton and Garrison LLP, John Breglio, Deborah Hartnett
Counsel .... Rosenberg & Estis
Counsel .... Andrew Lance, Gibson, Dunn, & Crutcher, LLP
Counsel .... Harry H. Weintraub, Glick and Weintraub, P.C.
Immigration Counsel .... Mark D. Koestler and Theodore Ruthizer
House Physicians .... Dr. Theodore Tyberg, Dr. Lawrence Katz
House Dentist .... Neil Kanner, D.M.D.
Insurance .... DeWitt Stern Group, Inc.
Accountant .... Lutz & Carr CPAs, LLP
Sponsorship .... The Marketing Group, Tanya Grubich, Laura Matalon, Anne Rippey, Erik Gensler
Advertising .... Eliran Murphy Group/ Denise Ganjou, Kara Eldridge
Events Photography .... Anita and Steve Shevett
Production Photographer .... Joan Marcus
Theatre Displays .... King Displays, Wayne Sapper

MANAGING DIRECTOR EMERITUS .... Ellen Richard

Roundabout Theatre Company
231 West 39th Street, New York, NY 10018
(212) 719-9393.

GENERAL PRESS REPRESENTATIVES
Adrian Bryan-Brown
Matt Polk Jessica Johnson Amy Kass

STAFF FOR *110 IN THE SHADE*

GENERAL MANAGER .... Sydney Beers
Company Manager .... Nancy Mulliner
Production Stage Manager .... Peter Hanson
Assistant Stage Manager .... Dan da Silva
Assistant Company Manager .... Dave Solomon
Assistant Director .... Matt Cowart
Assistant to the Director .... Will Nunziata
SSDC Observer .... Kitt Lavoie
Assistant Choreographer .... Caitlin Carter
Assistant Technical Supervisor .... Elisa Kuhar
Associate Scenic Designer .... Jenny Sawyers
Assistant Scenic Designer .... Tobin Ost
Assistant to the Scenic Designer .... Kanae Heike
Associate Costume Designer .... Matthew Pachtman
Assistant to the Costume Designer .... Sarah Sophia Turner
Associate Lighting Designer .... Ben Krall
Assistant Lighting Designer .... Caroline Chao
Associate Sound Designer .... Phillip Scott Peglow
Synthesizer Programmer .... Bruce Samuels
Production Carpenter .... Dan Hoffman
Production Electrician .... Josh Weitzman
Assistant Production Electrician .... John Wooding
Production Properties Coordinator .... Kathy Fabian, Propstar Inc.
Assistant Production Properties .... Carrie Mossman, Carrie Hash
Wardrobe Supervisor .... Nadine Hettel
Dressers .... Steven R. Cozzi, Joe Godwin, Yleana Nunez
Hair and Wig Supervisor .... Daryl Terry
Hair and Wig Stylist .... Kat Ventura
Make-up Design .... Angelina Avallone
Production Sound Engineer .... David Gotwald
Automation Operator .... Paul Ashton
Head Follow Spot Operator .... John Wooding
Properties Running Crew .... Erin Delaney, Daniel Mendeloff
Follow Spot Operators .... Dorian Fuchs, Dan Schultheis
Flyman .... Steve Jones
Moving Light Programmer .... Victor Seastone
Conventional Light Programmer .... Jessica Morton
Deck Sound .... Larry White
Deck Electrician .... Al Talbot
Local One IATSE Apprentice .... Dan Schultheis
Production Assistants .... Kathryn McKee, Rachel Bauder
Physical Therapy .... Encore Physical Therapy P.C.
Scenery Constructed, Automated, and painted by .... Hudson Scenic Studio, Inc.
Lighting Equipment Provided by .... PRG, Production Resource Group
Sound Equipment Provided by .... Sound Associates, Inc.
Specialty Prop Construction .... Craig Grigg and Plumb Square
Rain Equipment by .... Jauchem & Meeh
Costumes executed by .... Euro Co Costumes, Barbara Matera, Ltd., Lynne Baccus, Luigi Custom Tailor, Arel Studios
Fabric Painting & Dyeing by .... Jeff Fender
Custom Footwear by .... T.O. Dey
Hosiery and Undergarments by .... Bra*Tenders
Natural herb cough drops courtesy of .... Ricola USA Inc.
Rehearsed at .... 115 W. 45th Street and the new 42nd Street Studios

STUDIO 54 THEATRE STAFF

Theatre Manager .... Matthew Armstrong
Box Office Manager .... Jaime Perlman
House Manager .... LaConya Robinson
Associate House Manager .... Jack Watanachaiyot
House Staff .... Elicia Edwards, Jason Fernandez, Jen Kneeland, Kate Longosky, Latiffa Marcus, Nicole Marino, Jonathan Martinez, Dana McCaw, Nicole Ramirez, Anthony Roman, Nick Wheatley, Stella Varriale
House Carpenter .... Dan Hoffman
House Electrician .... Josh Weitzman
House Properties .... Lawrence Jennino
Security .... Gotham Security
Maintenance .... Ralph Mohan, Maman Garba
Lobby Refreshments by .... Sweet Concessions
Merchandise .... Marquee Merchandise LLC/ Matt Murphy

110 in the Shade

Scrapbook

Photos by Aubrey Reuben

1. Lyricist Tom Jones arrives at Studio 54 on opening night.
2. John Cullum at the cast party.
3. (L-R:) Steve Kazee and Christopher Innvar.
4. Carla Duren at Studio 54.
5. Curtain call on opening night.

Correspondent: Bobby Steggert, "Jimmy Curry"

Opening Night Gift: Director Lonny Price gave us a t-shirt with a picture of him posing in the same exact position as Audra in the show's poster: naked from the shoulders up, head tilted toward the rain. Instead of an orange background, there were white bathroom tiles. This masterpiece was titled *110 in the Shower*, and surely, if we ran long enough to have a softball team, it would be our uniform.

Most Exciting Celebrity Visitor: Karen Ziemba, who played Lizzie at New York City Opera and obviously someone to whom the show is very special, came backstage and was a wonderful and gracious supporter of our production.

Special Backstage Rituals: Heat being a major theme of our show, we need to appear as sweaty as possible when on stage, so before each show, we slather ourselves with baby oil. We then use one of the many strategically placed off-stage spray bottles to cover ourselves in water. If you listen closely in between lines, you can hear the "sh-sh-sh" just before a new character makes their entrance.

Cast Tradition: Anyone who's anyone spends their Wednesday and Saturday breaks playing poker in Steve Kazee's dressing room. The stakes are usually pretty low as far as money goes, but extremely high as far as winning goes. Just a word to the wise: don't bluff a bad hand to the girls in the cast. They'll mess you up.

Favorite Cast Game: Though drinking doesn't actually happen on the premises, our hypothetical drinking game is as follows: every time a character addresses another character by his name, you take a shot. One of the first scenes in the show begins: "Hey File," "Hey Jim," "Hey File," "Hey Noah," "Hey File," "Hey H.C." As you can see, we'd be pretty drunk pretty soon (hypothetically, of course).

Favorite Moment During Each Performance: Not only is it the obvious climax of the show, but it's a chance for the water to wash all that crap off! It never seems to lose its magic either, and is quite a cathartic experience each performance.

Favorite Off-Site Hangout: We all go to Xing, an Asian fusion place on Ninth Avenue and 52nd. They love our cast and give us plates and plates of free food, and half-price drinks. Our cast drink is probably the "Electric Karma," which you get to drink out of Buddha's belly.

Company In-Jokes: During "Little Red Hat" Carla Duren and I have a moment when we jump behind this big ramp on the stage and then, a couple of seconds later, pop up again. Audra and Steve are waiting under the ramp for the next scene, and unseen by anyone but us, they find incredibly creative (and sometimes disturbing) ways of trying to make us laugh (use your imaginations). It has been an eye-opening education to say the least.

Embarrassing Moments: Curtain calls take place on a wet raked stage, and I hold the record of having fallen on my butt twice in the first week of performances.

Coolest Thing About Being in This Show: Our cast is clearly biracial, with a lot of non-traditional casting, and we've never even noticed or questioned it. We've created a community of people where race doesn't come into the picture, and as a result, I think, the audience just accepts it as the reality of the world. In my opinion, it's how all shows should be cast.

The Pajama Game

First Preview: January 19, 2006. Opened: February 23, 2006.
Closed: June 17, 2006 after 41 Previews and 129 Performances.

PLAYBILL

CAST

(in order of appearance)

Factory Workers:

Prez .... PETER BENSON
Mae .... JOYCE CHITTICK
Virginia .... BRIDGET BERGER
Charlie .... STEPHEN BERGER
Martha .... KATE CHAPMAN
Brenda .... PAULA LEGGETT CHASE
Poopsie .... JENNIFER CODY
Lewie .... DAVID EGGERS
Cyrus .... MICHAEL HALLING
Carmen .... BIANCA MARROQUIN
Jake .... VINCE PESCE
Joe .... DEVIN RICHARDS
Ralph .... JEFFREY SCHECTER
Shirley .... DEBRA WALTON

Hines .... MICHAEL McKEAN
Mr. Hasler .... RICHARD POE
Gladys .... MEGAN LAWRENCE
Mabel .... ROZ RYAN
Ganzenlicker/Pop .... MICHAEL McCORMICK
Sid Sorokin .... HARRY CONNICK, JR.
Babe Williams .... KELLI O'HARA

TIME:

1954

PLACE:

Cedar Rapids, Iowa

Continued on next page

40TH ANNIVERSARY SEASON

ROUNDABOUTTHEATRECOMPANY

TODD HAIMES, Artistic Director
HAROLD WOLPERT, Managing Director
JULIA C. LEVY, Executive Director

By Special Arrangement with Jeffrey Richards, James Fuld, Jr., and Scott Landis

Present

Harry Connick, Jr.
Kelli O'Hara Michael McKean

in

THE PAJAMA GAME

Book by George Abbott and Richard Bissell
Music & Lyrics by Richard Adler and Jerry Ross
Based on the Novel *"7 ½ Cents"* by Richard Bissell
Book Revisions for this Production by Peter Ackerman

Peter Benson Joyce Chittick Megan Lawrence
Michael McCormick Richard Poe Roz Ryan

Bridget Berger Stephen Berger Kate Chapman Paula Leggett Chase Jennifer Cody
David Eggers Michael Halling Bianca Marroquin Michael O'Donnell Vince Pesce
Devin Richards Jeffrey Schecter Amber Stone Debra Walton

Set Design Derek McLane
Costume Design Martin Pakledinaz
Lighting Design Peter Kaczorowski
Sound Design Brian Ronan

Production Stage Manager David O'Brien
Hair & Wig Design Paul Huntley
Music Coordinator Seymour Red Press
Casting Jim Carnahan, C.S.A.

Associate Director Marc Bruni
Associate Choreographer Vince Pesce
Musical Director Rob Berman
Technical Supervisor Steve Beers
General Manager Sydney Beers

Press Representative Boneau/Bryan-Brown
Director of Marketing David B. Steffen
Founding Director Gene Feist
Associate Artistic Director Scott Ellis

Orchestrations
Dick Lieb and Danny Troob

Musical Supervisor/Vocal and Dance Arranger
David Chase

Directed and Choreographed by
Kathleen Marshall

Major support for this production provided by The Kaplen Foundation and JPMorgan Chase

Roundabout Theatre Company is a member of the League of Resident Theatres. www.roundabouttheatre.org

6/17/06

Photo by Joan Marcus

The cast performs "Hernando's Hideaway."

The Pajama Game

MUSICAL NUMBERS

ACT ONE

Overture	The Orchestra
"Racing with the Clock"	Factory Workers
"A New Town Is a Blue Town"	Sid
"I'm Not at All in Love"	Babe, Factory Girls
"I'll Never Be Jealous Again"	Hines, Mabel
"Hey There"	Sid
"Racing with the Clock" (Reprise)	Factory Workers
"Sleep Tite"	Joe, Brenda, Martha, Cyrus
"Her Is"	Prez, Gladys
"Once-a-Year-Day"	Sid, Babe, Company
"Her Is" (Reprise)	Prez, Mae
"Small Talk"	Sid, Babe
"There Once Was a Man"	Sid, Babe
"Hey There" (Reprise)	Sid

ACT TWO

"Steam Heat"	Mae, Lewie, Jake
"The World Around Us"	Sid
"Hey There" (Reprise) / "If You Win, You Lose" *	Babe, Sid
"Think of the Time I Save"	Hines, Factory Girls
"Hernando's Hideaway"	Gladys, Sid, Company
"The Three of Us" *	Hines, Gladys
"Seven and a Half Cents"	Prez, Babe, Factory Workers
"There Once Was a Man" (Reprise)	Babe, Sid
"The Pajama Game"	Full Company

* "If You Win, You Lose" and "The Three of Us" – music and lyrics by Richard Adler

Photo by Joan Marcus

The cast performs "Seven and a Half Cents."

Cast Continued

UNDERSTUDIES

For Babe:
BRIDGET BERGER

For Mr. Hasler, Ganzenlicker, Pop:
STEPHEN BERGER

For Mabel:
KATE CHAPMAN

For Gladys:
JENNIFER CODY

For Sid:
MICHAEL HALLING

For Hines:
MICHAEL McCORMICK

For Prez:
JEFFREY SCHECTER

For Mae:
DEBRA WALTON

SWINGS

MICHAEL O'DONNELL, AMBER STONE

Production Stage Manager:
DAVID JOHN O'BRIEN

Assistant Stage Managers:
STEPHEN R. GRUSE, LESLIE C. LYTER

ORCHESTRA

Conductor: ROB BERMAN
Associate Conductor: CHRIS FENWICK

Violin: MARILYN REYNOLDS
Cello: BETH STURDEVANT
Reeds: STEVE KENYON, JOHN WINDER
Trumpet: ROGER INGRAM, CHRISTIAN JAUDES
Trombone: JOHN ALLRED, JOE BARATI
Guitar: JIM HERSHMAN
Piano: CHRIS FENWICK
Bass: NEAL CAINE
Drums/Percussion: PAUL PIZZUTI

Synthesizer Programmer: ANDY BARRETT
Music Coordinator: SEYMOUR "RED" PRESS

The Pajama Game

Harry Connick, Jr.
Sid Sorokin

Kelli O'Hara
Babe Williams

Michael McKean
Hines

Peter Benson
Prez

Joyce Chittick
Mae

Megan Lawrence
Gladys

Michael McCormick
Ganzenlicker/Pop

Richard Poe
Mr. Hasler

Roz Ryan
Mabel

Bridget Berger
Virginia

Stephen Berger
Charlie

Kate Chapman
Martha

Paula Leggett Chase
Brenda

Jennifer Cody
Poopsie

David Eggers
Lewie,
Dance Captain

Michael Halling
Cyrus

Bianca Marroquin
Carmen

Michael O'Donnell
Swing

Vince Pesce
Associate
Choreographer, Jake

Devin Richards
Joe

Jeffrey Schecter
Ralph

Amber Stone
Swing

Debra Walton
Shirley

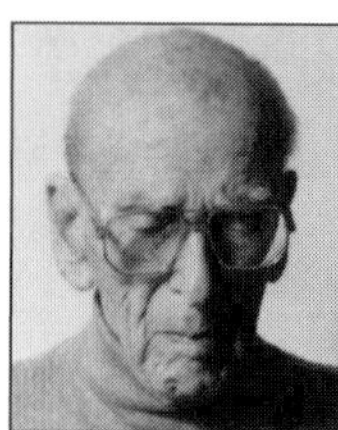
George Abbott
Book

Richard Adler
Music & Lyrics

Kathleen Marshall
Director &
Choreographer

Dick Lieb
Orchestrator

Danny Troob
Orchestrator

Derek McLane
Set Design

Martin Pakledinaz
Costume Design

Peter Kaczorowski
Lighting Design

Brian Ronan
Sound Design

Seymour Red Press
Music Coordinator

Rob Berman
Music Director/
Conductor

Paul Huntley
Wig Design

The Pajama Game

Marc Bruni
Associate Director

Jim Carnahan
Casting

Jeffrey Richards
Associate Producer

James Fuld, Jr.
Associate Producer

Gene Feist
Founding Director, Roundabout Theatre Company

Todd Haimes
Artistic Director, Roundabout Theatre Company

BOX OFFICE
(L-R):
Robert Morgan and Mead Margulies

Photos by Ben Strothmann

STAGE CREW
Front Row (L-R): Leslie C. Lyter, David John O'Brien, Stephen Gruse.
Second Row (L-R): Patty McKeever, Tammy Kopko, Susan Fallon, Jackie Freeman, Julie Hilimire, Victoria Grecki.
Third Row (L-R): Eddie Camacho, Bruce Harrow, Melissa Crawford, Thom Carlson, Brandon Claflin, Nellie LaPorte, Anne Ezell.
Fourth Row (L-R): Nelson Vaughn, Glenn Merwede, Chris Mattingly, Jeremy Lewit, Andrew Forste, Jill Anania.
Back Row (L-R): Mike Farfalla, Benjamin Barnes, Jefferson Rowland, Barb Bartel, Sean Haines, Dann Wojnar and Brian Maiuri.

The Pajama Game

ROUNDABOUT THEATRE COMPANY STAFF

ARTISTIC DIRECTOR .... **TODD HAIMES**
MANAGING DIRECTOR .... **HAROLD WOLPERT**
EXECUTIVE DIRECTOR .... **JULIA C. LEVY**
ASSOCIATE ARTISTIC DIRECTOR ... **SCOTT ELLIS**

ARTISTIC STAFF

DIRECTOR OF ARTISTIC DEVELOPMENT/ DIRECTOR OF CASTING .... **Jim Carnahan**
Artistic Consultant .... Robyn Goodman
Resident Director .... Michael Mayer
Associate Artists .... Scott Elliott, Doug Hughes, Bill Irwin, Joe Mantello
Consulting Dramaturg .... Jerry Patch
Artistic Assistant .... Jill Rafson
Casting Director .... Mele Nagler
Casting Associate .... Carrie Gardner
Casting Assistant .... Kate Schwabe
Casting Assistant .... Stephen Kopel
Artistic Intern .... Rachel Balik

---

EDUCATION STAFF

EDUCATION DIRECTOR ... **Margie Salvante-McCann**
Director of Instruction and Curriculum Development .... Renee Flemings
Education Program Associate .... Stacey L. Morris
Education Program Associate .... Carrie Soloman
Education Coordinator .... Jennifer DeBruin
Education Interns .... Allison Baucom, Molly Glenn
Education Dramaturg .... Ted Sod
Teaching Artists .... Phil Alexander, Tony Angelini, Cynthia Babak, Victor Barbella, Brigitte Barnett-Loftis, Caitlin Barton, Joe Basile, LaTonya Borsay, Bonnie Brady, Lori Brown-Niang, Michael Carnahan, Stella Cartaino, Joe Clancy, Melissa Denton, Joe Doran, Katie Down, Tony Freeman, Aaron Gass, Katie Gorum, Sheri Graubert, Adam Gwon, Susan Hamburger, Karla Hendrick, Lisa Renee Jordan, Alvin Keith, Rebecca Lord, Robin Mates, Erin McCready, Jordana Oberman, Andrew Ondrecjak, Laura Poe, Nicole Press, Jennifer Rathbone, Chris Rummel, Drew Sachs, Anna Saggese, Robert Signom, David Sinkus, Derek Straat, Vickie Tanner, Olivia Tsang, Jennifer Varbalow, Leese Walker, Eric Wallach, Diana Whitten, Gail Winar

---

ADMINISTRATIVE STAFF

GENERAL MANAGER .... **Sydney Beers**
Associate Managing Director .... Greg Backstrom
General Manager, Steinberg Center .... Rebecca Habel
General Counsel .... Nancy Hirschmann
Human Resources Manager .... Stephen Deutsch
MIS Director .... Jeff Goodman
Facilities Manager .... Abraham David
Manager of Corporate and Party Rentals ..... Jetaun Dobbs
Office Manager .... Scott Kelly
Assistant to the General Manager .... Maggie Cantrick
Management Associate .... Tania Camargo
MIS Assistant .... Micah Kraybill
Receptionists .... John Haynes, Elisa Papa, Allison Patrick, Monica Sidorchuk
Messenger .... Robert Weisser
Management Intern .... Michelle Bergmann

FINANCE STAFF

CONTROLLER .... **Susan Neiman**
Assistant Controller .... John LaBarbera
Accounts Payable Administrator .... Frank Surdi
Customer Service Coordinator .... Trina Cox
Business Office Associate .... David Solomon
Financial Associate .... Yonit Kafka
Business Intern .... Virginia Graham

DEVELOPMENT STAFF

DIRECTOR OF DEVELOPMENT ...... **Jeffory Lawson**
Director, Institutional Giving .... Julie K. D'Andrea
Director, Individual Giving .... Julia Lazarus
Director, Special Events .... Steve Schaeffer
Manager, Donor Information Systems .... Tina Mae Bishko
Capital Campaign Manager .... Mark Truscinski
Manager, Friends of Roundabout .... Jeff Collins
External Affairs Associate .... Robert Weinstein
Patrons Services Liaison .... Dawn Kusinski
Development Assistant .... Chelsea Glickfield
Individual Giving Assistant .... Dominic Yacobozzi
Special Events Assistant .... Ginger Vallen
Development Assistant .... Elissa Sussman
Special Events Intern .... Casey Cipriani
Development Intern .... Trey Gilpin

MARKETING STAFF

DIRECTOR OF MARKETING .... **David B. Steffen**
Marketing/ Publications Manager .... Margaret Casagrande
Assistant Marketing Director .... Sunil Ayyagari
Marketing Assistant .... Stefanie Schussel
Website Consultant .... Keith Powell Beyland
DIRECTOR OF TELESALES SPECIAL PROMOTIONS .... **Daniel Weiss**
Telesales Manager .... Anton Borissov
Telesales Office Coordinator .... J.W. Griffin
Marketing Intern .... Carla Borras

---

TICKET SERVICES STAFF

DIRECTOR OF SALES OPERATIONS .... **Jim Seggelink**
Ticket Services Manager .... Ellen Holt
Subscription Manager .... Charlie Garbowski, Jr.
Box Office Managers .... Edward P. Osborne, Jaime Perlman, Jessica Bowser
Group Sales Manager .... Jeff Monteith
Assistant Box Office Managers .... Paul Caspary, Steve Howe, Robert Morgan
Assistant Ticket Services Managers .... Robert Kane, David Meglino, Ethan Ubell
Assistant Director of Sales Operations .... Nancy Mulliner
Ticket Services .... Solangel Bido, Jessie Blum, Jacob Burstein-Stan, William Campbell, David Carson, Lauren Cartelli, Andrew Clements, Johanna Comanzo, Nisha Dhruna, Adam Elsberry, Scott Falkowski, John Finning, Catherine Fitzpatrick, Katrina Foy, Tova Heller, Dottie Kenul, Alexander LaFrance, Krystin MacRitchie, Mead Margulies, Chuck Migliaccio, Carlos Morris, Nicole Nicholson, Adam Owens, Thomas Protulipac, Jackie Rocha, Heather Siebert, Monté Smock, Lillian Soto, Greg Thorson, Pam Unger, Tiffany Wakely
Ticket Services Interns .... Rachel Bauder, Elisa Mala

---

SERVICES

Counsel .... Jeremy Nussbaum, Cowan, Liebowitz & Latman, P.C.
Counsel .... Rosenberg & Estis
Counsel .... Rubin and Feldman, P.C.
Counsel .... Andrew Lance, Gibson, Dunn, & Crutcher, LLP
Counsel .... Harry H. Weintraub, Glick and Weintraub, P.C.
Immigration Counsel .... Mark D. Koestler and Theodore Ruthizer
House Physicians .... Dr. Theodore Tyberg, Dr. Lawrence Katz
House Dentist .... Neil Kanner, D.M.D.
Insurance .... DeWitt Stern Group, Inc.
Accountant .... Brody, Weiss, Zucarelli & Urbanek CPAs, P.C.
Advertising .... Eliran Murphy Group/ Denise Ganjou, Katie Koch
Events Photography .... Anita and Steve Shevett
Production Photographer .... Joan Marcus
Theatre Displays .... King Displays, Wayne Sapper

MANAGING DIRECTOR EMERITUS .... ELLEN RICHARD

Roundabout Theatre Company
231 West 39th Street, New York, NY 10018
(212) 719-9393.

GENERAL PRESS REPRESENTATIVES
BONEAU / BRYAN-BROWN
Adrian Bryan-Brown　Matt Polk
Jessica Johnson　Shanna Marcus

CREDITS FOR *THE PAJAMA GAME*

GENERAL MANAGER .... Sydney Beers
Company Manager .... Denys Baker
Production Stage Manager .... David John O'Brien
Assistant Stage Managers .... Stephen R. Gruse, Leslie C. Lyter
Assistant to the Director .... Jenny Hogan
Dance Captain .... David Eggers
Assistant Technical Supervisor .... Elisa Kuhar
Associate Set Designer .... Shoko Kambara
Assistant Costume Designer .... Martin Lopez
Associate Lighting Designer .... Karen Spahn
Assistant Lighting Designer .... Jen Schriever
Assistant Sound Designer .... Mike Creason
Make-Up Design .... Angelina Avallone
Production Carpenter .... Glenn Merwede
Production Electrician .... Brian Maiuri
House Properties .... Andrew Forste
Wardrobe Supervisor .... Susan J. Fallon
House Sound Engineer .... Dann Wojnar
Hair and Wig Supervisor .... Manuela LaPorte
Production Properties .... Al Steiner
Production Sound Engineer .... Mike Farfalla
Deck Electrician .... Barb Bartel
Moving Light Programmer .... Josh Weitzman
Follow Spot Operators .... Benjamin Barnes, David Sean Haines, Jeff Rowland
Automation Operator .... Paul Ashton
Flyman .... Jeremy Lewit

The Pajama Game

Deck Stagehand .... Chris Mattingly
Properties .... Nelson Vaughn
Local One IATSE Apprentice .... Jill Anania
Dressers .... Thom Carlson, Jackie Freeman, Vicki Grecki, Bruce Harrow, Julie Hilimire, Tammy Kopko, Patty McKeever
Day Workers .... Elizabeth Barton, Melissa Crawford
Hair and Wig Assistant .... Brandon Scott Claflin
Assistant to Mr. Connick, Jr. .... Stephanie Conway
Hairstylist for Mr. Connick, Jr. .... Martial Corneville
Company Management Assistant .... Sherra Johnston
Costume Assistant to Mr. Pakledinaz ... Courtney McClain
Costume Intern .... Jessica Lustig
Assistant to Martin Pakledinaz .... Wendy Hill
Copyist .... Anixter Rice Music Service
Production Assistant .... Gregory T. Livoti
SDCF Observer .... Wendy Seyb
Company Orthopedist .... Dr. Phillip Bauman
Company Physical Therapist .... Physio Arts
Scenery Fabricated, Painted and Automated by ...... Hudson Scenic Studio
Properties Fabricated by .... Birch Street Design, Cigar Box Studios, Factory at 54
Lighting Equipment by . PRG, Production Resource Group
Sound Equipment Provided by .... Sound Associates
Mr. Connick Jr.'s Costumes Executed by .... Barbara Matera Ltd.
Costumes Executed by .... Carelli Costumes Inc.; Eric Winterling, Inc.; Marc Happel; Paul Chang Custom Tailors; Studio Rouge; Timberlake Studios, Inc.
Screen Printing & Fabric Dyeing by ... Gene Mignola, Inc.
Shoes by .... Celebrity Ballroom Dance Shoes, J.C. Theatrical & Custom Footwear Inc., LaDuca Shoes, T.O. Dey Shoes, WorldTone
Embroidery by .... Vogue Too
Custom Knitwear by .... C.C. Wei
Assorted Millinery by .... Arnold Levine and Arnold Hatters, Inc.
Vintage Eyewear by .... Fabulous Fanny's
Transportation Provided by .... John Walker
Onstage Merchandising .... George Fenmore/ More Merchandising International
Merchandising .... Max Merchandising, LLC/ Randi Grossman

SPECIAL THANKS

Special thanks to Altenburg Piano House, Anheuser-Busch Companies, Bra*Tenders, Channel Manufacturing Inc., Diamond Brands Inc., Nestle Confections and Snacks, Emeco: The Aluminum Chair Co., Lakeside Manufacturing Inc., N.G. Slater Corp., The Homer Laughlin China Co., Spalding Division, Russell Corp., United Thread Mills Corp., Westbridge PET Containers and Zippo Manufacturing Co., Keen Gat.

Stock and amateur rights for *The Pajama Game* are available through Music Theatre International, New York, NY. www.mtishows.com

AMERICAN AIRLINES THEATRE STAFF

General Manager .... Sydney Beers
House Carpenter .... Glenn Merwede
House Electrician .... Brian Maiuri
Wardrobe Supervisor .... Susan J. Fallon
Box Office Manager .... Edward P. Osborne
House Manager .... Stephen Ryan
Associate House Manager .... Zipporah Aguasvivas
Head Usher .... Edwin Camacho
House Staff .... Peter Breaden, Oscar Castillo, Ilia Diaz, Anne Ezell, Vince Allen Rawles, Jacklyn Rivera, Tiesha Rivera
Security .... Julious Russell
Additional Security Provided by .... Gotham Security
Maintenance .... Chucke Fernandez, Ron Henry, Kenrick Johnson, Maggie Western
Lobby Refreshments .... Sweet Concessions

Kelli O'Hara and Harry Connick, Jr. sing "There Once Was a Man."

Photo by Joan Marcus

The Phantom of the Opera

First Preview: January 9, 1988. Opened: January 26, 1988.
Still running as of May 31, 2007.

PLAYBILL®

CAST

The Phantom of the Opera ... HOWARD McGILLIN
Christine Daaé ... REBECCA PITCHER
Christine Daaé (at certain performances) ... JENNIFER HOPE WILLS
Raoul, Vicomte de Chagny ... MICHAEL SHAWN LEWIS
Carlotta Giudicelli ... PATRICIA PHILLIPS
Monsieur André ... GEORGE LEE ANDREWS
Monsieur Firmin ... DAVID CRYER
Madame Giry ... MARILYN CASKEY
Ubaldo Piangi ... ROLAND RUSINEK
Meg Giry ... HEATHER McFADDEN
Monsieur Reyer/Hairdresser (*Il Muto*) ... PETER LOCKYER
Auctioneer ... CARRINGTON VILMONT
Jeweler (*Il Muto*) ... FRANK MASTRONE
Monsieur Lefèvre/Firechief ... KENNETH KANTOR
Joseph Buquet ... RICHARD POOLE
Don Attilio (*Il Muto*) ... GREGORY EMANUEL RAHMING
Passarino (*Don Juan Triumphant*) ... CARRINGTON VILMONT
Slave Master (*Hannibal*)/Solo Dancer (*Il Muto*) ... DANIEL RYCHLEC
Flunky/Stage Hand ... HARLAN BENGEL
Page (*Don Juan Triumphant*) ... KRIS KOOP
Porter/Fireman ... JIMMY SMAGULA
Spanish Lady (*Don Juan Triumphant*) ... SALLY WILLIAMS
Wardrobe Mistress/Confidante (*Il Muto*) ... TREGONEY SHEPHERD
Princess (*Hannibal*) ... SUSAN OWEN

MAJESTIC THEATRE
247 West 44th Street
A Shubert Organization Theatre
Gerald Schoenfeld, *Chairman* **Philip J. Smith,** *President*
Robert E. Wankel, *Executive Vice President*

CAMERON MACKINTOSH and
THE REALLY USEFUL THEATRE COMPANY, INC.
present

The
PHANTOM
of the
OPERA™

starring
HOWARD McGILLIN
REBECCA PITCHER
MICHAEL SHAWN LEWIS

GEORGE LEE ANDREWS DAVID CRYER PATRICIA PHILLIPS
MARILYN CASKEY ROLAND RUSINEK HEATHER McFADDEN

At certain performances
JENNIFER HOPE WILLS
plays the role of "Christine"

Music by
ANDREW LLOYD WEBBER
Lyrics by CHARLES HART
Additional lyrics by RICHARD STILGOE
Book by RICHARD STILGOE & ANDREW LLOYD WEBBER
Based on the novel 'Le Fantôme de L'Opéra' by GASTON LEROUX
Production Design by MARIA BJÖRNSON Lighting by ANDREW BRIDGE
Sound by MARTIN LEVAN Musical Supervision & Direction DAVID CADDICK
Musical Director DAVID LAI Production Supervisor PETER von MAYRHAUSER
Orchestrations by DAVID CULLEN & ANDREW LLOYD WEBBER
Casting by TARA RUBIN CASTING Original Casting by JOHNSON-LIFF ASSOCIATES
General Management ALAN WASSER
Musical Staging & Choreography by GILLIAN LYNNE
Directed by HAROLD PRINCE

10/2/06

Madame Firmin ... MELODY RUBIE
Innkeeper's Wife (*Don Juan Triumphant*) ... WREN MARIE HARRINGTON
Marksman ... STEPHEN R. BUNTROCK
The Ballet Chorus of the Opéra Populaire ... EMILY ADONNA, KARA KLEIN, GIANNA LOUNGWAY, MABEL MODRONO, JESSICA RADETSKY, CARLY BLAKE SEBOUHIAN, DIANNA WARREN
Ballet Swing ... HARRIET CLARK
Swings ... SCOTT MIKITA, JAMES ROMICK, JANET SAIA

Continued on next page

Photo by Joan Marcus

Howard McGillin as The Phantom with Jennifer Hope Wills as Christine.

The Phantom of the Opera

SCENES & MUSICAL NUMBERS

PROLOGUE

The stage of the Paris Opéra House, 1911

OVERTURE

ACT ONE—PARIS 1881

Scene 1—The dress rehearsal of *Hannibal*
"Think of Me" .... Carlotta, Christine, Raoul
Scene 2—After the Gala
"Angel of Music" .... Christine and Meg
Scene 3—Christine's dressing room
"Little Lotte/The Mirror" (Angel of Music) .... Raoul, Christine, Phantom
Scene 4—The Labyrinth underground
"The Phantom of the Opera" .... Phantom and Christine
Scene 5—Beyond the lake
"The Music of the Night" .... Phantom
Scene 6—Beyond the lake, the next morning
"I Remember/Stranger Than You Dreamt It" .... Christine and Phantom
Scene 7—Backstage
"Magical Lasso" .... Buquet, Meg, Madame Giry and Ballet Girls
Scene 8—The Managers' office
"Notes/Prima Donna" .... Firmin, André, Raoul, Carlotta, Giry, Meg, Piangi and Phantom
Scene 9—A performance of *Il Muto*
"Poor Fool, He Makes Me Laugh" .... Carlotta and Company
Scene 10—The roof of the Opéra House
"Why Have You Brought Me Here/Raoul, I've Been There" .... Raoul and Christine
"All I Ask of You" .... Raoul and Christine
"All I Ask of You" (Reprise) .... Phantom

ENTR'ACTE

ACT TWO—SIX MONTHS LATER

Scene 1—The staircase of the Opéra House, New Year's Eve
"Masquerade/Why So Silent" .... Full Company
Scene 2—Backstage
Scene 3—The Managers' office
"Notes/Twisted Every Way" ... André, Firmin, Carlotta, Piangi, Raoul, Christine, Giry and Phantom
Scene 4—A rehearsal for *Don Juan Triumphant*
Scene 5—A graveyard in Peros
"Wishing You Were Somehow Here Again" .... Christine
"Wandering Child/Bravo, Bravo" .... Phantom, Christine and Raoul
Scene 6—The Opéra House stage before the Premiere
Scene 7—*Don Juan Triumphant*
"The Point of No Return" .... Phantom and Christine
Scene 8—The Labyrinth underground
"Down Once More/Track Down This Murderer" .... Full Company
Scene 9—Beyond the lake

Cast Continued

UNDERSTUDIES

For the Phantom: STEPHEN R. BUNTROCK, PETER LOCKYER, JAMES ROMICK
For Christine: KRIS KOOP, SUSAN OWEN
For Raoul: STEPHEN R. BUNTROCK, PETER LOCKYER, JAMES ROMICK, CARRINGTON VILMONT
For Firmin: KENNETH KANTOR, GREGORY EMANUEL RAHMING, JAMES ROMICK
For André: PETER LOCKYER, SCOTT MIKITA, RICHARD POOLE, JAMES ROMICK
For Carlotta: WREN MARIE HARRINGTON, KRIS KOOP, MELODY RUBIE, JANET SAIA
For Mme. Giry: KRIS KOOP, JANET SAIA, SALLY WILLIAMS
For Piangi: PETER LOCKYER, JOHN WASINIAK, JIMMY SMAGULA
For Meg Giry: POLLY BAIRD, KARA KLEIN, CARLY BLAKE SEBOUHIAN
For Slavemaster: HARLAN BENGEL
For Solo Dancer (*Il Muto*): HARLAN BENGEL
Dance Captain: HARRIET CLARK
Assistant Dance Captain: HEATHER McFADDEN

ORCHESTRA

Conductors: DAVID CADDICK, KRISTEN BLODGETTE, DAVID LAI, TIM STELLA, NORMAN WEISS
Violins: JOYCE HAMMANN (Concert Master), JAN MULLEN, ALVIN E. ROGERS, GAYLE DIXON, KURT COBLE, KAREN MILNE
Violas: STEPHANIE FRICKER, VERONICA SALAS
Cellos: TED ACKERMAN, KARL BENNION
Bass: MELISSA SLOCUM
Harp: HENRY FANELLI
Flute: SHERYL HENZE
Flute/Clarinet: ED MATTHEW
Oboe: MELANIE FELD
Clarinet: MATTHEW GOODMAN
Bassoon: ATSUKO SATO
Trumpets: LOWELL HERSHEY, FRANCIS BONNY
Bass Trombone: WILLIAM WHITAKER
French Horns: DANIEL CULPEPPER, DAVID SMITH, PETER REIT
Percussion: ERIC COHEN, JAN HAGIWARA
Keyboards: TIM STELLA, NORMAN WEISS

The Phantom of the Opera

Howard McGillin
The Phantom of the Opera

Rebecca Pitcher
Christine Daaé

Michael Shawn Lewis
Raoul, Vicomte de Chagny

George Lee Andrews
Monsieur André

David Cryer
Monsieur Firmin

Patricia Phillips
Carlotta Giudicelli

Marilyn Caskey
Madame Giry

Roland Rusinek
Ubaldo Piangi

Heather McFadden
Meg Giry

Jennifer Hope Wills
Christine Daaé at certain performances

Emily Adonna
Ballet Chorus

Harlan Bengel
Flunky/Stagehand

Stephen R. Buntrock
Marksman

Harriet Clark
Dance Captain/ Swing

Wren Marie Harrington
Innkeeper's Wife

Kenneth Kantor
Monsieur Lefèvre/ Firechief

Kris Koop
Page

Peter Lockyer
Jeweler

Gianna Loungway
Ballet Chorus

Scott Mikita
Swing

Mabel Modrono
Ballet Chorus

Susan Owen
Princess

Richard Poole
Monsieur Reyer/ Hairdresser

Jessica Radetsky
Ballet Chorus

Gregory Emanuel Rahming
Don Attilio

James Romick
Swing

Melody Rubie
Madame Firmin

Daniel Rychlec
Slave Master/ Solo Dancer

Janet Saia
Swing

Carly Blake Sebouhian
Ballet Chorus

Tregoney Shepherd
Wardrobe Mistress/ Confidante

Jimmy Smagula
Porter/Fireman

Carrington Vilmont
Auctioneer/ Passarino

Dianna Warren
Ballet Chorus

Sally Williams
Spanish Lady

The Phantom of the Opera

Andrew Lloyd Webber
Composer/Book/ Co-Orchestrator

Harold Prince
Director

Charles Hart
Lyrics

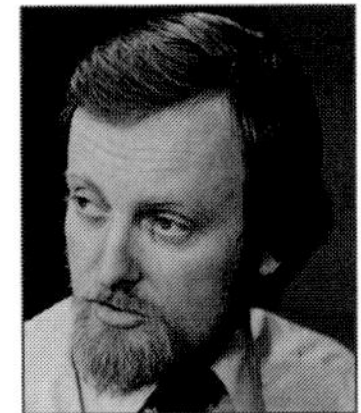
Richard Stilgoe
Book and Additional Lyrics

Gillian Lynne
Musical Staging and Choreography

Maria Björnson (1949-2002)
Production Design

Andrew Bridge
Lighting Designer

Martin Levan
Sound Designer

David Caddick
Musical Supervision and Direction

Kristen Blodgette
Associate Musical Supervisor

David Cullen
Co-Orchestrator

Ruth Mitchell (1919-2000)
Assistant to Mr. Prince

Denny Berry
Production Dance Supervisor

Craig Jacobs
Production Stage Manager

Bethe Ward
Stage Manager

David Lai
Musical Director

Peter von Mayrhauser
Production Supervisor

Vincent Liff and Geoffrey Johnson, Johnson-Liff Associates
Original Casting

Tara Rubin Casting
Casting

Alan Wasser Associates
General Manager

Cameron Mackintosh
Producer

Dara Adler
The Ballet Chorus of the Opéra Populaire

Julianne Cavendish
The Ballet Chorus of the Opéra Populaire

Julie Hanson
Christine Daaé

Jack Hayes
Flunky, Stage Hand, Slave Master ("Hannibal"), Solo Dancer ("Il Muto")

Michael McCoy
Joseph Buquet

Richard Warren Pugh
Joseph Buquet

Fred Rose
Jeweler ("Il Muto")

Julie Schmidt
Carlotta Giudicelli, Madame Firmin, Swing

Mary Leigh Stahl
Wardrobe Mistress, Confidante ("Il Muto")

Stephen Tewksbury
Joseph Buquet

The Phantom of the Opera

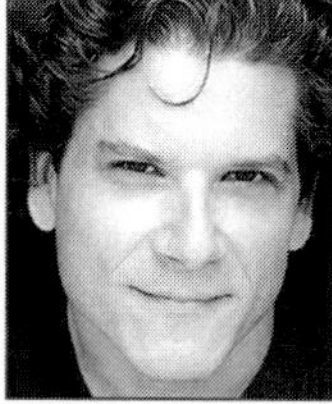
Michael Babin
Marksman, Swing

Katie Banks
Wardrobe Mistress, Confidante ("Il Muto")

Kyle DesChamps
Slave Master ("Hannibal")

Sara Jean Ford
Christine Daaé

Julie Hanson
Christine Daaé

Jack Hayes
Flunky, Stage Hand, Solo Dancer ("Il Muto")

Gary Mauer
The Phantom of the Opera

Jason Mills
Auctioneer, Passarino ("Don Juan Triumphant")

Justin Peck
Flunky, Stage Hand, Slave Master ("Hannibal"), Solo Dancer ("Il Muto")

Corbin Popp
Flunky, Stage Hand, Solo Dancer ("Il Muto"), Slave Master ("Hannibal")

Anne Runolfsson
Carlotta Giudicelli

Daniel Rychlec
Slave Master ("Hannibal")

Paul A. Schaefer
Marksman

Julie Schmidt
Carlotta Giudicelli, Princess ("Hannibal"), Spanish Lady (Don Juan Triumphant"), Wardrobe Mistress, Confidante ("Il Muto"), Swing

Jim Weitzer
Swing

Photo by Ben Strothmann

FRONT OF HOUSE STAFF

Front Row (L-R):
Denise Reich, Ron Raz, Peter Kulok, Dorothy Curich, Lucia Cappelletti.

Middle Row (L-R):
Miriam Silver, Devin Harjes, Perry Dell'Aquila, Joan Thorn, James Muro, Grace Price, Angelique James, Shellee Williams, Vereita Austin, Vanessa Edenfield, Sylvia Bailey, Cynthia Carlin.

Back Row (L-R):
Alexi Melvin, Amy Prokop, Anthony Stavick, Brian Zupanick, Emilio Benoit, Luciana Lenihan, Rodney Duncan, Danielle Bararducci and Maria Rodriguez.

The Phantom of the Opera

Photos by Ben Strothmann

STAGEHANDS AND STAGE MANAGERS
Front Row Seated (L-R):
Karen Parlato, Giancarlo Cottignoli, Ed Griffenkranz, Alan Lampel, Craig Evans.

Middle Row Kneeling (L-R):
Bill Kazdan, Brendan Smith, Brian Westmoreland, Brian Colonna, Daniel Dashman, Fred Smith.

Back Row Standing (L-R):
Matt Maloney, Matt Mezick, John Hulbert, Michael Eisenberg, Rob Wallace, Jack Farmer, Frank Dwyer.

WARDROBE, HAIR AND MAKE-UP
Front Row (L-R):
Mary Lou Rios, Anna McDaniel, Margie Marchionni.

Middle Row (L-R):
Ron Blakely, Thelma Pollard, Erika Smith, Pearleta Price.

Back Row (L-R):
Andrew Nelson, Bob Miller, Michael Jacobs, Bill Hubner.

ORCHESTRA
First Row (L-R):
Matt Goodman, David Lai, Stephanie Baer, Kathy Kienke, Karl Bennion, Patrissa Tomassini.

Second Row (L-R):
Gayle Dixon, Henry Fanelli, Sandra Billingslea, Karen Milne, Jan Mullen, Joyce Hammann, Alvin Rogers.

Third Row (L-R):
Bill Whitaker, Lorraine Cohen, Melanie Feld, Lowell Hershey, Ako Sato, Eddie Malave, Roger Mahadeen.

Fourth Row (L-R):
Sheryl Henze, Melissa Slocum, Ed Matthew, Norman Weiss.

STAFF FOR *THE PHANTOM OF THE OPERA*

General Manager
ALAN WASSER

General Press Representative
THE PUBLICITY OFFICE
Marc Thibodeau Bob Fennell
Michael S. Borowski Candi Adams

Assistant to Mr. Prince
RUTH MITCHELL

Production Supervisor
PETER von MAYRHAUSER

Production Dance Supervisor
DENNY BERRY

Associate Musical Supervisor
KRISTEN BLODGETTE

ASSOCIATE GENERAL MANAGER .... ALLAN WILLIAMS
TECHNICAL PRODUCTION MANAGERS ...... JOHN H. PAULL III, JAKE BELL
COMPANY MANAGER .... ROBERT NOLAN
PRODUCTION STAGE MANAGER .... CRAIG JACOBS

The Phantom of the Opera

Stage Managers .... Bethe Ward, Brendan Smith

U.S. Design Staff

ASSOCIATE SCENIC DESIGNER .... DANA KENN
ASSOCIATE COSTUME DESIGNER .... SAM FLEMING
ASSOCIATE LIGHTING DESIGNER .... DEBRA DUMAS
ASSISTANT SOUND DESIGNER ...... JON WESTON
Assistants to the Scenic Designer .... Paul Kelly, Paul Weimer, Steven Saklad
Assistants to the Costume Designer ...... David Robinson, Marcy Froehlich
Assistant to the Lighting Designer .... Vivien Leone
Assistants to the Sound Designer .... James M. Bay, Joan Curcio

U.K. Design Staff

PRODUCTION TECHNICAL CONSULTANT .... MARTYN HAYES ASSOCIATES
ASSOCIATE SCENIC DESIGNER .... JONATHAN ALLEN
ASSOCIATE COSTUME DESIGNER .... SUE WILLMINGTON
ASSOCIATE LIGHTING DESIGNER .... HOWARD EATON
Automation Consultant .... Michael Barnet
Draperies Consultant .... Peter Everett
Sculptures Consultant .... Stephen Pyle
Sound Consultant .... Ralph Colhns

ASSISTANT TO GILLIAN LYNNE .... NAOMI SORKIN
Associate Manager .... Thom Mitchell
Associate Company Manager .... Chris D'Angelo
Casting Associate .... Ron LaRosa
Dance Captain .... Harriet Clark
Production Carpenter .... Joseph Patria
Production Electrician .... Robert Fehribach
Production Propertyman .... Timothy Abel
Production Sound Operator .... Steve Kennedy
Production Wig Supervisor .... Leone Gagliardi
Production Make-up Supervisor .... Thelma Pollard
Make-up Assistants .... Pearleta N. Price, Shazia J. Saleem
Head Carpenter .... Russell Tiberio III
Automation Carpenters .... Santos Sanchez, Michael Girman
Assistant Carpenter .... Giancarlo Cottignoli
Flyman .... Daryl Miller
Head Electrician .... Alan Lampel
Assistant Electrician .... Joe Golz
Head Props .... Matthew Mezick
Asst. Props./Boat Captain .... Joe Caruso
Sound Operators .... Charlie Grieco, Jason McKenna, Jason Strangfeld
Wardrobe Supervisor .... Scott Westervelt
Assistant Wardrobe Supervisor .... Robert Strong Miller
Hair Supervisor .... Leone Gagliardi
Hairdressers .... Charise Champion, Lisa Harrell, Anna Hoffman, Kelly Reed
Production Costume Design Assistant .. Cynthia Hamilton
Production Sound Design Assistant .... Larry Spurgeon

Associate Conductor .... Tim Stella
Assistant Conductor .... Norman Weiss
Musical Preparation Supervisor (U.S.) .... Chelsea Music Service, Inc
Synthesizer Consultant .... Brett Sommer Music Technologies Inc.

Assistants to the Gen. Mgr. .... Jenny Bates, Christopher Betz, Jason Hewitt, Temah Higgins, Jake Hirzel, Bill Miller, Jennifer Mudge, Steven Schnepp
Lighting Intern .... Wendy Bodzin

Legal Counsel .... S. Jean Ward, Frankfurt Garbus Kurnit Klein & Selz, P.C.
Legal Advisor to The Really Useful Company .... Brooks & Distler, Marsha Brooks
Accounting .... Rosenberg, Neuwirth and Kutchner/ Christopher A. Cacace
Logo Design and Graphics .... Dewynters Plc London
Merchandising .... Dewynters Advertising Inc.
Advertising .... Serino Coyne Inc./ Greg Corradetti, Andrea Prince, Natalie Serota
Marketing/Promotions ..... Hugh Hysell Communications/ Hugh Hysell, Michael Redman, Matt Sicoli
Press Intern .... Matthew Fasano
Displays .... King Displays, Wayne Sapper
Insurance (U.S.) .... DeWitt Stern Group/ Peter K. Shoemaker
Insurance (U.K.) .... Walton & Parkinson Limited/ Richard Walton
Banking .... Commerce Bank/Barbara von Borstel
Customs Broker (U.S.) .... T.L. Customs House Brokers, Inc.
Customs Broker (U.K.) .... Theatours, Ltd.
Payroll Service .... Castellana Services, Inc.

Original Production Photographer .... Clive Barda
Additional Photography .... Joan Marcus Bob Marshak, Peter Cunningham
House Manager .... Peter Kulok

Special thanks to
MCNABB & ASSOCIATES
Jim McNabb

CREDITS AND ACKNOWLEDGMENTS

Scenic construction and boat automation by Hudson Scenic Studios. Scenery automation by Jeremiah J. Harris Associates, Inc./East Coast Theatre Supply, Inc. Scenery painted by Nolan Scenery Studios. Set and hand properties by McHugh Rollins Associates, Inc. Sculptural elements by Costume Armour. "Opera Ball" newell post statues and elephant by Nino Novellino of Costume Armour. Proscenium sculptures by Stephen Pyle. Draperies by I. Weiss and Sons, Inc. Soft goods provided by Quartet Theatrical Draperies. Safety systems by Foy Lighting equipment and special lighting effects by Four Star Lighting, Inc. Sound equipment and technical service provided by Masque Sound and Recording Corp. Special effects designed and executed by Theatre Magic, Inc., Richard Huggins, President. Costumes executed by Barbara Matera, Ltd. Costumes for "Hannibal" and "Masquerade" executed by Parsons/Meares, Ltd. Men's costumes by Vincent Costumes, Inc. Costume crafts for "Hannibal" and "Masquerade" by Janet Harper and Frederick Nihda. Fabric painting by Mary Macy. Additional costumes by Carelli Costumes, Inc. Costume accessories by Barak Stribling. Hats by Woody Shelp. Millinery and masks by Rodney Gordon. Footwear by Sharlot Battin of Montana Leatherworks, Ltd. Shoes by JC Theatrical and Costume Footwear and Taffy's N.Y. Jewelry by Miriam Haskell Jewels. Eyeglasses by H.L. Purdy. Wigs by The Wig Party. Garcia Vega cigars used. Make-Up consultant Kris Evans. Emer'gen-C super energy booster provided by Alacer Corp.

Champagne courtesy of
Champagne G.H. Mumm

Furs by Christie Bros.

Shoes supplied by Peter Fox Limlted

"The Phantom" character make-up created and designed by Christopher Tucker

Magic Consultant—Paul Daniels

CAMERON MACKINTOSH, INC.

Joint Managing Directors .... Nicholas Allott & Matthew Dalco
Production Associate .... Shidan Majidi

---

THE REALLY USEFUL COMPANY INC

Public Relations .... BROWN LLOYD JAMES/ PETER BROWN

THE REALLY USEFUL GROUP LIMITED

Directors .... THE LORD LLOYD-WEBBER, WILLIAM TAYLOR, JONATHAN HULL, JONATHAN WHEELDON

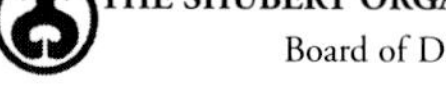

THE SHUBERT ORGANIZATION, INC.
Board of Directors

Gerald Schoenfeld
Chairman

Philip J. Smith
President

Wyche Fowler, Jr.

John W. Kluge

Lee J. Seidler

Michael I. Sovern

Stuart Subotnick

Robert E. Wankel
Executive Vice President

Peter Entin
Vice President
Theatre Operations

Elliot Greene
Vice President
Finance

David Andrews
Vice President
Shubert Ticketing Services

John Darby
Vice President
Facilities

D.S. Moynihan
Vice President – Creative Projects

The Phantom of the Opera

Scrapbook

Correspondents: Kris Koop Ouellette, Ensemble and Understudy for "Christine," "Carlotta" and "Madame Giry." Backstage photos by Antoinette Martinez.

Who Has Done the Most Shows: George Lee Andrews has been submitted to the "Guinness Book of World Records" for consideration as the actor who has played the most performances in the same Broadway show, ever! George, an original company member, has worked his way from role to role for all 19 years of *Phantom*'s record-breaking run on Broadway.

We must also mention Mary Leigh Stahl, original cast member, who retired from her position in the ensemble of *Phantom* this past year. We will never be able to recapture her class or her sass. We love you Mary Leigh!

"Easter Bonnet" Sketch: "The Longest Running Actor on Broadway," starring George Lee Andrews.

Special Backstage Rituals: 1: New to the cast, Jennifer Hope Wills (Christine) enjoys learning yoga stretches from our long-running Raoul, Michael Shawn Lewis, followed by a healthy sip of hot tea, and an even healthier bite of dark chocolate. The stretching, the tea and the chocolate combine to make a magical performance on stage.

2: There is also a ritual "Spanking of the Raoul and the Raoul Dresser" performed by various members of the female ensemble following the sitzprobe scene. This has grown into quite a production and is sometimes lightly choreographed. Every Raoul Understudy is taught this ritual while trailing for the first time, as we've come to consider it as part of his actual backstage blocking. Most are fearful at first, but then they learn to love it!

3: Craig Jacobs, Stage Manager, performs the ritual of taking any vacation request and ceremoniously placing it in the garbage can at the very moment it is received. Whether CJ trashes our requests with a smirk or a glowering stare of (feigned) contempt behind his eyeglasses, we all still manage to get some well-deserved time off.

4: Each Halloween season, we not only host Trick or Treat for all of the kiddies associated with the company, but we also produce an eerily-themed wall of photographs. Dan Rychlec, Slave Master, creates the theme and everyone in the cast, crew, orchestra and front-of-house is welcome to participate. This past Halloween, Lisa Brownstein of the Wardrobe Department took top honors, posing as a zombie seated before her television, playing a video game while simultaneously eating her own intestines. That's entertainment!

5: George Lee Andrews celebrates his Birthday each year with a jog throughout the theatre, making sure to greet everyone in the building as he goes along. This past year, his entire family followed along to cheer him on.

Favorite Moment During Each Performance: It appears that quite a few of us have selected the same moment…when we all gather on the "Masquerade" staircase facing upstage, and slowly, dramatically turn around and sing the final verse. As stated by Jennifer Hope Wills, "I really feel the excitement of being on Broadway" at that moment.

Favorite In-Theatre Gathering Place: Without question, the Stage Managers' Office, which is the size of your average public restroom stall (but smells much better…usually). The office temperature is kept well below freezing 365 days of the year, and it is often referred to as the "Meat Locker" because of that fact. Some believe that the temperature is kept so low there to give actors some relief in their heavy wool costumes, while others are convinced it's to preserve the candy supply.

Favorite Off-Site Hangout: Though too teeny in which to actually do much hanging out, we spend an extraordinary amount of time at Amy's Bread on Ninth Avenue. We swear that we go there because of the delicious coffee, but it's really more about their amazing cakes…AND scrumptious cookies...Oh, Dear Lord, and the bread. YUMMY! It's risky to haunt this place as frequently as we do, because no opera is ever really over until the FAT LADY sings…and if we don't stick to just the coffee, there's going to be a whole bunch of fat (and happy) ladies singing!

"Carols for a Cure" Carol: "Have Yourself a Merry Little Christmas."

Favorite Snack Food: One of our most delicious treats is homemade shortbread, delivered in person by Helen and Charlie, two faithful members of the Phantom family and leaders of the James Romick Fan Club.

We also had a brief fascination with Utz's Cheese Balls. Dick Miller had a giant container of these treats in his office, and a contest developed between cast members to see how many of the

Photos by Antoinette Martinez

1. Original cast member George Lee Andrews gets into an appropriately gothic mood in front of the stage-right call board at the Majestic Theatre at the "places" call for the top of the show

2. Gregory Rahming, in costume as the Old Man in the "Il Muto" scene, takes a break in the carpenters' room.

The Phantom of the Opera

Scrapbook

Photos by Antoinette Martinez

1. In the stage-right quick-change area, Kara Klein (L) pretends to sleep while waiting to get into her "Il Muto" costume. Dan Rychlec (R) tries to get as close as possible without touching her.
2. Yearbook Correspondent Kris Koop Ouellette in the wig room, getting into costume as a Wild Woman in the "Hannibal" scene.

puffed cheese balls one could cram into one's mouth at one time. No chewing, no swallowing. Very sophisticated, really. Stephen R. Buntrock and Michael Shawn Lewis were both leaders of the pack, but we all had to quit the game because of the painful lacerations that the cheese balls would create inside our cheeks and on the roof of our mouths. Apparently, Utz Cheese Balls are meant to be savored singly, not stuffed into the mouth, up to 30-plus at a time.

Favorite Therapy: After giving this a lot of thought, I believe I speak for us all when I say that RETAIL THERAPY is our true favorite. We do love our clothes...our shoes...our computers and gadgets...our excursions to Home Depot and Staples alike. Oh, and the flat screen TV obsession has hit us hard. There's something about job security in the theatre...we ARE in the longest running show in Broadway history, and we still sell out at the Box Office all the time. AND we're doing our small part to boost the economy. (At least that's what I tell my husband... Hi Steve.)

Memorable Ad-Libs: The honors for Onstage Ad-Lib belong solely to Ken Kantor, in the role of retiring Theatre Manager, Monsieur LeFèvre. On three separate performances, Ken mis-delivered his retiring speech in spectacular form, and received no support from his tickled cast-mates. We all just made direct eye contact with him, giggling aloud, and watching this dear man squirm. A slow-motion play-by-play of one of the ad-libs goes a little something like this...(read everything in italics in a hushed whisper, like a commentator on a golf course):

Ken: "You all may have perhaps already met Monsieur Firmin and Monsieur André."

(Okay, let's pause right here, because that line has already been delivered earlier in the scene. A light of recognition, then confusion plays across Ken's eyes. He cocks his head to one side. We all freeze for an awkward moment and watch in bemused horror as he continues.)

"And you may also have heard of... the possibility...that I might be...considering [strangled pause] LEAVING."

(We notice a furrowed brow as Ken continues to fish for the lost words...imminent retirement. Not going to happen today. He continues...)

"Well...[stammering] THESE [???] were all TRUE!" *(At this point, Ken does a quick yet deep plie, or in the Yiddish, Ken 'plotzed'. And yet, he crashed through the rest of his misspoken speech in the key of GUSTO!)*

"And I now have the great pleasure to introduce you—AGAIN—to Monsieur Richard Firmin and Monsieur Gilles André, who now own the Opera Populaire."

(We all clapped so hard for the new managers, that Ken got a chance to catch his breath and get back on track...but this speech tortured him for another two performances after THAT!)

Backstage Ad-Lib honors go to Peter Lockyer, for the following:

"Scott, do you bend over and finish with your finger?"

(Alright, get your mind out of the gutter! The two were trying to determine the best way to quietly close a trap door on the travelator, as letting it slam had been startling the Phantom during one of his tirades. Geez Louise.)

Memorable Press Encounter: We must pay tribute to our dear, departed friend and press agent, Bob Fennell. He strode into every situation on those long, long legs, bringing with him a calm and ease—and a bone-dry sense of humor and great wit. We are heartbroken to have lost him so young, and we are all eternally grateful for his amazing contribution to *The Phantom of the Opera*'s overall success.

Fastest Costume Change: Christine still wins this one, with approximately thirty seconds to get out of her "Don Juan" dress and cape and into the wedding dress for the Final Lair scene. She must escape the boat the moment it is out of audience view, even though it's still moving. Christine whips her cape fasteners open, runs into the quick-change room Stage Left and lets the Wardrobe professionals do their thing. It is the job of one crew member to hold her long wig-hair out of the way while another unzips the first dress, then several hands steady her as she steps into the next dress, quickly zipped up by Erna Diaz, the one and only original Christine Dresser, who then fastens the giant bow that drapes the back of the dress. There's not even time for Christine to grab a sip of water or a peek in the mirror before she's back in the wing, being dragged onstage by the Phantom!

Catchphrases Only the Company Would Recognize: "Whoosh" (referring to a move in the curtain call, and now, following numerous revisions to the curtain call choreography, "Be careful what you whoosh for.")

"You can all be seen, and that's a compliment." (Peter von Mayrhauser to the ensemble at a rehearsal, originally. We all repeat the phrase any time somebody screws up, even a little bit.)

The Phantom of the Opera
Scrapbook

Photos by Antoinette Martinez

1. (L-R): Harriet Clark, Emily Adonna, and Mabel Modrono pose in their "Masquerade" costumes in their dressing room.
2. (L-R): Kristina Miller and Michael Shawn Lewis ("Raoul") in the carpenters' room. Lewis demonstrates the technique that won him the company's cheese ball eating contest.
3. (L-R): David Gaschen and Susan Owen get into character at the "places" call for the top of the show, stage right.

"Secure the goat!" Richard Poole as Monsieur Reyer as part of the post-*Hannibal* hubbub.

Memorable Directorial Quotes: 1). "Stephen, please keep your backstage voice small and unimportant, much like your performance." (Spoken jokingly by Craig Jacobs to Stephen R. Buntrock on Stage Right.)

2). "Patricia Phillips, you are the best 'frog' ever..." (Hal Prince, over the PA system backstage, mid-performance, referring to the Diva's divine "ribbit" in *Il Muto*.) What Patricia THOUGHT the 'Prince' said of her frog: "Patricia Phillips, you are the best BROAD ever..."

Embarrassing Moment: Jennifer Hope Wills' boob burst out of her bustier during the Hannibal Ballet and the audience got more bang for their buck.

Coolest Thing About Being in This Show: There's nothing cooler than knowing that we are part of a continuing legend in musical theatre history, breaking a new record with every performance, setting the bar higher and higher and higher for every other show that will ever play on Broadway. We take great pride in the hard work we do every day to deserve such a distinction. From the lowliest chorus person to the Phantom himself; from brand new orchestra "sub" to "I played this show on Opening Night and I'm still here"; to original members of the crew who fathered our new crew members, and work alongside them to this day...we've got the best damn jobs on Broadway.

"Gypsy of the Year" Sketch: Sally Williams, along with the help of Jimmy Smagula, sharing a fit of brilliance, wrote the comedy sketch "Majestic Gardens." They spoofed the new Broadway hit, *Grey Gardens*, moving the characters from that play out of their decrepit, condemnable set and into the Majestic Theatre (home to our show for 19 years and counting). The skit suggested that the women and their feral cats would feel comfortable in the squalor of the Majestic Theatre's backstage areas which have withstood the likes of sewage backups, outright floods, and a healthy serving of mouse poop. The skit got a great response from the audience, and though we didn't receive an award for all of their hard work, we did deserve near-to-the-top honors for our fundraising effort. We do love our BC/EFA!!!

On a Serious Note: We dedicated our "Gypsy" skit, and we dedicate this installment of *The Playbill Broadway Yearbook*, to those we've loved and lost in this triumphant and tragic year. In loving memory of: Olive Miller, Joanie Koop, Lena Pollard, Richard Warren Pugh (original cast member), Patrick Quinn, Bob Fennell, El Dora Anteau, Rosalee Pollard, Margaret Rose Marchionni, Dolly Caskey, Lois Stahl, Ruth Rabinoff Arnold, Mark Slavinsky, Timothy Albrecht...and always, our beloved Barbara-Mae Phillips.

The Pirate Queen

First Preview: March 6, 2007. Opened: April 5, 2007.
Still running as of May 31, 2007.

PLAYBILL

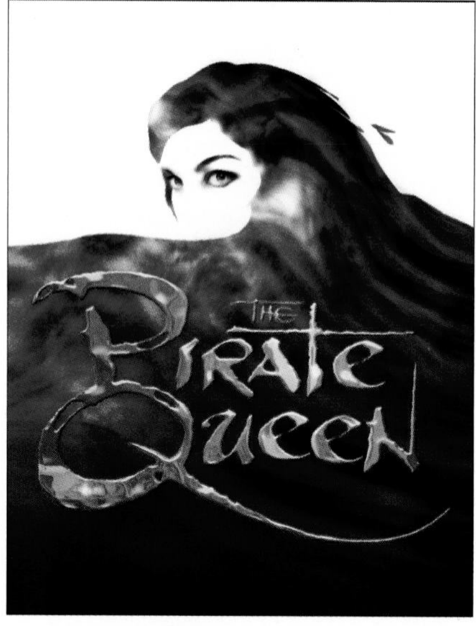

HILTON THEATRE
A CLEAR CHANNEL THEATRE

RIVERDREAM
UNDER THE DIRECTION OF
MOYA DOHERTY JOHN McCOLGAN
PRESENTS
BOUBLIL & SCHÖNBERG'S

BOOK BY
ALAIN BOUBLIL CLAUDE-MICHEL SCHÖNBERG
and RICHARD MALTBY, JR.

MUSIC BY
CLAUDE-MICHEL SCHÖNBERG

LYRICS BY
ALAIN BOUBLIL RICHARD MALTBY, JR. JOHN DEMPSEY

BASED UPON THE NOVEL, "GRANIA – SHE KING OF THE IRISH SEAS" BY MORGAN LLYWELYN

STARRING
Stephanie J. Block Hadley Fraser
Linda Balgord Marcus Chait Jeff McCarthy William Youmans

WITH
Nick Adams, Richard Todd Adams, Caitlin Allen, Steven Barath, Sean Beglan, Timothy W. Bish, Jerad Bortz, Troy Edward Bowles, Grady McLeod Bowman, Rachel Bress, Don Brewer, Kimilee Bryant, Alexis Ann Carra, Noelle Curran, Bobbie Ann Dunn, Brooke Elliott, Christopher Garbrecht, Eric Hatch, Cristin J. Hubbard, David Koch, Timothy Kochka, Jamie LaVerdiere, Joseph Mahowald, Tokiko Masuda, Christopher Grey Misa, Padraic Moyles, Brian O'Brien, Kyle James O'Connor, Michael James Scott, Greg Stone, Katie Erin Tomlinson, Daniel Torres, Áine Uí Cheallaigh, Kathy Voytko, Jennifer Waiser, Briana Yacavone

SCENIC DESIGN
EUGENE LEE

COSTUME DESIGN
MARTIN PAKLEDINAZ

LIGHTING DESIGN
KENNETH POSNER

SOUND DESIGN
JONATHAN DEANS

HAIR DESIGN
PAUL HUNTLEY

SPECIAL EFFECTS DESIGN
GREGORY MEEH

AERIAL SEQUENCE DESIGN
PAUL RUBIN

MAKE-UP DESIGN
ANGELINA AVALLONE

SCENIC DESIGN ASSOCIATE
EDWARD PIERCE

FIGHT DIRECTOR
J. STEVEN WHITE

ASSOCIATE DIRECTOR
TARA YOUNG

ASSOCIATE CHOREOGRAPHER
RACHEL BRESS

CASTING
TARA RUBIN CASTING

PRODUCTION MANAGER
PETER W. LAMB

PRODUCTION STAGE MANAGER
C. RANDALL WHITE

MUSICAL COORDINATOR
MSI/SAM LUTFIYYA

MARKETING
TMG-THE MARKETING GROUP

GENERAL PRESS REPRESENTATIVE
BONEAU BRYAN-BROWN

ASSOCIATE PRODUCER
DANCAP PRODUCTIONS, INC.

EXECUTIVE PRODUCER (DEVELOPMENT)
RONAN SMITH

EXECUTIVE PRODUCER
EDGAR DOBIE

GENERAL MANAGEMENT
THEATRE PRODUCTION GROUP LLC

ORCHESTRATIONS, VOCAL ARRANGEMENTS, MUSICAL SUPERVISION & DIRECTION
JULIAN KELLY

ARTISTIC DIRECTOR
JOHN McCOLGAN

IRISH DANCE CHOREOGRAPHER
CAROL LEAVY JOYCE

MUSICAL STAGING
GRACIELA DANIELE

DIRECTED BY
FRANK GALATI

THE PRODUCERS WISH TO EXPRESS THEIR APPRECIATION TO THEATRE DEVELOPMENT FUND FOR ITS SUPPORT OF THIS PRODUCTION.

4/5/07

CAST

(in order of appearance)

Grace (Grania) O'Malley ... STEPHANIE J. BLOCK
Tiernan ... HADLEY FRASER*
Dubhdara ... JEFF McCARTHY
Evleen ... ÁINE UÍ CHEALLAIGH*
Queen Elizabeth I ... LINDA BALGORD
Sir Richard Bingham ... WILLIAM YOUMANS
Donal O'Flaherty ... MARCUS CHAIT
Chieftain O'Flaherty ... JOSEPH MAHOWALD
Majella ... BROOKE ELLIOTT
Eoin ... (Wed. mat., Thurs., Sat. eve. & Sun. mat.) CHRISTOPHER GREY MISA
Eoin ... (Tues., Wed. eve., Fri. & Sat. mat.) STEVEN BARATH
Ensemble ... NICK ADAMS, RICHARD TODD ADAMS, CAITLIN ALLEN, SEAN BEGLAN, JERAD BORTZ, TROY EDWARD BOWLES, GRADY McLEOD BOWMAN, ALEXIS ANN CARRA, NOELLE CURRAN, BOBBIE ANN DUNN, BROOKE ELLIOTT, CHRISTOPHER GARBRECHT, ERIC HATCH, CRISTIN J. HUBBARD, DAVID KOCH, TIMOTHY KOCHKA, JAMIE LAVERDIERE, JOSEPH MAHOWALD, TOKIKO MASUDA, PADRAIC MOYLES, BRIAN O'BRIEN, KYLE JAMES O'CONNOR, MICHAEL JAMES SCOTT, GREG STONE, KATIE ERIN TOMLINSON, DANIEL TORRES, JENNIFER WAISER, BRIANA YACAVONE

Continued on next page

(L-R): Stephanie J. Block, Jeff McCarthy and Marcus Chait

Photo by Joan Marcus

The Pirate Queen

SCENES AND MUSICAL NUMBERS

Time: Late sixteenth century
Place: Ireland and England

ACT 1

	Prologue	Grace, Tiernan
SCENE 1	"The Pirate Queen"	Dubhdara, Tiernan, Grace, Evleen, Oarsmen and Company
	"Woman"	Grace
SCENE 2	"The Storm"	Company
	"My Grace"	Dubhdara and Grace
SCENE 3	"Here on This Night"	Grace, Tiernan, Crew
SCENE 4	"The First Battle"	Grace, Tiernan, Dubhdara and Company
SCENE 5	"The Waking of the Queen"	Elizabeth, Ladies-in-Waiting
	"Rah-Rah, Tip-Top"	Elizabeth, Bingham, Lords and Ladies-in-Waiting
SCENE 6	"The Choice Is Mine"	Grace, Dubhdara, Chieftain O'Flaherty, Tiernan, Donal and Company
	"The Bride's Song"	Grace, Evleen, Women
SCENE 7	"Boys'll Be Boys"	Donal, Mates and Barmaids
SCENE 8	"The Wedding"	Grace, Tiernan, Donal, Dubhdara, Chieftain O'Flaherty, Evleen and Company
SCENE 9	"I'll Be There"	Tiernan
SCENE 10	"Boys'll Be Boys" (Reprise)	Donal and Mates, Grace, Chieftain O'Flaherty
SCENE 11	"Trouble at Rockfleet"	Grace, Tiernan, Donal, Bingham and Company
SCENE 12	"A Day Beyond Belclare"	Grace, Tiernan, Donal and Company
SCENE 13	"Go Serve Your Queen"	Elizabeth and Bingham
SCENE 14	"Dubhdara's Farewell"	Dubhdara and Grace
	"Sail to the Stars"	Grace, Tiernan, Donal, Evleen and Company

ACT 2

	Entr'Acte	
SCENE 1	"It's a Boy"	Grace, Tiernan, Donal, Evleen, Majella and Sailors
SCENE 2	"Enemy at Port Side"	Grace, Tiernan, Donal, Evleen, Majella and Sailors
	"I Dismiss You"	Grace, Donal and Sailors
SCENE 3	"If I Said I Loved You"	Tiernan and Grace
SCENE 4	"The Role of the Queen"	Elizabeth, Bingham, Lords and Ladies-in-Waiting
SCENE 5	"The Christening"	Evleen, Grace, Tiernan and Company
	"Let a Father Stand By His Son"	Donal, Grace, Bingham, Tiernan, Evleen and Company
SCENE 6	"Surrender"	Bingham, Tiernan, Elizabeth and Company
SCENE 7	"She Who Has All"	Elizabeth and Grace
SCENE 8	"Lament"	Grace, Majella, Eoin and Company
SCENE 9	"The Sea of Life"	Grace and Company
SCENE 10	"Terra Marique Potens"	Elizabeth, Grace, Bingham
	"Woman to Woman"	Elizabeth and Grace
	"Behind the Screen"	Company
	"Grace's Exit"	Elizabeth, Grace, Bingham and Company
SCENE 11	Finale	Grace, Tiernan and Company

Cast Continued

UNDERSTUDIES

For Grace: KATIE ERIN TOMLINSON
For Tiernan: JAMIE LAVERDIERE, GREG STONE
For Queen Elizabeth I: KIMILEE BRYANT, CRISTIN J. HUBBARD
For Donal: RICHARD TODD ADAMS, DANIEL TORRES
For Bingham: RICHARD TODD ADAMS, JOSEPH MAHOWALD
For Dubhdara: CHRIS GARBRECHT, JOSEPH MAHOWALD
For Evleen: BROOKE ELLIOTT
For Majella: KIMILEE BRYANT

STANDBY

For Grace: KATHY VOYTKO

SWINGS

TIMOTHY W. BISH, RACHEL BRESS, DON BREWER, KIMILEE BRYANT

Dance Captain: RACHEL BRESS
Fight Captain, Assistant Dance Captain: TIMOTHY W. BISH
Assistant Dance Captain: PADRAIC MOYLES

Production Stage Manager: C. RANDALL WHITE
Stage Manager: KATHLEEN E. PURVIS

* Hadley Fraser and Áine Uí Cheallaigh are appearing with the permission of Actors' Equity Association. The producers gratefully acknowledge Actors' Equity Association for its assistance with this production.

ORCHESTRA

Musical Director/Conductor: JULIAN KELLY
Associate Musical Director: BRIAN CONNOR
Keyboard I: BRIAN CONNOR
Keyboard II/Assistant Conductor: JOSHUA ROSENBLUM
Fiddle/Violin: LIZ KNOWLES
Uilleann Pipes/Whistles: KIERAN O'HARE
Soprano Sax/Clarinet: KENNETH EDGE
Horn: NEIL KIMEL
Harp/Gaelic Harp: KIRSTEN AGRESTA
Guitars/Banjo: STEVE ROBERTS
Electric Bass: MICHAEL PEARCE
Percussion: DAVE ROTH
Drums/Bodhran: FRANK PAGANO
Music Coordinator: SAM LUTFIYYA/ MUSIC SERVICES INTERNATIONAL

Additional choreography by MARK DENDY

The Pirate Queen

Stephanie J. Block
Grace "Grania" O'Malley

Hadley Fraser
Tiernan

Linda Balgord
Queen Elizabeth I

Marcus Chait
Donal

Jeff McCarthy
Dubhdara

William Youmans
Bingham

Nick Adams
Ensemble

Richard Todd Adams
Ensemble

Caitlin Allen
Ensemble

Steven Barath
Eoin at certain performances

Sean Beglan
Ensemble

Timothy W. Bish
Assistant Fight Director/Fight Captain/Assistant Dance Captain/ Swing

Jerad Bortz
Ensemble

Troy Edward Bowles
Ensemble

Grady McLeod Bowman
Ensemble

Rachel Bress
Associate Choreographer/ Dance Captain/ Swing

Don Brewer
Swing

Kimilee Bryant
Swing

Alexis Ann Carra
Ensemble

Noelle Curran
Ensemble

Bobbie Ann Dunn
Ensemble

Brooke Elliott
Ensemble, Majella

Christopher Garbrecht
Ensemble

Eric Hatch
Ensemble

Cristin J. Hubbard
Ensemble

David Koch
Ensemble

Timothy Kochka
Ensemble

Jamie LaVerdiere
Ensemble

Joseph Mahowald
Chieftain O'Flaherty, Ensemble

Tokiko Masuda
Ensemble

Christopher Grey Misa
Eoin at certain performances

Padraic Moyles
Ensemble, Assistant Dance Captain

Brian O'Brien
Ensemble

Kyle James O'Connor
Ensemble

Michael James Scott
Ensemble

The Pirate Queen

Greg Stone
Ensemble

Katie Erin Tomlinson
Ensemble

Daniel Torres
Ensemble

Áine Uí Cheallaigh
Evleen

Kathy Voytko
Standby Grace

Jennifer Waiser
Ensemble

Briana Yacavone
Ensemble

Alain Boublil
Book and Lyrics

Claude-Michel Schönberg
Book and Music

Richard Maltby, Jr.
Book and Lyrics

Frank Galati
Director

Graciela Daniele
Musical Staging

Carol Leavy Joyce
Irish Dance Choreographer

Eugene Lee
Scenic Design

Martin Pakledinaz
Costume Design

Kenneth Posner
Lighting Design

Jonathan Deans
Sound Design

Paul Huntley
Wig Designer

Paul Rubin
Aerial Effects Design

Angelina Avallone
Makeup Design

J. Steven White
Fight Director

Tara Young
Associate Director

Tara Rubin,
Tara Rubin Casting
Casting

Ronan Smith
Executive Producer, Development

Edgar Dobie
Executive Producer

Moya Doherty
Producer

John McColgan
Producer and Artistic Director

Jeff Williams
Swing

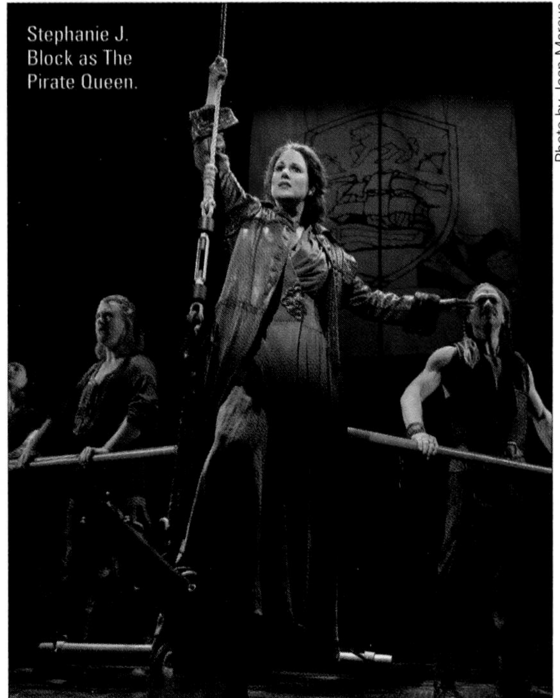
Stephanie J. Block as The Pirate Queen.

Photo by Joan Marcus

The Pirate Queen

Photos by Ben Strothmann

FRONT OF HOUSE STAFF
Front Row (L-R): Kirssy Toribio (Head Usher), Errol Whittington (Head Usher), Edward Griggs (Usher), Mr. Kennedy (Usher), Denise Williams (Usher), Adam Sarsfield (Usher), D. Lloyd (Head Usher).

Second Row (L-R): Billy Pena (Usher), Lisa Lopez (Usher), D. Langenfield (Usher), Juana Rivas (Usher), Mike Chaves (Usher), S. Wilson (Usher), Alicia Wright (Usher), P. Fetini (Usher), Sharon Hawkins (Usher).

Back Row (L-R): Alan Toribio (Usher), J. Blaustein (Usher), K. Fuller (Usher), C. Kayser (Usher), M. Bell (Usher), K. Murry (Usher).

STAGE CREW
Seated (L-R): Steven Kirkham, Lair Max Paulsen, Bobbi Morse, Mickey Abbate, Billy Hipkins, Shannon Quinones, Tree Sarvay, Sandra M. Franck.

Second Row (L-R): Jillian Beglan, Michael Louis, Robin Cook, Shannon Dunn, Vincent Berardi, Michael Wilhoite, Charlene Speyerer, Pam Hughes.

Standing (L-R): Arlene Watson, Kurt Kielmann, Danny Mura, Gregory Holtz, C. Randall White, Gary Seibert, Emily Ockenfels, Reginald Vessey, Donna Holland, Paul Verity, Vanessa Valeriano, Keith Caggiano, John Gibson, Chris Keene, Tommy McDonough, Dan C. Hochstine, Jeff Facinelli, Greg Fedigan, Mike Bernstein, Jimmy Harris, Walter Mazurek.

The Pirate Queen

Photo by Ben Strothmann

CAST AND CREW

Seated (L-R): Linda Balgord, Steven Kirkham, Cristin J. Hubbard, Briana Yacavone, Stephanie J. Block, Tara Young, Marcus Chait, Grady Bowman, Sandra M. Franck, Michael Wilhoite, William Youmans.

Second Row (L-R): Jason D. Shur, Bobbi Morse, John R. Gibson, Caitlin Allen, Tokiko Masuda, Michael James Scott, Noelle Curran, Kimilee Bryant, Timothy W. Bish, Jamie La Veriere, Charlene Speyerer, Kathy Voytko, Alexis Ann Carra, Hadley Fraser, Jeff McCarthy, John McColgan.

Third Row (L-R): Sean Beglan, Brooke Elliott, Bobbie Ann Dunn, Nick Adams, Troy Edward Bowles, Joseph Mahowald, Kyle James O'Connor, Richard Todd Adams, Jeff Williams.

Fourth Row (L-R): Tonya Bodison, Therese Ducey, Padriac Moyles, Rachel Bress, Daniel Torres, Brian O'Brien, Jerad Bortz, Eric Hatch, Áine Uí Cheallaigh, Walter Mazurek, Jillian Beglan, Emily Ockenfels.

Fifth Row (L-R): Pam Hughes, Carrie Phillips, Gregory Holtz, Katie Erin Tomlinson, Lair Max Paulsen, Vanessa Valeriano, David Koch, Mickey Abbate, Shannon Munn, Tree Sarvay, Billy Hipkins, Shannon Quinones, Donna Holland, Gary Seibert, Paul Verity, Michael Bernstein, Dan C. Hochstine, Edgar Dobie.

Last Row (L-R): Elizabeth Talmadge, Keith Caggiano, Michael Louis, Danny Mura, Robin Cook, Kurt Kielmann (Hidden), Arlene Watson, Joshua Rosenblum, Christopher Garbrecht, Vincent Berardi, Jim Brandeberry (Hidden), Jeff Facinelli, Kris Keene, Tommy McDonough (Hidden), Jimmy Harris (Hidden), C. Randall White (Hidden).

STAFF FOR *THE PIRATE QUEEN*

RIVERDREAM
Moya Doherty, Managing Producer
John McColgan, Managing Producer
Edgar Dobie, Executive Producer (North America)
Ronan Smith, Executive Producer (Dublin)
Paula Burke, Executive Manager
Louise Byrne, Production Coordinator
Majella Cuttle, Executive Assistant
Wendy Mau, Assistant to Edgar Dobie
Nicholas Morgenstern, Production Assistant

GENERAL MANAGEMENT
THEATRE PRODUCTION GROUP, LLC
Frank P. Scardino

COMPANY MANAGER
Jim Brandeberry

PRODUCTION MANAGER
Peter W. Lamb

GENERAL PRESS REPRESENTATIVE
BONEAU/BRYAN-BROWN
Adrian Bryan-Brown Matt Polk
Steven Padla Jessica Johnson Amy Kass

PRODUCTION STAGE MANAGER .... C. RANDALL WHITE
Stage Manager .... Kathleen E. Purvis
Assistant Stage Managers .... Sandra M. Franck, Charlene Speyerer, Michael Wilhoite
Assistant Company Manager .... Elizabeth M. Talmadge
Associate Director .... Tara Young
Associate Choreographer .... Rachel Bress
Assistant to the General Manager .... Tegan Meyer
Associate Scenic Designer .... Edward Pierce
1st Assistant Scenic Designer .... Nick Francone
2nd Assistant Scenic Designer .... Jen Price
Scenic Design Studio Assistants .... Arielle Schiff, Tristan Jeffers
Scenic Design Intern .... Iryna Clark
Associate Lighting Designers .... Philip Rosenberg, Patricia Nichols
Assistant Lighting Designer .... Aaron Spivey
Associate Costume Designer .... MaryAnn D. Smith
1st Assistant Costume Designer .... Courtney McClain
2nd Assistant Costume Designer .... Randall E. Klein
Assistant to the Costume Designer .... Erin Murphy
Costume Rendering Assistant .... William Beilke
Costume Student Intern .... Sarah Pauker
Assistant Sound Designer .... Brian Hsieh
Automated Lighting Programmer .... David Arch
Art Design Concept by ... The Apartment Creative Agency
Art Design Development and implementation by .... Zeus Creative Dublin
Special Effects Assistant .... Jeremy Chernick
Assistant Fight Director .... Timothy W. Bish
Electronic Music Programmer .... Brett Alan Sommer, Jim Harp
Music Copying & Preparation .... Mark Cumberland for Hotstave LTD
Additional Music Preparation .. Anixter Rice Music Service
Irish Music Consultant .... David Downes
Production Carpenter .... Don S. Gilmore
Head Carpenter .... Jim Kane

The Pirate Queen

Assistant Carpenters .... Eric E. Smith, Scott "Gus" Poitras
Production Electrician .... Michael S. LoBue
Head Electrician .... Jon Mark Davidson
Advance Electrician .... Jody Durham
Automated Lighting Programmer (Chicago) .... Timothy F. Rogers
Assistant Electricians .... Adam Biscow, Andrew J. Bynum, Thomas Galinski, Jr.
Production Sound .... Garth Helm
Head Sound .... Simon Matthews
Assistant Sound .... Daniel C. Hochstine
Production Property Master .... Joseph P Harris, Jr.
Head Property Man .... Michael Bernstein
Assistant Property Man .... Reginald Vessey
Wardrobe Supervisor .... Robert Guy
Assistant Wardrobe Supervisor .... Michael Louis
Dressers .... Gilbert Aleman, Vincent Berardi, Renee Borys, Bobby Condon, Robin Cook, Donna Holland, Gregory Holtz, Billy Hipkins, Pam Hughes, Kurt Kielmann, Estella Marie, Walter Mazurek, Bobbi Morse, Shannon Munn, Danny Mura, Emily Ockenfels, Carrie Phillips, Shannon Quinones, Tree Sarvay, Gary Seibert, Vanessa Valeriano, Arlene Watson
Hair and Makeup Supervisor .... Edward J. Wilson
Assistant Hair and Makeup Supervisor .... Steven Kirkham
Hair Stylists .... Lair Max Paulsen, Therese Dacey, Jason D. Shur, Tonya Bodison
Advertising .... SpotCo/Drew Hodges, Jim Edwards, Jim Aquino, Darius Suyama
Marketing .... TMG - The Marketing Group/ Laura Matalon, Tanya Grubich, Anne Rippey, Victoria Cairl, Ronni Seif, Meghan Zaneski, Allison Cabellon
Web Design/Internet Marketing .... Situation Marketing/ Damian Bazadona, Chris Powers, Joey Oliva
Souvenir Merchandise designed and created by .... The Araca Group
Castcom Producer .... Rachel O'Connor
Castcom Editor .... Andrew Robert Thomas
Casting .... Tara Rubin Casting
Casting Directors: Tara Rubin, Dunja Vitolic
Casting Associates: Eric Woodall, Laura Schutzel, Merri Sugarman
Casting Assistants: Rebecca Carfagna, Jeff Siebert
Production Assistants .... Christopher Munnell, Eva L. Hare
SDCF Observer .... Selda Sahin
Legal Counsel .... Levine, Plotkin & Menin, LLP/ Loren H. Plotkin, Susan Mindell
Accountants .... Fried & Kowgios CPAs LLP/ Robert Fried, Sarah Galbraith
Banking .... Commerce Bank / Barbara von Borstel, Ashley Elezi
Insurance .... AON Entertainment Insurance/ Claudia Kaufman
Payroll .... Castellana Services, Inc
Production Photographer .... Joan Marcus
Rehearsal Studio .... The New 42nd St. Studios
Travel Agent .... Protravel Incorporated, Beverly Hills
Housing Broker .... Marie-Claire Martineau, Maison International, Ltd.
Hotel Accommodations .... Road Concierge Inc.
Ground Transportation .... Hollywood Limousine

Makeup Provided by M.A.C Cosmetics

Scenery built by F&D Scene Changes; Show Control; and Scenic Motion Control featuring Stage Command Systems® by Scenic Technologies, a division of Production Resource Group LLC, New Windsor, NY. Lighting equipment and special lighting effects by PRG Lighting. Sound equipment from PRG Audio. Special effects by Jauchem & Meeh Inc. Faux-Fire by Technifex Inc. Costume Shops: Eric Winterling, Inc.; Tricorne, Inc.; Euro Co. Costumes; Carelli Costumes Inc.; Donna Langman Costumes; Seams Unlimited, Ltd. Armor by Costume Armour, Inc. Millinery by Lynne Mackey Studio; Arnold S. Levine, Inc.; Rodney Gordon, Inc. Queen Elizabeth's specialty collars by Killer Theatrical Crafts. Printing and dyeing by Gene Mignola, Inc. Dyeing and distressing by Izquierdo Studios, Ltd.; Dye-namix Inc.; Asiatico Studio. Footwear by Handmade Shoes/Fred Longtin; Pluma Handmade Dance Footwear; J.C. Theatrical and Custom Footwear; Harr Theaterschuhe; Capezio. Specialty jewelry by Lawrence Vrba. Celtic jewelry by Christine McPartland. Celtic embroidery by Robert W. Trump. Specialty gloves by Bionic Glove Technology. Props constructed by Cigar Box Studios Inc., Paragon Innovation Group Inc., The Spoon Group, John Creech Design & Production, Peter Sarafin, Beyond Imagination, Portafiori Flowers. Additional scenery built by Hawkeye Scenic Studios, Inc. Throat lozenges provided by Ricola. Special thanks to Ayotte Drums for building the drums, Axis Percussion for supplying the drum hardware, Lyon-Healy Harps for their generosity in coordinating the harps and TOP HAT Amplification for building the guitar amps used in this production.

Flying by Foy.

---

www.thepiratequeen.com

HILTON THEATRE STAFF

General Manager .... Micah Hollingworth
Assistant General Manager .... Teresa Ryno
Facility Manager .... Jeff Nuzzo
House Manager .... Emily Fisher
Box Office Treasurer .... Peter Attanasio Jr.
Head Carpenter .... James C. Harris
Head Electrician .... Art J. Friedlander
Head of Properties .... Joseph P. Harris Jr.
Head of Sound .... John R. Gibson
Asst. Facility Manager .... Michael Leach
Asst. Box Office Treasurer .... Spencer Taustine
Staff Accountant .... Carmen Martinez
Payroll Administrator .... Tiyana Works
Shipping/Receiving .... Dinara Kratsch
Administrative Assistant .... Jenny Kirlin

Hilton Theatre – A Live Nation Venue

LIVE NATION

President and Chief Executive Officer .... Michael Rapino

---

LIVE NATION – VENUES

President and CEO, Venues and Alliances .... Bruce Eskowitz
CFO .... Alan Ridgeway
Vice-President, Finance .... Kathy Porter
Executive Vice President .... Ned Collett
Senior Vice President NY and CT Venues .... John Huff
Director of Labor Relations .... Chris Brockmeyer

LIVE NATION – THEATRICAL

Chairman, Global Theatre .... David Ian
CEO Theatrical, North America .... Steve Winton
President and COO, North America .... David M. Anderson
CFO, North America .... Paul Dietz
Senior Vice President, Producing .... Jennifer Costello
Executive Vice President/CMO .... Susie Krajsa
Senior Vice President, Operations .... Dan Swartz
Senior Vice President, Business Affairs .... David Lazar
Senior Vice President, Sales and Ticketing .... Courtney Pierce
Vice President, Finance .... Chante Moore
Vice President, Programming .... Alison Spiriti

Live Nation is a leading live content and distribution company focused on creating superior experiences for artists, performers, corporations and audiences. Live Nation owns, operates or has booking rights for 150 venues worldwide and has promoted or produced more than 20,000 events in 2005 and 2006. Current producing credits include *The Producers, Hairspray* and *Spamalot* on Broadway; an all-new production of Andrew Lloyd Webber's *The Phantom of the Opera* at the Venetian in Las Vegas; and national tours of Dora the Explorer Live! and Barbie Live in Fairytopia. The theatrical division also presents Broadway Across America, www.BroadwayAcrossAmerica.com, an annual subscription series of top Broadway shows and theatrical entertainment in more than 50 markets across North America. Live Nation is listed on the New York Stock Exchange, trading under the symbol "LYV". More information about Live Nation and its businesses is available at www.LiveNation.com.

Photo by Joan Marcus

Linda Balgord as Queen Elizabeth I

The Pirate Queen
Scrapbook

Correspondent: Marcus Chait, "Donal"
Memorable Opening Night Faxes: We got a nice good-luck fax from one of the companies of *Riverdance*. A lot of the people in our show have done *Riverdance*. The Irish dancers in our show have all been in various productions of *Riverdance* all over the world, so it was nice to have their support. It's a nice tradition that you get faxes from most of the other Broadway shows wishing happy opening to their friends. It's a great reminder of how small and tight and supportive the community is, especially on nights like that.
Opening Night Gifts: There's a young artist named Matt Logan who is trying to follow in the footsteps of caricaturist Al Hirschfeld, and Stephanie Block commissioned him to make a piece for our cast, then had it framed and gave copies to everyone. It's quite extraordinary. I always thought it would be a great honor to appear in a Hirschfeld, but sadly he died just before my first Broadway show, *Urban Cowboy*. So this caricature was a really special gift. Our producers (the most supportive people I've every worked for) have given us so many incredible gifts, it's overwhelming. For our Chicago opening they commissioned some of Ireland's most respected artists who made us some incredible paintings. For the Broadway opening they gave us framed copies of our Playbill alongside pictures of our characters, which I have hanging in my dressing room. Our producers also gave us a gorgeous Waterford crystal clock inscribed with the title of show and opening night date. Claude-Michel Schönberg and Alain Boublil gave us sessions of Reflexology therapy. My dressing room was like a greenhouse full of flowers from family and friends.
Most Exciting Celebrity Visitors and What They Said/Did: Hillary Clinton was pretty spectacular. She was so engaging and genuinely interested in what we do. She was so impressed with the character of Grace O'Malley that she wanted to trace her DNA to see if she might somehow be related to her! Whatever your political views might be, you could see in two seconds why she and her husband are such successful politicians. Rosie O'Donnell came to the show and brought all of her kids. One of them told her it was their favorite show they'd ever seen, which was obviously nice to hear. Rosie put us on The View and has been very supportive of the show. We also got a visit from the President of Ireland, and had a photo taken with her. A lovely/classy woman, to say the least.
Who Got the Gypsy Robe: Brian O'Brien.
Actor Who Performed the Most Roles in This Show: I think one of our swings, Tim Bish, has gone on for nine roles. Our swings have one of the toughest jobs in the business, with all the dancing and fight choreography. We also had a really bad case of flu that went through the cast during previews, so swings and understudies were on quite often and with limited rehearsal. I have GREAT respect for people who can do that job. I have trouble remembering my one role!

Photos by Aubrey Reuben

1. Linda Balgord in her dressing room with a Queen Elizabeth doll.
2. Librettist/co-lyricist Richard Maltby Jr. at the premiere.
3. (L-R): Choreographer Mark Morris, costume designer Martin Pakledinaz and fellow costume designer Susan Hilferty at the opening.

Actor Who Has Done the Most Shows in Their Career: Jeff McCarthy, Linda Balgord and Bill Youmans have all made very impressive careers in this difficult business and I have great respect for all that they've accomplished.
Special Backstage Rituals: Before the curtain goes up, everyone holds hands in a circle and we send a pulse of energy around by squeezing the hand of the person next to us. The pulse goes in both directions so whoever gets the double-squeeze on both hands at the same time, everyone runs up to that person and gives them a hug. It blesses the show. We also like to rub Grady's bald head for good luck!
Favorite Moment During Each Performance: I really look forward to two moments. First is my fight with Hadley at the end of the show. We worked really hard to stage that fight and make it look as dangerous and exciting as possible, and it takes pretty much everything we have physically to get through it. Ironically we've become very close friends even though we play rivals fighting over the same woman. I wish he'd let me win once in a while!
My other favorite moment is "I Dismiss You" in which Stephanie and I officially end our marriage after telling one another what we really think of each other. Any frustration or angst I'm having in my real life, I have three minutes to get it all out and unload it on Steph. As for SJB, we call her "150 Percent Block" because she always give everything she has to each performance. No matter how tired you might be, you have to step up your game when The Pirate Queen herself is giving 150 percent.
Favorite In-Theatre Gathering Place: We're kind of spread out at the Hilton, so there is no one gathering place. However, Hadley and I maintain an open door policy at our dressing room, and it has become a nice social place to hang out. Most of the cast has very little down time during the show, as they're either on stage or changing clothes, so our real meeting place is on stage every night.
Favorite Off-Site Hangout: The ballfields of Central Park where we play in the Broadway Show League every Thursday afternoon. We have a strong team this year and a great cheerleading squad led by Mr. Michael James Scott!
Favorite Snack Food: Every Sunday afternoon is "Potluck Sunday" where we're all supposed to bring a dish of some kind to share with one another. But I've noticed that usually the dressers bring the food and the actors are the ones who eat it! We also have great times on people's birthdays where we get a cake for whomever is celebrating. Our cast and crew loves us some cake and it disappears rather quickly.
Favorite Therapy: With all the fighting and dancing on that raked stage, the physical therapy list goes up Sunday night and is filled up before Tuesday. Heidi is our PT and we'd be in big trouble without her.
Audience Noise Issues: Now that the audience

The Pirate Queen
Scrapbook

is allowed to eat in the theatre we constantly hear people unwrapping things. I've found that the best way to deal with this issue is to just stare the culprit down until they stop. But some are clueless and continue unwrapping. If you have to eat in the theater, at least do it quietly ...please?!?

Memorable Fan Encounters: Stephanie has a group of fans called the "Blockheads" who have been following her since she was in *Wicked* and *Boy From Oz,* and they have now adopted the cast of *The Pirate Queen* as their own. They are truly incredible. They send us flowers, t-shirts, cookies, tea, plaques, you name it. One woman made me my own action figure! It's made of clay and has a costume that looks exactly like mine.

Fastest Costume Change: Joe Mahowald goes from being an English lord to Chieftain O'Flaherty, and he has to change everything, including his wig. One night he didn't make it in time and we pirates were left onstage in a very intense staring contest...while trying our best not to laugh.

Busiest Day at the Box Office: The day after reviews came out.

Who Wore the Heaviest/Hottest Costume: Linda Balgord has one dress that weighs 45 lbs. I don't know how she makes it up the stairs.

Who Wore the Least: Nick Adams, Eddie Bowles and Brian O'Brien's pirate outfits are quite revealing.

Catchphrases Only the Company Would Recognize: In a word, "SENSIBLE."

Best In-House Parody Lyrics: After the Christening when we go into "Let A Father Stand By His Son," the music gets very eerie and offstage some people sing "Spooky, spooky, spooo-ooky," along with it.

When Lord Bingham asks Hadley, "Who are you?" He says, "My name is Tiernan of the Clan O'Malley." Offstage, we have various profane and obscene names as to who he really is. And our favorite: instead of "Let's have a chair set down for Grace" we replace the name "Grace" with "Laquisha."

Memorable Directorial Notes: Frank loves to quote very deep intellectual passages from various authors none of us ever heard of. He delivers these quotes as if he expects us all to have read them. We learned to nod and smile.

Every note session would begin with him addressing us as "Dear Ones...."

Understudy Anecdote: At one preview Kathy Voytko was in the audience watching the show, and suddenly she got word that Stephanie couldn't continue. She ran backstage, threw on Stephanie's clothes, makeup and wig and ran on like a champ.

Ghostly Encounters: When Michael Riedel and Ben Brantley were here.

Coolest Thing About Being in This Show: Working for such incredible producers alongside such a supportive cast and crew.

Photos by Aubrey Reuben

Photo by David Gewirtzman

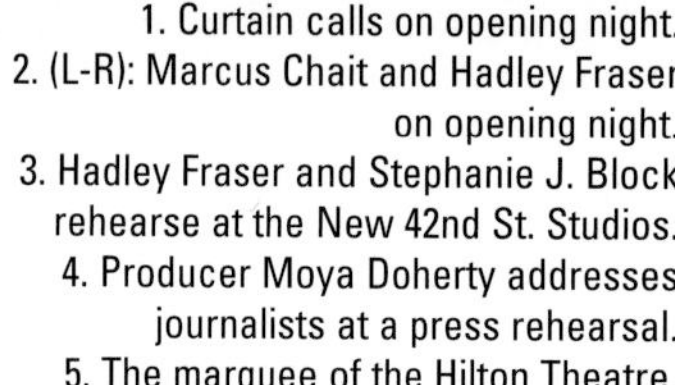

1. Curtain calls on opening night.
2. (L-R): Marcus Chait and Hadley Fraser on opening night.
3. Hadley Fraser and Stephanie J. Block rehearse at the New 42nd St. Studios.
4. Producer Moya Doherty addresses journalists at a press rehearsal.
5. The marquee of the Hilton Theatre.

Prelude to a Kiss

First Preview: February 17, 2007. Opened: March 8, 2007.
Closed: April 29, 2007 after 23 Previews and 61 Performances.

PLAYBILL

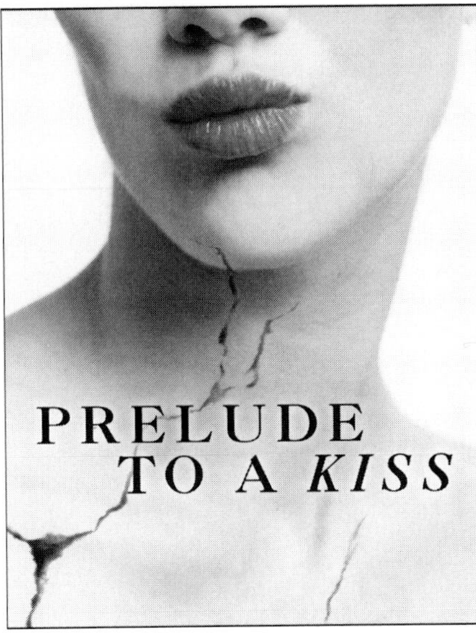

AMERICAN AIRLINES THEATRE

ROUNDABOUTTHEATRECOMPANY

Todd Haimes, Artistic Director
Harold Wolpert, Managing Director
Julia C. Levy, Executive Director
Presents

John Mahoney
Annie Parisse Alan Tudyk
in

PRELUDE TO A *KISS*

by
Craig Lucas
with
Robin Bartlett James Rebhorn

Francois Battiste, Brandon J. Dirden, MacIntyre Dixon, Marceline Hugot, Susan Pellegrino, Matthew Rauch, John Rothman, Karen Walsh

Set Design Santo Loquasto
Costume Design Jane Greenwood
Lighting Design Donald Holder
Original Music & Sound Design John Gromada
Hair & Wig Design Tom Watson
Production Stage Manager Leslie C. Lyter
Casting Jim Carnahan, C.S.A. Mele Nagler, C.S.A.
Technical Supervisor Steve Beers
General Manager Sydney Beers
Press Representative Boneau/Bryan-Brown
Director of Marketing & Sales Promotion David B. Steffen
Director of Development Jeffory Lawson
Founding Director Gene Feist
Associate Artistic Director Scott Ellis

Directed by
Daniel Sullivan

Lead support provided by our Play Production Fund partners:
Steven and Liz Goldstone, The Blanche and Irving Laurie Foundation, Mary and David Solomon

Roundabout Theatre Company is a member of the League of Resident Theatres.
www.roundabouttheatre.org

3/8/07

CAST

(in order of appearance)

Old Man .... JOHN MAHONEY
Peter .... ALAN TUDYK
Rita .... ANNIE PARISSE
Taylor .... MATTHEW RAUCH
Tom .... FRANCOIS BATTISTE
Dr. Boyle .... JAMES REBHORN
Mrs. Boyle .... ROBIN BARTLETT
Minister .... MACINTYRE DIXON
Uncle Fred .... JOHN ROTHMAN
Aunt Dorothy .... MARCELINE HUGOT
Jamaican Waiter .... FRANCOIS BATTISTE
Leah .... MARCELINE HUGOT
Ensemble .... BRANDON J. DIRDEN, SUSAN PELLEGRINO, KAREN WALSH

TIME and PLACE

Present: New York City

UNDERSTUDIES

For Tom/Jamaican Waiter/Taylor/Minister: BRANDON J. DIRDEN
For Old Man/Uncle Fred: MACINTYRE DIXON
For Aunt Dorothy/Leah/Mrs. Boyle: SUSAN PELLEGRINO
For Peter: MATTHEW RAUCH
For Dr. Boyle: JOHN ROTHMAN
For Rita: KAREN WALSH

Production Stage Manager: LESLIE C. LYTER
Stage Manager: JONATHAN DONAHUE

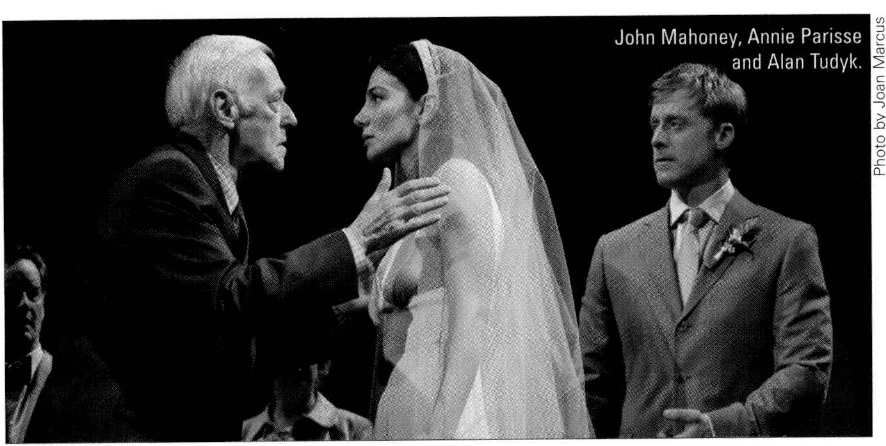

John Mahoney, Annie Parisse and Alan Tudyk.

Photo by Joan Marcus

Prelude to a Kiss

John Mahoney
Old Man

Annie Parisse
Rita

Alan Tudyk
Peter

Robin Bartlett
Mrs. Boyle

James Rebhorn
Dr. Boyle

Francois Battiste
Tom, Jamaican Waiter

Brandon J. Dirden
Ensemble

MacIntyre Dixon
Minister

Marceline Hugot
Aunt Dorothy, Leah

Susan Pellegrino
Ensemble

Matthew Rauch
Taylor

John Rothman
Uncle Fred

Karen Walsh
Ensemble

Craig Lucas
Playwright

Daniel Sullivan
Director

Santo Loquasto
Set Design

Jane Greenwood
Costume Design

Donald Holder
Lighting Design

John Gromada
Original Music and Sound Design

Tom Watson
Hair and Wig Design

Jim Carnahan
Casting

Gene Feist
Founding Director, Roundabout Theatre Company

Todd Haimes
Artistic Director, Roundabout Theatre Company

DOORMAN
Adolf Torres

Photos by Ben Strothmann

BOX OFFICE
(L-R): Heather Siebert (Ticket Services), Robert Morgan (Assistant Box Office Manager) and Mead Margulies (Ticket Services).

Prelude to a Kiss

HOUSE STAFF
(L-R): Zipporah Aguasvivas (Associate House Manager), Idair Melendez (House Staff), Peter Breaden (House Staff), Jacklyn Rivera (House Staff), Adam Wier (House Staff), and Rebecca Knell (House Staff).

Photos by Ben Strothmann

CREW
Kneeling (L-R): Chris Mattingly (Flyman), Susan J. Fallon (Wardrobe Supervisor), Victoria Grecki (Dresser), Nichole Jennino (Company Manager), Julie Hilimire, Leslie C. Lyter (Production Stage Manager), Nelson Vaughn (Properties), Jill Anania (Deck Electrician), Barb Bartel (Moving Light Technician), Hal Fraser (Deck Carpenter).

Standing (L-R): Jonathan Donahue (Stage Manager), Susan Kroeter, James Wilkinson, Melissa Crawford (Wardrobe Day Worker), Benjamin Barnes, Dann Wojnar (Sound Engineer), paper Tom Aldredge, Jefferson Rowland (Spot Operator), Brian Maiuri (Production Electrician), Glenn Merwede (Production Carpenter and Automation) and Andrew Forste (Properties Running).

ROUNDABOUT THEATRE COMPANY STAFF

ARTISTIC DIRECTOR . . . . TODD HAIMES
MANAGING DIRECTOR . . . . . HAROLD WOLPERT
EXECUTIVE DIRECTOR . . . . JULIA C. LEVY
ASSOCIATE ARTISTIC DIRECTOR . . SCOTT ELLIS

ARTISTIC STAFF

DIRECTOR OF ARTISTIC DEVELOPMENT/ DIRECTOR OF CASTING . . . . JIM CARNAHAN
Artistic Consultant . . . . Robyn Goodman
Associate Artists . . . . Scott Elliott, Doug Hughes, Bill Irwin, Joe Mantello, Mark Brokaw, Kathleen Marshall
Consulting Dramaturg . . . . Jerry Patch
Artistic Associate . . . . Jill Rafson
Casting Director . . . . Mele Nagler
Senior Casting Associate . . . . Carrie Gardner
Casting Associate . . . . Kate Schwabe
Casting Associate . . . . Stephen Kopel
Artistic Intern . . . . Michelle Lehrman

EDUCATION STAFF

EDUCATION DIRECTOR . . Margie Salvante-McCann
Director of Instruction and Curriculum Development . . . . Reneé Flemings
Education Program Manager . . . . David A. Miller
Education Associate . . . . Jennifer DeBruin
Education Assistant . . . . Allison Baucom
Education Dramaturg . . . . Ted Sod
Teaching Artists . . . . Phil Alexander, Cynthia Babak, Victor Barbella, LaTonya Borsay, Rob Bronstein, Lori Brown-Niang, Miss Stella, Hamilton Clancy, Joe Doran, Katie Down, Amy Fortoul, Tony Freeman, Sheri Graubert, Matthew Gregory, Adam Gwon, Karla Hendrick, Jim Jack, Lisa Renee Jordan, Alvin Keith, Jonathan Lang, Rebecca Lord, Tami Mansfield, Erin McCready, Jordana Oberman, Evan O'Brient, Deirdre O'Connor, Andrew Ondrecjak, Laura Poe, Alexa Polmer-Spencer, Nicole Press, Jennifer Rathbone, Leah Reddy, Amanda Rehbein, Taylor Ruckel, Chris Rummel, Cassy Rush, Drew Sachs, Nick Simone, Derek Straat, Daniel Robert Sullivan, Vickie Tanner, Olivia Tsang, Cristina Vaccaro, Jennifer Varbalow, Leese Walker, Eric Wallach, Gail Winar
Education Interns . . . . Anna Jamie Scanlon, Morgan Tylar Waite

ADMINISTRATIVE STAFF

GENERAL MANAGER . . . . Sydney Beers
Associate Managing Director . . . . Greg Backstrom
General Manager, Steinberg Center . . . . . . Rebecca Habel
General Counsel . . . . Nancy Hirschmann
Human Resources Manager . . . . Stephen Deutsch
MIS Director . . . . Jeff Goodman
Facilities Manager . . . . Abraham David
Manager of Corporate and Party Rentals . . . Jetaun Dobbs
Office Manager . . . . Scott Kelly

Prelude to a Kiss

Database Manager .... Dollye Evans
Assistant to the General Manager .... Maggie Cantrick
Management Associate .... Tania Camargo
MIS Assistant .... Micah Kraybill
Receptionists .... Dena Beider, Raquel Castillo, Elisa Papa, Allison Patrick, Monica Sidorchuk
Messenger .... Robert Weisser
Management Intern .... Alanna Degner

FINANCE STAFF

DIRECTOR OF FINANCE .... Susan Neiman
Assistant Controller .... John LaBarbera
Accounts Payable Administrator .... Frank Surdi
Business Office Associate .... David Solomon
Financial Associate .... Yonit Kafka
Business Office Assistant .... Joshua Cohen
Business Interns .... Li Shen, Richard Patterson

DEVELOPMENT STAFF

DIRECTOR OF DEVELOPMENT ..... Jeffory Lawson
Director, Institutional Giving .... Julie K. D'Andrea
Director, Individual Giving .... Julia Lazarus
Director, Special Events .... Steve Schaeffer
Manager, Donor Information Systems .... Tina Mae Bishko
Corporate Relations Manager .... Sara Bensman
Manager, Individual Giving .... Kara Kandel
Telefundraising Manager .... Douglas Sutcliffe
External Affairs Associate .... Robert Weinstein
Special Events Associate .... Ginger Vallen
Institutional Giving Associate .... Sarah Krasnow
Individual Giving Associate .... Kate Bartoldus
Patrons Services Assistant .... John Haynes
Development Assistants .... Jillian Brewster, Christopher Taggart
Individual Giving Intern .... Christopher DeRoche
Special Events Intern .... Erica Rotstein

MARKETING STAFF

DIRECTOR OF MARKETING AND SALES PROMOTION .... David B. Steffen
Marketing/Publications Manager ..... Margaret Casagrande
Assistant Director of Marketing .... Sunil Ayyagari
Marketing Assistant .... Stefanie Schussel
Website Consultant .... Keith Powell Beyland
DIRECTOR OF TELESALES SPECIAL PROMOTIONS .... Daniel Weiss
Telesales Manager .... Anton Borissov
Telesales Office Coordinator .... J.W. Griffin
Marketing Intern .... Trina McCarron

TICKET SERVICES STAFF

DIRECTOR OF SALES OPERATIONS . Jim Seggelink
Ticket Services Manager .... Ellen Holt
Subscription Manager .... Charlie Garbowski, Jr.
Box Office Managers .... Edward P. Osborne, Jessica Bowser
Group Sales Manager .... Jeff Monteith
Assistant Box Office Managers .... Andrew Clements, Krystin MacRitchie, Robert Morgan
Assistant Ticket Services Managers .... Robert Kane, Ethan Ubell, Carlos Morris
Customer Services Coordinator .... Trina Cox
Ticket Services .... Rachel Bauder, Solangel Bido, Jessie Blum, Jacob Burstein-Stern, William Campbell, Lauren Cartelli, David Carson, Nisha Dhruna, Adam Elsberry, Lindsay Ericson, John Finning, Catherine Fitzpatrick, James Graham, Tova Heller, Dorothea J. Kenul, Bill Klemm, Elisa Mala, Mead Margulies, Chuck Migliaccio, Nicole Nicholson, Bekah Nutt, Adam Owens, Ethan Paulini, David Pittman, Thomas Protulipac, Kate Regan, Jackie Rocha, Heather Siebert, Lillian Soto, DJ Thacker, Farra Ungar, Pam Unger, Thomas Walsh
Ticket Services Intern .... Heather Forman

SERVICES

Counsel .... Paul, Weiss, Rifkind, Wharton and Garrison LLP, John Breglio, Deborah Hartnett
Counsel .... Rosenberg & Estis
Counsel .... Andrew Lance, Gibson, Dunn, & Crutcher, LLP
Counsel .... Harry H. Weintraub, Glick and Weintraub, P.C.
Immigration Counsel .... Mark D. Koestler and Theodore Ruthizer
House Physicians .... Dr. Theodore Tyberg, Dr. Lawrence Katz
House Dentist .... Neil Kanner, D.M.D.
Insurance .... DeWitt Stern Group, Inc.
Accountant .... Lutz & Carr CPAs, LLP
Sponsorship .... The Marketing Group, Tanya Grubich, Laura Matalon, Anne Rippey, Erik Gensler
Advertising .... Eliran Murphy Group/ Denise Ganjou, Kara Eldridge
Events Photography .... Anita and Steve Shevett
Production Photographer .... Joan Marcus
Theatre Displays .... King Displays, Wayne Sapper
Merchandising .... Max Merchandising, LLC/ Randi Grossman

MANAGING DIRECTOR EMERITUS .... Ellen Richard

Roundabout Theatre Company
231 West 39th Street, New York, NY 10018
(212) 719-9393.

GENERAL PRESS REPRESENTATIVES

Adrian Bryan-Brown
Matt Polk Jessica Johnson Amy Kass

STAFF FOR *PRELUDE TO A KISS*

GENERAL MANAGER .... Sydney Beers
Company Manager .... Nichole Jennino
Production Stage Manager .... Leslie C. Lyter
Stage Manager .... Jonathan Donahue
Assistant Director .... Jonathan Solari
Associate Scenic Designer .... Jenny B. Sawyers
Assistant Costume Designers .... Camille Assaf, Amela Baksic
Assistant Lighting Designer .... Caroline Chao
Assistant to the Lighting Designer .... Rebecca Makus
Assistant Sound Designer .... Ryan Rumery
Fight Consultant .... J. Steven White
Assistant Technical Supervisor .... Elisa Kuhar
Production Carpenter and Automation .... Glenn Merwede
Properties Running .... Andrew Forste
Flyman .... Chris Mattingly
Deck Carpenter .... Hal Fraser
Properties .... Nelson Vaughn
Production Electrician .... Brian Maiuri
Sound Engineer .... Dann Wojnar
Deck Electrician .... Jill Anania
Moving Light Technician .... Barb Bartel
Spot Operator .... Jeff Rowland
Production Properties Coordination .... Kathy Fabian
Assistant Production Properties .... Melanie Mulder
Wardrobe Supervisor .... Susan J. Fallon
Wardrobe Day Worker .... Melissa Crawford
Dressers .... Julie Hilimire, Victoria Grecki
Hair and Wig Supervisor .... Manuela LaPorte
Production Assistant .... Courtney B. James
Scenery Constructed by .... Great Lakes Scenic Studios
Show Control and Scenic Motion Control featuring Command Systems® by .... Scenic Technologies, a division of Production Resource Group, LLC, New Windsor, NY
Sound Equipment provided by .... Sound Associates
Additional Props built by .... Craig Grigg
Lighting Equipment provided by .... PRG Lighting
Special thanks to .... Karen Spahn

Produced through special arrangement with Broadway Play Publishing Inc. The script to this play may be purchased from BPPI at www.BroadwayPlayPubl.com.

AMERICAN AIRLINES THEATRE STAFF

General Manager .... Sydney Beers
House Carpenter .... Glenn Merwede
House Electrician .... Brian Maiuri
House Properties .... Andrew Forste
Local One IATSE Apprentice .... Jill Anania
Wardrobe Supervisor .... Susan J. Fallon
Box Office Manager .... Ted Osborne
House Manager .... Steve Ryan
Associate House Manager .... Zipporah Aguasvivas
Head Usher .... Edwin Camacho
House Staff .... Jacklyn Rivera, Ilia Diaz, Peter Breaden, Anne Ezell, Adam Wier, Elsie Jamin-Maguire, Idair Melendez, Jose Vazquez, Maria Gerhard, Jessica Porcelli, Rebecca Knell, Stephen Fontana
Security .... Julious Russell
Additional Security provided by .... Gotham Security
Maintenance .... Willie Philips, John Sainz, Madala Western
Lobby Refreshments .... Sweet Concessions

CREDITS

Prelude to a Kiss was commissioned and first produced by South Coast Repertory in Costa Mesa, California, on January 15, 1988. It was subsequently produced in New York City by Circle Repertory Theatre on March 14, 1990, and premiered on Broadway in a production produced by Christopher Gould, Suzanne Golden and Dodger Productions on May 1, 1990.

The lyrics to "Prelude to a Kiss," words by Irving Gordon and Irving Mills, music by Duke Ellington, are copyright © 1938 (renewed 1965) and assigned to Famous Music Corporation and EMI Mills Music Inc.

Prelude to a Kiss

Scrapbook

Company members at a press conference. Seated (L-R): Annie Parisse, Marceline Hugot and Robin Bartlett. Standing (L-R): Alan Tudyk, Matthew Rauch, John Mahoney, John Rothman, James Rebhorn, MacIntyre Dixon and Francois Battiste.

Correspondent: Matt Rauch, "Taylor" and cover for Alan Tudyk.

Memorable Opening Night Notes: I got three fantastic cards from Dan Sullivan, Craig Lucas and Todd Haimes that really made me feel welcome here. But the best of all was the one from my mom and dad, saying, "To our Broadway Baby."

Opening Night Gifts: Craig gave each of us gifts that were beautifully thought out. Not odd, but unusual: Rebhorn got a silver bowl; I got an African tray. I'll certainly never forget that these came from Craig. Roundabout gave us a silver framed picture of the entire cast.

Most Exciting Celebrity Visitors: Brian Stokes Mitchell, Sam Rockwell, Richard Kind and a couple of the people from "Frasier" to see John Mahoney.

Actor Who Performed the Most Roles in This Show: My standby, Brandon Dirden. He appears in three separate roles on stage and covers three or four of the other male characters.

Who Has Done the Most Shows in Their Career: Mac Dixon has done like 30 Broadway shows alone. He's been working 50 years and is an amazing guy.

Special Backstage Rituals: We have a lot of funny rituals. It's basically a three-character play, especially in the second act, so when the rest of us are finished at 9:30 we go down to my and Jim Rebhorn's dressing room and drink wine and tell jokes until we come up for curtain calls a little after 10. It has a really nice communal feeling. We also have incredible Sunday brunches run by the fantastic Susan Fallon. It's a great way to finish the week as a team.

Francois Battiste and I have our own ritual. Just before we walk onstage for the wedding sequence we look at each other and smile and remind each other "Wow, we're doing a Broadway show!" We worked very hard for years to be here and we feel very blessed.

Favorite Moments During Each Performance: Offstage: My favorite moment is that moment with Francois. I understudied on Broadway ten years ago but was not actually in the show. So this feels like my Broadway debut and there are five others in the cast who are also making their Broadway debuts, so it's very exciting for us. It's a nice human moment, and I'll miss it when the run ends.

Onstage: Jim Rebhorn swatting imaginary mosquitoes in the barbecue scene, which I'm not sure anyone else notices. It's very funny.

Favorite Off-Site Hangout: Some go to Bar Centrale. As a cast we tend to go to a place like West Bank because we're a big group, even though we know that's kind of the Off-Broadway place to go. They also have a new chef, so the food is good. We have a few drinks and enjoy each other's company.

Favorite Snack Food: Ricolas, we have thousands of them! There's also a plethora of Hershey's kisses back here. Marceline Hugot's husband is a chef and he makes these really terrific salted nuts and peanut brittle. That stuff disappears in about 32 seconds. We also get to eat onstage as part of the play. They put out butter pretzels and strawberries in the party scene.

Mascot: The Doll of Moses—It's a talking Moses doll that speaks in Bible passages and looks exactly like director Dan Sullivan.

Favorite Therapies: Ricola and our Sunday brunch.

Memorable Ad-Lib/Cell Phone Story: We've had a plague of cell phones. It's been shocking to me. One night was particularly bad, Alan was in the middle of one of his monologues and this one phone just started ringing and ringing. Alan tried to work it into the show: "...and then a phone started ringing. But it was important because someone was waiting on a liver." The audience chuckled. And then it stopped and it was OK.

Fastest Costume Change: Alan and Annie have a 20-second change. When I had to do it I was shocked at how fast it was.

Memorable Directorial Note/Nickname: Right before tech, Dan Sullivan said, "This is Broadway Dan talking, and I'm telling you that you should pause there because there's going to be a laugh." After that we all called him "Broadway Dan."

Understudy Anecdote: I was shooting a movie on Roosevelt Island during the day and I was sitting in the makeup chair when I got a message: You're going on for Alan tonight! I was thinking, "You've got to get me off of this set! Find my script!" That was a hectic day. I got released at 6 PM, got to the theatre at 6:45 and went on for Alan at 8. Everyone in this cast has gotten sick. I went on three times for Alan, and I had walking pneumonia. I've learned that there are two ways to understudy: looking good and looking like an idiot. Understudying can be a terrifying experience if you're not prepared, but it can really be a kick if you are. Lesson: Be prepared.

Superstitions That Turned Out To Be True: There's a superstition about understudies: one of you ALWAYS goes on—and in the most unexpected way. We've also had people say the title of the Scottish Play, and we made them walk out of the dressing room, turn around three times, and spit.

Coolest Thing About Being in This Show: Working on Broadway is just really cool. Actors work their whole careers to get here. It's been ten years for me. You really have to enjoy it when it happens. People just light up when you tell them you're in a Broadway show. It's a real point of pride. When I come up out of the subway in Times Square and know that I'm going to work, I get tremendous pleasure out of it every day.

The Producers

First Preview: March 21, 2001. Opened: April 19, 2001.
Closed: April 22, 2007 after 33 Previews and 2,502 Performances.

PLAYBILL

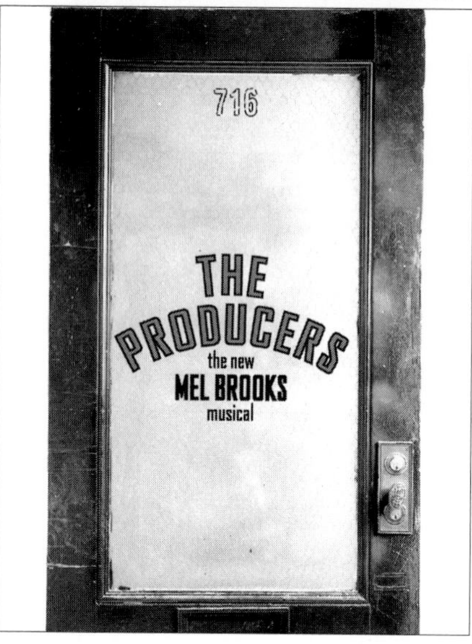

ST. JAMES THEATRE
A JUJAMCYN THEATRE
ROCCO LANDESMAN
PRESIDENT

PAUL LIBIN
PRODUCING DIRECTOR

JACK VIERTEL
CREATIVE DIRECTOR

Rocco Landesman Live Nation The Frankel • Baruch • Viertel • Routh Group
Bob and Harvey Weinstein Rick Steiner Robert F.X. Sillerman Mel Brooks
In Association with James D. Stern/Douglas Meyer
present

Tony Danza Roger Bart
in

THE PRODUCERS

the new
Mel Brooks
musical

Book by Mel Brooks and Thomas Meehan Music and Lyrics by Mel Brooks
and by Special Arrangement with StudioCanal
also starring
Brad Musgrove Bill Nolte Lee Roy Reams Angie Schworer
With
Madeleine Doherty Kathy Fitzgerald Eric Gunhus
Kevin Ligon Peter Marinos Christina Marie Norrup

Philip Michael Baskerville Jim Borstelmann Angie C. Creighton James Gray Justin Greer
Kimberly Hester Stacey Todd Holt Shauna Hoskin Kimberly Catherine Jones Chris Klink
Katrina Loncaric Liz McKendry Will Taylor Wendy Waring Ashley Yeater Courtney Young

Scenery Designed by Robin Wagner
Costumes Designed by William Ivey Long
Lighting Designed by Peter Kaczorowski

Sound Designed by Steve C. Kennedy
Casting by Tara Rubin Casting
Original Casting by Johnson-Liff Associates

Associate Director Steven Zweigbaum
Associate Choreographer Warren Carlyle
Wigs & Hair Designed by Paul Huntley

Music Direction and Vocal Arrangements by Patrick S. Brady
Orchestrations by Doug Besterman
Music Coordinator John Miller

General Management Richard Frankel Productions Laura Green
Technical Supervisor Juniper Street Productions
Press Representative Barlow • Hartman
Associate Producers Frederic H. and Rhoda Mayerson Jennifer Costello

Musical Arrangements and Supervision by
Glen Kelly

Direction and Choreography by
Susan Stroman

Grammy Award-winning Original Broadway Cast Recording Available On Sony Classical

LIVE BROADWAY

12/18/06

CAST

(in order of appearance)

The Usherettes ....CHRISTINA MARIE NORRUP, ASHLEY YEATER
Max Bialystock ....TONY DANZA
Leo Bloom ....ROGER BART
Hold-me Touch-me ....MADELEINE DOHERTY
Mr. Marks ....KEVIN LIGON
Franz Liebkind ....BILL NOLTE
Carmen Ghia ....BRAD MUSGROVE
Roger DeBris ....LEE ROY REAMS
Bryan ....PETER MARINOS
Kevin ....KEVIN LIGON
Scott ....JIM BORSTELMANN
Shirley ....KATHY FITZGERALD
Ulla ....ANGIE SCHWORER
Lick-me Bite-me ..CHRISTINA MARIE NORRUP
Kiss-me Feel-me ....KATHY FITZGERALD
Jack Lepidus ....PETER MARINOS
Donald Dinsmore ....JIM BORSTELMANN
Jason Green ....KEVIN LIGON
Lead Tenor ....ERIC GUNHUS
Sergeant ....KEVIN LIGON
O'Rourke ....WILL TAYLOR
O'Riley ....CHRIS KLINK
O'Houllihan ..PHILIP MICHAEL BASKERVILLE
Guard ....JIM BORSTELMANN
Bailiff ....WILL TAYLOR
Judge ....PETER MARINOS
Foreman of Jury ....KATHY FITZGERALD
Trustee ....KEVIN LIGON

Continued on next page

Photo by Paul Kolnik

Tony Danza (L) as Max Bialystock sings "The King of Broadway," accompanied by Jim Borstelmann.

The Producers

SCENES

ACT ONE

New York, 1959

Scene 1: Shubert Alley
"Opening Night" .... The Ensemble
"The King of Broadway" .... Max & Ensemble
Scene 2: Max's Office, June 16, 1959
"We Can Do It" .... Max & Leo
Scene 3: The Chambers Street Offices of Whitehall and Marks
"I Wanna Be A Producer" .... Leo & The Accountants
Scene 4: Max's Office
"We Can Do It" (Reprise) .... Max & Leo
Scene 5: Max's Office Early the Following Morning
Scene 6: The Rooftop of a Greenwich Village Apartment Building
"In Old Bavaria" .... Franz
"Der Guten Tag Hop Clop" .... Franz, Max, Leo
Scene 7: The Living Room of Renowned Theatrical Director Roger DeBris' Elegant Upper East Side Townhouse on a Sunny Tuesday Afternoon in June
"Keep It Gay" .... Roger, Carmen, Bryan, Kevin, Scott, Shirley, Max, Leo
Scene 8: Max's Office
"When You Got It, Flaunt It" .... Ulla
Scene 9: Little Old Lady Land
"Along Came Bialy" .... Max, Little Old Ladies
"Act One Finale" .... Max, Leo, Franz, Ulla, Roger, Carmen, Bryan, Kevin, Scott, Shirley, Ensemble

ACT TWO

Scene 1: Max's Office, late morning, a few weeks later
"That Face" .... Leo, Ulla, Max
Scene 2: The Bare Stage of a Broadway Theatre
"Haben Sie Gehoert Das Deutsche Band?" .... Jason, Franz
Scene 3: Shubert Alley
"Opening Night" (Reprise) .... The Usherettes
"You Never Say 'Good Luck' On Opening Night" .... Roger, Max, Carmen, Franz, Leo
Scene 4: The Stage of The Shubert Theatre
"Springtime For Hitler" .... Lead Tenor, Roger, Ulla, Ensemble
Scene 5: Max's Office, later that night
"Where Did We Go Right?" .... Max, Leo
Scene 6: The Holding Cell of a New York Courthouse, ten days later.
"Betrayed" .... Max
Scene 7: A New York Courtroom
" 'Til Him" .... Leo, Max
Scene 8: Sing Sing
"Prisoners Of Love" .... The Convicts
Scene 9: The Stage of The Shubert Theatre
"Prisoners Of Love" (continued) .... Roger, Ulla, The Ensemble
Scene 10: Shubert Alley
"Prisoners of Love (Reprise): Leo and Max" .... Leo, Max
Curtain Call
"Goodbye!" .... The Company

Cast Continued

THE ENSEMBLE

PHILIP MICHAEL BASKERVILLE, JIM BORSTELMANN, MADELEINE DOHERTY, KATHY FITZGERALD, ERIC GUNHUS, KIMBERLY HESTER, SHAUNA HOSKIN, KIMBERLY CATHERINE JONES, CHRIS KLINK, KEVIN LIGON, KATRINA LONCARIC, PETER MARINOS, CHRISTINA MARIE NORRUP, WILL TAYLOR, WENDY WARING, ASHLEY YEATER

SWINGS

ANGIE C. CREIGHTON, JAMES GRAY, JUSTIN GREER, STACEY TODD HOLT, LIZ McKENDRY, COURTNEY YOUNG

DANCE CAPTAINS

JUSTIN GREER, COURTNEY YOUNG

UNDERSTUDIES

Max Bialystock: KEVIN LIGON, BILL NOLTE
Leo Bloom: JUSTIN GREER, STACEY TODD HOLT
Franz Liebkind: JIM BORSTELMANN, KEVIN LIGON
Carmen Ghia: JUSTIN GREER, STACEY TODD HOLT
Roger DeBris: JIM BORSTELMANN, KEVIN LIGON
Ulla: KATRINA LONCARIC, WENDY WARING

ORCHESTRA

Conductor: PATRICK S. BRADY
Associate Conductor: DAVID GURSKY
Woodwinds: VINCENT DELLA ROCCA, STEVEN J. GREENFIELD, JAY HASSLER, ALVA F. HUNT, FRANK SANTAGATA
Trumpets: NICK MARCHIONE, FRANK GREENE, DAVID ROGERS
Tenor Trombones: DAN LEVINE, TIM SESSIONS
Bass Trombone: CHRIS OLNESS
French Horn: NANCY BILLMAN
Concert Master: RICK DOLAN
Violins: ASHLEY D. HORNE, LOUISE OWEN, KAREN M. KARLSRUD, HELEN KIM
Cello: LAURA BONTRAGER
Harp: ANNA REINERSMAN
String Bass: ROBERT RENINO
Drums: LARRY LELLI
Percussion: BENJAMIN HERMAN
Keyboard: DAVID GURSKY
Music Coordinator: JOHN MILLER
Additional Orchestrations: LARRY BLANK

The Producers

Tony Danza
Max Bialystock

Roger Bart
Leo Bloom

Brad Musgrove
Carmen Ghia

Bill Nolte
Franz Liebkind

Lee Roy Reams
Roger DeBris

Angie Schworer
Ulla

Madeleine Doherty
Hold-me Touch-me

Kathy Fitzgerald
Shirley, Kiss-me Feel-me, Foreman of Jury

Eric Gunhus
Lead Tenor

Kevin Ligon
Mr. Marks, Kevin, Jason Green, Sergeant, Trustee

Peter Marinos
Bryan, Jack Lepidus, Judge

Christina Marie Norrup
Usherette, Lick-me Bite-me

Philip Michael Baskerville
O'Houllihan

Jim Borstelmann
Blind Violinist, Scott, Donald Dinsmore, Guard

Angie C. Creighton
Swing

James Gray
Swing

Justin Greer
Dance Captain, Swing

Kimberly Hester
Ensemble

Stacey Todd Holt
Swing

Shauna Hoskin
Ensemble

Kimberly Catherine Jones
Ensemble

Chris Klink
O'Riley

Katrina Loncaric
Ensemble

Liz McKendry
Swing

Will Taylor
O'Rourke, Bailiff

Wendy Waring
Ensemble

Ashley Yeater
Usherette

Courtney Young
Resident Choreographer, Swing

Mel Brooks
Book, Composer & Lyricist, Producer

Thomas Meehan
Book

Susan Stroman
Director/ Choreographer

Robin Wagner
Set Design

William Ivey Long
Costume Designer

Peter Kaczorowski
Lighting Designer

Steve Canyon Kennedy
Sound Designer

The Producers

Tara Rubin
Casting

Vincent Liff and Geoffrey Johnson, Johnson-Liff Associates
Original Casting

Lisa Shriver
Assistant Choreographer

Paul Huntley
Wig and Hair Design

Doug Besterman
Orchestrations

John Miller
Music Coordinator

Laura Green, Richard Frankel Productions
General Management

Guy Kwan, John Paull, Hillary Blanken, Kevin Broomell, Ana Rose Greene, Juniper Street Productions
Technical Supervisor

Rocco Landesman
Producer

Richard Frankel, The Baruch•Viertel• Routh•Frankel Group
Producer

Steven Baruch, The Baruch•Viertel• Routh•Frankel Group
Producer

Thomas Viertel, The Baruch•Viertel• Routh•Frankel Group
Producer

Marc Routh, The Baruch•Viertel• Routh•Frankel Group
Producer

Bob Weinstein
Producer

Harvey Weinstein
Producer

Rick Steiner
Producer

Robert F.X. Sillerman
Producer

Douglas L. Meyer
Producer

Frederic H. Mayerson
Associate Producer

Rhoda Mayerson
Associate Producer

Melanie Allen
Ensemble

Gary Beach
Roger DeBris

Pamela Dayton
Foreman of Jury, Kiss-me Feel-me, Shirley, Ensemble

John Treacy Egan
Max Bialystock

Hunter Foster
Leo Bloom

Robert H. Fowler
O'Houllihan, Ensemble

Renée Klapmeyer
Ensemble

Jason Patrick Sands
Swing

John Treacy Egan
Max Bialystock

Hunter Foster
Leo Bloom

Robert H. Fowler
Ensemble

The Producers

Sarrah Strimel
Ensemble

Photos by Ben Strothmann

FRONT OF HOUSE
Kneeling (L-R): Cindy Lopiano, Russ Buenteo, Margaret McElroy, Ashley Devlin, Jim Barry.

Standing (L-R): Catherine Junior, Lenny Baron, Henry Menedez, Scott Rippe, Donna Van Der Linden, Erica Jones, Henry Linton, James Cline, Nicolette Capra and Heather Jewels.

USHERS and CONCESSIONAIRES
Front of Bar (L-R):
Francisco Medina, Liz Botros, Victor Beaulieu, Danny Duran.

Behind Bar (L-R):
Joe Laureano, Jovan Jackson, Josh Herod, Amanda Dunlap and Albert Kim.

WARDROBE
Kneeling (L-R): Roy Seiler, Herb Ouelette.

Middle Row (L-R): Maura Clifford, Terry LaVada, Jessica Dermody, unknown, Mary Kay Yezerski, unknown.

Back Row (L-R): Dennis Birchall, Vanessa Misty Fernandez, Theodore Katsoulogia, Julie Alderfer, Adam Ghadet, Shanah Kendall, Anna Hoffman, Jessica Minczeski, and Cara Hannah.

DOORMAN
Adam Hodzic

BOX OFFICE
(L-R): Carmine Loiacono, Vinny Sclafani and Michael Milione.

Photos by Ben Strothmann

STAGE MANAGER
Ira Mont

ORCHESTRA
Front Row, Sitting (L-R): Daniel Levine, Rick Dolan, Ben Herman.

Second Row, Kneeling (L-R): Frank Santagata, Connie Holperin, Steve Greenfield, Chris MacDonnell.

Standing (L-R): Jay Hassler, Tim Sessions, John Arbo and Greg Dlugos.

CARPENTRY AND ELECTRICS
Sitting and Kneeling (L-R): Jack Cennamo, Tom Maloney, David Gotwald, Sue Pelkofer, Bob Colgan, Julia Rubin, Bob Miller.

Back Row (L-R): Richard Anderson, Jeff Wondsel, James Devins, Tommy Thompson, Tom Ferguson, Ryan McDonough, Richard Prisco, Joe Pearson, Tim McDonough and Tim Mack. Jr.

STAFF FOR *THE PRODUCERS*

GENERAL MANAGEMENT
RICHARD FRANKEL PRODUCTIONS
Richard Frankel Marc Routh Laura Green
Rod Kaats Jo Porter Joe Watson

COMPANY MANAGER
Kathy Lowe
Associate Company Manager . . . . .Jackie Newman

GENERAL PRESS REPRESENTATIVE
BARLOW • HARTMAN
John Barlow Michael Hartman
Wayne Wolfe Andrew Snyder

CASTING
TARA RUBIN CASTING
Tara Rubin, CSA
Dunja Vitolic Eric Woodall Laura Schutzel
Mona Slomsky Rebecca Carfagna Jeff Siebert

Production Stage Manager . . . . .Steven Zweigbaum
Stage Manager . . . . .Ira Mont
Assistant Stage Managers . . . . .Ara Mark, Joseph Sheridan
Associate Choreographer . . . . .Warren Carlyle
Assistant Director . . . . .Scott Bishop
Assistant Choreographer . . . . .Lisa Shriver
Resident Choreographer . . . . .Courtney Young
Dance Captain . . . . .Justin Greer

The Producers

Technical Supervisor .... Juniper Street Productions/ Hillary Blanken, John H. Paul III
Technical Associates .... Kevin Broomell, Lonnie Goertz, Guy Kwan
Associate Set Designer .... David Peterson
Assistant Set Designers .... Atkin Pace, Thomas Peter Sarr
Associate Costume Designer .... Martha Bromelmeier
Assistant Costume Designer .... Tom Beall
Assistants to William Ivey Long .... Laura Oppenheimer, Heather Bair
Automated Light Programmer .... Josh Weitzman
First Assistant Lighting Designer .... Paul Miller
Assistant Lighting Designers .... Mick Addison Smith, Philip S. Rosenberg
Associate Sound Designer .... John Shivers
Supervising Production Carpenter .... Joe Patria
Head Carpenter .... Jack Cennamo
Assistant Carpenters .... Michael Cennamo, J. Marvin Crosland, Guy Patria, Richard Patria
Supervising Production Electrician .... Rick Baxter
Head Electrician .... Joe Pearson
Assistant Electrician .... Tom Ferguson
Head Sound Engineer .... David Gotwald
Assistant Sound Engineer .... Scott Silvian
Supervising Property Master .... Laura Koch
Head Property Master .... Tom Thomson
Production Wardrobe Supervisor ...... Douglas C. Petitjean
Wardrobe Supervisor .... Deidre LaBarre
Assistant Wardrobe Supervisor .... Jessica Minczeski
Mr. Danza's Dresser .... Terry LaVada
Mr. Bart's Dresser .... Scotty Cain
Dressers .... Dennis Birchall, Maura Clifford, Jessica Dermody, Dorothy Dicomo, Misty Fernandez, Ron Fleming, Adam Girardet, Lisa Marie Grosso, Constance Holperin, Shannon Munn, Herb Ouellette, Cesar Porto, Katherine Powers, John Rinaldi, Roy Seiler, Martha Smith, Ron Taggert
Wig Supervisor .... Ron Mack
Assistant Wig Supervisor .... Shanah-Ann Kendall
Wig Stylists .... Danielle Caputo, Cara Hannah, Anna Hoffman

---

Make-Up Design .... Randy Houston Mercer

Music Coordinator .... John Miller
Assistant Music Coordinator .... Todd Cutrona
Assistant to Mr. Miller .... Kelly M. Rach
Associate Conductor .... David Gursky
Synthesizer Programming .... Music Arts Technologies, Brett Sommer
Rehearsal Drummer .... Cubby O'Brien
Music Preparation .... Miller Music Services

Additional Orchestrations .... Larry Blank

---

Make-Up Consultant .... Melissa Silver
Physical Therapy Services .... PhysioArts
Associate to Mr. Brooks .... Leah Zappy
Asst. to Mr. Landesman .... Nicole Kastrinos
Assts. to Mr. Sillerman .... Gini Smythe, Matthew Morse, Manuela Perea
Asst. to Mr. Steiner .... Kathy Wall
Asst. to Mr. Stern .... Debbie Bisno, Leah Callaghan
Asst. to Mr. Baruch .... Sonja Soper
Asst. to Mr. Viertel .... Tania Senewiratne
Management Assistant .... Eric Cornell
Production Assistants .... Kate Sullivan, Donald Fried, Adam M. Muller, Erin J. Riggs, Leah Richardson, Sharon Del Pilar
Advertising .... Serino Coyne, Inc., Nancy Coyne, Sandy Block, Thomas Mygatt, Craig Sabbatino
Promotions/Marketing .... The Marketing Group
Photographers .... Paul Kolnik, Norman Jean Roy
Theatre Displays .... King Displays
Insurance .... DeWitt Stern Group
Legal Counsel .... Elliot Brown, Jason Baruch, Franklin Weinrib, Rudell & Vassallo, P.C.; Alan U. Schwartz; Greenberg Traurig, LLP
Banking .... Chase Manhattan Bank/ Stephanie Daulton, Michele Gibbons
Payroll Service .... Castellana Service, Inc.
Accounting .... Fried and Kowgios Partners, LLP
Travel Agencies .... JMC Travel, Navigant International
Exclusive Tour Direction .... On The Road, The Booking Group
On-Stage Merchandising .... George Fenmore/ More Merchandising International
Concessions .... Live Nation, Theatrical Merchandising
New York Rehearsals .... The New 42nd Street Studios
Opening Night Coordinator .... Tobak-Lawrence Events and Promotions/ Suzanne Tobak, Michael Lawrence, Jennifer Falik, Rebakah Sale

---

Group Sales .... Show Tix (212) 302-7000

RICHARD FRANKEL PRODUCTIONS STAFF

Finance Director .... **Michael Naumann**
Assistant to Mr. Frankel .... Jeff Romley
Assistant to Mr. Routh .... Seth Soloway
Assistant to Ms. Green .... Joshua A. Saletnik
Assistant Finance Director .... John DiMeglio
Information Technology Manager .... Roddy Pimentel
Management Assistant .... Heidi Schading
Accounting Assistant .... Heather Le Blanc
Accounting Assistant .... Nicole O'Bleanis
National Sales and Marketing Director .. **Ronni Mandell**
Marketing Manager .... Melissa Marano
Director of Business Affairs .... **Michael Sinder**
Office Manager .... **Lori Steiger-Perry**
Assistant Office Manager .... Stephanie Adamczyk
Receptionists .... Kathleen Kiernan, Matt Posner
Interns .... Kristi Bergman, Ashley Berman, Kevin Condardo, Yie Foong, Annie Grappone, Julie Griffith, Christina Macchia, Anthony Nunziata, Will Nunziata, Kimberly Jade Tompkins

---

LIVE NATION, THEATRICAL DIVISION

David Ian, Steve Winton, David Anderson

Wendy Connor, Jennifer Costello, Jennifer DeLange, Paul Dietz, Susie Krajsa, David Lazar, Courtney Pierce, Alison Spiriti, Dan Swartz

Make-Up courtesy of MAC Cosmetics

CREDITS AND ACKNOWLEDGEMENTS

Scenery and scenic effects built, painted, electrified and automated by Showmotion, Inc., Norwalk, CT; Scenery fabrication by Entolo/Scenic Technologies, a division of Production Resource Group, L.L.C., New Windsor, NY; Additional scenery built by Hudson Scenic Studios; Scenery automation by Showmotion, Inc., using the Autocue Computerized Motion Control System; Show control and scenic motion control featuring Stage Command Systems by Entolo, a division of Production Resource Group, L.L.C., New Windsor, NY; Soft goods by I. Weiss, New York; Water fountain effect by Waltzing Waters; Stormtrooper puppets designed and fabricated by Eoin Sprott; Tanks and pigeon puppets designed and fabricated by Jerard Studio; Lighting equipment from Fourth Phase New Jersey; Sound equipment from ProMix.; Costumes by Euro Co., Timberlake Studios, Inc., Tricorne New York City, Jennifer Love Costumes; Tailoring by Scafatti Custom Tailors; Shoes by LaDuca Shoes NYC, T.O. Dey; Hosiery provided by Hue; Specialty props fabricated by Prism Production Services, Rahway, N.J.; Max's office furniture, the script stacks and Roger's furniture by the Rabbit's Choice; Assorted hand props by Jennie Marino, Moon Boot Prod.; Vintage lighting fixture courtesy of Four Star Lighting; MP40 Schmeissers machine guns by Costume Armour; Walkers through J & J Medical Supplies, Teaneck, NJ; Champagne by Mumm's; Krylon spray paint by Siperstein's Paints; Custom shirts by Cego; Millinery by Rodney Gordon and Henry Ewoskio; Showgirl specialty costumes by Martin Adams; Set poster art by Jim Miller; Lozenges provided by Ricola, Inc.; Parker jotter pens courtesy of the Parker Corporation. The use of Village People characters and costumes is by kind courtesy and permission of Can't Stop Productions Inc. and Scorpio Music S.A. The name Village People and the trade-dress of the Village People are registered trademarks.

MUSIC CREDITS

Words and Music by Mel Brooks. Songs published by Mel Brooks Music, except for "Have You Ever Heard the German Band," "Springtime for Hitler" and "Prisoners of Love," published by Legation Music Corp.

JUJAMCYN THEATERS

ROCCO LANDESMAN
President

PAUL LIBIN
Producing Director

JACK VIERTEL
Creative Director

JERRY ZAKS
Resident Director

JORDAN ROTH
Resident Producer

DANIEL ADAMIAN
General Manager

JENNIFER HERSHEY
Director of Operations

MEREDITH VILLATORE
Chief Financial Officer

STAFF FOR THE ST. JAMES THEATRE

Manager .... Daniel Adamian
Treasurer .... Vincent Sclafani
Carpenter .... Timothy McDonough
Propertyman .... Barnett Epstein
Electrician .... Albert Sayers

The Producers
SCRAPBOOK

1. Mel Brooks chokes up during his curtain speech with Susan Stroman at the final performance.
2. Composer/lyricist Brooks with director Stroman and co-librettist Thomas Meehan on the St. James Theatre stage after the final performance.

Photos by Aubrey Reuben

Correspondent: Kathy Fitzgerald, "Shirley"

The Last Performance: I got *The Producers* in the summer of 2000. My baby, Hope, was about 11 months old. She has completely been brought up in this company. So when we got on the train April 22, 2007, to go to the last performance of the show she...*we* both were pretty sad.

We ran into Bill Nolte (Franz Liebkind) and he asked Hope what her favorite memory of the show was. She said going into the showgirls' room to play with a big stuffed bear. We got to the theatre, there was an excited buzz—strange on a closing, but it was still a major event.

We all were called to the stage to rehearse the bows for the end of the show with Stro and Mel. There were flowers and little blue Tiffany bags. We all got into costume and met on the stage before the curtain went up for the last time. We all formed a circle. Some people were crying. I started to cry and then tried to stop by talking about *Coram Boy,* a beautiful show a lot of us had just seen which was amazingly sad. I just kept talking about it to stop the tears. It worked!

During the first number I kept getting choked up and thought I would have to stop singing. The audience that day was so with us, screaming with every joke, that we felt like comedy rock stars. My husband and daughter were in the box seats and I couldn't help playing to them. Hope (now 7) was beaming and singing along with every word. I was trying to memorize as many laughs and moments as I could.

Before I knew it, the show was over. At the curtain call Mel, Stro and Tom Meehan came up to the stage and thanked everyone. All the backstage crew came on stage. Most of them had been there the whole six years. I overheard the prop guy, Barney, say, "I thought that we'd get a reprieve from the Governor!" We sang the "Goodbye" song one last time, the curtain came down and then everyone pretty much was hugging and crying.

Everyone changed their clothes and came back on stage for a champagne toast. Mel passed by me and I told him that I loved him. He said "I love you more" and then added, "You were pretty good tonight!"

Stro made a toast: "Treasure every day every moment. I love all of us, and everyone like us."

How beautifully put and how very true.

What a ride this has been. We've been though births and deaths, 9/11, the musicians' strike, the blackout, and we kept making people laugh all the way through it. How lucky for all of us.

I'm so thankful for this fabulous life experience but mostly that my daughter has had the opportunity to be around these wonderful, wonderful people.

Here's to us.

Radio Golf

First Preview: April 20, 2007. Opened: May 8, 2007.
Still running as of May 31, 2007.

PLAYBILL

AUGUST WILSON
1945 - 2005

CORT THEATRE
138 West 48th Street
A Shubert Organization Theatre
Gerald Schoenfeld, *Chairman* **Philip J. Smith,** *President*

Robert E. Wankel, *Executive Vice President*

JUJAMCYN THEATERS MARGO LION JEFFREY / JERRY RICHARDS FRANKEL TAMARA / WENDELL TUNIE PIERCE
FRAN KIRMSER BUNTING MANAGEMENT GROUP GEORGIA FRONTIERE / OPEN PICTURES
LAUREN / STEVEN DOLL GREIL & THE AW GROUP WONDER CITY, INC. / TOWNSEND TEAGUE

IN ASSOCIATION WITH

JACK VIERTEL and GORDON DAVIDSON

PRESENT

HARRY LENNIX TONYA PINKINS
ANTHONY CHISHOLM JOHN EARL JELKS

IN

AUGUST WILSON'S
RADIO GOLF

AND INTRODUCING
JAMES A. WILLIAMS
AS ROOSEVELT HICKS

SCENIC DESIGN BY **DAVID GALLO**
COSTUME DESIGN BY **SUSAN HILFERTY**
LIGHTING DESIGN BY **DONALD HOLDER**
MUSIC COMPOSED & ARRANGED BY **DAN MOSES SCHREIER**

DRAMATURG **TODD KREIDLER**
CASTING **STANCZYK / CHERPAKOV CASTING**

PRODUCTION MANAGEMENT **AURORA PRODUCTIONS**
PRODUCTION STAGE MANAGER **NARDA E. ALCORN**
EXECUTIVE PRODUCER **NICOLE KASTRINOS**

GENERAL MANAGEMENT **101 PRODUCTIONS, LTD**
PRESS REPRESENTATIVE **BARLOW • HARTMAN**
MARKETING **TMG THE MARKETING GROUP**

DIRECTED BY
KENNY LEON

August Wilson's RADIO GOLF was first produced by Yale Repertory Theatre, New Haven, CT in April 2005.
It was subsequently produced at Mark Taper Forum in Los Angeles, CA; Seattle Repertory Theatre in Seattle, WA; Centerstage in Baltimore, MD; Huntington Theatre in Boston, MA; Goodman Theatre in Chicago, IL; and McCarter Theatre in Princeton, NJ.

The Producers wish to express their appreciation to the Theatre Development Fund for its support of this production.

LIVE BROADWAY

5/8/07

CAST

(in order of appearance)

Mame Wilks .... TONYA PINKINS
Harmond Wilks .... HARRY LENNIX
Roosevelt Hicks .... JAMES A. WILLIAMS
Sterling Johnson .... JOHN EARL JELKS
Elder Joseph Barlow ..... ANTHONY CHISHOLM

SETTING

The Hill District, Pittsburgh, Pennsylvania, 1997. The office of Bedford Hills Redevelopment, Inc., in a storefront on Centre Avenue.

STANDBYS

Standby for Mame Wilks:
ROSALYN COLEMAN
Standby for Harmond Wilks and Roosevelt Hicks:
BILLY EUGENE JONES
Standby for Elder Joseph Barlow and Sterling Johnson:
CEDRIC YOUNG

Photo by Carol Rosegg

(L-R): John Earl Jelks and Anthony Chisholm

2006-2007 AWARD

New York Drama Critics' Circle Award
Best American Play

Radio Golf

Harry Lennix
Harmond Wilks

Tonya Pinkins
Mame Wilks

Anthony Chisholm
Elder Joseph Barlow

John Earl Jelks
Sterling Johnson

James A. Williams
Roosevelt Hicks

Rosalyn Coleman
Standby Mame Wilks

Billy Eugene Jones
Standby
Harmond Wilks,
Roosevelt Hicks

Cedric Young
Standby
Elder Joseph Barlow,
Sterling Johnson

August Wilson
Playwright,
1945-2005

Kenny Leon
Director

David Gallo
Scenic Design

Susan Hilferty
Costume Design

Donald Holder
Lighting Design

Dan Moses Schreier
Music Composition
and Arrangement

Derrick Sanders
Assistant Director

Charlie Smith
Associate Scenic
Designer

Rocco Landesman,
President,
Jujamcyn Theaters
Producer

Margo Lion
Producer

Jeffrey Richards
Producer

Jerry Frankel
Producer

Tamara Tunie
Producer

Lauren Doll
Producer

John O'Boyle,
Wonder City, Inc.
Producer

Lauren Stevens,
Wonder City, Inc.
Producer

Ricky Stevens,
Wonder City, Inc.
Producer

Jack Viertel
Producer

Gordon Davidson
Producer

HEAD PROPS
Lonnie Gaddy

USHER
Jeanine Buckley

Photos by Ben Strohmann

Radio Golf

STAGE CREW

(L-R): Dylan Foley (Production Props Supervisor),
Eileen Miller (Wardrobe Supervisor),
Lonnie Gaddy (Head Props),
Narda E. Alcorn (Production Stage Manager),
Marion Friedman (Stage Manager),
Scott DeVerna (Production Electrician),
Chris Morey (Company Manager),
David Ruble (Dresser)
and Phil Lojo (Head Sound Engineer).

BOX OFFICE

(L-R):
Diane Heatherington (Head Treasurer),
Joshua Skidmore (Assistant Treasurer).

Photos by Ben Strothmann

FRONT OF HOUSE

(L-R): Miguel (Security Officer), Lea Lefler, William Denson (Chief Usher), Robert Evans, Shanette Santos and Danielle Smith.

Radio Golf

STAFF FOR *RADIO GOLF*

GENERAL MANAGEMENT
101 PRODUCTIONS, LTD.
Wendy Orshan Jeffrey M. Wilson
David Auster

COMPANY MANAGER
Chris Morey

GENERAL PRESS REPRESENTATIVE
BARLOW•HARTMAN INC.
John Barlow Michael Hartman
Dennis Crowley Michelle Bergmann

PRODUCTION MANAGEMENT
AURORA PRODUCTIONS, INC.
Gene O'Donovan, W. Benjamin Heller II,
Bethany Weinstein, Melissa Mazdra,
Meghan Von Vett

MARKETING
IMAGES USA
Ricki Fairley-Brown
Hank Ernst Andrew Ledgister

WALKER INT'L COMMUNICATIONS GROUP
Donna Walker-Kuhne Natalie Clarke

BROTHERS AND SISTERS MARKETING
Irene Gandy

SITUATION MARKETING
Damian Bazadona Jimmy Lee
Jennifer Elston Ian Bennett Matt Healy

TMG — THE MARKETING GROUP
Tanya Grubich Laura Matalon
Anne Rippey Daya Wolterstorff Allison Cabellon

CASTING
Stanczyk/Cherpakov Casting
Laura Stanczyk, CSA Howie Cherpakov, CSA

Original Casting by Harriett Bass

Assistant Director .... **Derrick Sanders**
Production Stage Manager .... Narda E. Alcorn
Stage Manager .... Marion Friedman
Associate Scenic Designer .... Charlie Smith
Associate Costume Designer .... Maiko Matsushima
Associate Lighting Designer .... Hilary Manners
Associate Sound Designer .... David Bullard

Vocal Coach .... Erin Annarella

Production Carpenter .... Ed Diaz
Production Props Supervisor .... Dylan Foley
Production Electrician .... Scott DeVerna
Production Sound Supervisor .... Jens McVoy
Head Properties .... Lonnie Gaddy
Wardrobe Supervisor .... Eileen Miller
Dresser .... David Ruble
Hair Supervisor .... Barbara Roman
Production Assistant .... Michael Zaleski

Legal Counsel .... Loeb & Loeb, LLP/ Seth Gelblum, Esq.
Accountant .... Fried & Kowgios, CPAs, LLP/ Robert Fried, CPA
Controller .... Joseph S. Kubala
Advertising .... SPOTCO/ Drew Hodges, Jim Edwards, Tom McCann, Stephen Sosnowski
Website Design .... Situation Marketing
Sponsorships .... Above the Title Entertainment/ Jed Bernstein
Assistant to the General Managers .... John Vennema
101 Productions, Ltd. Staff .... Denys Baker, Ashley Berman, Katharine Croke, Barbara Crompton, Laura Dickinson, Sherra Johnston, Emily Lawson, Heidi Neven, Kyle Pickles, Mary Six Rupert, Evan Storey
101 Productions, Ltd. Intern .... Stewart Miller
Radio Golf Intern .... Jeremy Scott
Press Associates .... Leslie Baden, Tom D'Ambrosio, Steve Dow, Carol Fineman, Bethany Larsen, Tom Prudenti, Ryan Ratelle, Kevin Robak, Matt Stapleton, Wayne Wolfe
Casting Assistant .... Daryl Eisenberg
Banking .... J.P. Morgan Chase Bank/ Michele Gibbons, Margaret Wong
Insurance .... DeWitt Stern Group, Inc./ Jennifer Brown
Risk Managers .... Stockbridge Risk Management, Inc./ Neil Goldstein
Theatre Displays .... King Displays, Inc.
Merchandising .... Max Merchandising, LLC/ Randi Grossman
Payroll Services .... Castellana Services, Inc.
Production Photography .... Carol Rosegg
Artwork Photography .... Henry Leutwyler
Group Sales .... Telecharge.com Group Sales (212) 239-6262
Rehearsal Space .... Roundabout Rehearsal Studios

For the Estate of August Wilson:
Constanza Romero, Executor
Dena Levitin, Executive Administrator

Travel for ***Radio Golf*** courtesy of Avocet Travel.
Tracey Mendelsohn Luciana Cherques

CREDITS

The scenery and props for Radio Golf were constructed by the production shops at the Seattle Repertory Theatre. Lighting equipment from PRG Lighting. Sound equipment from PRG Sound.

To learn more about the production, please visit
RadioGolfOnBroadway.com

MUSIC CREDITS

"Blue Skies," music and lyrics by Irving Berlin. This selection is used by special arrangement with The Rodgers and Hammerstein Organization, on behalf of the Estate of Irving Berlin; all rights reserved. "Fuck tha Police" by Andre Young, O'Shea Jackson and L. G. Patterson. Used by permission of Ruthless Attack Muzick. "Me Against the World" by Tupac Amaru Shakur, Yafeu A. Fula, Malcolm Greenidge, Leon Ware, Minnie Riperton, Richard Rudolph, Burt Bacharach, Hal David, Carsten Schack and Kenneth Karlin. Used by permission of Songs of Universal, Inc. on behalf of itself and Joshua's Dream Music/Universal Music Corp., Yaki Kadafi Music, Thug Nation Music, Foxbeat Music, EMI Blackwood Music Inc., Warner Chappell Music and Casa David. "My Lovin' (You're Never Gonna Get It)" by Denzil Foster and Thomas McElroy. Published By EMI Blackwood Music Inc. "You Make Me Wanna" By Jermaine Dupri, Manuel Seal, Usher Raymond. Used by permission of EMI April Music Inc. and BMG Music Publishing. Music clearance by BZ/Rights & Permissions, Inc.

SPECIAL THANKS

Thanks to Eric Schnall. Kenny would like to thank all of the actors, designers, regional theatres and theatre lovers in the wonderful cities of New Haven, Los Angeles, Seattle, Baltimore, Boston, Chicago and Princeton for their remarkable contributions to August Wilson's RADIO GOLF along its journey to Broadway.

THE SHUBERT ORGANIZATION, INC.
Board of Directors

Gerald Schoenfeld Chairman
Philip J. Smith President
Wyche Fowler, Jr.
John W. Kluge
Lee J. Seidler
Michael I. Sovern
Stuart Subotnick

Robert E. Wankel
Executive Vice President

Peter Entin Vice President – Theatre Operations
Elliot Greene Vice President – Finance
David Andrews Vice President – Shubert Ticketing Services
John Darby Vice President – Facilities

D.S. Moynihan
Vice President – Creative Projects

CORT THEATRE

House Manager .... Joseph Traina

Photo by Carol Rosegg

(L-R): Tonya Pinkins and Harry Lennix

Radio Golf

SCRAPBOOK

Correspondent: James A. Williams, "Roosevelt Hicks"
Actor Who Has Done the Most Shows in His Career: Anthony Chisholm.
Favorite Therapy: Breathe Easy Tea.
Record Number of Cell Phone Rings During a Performance: Too many to count!
Memorable Stage Door Fan Encounter: First stage door fan—It's my first Broadway show!
Who Wore the Heaviest/Hottest Costume: Anthony Chisholm.
Catchphrases Only the Company Would Recognize: "Let's Do What We Do!" "Chunk It Up There."
Nicknames: "Harry The King," "Silk," "El Magnifico."
Embarrassing Moments: Walked onstage without the keys and had to ad-lib.
Superstitions That Turned Out To Be True: Whenever the Assistant Stage Manager wears red shoes we have a great show.
Coolest Thing About Being in This Show: Completing August Wilson's play cycle.

Photos by Aubrey Reuben

Photo by David Gewirtzman

1. (L-R): Director Kenny Leon and cast members Anthony Chisholm, Tonya Pinkins, John Earl Jelks, James A. Williams and Harry Lennix at the opening night party at Bond 45.
2. The marquee of the Cort Theatre.
3. (L-R): Constanza Romero and Azula Wilson, respectively widow and daughter of playwright August Wilson, at the premiere.
4. Producer Wendell Pierce (R) with guest Tracie Thoms at Bond 45.
5. (L-R): Guests Leslie Uggams and Phylicia Rashad.
6. (L-R): Pinkins with producer Tamara Tunie.

Rent

First Preview: April 16, 1996. Opened: April 29, 1996.
Still running as of May 31, 2007.

PLAYBILL

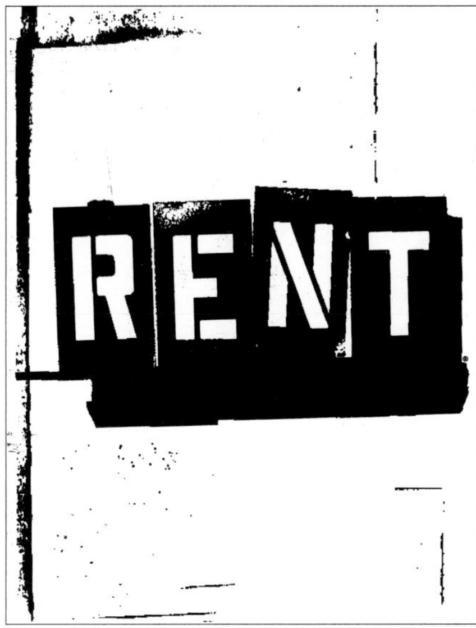

CAST

(in order of appearance)

Roger Davis .... TIM HOWAR
Mark Cohen .... CHRISTOPHER J. HANKE
Tom Collins .... DESTAN OWENS
Benjamin Coffin III .... D'MONROE
Joanne Jefferson .... NICOLE LEWIS
Angel Schunard .... JUSTIN JOHNSTON
Mimi Marquez .... JAIME LEE KIRCHNER
Maureen Johnson .... AVA GAUDET
Mark's mom and others .... HAVEN BURTON
Christmas caroler, Mr. Jefferson, a pastor,
and others .... MARCUS PAUL JAMES
Mrs. Jefferson, woman with bags,
and others .... FRENCHIE DAVIS
Gordon, the man, Mr. Grey,
and others .... LUTHER CREEK
Steve, man with squeegee, a waiter,
and others .... ANDY SEÑOR
Paul, a cop, and others .... SHAUN EARL
Alexi Darling, Roger's mom,
and others .... MAYUMI ANDO

Continued on next page

NEDERLANDER THEATRE

UNDER THE DIRECTION OF
JAMES M. NEDERLANDER AND JAMES L. NEDERLANDER

Jeffrey Seller Kevin McCollum Allan S. Gordon
and New York Theatre Workshop

present

Book, Music and Lyrics by
Jonathan Larson

Mayumi Ando Haven Burton Luther Creek Frenchie Davis
D'Monroe Shaun Earl Ava Gaudet Christopher J. Hanke
Tim Howar Marcus Paul James Justin Johnston
Jaime Lee Kirchner Nicole Lewis Destan Owens Andy Señor
Karmine Alers Crystal Monée Hall Owen Johnston II
Philip Dorian McAdoo Moeisha McGill Kyle Post

Set Design Paul Clay | Costume Design Angela Wendt | Lighting Design Blake Burba | Sound Design Kurt Fischer

Original Concept/Additional Lyrics Billy Aronson | Musical Arrangements Steve Skinner | Dramaturg Lynn M. Thomson

Casting Telsey + Company | Publicity Richard Kornberg/Don Summa

Music Director David Truskinoff | Production Stage Manager John Vivian

General Manager John Corker | Technical Supervision Unitech Productions, Inc.

Music Supervision and Additional Arrangements Tim Weil | Choreography Marlies Yearby

Director
Michael Greif

Original cast recording available on DreamWorks Records' CD's and cassettes

10/2/06

(L-R): Christopher J. Hanke and Tim Howar as Mark and Roger.

Photo by Joan Marcus

MUSICAL NUMBERS

ACT ONE

“Tune Up”/”Voice Mail #1” .... Mark, Roger, Mrs. Cohen, Collins, Benny
“Rent” .... The Company
“You Okay Honey?” .... Angel, Collins
“One Song Glory” .... Roger
“Light My Candle” .... Roger, Mimi
“Voice Mail #2” .... Mr. & Mrs. Jefferson
“Today 4 U” .... Angel
“You'll See” .... Benny, Mark, Collins, Roger, Angel
“Tango: Maureen” .... Mark, Joanne
“Life Support” .... Paul, Gordon, The Company
“Out Tonight” .... Mimi
“Another Day” .... Roger, Mimi, The Company
“Will I?” .... Steve, The Company
“On the Street” .... The Company
“Santa Fe” .... Collins and The Company
“I'll Cover You” .... Angel, Collins
“We're Okay” .... Joanne
“Christmas Bells” .... The Company
“Over the Moon” .... Maureen
“La Vie Boheme”/“I Should Tell You” .... The Company

ACT TWO

“Seasons of Love” .... The Company
“Happy New Year”/“Voice Mail #3” .... Mimi, Roger, Mark, Maureen, Joanne, Collins, Angel, Mrs. Cohen, Alexi Darling, Benny, The man
“Take Me or Leave Me” .... Maureen, Joanne
“Without You” .... Roger, Mimi
“Voice Mail #4” .... Alexi Darling
“Contact” .... The Company
“I'll Cover You: Reprise” .... Collins, The Company
“Halloween” .... Mark
“Goodbye, Love” .... Mark, Mimi, Roger, Maureen, Joanne, Collins, Benny
“What You Own” .... Pastor, Mark, Collins, Benny, Roger
“Voice Mail #5” .... Roger's Mom, Mimi's Mom, Mr. Jefferson, Mrs. Cohen
“Your Eyes”/“Finale” .... Roger, The Company

The cast sings “La Vie Boheme.”

Photo by Joan Marcus

Cast Continued

UNDERSTUDIES

For Roger:
LUTHER CREEK, OWEN JOHNSTON II, KYLE POST
For Mark:
LUTHER CREEK, KYLE POST
For Tom Collins:
MARCUS PAUL JAMES, PHILIP DORIAN McADOO
For Benjamin:
MARCUS PAUL JAMES, PHILIP DORIAN McADOO
For Joanne:
FRENCHIE DAVIS, CRYSTAL MONÉE HALL, MOEISHA McGILL
For Angel:
SHAUN EARL, OWEN JOHNSTON II, ANDY SEÑOR
For Mimi:
KARMINE ALERS, AVA GAUDET, MOEISHA McGILL
For Maureen:
KARMINE ALERS, HAVEN BURTON

SWINGS

KARMINE ALERS, CRYSTAL MONÉE HALL, OWEN JOHNSTON II, PHILIP DORIAN McADOO, MOEISHA McGILL, KYLE POST

DANCE CAPTAIN

OWEN JOHNSTON II

THE BAND

Conductor, Keyboards:
DAVID TRUSKINOFF
Bass:
STEVE MACK
Guitar:
BOBBY BAXMEYER
Drums:
JEFF POTTER
Keyboards, Guitar:
JOHN KORBA

FILM BY

Tony Gerber

Rent

Mayumi Ando
Ensemble

Haven Burton
Ensemble

Luther Creek
Ensemble

Frenchie Davis
Ensemble

D'Monroe
Benny

Shaun Earl
Ensemble

Ava Gaudet
Maureen

Christopher J. Hanke
Mark

Tim Howar
Roger

Marcus Paul James
Ensemble

Justin Johnston
Angel

Jaime Lee Kirchner
Mimi

Nicole Lewis
Joanne

Destan Owens
Collins

Andy Señor
Ensemble

Karmine Alers
Understudy

Crystal Monée Hall
Understudy

Owen Johnston II
Understudy

Philip Dorian McAdoo
Understudy

Moeisha McGill
Understudy

Kyle Post
Understudy

Jonathan Larson
Book, Music, Lyrics

Michael Greif
Director

Marlies Yearby
Choreography

Billy Aronson
Original Concept and Additional Lyrics

John Corker
General Manager

David Santana
Wig, Hair and Make-up Design

Bernard Telsey, Telsey + Company
Casting

Richard Kornberg & Associates
Press Representative

Brian Lynch, Unitech Productions, Inc.
Technical Supervision

Jeffrey Seller
Producer

Kevin McCollum
Producer

Allan S. Gordon
Producer

James C. Nicola, Artistic Director New York Theatre Workshop
Producer

Rent

Justin Brill
Swing

Matt Caplan
Mark Cohen

Robin De Jesús
Steve, man with squeegee, a waiter, and others

Keena J. Ramsey
Joanne Jefferson

Antonique Smith
Mimi Marquez

Maggie Benjamin
Maureen Johnson

Matt Caplan
Mark Cohen

T.V. Carpio
Alexi Darling, Roger's mom, and others

Dana Dawson
Swing

Tonya Dixon
Joanne Jefferson

Mark Richard Ford
Tom Collins

Tamyra Gray
Mimi Marquez

Nicolette Hart
Maureen Johnson

Troy Horne
Tom Collins

Telly Leung
Steve, man with squeegee, a waiter, and others

Todd E. Pettiford
Swing

Antonique Smith
Mimi Marquez

Gwen Stewart
Mrs. Jefferson, woman with bags, and others

Maia Nkenge Wilson
Mrs. Jefferson, woman with bags, and others

Photo by Melissa Merlo

PROPS AND CARPENTRY
(L-R): Billy Wright (House Prop Man), Joe Ferreri, Sr. (House Carpenter), Jan Marasek (Production Prop Man) and Joe Ferreri, Jr. (Assistant House Carpenter).

Rent

Photos by Melissa Merlo

BOX OFFICE
(L-R): Jim Burns (Ticket Seller), Russell Hammel (Ticket Seller).
Not Pictured: Scott Kenny (Ticket Seller) and Gary Kenny (Treasurer).

BARTENDERS
(L-R): Chris Ullness and Michael Rios.

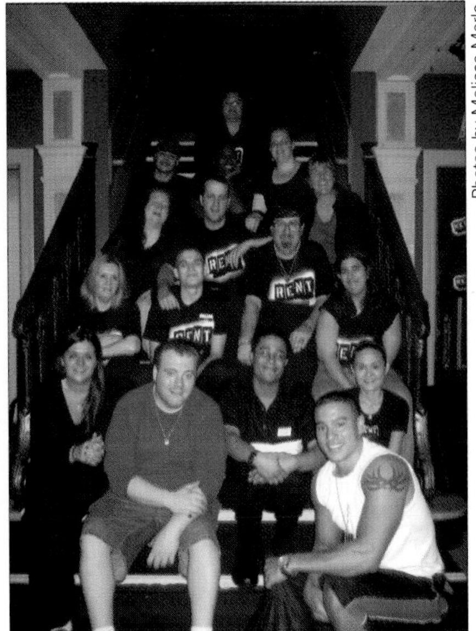

FRONT OF HOUSE STAFF
Front Row (L-R): Katie Spillane (Usher), Derek King (Audience Coordinator), Joaquin Quintana (Audience Coordinator), Angel Serrano (Usher), Cecille Metzler (Merchandising).

Second Row (L-R): Lee Bonacci (Usher), John Cuevas (Usher), Mike Angelino (Usher), Toni Ostini (Head Merchandiser).

Third Row (L-R): Kim Holmes (Ticket Taker), Terrence Cummiskey (Ticket Taker), Trish Ryan (Head Usher).

Back Row (L-R): Marion Pichardo (Usher), Renee Fleetwood (Usher), Grace Kong (Usher) and Heather (Usher).

BAND
(L-R): David Truskinoff (Music Director), John Korba (2nd Keyboard & Guitar), Jeff Potter (Percussion), Steve Mack (Bass) and Bob Baxmeyer (Guitar).

WARDROBE DEPARTMENT
(L-R): Cleo Matheos (Dresser), Roberta Christy (Associate Wardrobe Supervisor) and Jackie Freeman (Dresser).
Not Pictured: Karen Lloyd, Tamara Kopko.

DOORMEN
Joe Santiago.

Not Pictured: Bob Garner.

STAGE MANAGEMENT
Front: John Vivian (Production Stage Manager).
Back Row (L-R): Justin Scribner (Assistant Stage Manager) and Crystal Huntington (Stage Manager).

SOUND DEPARTMENT
(L-R): Susan Ash (Sound Board Operator), Greg Freedman (Sound Board Operator) and Aaron Straus (Deck Electrician).

Photos by Melissa Merlo

ELECTRICS
(L-R): Holli Shevett (Sound Board Operator), Stephen Clem (Console Operator) and Cliff Russell (Spot Operator). Not Pictured: Tom O'Neill and Richie Beck.

STAFF FOR *RENT*

GENERAL MANAGER
JOHN CORKER

GENERAL PRESS REPRESENTATIVE
RICHARD KORNBERG & ASSOCIATES
RICHARD KORNBERG, CARRIE FRIEDMAN

Telsey + Company, C.S.A.:
Bernie Telsey, Will Cantler, David Vaccari,
Bethany Knox, Craig Burns,
Tiffany Little Canfield, Stephanie Yankwitt,
Carrie Rosson, Justin Huff, Joe Langworth

COMPANY MANAGER .... **NICK KALEDIN**

PRODUCTION STAGE MANAGER .... **JOHN VIVIAN**

Stage Manager .... Crystal Huntington
Assistant Stage Manager .... Ryan J. Bell
Technical Supervision .... Unitech Productions, Inc. Brian Lynch, Ken Keneally, Manuel Becker & Jack Culver
Assistant Director .... Martha Banta
Resident Assistant Director .... Evan Ensign
Associate Conductor .... John Korba
Company Manager Associates .... Andrew Jones, Ginger Montel
Wig, Hair and Make-Up Designer .... David Santana
Assistant Costume Designer .... Lisa Zinni
Wardrobe Supervisors .... Karen Lloyd, Roberta Christy
Hair and Make-Up Supervisor .... David Santana
House Manager .... Louise Angelino
Treasurer .... Gary Kenny
House Electrician .... Richard J. Beck
Console Operator .... Stephen Clem
Follow Spot Operators .... Tom O'Neill, Holli Shevett
Sound Board Operators .... Susan Ash, Greg Freedman
Deck Electrician .... Emile LaFargue
House Carpenter .... Joe Ferreri
Assistant House Carpenter .... Joe Ferreri, Jr.
House Prop Master .... Billy Wright
Prop Master .... Jan Marasek
Assistant House Prop Master .... William T. Wright
Dressers .... Elizabeth Floyd, Tamara Kopko, Cleo Matheos
Wardrobe Daywork .... Paula Inocent
Costume Construction .... Marybeth Regan
Assistant to Messrs. Seller & McCollum .... Ryan Hill
Assistant to John Corker .... Kim Vasquez
Receptionist .... Caitlyn Thomson
Office Intern .... Erin Ashland
Dramaturg .... Lynn M. Thomson
Front of House/Lobby Creative Assistant .... Jamie Leo
Lobby Ceiling Murals .... Billy Miller
Music Preparation .... Eva Gianono
Marketing .... TMG-The Marketing Group/ Tanya Grubich, Laura Laponte, Laura Matalon, Anne Rippey
Advertising .... SpotCo Peter Milano, Jim McNicholas
Education Program .... Students Live!/ Amy Weinstein, President Kathy Fiorito, Petol Weekes
Merchandising .... Max Merchandising, LLC/ Toni Ostini, Manager
Title Treatment Design .... Spot Design
Poster Artwork .... Amy Guip
Legal Counsel .... Levine Plotkin & Menin, LLP/ Loren H. Plotkin
Accounting .... Lutz & Carr
Insurance .... DeWitt Stern Group
Banking .... JP Morgan
Payroll Service .... ADP
Production Photographers .... Joan Marcus/ Carol Rosegg
Theatre Displays .... King Display
Product Placement .... George Fenmore/ More Merchandising Internat'l

New York Theatre Workshop

Artistic Director	Managing Director
James C. Nicola	Lynn Moffat

The Producing Office
Kevin McCollum Jeffrey Seller
John Corker

Allan S. Gordon Productions
Allan S. Gordon
Elan Vital McAllister
Anne Caruso David R. Gerson

Credits
Scenery by Hudson Scenic Inc. Lighting equipment by PRG Lighting. Sound equipment by PRG Audio. Drums by Pearl Drums. Bed linens by Martex. Additional musical instruments courtesy of Sam Ash Music Stores. Motorcycle helmets courtesy of Bell Helmets. 16 mm Projectors by Elmo Mfg. Corp. Acrylic drinkware by US Acrylic, Inc. Candles courtesy of Will & Baumer, Inc. Diamond Brand matches used. Some skin care and hair products provided by Kiehl's. Guitar strings supplied by D'Addario & Co. Some denim wear by Lee Apparel and Rider. Make-up provided by Francois Nars. Tattoos by Temptu Marketing. Throat lozenges provided by Ricola, Inc. Plastic cups by Polar Plastic, Inc. Emer'gen-C Super Energy Booster provided by Alacer Corp.

Special Thanks to:
Allan and Nanette Larson; Julie Larson; Victoria Leacock.

"White Christmas" used by arrangement with the Irving Berlin Music Company. "Do You Know the Way to San Jose," written by Burt Bacharach and Hal David, used by permission of Casa David and New Hidden Valley Music. "The Christmas Song (Chestnuts Roasting on an Open Fire)" by Mel Torme and Robert Wells, used by permission of Edwin H. Morris & Company, a division of MPL Communications, Inc. "Rudolph the Red-Nosed Reindeer" written by Johnny Marks used by permission of St. Nicholas Music, Inc.

N
NEDERLANDER

Chairman .... **James M. Nederlander**
President .... **James L. Nederlander**

Executive Vice President
Nick Scandalios

Vice President Corporate Development	Senior Vice President Labor Relations
Charlene S. Nederlander	**Herschel Waxman**

Vice President	Chief Financial Officer
Jim Boese	**Freida Sawyer Belviso**

Rent

SCRAPBOOK

Photo by Aubrey Reuben

Cast members at the September 2006 "Broadway on Broadway" event in Times Square. Back row (L-R): D'Monroe, Christopher Hanke, Destan Owens, Shaun Earl, Justin Johnston, Marcus Paul James, Tim Howar. Middle Row: Nicole Lewis, Ava Gaudet, Karmine Alers, Jaime Lee Kirchner, Robin deJesus, Frenchie Davis. Front Row (L-R): Haven Burton and Luther Creek.

Correspondent: Luther Creek, "Gordon"

Memorable Directorial Encounter: After eleven years, Director Michael Greif called a rehearsal with full cast and crew to re-stage a moment toward the end of Act I. Each of us was bewildered and tickled that we would be asked to do something new!

Anniversary Party: The ten-year *Rent* anniversary! A benefit was thrown to support the charity Friends In Deed, which Jonathan Larson had utilized before his death, and is, in part, inspiration for one of the scenes in *Rent*. The reunion of most of the original company was followed with a gathering at Cipriani.

Most Exciting Celebrity Visitor: Laurence Fishburne, who brought his daughter to see the show for her birthday. He came backstage and was complimentary, kind and gracious as we each offered our admiration for his work.

"Gypsy of the Year" Sketch: "Hopeful." Philip McAdoo, Haven Burton, Crystal Moneé Hall, and Marcus Paul James worked extensively with a group of students who wrote the text of the performance.

"Carols for a Cure" Carol: "Angels We Have Heard on High (on a theme by Jonathan Larson)."

Actor Who Performed the Most Roles in This Show: We had a half-joke at the theatre, that if everyone in the building were to call out on one of those incredible summer afternoons, that, instead of canceling the show, Karmine Alers would be called in to play every single role. It seems she has played nearly everything, and has only narrowly avoided playing opposite herself!

Who Has Done the Most Shows: We have several faithfuls, but Shaun Earl makes a clean finish ahead in the diligent worker category, while Justin Johnston is racing to a close second.

Special Backstage Rituals: This current ensemble has a few favorite understage moments where the creative dancing is much more stylized than would be appropriate in our East Village onstage world. "So Swift" is the echo heard, while as many of the company as are available trail behind in a canon of modern movement. Fools.

Favorite Moment: Most of us still take pleasure in the simple things in life. Who doesn't love to watch someone who absolutely cannot clap in time? There's a tremendous simplicity in that. At the top of Act II, our entire company faces the audience in a bonding and spiritual celebration of life. Many a rush-seat clapping enthusiast offers that animated passion, without the skill to match the rhythm. Ah, live theatre.

Favorite In-Theatre Gathering Place: The greenroom. It's our game room, dining room, and laboratory of silliness.

Favorite Off-Site Hangouts: Recently, it has been Tony's Di Napoli, Marseille, and the wild and wonderful Chez Josephine.

Favorite Therapy: Water, water and more water.

Memorable Ad-Lib: Maggie Benjamin improvised at the end of the show when an understudy 'Mimi' hadn't quite made it to the stage for her entrance. "Mark! Roger! Anyone! Help! It's Mimi, (we found her somewhere in the park)!," before the poor girl came literally crawling on.

Audience Distractions: Not too many cell rings, and we usually have a fair amount of flash photos, but just last week, we were surprised to begin the show with our audience-direct title song, and find two young girls eating full take-out dinner in the front row. Their set-up included various containers and utensils, and they kept reaching to the floor for another and swapping items back and forth. So odd.

Memorable Press Encounter: Following the Ten-Year Anniversary Benefit performance, a photo appeared in *The New York Times* with the image of about seventy cast members past and present from a single moment on the Nederlander stage the evening before. It was a thrilling reminder of how many wonderful, enduring friendships have been fostered through *Rent*, onstage and off.

Memorable Stage Door Fan Encounter: For Halloween this year, two teenage fans dressed up, not as characters from the show, but as actress Haven Burton, and myself! They were very charming and devoted. Haven exclaimed, "They look better as us than we do!" Perhaps we need better self-costumes.

Fastest Costume Change: Ah-ha! Swing Justin Brill was on for his first performance as 'Gordon,' and the call was places. Suddenly, when our actor playing 'Mark' didn't arrive at about five minutes after places, it was realized he might not be coming at all. He was called at home, and it seems he didn't know of the added performance and changed time, and was comfortably at home in Brooklyn. Justin was told to change into his 'Mark' attire and went on to his debut in a role he had scarcely rehearsed for!

Busiest Day at the Box Office: Christmas Eve.

Heaviest/Hottest Costume: The contest is on. Almost the entire company wears winter coats, scarves and all—often under-dressed in another costume.

Who Wore the Least: Following a quick-change into "Contact," one actress entered, but had neglected to under-dress her next costume. She stood onstage for a scene and a half in nothing but a small shirt, tights and underwear.

Orchestra Member Who Played the Most Performances Without a Sub: Steve Mack, bass.

In-House Parody Lyrics: My goodness there are so many. Perhaps, "Her femur's breaking."

Memorable Directorial Note: If I may paraphrase an in-house note from management: "Be on stage right # 4, facing left, right hand on her left shoulder. Sing."

Company In-Joke: "Lipsynch Ah Fantasia!"

Understudy Anecdote: One of our male swings, Kyle Post, making his Broadway debut in *Rent*, was on for 'Mark Cohen' on Christmas Eve, and had the pleasure of saying the opening line, "We begin on Christmas Eve."

Embarrassing Moment: "T.V. did it!"

Coolest Thing About Being in This Show: The show's message. It has been a wild and tumultuous year, and it has been very rewarding to have the opportunity to remind people of the power they have to live in the moment and to help teach tolerance and love.

Also: I think it's lovely to remember, especially at such a difficult time in the social and political energy of the world, that we have an incredible opportunity as artists to speak for those who may not have the opportunity to speak for themselves. I feel lucky to be part of such a platform of possibilities. May there be inspired justice, love, dignity and peace for everyone!

Special Thank-You: To Haven Burton, who was kind to assist me in filling in some details of a few moments of the last year.

Shining City

First Preview: April 20, 2006. Opened: May 9, 2006.
Closed: July 16, 2006 after 21 Previews and 80 Performances.

PLAYBILL

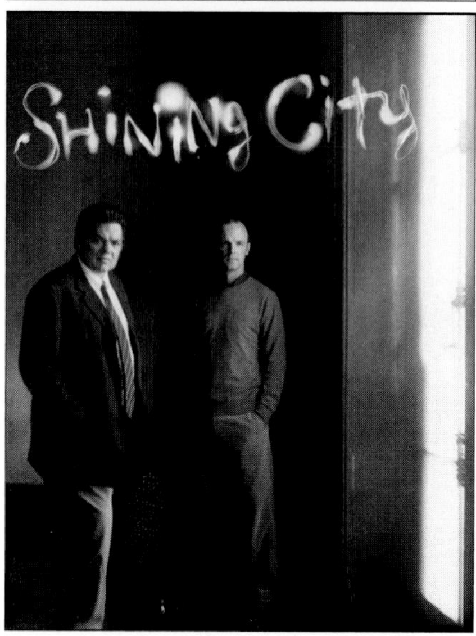

BILTMORE THEATRE

MANHATTAN THEATRE CLUB

Artistic Director
LYNNE MEADOW

Executive Producer
BARRY GROVE

By Special Arrangement with

SCOTT RUDIN **ROGER BERLIND** **DEBRA BLACK**

Presents

by

CONOR McPHERSON

with

BRÍAN F. O'BYRNE **OLIVER PLATT**
MARTHA PLIMPTON **PETER SCANAVINO**

Scenic Design
SANTO LOQUASTO

Costume Design
KAYE VOYCE

Lighting Design
CHRISTOPHER AKERLIND

Sound Design
OBADIAH EAVES

Dialect Coach
DEBORAH HECHT

Production Stage Manager
BARCLAY STIFF

Directed by

ROBERT FALLS

Casting
NANCY PICCIONE/ DAVID CAPARELLIOTIS

Director of Artistic Operations
MANDY GREENFIELD

Production Manager
RYAN MCMAHON

Director of Development
JILL TURNER LLOYD

Director of Marketing
DEBRA A. WAXMAN

Press Representative
BONEAU/ BRYAN-BROWN

General Manager
FLORIE SEERY

Director of Artistic Development
PAIGE EVANS

Director of Artistic Production
MICHAEL BUSH

SHINING CITY was first presented by The Royal Court Theatre, London and The Gate Theatre, Dublin on June 4, 2004.
Manhattan Theatre Club wishes to express its appreciation to Theatre Development Fund for is support of this production.

7/16/06

CAST

(in order of appearance)

Ian .... BRÍAN F. O'BYRNE
John .... OLIVER PLATT
Neasa .... MARTHA PLIMPTON
Laurence .... PETER SCANAVINO

PLACE

An office in Dublin.

TIME

Present. Roughly two months separate each scene.

Stage Manager: Francesca Russell

UNDERSTUDIES

For Ian/Laurence: CHRIS GENEBACH
For Neasa: FIANA TOIBIN

Martha Plimpton and Brian F. O'Byrne

Photo by Joan Marcus

Shining City

Brían F. O'Byrne
Ian

Oliver Platt
John

Martha Plimpton
Neasa

Peter Scanavino
Laurence

Chris Genebach
Understudy for Ian, Laurence

Fiana Toibin
Understudy for Neasa

Robert Falls
Director

Conor McPherson
Playwright

Santo Loquasto
Scenic Design

Kaye Voyce
Costume Design

Christopher Akerlind
Lighting Design

Obadiah Eaves
Scenic Designer

Lynne Meadow
Artistic Director, Manhattan Theatre Club, Inc.

Barry Grove
Executive Producer, Manhattan Theatre Club, Inc.

CRREW AND FRONT OF HOUSE STAFF

Front Row (L-R): Tevy Bradley (Assistant Box Office Treasurer), Valerie D. Simmons (Theatre Manager), Johannah-Joy Magyawe (Assistant Theatre Manager), Francesca Russell (Stage Manager) and David Dillon (Box Office Treasurer).

Second Row (L-R): Ingrid Pohle, Sue Poulin (Apprentice), Miranda Scopel, Tim Walters (Head Propertyman), Tracey Boone (Dresser), Angela Simpson (Wardrobe Supervisor), Walter Cordero, Catherine Burke and Wendy Wright.

Back Row (L-R): Barclay Stiff (Production Stage Manager), Louis Shapiro (Sound Engineer), Jeff Dodson (Master Electrician), Taurance Williams, Daniel Kerrigan (Apprentice), Jackson Ero, Edward Brashear, Bruce Dye, Patricia Polhill and Beren Willwerth.

Photo by Ben Strothmann

Photo courtesy of Barclay Stiff

SCRAPBOOK

(L-R): Oliver Platt, Martha Plimpton and Brían F. O'Byrne in rehearsal.

Photo by Aubrey Reuben

Oliver Platt and *Chicago*'s Lillias White take part in the summer 2006 "Stars in the Alley" event.

Shining City

MANHATTAN THEATRE CLUB STAFF

Artistic Director .... **Lynne Meadow**
Executive Producer .... **Barry Grove**
General Manager .... **Florie Seery**
Director of Artistic Production .... **Michael Bush**
Director of Artistic Development .... **Paige Evans**
Director of Artistic Operations .... **Mandy Greenfield**
Artistic Associate/
Assistant to the Artistic Director .... Amy Gilkes Loe
Artistic Assistant .... Kacy O'Brien
Director of Casting .... **Nancy Piccione**
Casting Director .... **David Caparelliotis**
Casting Assistant .... Kristin Svenningsen
Literary Manager .... **Emily Shooltz**
Play Development Associate/
Sloan Project Manager .... Aaron Leichter
Play Development Assistant .... Annie MacRae
Director of Musical Theatre .... **Clifford Lee Johnson III**
Artistic Consultant .... Ethan Youngerman
Director of Development .... **Jill Turner Lloyd**
Director, Corporate Relations .... Karen Zornow Leiding
Director, Individual Giving .... Casey Reitz
Director, Special Events .... Allison Gutstein
Director, Foundation and
Government Relations .... Josh Jacobson
Senior Development Associate,
Individual Giving .... Antonello Di Benedetto
Development Associate/
Foundation & Gov't Relations .... Andrea Gorzell
Development Associate/
Planning & Projects .... Liz Halakan
Development Associate/
Corporate Relations .... Jessica Sadowski
Development Database
Coordinator .... Rey Pamatmat
Patrons' Liaison .... Sage Young
Director of Marketing .... **Debra A. Waxman**
Marketing Manager .... Dale Edwards
Marketing Associate/
Website Manager .... Ryan M. Klink
Director of Finance .... **Jeffrey Bledsoe**
Business Manager .... Holly Kinney
HR/Payroll Manager .... Darren Robertson
Senior Business Associate
& HR Coordinator .... Denise L. Thomas
Business Assistant .... Adam Cook
Manager of Systems Operations .... Avishai Cohen
Systems Analyst .... Andrew Dumawal
Associate General Manager .... **Lindsey T. Brooks**
Company Manager/New York City Center .... Erin Moeller
Assistant to the Executive Producer .... Bonnie Pan
Director of Subscriber Services .... **Robert Allenberg**
Associate Subscriber Services Manager ...... Andrew Taylor
Subscriber Services Representatives .... Mark Bowers, Alva Chinn, Rebekah Dewald, Matthew Praet, Rosanna Consalvo Sarto
Director of Telesales and Telefunding ..... **George Tetlow**
Assistant Manager .... Terrence Burnett
Director of Education .... **David Shookhoff**
Asst. Director of Education/Coordinator,
Paul A. Kaplan Theatre
Management Program .... Amy Harris
Education Assistants .... Kayla Cagan, Sarah Ryndak
MTC Teaching Artists .... Stephanie Alston, David Auburn, Michael A. Bernard, Carl Capotorto, Chris Ceraso, Charlotte Colavin, Gilbert Girlon, Andy Goldberg, Elise Hernandez, Jeffrey Joseph, Kate Long, Lou Moreno, Michaela Murphy, Melissa Murray, Angela Pietropinto, Alfonso Ramirez, Carmen Rivera, Judy Tate, Candido Tirado, Joe White
Theatre Management Interns .... Maureen Cavanaugh, Kyle Frisina, Meghan Goria, Charles Graytok, Wade T. Handy, Amanda Johnson, Katie Liberman, Samantha Mascali, Rebecca Roffman, Miranda Scopel, Natalie Silva, Whitney Skold, Shayla Titley

---

The Paul A. Kaplan Theatre Management Program, MTC's internship program, is designed to train the next generation of theatre leaders.

Randy Carrig Casting Intern .... Drew Ross
Reception/Studio Manager .... Lauren Butler
Production Manager .... **Ryan McMahon**
Associate Production Manager .... Bridget Markov
Assistant Production Manager .... Ian McNaugher
Technical Director .... **William Mohney**
Assistant Technical Director .... Peter Gilchrist
Shop Foreman .... Shayne Izatt
Assistant Shop Foreman .... Nicholas Morales
Carpenter .... Brian Corr
Scenic Painting Supervisor .... **Jenny Stanjeski**
Lights and Sound Supervisor .... **Matthew T. Gross**
Properties Supervisor .... **Scott Laule**
Assistant Properties Supervisor .... Dana Lewman
Props Carpenter .... Peter Grimes
Costume Supervisor .... **Erin Hennessy Dean**
Assistant Costume Supervisor .... Michelle Sesco

GENERAL PRESS REPRESENTATIVES
BONEAU/BRYAN-BROWN
Chris Boneau Jim Byk
Aaron Meier Heath Schwartz

Script Readers .... Sadie Foster, Liz Jones, Lara Mottolo, Mark von Sternberg, Michelle Tattenbaum, Kathryn Walat, Ethan Youngerman
Musical Theatre Reader .... Emily King

SERVICES

Accountants .... ERE, LLP
Advertising .... SpotCo/ Drew Hodges, Jim Edwards, Tom McCann, Aaliytha Davis
Marketing Consultants .... The Marketing Group/ Tanya Grubich, Laura Matalon, Trish Santini, Bob Bucci, Amber Glassberg, Liz Miller
Web Design .... Pilla Marketing Communications
Legal Counsel .... John Breglio, Deborah Hartnett/ Paul, Weiss, Rifkind, Wharton and Garrison LLP
Real Estate Counsel .... Marcus Attorneys
Labor Counsel .... Harry H. Weintraub/ Glick and Weintraub, P.C.
Immigration Counsel .... Theodore Ruthizer/ Kramer, Levin, Naftalis & Frankel, LLP
Special Projects .... Elaine H. Hirsch
Insurance .... DeWitt Stern Group Inc./ Anthony Pittari
Opening Night Coordination .... Joanna B. Koondel, Suzanne Tobak/ Tobak Lawrence Company
Maintenance .... Reliable Cleaning
Production Photographer .... Joan Marcus
Cover Photo .... Frank Ockenfels 3
Cover Design .... SpotCo
Theatre Displays .... King Display

For more information visit
www.ManhattanTheatreClub.com

PRODUCTION STAFF FOR *SHINING CITY*

Company Manager .... **Denise Cooper**
Production Stage Manager .... **Barclay Stiff**
Stage Manager .... Francesca Russell
Assistant Director .... Henry Wishcamper
Associate Scenic Designer .... Jenny B. Sawyers
Assistant Scenic Designer .... Wilson Chin
Assistant Costume Designer .... Sarah Laux
Assistant Lighting Designer .... Michael Spadaro
Assistant Sound Designer .... Mark Huang
Wigs .... Tom Watson
Hair & Make-Up Supervisor .... Marion M. Geist
Dresser .... Tracey Boone
Lighting Programmer .... Marc Polimeni
Production Assistant .... Kyle Gates

CREDITS

Scenic elements by Showman Fabricators, Inc. Backdrop by USA Image Technologies, Inc. Lighting equipment provided by PRG Lighting. Sound equipment provided by Masque Sound. Natural herbal cough drops courtesy of Ricola USA.

MUSIC CREDITS

"**Polly Come Home,**" written and performed by Gene Clark. All rights owned or administered by ©Irving Music, Inc./BMI. Used by permission. "**Through the Morning, Through the Night,**" written and performed by Gene Clark. All rights owned or administered by ©Irving Music, Inc./BMI. Used by permission. "**Fair and Tender Ladies,**" written and performed by Gene Clark. Published by GENE CLARK MUSIC (BMI), administered by Bug. "**Razor Love,**" written and performed by Neil Young. Published by Silver Fiddle Music.

SPECIAL THANKS

Hudson Photographic, Downtime Productions

MANHATTAN THEATRE CLUB/
BILTMORE THEATRE STAFF

Theatre Manager .... **Valerie D. Simmons**
Assistant House Manager .... Johannah-Joy Magyawe
Box Office Treasurer .... **David Dillon**
Assistant Box Office Treasurers .... Tevy Bradley, Stephanie Valcarcel
Head Carpenter .... Chris Wiggins
Head Propertyman .... Timothy Walters
Sound Engineer .... Louis Shapiro
Master Electrician .... Jeff Dodson
Wardrobe Supervisor .... Angela Simpson
Apprentices .... Daniel Kerrigan, Sue Poulin
Engineers .... Deosarran, Richardo Deosarran, Byron Johnson
Security .... OCS/Initial Security
Lobby Refreshments .... Sweet Concessions

Spring Awakening

First Preview: November 16, 2006. Opened: December 10, 2006.
Still running as of May 31, 2007.

PLAYBILL

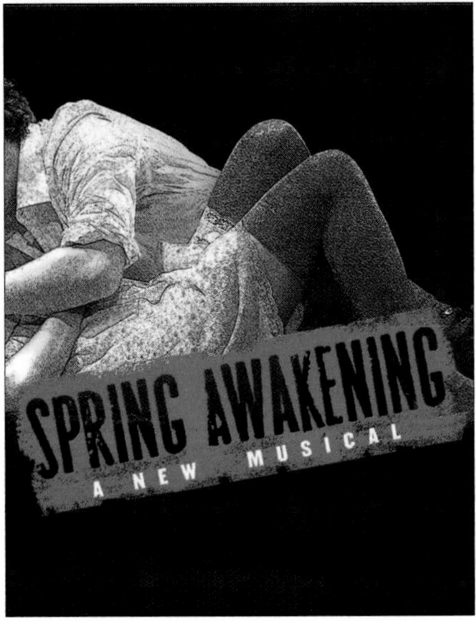

EUGENE O'NEILL THEATRE
A JUJAMCYN THEATRE
ROCCO LANDESMAN
PRESIDENT

PAUL LIBIN
PRODUCING DIRECTOR

JACK VIERTEL
CREATIVE DIRECTOR

IRA PITTELMAN TOM HULCE JEFFREY RICHARDS JERRY FRANKEL
ATLANTIC THEATER COMPANY
Jeffrey Sine Freddy DeMann Max Cooper
Mort Swinsky/Cindy and Jay Gutterman/Joe McGinnis/Judith Ann Abrams
ZenDog Productions/CarJac Productions
Aron Bergson Productions/Jennifer Manocherian/Ted Snowdon
Harold Thau/Terry Schnuck/Cold Spring Productions
Amanda Dubois/Elizabeth Eynon Wetherell
Jennifer Maloney/Tamara Tunie/Joe Cilibrasi/StyleFour Productions
present

Book & Lyrics by
Steven Sater

Music by
Duncan Sheik

Based on the play by
Frank Wedekind

with
Skylar Astin Gerard Canonico Lilli Cooper Jennifer Damiano Rob Devaney
Christine Estabrook John Gallagher, Jr. Gideon Glick Jonathan Groff Robert Hager
Brian Charles Johnson Frances Mercanti-Anthony Lea Michele Lauren Pritchard Krysta Rodriguez
Stephen Spinella Phoebe Strole Jonathan B. Wright Remy Zaken

Scenic Design
Christine Jones

Costume Design
Susan Hilferty

Lighting Design
Kevin Adams

Sound Design
Brian Ronan

Orchestrations
Duncan Sheik

Vocal Arrangements
AnnMarie Milazzo

Additional Arrangements
Simon Hale

Music Coordinator
Michael Keller

Casting
Jim Carnahan, C.S.A.
Carrie Gardner

Fight Direction
J. David Brimmer

Production Stage Manager
Heather Cousens

Associate Producers
Joan Cullman Productions
Patricia Flicker Addiss

Technical Supervision
Neil A. Mazzella

General Management
Abbie M. Strassler

Press Representative
Jeffrey Richards Associates

Music Director
Kimberly Grigsby

Choreography
Bill T. Jones

Directed by
Michael Mayer

Originally produced by the Atlantic Theater Company by special arrangement with Tom Hulce & Ira Pittelman.
The producers wish to express their appreciation to the Theatre Development Fund for its support of this production.

LIVE BROADWAY

12/10/06

CAST

(in order of speaking)

Wendla .... LEA MICHELE
The Adult Women .... CHRISTINE ESTABROOK
Martha .... LILLI COOPER
Ilse .... LAUREN PRITCHARD
Anna .... PHOEBE STROLE
Thea .... REMY ZAKEN
The Adult Men .... STEPHEN SPINELLA
Otto .... BRIAN CHARLES JOHNSON
Hanschen .... JONATHAN B. WRIGHT
Ernst .... GIDEON GLICK
Georg .... SKYLAR ASTIN
Moritz .... JOHN GALLAGHER, JR.
Melchior .... JONATHAN GROFF
Ensemble .... GERARD CANONICO, JENNIFER DAMIANO, ROBERT HAGER, KRYSTA RODRIGUEZ

TIME/PLACE

The play is set in a provincial German town in the 1890s.

(L-R): Jonathan Groff (seated), John Gallagher, Jr., Jonathan B. Wright, Skylar Astin and Gideon Glick

Photo by Joan Marcus

Continued on next page

Spring Awakening

MUSICAL NUMBERS

ACT ONE

"Mama Who Bore Me"	Wendla
"Mama Who Bore Me" (Reprise)	Girls
"All That's Known"	Melchior
"The Bitch of Living"	Moritz with Boys
"My Junk"	Girls and Boys
"Touch Me"	Boys and Girls
"The Word of Your Body"	Wendla, Melchior
"The Dark I Know Well"	Martha, Ilse with Boys
"And Then There Were None"	Moritz with Boys
"The Mirror-Blue Night"	Melchior with Boys
"I Believe"	Boys and Girls

ACT TWO

"The Guilty Ones"	Wendla, Melchior with Boys and Girls
"Don't Do Sadness"	Moritz
"Blue Wind"	Ilse
"Left Behind"	Melchior
"Totally Fucked"	Melchior with Full Company
"The Word of Your Body" (Reprise)	Hanschen, Ernst with Boys and Girls
"Whispering"	Wendla
"Those You've Known"	Moritz, Wendla, Melchior
"The Song of Purple Summer"	Full Company

(L-R): Lea Michele and Jonathan Groff

Photo by Joan Marcus

Cast Continued

UNDERSTUDIES

For Melchior:
ROBERT HAGER, JONATHAN B. WRIGHT

For Moritz:
GERARD CANONICO,
BRIAN CHARLES JOHNSON

For Georg:
GERARD CANONICO, ROBERT HAGER,
BRIAN CHARLES JOHNSON

For Hanschen, Otto, Ernst:
GERARD CANONICO, ROBERT HAGER

For Adult Men:
ROB DEVANEY

For Wendla:
KRYSTA RODRIGUEZ, PHOEBE STROLE

For Ilse:
KRYSTA RODRIGUEZ, PHOEBE STROLE

For Anna, Martha, Thea:
JENNIFER DAMIANO, KRYSTA RODRIGUEZ

For Adult Women:
FRANCES MERCANTI-ANTHONY

Swings:
ROB DEVANEY,
FRANCES MERCANTI-ANTHONY

THE BAND

Conductor/Keyboards:
KIMBERLY GRIGSBY
Guitars:
THAD DeBROCK
Bass:
GEORGE FARMER
Associate Conductor/Drums:
TREY FILES
Cello:
BENJAMIN KALB
Violin/Guitar:
OLIVIER MANCHON
Viola:
HIROKO TAGUCHI

Spring Awakening

Skylar Astin
Georg

Gerard Canonico
Ensemble

Lilli Cooper
Martha

Jennifer Damiano
Ensemble

Rob Devaney
Understudy Adult Men

Christine Estabrook
Adult Women

John Gallagher, Jr.
Moritz

Gideon Glick
Ernst

Jonathan Groff
Melchior

Robert Hager
Ensemble

Brian Charles Johnson
Otto

Frances Mercanti-Anthony
Understudy Adult Women

Lea Michele
Wendla

Lauren Pritchard
Ilse

Krysta Rodriguez
Ensemble

Stephen Spinella
Adult Men

Phoebe Strole
Anna

Jonathan B. Wright
Hanschen

Remy Zaken
Thea

Steven Sater
Book & Lyrics

Duncan Sheik
Music

Michael Mayer
Director

Bill T. Jones
Choreographer

Frank Wedekind
Author

Christine Jones
Set Designer

Susan Hilferty
Costume Designer

Kevin Adams
Lighting Designer

Kimberly Grigsby
Music Director

Deborah Abramson
Associate Musical Director

AnnMarie Milazzo
Vocal Arrangements

Simon Hale
String and Additional Orchestrations

Michael Keller
Music Coordinator

J. David Brimmer
Fight Director, SAFD

Neil A. Mazzella
Technical Supervision

Jim Carnahan
Casting

Spring Awakening

Ira Pittelman
Producer

Tom Hulce
Producer

Jeffrey Richards
Producer

Jerry Frankel
Producer

Neil Pepe,
Artistic Director, Atlantic Theater Company

Andrew D. Hamingson,
Managing Director, Atlantic Theater Company

Freddy DeMann
Producer

Morton Swinsky
Producer

Jay and Cindy Gutterman
Producer

Joe McGinnis
Producer

Judith Ann Abrams
Producer

Pun Bandhu,
ZenDog Productions
Producer

Marc Falato,
ZenDog Productions
Producer

Carl Moellenberg,
CarJac Productions
Producer

Tracy Aron
Producer

Stefany Bergson
Producer

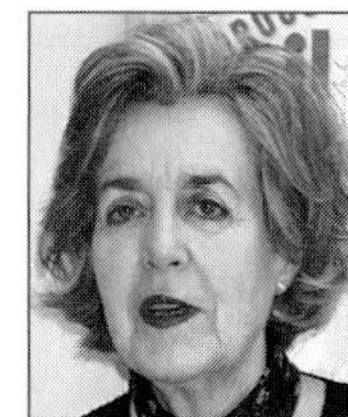

Jennifer Manocherian
Producer

Ted Snowdon
Producer

Harold Thau
Producer

Terry E. Schnuck
Producer

Robert Bailenson
Producer

Jennifer Maloney
Producer

Tamara Tunie
Producer

Joseph Cilibrasi
Producer

John Styles,
Stylefour Productions
Producer

Dave Clemmons,
Stylefour Productions
Producer

Pat Flicker Addiss
Associate Producer

Matt Doyle
Swing

Ken Marks
Swing

Spring Awakening

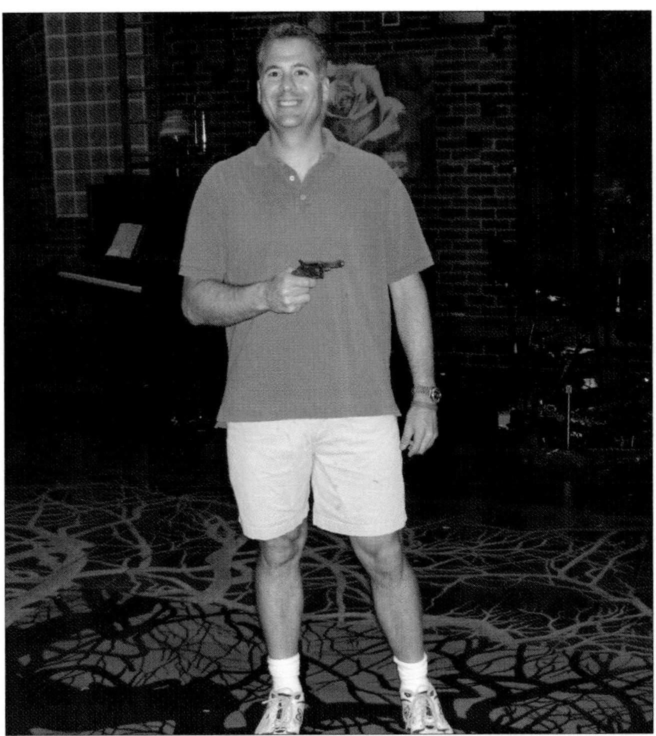

PROPS
Chris Beck

Photos by David Gewirtzman

BAND
Front Row (L-R): Olivier Manchon (Violin/Guitar), Trey Files (Drums), Hiroko Taguchi (Viola), Ben Kalb (Cello).
Back Row (L-R): George Farmer (Bass), Thad DeBrock (Guitar), and Kimberly Grigsby (Conductor/Music Director).

STAGE AND COMPANY MANAGEMENT
Front Row (L-R): Chris Recker (Assistant Company Manager), John Gendron (Company Manager).
Back Row (L-R): Richard Rauscher (Stage Manager), Heather Cousens (Production Stage Manager), Bethany Russell (Assistant Stage Manager).

WARDROBE
(L-R): Susan Checklick (Supervisor), Cathy Cline (Dresser), Sue Stepnik (Dresser), Deb Black (Dresser) and Danny Paul (Dresser).

Spring Awakening

Photos by David Gewirtzman

FRONT OF HOUSE STAFF

Seated (L-R): Bruce Lucoff (Usher), Christine Ehren (Doorperson), Irene Vincent (Usher), Dorothy Lennon (Usher), Andrea Sherman (Sub Usher), Barbara Carroll (Sub Usher), Hal Goldberg (Theatre Manager).

Standing (L-R): Scott Rippe (Sub Usher), Verna Hobson (Usher), Saime Hodzic (Usher Director), Larry Summers (Security), Cynthia Lopiano (Sub Usher), James Kline (Sub Usher), Sandra Palmer (Sub Usher), Elise Gainer (Sub Usher) and Nicole Tessier (Assistant Theatre Manager).

ELECTRICS/SOUND

Front Row (L-R): Francis Elers (Production Sound Engineer), Tommy Grasso (Deck Sound), Al Sayers (Electrician).

Back Row (L-R): Craig Van Tassel (Deck Sound), Michele Gutierrez (Front Light Operator), Todd D'Aiuto (Production Electrician) and James Gardner (Electrician).

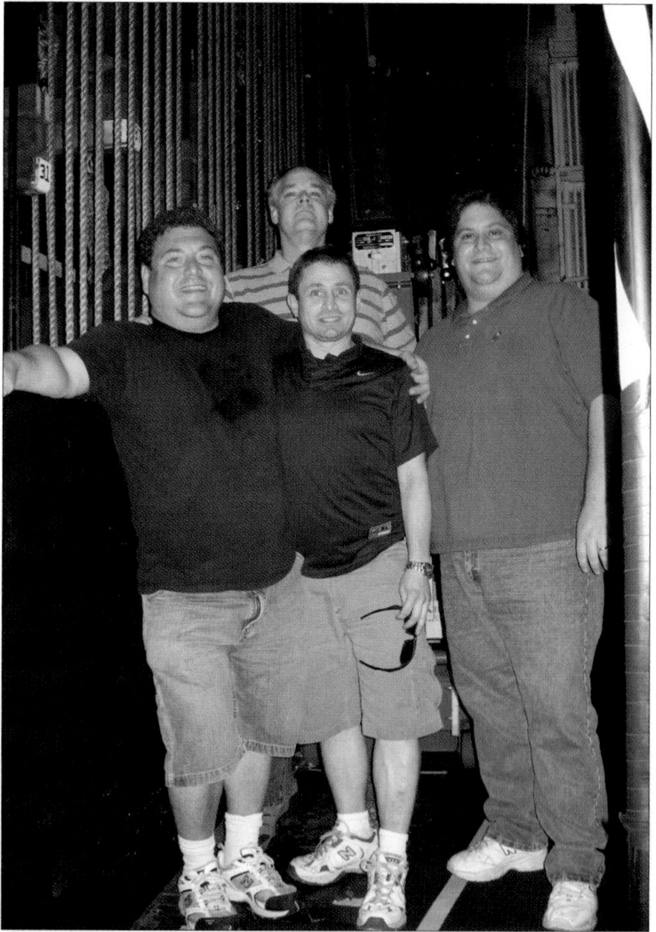

CARPENTERS

Front Row (L-R): Kevin Maher (Flyman), Tom Sherman (Automation), Guy Patria (Automation).

Back Row: Donnie Robinson (Head Carpenter).

Spring Awakening

2006-2007 AWARDS

TONY AWARDS
Best Musical
Best Book of a Musical
(Steven Sater)
Best Original Score
(Duncan Sheik and Steven Sater)
Best Featured Actor in a Musical
(John Gallagher, Jr.)
Best Direction of a Musical
(Michael Mayer)
Best Choreography
(Bill T. Jones)
Best Orchestrations
(Duncan Sheik)
Best Lighting Design of a Musical
(Kevin Adams)

DRAMA DESK AWARDS
Outstanding Musical
Outstanding Music
(Duncan Sheik)
Outstanding Lyrics
(Steven Sater)
Outstanding Director of a Musical
(Michael Mayer)

DRAMA CRITICS' CIRCLE AWARD
Best Musical

OUTER CRITICS CIRCLE AWARDS
Outstanding New Broadway Musical
Outstanding New Score
(Duncan Sheik and Steven Sater)
Outstanding Director of a Musical
(Michael Mayer)

DRAMATISTS GUILD AWARD
Hull-Warriner Award
(Steven Sater and Duncan Sheik)

DRAMA LEAGUE AWARDS
Distinguished Production of a Musical
Julia Hansen Award for Excellence in Directing (Michael Mayer)

THEATRE WORLD AWARD
Outstanding Broadway Debut
(Jonathan Groff)

OBIE AWARD
Choreography
(Bill T. Jones)

STAFF FOR *SPRING AWAKENING*

GENERAL MANAGEMENT
IRON MOUNTAIN PRODUCTIONS

GENERAL MANAGER
ABBIE M. STRASSLER

COMPANY MANAGER
JOHN E. GENDRON

GENERAL PRESS REPRESENTATIVE
JEFFREY RICHARDS ASSOCIATES/IRENE GANDY
Christopher Hanley   Michael Dressel
Hannah Oberman-Breindel   JC Cassis

MARKETING AND PROMOTIONS
Situation Marketing
Damian Bazadona   Steve Tate

Production Stage Manager ....Heather Cousens
Stage Manager ....Rick Steiger
Assistant Stage Manager ....Bethany Russell
Assistant Company Manager ....Scott Turowsky
Dance Captain ....Lauren Pritchard
Fight Captain ....Brian Charles Johnson
National Marketing Consultants ....Susan Blond, Simone Smalls, Liza Bychkov
National Press Consultants ....Rubenstein Communications, Inc./ Amy Jacobs, Andy Shearer, Alice McGillion
Associate Technical Supervision ....Sam Ellis
Assistant Director ....Beatrice Terry
Assistant Choreographer ....Miguel Anaya, Jr.
Associate Music Director ....Deborah Abramson
Associate Set Designer ....Edward Coco
Associate Costume Designer ....Maiko Matsushima
Associate Lighting Designer ....Aaron Sporer
Moving Light Programmer ....Bobby Harrell
Conventional Light Programmer ....Neil McShane
Assistant Sound Designer ....David Stollings
Scenic Assistants ....Tim McNath, Akiko Kosaka, Amy Rubin, Rob Monaco, Sarah Walsh
Costume Assistant ....Marina Reti
Head Carpenter ....Donald Robinson
Fly Automation ....Kevin Maher
Deck Automation ....Thomas Sherman
Production Electrician ....Todd D'Aiuto
Head Electrician ....Greg Husinko
Front Light Operators ....Michele Gutierrez, David Holliman
Properties Coordinator ....Kathy Fabian/Propstar
Assistant Properties Coordinators ....Peter Sarafin, Carrie Mossman, Carrie Hash
Production Properties ....Christopher Beck
Production Sound Engineer ....Francis Elers
Sound System Engineer ....Mike Farfalla
Deck Sound ....Craig Van Tassel
Wardrobe Supervisor ....Susan Checklick
Dressers ....Cathy Cline, Karen L. Eifert, Paul Ludick, Gayle Palmieri
Hair Consultant ....Rufus Mayhem
Hair Supervisor ....Nathaniel Hathaway
Music Copyist ....Steven M. Alper
Production Assistants ....Maura Farver, Adam Grosswirth
Management Associate ....Mike Salonia
Assistant to Mr. Hulce ....Christopher Maring
Banking ....JP Morgan Chase/Richard Callian
Payroll ....Castellana Services, Inc./Lance Castellana
Accountant ....Fried & Kowgios Partners CPA's LLP/ Robert Fried, CPA
Comptroller ....Sarah Galbraith
Insurance ....Tanenbaum Harber of Florida/ Carol Bressi-Cilona
Legal Counsel ....Lazarus & Harris, LLP/ Scott R. Lazarus, Esq., Robert C. Harris, Esq.
Tutoring ....On Location Education
Merchandising ....Max Merchandising
Advertising ....Serino Coyne, Inc.
Website Design/ Web Marketing ....Situation Marketing/ Damian Bazadona, Steve Tate
Production Photographer ....Joan Marcus
Additional Photography ....Doug Hamilton
Travel Agency ....Tzell Travel/The "A" Team
Opening Night Coordination ....Tobak Lawrence Company/ Suzanne Tobak, Michael P. Lawrence
Mascots ....Lottie and Skye

ATLANTIC THEATER COMPANY STAFF
Artistic Director ....Neil Pepe
Managing Director ....Andrew D. Hamingson
School Director ....Mary McCann
General Manager ....Melinda Berk
Associate Artistic Director ....Christian Parker
Development Director ....Erika Mallin
Development Associate ....Rose Yndigoyen
Development Associate ....Katherine Jaeger
Production Manager ....Lester Grant
Marketing Director ....Jodi Sheeler
Membership Coordinator ....Sara Montgomery
Operations Manager ....Anthony Francavilla
Company Manager ....Nick Leavens
Executive Assistant ....Laura Savia
Business Manager ....Hilary O'Connor

CREDITS AND ACKNOWLEDGEMENTS

Scenery and automation by Hudson Scenic Studio, Inc. Lighting equipment from Hudson Sound and Light LLC. Sound equipment by Masque Sound. Costumes constructed by Eric Winterling Inc. Hosiery and undergarments provided by Bra*Tenders. Wigs by Paul Huntley. Specialty props construction by Tom Carroll Scenery Inc., Plumb Square, Ann Guay Inc. Custom framing by The Great Frame Up. Flame proofing by Turning Star. Piano provided by Beethoven Pianos. Guitars supplied courtesy of Lou Vito, Artist Relations East Coast Fender Musical Instruments. Natural herb cough drops courtesy of Ricola USA, Inc. Rehearsed at the New 42nd Street Studios. Special thanks to the staff and crew at the Atlantic Theater Company and Daniel Schmeder.

Originally commissioned and developed by La Jolla Playhouse, ***Spring Awakening*** was further developed, in part, with the assistance of the Sundance Institute Theatre Lab, the Roundabout Theatre Company and the American Songbook Series at Lincoln Center for the Performing Arts. Special thanks to Anne Hamburger, Robert Blacker, Todd Haimes, Jon Nakagawa and the staff and crew of the Atlantic Theater Company.

www.springawakening.com

JUJAMCYN THEATERS

ROCCO LANDESMAN
President

PAUL LIBIN
Producing Director

JACK VIERTEL
Creative Director

JERRY ZAKS
Resident Director

JORDAN ROTH
Resident Producer

DANIEL ADAMIAN
General Manager

JENNIFER HERSHEY
Director of Operations

MEREDITH VILLATORE
Chief Financial Officer

Spring Awakening
Scrapbook

Photos by Aubrey Reuben

Correspondent: Heather Cousens, Production Stage Manager
Opening Night Gifts: *Spring Awakening* condoms, *Spring Awakening* temporary tattoos.
Most Exciting Celebrity Visitors: Václav Havel, Steven Spielberg, Zach Braff, Liza Minnelli.
Who Got the Gypsy Robe: Krysta Rodriguez.
Actor Who Performed the Most Roles in This Show: Krysta Rodriguez.
Special Backstage Rituals: 1. Practicing Mama Bergman's first entrance.
2. Stagehand/actor/SM rock-out during "Sadness."
3. Fight call cheer.
Favorite Moment During Each Performance: We like them all.
Favorite In-Theatre Gathering Place: Stage-left wing.
Favorite Off-Site Hangouts: Luxia, Pigalle.
Favorite Snack Foods: Green M&Ms. Skylar's mom bakes us enormous cookies. *Whatever* Bethany bakes for us!
Mascot: A krait (a very poisonous snake).
Favorite Therapy: Arnica.
Most Memorable Ad-Lib: "ALL THINGS…"
Catchphrases Only the Company Would Recognize: "Eew! Heinous!"
Memorable Stage Door Fan Encounters: The people who bake us cookies.
Latest Audience Arrival: Try not to notice!
Record Number of Cell Phone Rings, Cell Phone Photos or Texting Incidents During a Performance: Try not to notice!
Memorable Directorial Notes: To pay attention to the sensitivity of various body parts. "You have a smile as big as Liza's. Use it."
Heaviest/Hottest Costumes: Dancing in the woolly schoolboy suits or Christine's period ensemble with corset and bustle.
Who Wore the Least: Wendla's top-of-show underclothes.

Photo by David Gewirtzman

1. Curtain call on opening night (L-R): Skylar Astin, Jonathan B. Wright, Robert Hager, Lilli Cooper, Krysta Rodriguez and Lauren Pritchard.
2. Choreographer Bill T. Jones on opening night.
3. John Gallagher Jr. (L) and Stephen Spinella arrive at the cast party.
4. The marquee of the Eugene O'Neill Theatre.

Spring Awakening
Scrapbook

Photos by Aubrey Reuben

Fastest Costume Change: Fifty-two seconds (Hanschen into "My Junk" nightgown).
Orchestra Member Who Played the Most Instruments: Thad DeBrock (lead guitarist) plays six guitars.
Best In-House Parody Lyric: "Don't touch me there; no, not like that!"
Company In-Jokes: Moritzisms; being "so his character." "Oh look, the red light's on."
Nicknames: "Gidge." "L.B." We have a lot of Johns, so it's "Groff," "Gallagher," "Jonny B," et cetera.
Embarrassing Moments: We don't get embarrassed. Not allowed to experience shame!
Coolest Thing About Being in This Show: Getting to rock out together every night!

1. At the cast party (L-R): Lilli Cooper, Gideon Glick, Stephen Spinella, Brian Charles Johnson, Jonathan B. Wright, Phoebe Strole, Krysta Rodriguez, Skylar Astin, Michael Mayer, Jennifer Damiano, Jonathan Groff and Remy Zaken.
2. Phoebe Strole and Remy Zaken.
3. Jonathan Groff and Lea Michele.
4. Director Michael Mayer, librettist/lyricist Steven Sater and composer Duncan Sheik.

Sweeney Todd

First Preview: October 3, 2005. Opened: November 3, 2005.
Closed: September 3, 2006 after 35 Previews 349 Performances.

PLAYBILL

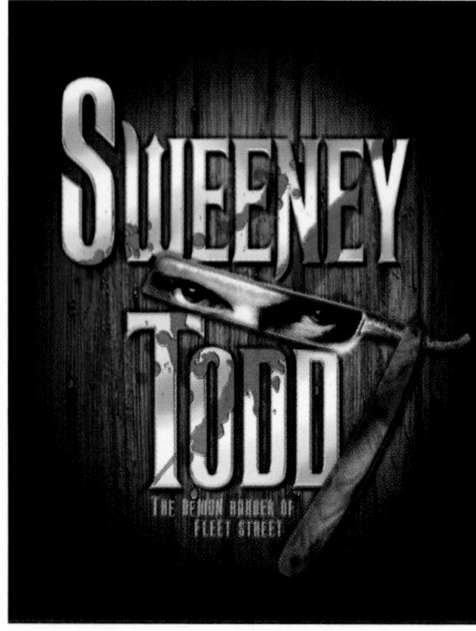

CAST

Mrs. Lovett ....PATTI LuPONE
Tuba, Orchestra Bells, Percussion

Sweeney Todd ....MICHAEL CERVERIS
Guitar, Orchestra Bells, Percussion

Judge Turpin ....MARK JACOBY
Trumpet, Orchestra Bells, Percussion

Pirelli ....DONNA LYNNE CHAMPLIN
Accordion, Keyboard, Flute

Tobias ....MANOEL FELCIANO
Violin, Clarinet, Keyboard

The Beadle ....ALEXANDER GEMIGNANI
Keyboard, Trumpet

Jonas Fogg ....JOHN ARBO
Bass

Beggar Woman ....DIANA DIMARZIO
Clarinet

Anthony ....BENJAMIN MAGNUSON
Cello, Keyboard

Johanna ....LAUREN MOLINA
Cello

Continued on next page

EUGENE O'NEILL THEATRE
A JUJAMCYN THEATRE
ROCCO LANDESMAN
PRESIDENT

PAUL LIBIN — PRODUCING DIRECTOR
JACK VIERTEL — CREATIVE DIRECTOR

TOM VIERTEL STEVEN BARUCH MARC ROUTH RICHARD FRANKEL
AMBASSADOR THEATRE GROUP ADAM KENWRIGHT TULCHIN/BARTNER/BAGERT

present

PATTI LuPONE MICHAEL CERVERIS

in

SWEENEY TODD
THE DEMON BARBER OF FLEET STREET

Music and Lyrics by
STEPHEN SONDHEIM

Book by
HUGH WHEELER

From an Adaptation by CHRISTOPHER BOND

Originally Directed on Broadway by HAROLD PRINCE

with

DONNA LYNNE CHAMPLIN MANOEL FELCIANO ALEXANDER GEMIGNANI
JOHN ARBO DIANA DIMARZIO BENJAMIN MAGNUSON LAUREN MOLINA
MERWIN FOARD DOROTHY STANLEY BENJAMIN EAKELEY ELISA WINTER
DAVID HESS STEPHEN McINTYRE JESSICA WRIGHT

and

MARK JACOBY

Lighting Design
RICHARD G. JONES

Sound Design
DAN MOSES SCHREIER

Wig & Hair Design
PAUL HUNTLEY

Resident Music Supervisor
MARY-MITCHELL CAMPBELL

Casting
BERNARD TELSEY CASTING

Music Coordinator
JOHN MILLER

General Management
RICHARD FRANKEL PRODUCTIONS, INC.
JO PORTER

Production Stage Manager
ADAM JOHN HUNTER

Press Representative
BARLOW•HARTMAN

Production Management
SHOWMAN FABRICATORS, INC.

Musical Supervision and Orchestrations by
SARAH TRAVIS

Directed and Designed by
JOHN DOYLE

Originally produced on Broadway by Richard Barr, Charles Woodward, Robert Fryer, Mary Lea Johnson, Martin Richards in association with Dean and Judy Manos.

Proudly sponsored by Fidelity Investments

The Producers wish to express their appreciation to the Theatre Development Fund for its support of this production. LIVE BROADWAY

9/3/06

Photo by Paul Kolnik

(L-R): Lauren Molina, Benjamin Magnuson, Alexander Gemignani, Patti LuPone, Michael Cerveris, Diana DiMarzio, Manoel Felciano, Mark Jacoby, John Arbo and Donna Lynne Champlin.

Sweeney Todd

MUSICAL NUMBERS

ACT I

"The Ballad of Sweeney Todd"	Company
"No Place Like London"	Anthony, Sweeney Todd, Beggar Woman
"The Barber and His Wife"	Sweeney Todd
"The Worst Pies in London"	Mrs. Lovett
"Poor Thing"	Mrs. Lovett
"My Friends"	Sweeney Todd, Mrs. Lovett
"Green Finch and Linnet Bird"	Johanna
"Ah, Miss"	Anthony, Beggar Woman
"Johanna"	Anthony
"Pirelli's Miracle Elixir"	Tobias, Sweeney Todd, Mrs. Lovett, Company
"The Contest"	Pirelli
"Johanna"	Judge Turpin
"Wait"	Mrs. Lovett
"Kiss Me"	Johanna, Anthony
"Ladies in Their Sensitivities"	The Beadle
"Quartet"	Johanna, Anthony, The Beadle, Judge Turpin
"Pretty Women"	Sweeney Todd, Judge Turpin
"Epiphany"	Sweeney Todd
"A Little Priest"	Sweeney Todd, Mrs. Lovett

ACT II

"God, That's Good!"	Tobias, Mrs. Lovett, Sweeney Todd, Company
"Johanna"	Anthony, Sweeney Todd, Johanna, Beggar Woman
"By the Sea"	Mrs. Lovett
"Not While I'm Around"	Tobias, Mrs. Lovett
"Parlor Songs"	The Beadle, Mrs. Lovett
"City on Fire!"	Tobias, Johanna, Anthony, Company
"Final Sequence"	Anthony, Beggar Woman, Sweeney Todd, Judge Turpin, Mrs. Lovett, Johanna, Tobias
"The Ballad of Sweeney Todd"	Company

Cast Continued

STANDBYS

For Sweeney Todd, Judge Turpin:
MERWIN FOARD,
Orchestra Bells, Percussion

For Mrs. Lovett, Pirelli:
DOROTHY STANLEY,
Violin, Keyboard, Orchestra Bells, Percussion

For Anthony, Tobias, The Beadle:
BENJAMIN EAKELEY,
Keyboard, Clarinet

For Johanna, Beggar Woman:
ELISA WINTER,
Cello, Accordion, Keyboard, Guitar

For Sweeney Todd, Judge Turpin, The Beadle, Jonas Fogg:
DAVID HESS,
Trumpet, Orchestra Bells, Percussion

For Jonas Fogg:
STEPHEN McINTYRE,
Bass, Cello

For Beggar Woman, Pirelli:
JESSICA WRIGHT,
Flute, Clarinet, Violin

Patti LuPone
Mrs. Lovett

Michael Cerveris
Sweeney Todd

Mark Jacoby
Judge Turpin

Donna Lynne Champlin
Pirelli

Manoel Felciano
Tobias

Alexander Gemignani
The Beadle

John Arbo
Jonas Fogg

Diana DiMarzio
Beggar Woman

Benjamin Magnuson
Anthony

Lauren Molina
Johanna

Merwin Foard
Standby for Sweeney Todd, Judge Turpin

Dorothy Stanley
Standby Mrs. Lovett, Pirelli

Benjamin Eakeley
Standby Tobias, Anthony, The Beadle

Elisa Winter
Standby Johanna, Beggar Woman

Sweeney Todd

David Hess
Standby Sweeney Todd, Judge Turpin, The Beadle, Fogg

Stephen McIntyre
Standby Fogg

Jessica Wright
Standby Beggar Woman, Pirelli

Stephen Sondheim
Music & Lyrics

John Doyle
Director and Designer

Sarah Travis
Musical Supervisor and Orchestrator

Mary-Mitchell Campbell
Resident Music Supervisor

Richard G. Jones
Lighting Designer

Dan Moses Schreier
Sound Designer

Paul Huntley
Wig & Hair Designer

Angelina Avallone
Make-up Designer

John Miller
Music Coordinator

Bernard Telsey Casting, C.S.A.
Casting

Ted LeFevre
Associate Set Designer

Paul Miller
Associate Lighting Designer

Tom Viertel,
The Viertel Baruch Routh Frankel Group
Producer

Steven Baruch,
The Viertel Baruch Routh Frankel Group
Producer

Marc Routh,
The Viertel Baruch Routh Frankel Group
Producer

Richard Frankel,
The Viertel Baruch Routh Frankel Group
Producer

Adam Kenwright
Producer

Darren Bagert
Producer

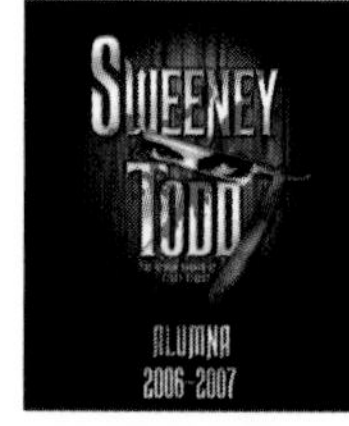

Judy Kaye
Mrs. Lovett

Photo by Ben Strothmann

FRONT OF HOUSE STAFF
Sitting (L-R):
Charlotte Brauer (Usher), Sarah Jane Runser (Merchandise Manager).
Second Row (L-R):
Bryon Vargas (Porter), Carmella Galante (Usher), Verna Hobson (Usher).
Back Row (L-R):
Dorothy Lennon (Usher), John Dapolito (Usher), Jim Higgins (Engineer), Adrian Atkinson-Bleakley (Usher), Christine Ehren (Stage Door), Lauren Vadino (House Manager) and Irene Vincent (Usher).

Sweeney Todd

STAGE CREW

Front Row (L-R): Penny Davis (Wardrobe Supervisor), Adam John Hunter (Production Stage Manager), Vanessa Anderson (Hair and Wig Supervisor).
Back Row (L-R): Todd D'Aiuto (Production Electrician), Christopher Cronin (Production Sound Engineer), Christopher Beck (Production Property Master), Patricia White (Ms. LuPone's Dresser), Donny Beck (Stagehand Emeritus), Kevin O'Brien (Dresser), Karen Zabinski (Deck Sound), Mary McGregor (Deck Electrician), Newton Cole (Stage Manager), Michelle Gutierrez (Board Operator) and Aja Kane (Assistant Stage Manager).

Photo by Ben Strothmann

STAFF FOR *SWEENEY TODD*

GENERAL MANAGEMENT
RICHARD FRANKEL PRODUCTIONS
Richard Frankel Marc Routh Jo Porter
Laura Green Rod Kaats Joe Watson

COMPANY MANAGER
Sammy Ledbetter
Associate Company Manager ..... Jason Pelusio

GENERAL PRESS REPRESENTATIVE
BARLOW•HARTMAN
John Barlow Michael Hartman
Leslie Baden

CASTING
BERNARD TELSEY CASTING, C.S.A.
Bernie Telsey Will Cantler David Vaccari
Bethany Knox Craig Burns
Tiffany Little Canfield Stephanie Yankwitt
Betsy Sherwood

Production Stage Manager ..... Adam John Hunter
Stage Manager ..... Newton Cole
Assistant Stage Manager ..... Aja Kane
Production Management ..... Showman Fabricators, Inc., Kai Brothers, Annie Jacobs
Associate Set Designer, Broadway Production ..... Ted LeFevre
Associate Costume Designer, Broadway Production ..... Patrick Chevillot
Make-Up Designer ..... Angelina Avallone
Assistant Costume Designer ..... Rosemary Lepre
Associate Lighting Designer, Broadway Production ..... Paul Miller
Associate Sound Designer, Broadway Production ..... David Bullard
Production Carpenter ..... Donald Robinson
Production Electrician ..... Todd D'Aiuto
Production Property Master ..... Christopher Beck
Board Operator ..... Michele Gutierrez
Production Sound Engineer ..... Christopher Cronin
Deck Sound ..... Karen Zabinski
Flyman ..... Kevin Mahr
Wardrobe Supervisor ..... Penny Davis
Dresser ..... Kevin O'Brien
Hair Design Assistant ..... Giovanna Calabretta
Ms. LuPone's Dresser ..... Pat White
Hair & Wig Supervisor ..... Vanessa Anderson

Assistant to Mr. Sondheim ..... Steven Clar
Assistant to John Miller ..... Tom Dannenbaum
Asst. to Mr. Baruch ..... Sonja Soper
Asst. to Mr. Viertel ..... Tania Senewiratne
Creative Director for Mr. Bagert ..... Russell Owen
Assistant to Mr. Bagert ..... Ryann Ferguson
Management Assistant ..... Tanase Popa
Production Assistants ..... Ryan J. Bell, Lauren Roth, David Redman Scott
Assistant to Mr. Cerveris ..... Meghan Ritchie
Advertising ..... Serino Coyne, Inc./ Sandy Block, Greg Corradetti, Craig Sabbatino, Natalie Serota
Press Associates ..... Dennis Crowley, Carol Fineman, Ryan Ratelle, Gerilyn Shur, Andrew Snyder, Wayne Wolfe
Press Office Manager ..... Bethany Larsen
Photography ..... Paul Kolnik, Nigel Parry
Web Designer ..... Simma Park
Theatre Displays ..... King Displays
Music Copying ..... Kaye-Houston Music/ Anne Kaye, Doug Houston
Insurance ..... DeWitt Stern Group/ Peter Shoemaker
Legal Counsel ..... Patricia Crown, Esq., Coblence & Associates
Banking ..... Chase Manhattan Bank/Michele Gibbons
Payroll Service ..... Castellana Services, Inc.
Accounting ..... Fried & Kowgios Partners, CPAs, LLP
Travel Agency ..... JMC Travel, Judith Marinoff
Exclusive Tour Direction ..... On the Road
New York Rehearsals ..... Ripley-Grier Studios
Opening Night Coordinator ..... Tobak-Lawrence Company Suzanne Tobak, Michael Lawrence

Group Sales ..... Show Tix (212) 302-7000

RICHARD FRANKEL PRODUCTIONS STAFF
Finance Director ..... Michael Naumann
Assistant to Mr. Frankel ..... Jeff Romley
Assistant to Mr. Routh ..... Michael Sag
Assistant to Ms. Porter ..... Myriah Perkins
Assistant Finance Director ..... Liz Hines
Information Technology Manager ..... Roddy Pimentel
Management Assistant ..... Heidi Schading
Finance Assistant ..... Heather LeBlanc
Finance Assistant ..... Nicole O'Bleanis
National Sales and Marketing Director ..... Ronni Mandell
Director of Business Affairs ..... Carter Anne McGowan
Marketing Manager ..... Melissa Marano
Office Manager ..... Lori Steiger-Perry
Office Manager ..... Stephanie Adamczyk
Receptionists ..... Meghan Lowery, Randy Rainbow
Interns ..... Benton Whitley, Danielle Toscano, Marc Paskin, Brent McCreary, Natalie Gilhome, Laurel Russell, Ellys Abrahms, Elizabeth Leavitt, Chelsea Amengual

AMBASSADOR THEATRE GROUP LTD.
Chairman ..... Sir Eddie Kulukundis, OBE
Deputy Chairman ..... Peter Beckwith
Managing Director ..... Howard Panter
Executive Director ..... Rosemary Squire
For ***Sweeney Todd*** New York:
Associate Producer ..... Angela Edwards
Business Affairs Manager ..... Diane Benjamin

CREDITS AND ACKNOWLEDGEMENTS
Scenery built and painted by Showmotion, Inc. Lighting equipment from PRG Lighting. Sound equipment from PRG Audio. Miss LuPone's costume built by Barbara Matera, Ltd. Special thanks to Novelet Knight, Steven Clar, Matthew Goldenberg, Grant A. Rice, Walter W. Kuehr, Charles Butler, Stas Iavorski, Daedalus Productions, The Spoon Group, Heidi Ettinger and Ian Goldrich.

www.SweeneyToddonBroadway.com

STAFF FOR EUGENE O'NEILL THEATRE
Manager ..... Hal Goldberg
Treasurer ..... Dean Gardner
Carpenter ..... Donald Robinson
Propertyman ..... Christopher Beck
Electrician ..... Todd D'Aiuto
Engineer ..... Padraig Mullen

JUJAMCYN THEATERS

ROCCO LANDESMAN
President

PAUL LIBIN — Producing Director
JACK VIERTEL — Creative Director
JERRY ZAKS — Resident Director
JORDAN ROTH — Resident Producer
DANIEL ADAMIAN — General Manager
JENNIFER HERSHEY — Director of Operations
MEREDITH VILLATORE
Chief Financial Officer

Sweeney Todd
SCRAPBOOK

Correspondent: Donna Lynne Champlin, "Pirelli"

Our producers generously gave us five weeks notice before the September 3 closing. We thought that would have been enough time to prepare emotionally for the ending of this magical year together. But now I realize that no amount of time would have sufficed to prepare us for the experience of our final performance.

From the first day of rehearsal, director John Doyle constructed *Sweeney Todd* to be a living, breathing, organic piece. Therefore we knew that it was completely acceptable for all of us to bring into our final show the awareness that this was our last time performing together and to embrace whatever that circumstance brought to our storytelling. As a result, most of us were on the brink of tears the entire time, and allowed the tears to flow freely when it felt right to do so.

Even before the curtain went up, the crowd was clapping and screaming. The audience was so supportive, so loving, so invested and so *engaged.* The energy was electrifying both on and off stage. The laughs were just as enormous as the silences. And while the show was always a powerful experience for us from the very first note of the opening ballad, the show's intensity was the strongest it had ever been. Sadly, the show flew by for all of us, especially since we were aware that every note we played was our last as a team.

On the final note of the last ballad, the door slammed and the lights went out. The crowd was going absolutely insane and we could hear them—but we couldn't, really. We all left the stage, put our instruments down and took our coats off in uncharacteristic silence. We lined up for curtain call, a time when we usually would crack jokes or laugh about whatever mishaps had happened that night. On the final night we all just exchanged teary glances, smiled weak smiles, and gave various one-armed hugs. It was, it seemed, the best we could do in that moment.

All I can say about bowing that night was that the wall of sound that came from the audience was like an emotional battering ram, in the best of ways. We were given a reception usually reserved for rock stars—almost unbearable in its overwhelming enthusiasm. And when Patti and Michael came out, it was absolutely deafening. As we all came together for our ensemble bow, so many flash bulbs went off it made the crowd look like one big mirror ball. Roses flew onto the stage floor from the orchestra, from the balcony, from everywhere. We brought out our brilliant understudies to share the glory.

Photo by Nigel Perry

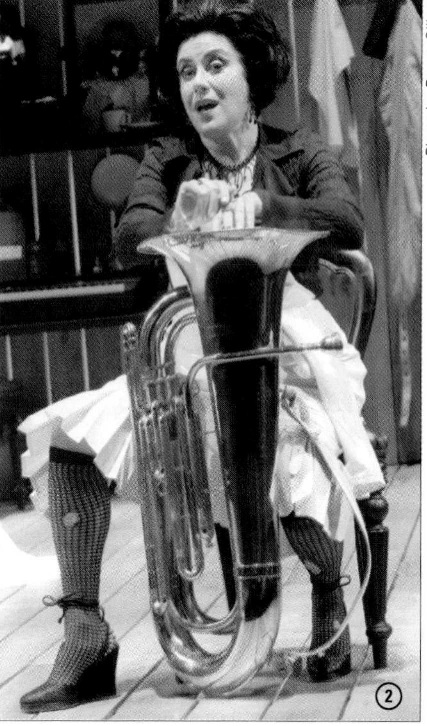

Photo by Bruce Glikas

1. Patti LuPone and Michael Cerveris pose in a meat locker for one of Nigel Perry's macabre press photos used early in the run.
2. Judy Kaye as Mrs. Lovett.

When Michael put his hand up to quiet the crowd, they just wouldn't have it. We all wept, as we just stood there for Lord knows how long and let it all wash over us.

Michael then said a few words about our experience and our wonderful fans, and then Patti said a few words, thanking especially Stephen Sondheim—who for the first time actually sat in a proper seat to watch the show (he usually stood in the back). Then we waved goodbye, waded through the flowers on the floor and made our way backstage.

We packed up our instruments in our cases to take home, hugged our producers who were waiting for us in the wings and went off to our dressing rooms. And it was over.

Or so we thought.

When we went out the stage door, there were hundreds of fans. We all knew that the show touched many people, in most cases quite viscerally, but the reception at the stage door was just unreal. I don't know what it was about our show that affected people so very deeply. I'm sure for everyone it was something different. But I suppose that shouldn't be surprising. That's the way John designed it to be.

Our *Sweeney* was indeed a once-in-a-lifetime experience. From the auditions, to the grueling yet addictive rehearsals, to the previews, to the opening, to the critical successes, to the marvelous fans, to all the awards we were so generously given, to the Tonys, to that miraculous closing performance...the experience was groundbreaking in every way.

And, while I will admit that the amount of physical and mental energy it took to do the show eight times a week sometimes seemed impossible, it was devastating to realize that we wouldn't see each other every day, or play this glorious score again, or even compose and orchestrate for various BC/EFA events.

We were more than just a company. We were more than a family, really. We were like a battalion that had gone through basic training together, followed by a full-scale year-long 'operation' where everyone's safety and success depended with absolute certainty on everyone else having their back. We formed a bond of trust and generosity by both circumstance and choice that I hope to know again in my career someday. And that is what we will miss the most, I believe: Each other, and the ensemble experience we forged night after night.

And with that, I would like to personally thank everyone who was involved with our show onstage and off, in every capacity. I have tried my best to put into words what it was like to be in this production of *Sweeney Todd*, but I know full well that there really are no words that will ever completely do it justice.

Talk Radio

First Preview: February 15, 2007. Opened: March 11, 2007.
Still running as of May 31, 2007.

PLAYBILL

LONGACRE THEATRE
220 West 48th Street
A Shubert Organization Theatre
Gerald Schoenfeld, *Chairman* Philip J. Smith, *President*
Robert E. Wankel, *Executive Vice President*

JEFFREY RICHARDS JERRY FRANKEL JAM THEATRICALS
FRANCIS FINLAY RONALD FRANKEL JAMES FULD, JR. STEVE GREEN JUDITH HANSEN
PATTY ANN LACERTE JAMES RILEY MARY LU ROFFE/MORT SWINSKY
SHELDON STEIN TERRI & TIMOTHY CHILDS/STYLEFOUR PRODUCTIONS
IRVING WELZER/HERB BLODGETT
present

LIEV SCHREIBER
in

TALK RAD!O

written by ERIC BOGOSIAN
created for the stage by ERIC BOGOSIAN and TAD SAVINAR

also starring

STEPHANIE MARCH PETER HERMANN MICHAEL LAURENCE
CHRISTINE PEDI BARBARA ROSENBLAT ADAM SIETZ
MARC THOMPSON KIT WILLIAMSON CORNELL WOMACK
and SEBASTIAN STAN

set design
MARK WENDLAND

costume design
LAURA BAUER

lighting design
CHRISTOPHER AKERLIND

sound design
RICHARD WOODBURY

casting
TELSEY + COMPANY

production stage manager
JANE GREY

press representative
JEFFREY RICHARDS ASSOC.
IRENE GANDY

general management
ALBERT POLAND

technical supervisor
NEIL A. MAZZELLA

directed by
ROBERT FALLS

Original New York Production by New York Shakespeare Festival Produced by Joseph Papp.
Originally produced at the Portland Center for Visual Arts through a grant from the National Endowment for the Arts.

TALK RADIO is presented in association with the Atlantic Theater Company

The producers wish to express their appreciation to Theatre Development Fund for its support of this production.

3/11/07

CAST

(in order of appearance)

Sid Greenberg .... ADAM SIETZ
Bernie .... CORNELL WOMACK
Spike .... KIT WILLIAMSON
Stu Noonan .... MICHAEL LAURENCE
Linda MacArthur .... STEPHANIE MARCH
Vince Farber .... MARC THOMPSON
Barry Champlain .... LIEV SCHREIBER
Dan Woodruff .... PETER HERMANN
Kent .... SEBASTIAN STAN
Dr. Susan Fleming .... BARBARA ROSENBLAT
Rachael .... CHRISTINE PEDI
Callers' Voices .... CHRISTINE PEDI, BARBARA ROSENBLAT, ADAM SIETZ, MARC THOMPSON, CORNELL WOMACK

TIME

Spring 1987

SETTING

Studio B of radio station WTLK in Cleveland, Ohio

Liev Schreiber as Barry Champlain.

Photo by Joan Marcus

Continued on next page

Talk Radio

Cast Continued

UNDERSTUDIES/STANDBYS

Standby for Liev Schreiber:
MICHAEL LAURENCE
For Dan Woodruff:
MICHAEL LAURENCE, LEE SELLARS
For Stu Noonan:
LEE SELLARS, CORNELL WOMACK
For Linda MacArthur, Rachael, Female Callers:
CHRISTY PUSZ
For Kent:
KIT WILLIAMSON
For Spike:
LEE SELLARS
For Sid Greenberg, Bernie, Vince Farber:
OLIVER VAQUER
For Dr. Susan Fleming:
CHRISTINE PEDI
For Male Callers:
ADAM SIETZ, MARC THOMPSON,
OLIVER VAQUER, CORNELL WOMACK

THIS PRODUCTION IS DEDICATED TO THE MEMORY OF JOSEPH PAPP.

2006-2007 AWARD

DRAMA LEAGUE AWARD
Distinguished Performance
(Liev Schreiber)

Sebastian Stan as Kent.

Photo by Joan Marcus

Liev Schreiber
Barry Champlain

Stephanie March
Linda MacArthur

Peter Hermann
Dan Woodruff

Michael Laurence
Stu Noonan

Sebastian Stan
Kent

Christine Pedi
Rachael, Female Callers

Barbara Rosenblat
Female Callers, Dr. Susan Fleming

Adam Sietz
Sid Greenberg, Male Callers

Marc Thompson
Vince Farber, Male Callers

Kit Williamson
Spike

Cornell Womack
Bernie, Male Callers

Christy Pusz
understudy Linda, Female Callers

Lee Sellars
understudy Dan Woodruff, Stu Noonan, Spike

Oliver Vaquer
understudy Sid Greenberg, Bernie, Male Callers

Eric Bogosian
Playwright

Robert Falls
Director

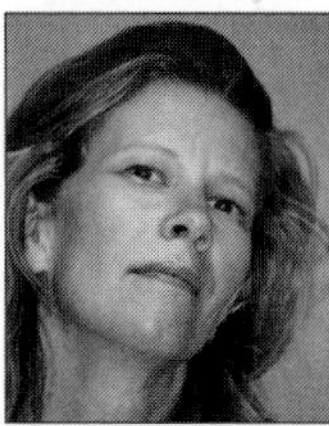

Laura Bauer
Costume Designer

Christopher Akerlind
Lighting Designer

Bernard Telsey/
Telsey + Company
Casting

Neil A. Mazzella
Technical Supervisor

Talk Radio

Albert Poland
General Manager

Jeffrey Richards
Producer

Jerry Frankel
Producer

James Fuld Jr.
Producer

James Riley
Producer

Mort Swinsky
Producer

Sheldon Stein
Producer

Irving Welzer
Producer

Herb Blodgett
Producer

John Styles/
Stylefour
Productions
Producer

Dave Clemmons/
Stylefour
Productions
Producer

Neil Pepe
Artistic Director,
Atlantic Theater
Company

Andrew D.
Hamingson
Managing Director,
Atlantic Theater
Company

STAGE MANAGEMENT
(L-R): Ben West (Production Assistant), Jane Grey (Production Stage Manager) and Matthew Farrell (Stage Manager).

Photos by Melissa Merlo

CREW
(L-R): Brad Robertson (Head Electrician), Valerie Spradling (Production Sound), Sandy Binion (Dresser) and Richard F. Rogers (House Electrician).

THE *TALK RADIO* FAMILY

Standing (L-R): Sebastian Stan, Sandy Binion, Rose Marie C. Cappelluti, Brad Robertson, Matthew Farrell, Valerie Spradling, Wilbur Graham, Chris White, John Lofgren.

Seated (L-R): Marc Thompson, Adam Sietz, Michael Laurence, Barbara Rosenblat, Jane Grey, Christine Pedi, Stephanie March, Liev Schreiber, Michael Altbaum, Oliver Vaquer.

Floor (L-R): Ben West and Christy Pusz.

Not Pictured: Kristine Bellerud, Peter Hermann, Regan Kimmel, Daniel Kuney, Bob Reilly, Richard F. Rogers, Lee Sellars, Kit Williamson and Cornell Womack.

Talk Radio

COMPANY MANAGER
Daniel Kuney

STAGE CREW
Standing (L-R): Richard F. Rogers (House Electrician), John Lofgren (House Prop Head), Wilbur Graham (Production Carpenter) and Brad Robertson (Head Electrician).
Seated: Valerie Spradling (Sound Engineer).

DOORMAN
Chris White

Photos by Melissa Merlo

STAFF FOR *TALK RADIO*

GENERAL MANAGEMENT
ALBERT POLAND

GENERAL PRESS REPRESENTATIVE
JEFFREY RICHARDS ASSOCIATES
IRENE GANDY
Mark Barber Matt Greenstein
Nicole Lee Elon Rutberg

CASTING
TELSEY + COMPANY, C.S.A.
Bernie Telsey, Will Cantler, David Vaccari, Bethany Knox, Craig Burns, Tiffany Little Canfield, Rachel Hoffman, Stephanie Yankwitt, Carrie Rosson, Justin Huff, Joe Langworth, Bess Fifer

COMPANY MANAGER
DANIEL KUNEY

PRODUCTION STAGE MANAGER .... JANE GREY
TECHNICAL SUPERVISOR ...... NEIL A. MAZZELLA
Stage Manager .... Matthew Farrell
Assistant Director .... José Zayas
Assistant Set Designer .... Rachel Nemec
Associate Costume Designer .... Bobby Tilley
Assistant Lighting Designer .... Ben Krall
Associate Sound Designer .... Jeremy Lee
Props Coordinator .... Kathy Fabian
Asst. Props Coordinator .... Carrie Hash
Assistant to Mr. Schreiber .... Roger Mendoza
Assistant to Mr. Richards .... Mark Barber
Assistant to Mr. Bogosian .... Nikole Beckwith
Assistant to Mr. Falls .... Julie Massey
Assistant to Mr. Poland .... Michael Altbaum
Associate Technical Supervisor .... Sam Ellis
Production Assistant .... Ben West
Production Interns .... KathrynAnn Pierroz, Jennifer Leigh Shipp
Sound Intern .... David Horowitz
Production Carpenter .... Adam Braunstein
Production Electrician .... James Maloney
Head Electrician .... Brad Robertson
Production Props .... John Lofgren
Production Sound .... Valerie Spradling
Wardrobe Supervisor .... Kristine Bellerud
Mr. Schreiber's Dresser .... Rose Marie C. Cappelluti
Dresser .... Sandy Binion
Dialect Coach .... Kate Maré
Advertising .... Serino Coyne, Inc./ Greg Corradetti, Ruth Rosenberg, Andrea Prince
Website Design/Web Marketing ...... Situation Marketing/ Damian Bazadona, Steve Tate
Merchandising .... Max Merchandising
Banking .... JP Morgan Chase/ Richard Callian, Michele Gibbons
Accountants .... Rosenberg, Neuwirth & Kuchner/ Mark A. D'Ambrosi, Jana M. Jevnikar
Insurance .... DeWitt Stern Group/ Peter Shoemaker, Stan Levine
Legal Counsel .... Lazarus & Harris, LLP/ Scott R. Lazarus, Esq., Robert C. Harris, Esq. Diane Viale
Payroll .... Castellana Services, Inc.
Production Photographer .... Joan Marcus
Car Services .... Elegant Limousine/Joe Cox
Company Mascots .... Lottie and Skye

CREDITS

Scenery constructed by Hudson Scenic Studio Inc. Lighting equipment from Hudson Sound and Light LLC. Sound equipment from Sound Associates, Inc. Costumes executed by John Kristiansen New York Inc. Rehearsed at New 42nd Street Studios. Natural herb cough drops courtesy of Ricola USA, Inc. Emergen-C super energy booster provided by Alacer Corp.

THE AUTHOR WOULD LIKE TO THANK EDWARD PRESSMAN, OLIVER STONE AND FRED ZOLLO FOR THEIR INVALUABLE COLLABORATION ON *TALK RADIO.*

SPECIAL THANKS
Rick Sordelet,
Bra*Tenders for hosiery and undergarments

www.talkradioonbroadway.com

THE SHUBERT ORGANIZATION, INC.
Board of Directors

Gerald Schoenfeld
Chairman

Philip J. Smith
President

Wyche Fowler, Jr.

John W. Kluge

Lee J. Seidler

Michael I. Sovern

Stuart Subotnick

Robert E. Wankel
Executive Vice President

Peter Entin
Vice President
Theatre Operations

Elliot Greene
Vice President
Finance

David Andrews
Vice President
Shubert Ticketing Services

John Darby
Vice President
Facilities

D.S. Moynihan
Vice President – Creative Projects

House Manager .... Joann Swanson

Talk Radio
Scrapbook

Correspondent: Jane Grey, Production Stage Manager
Opening Night Gifts: '80s-style transistor radios from Liev, miniature telephones from Peter, soup and cheddar cheese crackers delivered by Matthew from one of the show's characters, a photograph of our company mascot on the set staging his own radio show, recordable microphone keychains from our producers, a "classic" thank-you from Eric, and "Twinkle Candy" from the folks at *Grey Gardens*.
Memorable Opening Night Letter: A detailed explanation of the lives of all of the on-stage characters, 20 years after the show.
Celebrity Visitors: Naomi Watts, Mariska Hargitay and Bobby Flay (many times to cheer on their sweethearts), Madonna (caused quite a stir), Paul Newman, Orlando Bloom, Stockard Channing, Neil Patrick Harris, Kathleen Turner, Joan Rivers, Hugh Jackman, Lucy Liu, Bernadette Peters, Joe Mantello, Peter Weller, Alan Alda, Natalie Portman, Anna Paquin, Cynthia Nixon, Kristin Davis, Christopher Meloni, Richard Belzer, Vincent D'Onofrio, Chris Noth, B.D. Wong – THEY ALL LOVED IT, no need to ask them, trust us.
Which Actor Performed the Most Roles: Barbara Rosenblat: Ruth, Cathleen, June, Agnes, Julia and Dr. Susan Fleming. (Honorable Mention to Marc Thompson for back-to-back callers: Bob and Chet).
Who Has Done the Most Shows: We're gonna go ahead and say Liev.
Favorite Moment: Jane Grey calling her "places-pep-talk-du-jour" which include a different contextual quote from the show at each performance.
Favorite Snack Food: Cupcakes, doughnuts, pretzels, jelly beans, Beard Poppa creampuffs, cookies (we're generally a healthy bunch).
Therapy: After this show, yes. COFFEE, Ricola, Throat Coat tea, honey, Sebastian's Herbal "Barnyard" Throat Spray that everyone has accidently used, crossword puzzles...did I say COFFEE?
Mascot: "Buster" the wonder pooch.
Memorable Ad-Lib: Sebastian Stan as Kent was about to light his cigarette during his line and Liev noticed that he had it in backwards and was about to light the filter. "Ya got that in backwards there, Kent," said Liev, to which Sebastian replied, "Oh. Thanks, Barry!" "No problem," said Liev. Sebastian flipped the cigarette around, lit it, and the scene went on.
Record Number of Cell Phone Rings: You'd have to ask Stephanie March–they're unfortunately always during her monologue.
Fastest Costume Change: Adam Sietz as Sid Greenberg: at the beginning of the scene he has no hat on. At the end: Hat! All without the help of a dresser. Unbelievable!
Who Wore the Heaviest/Hottest Costume: Between the leather jackets and the Cosby sweaters it's hard to say.

Photos by Aubrey Reuben

1. (L-R): Star Liev Schreiber, director Robert Falls and playwright Eric Bogosian on opening night.
2. (L-R): Cast members Kit Williamson and Christine Pedi at the opening night party at Bar Americain.
3. Stephanie March at the cast party.

Memorable Directorial Note: "Wouldn't it be great if he, like, came in and just threw up?! Yeah! I wanna see that. Sebastian, why don't you try that." – Robert Falls
Catchphrases Only the Company Would Recognize: "Haccamo." "There are no pets allowed in the Champagne Cocktail." "Lock and Load." "How many pairs of shoes do you have?" "Niiiiiiiiiice." "Monkey Boy." "I got bigger fish to fry than 'Debi-luh.'" "Did I tell you the one about the ...'Yes, Adam, you did.'"
Company In-Jokes: Christy Pusz announcing herself as a man. "Vince Farber." Peter Hermann's "light" reading. How many paint rollers does it takes to apply Stephanie's eye shadow? "You sit here, Sebastian." "Blumpkins & Warm Normans." Vince Farber reads cut callers' obits over the P.A. system. "No seriously: How many pairs of shoes do you have?"
Sweethearts Within the Company: We're all sweet on each other.
Superstitions That Turned Out To Be True: If you hire a Romanian kid, you get great reviews.
Embarrassing Moments: Liev threw his index cards in the air scattering them about except for one. Unbeknownst to Liev the solitary card landed in his headphones and stuck straight up dubbing him: Barry "Pocahontas" Champlain. Stephanie March plucked it out during her exit cross. Adam Sietz stepped on Christy Pusz's boot heel causing her to step out of her shoe for the curtain call. Liev was nice enough to grab it on his way off stage after the company bow.

Tarzan

First Preview: March 24, 2006. Opened: May 10, 2006.
Still running as of May 31, 2007.

PLAYBILL®

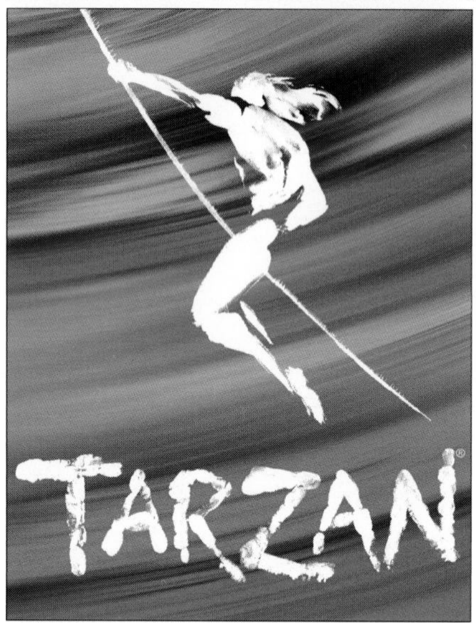

CAST

(in order of appearance)

Kerchak ....SHULER HENSLEY
Kala ....MERLE DANDRIDGE
Young Tarzan ....DYLAN RILEY SNYDER
or ALEX RUTHERFORD
Terk ....CHESTER GREGORY II
Tarzan ....JOSH STRICKLAND
Jane Porter ....JENN GAMBATESE
Professor Porter ....TIM JEROME
Mr. Clayton ....MICHAEL HOLLICK
Snipes ....HORACE V. ROGERS

Ensemble ....MARCUS BELLAMY, CELINA CARVAJAL, DWAYNE CLARK, KEARRAN GIOVANNI, KARA MADRID, KEVIN MASSEY, ANASTACIA McCLESKEY, RIKA OKAMOTO, MARLYN ORTIZ, JOHN ELLIOTT OYZON, ANDY PELLICK, STEFAN RAULSTON, HORACE V. ROGERS, SEAN SAMUELS, NIKI SCALERA

SWINGS

VEN DANIEL, VERONICA deSOYZA, ALAYNA GALLO, JESLYN KELLY, JOSHUA KOBAK, WHITNEY OSENTOSKI, ANGELA PHILLIPS, NICK SANCHEZ, NATALIE SILVERLIEB, JD AUBREY SMITH

Dance Captain ....MARLYN ORTIZ

Continued on next page

RICHARD RODGERS THEATRE

UNDER THE DIRECTION OF JAMES M. NEDERLANDER AND JAMES L. NEDERLANDER

DISNEY THEATRICAL PRODUCTIONS
under the direction of
Thomas Schumacher

presents

TARZAN®

Music and Lyrics by
PHIL COLLINS

Book by
DAVID HENRY HWANG

with
JOSH STRICKLAND JENN GAMBATESE
MERLE DANDRIDGE CHESTER GREGORY II
MICHAEL HOLLICK TIM JEROME
ALEX RUTHERFORD DYLAN RILEY SNYDER
and
SHULER HENSLEY

DARRIN BAKER MARCUS BELLAMY CELINA CARVAJAL DWAYNE CLARK VEN DANIEL VERONICA deSOYZA
ALAYNA GALLO KEARRAN GIOVANNI JESLYN KELLY JOSHUA KOBAK KARA MADRID KEVIN MASSEY
ANASTACIA McCLESKEY RIKA OKAMOTO MARLYN ORTIZ WHITNEY OSENTOSKI JOHN ELLIOTT OYZON
ANDY PELLICK ANGELA PHILLIPS STEFAN RAULSTON HORACE V. ROGERS SEAN SAMUELS
NICK SANCHEZ NIKI SCALERA NATALIE SILVERLIEB JD AUBREY SMITH

Based on the story *Tarzan of the Apes* by
EDGAR RICE BURROUGHS
and the Disney film *Tarzan*®
Screenplay by
TAB MURPHY, BOB TZUDIKER & NONI WHITE
Directed by
KEVIN LIMA & CHRIS BUCK

Scenic and Costume Design
BOB CROWLEY

Lighting Design
NATASHA KATZ

Sound Design
JOHN SHIVERS

Hair Design
DAVID BRIAN BROWN

Make-Up Design
NAOMI DONNE

Soundscape
LON BENDER

Special Creatures
IVO COVENEY

Fight Direction
RICK SORDELET

Vocal Arrangements
PAUL BOGAEV

Dance Arrangements
JIM ABBOTT

Orchestrations
DOUG BESTERMAN

Music Director
JIM ABBOTT

Music Coordinator
MICHAEL KELLER

Casting
TELSEY + COMPANY

Production Stage Manager
FRANK LOMBARDI

Technical Supervisor
TOM SHANE BUSSEY

Press Representative
BONEAU/BRYAN-BROWN

Associate Director
JEFF LEE

Associate Producer
MARSHALL B. PURDY

Production Supervisor
CLIFFORD SCHWARTZ

Aerial Design by
PICHÓN BALDINU

Music Produced by
PAUL BOGAEV

Choreography by
MERYL TANKARD

Direction by
BOB CROWLEY

Disney BROADWAY

10/2/06

Sean Samuels swings across the stage as part of the ape ensemble.

Photo by Heinz Kluetmeier

Tarzan

MUSICAL NUMBERS

ACT I

"Two Worlds"	Voice of Tarzan, Ensemble
"You'll Be in My Heart"	Kala, Ensemble
"Jungle Funk"	Instrumental
"Who Better Than Me?"	Terk, Young Tarzan
"No Other Way"	Kerchak
"I Need to Know"	Young Tarzan
"Son of Man"	Terk, Tarzan, Ensemble
"Son of Man" (Reprise)	Terk, Tarzan, Ensemble
"Sure As Sun Turns to Moon"	Kala, Kerchak
"Waiting for This Moment"	Jane, Ensemble
"Different"	Tarzan

ACT II

"Trashin' the Camp"	Terk, Ensemble
"Like No Man I've Ever Seen"	Jane, Porter
"Strangers Like Me"	Tarzan, Jane, Ensemble
"For the First Time"	Jane, Tarzan
"Who Better Than Me?" (Reprise)	Terk, Tarzan
"Everything That I Am"	Voice of Young Tarzan, Tarzan, Kala, Ensemble
"You'll Be in My Heart" (Reprise)	Tarzan, Kala
"Sure As Sun Turns to Moon" (Reprise)	Kala
"Two Worlds" (Finale)	Ensemble

Instrumental score for "Two Worlds" and "Meeting the Family" based on the original score by Mark Mancina, written for the Disney film TARZAN®.

Josh Strickland as Tarzan battles John Elliott Oyzon as the leopard.

Photo by Joan Marcus

Cast Continued

STANDBYS AND UNDERSTUDIES

Standby for Kerchak and Porter:
DARRIN BAKER

Understudies:
For Tarzan:
JOSHUA KOBAK, KEVIN MASSEY
For Jane:
CELINA CARVAJAL, NIKI SCALERA, NATALIE SILVERLIEB
For Kerchak:
MICHAEL HOLLICK, HORACE V. ROGERS
For Kala:
KEARRAN GIOVANNI, NATALIE SILVERLIEB
For Terk:
DWAYNE CLARK, NICK SANCHEZ
For Clayton:
JOSHUA KOBAK
For Porter:
MICHAEL HOLLICK

SPECIALTIES

Waterfall Ribbon Dancer:
KARA MADRID
Lead Son of Man Vocals:
HORACE V. ROGERS
Moth:
ANDY PELLICK

ORCHESTRA

Conductor: JIM ABBOTT
Associate Conductor: ETHAN POPP
Synthesizer Programmer: ANDREW BARRETT

Keyboard 1: JIM ABBOTT
Keyboard 2: ETHAN POPP
Keyboard 3: MARTYN AXE
Drums: GARY SELIGSON
Percussion: ROGER SQUITERO, JAVIER DIAZ
Bass: HUGH MASON
Guitar: JJ McGEEHAN
Cello: JEANNE LeBLANC
Flutes: ANDERS BOSTRÖM
Reeds: CHARLES PILLOW
Trumpet: ANTHONY KADLECK
Trombone: BRUCE EIDEM
French Horn: THERESA MacDONNELL

Music Coordinator: MICHAEL KELLER

Tarzan

Josh Strickland
Tarzan

Jenn Gambatese
Jane

Merle Dandridge
Kala

Shuler Hensley
Kerchak

Chester Gregory II
Terk

Michael Hollick
Clayton

Timothy Jerome
Professor Porter

Alex Rutherford
Young Tarzan

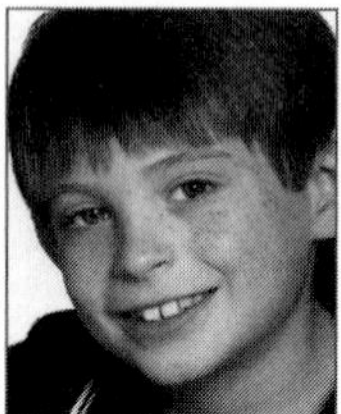
Dylan Riley Snyder
Young Tarzan

Darrin Baker
Standby for Kerchak and Porter

Marcus Bellamy
Ensemble

Celina Carvajal
Ensemble

Dwayne Clark
Ensemble

Ven Daniel
Swing

Veronica deSoyza
Swing

Alayna Gallo
Swing

Kearran Giovanni
Ensemble

Jeslyn Kelly
Swing

Joshua Kobak
Swing

Kara Madrid
Ensemble

Kevin Massey
Ensemble

Anastacia McCleskey
Ensemble

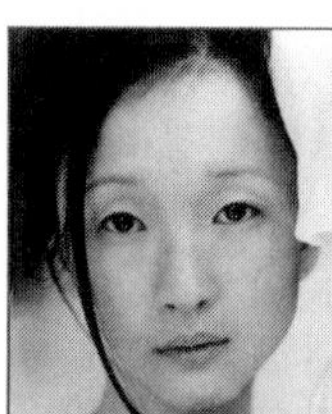
Rika Okamoto
Ensemble

Marlyn Ortiz
Ensemble

Whitney Osentoski
Swing

John Elliott Oyzon
Ensemble

Andy Pellick
Ensemble

Angela Phillips
Swing/Assistant Aerial Designer

Stefan Raulston
Ensemble

Horace V. Rogers
Snipes/Ensemble

Sean Samuels
Ensemble

Nick Sanchez
Swing

Niki Scalera
Ensemble

Natalie Silverlieb
Swing

JD Aubrey Smith
Swing

Tarzan

Phil Collins
Music/Lyrics

David Henry Hwang
Book

Bob Crowley
Director/Scenic and Costume Design

Meryl Tankard
Choreography

Pichón Baldinu
Aerial Design

Natasha Katz
Lighting Design

John Shivers
Sound Design

David Brian Brown
Hair Design

Naomi Donne
Makeup Design

Lon Bender
Soundscape

Ivo Coveney
Special Creatures

Rick Sordelet
Fight Director

Paul Bogaev
Music Producer/ Vocal Arrangements

Jim Abbott
Music Director/ Dance Arrangements

Doug Besterman
Orchestrator

Michael Keller
Music Coordinator

Andrew Barrett
Synthesizer Programmer

Bernard Telsey, Telsey + Company
Casting

Jeff Lee
Associate Director

Clifford Schwartz
Production Supervisor

Thomas Schumacher, Director Disney Theatrical Productions
Producer

Donnie Keshawarz
Mr. Clayton

Daniel Manche
Young Tarzan

Rachel Stern
Swing

Christopher Carl
Standby for Kerchak, Porter and Clayton

Andrea Dora
Ensemble

Robert Evan
Kerchak

Gregory Haney
Ensemble

Jonathan Johnson
Moth Specialty, Ensemble

Donnie Keshawarz
Mr. Clayton

Allison Thomas Lee
Swing

Nicholas Rodriguez
Ensemble

Tarzan

BOX OFFICE
(L-R): Ken Klein and Corinne Parker-Dorso.

Photos by Ben Strothmann

STAGE MANAGEMENT
In Front: Tanya Gillette (Assistant Stage Manager).

(L-R): Allison A. Lee, Kenneth J. McGee (Assistant Stage Manager), Robert M. Armitage (Assistant Stage Manager) and Frank Lombardi (Production Stage Manager).

COMPANY MANAGEMENT
(L-R): Eduardo Castro (Associate Company Manager) and Francesca Panagopoulos.

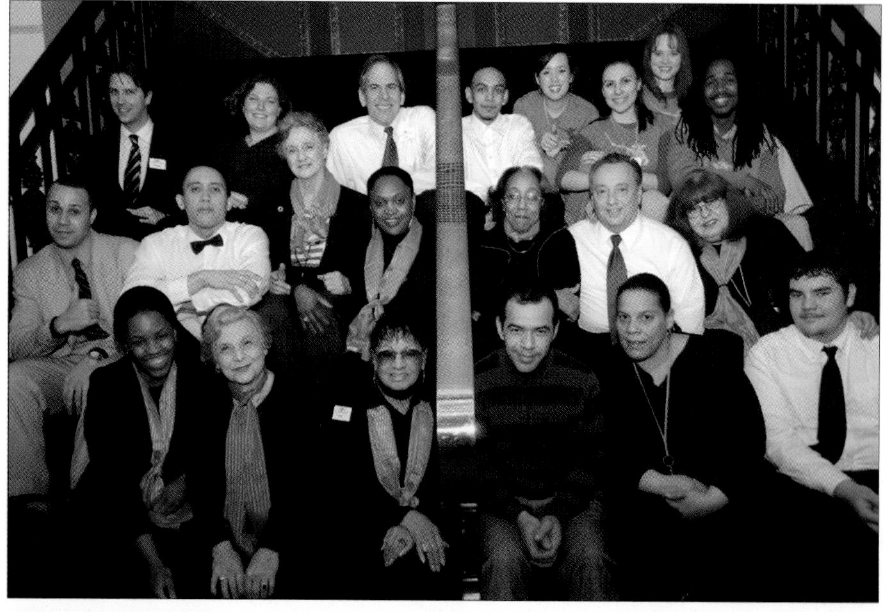

FRONT OF HOUSE STAFF
Front Row (L-R): Nadiah Earle, Frances Eppy, Carmen Frank, Rafael Ortiz, Roseanne Kelly, William Phelan.

Middle Row (L-R): Jose Rivera, Wayne Cameron, Dorothy Darby, Dianne Hosang, Beverly Thornton, Joseph Melchiorre, Maureen Babreo.

Back Row (L-R): Timothy Pettolina (House Manager), Jamie Sponcil, Robert Rea, Frank Almiron, Nicole Pasquale, Lucy Horton, Julia McDarris and Michael Stalling.

Tarzan

STAGE CREW

Front Row (L-R): Charlene Belmond (Assistant Hair Supervisor), Margo Lawless (Dresser), Mike Kearns (Assistant Carpenter), Sonia Rivera (Hair Supervisor), Franklin Hollenbeck, Dan Tramontozzi (Sound Engineer), Eric Nahaczewski.

Second Row (L-R): Paul Curran (Assistant Carpenter), Denise Grillo (Production Props), Nanette Golia (Wardrobe Supervisor), Melanie McClintock (Dresser), Beth Frank (Physical Therapy), Dawn Reynolds, Margaret Kurz (Assistant Wardrobe Supervisor).

Third Row (L-R): Vivienne Crawford (Dresser), Denise Ozker, Christina Grant (Makeup Supervisor), Jorge Vargas (Assistant Makeup Supervisor), Theresa Distasi, Kevin Crawford (Assistant Props), Lisa Preston (Dresser), Don McCarty, David Dignazio.

Back Row (L-R): Robert Terrill, Jr., Andrew Trotto, Randy Zaibek (Head Electrician/Light Board Operator), Hugh Mason, Frank Illo, Walter Bullard, Joseph De Paulo, Ronald Knox, Thomas Maher, Robert Kelly.

STAFF FOR *TARZAN*®

COMPANY MANAGER ....RANDY MEYER
Associate Company Manager ....Eduardo Castro
Assistant to the Associate Producer ....Janine McGuire
Show Accountant ....Jodi Yeager

Assistant Choreographer ....Leonora Stapleton
Assistant Aerial Designer ....Angela Phillips

"Son of Man" Animated Sequence ....Little Airplane Productions, Inc.

GENERAL PRESS REPRESENTATIVE
BONEAU/BRYAN-BROWN
Chris Boneau
Jim Byk Matt Polk Juliana Hannett

Production Stage Manager ....Frank Lombardi
Stage Manager ....Julia P. Jones
Assistant Stage Managers ....Robert M. Armitage, Tanya Gillette, Kenneth J. McGee
Dance Captain ....Marlyn Ortiz
Assistant Dance Captain ....Stefan Raulston
Fight Captain ....Stefan Raulston
Production Assistants ....Ryan J. Bell, Sara Bierenbaum

Associate Scenic Designer ....Brian Webb
Scenic Design Associate ....Rosalind Coombes
Assistant Scenic Designer ....Frank McCullough
Associate Costume Designer ....Mary Peterson
Assistant Costume Designer ....Daryl Stone
Associate Lighting Designer ....Yael Lubetzky
Assistant Lighting Designer ....Aaron Spivey
Automated Lighting Programmer ....Aland Henderson
Automated Lighting Tracker ....Jesse Belsky
Assistant to Lighting Designer ....Richard Swan
Associate Sound Designer ....David Patridge
Assistant Sound Designer ....Jeremy Lee
LCS Sound System Programmer ....Garth Hemphill
"Son of Man" Visual Development ....Kevin Harkey
Hand Lettering of Show Scrim .....Harriet Rose Calligraphy & Design

Technical Supervisor ....Tom Shane Bussey
Associate Technical Supervisor ....Rich Cocchiara
Assistant Technical Supervisor ....Matt Richman
Technical Production Assistant ....Noelle Font
Production Carpenter ....Jeff Goodman
Assistant Carpenter ....Mike Kearns
Assistant Carpenter/Foy Operator ....Richard Force
Scenic Automation ....Dave Brown
Deck Automation ....Mike Fedigan
Assistant Carpenter ....Kirk Aengenheyster
Assistant Carpenter ....Will Carey
Assistant Carpenter ....Paul Curran
Assistant Carpenter ....Thorvald Jacobson
Harness Construction ....Dany Conde
Production Electrician ....Jimmy Fedigan
Head Electrician/Light Board Operator ......Randy Zaibek
Lead Follow Spot Operator ....Andrew Dean
Moving Light Technician ....Derek Healy
Pyrotechnician ....Norman Ballard
Production Props ....Denise J. Grillo
Assistant Props ....Kevin Crawford
Props Shopper ....Kate Foster
Production Sound ....David Patridge
Sound Engineer ....Dan Tramontozzi
Atmospheric Effects ....Chic Silber
Associate to Mr. Silber ....Aaron Waitz
Wardrobe Supervisor ....Nanette Golia
Assistant Wardrobe Supervisor ....Margaret Kurz
Dressers ....Vivienne Crawford, Jay Gill, Margo Lawless, Lisa Preston, Melanie McClintock, David Turk
Hair Supervisor ....Sonia Rivera
Assistant Hair Supervisor ....Charlene Belmond

Tarzan

Hairdresser ....Enrique Vega
Makeup Supervisor ....Christina Grant
Assistant Makeup Supervisor ....Jorge Vargas

Music Copyist ....Russell Anixter, Donald Rice/
Anixter Rice Music Service
Synthesizer Programming ....Andrew Barrett
Synthesizer Programming Assistant ....Anders Boström
Electronic Drum Arrangements ....Gary Seligson
Rehearsal Drummer ....Gary Seligson
Rehearsal Pianist ....Ethan Popp
Music Production Assistant ....Brian Allan Hobbs

Telsey + Company, C.S.A.:
Bernie Telsey C.S.A., Will Cantler, David Vaccari,
Bethany Knox, Craig Burns,
Tiffany Little Canfield, Stephanie Yankwitt,
Carrie Rosson, Justin Huff, Joe Langworth

DIALOGUE & VOCAL COACH ....DEBORAH HECHT

Web Design Consultant ....Joshua Noah
Advertising ....Serino Coyne, Inc.
Production Photography ....Joan Marcus
Acoustic Consultant.............Paul Scarbrough/a.'ku.stiks
Structural Engineering Consultant ....Bill Gorlin, McLaren, P.C.
Production Travel ....Jill L. Citron
Payroll Manager ....Cathy Guerra, Johnson West
Children's Tutoring ....On Location Education/
Maryanne Keller
Physical Therapy ....Neuro Tour Physical Therapy, Inc./
Beth Frank, DPT
Medical Consultant ....Jordan Metzl, MD
Chaperone ....Robert Wilson
Assistant to Phil Collins ....Danny Gillen
Assistant to Bob Crowley ....Fred Hemminger
Press Assistant ....Matt Ross

CREDITS

Scenery by Hudson Scenic Studio, Inc., Scenic Technologies, a division of Production Resource Group, LLC, New Windsor, NY; Dazian Fabrics; CMEANN Productions, Inc.; Stone Pro Rigging, Inc. Automation by Foy Inventerprise, Inc.; Hudson Scenic Studio, Inc., Show control and scenic motion control featuring Stage Command Systems® by Scenic Technologies, a division of Production Resource Group, LLC, New Windsor, NY. Lighting equipment by PRG Lighting. Sound equipment by Masque Sound. Costumes by Donna Langman Costumes; Tricorne, Inc.; DerDau; G! Willikers!; Pluma; Hochi Asiatico; Gene Mignola. Millinery provided by Rodney Gordon. Wigs provided by Ray Marston Wig Studio Ltd. Props by Paragon; Rabbit's Choice; Jauchem and Meeh; Randy Carfagno; ICBA, Inc.; John Creech Design & Production; Camille Casaretti, Inc.; Steve Johnson; Jerard Studios, Trashin' the Camp furniture fabric by Old World Weavers, division of Stark Carpet. Special effects equipment by Jauchem & Meeh, Inc. Firearms by Boland Production Supply, Inc. Soundscape by Soundelux. Atmospheric effects equipment provided by Sunshine Scenic Studios and Aztec Stage Lighting. Acoustic drums by Pearl Drums. Rehearsal catering by Mojito Cuban Cuisine. Ricola natural herb cough drops courtesy of Ricola USA, Inc.

Make-Up provided by M•A•C

TARZAN® rehearsed at Studio 2, Steiner Studios
Brooklyn Navy Yard and New 42nd Street Studios.

SPECIAL THANKS

James M. Nederlander; James L. Nederlander; Nick Scandalios; Herschel Waxman; Jim Boese; David Perry of the Nederlander Organization and Ojala Producciones, S. A.; Siam Productions, LLC

NEDERLANDER

Chairman ....James M. Nederlander
President ....James L. Nederlander

Executive Vice President
Nick Scandalios

Vice President
Corporate Development
Charlene S. Nederlander

Senior Vice President
Labor Relations
Herschel Waxman

Vice President
Jim Boese

Chief Financial Officer
Freida Sawyer Belviso

HOUSE STAFF FOR THE RICHARD RODGERS THEATRE

House Manager ....Timothy Pettolina
Box Office Treasurer ....Fred Santore Jr.
Assistant Treasurer ....Daniel Nitopi
Electrician ....Steve Carver
Carpenter ....Kevin Camus
Propertymaster ....Steve DeVerna
Engineer ....Sean Quinn

DISNEY THEATRICAL PRODUCTIONS

President ....Thomas Schumacher
SVP & General Manager ....Alan Levey
SVP, Managing Director & CFO ....David Schrader

Senior Vice President, Creative Affairs .....Michele Steckler
Senior Vice President, International ....Ron Kollen
Vice President, International Marketing .....Fiona Thomas
Vice President, Operations ....Dana Amendola
Vice President, Labor Relations ....Allan Frost
Vice President, Domestic Touring ....Jack Eldon
Director, Domestic Touring.............Michael Buchanan
Vice President, Theatrical Licensing.........Steve Fickinger
Director, Human Resources ....June Heindel
Manager, Labor Relations..................Stephanie Cheek
Manager, Human Resources ....Cynthia Young
Manager, Information Systems ....Scott Benedict
Senior Computer Support Analyst.......Kevin A. McGuire

Production

Executive Music Producer ....Chris Montan
Vice President, Creative Affairs ....Greg Gunter
Vice President, Physical Production ....John Tiggeloven
Senior Manager, Safety ....Canara Price
Manager, Physical Production ....Karl Chmielewski
Purchasing Manager.......................Joseph Doughney
Staff Associate Designer ....Dennis W. Moyes
Staff Associate Dramaturg.....................Ken Cerniglia

Marketing

Vice President, Broadway ....Andrew Flatt
Manager, Broadway ....Michele Groner
Manager, Broadway ....Leslie Barrett
Website Manager ....Eric W. Kratzer
Assistant Manager, Communications ....Dana Torres

Sales

Vice President, Ticketing ....Jerome Kane
Manager, Group Sales ....Jacob Lloyd Kimbro
Assistant Manager, Group Sales.......................Juil Kim
Group Sales Representative ....Jarrid Crespo

Business and Legal Affairs

Senior Vice President ....Jonathan Olson
Vice President ....Robbin Kelley
Director ....Harry S. Gold
Attorney ....Seth Stuhl
Paralegal/Contract Administration ....Colleen Lober

Finance

Director.....................................Joe McClafferty
Senior Manager, Finance ....Dana James
Manager, Finance ....Justin Gee
Manager, Finance ....John Fajardo
Production Accountants ....Joy Brown, Nick Judge,
Barbara Toben, Jodi Yaeger
Assistant Production Accountant ....Darrell Goode
Senior Financial Analyst ....Tatiana Bautista
Analyst ....Liz Jurist

Controllership

Director, Accounting ....Leena Mathew
Manager, Accounting ....Erica McShane
Senior Analysts ....Stephanie Badie,
Mila Danilevich,
Adrineh Ghoukassian
Analysts ....Ken Herrell, Bilda Donado

Administrative Staff

Dusty Bennett, Jane Buchanan, Craig Buckley, Lauren Daghini, Jessica Doina, Cristi Finn, Cristina Fornaris, Dayle Gruet, Gregory Hanoian, Jonathan Hanson, Jay Hollenback, Connie Jasper, Kerry McGrath, Lisa Mitchell, Ryan Pears, Flora Rhim, Roberta Risafi, Bridget Ruane, Kisha Santiago, David Scott, Andy Singh

BUENA VISTA THEATRICAL MERCHANDISE, L.L.C.

Vice President ....Steven Downing
Merchandise Manager..........................John F. Agati
Operations Manager ....Shawn Baker
Assistant Manager, Inventory ....Suzanne Jakel
Associate Buyer..............................Violeta Burlaza
Retail Supervisor.............................Mark Nathman
On-site Retail Manager ....Jamie Sponcil
On-site Assistant Retail Manager..........Seth Augspurger

Disney Theatrical Productions • 1450 Broadway
New York, NY 10018

guestmail@disneytheatrical.com

Tarzan
Scrapbook

Correspondent: Josh Strickland, "Tarzan"
Memorable Opening Night Letter: Phil Collins wrote each person in the cast a congratulatory letter that he gave us on Opening Night. Everyone was really moved by it. It was such an honor to work with him and have him be so involved in the creation of the show.
Opening Night Gifts: My favorites were a costume sketch from Bob Crowley and a photo that Patti LuPone sent me—she took a picture of herself holding up my photo in The New York Times and included a very sweet note.
Most Exciting Celebrity Visitor: Hugh Jackman came and I missed him! But, I was there to meet Ewan McGregor who brought his family to the show and they had a great time.
"Carols for a Cure" Song: An original Hanukah song called "Shine On" which was written by cast members Natalie Silverlieb and John Elliott Oyzon.
Actor Who Performed the Most Roles: Kara Madrid.
Who Has Done the Most Shows in Their Career: Tim Jerome (Professor Porter).
Special Backstage Ritual: The company holds a prayer circle backstage before every performance.
Favorite Moment: When all the apes fly towards the audience during the curtain call. I don't get to participate in that, but it is so much fun to watch the cast interact with the audience.
Favorite In-Theatre Gathering Place: The hair and makeup room.
Favorite Off-Site Hangout: Joshua Tree.
Favorite Snack Food: Candy—there's always some candy somewhere in the theatre.
Favorite Therapy: Massages! Getting massages from our wonderful physical therapists is everyone's favorite.
Memorable Ad-Lib: Chester Gregory is always doing something different and fun with his character (Terk).
Record Number of Cell Phone Rings, Cell Phone Photos or Texting Incidents: I've lost count – people are always doing it.
Memorable Press Encounter: "The View." The first time I got to perform "Who Better Than Me" with Phil Collins and that was amazing. Later on, Chester and the company performed "Trashin' the Camp" and I got to hang out and cheer them on.
Stage Door Fan Encounter: I got asked to prom on several occasions by teenage fans.
Heaviest/Hottest Costume: Jenn—as Jane she keeps a special effect in one of her costumes that weighs 30 pounds.
Who Wore the Least: Me!
Catchphrases Only the Company Would Recognize: "Tarzan 2006 y'all."
Coolest Things About Being in This Show: Being able to make my Broadway debut as an iconic character like Tarzan. And getting to fly over the audience every night isn't half bad either!

Photos by Aubrey Reuben

1. (L-R): Jenn Gambatese, composer Phil Collins and Josh Strickland at the launch of the Grammy SoundChecks program at the Richard Rodgers Theatre.

2. Disney meets Disney as Strickland joins *Mary Poppins* star Ashley Brown at "When Hollywood Met Broadway: Great Songs from Stage and Screen," the 22nd Annual Benefit Gala for the Drama League at the Rainbow Room at Rockefeller Plaza February 5.

3. Gambatese and Strickland at the September 2006 "Broadway on Broadway" event in Times Square.

Three Days of Rain

First Preview: March 28, 2006. Opened: April 19, 2006.
Closed: June 18, 2006 after 26 Previews and 70 Performances.

PLAYBILL

BERNARD B. JACOBS THEATRE
242 West 45th Street
A Shubert Organization Theatre
Gerald Schoenfeld, *Chairman* **Philip J. Smith,** *President*

Robert E. Wankel, *Executive Vice President*

MARC PLATT DAVID STONE THE SHUBERT ORGANIZATION

present

JULIA ROBERTS PAUL RUDD BRADLEY COOPER

in

THREE DAYS OF RAIN

by

RICHARD GREENBERG

set and costume design
SANTO LOQUASTO

lighting design
PAUL GALLO

original music and sound design
DAVID VAN TIEGHEM

casting
BERNARD TELSEY CASTING

rain
JAUCHEM & MEEH

hair design
LYNDELL QUIYOU

production stage manager
WILLIAM JOSEPH BARNES

production management
AURORA PRODUCTIONS

press representative
THE PUBLICITY OFFICE

general management
STUART THOMPSON PRODUCTIONS/
JAMES TRINER

directed by
JOE MANTELLO

Originally produced in New York City by the Manhattan Theatre Club on October 21, 1997
Commissioned and first produced by South Coast Repertory

6/18/06

CAST
(in order of appearance)

ACT I
An unoccupied loft space in downtown Manhattan.
1995.

Walker .... PAUL RUDD
Nan .... JULIA ROBERTS
Pip .... BRADLEY COOPER

ACT II
The same space. 1960.

Theo .... BRADLEY COOPER
Lina .... JULIA ROBERTS
Ned .... PAUL RUDD

UNDERSTUDIES
Understudy for Walker/Ned and Pip/Theo:
MICHAEL DEMPSEY

Understudy for Nan/Lina:
MICHELLE FEDERER

(L-R) Bradley Cooper and Julia Roberts
Photo by Joan Marcus

Three Days of Rain

Julia Roberts
Nan/Lina

Paul Rudd
Walker/Ned

Bradley Cooper
Pip/Theo

Michael Dempsey
Understudy for Walker/Ned and Pip/Theo

Michelle Federer
Understudy for Nan/Lina

Richard Greenberg
Playwright

Joe Mantello
Director

Santo Loquasto
Set and Costume Design

Paul Gallo
Lighting Designer

Bernard Telsey Casting, C.S.A
Casting

Stuart Thompson Productions
General Manager

Marc Platt
Producer

David Stone
Producer

Gerald Schoenfeld, The Shubert Organization
Producer

DOORMAN
Jerry Klein (Night Doorman)

STAGE MANAGEMENT
(L-R): Tim Semon (Stage Manager) and Billy Barnes (Production Stage Manager).

GENERAL MANAGEMENT
James Triner
(Associate General Manager)

Photos by Ben Strothmann

Three Days of Rain

Photos by Ben Strothmann

FRONT OF HOUSE STAFF
Front Row (L-R): Roxanne Gayol (Usher), Sean Cutler (Ticket Taker), Martha Rodriguez (Usher), Rosa Pesante (Usher), Carrie Hart (Usher).

Middle Row (L-R): A. Pollock (Usher), John Minore (Director), Billy Mitchell (Manager), Patanne McEvoy (Usher), Daria Cherny (Usher).

Back Row (L-R): Al Peay (Usher), Paul Alonzo (Security), Eva Laskow (Chief Usher) and Anthony Tronchin (Usher).

STAGE CREW
Front Row (L-R): Michael Van Praagh (House Carpenter), Edward Ruggiero (House Flyman), Fred Ricci (Head House Propman), Daniel E. Carpio (House Propman), Michael LoBue (Production Electrician), Christopher Sloan (Production Sound Engineer).

Back Row (L-R): Freddy Mecionis (House Propman), Abe Morrison (Production Props) and Herbert Messing (House Electrician).

Three Days of Rain

WARDROBE AND HAIR DEPARTMENT
(L-R): Lyndell Quiyou (Hair Designer) and Barry Doss (Wardrobe).

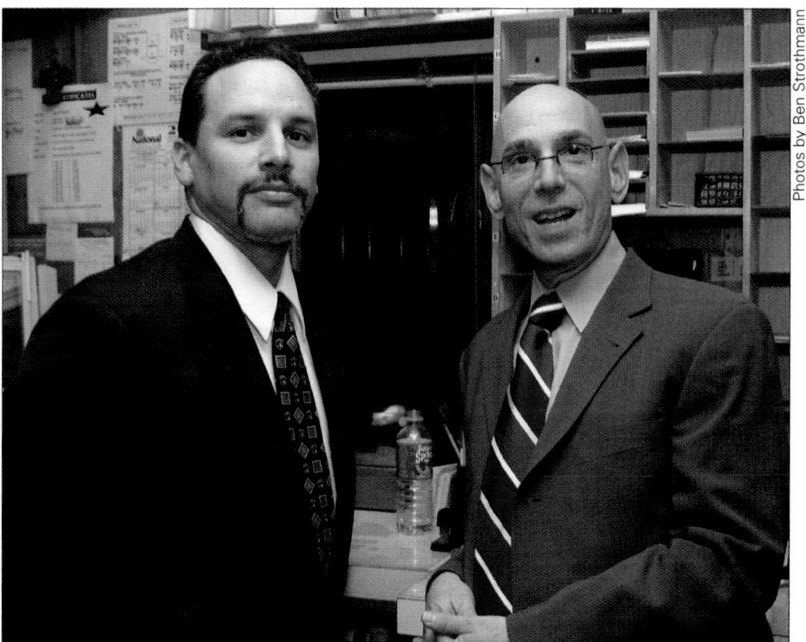

Photos by Ben Strothmann

BOX OFFICE
(L-R): Jose Hernandez (Assistant Treasurer) and Howard Fox (Treasurer).

STAFF FOR *THREE DAYS OF RAIN*

GENERAL MANAGEMENT
STUART THOMPSON PRODUCTIONS
Stuart Thompson Caroline Prugh James Triner

GENERAL PRESS REPRESENTATIVE
THE PUBLICITY OFFICE
Bob Fennell Marc Thibodeau
Candi Adams Michael S. Borowski

CASTING
BERNARD TELSEY CASTING, C.S.A.:
Bernie Telsey, Will Cantler, David Vaccari, Bethany Knox, Craig Burns, Tiffany Little Canfield, Stephanie Yankwitt, Betsy Sherwood, Carrie Rosson, Justin Huff

PRODUCTION MANAGEMENT
AURORA PRODUCTIONS INC.
Gene O'Donovan W. Benjamin Heller II
Bethany Weinstein Hilary Austin

Production Stage Manager .... William Joseph Barnes
Stage Manager .... Timothy R. Semon
Assistant Director .... Michael Silverstone
Associate Set Designer .... Jenny Sawyers
Assistant Set Designer .... Wilson Chin
Assistant Costume Designer .... Matthew Pachtman
Associate Lighting Designer .... Paul Miller
Associate Sound Designer .... Jill BC Du Boff
Production Carpenter .... Donald "Buck" Roberts
Production Electrician .... Michael LoBue
Production Props .... Abraham Morrison
Production Sound .... Christopher Sloan
Wardrobe Supervisor .... Kristine Bellerud
Dresser .... Barry Doss
Production Assistant .... Maura Farver
General Management Assistant .... Megan Curran
Management Intern .... Jeremy Blocker
Production Intern .... Michelle Shannon
Press Assistant .... Matt Fasano
Banking .... JP Morgan Chase/Michele Gibbons
Payroll .... Castellana Services, Inc./ Lance Castellana
Accountant .... Fried & Kowgios CPA's LLP/ Robert Fried, CPA
Controller .... Joseph S. Kubala
Insurance .... DeWitt Stern Group, Inc./ Jolyon F. Stern, Peter Shoemaker, Anthony L. Pittari
Legal Counsel .... Schrek Rose Dapello & Adams LLP/ Nancy A. Rose
Advertising .... Serino Coyne, Inc./ Greg Corradetti, Ruth Rosenberg, Joaquin Esteva, Hunter Robertson
Opening Night Coordination .... Tobak Lawrence Company/ Joanna B. Koondel, Suzanne Tobak

Ms. Roberts' makeup designed by Richard Dean.

MARC PLATT PRODUCTIONS
President: Abby Wolf-Weiss
Adam Siegel, Lynda Brendish, Nicole Brown, Jared LeBoff, Joey Levy, Chris Kuhl, Nik Mavinkurve

STONE PRODUCTIONS
Associate: Patrick Catullo

CREDITS
Scenery and scenic effects built and painted by Showmotion, Inc., Norwalk, CT. Scenic paintings by Scenic Art Studios, Inc. Lighting equipment from PRG Lighting. Sound equipment from PRG Audio. Costumes by Euro Co. Costumes, Inc. Dyeing by Dye-Namix and Gene Mignola Inc. Military clothing provided by Kaufman's Army & Navy. Furniture construction by Craig Grigg. Journals by Jeremy Chernick. Plants by Modern Artificial. Ricola natural herbal cough drops courtesy of Ricola USA, Inc. Emer'gen-C provided by Alacer Corp. Rehearsed at the Lawrence A. Wien Center for Dance and Theater.

MUSIC CREDITS
"Sakeena's Vision" (Wayne Shorter) used by permission of EMI Unart Catalog, Inc.

THE SHUBERT ORGANIZATION, INC.
Board of Directors

Gerald Schoenfeld Chairman
Philip J. Smith President

Wyche Fowler, Jr. **John W. Kluge**
Lee J. Seidler **Michael I. Sovern**
Stuart Subotnick

Robert E. Wankel
Executive Vice President

Peter Entin Vice President - Theatre Operations
Elliot Greene Vice President - Finance

David Andrews Vice President - Shubert Ticketing Services
John Darby Vice President - Facilities

D.S. Moynihan
Vice President – Creative Projects

House Manager .... William Mitchell

The Threepenny Opera

First Preview: March 24, 2006. Opened: April 20, 2006.
Closed: June 25, 2006 after 32 Previews and 77 Performances.

PLAYBILL

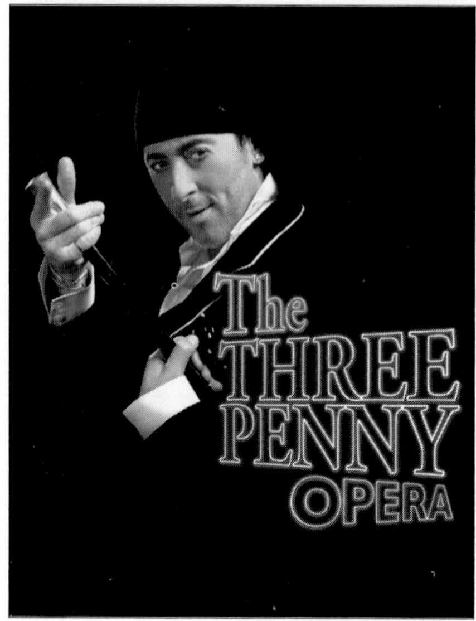

ROUNDABOUTTHEATRECOMPANY

TODD HAIMES, Artistic Director
HAROLD WOLPERT, Managing Director
JULIA C. LEVY, Executive Director

Present

Alan Cumming Jim Dale Ana Gasteyer Cyndi Lauper Nellie McKay

in

The THREEPENNY OPERA

By Bertolt Brecht *and* Kurt Weill

In a New Translation by Wallace Shawn

Based on Elisabeth Hauptmann's German Translation of John Gay's *The Beggar's Opera*.

with

Christopher Innvar Carlos Leon Brian Charles Rooney

Adam Alexi-Malle Terry Burrell Brian Butterick David Cale
Romain Frugé John Herrera Nehal Joshi Christopher Kenney
Deborah Lew Valisia Lekae Little Maureen Moore
Brooke Sunny Moriber Kevin Rennard Lucas Steele

Set Design Derek McLane
Costume Design Isaac Mizrahi
Lighting Design Jason Lyons
Sound Design Ken Travis

Hair & Wig Design Paul Huntley
Original Orchestrations Kurt Weill
Music Coordinator John Miller
Production Stage Manager Peter Hanson

Casting Jim Carnahan, C.S.A.
Technical Supervisor Steve Beers
General Manager Sydney Beers

Press Representative Boneau/Bryan-Brown
Director of Marketing David B. Steffen
Founding Director Gene Feist
Associate Artistic Director Scott Ellis

Music Director Kevin Stites

Choreographed by Aszure Barton

Directed by Scott Elliott

Lead support provided by our Musical Theatre Fund partners;
The Kaplen Foundation, John and Gilda McGarry, Tom and Diane Tuft.

Major support for this production provided by The Blanche and Irving Laurie Foundation, the National Endowment for the Arts, and the Eleanor Naylor Dana Charitable Trust.

Roundabout Theatre Company is a member of the League of Resident Theatres. www.roundabouttheatre.org

6/25/06

CHARACTERS

(in order of appearance)

Jenny .... CYNDI LAUPER
Smith .... JOHN HERRERA
Walter/Betty .... MAUREEN MOORE
Jimmy/Dolly .... BROOKE SUNNY MORIBER
Rev. Kimball/Eunice .... TERRY BURRELL
Robert .... ROMAIN FRUGÉ
Vixen .... DEBORAH LEW
Matthew .... DAVID CALE
Macheath .... ALAN CUMMING
Mr. Peachum .... JIM DALE
Beggar/Beatrice .... BRIAN BUTTERICK
Filch .... CARLOS LEON
Mrs. Peachum .... ANA GASTEYER
Polly Peachum .... NELLIE McKAY
Jacob .... ADAM ALEXI-MALLE
Eddie .... KEVIN RENNARD
Tiger Brown .... CHRISTOPHER INNVAR
Bruno/Molly .... CHRISTOPHER KENNEY
Harry/Velma .... LUCAS STEELE
Lucy Brown .... BRIAN CHARLES ROONEY
Policemen and Beggars .... MAUREEN MOORE, BROOKE SUNNY MORIBER, TERRY BURRELL, ROMAIN FRUGÉ, DEBORAH LEW, BRIAN BUTTERICK, CARLOS LEON, ADAM ALEXI-MALLE, KEVIN RENNARD, CHRISTOPHER KENNEY, LUCAS STEELE

Continued on next page

Alan Cumming and Cyndi Lauper

Photo by Joan Marcus

The Threepenny Opera

SCENES / MUSICAL NUMBERS

OVERTURE .... The Orchestra

PROLOGUE
"Song of the Extraordinary Crimes of Mac the Knife" .... Jenny and the Company

SCENE 1 – Wardrobe Department of Peachum's Begging Business
"Peachum's Morning Hymn" .... Mr. Peachum
"The 'Rather Than' Song" .... Mr. & Mrs. Peachum
SCENE 2 – An Empty Stable
"Wedding Song" .... Matthew and the Gang
"Pirate Jenny" .... Polly
"The Army Song" .... Macheath, Tiger, Polly and the Gang
"Wedding Song" reprise .... Matthew and the Gang
"Love Song" .... Macheath and Polly
SCENE 3 – Peachum's Wardrobe Department
"The 'No' Song" .... Polly
"Certain Things Make Our Life Impossible" .... Mr. Peachum, Mrs. Peachum and Polly
SCENE 4 – The Stable
"Goodbye" .... Macheath
"Polly's Song" .... Polly

INTERMISSION

INTERLUDE – A Street
"The Ballad of the Overwhelming Power of Sex" .... Mrs. Peachum
SCENE 5 – A Brothel in Turnbridge
"The Ballad of the Pimp" .... Macheath and Jenny
SCENE 6 – The Prison of the Old Bailey
"The Ballad of the Happy Life" .... Macheath
"The Jealousy Duet" .... Lucy and Polly
"How Do Humans Live?" .... Mac, Mrs. Peachum and Company
SCENE 7 – Peachum's Wardrobe Department
"The Ballad of the Overwhelming Power of Sex" reprise .... Mrs. Peachum
"The Song of Inadequacy of Human Striving" .... Mr. Peachum
"The Song of Inadequacy of Human Striving" reprise .... Mr. Peachum
"Solomon Song" .... Jenny
SCENE 8 – Lucy Brown's Bedroom, an Attic in the Old Bailey
"Lucy's Aria" .... Lucy
SCENE 9 – The Death Cell
"Cry from the Grave" .... Macheath
"The Ballad in which Macheath asks Everyone's Forgiveness" .... Macheath
"Finale" .... Company

Photo by Joan Marcus

(L-R): Ana Gasteyer, Nellie McKay and Jim Dale

Cast Continued

SWINGS
NEHAL JOSHI, VALISIA LEKAE LITTLE

UNDERSTUDIES
For Mac:
ROMAIN FRUGÉ

For Jenny:
MAUREEN MOORE

For Polly:
BROOKE SUNNY MORIBER

For Mrs. Peachum:
TERRY BURRELL

For Mr. Peachum:
DAVID CALE

For Lucy:
LUCAS STEELE

For Filch:
ADAM ALEXI-MALLE

For Tiger:
JOHN HERRERA

Production Stage Manager: PETER HANSON
Stage Manager: JON KRAUSE

ORCHESTRA
Conductor: KEVIN STITES
Associate Conductor: PAUL RAIMAN

Reeds:
EDDIE SALKIN, ROGER ROSENBERG
Trumpets:
TIM SCHADT, MATT PETERSON
Tenor Trombone:
MIKE CHRISTIANSON
Cello, Accordion:
CHARLES DUCHATEAU
Guitar, Hawaiian Guitar, Banjo, Mandolin:
GREG UTZIG
Harmonium, Celeste, Piano:
PAUL RAIMAN
Percussion/Drums:
CHARLES DESCARFINO
String Bass:
RICHARD SARPOLA

Music Coordinator: JOHN MILLER

The Threepenny Opera

Alan Cumming
Macheath

Jim Dale
Mr. Peachum

Ana Gasteyer
Mrs. Peachum

Cyndi Lauper
Jenny

Nellie McKay
Polly Peachum

Christopher Innvar
Tiger Brown

Carlos Leon
Filch

Brian Charles Rooney
Lucy Brown

Adam Alexi-Malle
Jacob

Terry Burrell
Rev. Kimball, Eunice

Brian Butterick
Beggar, Beatrice

David Cale
Matthew

Romain Frugé
Robert

John Herrera
Smith

Nehal Joshi
Swing

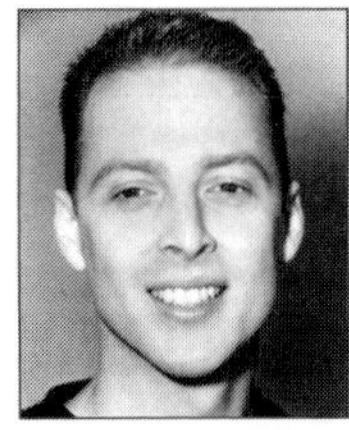
Christopher Kenney
Bruno, Molly

Deborah Lew
Vixen

Valisia Lekae Little
Dance Captain/ Swing

Maureen Moore
Walter, Betty

Brooke Sunny Moriber
Jimmy, Dolly

Kevin Rennard
Eddie

Lucas Steele
Harry, Velma

Bertolt Brecht
Book and Lyrics

Kurt Weill
Music

Wallace Shawn
New Translation

Scott Elliott
Director

Aszure Barton
Choreographer

Derek McLane
Set Design

Isaac Mizrahi
Costume Design

Jason Lyons
Lighting Design

Ken Travis
Sound Design

John Miller
Music Coordinator

Paul Huntley
Hair and Wig Design

Jon Krause
Stage Manager

Marie Masters
Associate Director

The Threepenny Opera

Jim Carnahan
Casting

Todd Haimes
Artistic Director, Roundabout Theatre Company

Gene Feist
Founding Director, Roundabout Theatre Company

Photos by Ben Strothmann

BOX OFFICE
(L-R): Krystin MacRitchie, Jaime Perlman (Treasurer), Adam Owens

FRONT OF HOUSE STAFF AND CREW
Front Row (L-R): Jack Watanachaiyot (Associate House Manager), Allyn Bard Rathus, Larry Jennino, Nichole Larson (Company Manager), Lindsay Ericson (Production Assistant), Erin Delaney (Follow Spot Operator), LaConya Robinson (House Manager), Nicole Ramirez (House Staff).

Second Row (L-R): Mary Jeanette Harrington, Edward Wilson (Hair, Wig, and Makeup Supervisor), Susan Cook (Dresser), Nadine Hettel (Wardrobe Supervisor), Jean Scheller (Props Crew), Stella Varriale (House Staff), Kristina Olsen.

Third Row (L-R): Jennifer Kneeland (House Staff), Kimberly Mark Sirota (Dresser), Kate Longosky (House Staff), Dana McCaw (House Staff), Kimberly Butler (Dresser), Joe Hickey (Dresser), Douglas Lombardi, Sue Pelkofer (Deck Electrician), Josh Weitzman (House Head Electrician), Dorian Fuchs (Follow Spot Operator), Roger Rosenberg, Jonathan Martinez.

Back Row (L-R): Anthony Roman (House Staff), Nick Wheatley (House Staff), Kurt Kielmann (Day Worker), Dan Mendeloff (Props Crew), Billy Lombardi (Automation), Rob Mannsman, Al Steiner (Props Crew), John Wooding (Head Follow Spot Operator and Assistant Production Electrician) and Peter Hanson.

ROUNDABOUT THEATRE COMPANY STAFF

ARTISTIC DIRECTOR..................TODD HAIMES
MANAGING DIRECTOR ....HAROLD WOLPERT
EXECUTIVE DIRECTOR ....JULIA C. LEVY
ASSOCIATE ARTISTIC DIRECTOR .....SCOTT ELLIS

ARTISTIC STAFF

DIRECTOR OF ARTISTIC DEVELOPMENT/ DIRECTOR OF CASTING ....Jim Carnahan
Artistic Consultant ....Robyn Goodman
Resident Director ....Michael Mayer
Associate Artists ....Scott Elliott, Doug Hughes, Bill Irwin, Joe Mantello
Consulting Dramaturg ....Jerry Patch
Artistic Assistant ....Jill Rafson
Casting Director ....Mele Nagler
Casting Associate ....Carrie Gardner
Casting Assistant ....Kate Schwabe
Casting Assistant ....Stephen Kopel
Artistic Intern ....Rachel Balik

EDUCATION STAFF

EDUCATION DIRECTOR.....Margie Salvante-McCann
Director of Instruction and Curriculum Development ....Renee Flemings
Education Program Associate ....Stacey L. Morris
Education Program Associate ....Carrie Soloman
Education Coordinator ....Jennifer DeBruin
Administrative Assistant for Education ....Allison Baucom
Education Intern ....Molly Glenn
Education Dramaturg ....Ted Sod
Teaching Artists ....Phil Alexander, Tony Angelini, Cynthia Babak, Victor Barbella, Brigitte Barnett-Loftis, Caitlin Barton, Joe Basile, LaTonya Borsay, Bonnie Brady, Lori Brown-Niang, Michael Carnahan, Stella Cartaino, Joe Clancy, Melissa Denton, Joe Doran, Katie Down, Tony Freeman, Aaron Gass, Katie Gorum, Sheri Graubert, Adam Gwon, Susan Hamburger, Karla Hendrick, Lisa Renee Jordan, Alvin Keith, Rebecca Lord, Robin Mates, Erin McCready, Jordana Oberman, Andrew Ondrecjak, Laura Poe, Nicole Press, Jennifer Rathbone, Chris Rummel, Drew Sachs, Anna Saggese, Robert Signom, David Sinkus, Derek Straat, Vickie Tanner, Olivia Tsang, Jennifer Varbalow, Leese Walker, Eric Wallach, Diana Whitten, Gail Winar

ADMINISTRATIVE STAFF

GENERAL MANAGER ....Sydney Beers
Associate Managing Director ....Greg Backstrom
General Manager, Steinberg Center ....Rebecca Habel
General Counsel ....Nancy Hirschmann
Human Resources Manager ....Stephen Deutsch
MIS Director ....Jeff Goodman
Facilities Manager ....Abraham David
Manager of Corporate and Party Rentals ....Jetaun Dobbs
Office Manager ....Scott Kelly
Assistant to the General Manager ....Maggie Cantrick
Management Associate ....Tania Camargo
MIS Assistant ....Micah Kraybill
Receptionists ....John Haynes, Elisa Papa, Allison Patrick, Monica Sidorchuk
Messenger ....Robert Weisser
Management Intern ....Michelle Bergmann

FINANCE STAFF

CONTROLLER .... Susan Neiman
Assistant Controller .... John LaBarbera
Accounts Payable Administrator .... Frank Surdi
Customer Service Coordinator .... Trina Cox
Business Office Associate .... David Solomon
Financial Associate .... Yonit Kafka
Business Intern .... Virginia Graham

DEVELOPMENT STAFF

DIRECTOR OF DEVELOPMENT ..... Jeffory Lawson
Director, Institutional Giving .... Julie K. D'Andrea
Director, Individual Giving .... Julia Lazarus
Director, Special Events .... Steve Schaeffer
Manager, Donor Information Systems .... Tina Mae Bishko
Capital Campaign Manager .... Mark Truscinski
Manager, Friends of Roundabout .... Jeff Collins
External Affairs Associate .... Robert Weinstein
Patrons Services Liaison .... Dawn Kusinski
Corporate Relations Manager .... Sara Bensman
Institutional Giving Associate .... Sarah Krasnow
Development Assistant .... Chelsea Glickfield
Individual Giving Assistant .... Dominic Yacobozzi
Special Events Assistant .... Ginger Vallen
Development Assistant .... Elissa Sussman
Special Events Intern .... Casey Cipriani
Individual Giving Intern .... Arielle Cahaner

MARKETING STAFF

DIRECTOR OF MARKETING .... David B. Steffen
Marketing/Publications Manager ..... Margaret Casagrande
Assistant Director of Marketing .... Sunil Ayyagari
Marketing Assistant .... Stefanie Schussel
Website Consultant .... Keith Powell Beyland
DIRECTOR OF TELESALES SPECIAL PROMOTIONS .... Daniel Weiss
Telesales Manager .... Anton Borissov
Telesales Office Coordinator .... J.W. Griffin
Marketing Intern .... Carla Borras

TICKET SERVICES STAFF

DIRECTOR OF SALES OPERATIONS .. Jim Seggelink
Ticket Services Manager .... Ellen Holt
Subscription Manager .... Charlie Garbowski, Jr.
Box Office Managers .... Edward P. Osborne, Jaime Perlman, Jessica Bowser
Group Sales Manager .... Jeff Monteith
Assistant Box Office Managers .... Andrew Clements, Steve Howe, Robert Morgan
Assistant Ticket Services Managers .... Robert Kane, David Meglino, Ethan Ubell
Assistant Director of Sales Operations ...... Nancy Mulliner
Ticket Services .... Solangel Bido, Jessie Blum, Jacob Burstein-Stan, William Campbell, Laura Carielli, David Carson, Johanna Comanzo, Nisha Dhruna, Adam Elsberry, Scott Falkowski, John Finning, Catherine Fitzpatrick, Katrina Foy, Tova Heller, Dottie Kenul, Alexander LaFrance, Krystin MacRitchie, Mead Margulies, Chuck Migliaccio, Carlos Morris, Nicole Nicholson, Adam Owens, Thomas Protulipac, Jackie Rocha, Heather Siebert, Monté Smock, Lillian Soto, Greg Thorson, Pam Unger, Tiffany Wakely
Ticket Services Interns .... Rachel Bauder, Elisa Mala

SERVICES

Counsel .... Jeremy Nussbaum, Cowan, Liebowitz & Latman, P.C.
Counsel .... Rosenberg & Estis
Counsel .... Rubin and Feldman, P.C.
Counsel .. Andrew Lance,Gibson, Dunn, & Crutcher, LLP
Counsel .. Harry H. Weintraub, Glick and Weintraub, P.C.
Immigration Counsel .... Mark D. Koestler and Theodore Ruthizer
House Physicians .... Dr. Theodore Tyberg, Dr. Lawrence Katz
House Dentist .... Neil Kanner, D.M.D.
Insurance .... DeWitt Stern Group, Inc.
Accountant .... Brody, Weiss, Zucarelli & Urbanek CPAs, P.C.
Advertising .... Eliran Murphy Group/ Denise Ganjou, Katie Koch
Events Photography .... Anita and Steve Shevett
Production Photographer .... Joan Marcus
Theatre Displays .... King Displays, Wayne Sapper

MANAGING DIRECTOR EMERITUS .... ELLEN RICHARD

Roundabout Theatre Company
231 West 39th Street, New York, NY 10018
(212) 719-9393.

GENERAL PRESS REPRESENTATIVES
BONEAU / BRYAN-BROWN
Adrian Bryan-Brown   Matt Polk
Jessica Johnson   Shanna Marcus

CREDITS FOR *THE THREEPENNY OPERA*

GENERAL MANAGER .... Sydney Beers
Company Manager .... Nichole Larson
Asst. to the Company Manager .... Allyn Bard Rathus
Production Stage Manager .... Peter Hanson
Stage Manager .... Jon Krause
Assistant Director .... Marie Masters
Assistant Choreographer .... William Briscoe
Associate Music Director/Rehearsal Pianist .... Paul Raiman
Assistant Technical Supervisor .... Elisa R. Kuhar
Assistant Set Designer .... Shoko Kambara
Assistant Costume Designer .... Courtney Logan
Second Assistant Costume Designer .... David Withrow
Associate Lighting Designer .... Jennifer Schriever
Assistant Lighting Designer .... Carrie Wood
Assistant to Jason Lyons .... Sandy Paul
Associate Sound Designer .... Tony Smolenski
Assistant Musical Coordinator .... Kelly M. Rach
Production Electrician .... Josh Weitzman
Head Followspot Operator and Assistant Production Electrician .... John Wooding
Moving Light Programmer .... Victor Seastone
Conventional Light Programmer .... Jessica Morton
Followspot Operators .... Erin Delaney, Dorian Fuchs
Production Sound Mixer .... Thomas Grasso
Deck Sound .... Greg Peeler
Deck Electrician .... Sue Pelkofer
Wardrobe Supervisor .... Nadine Hettel
Production Properties .... Al Steiner
Props Crew .... Al Steiner, Dan Mendeloff, Jean Scheller
Production Head Carpenter .... Dan Hoffman
Head Flyman .... Steve Jones
Automation .... Billy Lombardi
Dressers .... Kimberly Butler, Susan Cook, Joe Hickey, Kimberly Mark Sirota
Day Workers .... Amanda Scott, Andrea Gonzalez, Kimberly Baird, Kurt Kielmann
Hair, Wig and Make-Up Supervisor ...... Edward J. Wilson
Assistant Hair Stylist .... Steven Kirkham
Production Assistants ...... Lindsay Ericson, Stephanie Cali
Music Copying .... Emily Grishman Music Preparation/ Katharine Edmonds
Physical Therapy .... Performing Arts Physical Therapy
Orthopedic Consultant .... Phillip Bauman, MD
Scenery Constructed by .... Showman Fabricators, Inc., NY
Computer Motion Control and Automation of Scenery by ...... Showman Fabricators, Inc.
Flying by .... Foy
Props Built by .... Gotham Scenic and Beyond Imagination
Soft Goods by .... RoseBrand
LED Sign Provided by ..... Trans-Lux Display Corporation
LED Sign Software .... Steve Weiss from C-Scape
Sound Equipment by .... Sound Associates
Shoes Made by .... T.O. Dey
Hats by .... Arnold Levine
Lighting Equipment from .... PRG Lighting
Costumes Built by .... Tricorne, Inc.
Make-Up Provided by .... M•A•C
Make-Up Designer .... Chantel Miller
Onstage Merchandising .... George Fenmore/ More Merchandising Int'l
Stainless Steel Toilet Courtesy of .... Bradley Corp.
Room Service Table by .... Forbes Industries
Mobile Computer Courtesy of .... Symbol Technologies, Inc.
Polyglass Plate Covers by .... Carlisle Sanitary Maintenance Products
Acrylic Drinkware by .... U.S. Acrylic, Inc.
Threepenny Opera Uses .... Baldwin Pianos
Music Instruments by .... Carroll Musical Instruments
Merchandising .... Max Merchandising/ Randi Grossman
Props Built by .... Gotham Scenic, Beyond Imagination and Craig Grigg

SPECIAL THANKS

Trash and Vaudeville, Tripp NYC; Bra*Tenders for hosiery and undergarments; Dr. Arthur Fisher and Sal Martella of Progressive Prosthetics; Kenny Greenberg from Krypton Neon; Ricola USA for supplying the company with cough drops.

STUDIO 54 THEATRE STAFF

Theatre Manager .... Tina Beck Carlson
House Manager .... LaConya Robinson
Associate House Manager .... Jack Watanachaiyot
Assistant House Manager .... Jay Watanachaiyot
House Staff .... Elicia Edwards, Jason Fernandez, Jen Kneeland, Kate Longosky, Latiffa Marcus, Nicole Marino, Jonathan Martinez, Dana McCaw, Nicole Ramirez, Anthony Roman, Nick Wheatley, Stella Varriale
House Head Electrician .... Josh Weitzman
House Head Carpenter .... Dan Hoffman
House Head Properties .... Lawrence Jennino
Security .... Gotham Security
Maintenance .... Ralph Mohan, Maman Garba, Willie Phillips
Lobby Refreshments by .... Sweet Concessions

The Times They Are A-Changin'

First Preview: September 25, 2006. Opened: October 26, 2006.
Closed: November 19, 2006 after 35 Previews and 28 Performances.

PLAYBILL

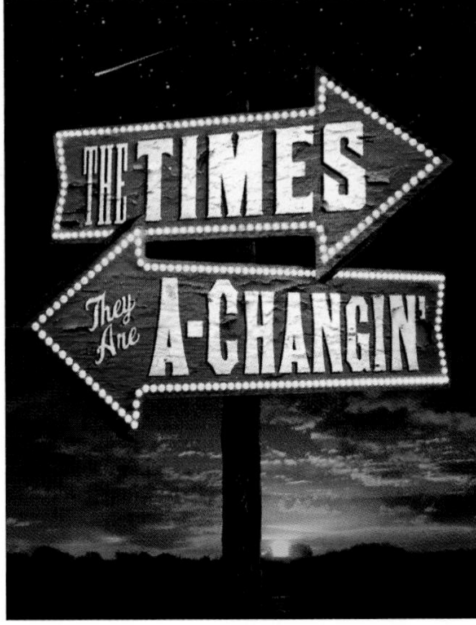

CAST

Coyote .... MICHAEL ARDEN
Captain Ahrab .... THOM SESMA
Cleo .... LISA BRESCIA

THE ENSEMBLE

LISA GAJDA, NEIL HASKELL,
JASON McDOLE,
CHARLIE NESHYBA-HODGES,
JONATHAN NOSAN,
JOHN SELYA, RON TODOROWSKI

SWINGS

ALEXANDER BRADY, ALAINE KASHIAN,
KEITH KÜHL, MARTY LAWSON,
JOSEPH PUTIGNANO, CARY TEDDER

DANCE CAPTAIN

ALEXANDER BRADY

STANDBYS

For Coyote:
JASON WOOTEN
For Captain Ahrab:
JOHN HERRERA
For Cleo:
KATIE KLAUS

SETTING

Sometime between awake and asleep.

Continued on next page

N BROOKS ATKINSON THEATRE
UNDER THE DIRECTION OF JAMES M. NEDERLANDER AND JAMES L. NEDERLANDER

JAMES L. NEDERLANDER
HAL LUFTIG/WARREN TREPP DEBRA BLACK EAST OF DOHENY RICK STEINER/MAYERSON BELL STATON GROUP
TERRY ALLEN KRAMER PATRICK CATULLO JON B. PLATT/ROLAND STURM
present

THE TIMES THEY ARE A-CHANGIN'

Conceived by **TWYLA THARP** *Music and Lyrics by* **BOB DYLAN**

Starring
MICHAEL ARDEN THOM SESMA
and
LISA BRESCIA

LISA GAJDA NEIL HASKELL JASON McDOLE
CHARLIE NESHYBA-HODGES JONATHAN NOSAN JOHN SELYA RON TODOROWSKI

ALEXANDER BRADY JOHN HERRERA ALAINE KASHIAN KATIE KLAUS
KEITH KÜHL MARTY LAWSON JOSEPH PUTIGNANO CARY TEDDER JASON WOOTEN

Scenic and Costume Design SANTO LOQUASTO *Lighting Design* DONALD HOLDER *Sound Design* PETER HYLENSKI

Orchestrations by MICHAEL DANSICKER AND BOB DYLAN *Music Director* HENRY ARONSON

Music Coordinator HOWARD JOINES *Casting by* JAY BINDER JACK BOWDAN/MEGAN LARCHE *Technical Supervisor* SMITTY

Production Stage Manager ARTHUR GAFFIN *Associate Producers* JESSE HUOT GINGER MONTEL RHODA MAYERSON *Resident Director* KIM CRAVEN

General Press Representative SHAFFER-COYLE PUBLIC RELATIONS *General Management* THE CHARLOTTE WILCOX COMPANY

Music Arranged, Adapted and Supervised by
MICHAEL DANSICKER

Directed and Choreographed by
TWYLA THARP

WORLD PREMIERE AT THE OLD GLOBE THEATRE San Diego, California
Artistic Director JACK O'BRIEN Executive Director LOUIS G. SPISTO
THE PRODUCERS WISH TO EXPRESS THEIR APPRECIATION TO THEATRE DEVELOPMENT FUND FOR ITS SUPPORT OF THIS PRODUCTION.

10/26/06

From Top:
Charlie Neshyba-Hodges
and Michael Arden.

Photo by Craig Schwartz

The Times They Are A-Changin'

Cast Continued

THE BAND

Conductor, Keyboards, Accordion, Percussion:
HENRY ARONSON

Guitars, Banjo, Dobro, Harmonica:
JOHN "J.J." JACKSON
Guitars, Banjo:
DAVE MacNAB
Electric and Upright Basses:
PAUL OSSOLA
Drums, Percussion:
BRIAN DOHERTY

Music Coordinator:
HOWARD JOINES

Thom Sesma as Captain Ahrab.
Photo by Craig Schwartz

Michael Arden
Coyote

Thom Sesma
Captain Ahrab

Lisa Brescia
Cleo

Lisa Gajda
Ensemble

Neil Haskell
Ensemble

Jason McDole
Ensemble

Charlie Neshyba-Hodges
Ensemble

Jonathan Nosan
Ensemble

John Selya
Ensemble

Ron Todorowski
Ensemble

Alexander Brady
Swing/ Dance Captain

John Herrera
Standby for Captain Ahrab

Alaine Kashian
Swing

Katie Klaus
Standby for Cleo

Keith Kühl
Swing

Marty Lawson
Swing

Joseph Putignano
Swing

Cary Tedder
Swing

Jason Wooten
Standby for Coyote

Twyla Tharp
Director/ Choreographer

The Times They Are A-Changin'

Bob Dylan
Music and Lyrics, Co-Orchestrator

Michael Dansicker
Musical Adaptation, Vocal and Dance Arranger, Co-Orchestrator, Musical Supervisor

Santo Loquasto
Scenic and Costume Design

Donald Holder
Lighting Design

Peter Hylenski
Sound Design

Henry Aronson
Musical Director/ Keyboards

Howard Joines
Musical Coordinator

Jay Binder C.S.A.
Casting

Jack Bowdan C.S.A.
Casting

Christopher C. Smith, Smitty/ Theatersmith, Inc.
Production Manager

Rhoda Mayerson
Associate Producer

Kim Craven
Resident Director/ Dance Supervisor

Charlotte Wilcox Company
General Manager

James L. Nederlander
Producer

Hal Luftig
Producer

Debra Black
Producer

Rick Steiner
Producer

Frederic H. Mayerson, Mayerson/Bell/ Staton Group
Producer

Marc Bell, Mayerson/Bell/ Staton Group
Producer

Dan Staton, Mayerson/Bell/ Staton Group
Producer

Terry Allen Kramer
Producer

Jon B. Platt
Producer

Jack O'Brien, Artistic Director, Old Globe Theatre
Regional Production

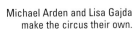

Caren Lyn Manuel
Cleo

2006 Bruce Glikas

Michael Arden and Lisa Gajda make the circus their own.

The Times They Are A-Changin'

STAGE & COMPANY MANAGEMENT
(L-R):
David Sugarman (Stage Manager), Justin Scribner (Assistant Stage Manager), Arthur Gaffin (Production Stage Manager), Jamie Greathouse (Production Assistant) and Alexandra Gushin (Associate Company Manager).

STAGE CREW
Front Row (L-R):
Joseph P. DePaulo (House Properties), Peter Iacoviello (Props), Mike "Jersey" Van Nest (Electrician), Gerry Griffin (Production Carpenter), Tom Lavaia (House Carpenter), Paul Delcioppo.

Second Row (L-R):
Jeff Lunsford (Production Flyman), Dorian Fuchs, Susanne Williams, Bill Staples, Jeff Koger.

Back Row (L-R):
Eric Castaldo (Properties), Richard Tyndall, Phillip Lojo (Production Sound Engineer), Neil Rosenberg (Production Props) and Brad Robertson (House Electrician).

Photos by Melissa Merlo

WARDROBE DEPARTMENT
Front Row (L-R):
Kathleen Gallagher (Wardrobe Supervisor), Amber Isaac (Assistant Wardrobe Supervisor), Erin Schindler (Dresser).

Back Row (L-R):
Rodney Sovar (Dresser), Maggie Horkey (Dresser), Joelyn Wilkosz (Dresser) and Ginene Licata (Dresser).

The Times They Are A-Changin'

Photo by Melissa Merlo

CAST & CREW
In Front (L-R): John Selya (Ensemble), Jason Wooten (Standby for "Coyote").

First Row (L-R): Keith Kühl (Swing), Lisa Gajda (Ensemble), Susanne Williams (Crew), Alexandra Gushin (Associate Company Manager), Lisa Brescia ("Cleo"), Thom Sesma ("Captain Ahrab"), Jonathan Nosan (Ensemble), Alaine Kashian (Swing), Joseph Putignano (Swing), Peter Iacoviello (Props).

Second Row (L-R): Jason McDole (Ensemble), Justin Scribner (Assistant Stage Manager), Alexander Brady (Swing/Dance Captain), Amber Isaac (Assistant Wardrobe Supervisor), Kathleen Gallagher (Wardrobe Supervisor), Charlie Neshyba-Hodges (Ensemble), Neil Haskell (Ensemble), Marty Lawson (Swing), Rodney Sovar (Dresser), Ginene Licata (Dresser), Erin Schindler (Dresser), Maggie Horkey (Dresser), Joe DePaulo (House Properties), Joelyn Wilkosz (Dresser), Thomas A. Lavaia (House Carpenter), Mike "Jersey" Van Nest (Electrician), Michael Attianese (Crew).

Back Row (L-R): Henry Aronson (Musical Director/Keyboards), Ron Todorowski (Ensemble), Arthur Graffin (Production Stage Manager), Eric Castaldo (Properties), David Sugarman (Stage Manager), Katie Klaus (Standby for "Cleo"), Phillip Lojo (Production Sound Engineer), John "J.J." Jackson (Guitar), Lazaro Arencibia (Hair Supervisor), Michael Arden ("Coyote"), Paul DelCioppo (Crew), Russ Beasley (Massage Therapist), Gerry Griffin (Crew), Richard Tyndall (Crew), Brad Robertson (Crew), Dorian Fuchs (Crew) and Bill Staples (Crew).

Photo by Robert Viagas

BAND
(L-R): John "J.J." Jackson (Guitars, Banjo, Dobro, Harmonica), Dave MacNab (Guitars, Banjo), Paul Ossola (Electric & Upright Basses), and Henry Aronson (Musical Director; Keyboards, Accordion, Percussion).

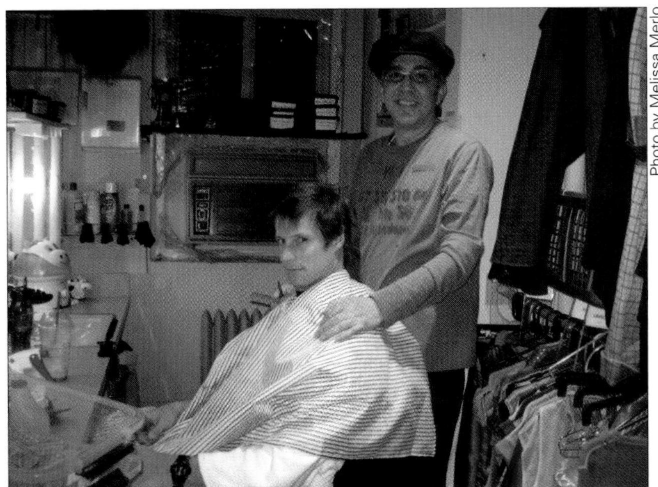

Photo by Melissa Merlo

HAIR DEPARTMENT
Lazaro Arencibia (Hair Supervisor) with John Selya (in the chair).

The Times They Are A-Changin'

BOX OFFICE
(L-R): Robert Wilamowski (Asst. Treasurer), Keshave Sattaur (Treasurer).

Photos by Melissa Merlo

FRONT OF HOUSE STAFF
Front Row (L-R): Barbara Carrellas (House Manager), Brenda Brauer (Chief Usher).
Second Row (L-R): Arlene Reilly, Marie Gonzalez, Timothy Newsome, Kathy Dib.
Back Row (L-R): Robert Banyai (Ticket-Taker), Kimberlee Imperato, Brenden Imperato, Joann Decicca.

STAFF FOR *THE TIMES THEY ARE A-CHANGIN'*

GENERAL MANAGEMENT
THE CHARLOTTE WILCOX COMPANY
Charlotte Wilcox
Matthew W. Krawiec Emily Lawson
Steve Supeck Margaret Wilcox Beth Cochran

GENERAL PRESS REPRESENTATIVE
Shaffer-Coyle Public Relations
Bill Coyle Jeremy Shaffer Adriana Douzos

COMPANY MANAGER
James Lawson

ASSOCIATE COMPANY MANAGER
Alexandra Gushin

CASTING
JAY BINDER CASTING
Jay Binder CSA
Jack Bowdan CSA, Mark Brandon, Megan Larche
Assistants: Nikole Vallins, Allison Estrin

PRODUCTION STAGE MANAGER .... **Arthur Gaffin**
Stage Manager ..... David Sugarman
Assistant Stage Manager ..... Justin Scribner
Dance Captain ..... Alexander Brady
Associate Set Designer ..... Wilson Chin
Associate Costume Designer ..... Matthew Pachtman
Assistant to the Costume Designer .... Sarah Sophia Turner
Associate Lighting Designer ..... Jeanne Koenig
Assistant Lighting Designers ..... Caroline Chao, Ben Krall, Hilary Manners, Carolyn Wong
Assistant Sound Designer ..... TJ McEvoy
Make-Up Designer ..... Angelina Avallone
Production Electrician ..... James Maloney
Production Carpenter ..... Gerard Griffin
Production Flyman ..... Jeffrey Lunsford
Head Electrician ..... Brad Robertson
Assistant Electrician ..... Michael Taylor
Associate Lighting Designer-
Automated Lighting ..... Aland Henderson
Production Properties ..... Neil Rosenberg
Properties ..... Eric Castaldo
Production Sound Engineer ..... Phillip Lojo
Wardrobe Supervisor ..... Kathleen Gallagher
Assistant Wardrobe Supervisor ..... Amber Isaac
Dressers ..... Maggie Horkey, Ginene M. Licata, Erin Schindler, Rodney Sovar, Joelyn R. Wilkosz
Hair Supervisor ..... Lazaro Arencibia
Production Assistants ..... Jamie Greathouse, James Valletti

Legal Counsel ..... Lazarus & Harris LLP/ Scott Lazarus, Esq., Robert C. Harris, Esq.
Accountants ..... Fried & Kowgios CPA's LLP/ Robert Fried, CPA
Controller ..... Sarah Galbraith
Advertising ..... SpotCo/ Drew Hodges, Jim Edwards, Jim Aquino, Y. Darius Suyama
Internet Marketing/
Website Design ..... Situation Marketing LLC/ Damian Bazadona, Ian Bennett, Sara Fitzpatrick, Samantha Mobarek, Chris Powers
Production Photography ..... Richard Termine, Bruce Glikas
Banking ..... J.P. Morgan Chase/ Michele Gibbons
Payroll Service ..... Castellana Services, Inc.
Opening Night Party .... The Really Spectacular Company/ Christopher Raphael
Physical Therapy ..... PhysioArts
Massage Therapist ..... Russell Beasley, LMT
Company Orthopedist ..... Dr. Phillip Bauman
Insurance Consultant ..... Stockbridge Risk Management/ Neil Goldstein
Air Travel Services ..... Tzell Travel Group

San Diego Design Assistants
Associate Set Designer ..... Jenny Sawyers
Assistant to the Set Designer ..... Amanda Stephens
Associate Costume Designer ..... Mitchell Bloom
Assistant to the Costume Designer ..... Charlotte Devaux

CREDITS

Scenery fabricated and painted by Hudson Scenic Studio, Inc.; Old Globe Theatre, San Diego. Automation provided by Hudson Scenic Studio, Inc. Soft Goods provided by I. Weiss. Costumes by the Old Globe Theatre, San Diego; Euro Co. Costumes; Barbara Matera Ltd.; Malabar Ltd.; Werner Russold; Mardana; Marc Happel; Barry Doss. Millinery by Leslie Norgate; Karen Rodd. Fabric Painting and Dyeing by Dye-Namix Inc.; Gene Mignola, Inc.; Jeff Fender. Built Props by Craig Grigg; Old Globe Theatre, San Diego; Aerostar International, Inc. Slide of Life designed and fabricated by Philippe Vercrusyssen. Lighting equipment from PRG Lighting. Sound equipment from PRO Audio. Circus consultation by Acroback, Inc. Special thanks to Bra*Tenders for hosiery and undergarments. Ricola natural herb cough drops courtesy of Ricola USA, Inc. Emergen-C super energy booster provided by Alacer Corp.

SPECIAL THANKS
Jason McDole,
Charlie Neshyba-Hodges and Joseph Putignano.

Thanks to Radu Physical Arts, Looking Glass Productions, Friends in High Places.

A portion of your ticket today goes towards the VH1 Save the Music Foundation's efforts to restore music education programs in America's public schools.

Instruments provided by Gibson Guitar and Slingerland Drums. Bass amplifier provided by Gallien-Krueger.

The Times They Are A-Changin'
rehearsed at AARON DAVIS HALL.

www.TimesTheyAreAChangin.com

NEDERLANDER

Chairman ..... **James M. Nederlander**
President ..... **James L. Nederlander**

Executive Vice President
Nick Scandalios

Vice President
Corporate Development
Charlene S. Nederlander

Senior Vice President
Labor Relations
Herschel Waxman

Vice President
Jim Boese

Chief Financial Officer
Freida Sawyer Belviso

STAFF FOR THE BROOKS ATKINSON THEATRE
House Manager ..... Barbara Carrellas
Treasurer ..... Keshave Sattaur
Assistant Treasurers ..... William Dorso, William O'Brien
House Carpenter ..... Thomas A. Lavaia
House Flyman ..... Joseph J. Maher
House Electrician ..... Manuel Becker
House Properties ..... Joseph P. DePaulo
Engineer ..... Kevin MacKay

The Times They Are A-Changin'

Scrapbook

Photo by Aubrey Reuben

Photo by Aubrey Reuben

Photo by Aubrey Reuben

Photo by Melissa Merlo

Photo by Melissa Merlo

Photo by Melissa Merlo

1. Cast members (L-R) Thom Sesma, Lisa Brescia and Michael Arden at the opening night party at Roseland.
2. Twyla Tharp takes her curtain call on opening night.
3. Cast members Lisa Gajda and John Selya at the cast party.
4. Artie Gaffin's backstage "Sugar Heaven No-No Box."
5. (L-R): Cary Tedder, Michael Arden, Jason Wooten and Katie Klaus as carnival slackers.
6. Backstage collection of tags with names bestowed on the dummy each night.

Correspondent: Thom Sesma, "Captain Ahrab"
Opening Night Gifts: Champagne Flutes, Backpacks, Dream/Eye Pillows, Trophies.
Most Exciting Celebrity Visitor and What They Said: #1: Bob Dylan: "You guys blow me away. A lot of people have covered my songs but I've never heard 'em sung better than here. I feel like I can retire now."
#2: A house party of Vietnam Vets who stayed for a talkback and shared their own stories about listening to Dylan out in the field during the war.
Who Got the Gypsy Robe: Lisa Gajda; Erin Schindler covered it with every lyric from the show.
Actor Who Performed the Most Roles: Josh Dean in San Diego.
Who Has Done the Most Shows: John Herrera.
Special Backstage Ritual: Pre-show "On The Pequod" word selection (a collective choice of a single word we would all focus on throughout that single performance, like "family," "horizon," "mystery" and the like).
Favorite Moments During Each Performance: Charlie Hodges' "Mr. Tambourine Man" solo; Lisa Gajda's Cinderella solo; Michael Arden singing "Dignity."
Favorite In-Theatre Gathering Place: Onstage vocal warm-up and Pequod ritual.
"Gypsy of the Year" Sketch: "Thou, Winter Wind" with Michael Arden, Charlie Neshyba-Hodges, Alaine Kashian and Marty Lawson.
Favorite Off-Site Hangout: Tony's DiNapoli!
Favorite Snack Food: Chocolate from Artie Gaffin's "Sugar Heaven No-No Box."
Mascot: Twyla Tharp.
Favorite Therapy: Russ Beasley, masseur extraordinaire.
Memorable Ad-Lib: When all three of Michael Arden's mics went out during "Like A Rolling Stone" and the entire audience sang all of the lyrics.
Texting Incident During a Performance: Two teenage girls (looked like sisters) sitting on opposite ends of the short second row texted each other during an entire performance, including through the bows.
Memorable Stage Door Fan Encounter: Every night we were greeted by parents in their 40s or 50s who brought their kids to introduce them to Dylan's music and the kids couldn't wait to hear more.
Fastest Costume Change: Charlie Hodges into finale costume.
Heaviest/Hottest Costume: John Selya and his skeleton puppet; Charlie Hodges and his one-man band suit.
Who Wore the Least: Jenn Colella in the parking lot of the Park Manor Hotel in San Diego.
Catchphrase Only the Company Would Recognize: "I think this is the one."
Orchestra Member Who Played the Most Instruments: John J.J. Jackson, guitarist extraordinaire played multiple guitars and harmonicas.
Memorable Directorial Note: "It's Melville!"
Company In-Joke: "It's Melville!"
Company Legends: Bob Dylan's visit; and the best swings in the history of Broadway.
Sweethearts Within the Company: Lisa Gajda and one very lucky John Selya.
Superstition That Turned Out To Be True: Never decorate your dressing room before opening night.
Coolest Thing About Being in This Show: That's simple. It was, is and always will be, being in this show, the coolest show ever.
Also: On the eve of opening night, the entire crew gathered onstage and presented Twyla Tharp a Local 1 jacket and made her an honorary member of the crew with a thunderous ovation. In our collective memories as a cast, no one of us had ever seen a director so honored.

Translations

First Preview: January 4, 2007. Opened: January 25, 2007.
Closed: March 11, 2007 after 24 Previews and 53 Performances.

PLAYBILL

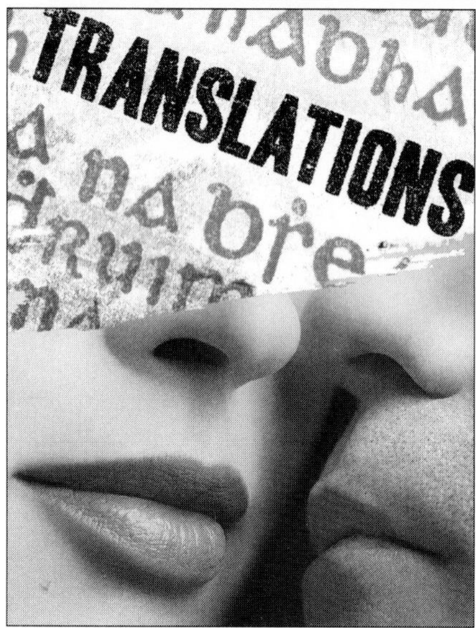

CAST

(in order of appearance)

Manus .... DAVID COSTABILE
Sarah .... MORGAN HALLETT
Jimmy Jack .... DERMOT CROWLEY
Maire .... SUSAN LYNCH
Doalty .... MICHAEL FITZGERALD
Bridget .... GERALDINE HUGHES
Hugh .... NIALL BUGGY
Owen .... ALAN COX
Captain Lancey .... GRAEME MALCOLM
Lieutenant Yolland .... CHANDLER WILLIAMS

SETTING

A hedge school in the townland of Baile Beag/Ballybeg, an Irish-speaking community in County Donegal.

Under British occupation since the 16th century, Ireland saw the rights and freedoms of its people slowly stripped away, despite continual uprisings. In 1845, the Great Famine decimated the Irish population, sowing the final seeds of unrest and rebellion that would overturn British rule.

ACT ONE

An afternoon in late August, 1833

ACT TWO

A few days later

ACT THREE

The evening of the following day

Continued on next page

BILTMORE THEATRE

MANHATTAN THEATRE CLUB AND McCARTER THEATRE CENTER

ARTISTIC DIRECTOR LYNNE MEADOW
EXECUTIVE PRODUCER BARRY GROVE
ARTISTIC DIRECTOR EMILY MANN
MANAGING DIRECTOR JEFFREY WOODWARD

PRESENT

TRANSLATIONS

BY

BRIAN FRIEL

WITH

NIALL BUGGY DAVID COSTABILE
ALAN COX DERMOT CROWLEY
MICHAEL FITZGERALD MORGAN HALLETT
GERALDINE HUGHES SUSAN LYNCH
GRAEME MALCOLM CHANDLER WILLIAMS

SCENIC & COSTUME DESIGN FRANCIS O'CONNOR
LIGHTING DESIGN DAVY CUNNINGHAM
SOUND DESIGN JOHN LEONARD

ORIGINAL MUSIC SAM JACKSON
PRODUCTION STAGE MANAGER RICHARD COSTABILE

DIRECTED BY

GARRY HYNES

CASTING LAURA STANCZYK NANCY PICCIONE/ DAVID CAPARELLIOTIS
DIRECTOR OF ARTISTIC OPERATIONS MANDY GREENFIELD
PRODUCTION MANAGER RYAN MCMAHON

DIRECTOR OF DEVELOPMENT JILL TURNER LLOYD
DIRECTOR OF MARKETING DEBRA A. WAXMAN
PRESS REPRESENTATIVE BONEAU/ BRYAN-BROWN

GENERAL MANAGER FLORIE SEERY
DIRECTOR OF ARTISTIC DEVELOPMENT PAIGE EVANS

FOR THE McCARTER THEATRE CENTER

PRODUCING DIRECTOR MARA ISAACS
DIRECTOR OF PRODUCTION DAVID YORK

Manhattan Theatre Club wishes to express its appreciation to Theatre Development Fund for its support of this production.

1/25/07

(L-R): Morgan Hallett and David Costabile as Sarah and Manus.

Photo by Joan Marcus

Translations

Cast Continued

Stage Manager ....KASEY OSTOPCHUCK

UNDERSTUDIES

For Manus, Doalty, Owen, Lieutenant Yolland:
JEREMY BOBB
For Sarah, Maire, Bridget:
DIANE LANDERS
For Jimmy Jack, Hugh, Captain Lancey:
KENNETH TIGAR

Niall Buggy and Susan Lynch are appearing with the permission of Actors' Equity Association pursuant to an exchange program between American Equity and UK Equity.

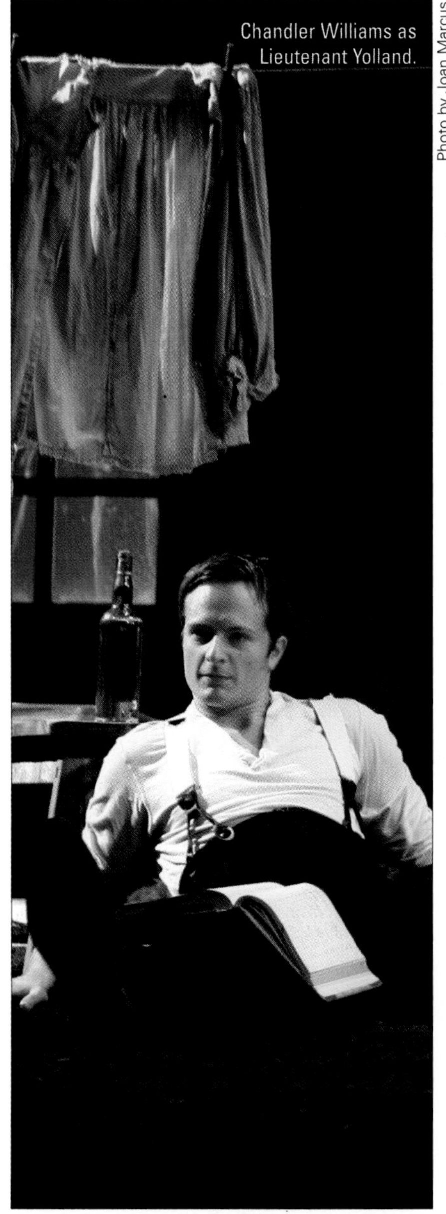
Chandler Williams as Lieutenant Yolland.
Photo by Joan Marcus

Niall Buggy
Hugh

Dermot Crowley
Jimmy Jack

David Costabile
Manus

Alan Cox
Owen

Michael FitzGerald
Doalty

Morgan Hallett
Sarah

Geraldine Hughes
Bridget

Susan Lynch
Maire

Graeme Malcolm
Captain Lancey

Chandler Williams
Lieutenant Yolland

Jeremy Bobb
Understudy for Manus, Doalty, Owen, Lieutenant Yolland

Kenneth Tigar
Understudy for Jimmy Jack, Hugh, Captain Lancey

Diane Landers
Understudy for Sarah, Maire, Bridget

Brian Friel
Playwright

Garry Hynes
Director

Emily Mann
Artistic Director, McCarter Theatre Center

Lynne Meadow
Artistic Director, Manhattan Theatre Club, Inc.

Barry Grove
Executive Producer, Manhattan Theatre Club, Inc.

Translations

Photos by Ben Strothmann

CREW
Front Row (L-R): Jeff Dodson (Master Electrician), Louis Shapiro (Sound Engineer), Angela Simpson (Wardrobe Supervisor), Kasey Ostopchuck (Stage Manager).

Back Row (L-R): Tim Walters (Head Propertyman), Patrick Murray (Flyman), Tim Hanlon (Dresser), Marc Grimshaw (IATSE Apprentice), Andrew Sliwinski (IATSE Apprentice), and Richard Costabile (Production Stage Manager).

FRONT OF HOUSE STAFF
Front Row (L-R): Wendy Wright (Head Usher), Pamela Gittlitz (Usher).

Second Row (L-R): Dinah Glorioso (Usher), Ben Tostado (Usher), Miranda Scopel (Assistant House Manager), Alana Samuels (Subscriber Services Liason).

Third Row (L-R): Ed Brashear (Ticket Taker), Russ Ramsey (Theatre Manager), Beren Willwerth (Sweet Concessions Manager), Jackson Ero (Usher) and Bruce Dye (Usher).

BOX OFFICE
(L-R): Dave Dillon and Jonathan Pate.

Translations

MANHATTAN THEATRE CLUB STAFF

Artistic Director .... **Lynne Meadow**
Executive Producer .... **Barry Grove**
General Manager .... **Florie Seery**
Director of Artistic Development .... **Paige Evans**
Director of Artistic Operations .... **Mandy Greenfield**
Artistic Consultant .... **Daniel Sullivan**
Director of Artistic Administration/
Assistant to the Artistic Director ... **Amy Gilkes Loe**
Associate Director of Artistic Operations ..... Lisa McNulty
Artistic Assistant .... Kacy O'Brien
Director of Casting .... **Nancy Piccione**
Casting Director .... **David Caparelliotis**
Casting Assistants .... Rebecca Atwood, Kristin Svenningsen
Literary Manager .... **Emily Shooltz**
Play Development Associate/
Sloan Project Manager .... Aaron Leichter
Play Development Assistant .... Annie MacRae
Director of
Musical Development .... **Clifford Lee Johnson III**
Director of Development .... **Jill Turner Lloyd**
Director, Special Events .... Allison Gutstein
Director, Foundation &
Government Relations .... Josh Jacobson
Director, Corporate Relations ...... Karen Zornow Leiding
Director, Individual Giving .... Jon W. Haddorff
Senior Development Associate,
Individual Giving .... Antonello Di Benedetto
Development Associate/
Foundation & Government Relations .. Andrea Gorzell
Development Associate/
Planning & Projects .... Liz Halakan
Development Associate/
Corporate Relations .... Jessica Sadowski
Development Database Coordinator .... Ann Mundorff
Patrons' Liaison .... Sage Young
Director of Marketing .... **Debra A. Waxman**
Marketing and Website Manager .... Ryan Klink
Marketing Associate .... Tom O'Connor
Director of Finance .... **Jeffrey Bledsoe**
Business Manager .... Holly Kinney
HR/Payroll Manager .... Darren Robertson
Senior Business Associate &
HR Coordinator .... Denise L. Thomas
Business Assistant .... Adam Cook
Manager of Systems Operations .... Avishai Cohen
Associate General Manager .... **Lindsey Brooks Sag**
Company Manager/ NY City Center .... Erin Moeller
General Management Assistant .... Laura Roumanos
Assistant to the Executive Producer .... Bonnie Pan
Director of Subscriber Services .... **Robert Allenberg**
Associate Subscriber Services Manager ...... Andrew Taylor
Subscriber Services Representatives .... Mark Bowers, Rebekah Dewald, Matthew Praet, Rosanna Consalva Sarto
Director of Telesales and Telefunding .... **George Tetlow**
Assistant Manager,
Telesales and Telefunding .... Terrence Burnett
Director of Education .... **David Shookhoff**
Asst. Director of Education/
Coordinator, Paul A. Kaplan
Theatre Management Program .... Amy Harris
Education Assistants .... Kayla Cagan, Sarah Ryndak
MTC Teaching Artists .... Stephanie Alston, David Auburn, Michael Bernard, Carl Capotorto, Chris Ceraso, Charlotte Colavin, Dominic Colon, Gilbert Girion, Andy Goldberg, Elise Hernandez, Jeffrey Joseph, Julie Leedes, Kate Long, Louis D. Moreno, Melissa Murray, Angela Pietropinto, Alfonso Ramirez, Carmen Rivera, Judy Tate, Candido Tirado, Joe White
Theatre Management Interns .... Nicky Barton, Stephanie Cowan, Ian Darrah, Jocelyn Florence, Jennifer Gibson, Diana Glazer, Charles Graytok, Cia Jordan, Lauren Kosteski, Kara McGann, Katie Murray, Alana Samuels, Hannah Shafran, Marielle Solan, Rachel Swan

---

The Paul A. Kaplan Theatre Management Program, MTC's internship program, is designed to train the next generation of theatre leaders.

Randy Carrig Casting Intern .... Shira Sandler
Reception/Studio Manager .... Lauren Butler
Production Manager .... **Ryan McMahon**
Associate Production Manager .... Bridget Markov
Assistant Production Manager .... Stephanie Madonna
Lights and Sound Supervisor .... **Matthew T. Gross**
Properties Supervisor .... **Scott Laule**
Assistant Properties Supervisor .... Julia Sandy
Props Carpenter .... Peter Grimes
Costume Supervisor .... **Erin Hennessy Dean**
Assistant Costume Supervisor .... Michelle Sesco

GENERAL PRESS REPRESENTATION
BONEAU/BRYAN-BROWN
Chris Boneau Jim Byk
Aaron Meier Heath Schwartz Christine Olver

Script Readers .... Erin Detrick, Liz Jones, Asher Richelli, Michelle Tattenbaum, Kathryn Walat, Ethan Youngerman
Musical Theatre Reader .... Emily King

SERVICES

Accountants .... ERE, LLP
Advertising .... SpotCo/ Drew Hodges, Jim Edwards, Ben Downing, Laura Price
Web Design .... Pilla Marketing Communications
Legal Counsel .... John Breglio, Deborah Hartnett/ Paul, Weiss, Rifkind, Wharton and Garrison LLP
Real Estate Counsel .... Marcus Attorneys
Labor Counsel .... Harry H. Weintraub/ Glick and Weintraub, P.C.
Immigration Counsel .... Theodore Ruthizer/ Kramer, Levin, Naftalis & Frankel, LLP
Special Projects .... Elaine H. Hirsch
Insurance .... DeWitt Stern Group, Inc./Anthony Pittari
Maintenance .... Reliable Cleaning
Production Photographer .... Joan Marcus
Cover Photo .... Henry Leutwyler
Cover Design .... SpotCo
Theatre Displays .... King Display

PRODUCTION STAFF FOR *TRANSLATIONS*

Company Manager .... **Seth Shepsle**
Production Stage Manager .... **Richard Costabile**
Stage Manager .... Kasey Ostopchuck
Drama League Assistant Director ... Gaye-Taylor Upchurch
Assistant Scenic Designer .... Peter R. Feuchtwanger
Assistant Lighting Designer .... Miriam Crowe
Dialect Consultant .... Charlotte Fleck
Hair/Makeup Supervisor .... Natasha Steinhagen
Dresser .... Tim Hanlon
Flyman .... Patrick Murray
Lighting Programmer .... Marc Polimeni
Production Assistant .... John Ferry

CREDITS

Lighting equipment provided by PRG Lighting. Sound equipment provided by Masque Sound. Natural herbal cough drops courtesy of Ricola USA.

SPECIAL THANKS

Showman Fabricators, Denise Cooper

For more information visit
www.ManhattanTheatreClub.com

MANHATTAN THEATRE CLUB/
BILTMORE THEATRE STAFF

Theatre Manager .... **Russ Ramsey**
Assistant House Manager .... Miranda Scopel
Box Office Treasurer .... **David Dillon**
Assistant Box Office Treasurers .... Tevy Bradley, Jonathan Pate
Head Carpenter .... Chris Wiggins
Head Propertyman .... Timothy Walters
Sound Engineer .... Louis Shapiro
Master Electrician .... Jeff Dodson
Wardrobe Supervisor .... Angela Simpson
Apprentices .... Marc Grimshaw, Andrew Sliwinski
Engineers .... Robert Allen, Richardo Deosarran, Byron Johnson
Security .... Initial Security
Lobby Refreshments .... Sweet Concessions

McCARTER THEATRE CENTER STAFF

General Manager .... Thomas J. Muza
Director of Play Development .... Douglas Langworthy
Literary Manager/
Dramaturg for Translations .... Carrie Hughes
Director of Artistic Administration .... Grace Shackney
Director of Development .... Mary T. Funsch, CFRE
Director of Marketing .... Barbara Andrews
Director of Public &
Community Relations .... Dan Bauer
Director of Education .... Christopher T. Parks
Director of Information Technology ...... Charlotte Hussey
Director of Ticketing Services .... Anne W. Gribbins
Technical Director .... Christopher Nelson
Costume Shop Manager .... Becca Pryce
Prop Master .... Michele Sammarco
Stage Supervisor .... Stephen Howe
Charge Scenic Artist .... Carrie Ballenger
Directing Assistant .... Michael Grayman

Translations
Scrapbook

Correspondent: Michael FitzGerald, "Doalty"
Opening Night Gifts: Production Stage Manager Richard Costabile made us a frame containing all our photos. Geraldine Hughes gave us all nice scarves. We got Swiss chocolate and all kinds of different treats like that.
Most Exciting Celebrity Visitors: On opening night Glenn Close came backstage with her whole entourage and was sitting in the men's dressing room—only I didn't know. I was taking a shower. When I emerged, I was very modestly dressed in nothing but a towel. I knew there were visitors in the dressing room, but I wasn't registering that one of them was Glenn Close. All I heard was a voice saying, "I think this young man wants us to leave." Later, Chandler Williams told me that the person who was talking was Glenn Close. That was my little faux pas. We also had visits from Angela Lansbury, Danny DeVito, Rhea Perlman, Kevin Spacey and Edward Norton. Norton was especially exciting because he's such a hero of mine.
Who Has Done the Most Shows in Their Career: Dermot Crowley is the eldest so I'm tempted to say him. But Niall Buggy is just one year younger, so those two, hands down, have done the most in terms of longevity.
Special Backstage Rituals: We congregate in the women's dressing room every night to shoot the breeze and have our playtime before we go on. There's a maternal vibe in there that helps us get in the mood.
Favorite Moment During Each Performance: That would have to be the First Act, before the Brits arrive. We're all in a very free-flowing ensemble playing. We achieve a sort of seamlessness in our playing, riffing off of each other, that is really pleasurable. I love to experience that as a performer.
Favorite Off-Site Hangout: Joe Allen, Bar Centrale and Angus McIndoe.
Favorite Snack Food: We have a jar of Reese's Pieces, Skittles and chocolate—all sorts of terrible temptations all in one jar. We all dip in there, to our shame. It sits in the Stage Manager's office, next to the computer, and we're all on the internet a lot.
Mascot: Dermot Crowley who play Jimmy-Jack has a snail named Legless the Snail. Legless sometimes goes missing and Dermot finds ransom notes under his door.
Favorite Therapies: A lot of Ricola and Emergen-C—it's great stuff! We keep ourselves healthy.
Memorable Ad-Libs: Part of the fun of the First Act is that liberties must be taken to add to the reality of the scene. We swap books, ad lib mouthing the times tables, various things to help the action.
Cell Phone Rings, Cell Phone Photos or Texting Incidents: It's not been too bad. We haven't had any major rudeness or ignorance.
Memorable Stage Door Fan Encounters: There are some very sweet people who remember you from shows you've done, lovely people. There are also autograph bounty hunters who want to get your autograph now before you become famous. Which is sort of a compliment, too. People are generally very nice.
Fastest Costume Change: When Morgan Hallett changes at the end of the love scene. She has about thirty seconds to get back into her dress from Boston for the next scene.
Busiest Day at the Box Office: The day the reviews came out we had lines stretching down the block.
Who Wore the Heaviest/Hottest Costume: Niall Buggy has the big overcoat—but, mind you it's freezing on that stage, so we could all do with a big coat.
Who Wore the Least: That would have to be me. In one scene I'm in breeches and a raggedy shirt, and that's about it.
Catchphrases Only the Company Would Recognize: "Mommy! You're turning me!" "See you in school!" "Stop the Lights!"—a la Bunny Carr.
Memorable Directorial Notes: "Would you ever see what it feels like to f*** off?" "Keep going, Bugs."
Understudy Anecdote: The house played a practical joke on Chandler one night. There was a note in the program that said, "At tonight's performance, the role usually played by Chandler Williams will be played by Ken Tigar." Chandler is 27 and Ken Tigar is about 60. So that would be quite a stretch.
Nicknames: Morgan is "El Muta." Niall Buggy is called "Bugs."
Embarrassing Moments: In the Princeton tryout, David Costabile was hijinking backstage and his breeches fell down, while he was doing a merry dance for Susan Lynch. He then spent the whole next scene trying not to let his pants fall down.
Coolest Thing About Being in This Show: Just being on Broadway. I think every actor would like to think they can get to Broadway at least once. To be able to do to it with such a successful show and such a great company is by far the coolest thing.

Photos by Aubrey Reuben

1. The cast at the opening night party at the Hard Rock Cafe.
2. (L-R): Amy Ryan, Geraldine Hughes, Patricia Clarkson on opening night.
3. Curtain call on opening night.

The 25th Annual Putnam County Spelling Bee

First Preview: April 15, 2005. Opened: May 2, 2005.
Still running as of May 31, 2007.

PLAYBILL

CIRCLE IN THE SQUARE
UNDER THE DIRECTION OF
THEODORE MANN and PAUL LIBIN

David Stone James L. Nederlander Barbara Whitman Patrick Catullo
Barrington Stage Company Second Stage Theatre

Present

The 25th Annual Putnam County
SPELLING BEE

Music & Lyrics by
WILLIAM FINN

Book By
RACHEL SHEINKIN

Conceived by
REBECCA FELDMAN

Additional Material by
JAY REISS

With
DERRICK BASKIN, DEBORAH S. CRAIG, BARRETT FOA, JOSH GAD, LISA HOWARD,
JOSE LLANA, SARAH SALTZBERG, GREG STUHR, JESSICA-SNOW WILSON
TODD BUONOPANE, MAURICE MURPHY, KATE WETHERHEAD, LISA YUEN

Set Design by
BEOWULF BORITT

Costume Design by
JENNIFER CAPRIO

Lighting Design by
NATASHA KATZ

Sound Design by
DAN MOSES SCHREIER

Orchestrations by
MICHAEL STAROBIN

Music Director & Dance Arrangements by
VADIM FEICHTNER

Vocal Arrangements by
CARMEL DEAN

Music Coordinator
MICHAEL KELLER

Press
THE PUBLICITY OFFICE

Casting
TARA RUBIN CASTING

Production Stage Manager
ANDREA "SPOOK" TESTANI

Production Manager
KAI BROTHERS

General Management
321 THEATRICAL MANAGEMENT

Choreographed by
DAN KNECHTGES

Directed by
JAMES LAPINE

Based on C-R-E-P-U-S-C-U-L-E, an original play by THE FARM.
Original Broadway Cast Recording on GHOSTLIGHT RECORDS.

10/2/06

CAST

(in alphabetical order)

Mitch Mahoney .... DERRICK BASKIN
Marcy Park .... DEBORAH S. CRAIG
Leaf Coneybear .... BARRETT FOA
William Barfee .... JOSH GAD
Rona Lisa Peretti .... LISA HOWARD
Olive Ostrovsky ...... JESSICA-SNOW WILSON
Chip Tolentino .... JOSE LLANA
Douglas Panch .... GREG STUHR
Logainne Schwartzandgrubenierre . . SARAH SALTZBERG

UNDERSTUDIES

For William Barfee:
TODD BUONOPANE
For Mitch Mahoney:
MAURICE MURPHY
For Leaf Coneybear, Chip Tolentino:
TODD BUONOPANE, MAURICE MURPHY
For Douglas Panch:
TODD BUONOPANE, MAURICE MURPHY
For Marcy Park:
LISA YUEN
For Olive Ostrovsky:
KATE WETHERHEAD, LISA YUEN
For Rona Lisa Peretti:
LISA YUEN
For Logainne Schwartzandgrubenierre:
KATE WETHERHEAD

Continued on next page

Photo by Joan Marcus

(L-R): Sarah Saltzberg, Jose Llana, Deborah S. Craig (Bottom), Josh Gad (Top), Barrett Foa and Jessica-Snow Wilson.

The 25th Annual Putnam County Spelling Bee

Cast Continued

Dance Captain: DERRICK BASKIN

MUSICIANS

Conductor/Piano:
VADIM FEICHTNER
Associate Conductor/Synthesizer:
CARMEL DEAN
Reed:
RICK HECKMAN
Cello:
AMY RALSKE
Drums/Percussion:
GLENN RHIAN
Music Coordinator:
MICHAEL KELLER

Music Copying:
EMILY GRISHMAN MUSIC PREPARATION
EMILY GRISHMAN/KATHARINE EDMONDS

Barrett Foa as Leaf Coneybear.

Photo by Joan Marcus

Derrick Baskin
Mitch Mahoney

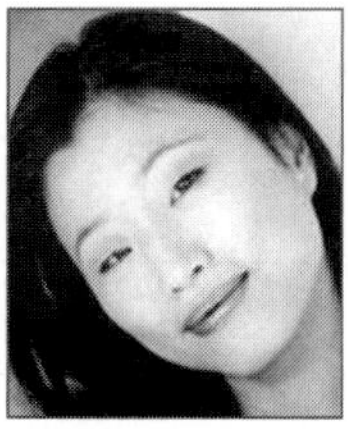
Deborah S. Craig
Marcy Park

Barrett Foa
Leaf Coneybear

Josh Gad
William Barfee

Lisa Howard
Rona Lisa Peretti

Jose Llana
Chip Tolentino

Sarah Saltzberg
Logainne Schwartzandgrubenierre

Greg Stuhr
Douglas Panch

Jessica-Snow Wilson
Olive Ostrovsky

Todd Buonopane
Understudy for Barfee, Coneybear, Chip, Mr. Panch

Maurice Murphy
Understudy for Coneybear, Mitch, Chip, Mr. Panch

Kate Wetherhead
Understudy for Olive, Marcy, Logainne

Lisa Yuen
Understudy for Olive, Marcy, Ms. Peretti

William Finn
Music/Lyrics

Rachel Sheinkin
Book

Rebecca Feldman
Conceiver

Jay Reiss
Additional Material

James Lapine
Director

Dan Knechtges
Choreographer

Darren Katz
Resident Director

The 25th Annual Putnam County Spelling Bee

Beowulf Boritt
Set Designer

Jennifer Caprio
Costume Designer

Natasha Katz
Lighting Designer

Dan Moses Schreier
Sound Designer

Marty Kopulsky
Hair and Wig Designer

Michael Starobin
Orchestrations

Vadim Feichtner
Musical Director/ Dance Arrangments

Carmel Dean
Vocal Arranger/ Associate Conductor/ Synthesizer

Michael Keller
Music Coordinator

Tara Rubin Casting
Casting

Marcia Goldberg, Nancy Nagel Gibbs and Nina Essman,
321 Theatrical Management
General Management

David Stone
Producer

James L. Nederlander
Producer

Barbara Whitman
Producer

Carole Rothman, Artistic Director, Second Stage Theatre
Producer

Jesse Tyler Ferguson
Leaf Coneybear

Celia Keenan-Bolger
Olive Ostrovsky

Kevin Smith Kirkwood
Understudy for Chip Tolentino, Mitch Mahoney

Jacqui Polk
Understudy for Olive Ostrovsky, Logainne Schwartzandgrubenierre

Lauren Worsham
Understudy for Olive Ostrovsky, Marcy Park

Aaron J. Albano
Chip Tolentino

Stanley Bahorek
Leaf Coneybear

Jenni Barber
Olive Ostrovsky

Cathryn Basile
Understudy for Marcy Park, Olive Ostrovsky, Rona Lisa Peretti

Elsa Carmona
Understudy for Rona Lisa Peretti

Jared Gertner
William Barfee

Brian Gonzales
Understudy for Leaf Coneybear, Chip Tolentino, Douglas Panch, William Barfee

Carly Hughes
Understudy for Marcy Park, Rona Lisa Peretti

James Monroe Inglehart
Mitch Mahoney

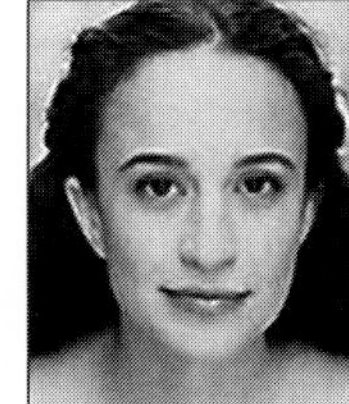
Sara Inbar
Logainne Schwartzandgrubenierre

Kevin Smith Kirkwood
Understudy for Mitch Mahoney, Chip Tolentino

Greta Lee
Marcy Park

The 25th Annual Putnam County Spelling Bee

Rory O'Malley
Understudy for Leaf Coneybear, Douglas Panch, William Barfee

Jacqui Polk
Understudy for Marcy Park, Olive Ostrovsky, Logainne Schwartzandgrubenierre

Mo Rocca
Douglas Panch

Jennifer Simard
Rona Lisa Peretti

Law Tarello
Understudy for Douglas Panch, William Barfee

WARDROBE

(L-R): Magie Dominic (Sub Dresser), Cleon Byerly (Dresser) and Yvonna Balfour (Wardrobe Supervisor).

Not Pictured: Susan Sigrist (Dresser).

BOX OFFICE

(L-R): Thomas Motylenski (Assistant Box Office Treasurer) and Ilene Towell (Box Office Treasurer).

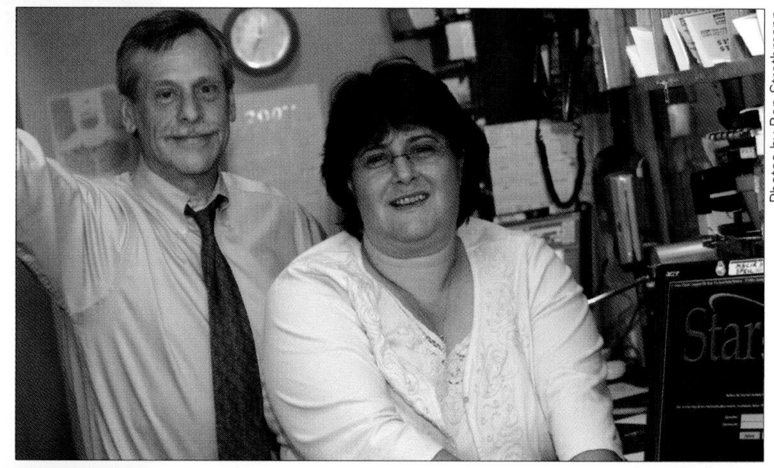

Photos by Ben Strothmann

ORCHESTRA

Top Row (L-R):
Sarah Carter (Sub Cello), Dennis Anderson (Sub Reeds), Carmel Dean (Associate Conductor/Synthesizer).

Bottom Row (L-R):
Vadim Feichtner (Conductor/Piano) and Glenn Rhian (Drums/Percussion).

Not Pictured: Amy Ralske (Cello) and Rick Heckman (Reeds).

The 25th Annual Putnam County Spelling Bee

Photos by Ben Strothmann

VOLUNTEER SPELLER WRANGLERS
Bottom Row (L-R): Dana Wickens, Irene Pastuszek.

Top Row (L-R): Jen Norton and Aaron Glick.

FRONT OF HOUSE STAFF
Front Row (L-R): Sophie Koufakis (Usher), Allyson Ansel (Porter), Stephen Winterhalter (Merchandise), Margarita Caban (Usher), Xavier Young (Usher).

Back Row (L-R): Shawn Fertitta (House Manager), Georgia Keghlian (Usher), Tammy Cummiskey (Usher), Michael Trupia (Usher) and Barbara Zavilowicz (Usher).

STAGE CREW
Front Row (L-R): Robert S. Lindsay (F.O.H. Sound Engineer), Bill Seelig (Flyman), Stephanie Vetter (Monitor Engineer), Stewart Wagner (Head Electrician).

Back Row (L-R):
Owen E. Parmele (Prop Master) and Robert Gordon (Head Carpenter).

COMPANY & STAGE MANAGERS
(Top-Bottom): Dan Shaheen (Sub Stage Manager), Lisa Koch Rao (Company Manager) and Kelly Hance (Stage Manager).

Not Pictured: Spook Testani (Production Stage Manager).

The 25th Annual Putnam County Spelling Bee

STAFF FOR *THE 25TH ANNUAL PUTNAM COUNTY SPELLING BEE*

GENERAL MANAGEMENT
321 THEATRICAL MANAGEMENT
Nancy Nagel Gibbs
Nina Essman Marcia Goldberg

GENERAL PRESS REPRESENTATIVE
THE PUBLICITY OFFICE
Bob Fennell Marc Thibodeau
Michael S. Borowski Candi Adams

MARKETING
THE ARACA GROUP
Clint Bond, Jr.
Kirsten Berkman

CASTING
TARA RUBIN CASTING
Tara Rubin, CSA
Dunja Vitolic, Eric Woodall, Laura Schutzel,
Mona Slomsky, Rebecca Carfagna, Jeff Siebert

COMPANY MANAGER .... **Lisa Koch Rao**

Resident Director .... Darren Katz
Production Stage Manager .... Andrea "Spook" Testani
Stage Manager .... Kelly Hance
Assistant Stage Manager .... Lisa Yuen
Management Assistant .... Jayna Neagle
Assistant Choreographer .... DJ Gray
Dance Captain .... Derrick Baskin
Associate Lighting Designer .... Philip Rosenberg
Assistant Set Designer .... Jo Winiarski
Assistant Costume Designer .... Brian Russman
Associate Sound Designer .... David Bullard
Assistant Lighting Designer .... John Viesta
Automated Lights Programmer .... Laura Frank
Production Managers .... Kai Brothers, Jason Block
Electrician .... Randall Zaibek
Flyman .... Billy Seelig
Monitor Engineer .... Stephanie Vetter
Wardrobe Supervisor .... Yvonna Balfour
Dressers .... Cleon Byerly, Susan Sigrist
Costume Assistant .... Jeffrey Hinchee
Set Design Assistants .... John Conners, Camille Connolly, Mike Wade
Synthesizer Programming .... Bruce Samuels
Music Preparation .... Emily Grishman
Advertising .... Serino Coyne, Inc./ Greg Corradetti, Ruth Rosenberg, Joaquin Esteva, Natalie Serota
Lobby Design .... Beowulf Boritt
Web Design .... Late August/Jeff Prout, Jeff Bowen
Merchandising .... The Araca Group/ Joseph Boyles, Peter Pegola, Anne MacLean, Karen Davidov, Zach Lezberg, Julie Monahan, Chet Unger
Volunteer Spellers Coordinators .... Erik Alden, Alan Arellano, Brooke Brod, Amy Kaissar, Jen Norton, Teresa Pond, Barbara Rubin
Lottery Coordinator .... Michelle Schechter
Production Assistant .... Benjamin J. Shuman
Legal Counsel .... Schreck, Rose & Dapello/ Nancy Rose
Accountant .... FK Partners CPA's LLP/ Robert Fried
Banking .... JP Morgan Chase/ Richard Callian, Michele Gibbons
Insurance .... AON/Albert G. Ruben Insurance/ George Walden, Claudia Kaufman
Payroll Service .... Castellana Services, Inc.
Production Photography .... Joan Marcus
Opening Night Coordination .... Tobak-Dantchik Events and Promotions, Inc./ Cathy Dantchik, Joanna B. Koondel

Group Sales Box Office
212.398.8383 / 800.223.7565

321 THEATRICAL MANAGEMENT
Beth Blitzer, Bob Brinkerhoff, Rachel Marcus, Amy Merlino, Jeanette Norton, Ted Rounsaville, Susan Sampliner, Greg Schaffert, Erica Lynn Schwartz, Ken Silverman, David Turner, Erica Whelan, Sarah Zeitler

SECOND STAGE THEATRE
Artistic Director: Carole Rothman;
Executive Director: Ellen Richard;
Associate Artistic Director: Christopher Burney;
Production Manager: Jeff Wild

Board of Trustees
Anthony C.M. Kiser, Co-Chairman; Stephen C. Sherrill, Co-Chairman; David A. Ackert, Elizabeth Berger, Tavener Holmes Berry, Maura Bulkeley, Jeffrey H. Bunzel, Sally Clement, Suzanne Schwartz Davidson, Fran Fergusson, Bambi de la Gueronniere, Richard C. Gay, Edward I. Herbst, Hamilton E. James, Wendy Evans Joseph, Steven B. Klinsky, George S. Loening, Patti LuPone, Timothy J. McClimon, Mary P. Moran, John Partilla, Kirk A. Radke, Lynne Randall, David Resnicow, Donna Rosen, Carole Rothman, Joshua Ruch, John R. Schmidt, Denise V. Seegal, Ann Tenenbaum, Michael Weinstein, Peter Weller, Herbert S. Winokur, Jr.

BARRINGTON STAGE COMPANY
Board of Trustees
Mary Ann Quinson, President; Richard Solar, Vice President/Treasurer; James A. Lapenn, Vice President; Marion Simon, Secretary; Julianne Boyd, Artistic Director; Sydelle Blatt, Reba Hough Evenchik, Chris Farrell, Jeananne Hauswald, Robin Kaplan, Dan Mathieu, Martha Piper, Sheila Richman, Ira Sarinsky, Susan R. Simon, Eda Sorokoff, Mark St. Germain, Tucker Welch, Eileen Young

The Barrington Stage Co. workshop of *The 25th Annual Putnam County Spelling Bee* was originally co-directed by Michael Barakiva and Rebecca Feldman.

CREDITS
Scenery constructed by Showman Fabricators. Lighting equipment by Production Resource Group. Costumes by Tricorne, Martin Izquierdo Studios, Matthew Hemesath and Donna Langman. Sound Equipment by Masque Sound. Props by Susan Barras. Ricola natural herb cough drops courtesy of Ricola USA, Inc. Water courtesy of FIJI Water. Apple & Eve 100% fruit juices used. Gummi Bears courtesy of Haribo Gold-Bears. Wise pretzels and chips used. Snack bags provided by Utz Quality Foods, Inc. Additional set and hand props courtesy of George Fenmore, Inc. Therapy services provided by Harkness Center for Dance Injuries at the Hospital for Joint Diseases Orthopaedic Institute. Piano by Steinway & Sons. Onstage merchandising by George Fenmore/More Merchandising International.

SPECIAL THANKS
Dana Harrel, Mimi Bilinski, Daniel Heffernan, Jim Mack. Steven, Mandy and Susan Fine. Bayside Elementary in Stevensville, MD. Robert Morris School, South Bound Brook, NJ. Ridgefield Park Public Schools.

www.spellingbeethemusical.com

CIRCLE IN THE SQUARE THEATRE
Thespian Theatre, Inc.
Under the direction of
Theodore Mann and Paul Libin

Vice President of Finance .... Susan Frankel
House Manager .... Richard D. Berg
Assistant House Manager .... Cody Perret
Head Carpenter .... Robert Gordon
Head Electrician .... Stewart Wagner
Prop Master .... Owen E. Parmele
FOH Sound Engineer .... Robert S. Lindsay
Box Office Treasurer .... Ilene Towell
Assistant to Paul Libin .... Patricia Michael
Assistant to Theodore Mann .... Holly Ricciuti

CIRCLE IN THE SQUARE THEATRE SCHOOL
Staff
President .... Paul Libin
Artistic Director .... Theodore Mann
Theatre School Director .... E. Colin O'Leary
Administrative Assistant .... Jonathan Kronenberger
Administrative Assistant .... David Pleva
Arts Education/Development .... Jonathan Mann
Development Associate .... Holly Ricciuti

The 25th Annual Putnam County Spelling Bee

Scrapbook

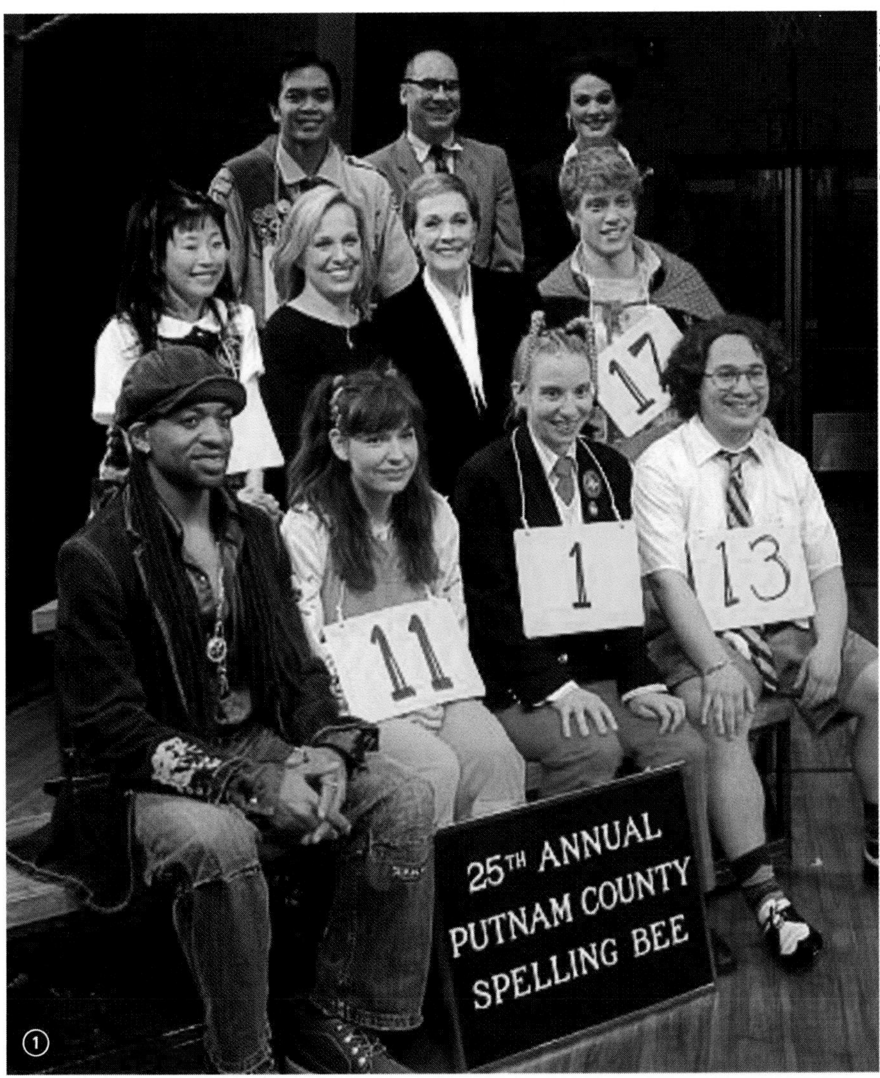

Photo by Rory O'Malley

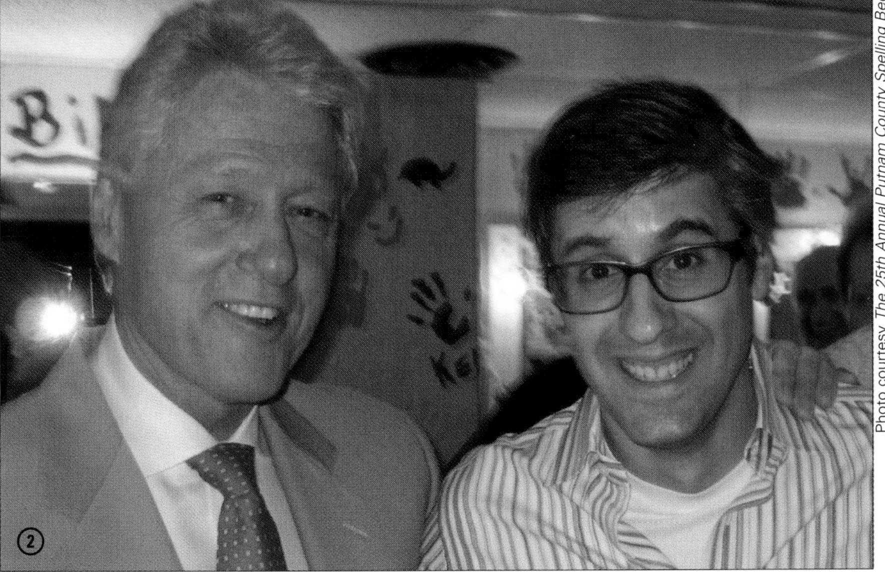

Photo courtesy *The 25th Annual Putnam County Spelling Bee*

Correspondent: Jacqui Polk, Understudy for "Logainne Schwartzandgrubenierre," "Marcy Park" and "Olive Ostrovsky."

Neat Gifts: Our prop master, Owen, is not only a master of the props but also of the culinary art of baking! For Josh Gad's happy trails he baked a beautiful loaf of bread in the shape of a foot! It was truly a magic foot that tasted unbelievable. And for Coco (Lisa Yuen) he baked a heart shaped cake that alternated chocolate and lemon (yellow flavors)...he called the cake "the heart of the bee," because she truly was! Sarah Saltzberg's mom is the best. She bakes loaves of pumpkin bread (with chocolate morsels) and banana bread. She also makes the best chicken salad EVER. It makes everyone very happy when Sarah's mom comes to visit!

Most Exciting Celebrity Visitors: Jesse Tyler Ferguson, the star of CBS's "The Class," came to the second half of the show! Teri Hatcher and Halle Berry both came to the show, however, no one could outshine the one and only JULIE ANDREWS!! She was absolutely perfect in every way...so gracious, kind, and the definition of a class act! It was an absolute blast to have her in the show; she made it impossible to watch anyone else!

Snack Foods: Jose is really good about bringing in snacks for everyone, usually doughnuts. Another day it was Oreos. We definitely love our sweets!

Mascot: Our mascot is Mr. Mousifer who happens to also be our biggest fan! Mr. Mousifer is a real mouse who lives in our greenroom. He likes to snack on our crumbs and does an occasional lap around the room and has even been know to run on people's feet. Mr. Mousifer was pretty terrifying at first but now that we have come to an understanding we really enjoy his presence and are grateful for his wisdom.

"Gypsy of the Year" Sketch: We sang "December's Other, Less Famous Holidays," a brilliant song that Sarah Saltzberg and Law Tarello wrote, which has been preserved forever on the "Carols for a Cure" CD. I wanted to take this time to clear some things up: #1 Katy Basile is neither gay nor Filipino. And #2 Rory O'Malley who played the Muslim is very obviously Jewish.

Understudy Anecdotes: Backstage during the show we have understudy parties. We paint, we have dips and chips, we play poker, and we play lots of practical jokes. None of which I can reveal for fear of embarrassing my fellow understudies!!

Some Crazy Catchphrases: "Banana wuuuuuut?!?!" "I'm jus' doin' my yob." "Saturday Night on Broadway!" "Pumpkin nut E. chip."

1. Julie Andrews (middle row, 2nd from right) with daughter Emma Walton Hamilton (middle row, 2nd from left) with the cast on "Kids' Night on Broadway."
2. Former President Bill Clinton visits Mo Rocca backstage at the Circle in the Square Theatre.

The Vertical Hour

First Preview: November 9, 2006. Opened: November 30, 2006.
Closed March 11, 2007 after 23 Previews and 117 Performances.

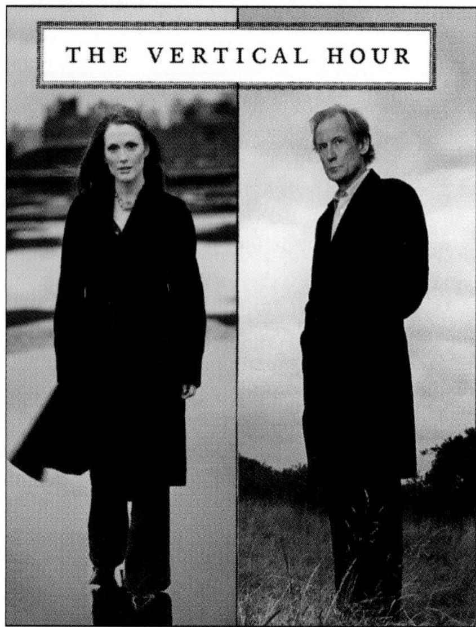

THE MUSIC BOX
THE ESTATE OF IRVING BERLIN AND THE SHUBERT ORGANIZATION, OWNERS
239 W. 45th STREET

SCOTT RUDIN ROBERT FOX NEAL STREET PRODUCTIONS
ROGER BERLIND DEBRA BLACK THE SHUBERT ORGANIZATION

present

JULIANNE MOORE BILL NIGHY

THE VERTICAL HOUR

By DAVID HARE

with

ANDREW SCOTT

DAN BITTNER RUTINA WESLEY

Set Design SCOTT PASK
Costume Design ANN ROTH
Lighting Design BRIAN MACDEVITT

Sound Design CHRISTOPHER CRONIN
Casting DANIEL SWEE
UK Casting Consultant ANNE MCNULTY

Production Stage Manager JAMES HARKER
Associate Director BT MCNICHOLL
Production Management AURORA PRODUCTIONS

Press Representative BARLOW·HARTMAN
General Management STUART THOMPSON PRODUCTIONS/ JAMES TRINER

Directed by
SAM MENDES

11/30/06

CAST

(in order of speaking)

Oliver Lucas .... BILL NIGHY
Nadia Blye .... JULIANNE MOORE
Dennis Dutton .... DAN BITTNER
Philip Lucas .... ANDREW SCOTT
Terri Scholes .... RUTINA WESLEY

SETTINGS

Scene One: An office at Yale University, day
Scene Two: A lawn on the Welsh borders, morning, two weeks later
Scene Three: Same, evening
Scene Four: Same, next day, just before dawn
Scene Five: An office at Yale University, three months later

STANDBYS

For Nadia Blye: JENNIFER ROSZELL
For Dennis Dutton and Philip Lucas: MATTHEW HUMPHREYS
For Oliver Lucas: STEVEN CROSSLEY
For Terri Scholes: CRYSTAL NOELLE

Bill Nighy and Andrew Scott appeared with the permission of Actors' Equity Association.

(L-R): Julianne Moore as Nadia Blye and Bill Nighy as Oliver Lucas

Photo by Paul Kolnik

The Vertical Hour

Julianne Moore
Nadia Blye

Bill Nighy
Oliver Lucas

Andrew Scott
Philip Lucas

Dan Bittner
Dennis Dutton

Rutina Wesley
Terri Scholes

Steven Crossley
Standby Oliver Lucas

Matthew Humphreys
Standby Dennis Dutton and Philip Lucas

Crystal Noelle
Standby Terri Scholes

Jennifer Roszell
Standby Nadia Blye

David Hare
Playwright

Sam Mendes
Director

Scott Pask
Set Design

Ann Roth
Costume Design

Brian MacDevitt
Lighting Design

Christopher Cronin
Sound Design

BT McNicholl
Associate Director

James Triner
Associate General Manager

Scott Rudin
Producer

Robert Fox
Producer

Roger Berlind
Producer

Debra Black
Producer

Gerald Schoenfeld, Chairman, The Shubert Organization
Producer

Photo by Ben Strothmann

STAGE CREW

First Row (L-R): Chris Cronin, Barry Doss, Dennis Maher.

Second Row (L-R): Abe Morrison, Kelly Smith, Laura Beattie.

Back Row (L-R): Jim Harker, Dave Cohen, Kim Garnett, Lee Iwanski, Carlos Jaramillo, Thea Gillies and Brian McGarity.

The Vertical Hour

FRONT OF HOUSE

Back Row (L-R): Joseph Amato, Jack Pisciotta, Matthew Wickert, Kenneth Kelly, Joseph Lopez, Thomas Cassano.

Middle Row (L-R): Michael Composto, Steven Staszewski, Nicholas Fusco.

Front Row: Jenna Scanlon and Jonathan Shulman (House Manager).

2006-2007 AWARD

THEATRE WORLD AWARD
Outstanding Broadway Debut (Bill Nighy)

Photos by Ben Strothmann

DOORMAN

Tim Barrett

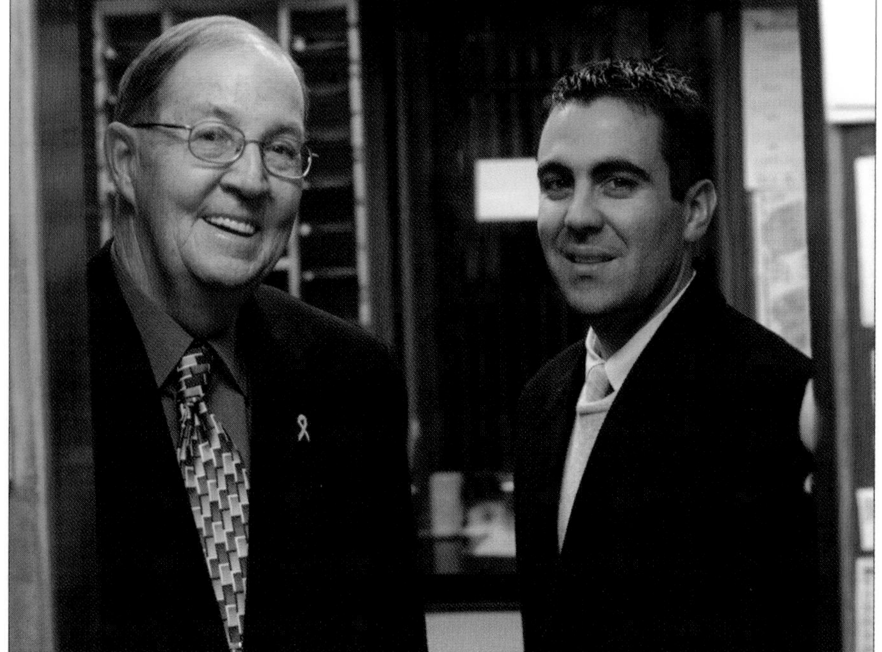

BOX OFFICE

(L-R): Robert D. Kelly
and Brendan C. Berberich.

The Vertical Hour

Scrapbook

Correspondent: Dan Bittner, "Dennis Dutton"

Memorable Note: A memorable note that we received not on opening night, but in January was from Joanne Woodward and Paul Newman wishing us the best and applauding David on writing about important issues of today with class.

Most Exciting Celebrity Visitor and What They Did/Said: There were many exciting guests, but Jane Fonda takes home the honor of most exciting celebrity visitor. She left everyone here blushing after she congratulated us on a job well done.

Special Backstage Rituals: Apart from our rigorous two-hour-long Yoga warmup, led by our very own Bill Nighy, the cast gets together on stage before each show to chat about our day. We cover everything from movies and politics to celebrity gossip and what Julianne Moore's kids are up to.

Favorite Moment During Each Performance (On Stage or Off): Listening to veteran stage actor Bill Nighy take on the "coughers" in the audience, by masterfully weaving the language of the play in and around coughing fits and nose blowing.

Catchphrases Only the Company Would Recognize: "Three million people have no access to sanitation."

Favorite Therapy: Ricola, and B-12 shots in the bum!

Company In-Jokes: "Ahhhhhhh, helloooo therrrrre" (in heavy Irish accent).

Superstitions That Turned Out To Be True: Eight shows a week is indeed a hard thing to do.

Photos by Aubrey Reuben

(L-R) Dan Bittner, Rutina Wesley, Andrew Scott, Julianne Moore and Bill Nighy at the opening night party at the Royalton Hotel.

STAFF FOR *THE VERTICAL HOUR*

GENERAL MANAGEMENT
STUART THOMPSON PRODUCTIONS
Stuart Thompson Caroline Prugh James Triner

COMPANY MANAGER
Chris Morey

PRESS REPRESENTATIVE
BARLOW•HARTMAN
John Barlow Michael Hartman
Dennis Crowley Ryan Ratelle

PRODUCTION MANAGEMENT
AURORA PRODUCTIONS INC.
Gene O'Donovan W. Benjamin Heller II
Bethany Weinstein Melissa Mazdra
Tuesday Curran

Production Stage Manager ..... James Harker
Stage Manager ..... Thea Bradshaw Gillies
Associate Scenic Designer ..... Orit Jacoby Carroll
Assistant Scenic Designer ..... Jeffrey Hinchee
Associate Costume Designer ..... Michelle Matland
Associate Lighting Designer ..... Jennifer Schriever
Production Carpenter ..... David M. Cohen
Production Electrician ..... Brian G.F. McGarity
Production Props ..... Abraham Morrison
Production Sound Operator ..... Bill Lewis
Wardrobe Supervisor ..... Douglas C. Petitjean
Dressers ..... Laura Beattie, Barry Doss
Hair Supervisor ..... Susan Schectar
Production Assistant ..... John Bantay
Assistants to Mr. Rudin ..... James P. Queen, Nathan Kelly
Assistant to Mr. Fox ..... Hannah Bower
Assistant to Mr. Mendes ..... Laurent Lambert
Assistant to Mr. Berlind ..... Jeffrey Hillock
Assistant to Ms. Black ..... Ana Pilar Camacho
Assistant to Mr. Hare ..... Susie Graves
Neal Street Productions Theater Producer ..... Beth Byrne
General Management Assistant ..... Megan Curren
Management Interns ..... Aaron Thompson, Megan Wildebour
Casting Associate ..... Camille Hickman
Banking ..... JP Morgan Chase/ Michele Gibbons
Payroll ..... Castellana Services, Inc.
Accountant ..... Fried & Kowgios CPA's LLP/ Robert Fried, CPA
Controller ..... Joseph S. Kubala
Insurance ..... Ventura Insurance Brokerage Inc.
Legal Counsel ..... F. Richard Pappas, Esq.
Advertising ..... SpotCo/ Drew Hodges, Jim Edwards, Jim Aquino, Stephen Sosnowski
Production Photographer ..... Michal Daniel
Immigration ..... Traffic Control Group, Inc.
Theatre Displays ..... King Displays, Inc.

Hair Designs by Alan D'Angerio

CREDITS

Scenery constructed by Showman Fabricators, Inc., Long Island City, NY. Computer motion control and automation of scenery and rigging by Showman Fabricators Inc. Lighting and sound equipment supplied by GSD Productions, Inc., West Hempstead, NY. Mr. Nighy's eyewear provided by Cutler and Gross, Ltd., London. Tree fabricated by Souvenir Scenic Studios, Ltd., London, England. Office furniture by Bergen Office Furniture. Apple laptop by Tekserve. Wine bottles by Palmbay Imports. Built props by Art Brasington and Craig Grigg. Rehearsal props by Spoon Group. Rehearsed at the New 42nd Street Studios.

STAFF FOR THE MUSIC BOX THEATRE

HOUSE MANAGER ..... Jonathan Shulman
Box Office Treasurer ..... Robert D. Kelly
Assistant Treasurers ..... Michael Taustine, Brendan Berberich, Victoria Radolinski
House Carpenter ..... Dennis Maher
House Electrician ..... F. Lee Iwanski
House Propertyman ..... Kim Garnett
Chief of Staff ..... Dennis Scanlon
Accountant ..... William C. Grother

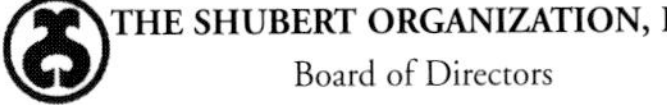

THE SHUBERT ORGANIZATION, INC.
Board of Directors

Gerald Schoenfeld
Chairman

Philip J. Smith
President

Wyche Fowler, Jr.

John W. Kluge

Lee J. Seidler

Michael I. Sovern

Stuart Subotnick

Robert E. Wankel
Executive Vice President

Peter Entin
Vice President
Theatre Operations

Elliot Greene
Vice President
Finance

David Andrews
Vice President
Shubert Ticketing Services

John Darby
Vice President
Facilities

D.S. Moynihan
Vice President – Creative Projects

The Wedding Singer

First Preview: March 30, 2006. Opened: April 27, 2006.
Closed: December 31, 2006 after 28 Previews and 285 Performances.

PLAYBILL®

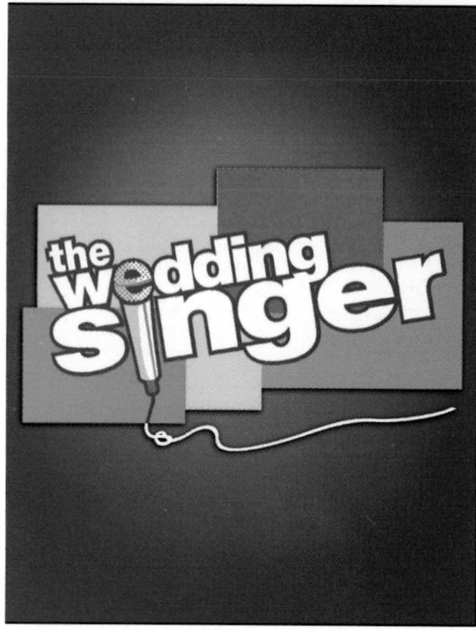

CAST

(in order of appearance)

Robbie Hart .... STEPHEN LYNCH
Sammy .... CONSTANTINE MAROULIS
George .... KEVIN CAHOON
Debbie .... ASHLEY AMBER
Harold .... NICK KENKEL
David .... DAVID JOSEFSBERG
Julia Sullivan .... LAURA BENANTI
Holly .... AMY SPANGER
Glen Guglia .... RICHARD H. BLAKE
Rosie .... RITA GARDNER
Linda .... FELICIA FINLEY
Angie .... ADINAH ALEXANDER
Mookie .... ERIC LaJUAN SUMMERS
Crystal .... TRACEE BEAZER
Donatella .... JOANNE MANNING
Shane .... MATT ALLEN
Bad Haircut Guy .... DAVID JOSEFSBERG
Sideburns Lady .... CHRISTINA SIVRICH
Trekkie .... MATTHEW STOCKE
Large Lady .... ADINAH ALEXANDER
China Clerk .... ADINAH ALEXANDER
Ricky .... ERIC LaJUAN SUMMERS
Bum .... PETER KAPETAN
Vegas Airlines
Ticket Agent .... ADINAH ALEXANDER
Impersonators .... TRACEE BEAZER,
PETER KAPETAN, JOANNE MANNING,
J. ELAINE MARCOS, T. OLIVER REID,
CHRISTINA SIVRICH, MATTHEW STOCKE

Continued on next page

AL HIRSCHFELD THEATRE
A JUJAMCYN THEATRE
ROCCO LANDESMAN
PRESIDENT

PAUL LIBIN, PRODUCING DIRECTOR — JACK VIERTEL, CREATIVE DIRECTOR

MARGO LION NEW LINE CINEMA THE ARACA GROUP
ROY FURMAN DOUGLAS L. MEYER / JAMES D. STERN
RICK STEINER / THE STATON BELL OSHER MAYERSON GROUP JAM THEATRICALS
in association with
JUJAMCYN THEATERS
and
JAY FURMAN MICHAEL GILL DR. LAWRENCE HOROWITZ RHODA MAYERSON
MARISA SECHREST GARY WINNICK DANCAP PRODUCTIONS, INC. ÉLAN V. MCALLISTER / ALLAN S. GORDON / ADAM EPSTEIN
present

the wedding singer

music by **MATTHEW SKLAR** — book by **CHAD BEGUELIN and TIM HERLIHY** — lyrics by **CHAD BEGUELIN**

BASED UPON THE NEW LINE CINEMA FILM
WRITTEN BY TIM HERLIHY

starring

STEPHEN LYNCH LAURA BENANTI
RICHARD H. BLAKE KEVIN CAHOON FELICIA FINLEY
AMY SPANGER TINA MADDIGAN
and
RITA GARDNER

ADINAH ALEXANDER MATT ALLEN ASHLEY AMBER TRACEE BEAZER
CARA COOPER NICOLETTE HART ANGELIQUE ILO DAVID JOSEFSBERG
PETER KAPETAN NICK KENKEL KEVIN KERN JOANNE MANNING
J. ELAINE MARCOS MICHAEL McGURK T. OLIVER REID
CHRISTINA SIVRICH MATTHEW STOCKE ERIC LAJUAN SUMMERS
and
CONSTANTINE MAROULIS

scenic design **SCOTT PASK** — costume design **GREGORY GALE** — lighting design **BRIAN MACDEVITT** — sound design **PETER HYLENSKI**

casting by **TELSEY + COMPANY** — hair design **DAVID BRIAN BROWN** — make-up design **JOE DULUDE II**

orchestrations **IRWIN FISCH** — incidental & dance music arranger **DAVID CHASE** — music director/conductor **JAMES SAMPLINER**

executive producer **MARK KAUFMAN** — production manager **JUNIPER STREET PRODUCTIONS** — associate choreographer **JOANN M. HUNTER** — production stage manager **ROLT SMITH**

press representative **RICHARD KORNBERG, DON SUMMA** — marketing **THE ARACA GROUP** — music coordinator **JOHN MILLER** — general management **THE CHARLOTTE WILCOX COMPANY**

choreographed by
ROB ASHFORD
directed by
JOHN RANDO

The world premiere of "The Wedding Singer" was produced with The 5th Avenue Theatre in Seattle, Washington, David Armstrong, Producing Artistic Director, Marilynn Sheldon, Managing Director.

Original Broadway Cast Recording on Masterworks Broadway, a division of Sony BMG Masterworks, an operating unit of Sony BMG Music Entertainment.

The producers wish to express their appreciation to Theatre Developement Fund for its support of this production. LIVE BROADWAY

10/2/06

The Company performs "All About the Green."

Photo by Joan Marcus

The Wedding Singer

SCENES AND MUSICAL NUMBERS

Ridgefield, NJ, 1985

ACT ONE

Scene 1: Reception Hall
"It's Your Wedding Day" .... Robbie and Company
"Someday" .... Julia
Scene 2: The Loading Dock
Scene 3: Robbie's Bedroom
"Someday" (Reprise) .... Robbie, Rosie
Scene 4: Reception Hall
"A Note From Linda" .... Linda
Scene 5: The Restaurant
"Pop" .... Holly, Julia, Angie and Company
Scene 6: Robbie's Bedroom
"Somebody Kill Me"* .... Robbie
"A Note From Grandma" .... Rosie
Scene 7: Reception Hall
"Casualty of Love" .... Robbie and Company
Scene 8: The Loading Dock
"Come Out of the Dumpster" .... Julia, Robbie
Scene 9: Reception Hall
"Today You Are a Man" .... Robbie, Sammy, George
"George's Prayer" .... George
Scene 10: The Mall
"Not That Kind of Thing" .... Robbie, Julia and Company
Scene 11: Holly's Closet/The Club
"Saturday Night in the City" .... Holly & Company

ACT TWO

Scene 1: Glen's Office
"All About the Green" .... Glen, Robbie and Company
Scene 2: Reception Hall
"Right in Front of Your Eyes" .... Holly, Sammy
Scene 3: Rosie's Porch
Scene 4: The Bar
"Single" .... Sammy, Robbie, George, Ricky, Bum and Men
Scene 5: Julia's Bedroom
"If I Told You" .... Robbie, Julia
Scene 6: Robbie's Bedroom
"Let Me Come Home" .... Linda
Scene 7: Reception Hall
"If I Told You" (Reprise) .... Robbie, Julia
"Move That Thang" .... Rosie, George
Scene 8: White House Wedding Chapel, Las Vegas
"Grow Old With You"* .... Robbie, Julia
Scene 9: Reception Hall
"It's Your Wedding Day" (Finale) .... The Company

* Written by Adam Sandler and Tim Herlihy

Cast Continued

Ensemble .... ADINAH ALEXANDER, MATT ALLEN, ASHLEY AMBER, TRACEE BEAZER, NICOLETTE HART, DAVID JOSEFSBERG, PETER KAPETAN, NICK KENKEL, JOANNE MANNING, J. ELAINE MARCOS, T. OLIVER REID, CHRISTINA SIVRICH, MATTHEW STOCKE, ERIC LaJUAN SUMMERS

SWINGS

ANGELIQUE ILO, KEVIN KERN, JOANNE MANNING, MICHAEL McGURK

Standby for Julia Sullivan: TINA MADDIGAN

UNDERSTUDIES

For Robbie Hart: KEVIN KERN, MATTHEW STOCKE
For Julia Sullivan: CHRISTINA SIVRICH
For Holly: CARA COOPER, NICOLETTE HART
For George: KEVIN KERN, ERIC LaJUAN SUMMERS
For Glen Guglia: KEVIN KERN, MATTHEW STOCKE
For Sammy: MATT ALLEN, DAVID JOSEFSBERG, MATTHEW STOCKE
For Linda: ASHLEY AMBER, NICOLETTE HART
For Rosie: ADINAH ALEXANDER, CHRISTINA SIVRICH

Dance Captains .... ANGELIQUE ILO, MICHAEL McGURK

ORCHESTRA

Conductor: JAMES SAMPLINER
Associate Conductor: JOHN SAMORIAN
Guitars: LARRY SALTZMAN, STEPHEN LYNCH, JOHN PUTNAM, GARY SIEGER
Keyboards: JAMES SAMPLINER, JOHN SAMORIAN, JON WERKING
Bass: IRIO O'FARRILL, CONSTANTINE MAROULIS
Drums: WARREN ODZE
Reeds: CLIFFORD LYONS, JACK BASHKOW
Trumpet: TREVOR NEUMANN
Percussion: JAMES SAPORITO
Music Coordinator: JOHN MILLER
Electronic Musical Instrument Programmer: IRWIN FISCH
Music Copying: EMILY GRISHMAN MUSIC PREPARATION/ EMILY GRISHMAN, KATHARINE EDMONDS

The Wedding Singer

Stephen Lynch
Robbie Hart

Laura Benanti
Julia Sullivan

Rita Gardner
Rosie

Richard H. Blake
Glen Guglia

Kevin Cahoon
George

Felicia Finley
Linda

Amy Spanger
Holly

Tina Maddigan
Standby
Julia Sullivan

Constantine Maroulis
Sammy

Adinah Alexander
Ensemble, Angie

Matt Allen
Ensemble

Ashley Amber
Ensemble

Tracee Beazer
Ensemble,
Impersonator

Cara Cooper
Ensemble

Nicolette Hart
Ensemble

Angelique Ilo
Dance Captain,
Swing

David Josefsberg
Ensemble, David

Peter Kapetan
Ensemble,
Impersonator

Nick Kenkel
Ensemble

Kevin Kern
Swing

Joanne Manning
Swing

J. Elaine Marcos
Ensemble,
Impersonator

Michael McGurk
Swing

T. Oliver Reid
Ensemble,
Impersonator

Christina Sivrich
Ensemble,
Impersonator

Matthew Stocke
Ensemble,
Impersonator

Eric LaJuan
Summers
Ensemble

Matthew Sklar
Composer

Chad Beguelin
Book/Lyrics

Tim Herlihy
Book

John Rando
Director

Rob Ashford
Choreographer

Scott Pask
Scenic Design

Gregory Gale
Costume Design

Brian MacDevitt
Lighting Design

The Wedding Singer

Peter Hylenski
Sound Designer

David Brian Brown
Wig/Hair Design

Joe Dulude II
Makeup Design

Bernard Telsey,
Telsey + Company
Casting

Richard Kornberg & Associates
Press Representative

Irwin Fisch
Orchestrator

James Sampliner
Music Director/ Conductor

John Miller
Music Coordinator

Charlotte Wilcox
General Manager

JoAnn M. Hunter
Associate Choreographer

Guy Kwan, John Paull III, Hillary Blanken, Kevin Broomell, Ana Rose Greene,
Juniper Street Productions
Production Manager

Jen Bender
Assistant Director

Margo Lion
Producer

Roy Furman
Producer

Douglas L. Meyer
Producer

Rick Steiner,
The Osher, Staton, Bell, Mayerson Group
Producer

John and Bonnie Osher,
The Osher, Staton, Bell, Mayerson Group
Producer

Dan Staton,
The Osher, Staton, Bell, Mayerson Group
Producer

Marc Bell,
The Osher, Staton, Bell, Mayerson Group
Producer

Frederic H. Mayerson,
The Osher, Staton, Bell, Mayerson Group
Producer

Rocco Landesman, President,
Jujamcyn Theaters
Producer

Michael Gill
Producer

Lawrence Horowitz, M.D.
Producer

Rhoda Mayerson
Associate Producer

Marisa Sechrest
Producer

Elan V. McAllister
Producer

Allan S. Gordon
Producer

Adam Epstein
Producer

Mark Kaufman
Executive Producer

David Armstrong,
5th Avenue Theatre
Presented World Premiere of
The Wedding Singer

Marilynn Sheldon,
5th Avenue Theatre
Presented World Premiere of
The Wedding Singer

The Wedding Singer

Andy Karl
David, Bad Haircut Guy, Ensemble

Spencer Liff
Harold, Ensemble

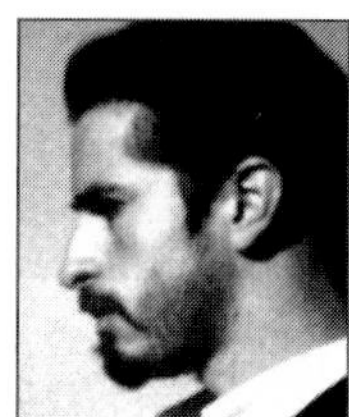
Matthew Saldivar
Sammy

David Eggers
Shane, Ensemble

Robyn Hurder
Donatella, Impersonator, Ensemble

Spencer Liff
Harold, Ensemble

Jon-Paul Mateo
Impersonator, Ensemble

Matthew Saldivar
Sammy

Dennis Stowe
Impersonator, Ensemble

HAIR
Front Row (L-R): Jodi Jackson, Sara Landbeck.

Back Row (L-R): June Kim, Joe Whitmeyer and Joel Hawkins.

Photos by Ben Strothmann

STAGE MANAGEMENT
(L-R): Julie Baldauff, Rolt Smith and Janet Takami.

The Wedding Singer

FRONT OF HOUSE STAFF
Front Row (L-R): Mary Marzin, Mrs. Carmel Robinson (House Manager), Julie Burnham, Lorraine Feeks, Alberta McJamee, Frances Cohen.

Middle Row (L-R): Tereso Avila, Roberto Ellington, Janice Rodriguez, Fernando Colon, Theresa Lopez.

Back Row (L-R): Donald L. Royal, Tristan Blacer, Henry Menendez, Bart Ryan and Hollis Miller.

Photos by Ben Strothmann

BOX OFFICE
(L-R): Dennis Vogelgesans and Linda Canavan.

WARDROBE
Front Row (L-R): Chastity Neutze, Jenny Barnes, Bill Huber, Karen McGovern, Tasha Cowd.

Back Row (L-R): Kelly Saxon (Assistant Supervisor), Shana Dunbar (Supervisor), Sarah Rochford, Tree Sarvay, Leslie Thompson, Jane Davis, Gina Gornik and Kay Gowenlock.

The Wedding Singer

CARPENTRY
In Dumpster (L-R):
Eric Yantz, Unknown, Tom Sherman.

Seated Front:
Hank Hale.

Standing Back (L-R):
Richie Fedeli and Billy Vandebogart.

ELECTRICS AND SOUND
Front Row (L-R):
Unknown, Eric Abbott, Dermot J. Lynch (House Electrician), Dan Ansbro.

Back Row (L-R):
Aaron Straus (Spot Operator), David Dignazio, Timothy F. Rogers and John Blixt.

Photos by Ben Strothmann

PROPS
(L-R):
Justin Sanok, Angelo Torre, Richard Horn and Sal Sclafani.

The Wedding Singer

Staff for *THE WEDDING SINGER*

GENERAL MANAGEMENT
THE CHARLOTTE WILCOX COMPANY
Charlotte Wilcox
Matthew W. Krawiec Emily Lawson
Steve Supeck Margaret Wilcox Beth Cochran

GENERAL PRESS REPRESENTATIVE
RICHARD KORNBERG & ASSOCIATES
Richard Kornberg Don Summa
Carrie Friedman

MARKETING
THE ARACA GROUP
Clint Bond, Jr. Kirsten Berkman Drew Padrutt
John Wiseman

COMPANY MANAGER
Edward Nelson

ASSOCIATE COMPANY MANAGER
Beverly Edwards

CASTING
Telsey + Company, C.S.A.:
Bernie Telsey, Will Cantler, David Vaccari,
Bethany Knox, Craig Burns,
Tiffany Little Canfield, Stephanie Yankwitt,
Carrie Rosson, Justin Huff, Joe Langworth

PRODUCTION MANAGEMENT
JUNIPER STREET PRODUCTIONS
Hillary Blanken Guy Kwan
Kevin Broomell Ana Rose Greene

PRODUCTION STAGE MANAGER .... Rolt Smith
Stage Manager .... Julie Baldauff
Assistant Stage Manager .... Janet Takami
Dance Captain .... Angelique Ilo
Assistant Dance Captain .... Michael McGurk
Associate Choreographer .... JoAnn M. Hunter
Assistant Director .... Jen Bender
Associate Scenic Designer .... Orit Jacoby Carroll
Assistant Scenic Designers .... Lauren Alvarez, Edmund LeFevre
Assistant to the Scenic Designer .... Jeff Hinchee
Associate Costume Designer .... Brian Russman
Assistant Costume Designer .... Janine Marie McCabe
Assistants to the Costume Designer .... Rachel Attridge, Tracey Herman, David Withrow
Associate Lighting Designer .... Charles Pennebaker
Assistant Lighting Designers .... Rachel Eichorn, Anne McMills
Automated Lighting Programmer .... Timothy F. Rogers
Assistant Sound Designer .... T.J. McEvoy
Associate Hair/Wig Designer .... Josh Marquette
Production Carpenter .... Tony Menditto
Production Electrician .... Dan Coey
Production Properties .... Joseph P. Harris Jr.
Head Carpenter .... Hank Hale
Assistant Carpenters .... Ian Michaud, Tom Sherman, Robert M. Hentze
Head Electrician .... Ron Martin
Assistant Electrician .... Eric Abbott
Head Properties .... Justin Sanok
Assistant Properties .... Angelo Torre
Head Sound .... David Dignazio
Assistant Sound .... Aaron Straus
Production Wardrobe Supervisor .... Shana Dunbar
Assistant Wardrobe Supervisor .... Kristin Gardner
Dressers .... Jenny Barnes, Tina Clifton, Tasha Cowd, Jane Davis, Kay Gowenlock, Paul Ludick, Ryan Rossetto, Tree Sarvay, Kelly Saxon, Leslie Thompson, Franc Weinperl, Chip White
Hair Supervisor .... Carole Morales
Assistant Hair Supervisor .... Tom Augustine
Hair Dressers .... Joel Hawkins, Jodi Jackson, Joe Whitmeyer
Associate Producer/Margo Lion Ltd. .... Lily Hung
Assistant to Executive Producer .... Alexandra Loewy
Assistant to Margo Lion Ltd. .... T. Rick Hayashi
Keyboard and Electronic Music Technician .... Scott Reisett
Press Intern .... Alyssa Hart
Assistants to the Araca Group .... Maryana Geller, Aaron Schwartzbord
MIDI Consultants .... Scott Riesett, Nick Vidar
Production Assistants .... Scott Rowen, Sara Sahin, Jamie Rose Thoma, Sunneva Stapleton
SSDC Observer .... Paul Stancato
Costume Intern .... Mike Kale
Dialogue Coach .... Deborah Hecht
Legal Counsel .... Feitelson, Lasky, Aslan & Couture/ Jerold L. Couture
Accountants .... Fried & Kowgios CPA's LLP/ Robert Fried, CPA
Controller .... Sarah Galbraith
Advertising .... Serino Coyne/ Greg Corradetti, Ruth Rosenberg, Andrea Prince, Natalie Serota
Group Sales .... Show Tix
Merchandise .... Araca Merch/ Anne MacLean, Philip McBride, Joey Boyles, Karen Davidov, Audra Ewing, Zach Lezberg, Julie Monahan, Bryan Pace, Peter Pergola
Website Design .... Situation Marketing LLC/ Damian Bazadona
Production Photography .... Joan Marcus
Additional Photography .... Bruce Glikas
Banking .... J.P. Morgan Chase
Payroll Service .... Castellana Services, Inc.
Insurance Consultant .... Stockbridge Risk Management/ Neil Goldstein
Theatre Displays .... King Displays
Air Travel Services .... Tzell Travel
Hotel and Ground Travel Services .... Road Rebel
Performing Arts Physical Therapy .... Dr. Phillip A. Bauman

Souvenir merchandise designed and created by
Araca Merch, LLC
www.aracamerch.com or (212) 869-0070

CREDITS

Scenery fabricated and painted by Hudson Scenic Studio, Inc. Scenery fabrication by Scenic Technologies, a division of Production Resource Group, LLC, New Windsor, NY. Show control and scenic motion control featuring stage command systems® by Scenic Technologies, a division of Production Resource Group, LLC, New Windsor, NY. Scenic elements by Cigar Box Studios, Spoon Group, Seattle Opera. Scenic elements painted by Scenic Arts Studio. Water effect by Jauchem and Meeh Inc. Drapery by I. Weiss. Costumes constructed by Barbara Matera Ltd.; Euro Co Costumes; Jennifer Love Costumes; John Kristiansen NY Inc.; Vanson Leather; Timberlake Studios; Rawhides Custom Leatherwear; TRICORNE, INC.; and Western Costume Co. Custom boots and shoes by Frederick Longtin Handmade Shoes; J.C. Theatrical & Custom Footwear; T.O. Dey Custom Shoes; Celebrity Dance Shoes; Elegance Dance Shoes; and Worldtone Dance Shoes. Custom veils and millinery by Rodney Gordon, Inc. Custom knitwear by C.C. Wei. Fabric painting by Hochi Asiatico. Custom jewelry by Martin Lopez and Larry Vrba. Sunglasses provided by Ray Ban. Custom Shirts by Sandy Perlmutter at Allmeier. Built props fabricated by Spoon Group. Floral arrangements by Portafiori Floral Design Studio. Tablecloth linens by Cloth Connection. Lighting equipment from PRG Lighting. Sound equipment from PRG Audio. Wigs by Ray Marston London. Throat lozenges provided by Ricola. Special thanks to Bra*Tenders for hosiery and undergarments. PONG™ classic arcade game and classic Atari video game images courtesy of Atari Interactive, Inc. © 2006 Atari Interactive, Inc. All rights reserved. Used with permission.

Makeup provided by M·A·C

Gibson guitars, Epiphone guitars and Slingerland Drums provided by Gibson Musical Instruments. Musical equipment provided by Alto Music; Yamaha Corporation of America. Receptors provided by Muse Research. Amp simulators provided by Line 6 Electronics.

The Wedding Singer
rehearsed at the New 42nd Street Studios.

JUJAMCYN THEATERS

ROCCO LANDESMAN
President

PAUL LIBIN Producing Director
JACK VIERTEL Creative Director
JERRY ZAKS Resident Director
JORDAN ROTH Resident Producer
DANIEL ADAMIAN General Manager
JENNIFER HERSHEY Director of Operations
MEREDITH VILLATORE Chief Financial Officer

Staff for the Al Hirschfeld Theatre

Manager .... Carmel Gunther
Treasurer .... Carmine La Mendola
Carpenter .... Joseph J. Maher, Jr.
Propertyman .... Sal Sclafani
Electrician .... Dermot J. Lynch
Engineer .... Vladimir Belenky

The Wedding Singer
Scrapbook

Correspondent: Eric LaJuan Summers, "Ensemble."
Memorable Gifts: Our opening night jacket. We always wear it and look like some sort of olympic team when we're together.
Most Exciting Celebrity Visitor: Adam Sandler, and he loved the show (the Seattle version, that is).
Actor Who Performed the Most Roles: White people (Kevin Kern); Black people (clearly Eric Summers)
Who Has Done the Most Shows: Probably Rita Gardner (she's old school like that).
Special Backstage Ritual: "1-2-3- WEDDING SINGER!" We chanted this before every single show (and sometimes events).
Favorite Moment: The opening. Christina Sivrich and I (Brianna and Ricky) are extremely dirty and have so much fun.
In-Theatre Gathering Place: Guy's ensemble room. That's where we hosted Saturday Night Dance Party. Every Saturday night performance at our 15-minute call we'd blast a song on the iPod and party like it was 1985!
Off-Site Hangout: Angus McIndoe (thanks Christina).
Favorite Snack Foods: Tequila (thanks Adinah).
Mascot: Sonny Lynch.
Favorite Therapy: Felicia's back massager. That thing will make you feel things you didn't know were possible. That and Vicodin (the show is hard on the body).
Memorable Ad-Lib: Joberg (David Josefsberg) backstage during "Someday." There was always an ad-lib going on.
Memorable Stage Door Fan Encounters: Every day we have someone doing something pretty odd. We even have people dressing up like our characters and waiting at the stage door, whether or not they see the show.
Fastest Costume Change: The Ensemble at intermission. Changing wigs, make-up, and club gear and getting into three-piece suits in 10 minutes is pretty fast.
Busiest Days at the Box Office: Right after our Tony Awards performance or "Today Show" appearance.
"Carols for a Cure" Carol: "The Hanukah Song."
Who Wore the Heaviest/Hottest Costume: Stocke and Peter during "Saturday Night."
Who Wore the Least: During rehearsal, probably Ashley. During the show, Felicia.
Catchphrases Only the Company Would Recognize: "Wickeet"; "Damn Damn Damn"; "Oh no no."
Sweethearts Within the Company: The now-engaged Felicia Finley and Paul Stancato. I can't tell any more than that or I'll be shot.
In-House Parody Lyrics: "Awkward, Linda makes me feel awkward" instead of "awesome." (But, then again, I only sing that to myself.)

Photo courtesy Eric LaJuan Summers

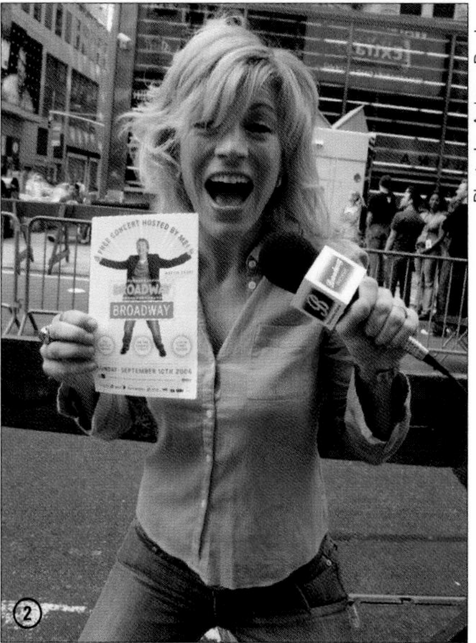

Photo by Aubrey Reuben

Photo courtesy Eric LaJuan Summers

1. The cast rehearses for the June 2006 Tony Awards broadcast on the stage of Radio City Music Hall.
2. Felicia Finley does a promo for "Broadway on Broadway."
3. The ensemble prepares to record the original cast album.

Memorable Directorial Note: I don't remember specific notes but John Rando gave the absolute best speeches in the world. That man can encourage you to do anything.
Company In-Jokes: Stephen excluding me (Eric Summers) from anything or just singling me out. Whenever he was interviewed and asked how he felt about the cast, he'd say he loved "everyone except Eric LaJuan Summers." OK, even I thought it was funny.
Company Legends: Rita Gardner.
Understudy Anecdote: Anyone who has seen the show knows that Holly (flawlessly played by *the* Amy Spanger) closes Act I by riding onstage on a go-go box and drenching herself with water in the middle of the dance floor *a la Flashdance*. Well, Robyn Hurder's first time on as Holly (two weeks after joining the show), the go-go platform did not come back out. So she jazz ran–yes jazz ran–across stage and jumped up to reach the pulley for the water, and continued hanging on it for a second or two before coming back down. None of us sang so much as just screamed in amazement that she made it out there. That was pretty amazing.
Nicknames: Jewberg (David Josefberg), Black (Eric LaJuan Summers), Kernel (Kevin Kern), DeLynchious (Stephen Lynch), Tiny (Tina Maddigan), Saldy (Matt Saldivar).
Embarrassing Moments: Me playing a woman (Tina Turner) or me playing the trumpet as George (I sucked at that).
Coolest Thing About Being in This Show: Truly having fun while putting your body through hell.

Wicked

First Preview: October 8, 2003. Opened: October 30, 2003.
Still running as of May 31, 2007.

PLAYBILL

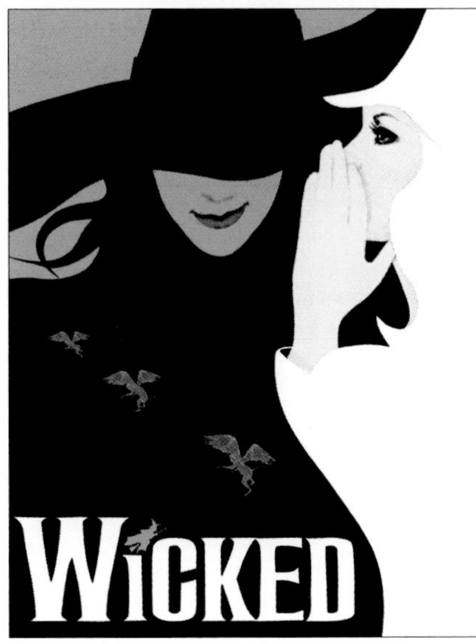

GERSHWIN THEATRE

UNDER THE DIRECTION OF
JAMES M. NEDERLANDER AND JAMES L. NEDERLANDER

Marc Platt
Universal Pictures
The Araca Group and Jon B. Platt
David Stone

present

Eden Espinosa **Kate Reinders**

WICKED

Music and Lyrics
Stephen Schwartz

Book
Winnie Holzman

Based on the novel by Gregory Maguire

Also Starring

Carol Kane
Derrick Williams

Jenna Leigh Green Logan Lipton Steven Skybell

Ioana Alfonso Sonshine Allen Clyde Alves Kevin Aubin Michael DeVries Lori Ann Ferreri Anthony Galde Rhett G. George Gaelen Gilliland Kristen Leigh Gorski Tiffany Haas Manuel I. Herrera Kenway Hon Wai K. Kua Barrett Martin Brandi Chavonne Massey Corinne McFadden-Herrera Clifton Oliver Eddie Pendergraft Alexander Quiroga Noah Rivera Kathy Santen Michael Seelbach Megan Sikora Terrance Spencer Heather Spore Katie Webber

and

David Garrison
as the Wizard

Settings Eugene Lee — Costumes Susan Hilferty — Lighting Kenneth Posner — Sound Tony Meola

Projections Elaine J. McCarthy — Wigs & Hair Tom Watson — Technical Supervisor Jake Bell

Music Arrangements Alex Lacamoire & Stephen Oremus — Music Director Robert Billig — Dance Arrangements James Lynn Abbott — Music Coordinator Michael Keller

Associate Set Designer Edward Pierce — Special Effects Chic Silber — Associate Choreographer Mark Myars — Associate Director Lisa Leguillou

Casting Telsey + Company — Production Stage Manager Thom Widmann — General Management 321 Theatrical Management — Press The Publicity Office — Executive Producers Marcia Goldberg & Nina Essman

Orchestrations
William David Brohn

Music Supervisor
Stephen Oremus

Musical Staging by
Wayne Cilento

Directed by
Joe Mantello

Grammy Award-winning Original Cast Recording on DECCA BROADWAY

10/2/06

THE CAST

(in order of appearance)

Glinda ..... KATE REINDERS
Witch's Father ..... MICHAEL DeVRIES
Witch's Mother ..... KATIE WEBBER
Midwife ..... KATHY SANTEN
Elphaba ..... EDEN ESPINOSA
Nessarose ..... JENNA LEIGH GREEN
Boq ..... LOGAN LIPTON
Madame Morrible ..... CAROL KANE
Doctor Dillamond ..... STEVEN SKYBELL
Fiyero ..... DERRICK WILLIAMS
Ozian Official ..... MICHAEL DeVRIES
The Wonderful Wizard of Oz . DAVID GARRISON
Chistery ..... MANUEL I. HERRERA
Monkeys, Students, Denizens of the Emerald City, Palace Guards and Other Citizens of Oz ..... IOANA ALFONSO, SONSHINE ALLEN, KEVIN AUBIN, MICHAEL DeVRIES, LORI ANN FERRERI, RHETT G. GEORGE, GAELEN GILLILAND, MANUEL I. HERRERA, KENWAY HON WAI K. KUA, BRANDI CHAVONNE MASSEY, CORINNE McFADDEN-HERRERA, BARRETT MARTIN, CLIFTON OLIVER, EDDIE PENDERGRAFT, ALEXANDER QUIROGA, NOAH RIVERA, KATHY SANTEN, MICHAEL SEELBACH, MEGAN SIKORA, HEATHER SPORE, KATIE WEBBER

Continued on next page

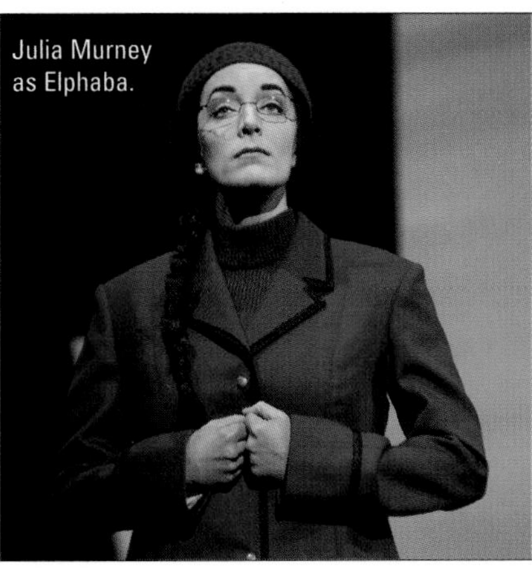
Julia Murney as Elphaba.

Kendra Kassebaum as Glinda.

Photos by Joan Marcus

Wicked

MUSICAL NUMBERS

ACT I

"No One Mourns the Wicked"	Glinda and Citizens of Oz
"Dear Old Shiz"	Students
"The Wizard and I"	Morrible, Elphaba
"What Is This Feeling?"	Galinda, Elphaba and Students
"Something Bad"	Dr. Dillamond and Elphaba
"Dancing Through Life"	Fiyero, Galinda, Boq, Nessarose, Elphaba and Students
"Popular"	Galinda
"I'm Not That Girl"	Elphaba
"One Short Day"	Elphaba, Glinda and Denizens of the Emerald City
"A Sentimental Man"	The Wizard
"Defying Gravity"	Elphaba, Glinda, Guards and Citizens of Oz

ACT II

"No One Mourns the Wicked" (reprise)	Citizens of Oz
"Thank Goodness"	Glinda, Morrible and Citizens of Oz
"The Wicked Witch of the East"	Elphaba, Nessarose and Boq
"Wonderful"	The Wizard and Elphaba
"I'm Not That Girl" (reprise)	Glinda
"As Long As You're Mine"	Elphaba and Fiyero
"No Good Deed"	Elphaba
"March of the Witch Hunters"	Boq and Citizens of Oz
"For Good"	Glinda and Elphaba
"Finale"	All

ORCHESTRA

Conductor: ROBERT BILLIG
Associate Conductor: DAVID EVANS

Concertmaster: CHRISTIAN HEBEL
Violin: VICTOR SCHULTZ
Viola: KEVIN ROY
Cello: DANNY MILLER
Harp: LAURA SHERMAN
Lead Trumpet: JON OWENS
Trumpet: TOM HOYT
Trombones: DALE KIRKLAND, DOUGLAS PURVIANCE
Flute: HELEN CAMPO
Oboe: TUCK LEE
Clarinet/Soprano Sax: JOHN MOSES
Bassoon/Baritone Sax/Clarinets: JOHN CAMPO
French Horns: THEO PRIMIS, CHAD YARBROUGH
Drums: MATT VANDERENDE
Bass: KONRAD ADDERLEY
Piano/Synthesizer: BEN COHN
Keyboards: PAUL LOESEL, DAVID EVANS
Guitars: RIC MOLINA, GREG SKAFF
Percussion: ANDY JONES

Music Coordinator: Michael Keller

Jayne Houdyshell as Madame Morrible.

Photo by Joan Marcus

Cast Continued

UNDERSTUDIES and STANDBYS

Standby for Glinda:
KATIE ADAMS
Standby for Elphaba:
SAYCON SENGBLOH

Understudy for Elphaba:
BRANDI CHAVONNE MASSEY
For Glinda:
MEGAN SIKORA
For Fiyero:
ANTHONY GALDE, CLIFTON OLIVER, MICHAEL SEELBACH
For the Wizard:
MICHAEL DeVRIES, ANTHONY GALDE
For Dr. Dillamond:
MICHAEL DeVRIES, ANTHONY GALDE
For Madame Morrible:
GAELEN GILLILAND, KATHY SANTEN
For Boq:
CLYDE ALVES, NOAH RIVERA
For Nessarose:
LORI ANN FERRERI, TIFFANY HAAS, MEGAN SIKORA
For Chistery:
CLYDE ALVES, KEVIN AUBIN
For Witch's Father and Ozian Official:
ANTHONY GALDE, ALEXANDER QUIROGA
For Witch's Mother:
LORI ANN FERRERI, KRISTEN LEIGH GORSKI
For Midwife:
LORI ANN FERRERI, TIFFANY HAAS, LORNA VENTURA

Swings:
ANTHONY GALDE, TIFFANY HAAS, TERRANCE SPENCER

Dance Captains/Swings: CLYDE ALVES, KRISTEN LEIGH GORSKI

Assistant Dance Captain:
CORINNE McFADDEN-HERRERA

Wicked

Eden Espinosa
Elphaba

Kate Reinders
Glinda

David Garrison
The Wizard

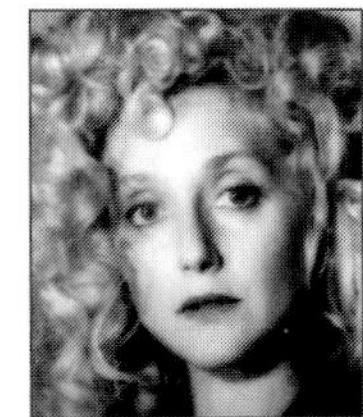
Carol Kane
Madame Morrible

Derrick Williams
Fiyero

Jenna Leigh Green
Nessarose

Logan Lipton
Boq

Steve Skybell
Dr. Dillamond

Katie Adams
Standby for Glinda

Saycon Sengbloh
Standby for Elphaba

Ioana Alfonso
Ensemble

Sonshine Allen
Ensemble

Clyde Alves
Swing;
Asst. Dance Captain

Kevin Aubin
Ensemble

Michael DeVries
Witch's Father/
Ozian Official

Lori Ann Ferreri
Ensemble

Anthony Galde
Swing

Gaelen Gilliland
Ensemble

Kristen Leigh Gorski
Swing;
Assistant
Dance Captain

Tiffany Haas
Swing

Manuel I. Herrera
Chistery

Kenway Hon Wai K.
Kua
Ensemble

Barrett Martin
Ensemble

Brandi Chavonne
Massey
Ensemble

Corinne McFadden-
Herrera
Ensemble/
Associate
Choreographer/
Asst. Dance Captain

Clifton Oliver
Ensemble

Eddie Pendergraft
Ensemble

Alexander Quiroga
Ensemble

Noah Rivera
Ensemble

Kathy Santen
Midwife

Michael Seelbach
Ensemble

Megan Sikora
Ensemble

Terrance Spencer
Swing

Heather Spore
Ensemble

Katie Webber
Witch's Mother

Wicked

Stephen Schwartz
Music and Lyrics

Winnie Holzman
Book

Joe Mantello
Director

Wayne Cilento
Musical Staging

Eugene Lee
Scenic Designer

Susan Hilferty
Costume Designer

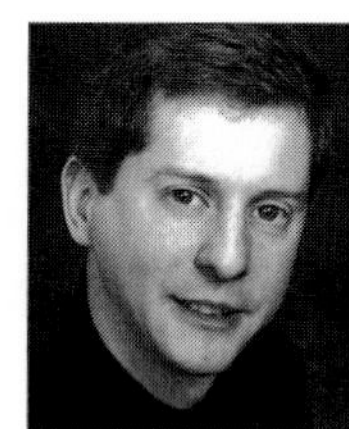
Kenneth Posner
Lighting Designer

Tony Meola
Sound Designer

Tom Watson
Wig and Hair Designer

Stephen Oremus
Music Supervisor/ Music Arrangements

William David Brohn
Orchestrations

Alex Lacamoire
Music Arrangements

Robert Billig
Music Director

Michael Keller
Music Coordinator

Chic Silber
Special Effects

Paul Rubin,
ZFX Flying Illusions
Flying Effects

Bernard Telsey,
Telsey + Company
Casting

Gregory Maguire
Author of Original Novel

Marcia Goldberg, Nancy Nagel Gibbs and Nina Essman,
321 Theatrical Management
General Management

Marc Platt
Producer

Jon B. Platt
Producer

David Stone
Producer

Stephen Lee Anderson
Swing

Jerad Bortz
Ensemble

Ben Cameron
Ensemble

Sarah Jane Everman
Ensemble

Adam Fleming
Ensemble

Zach Hensler
Ensemble

Kisha Howard
Ensemble

Reed Kelly
Ensemble

Sean McCourt
Doctor Dillamond, Witch's Father

Mark Myars
Dance Captain/ Swing

Wicked

Jan Neuberger
Ensemble, Midwife

Walter Winston Oneil
Understudy for Boq

Carson Reide
Swing

Adam Sanford
Ensemble

Robb Sapp
Boq

Phillip Spaeth
Chistery, Ensemble

Eric Stretch
Dance Captain, Swing

Charlie Sutton
Ensemble

Marty Thomas
Ensemble

Brooke Wendle
Ensemble

Briana Yacavone
Ensemble

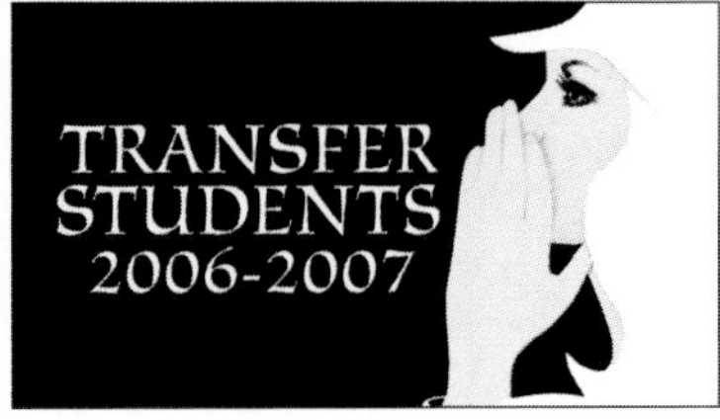

Sebastian Arcelus
Fiyero

Brad Bass
Ensemble

Lisa Brescia
Standby Elphaba

Crista Candler
Nessarose

Kathy Deitch
Ensemble

Kristina Fernandez
Ensemble, Swing, Dance Captain

Ana Gasteyer
Elphaba

Lauren Gibbs
Ensemble

Todd Hanebrink
Ensemble

Zach Hensler
Ensemble

Afra Hines
Swing

Jayne Houdyshell
Madame Morrible

Kendra Kassebaum
Glinda

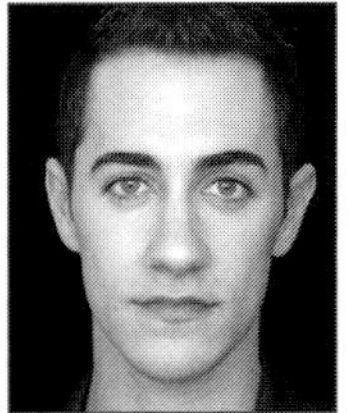
Reed Kelly
Ensemble

Ryan Patrick Kelly
Swing

Allison Leo
Swing

Caissie Levy
Ensemble

Alli Mauzey
Standby Glinda

Julia Murney
Elphaba

Lindsay K. Northen
Ensemble

Brandon Cristopher O'Neal
Ensemble

Adam Sanford
Swing

Wicked

Brian Slaman
Ensemble

Charlie Sutton
Ensemble

Katherine Tokarz
Swing

Shanna VanDerwerker
Ensemble, Swing

Jonathan Warren
Chistery, Ensemble

HAIR & MAKEUP DEPARTMENT
Front Row (L-R): Nora Martin (Assistant Hair Supervisor), Jimmy Cortés (Makeup Supervisor), Rob Greene (Hairdresser).

Back Row (L-R): Ryan P. McWilliams (Hairdresser) and Chris Clark (Hair Supervisor).

DOORMAN
Eddie Moreira

Photos by Ben Strothmann

STAGE AND COMPANY MANAGEMENT
Front Row (L-R): Susan Sampliner (Company Manager), Chris Zaccardi (Assistant Stage Manager), Christy Ney (Assistant Stage Manager).
Back Row (L-R): Bob Brinkerhoff (Associate Company Manager), Chris Jamros (Production Stage Manager), Jennifer Marik (Stage Manager).

FRONT OF HOUSE STAFF
First Row (L-R): Lary Ann William (Matron), Jean Logan (Usher), Albert Cruz (Usher), José Rodriguez (Usher), James Gunn (Usher).
Second Row (L-R): Rick Kaye (Manager), Dwayne Mann (Associate Manager), Miguel Buelto (Porter), Carlos Buelto (Porter), Ivan Rodriguez (Usher), Maria Szymanski (Usher).
Third Row (L-R): Mariana Casanova (Usher), Peggy Boyles (Usher), Betty Friar (Usher), Siobhan Dunne (Usher), Sharon Nelson (Usher), Edda Sorrentino (Usher), Joyce Pena (Usher), David Pena (Usher).
Fourth Row (L-R): Lorriane Lowrey (Ticket Taker), Kathleen White (Usher), Gregory Woolard (Usher), Eileen Roig (Usher), Carmen Rodriguez (Usher), Philippa Koopman (Usher), Joe Ortenzio (Usher), Michele Belmond (Usher), Brenda Denaris (Usher).

Wicked

STAGE CREW
Front Row (L-R): Joe Schwarz, Danny Viscarto, C. Mark Overton, Jack Babin, John Curvan.

Second Row (L-R): Dennis (last name unknown), Kevin Anderson, Dennis Fox, Brendan Quigley, John Riggins.

Back Row (L-R): Jeff Sigler, Frank Illo, John Gentile, Bruce Moore, Chris Riggins, Mickey Fox, Brian McDunna, Bobby Bullard, Jordan Pankin, unknown, Henry Brisen, William Breidenbach and Valerie Gilmore.

WARDROBE DEPARTMENT
Front Row (L-R):
Kevin Hucke (Dresser), Kathe Mull (Dresser), Christina Cocchiara (Stitcher), Randy Witherspoon (Dresser).

Middle Row (L-R):
Barry Doss (Stitcher), Nancy Lawson (Dresser), Dianne Hylton (Dresser), James Byrne (Dresser).

Back Row (L-R):
Jason Viarengo (Dresser), Michael Michalski (Dresser), Trent Armstrong (Assistant Wardrobe Supervisor), Bobbye Sue Albrecht (Dresser), Judy Kahn (Day Worker), Barbara Rosenthal (Dresser) and Laurel Parrish (Dresser).

Photos by Ben Strothmann

ORCHESTRA
First Row (L-R):
John Campo (Reed 4), Greg Skaff (Guitar 2), Misty Pereira (Substitute French Horn 2), David Evans (Associate Conductor), Leona Nadj (Substitute Violin 2), Laura Sherman (Harp), Cathy Gerardi (Reed 1 Substitute).

Second Row (L-R):
Konrad Adderley (Bass), Ben Cohn (Keyboard 1), Don Batchelder (Substitute Trumpet), Kevin Osborne (Substitute Trombone 1), Theo Primus (French Horn 1), John Moses (Reed 3), Joel Shelton (Substitute Bass Trombone), Eric Poland (Substitute Drums), Chad Yarbrough (French Horn 2), Ric Molina (Guitar 1) and Andy Jones (Percussion).

STAFF FOR *WICKED*

GENERAL MANAGEMENT
321 THEATRICAL MANAGEMENT
Nina Essman Nancy Nagel Gibbs
Marcia Goldberg

GENERAL PRESS REPRESENTATIVE
THE PUBLICITY OFFICE
Bob Fennell Marc Thibodeau
Michael S. Borowski Candi Adams

CASTING
Telsey + Company, C.S.A.:
Bernie Telsey, Will Cantler, David Vaccari, Bethany Knox, Craig Burns, Tiffany Little Canfield, Stephanie Yankwitt, Carrie Rosson, Justin Huff, Joe Langworth

TECHNICAL SUPERVISION
JAKE BELL PRODUCTION SERVICES LTD.

COMPANY MANAGERS ....SUSAN SAMPLINER, AMY MERLINO COEY

Stage Manager ....Chris Jamros
Assistant Stage Managers ....Jennifer Marik, Matthew Aaron Stern
Associate Company Manager....Robert Brinkerhoff
Associate Choreographer ....Mark Myars
Assistant Choreographer ....Corinne McFadden-Herrera
Assistant Dance Captains ....Clyde Alves, Kristen Leigh Gorski, Corinne McFadden-Herrera
Assistant to Mr. Schwartz....Michael Cole
Assistant Scenic Designer ....Nick Francone
Dressing/Properties ....Kristie Thompson
Scenic Assistant ....Christopher Domanski
Oz Map Design ....Francis Keeping
Draftsman ....Ted LeFevre
Set Model Construction ....Miranda Hardy
Associate Costume Designers ....Michael Sharpe, Ken Mooney
Assistant Costume Designers ....Maiko Matsushima, Amy Clark
Costume Coordinator ....Amanda Whidden
Associate Lighting Designer ....Karen Spahn
Associate Lighting Designer/ Automated Lights ....Warren Flynn
Assistant Lighting Designer ....Ben Stanton
Lighting Assistant ....Jonathan Spencer
Associate Sound Designer ....Kai Harada
Sound Assistant ....Shannon Slaton
Projection Programmer ....Mark Gilmore
Assistant Projection Designers ....Jenny Lee, Michael Patterson, Jacob Daniel Pinholster
Projection Animators ....Gareth Smith, Ari Sachter Zeltzer
Special Effects Associate ....Aaron Waitz
Associate Hair Designer ....Charles LaPointe
Fight Director ....Tom Schall
Production Carpenter ....Rick Howard
Head Carpenter ....C. Mark Overton
Deck Automation Carpenter ....William Breidenbach
Production Electrician ....Robert Fehribach
Head Electrician ....Pat Gilmore
Deck Electrician/ Moving Light Operator ....Brendan Quigley
Follow Spot Operator ....Valerie Gilmore
Production Properties ....George Wagner
Property Master ....Joe Schwarz
Assistant Property Master ....John Gentile
Production Sound Engineer....Douglas Graves
Sound Engineer ....Jordan Pankin
Assistant Sound Engineer ....Jack Babin
Production Wardrobe Supervisor ....Alyce Gilbert
Assistant Wardrobe Supervisor ....Trent Armstrong
Dressers ....Bobbye Sue Albrecht, Artie Brown, Kevin Hucke, Dianne Hylton, Kim Kaldenberg, Michael Michalski, Kathe Mull, Gayle Palmieri, Laurel Parrish, Barbara Rosenthal, Jason Viarengo, Randy Witherspoon
Hair Supervisor ....Chris Clark
Assistant Hair Supervisor ....Nora Martin
Hairdressers ....Beverly Belletieri, Ryan McWilliams
Makeup Design ....Joseph Dulude II
Makeup Supervisor ....Jimmy Cortes
Music Preparation Supervisor ....Peter R. Miller, Miller Music Service
Synthesizer Programming ....Andrew Barrett for Lionella Productions, Ltd.
Rehearsal Pianists ....Randy Cohen, Ben Cohn, Matthew Doebler, Matthew Gallagher, Paul Masse
Rehearsal Drummer ....Gary Seligson
Music Intern ....Joshua Salzman
Assistant to the General Managers ....Rachel Marcus
Production Assistants ....Timothy R. Semon, David Zack
Advertising ....Serino Coyne/Greg Corradetti, Joaquin Esteva, Ruth Rosenberg, Hunter Robertson
Marketing ....Betsy Bernstein
Website/Internet Marketing ....Late August Design/ Jeff Prout, Jeff Bowen
Merchandising ....The Araca Group/Clint Bond, Jr., Karen Davidov, Julie Monahan, James M. Pellechi, Jr., Meredith Toole
Theatre Display ....King Displays
Group Sales ....Group Sales Box Office/ Stephanie Lee (800-223-7565)
Banking ....JP Morgan Chase Bank/Michele Gibbons
Payroll ....Castellana Services, Inc.
Accountant ....Robert Fried, C.P.A.
Comptroller ....Lawrence Anderson
Insurance ....AON/Albert G. Ruben Insurance
Legal Counsel ....Loeb & Loeb/Seth Gelblum
Legal Counsel for Universal Pictures ....Keith Blau
Physical Therapy ....P.T. Plus, P.C./Marc Hunter-Hall
Orthopaedist ....David S. Weiss, MD
Onstage Merchandising ....George Fenmore, Inc.

Makeup provided by MAC Cosmetics

MARC PLATT PRODUCTIONS
Adam Siegel, Greg Lessans, Joey Levy, Jared Leboff, Chris Kuhl, Nik Mavinkurve

STONE PRODUCTIONS
Associate: Patrick Catullo

UNIVERSAL PICTURES
President & COO, Universal Studios, Inc. ....Ron Meyer
Chairman ....Marc Shmuger
Co-Chairman ....David Linde
President of Marketing ....Adam Fogelson
Co-President of Marketing ....Eddie Egan
Co-President, Production & EVP, Universal Pictures ....Jimmy Horowitz

Grand Hyatt New York is the official hotel partner of ***Wicked***.

For additional ***WICKED*** merchandise, please visit www.wickedthemusical.com

CREDITS

Scenery built by F&D Scene Changes, Calgary, Canada. Show control and scenic motion control featuring Stage Command Systems© and scenery fabrication by Scenic Technologies, a division of Production Resource Group, New Windsor, NY. Lighting and certain special effects equipment from Fourth Phase and sound equipment from ProMix, both divisions of Production Resource Group LLC. Other special effects equipment by Sunshine Scenic Studios and Aztec Stage Lighting. Video projection system provided by Scharff Weisberg Inc. Projections by Vermilion Border Productions. Costumes by Euroco Costumes, Barbara Matera Ltd., Parsons-Meares Ltd., Scafati, TRICORNE New York City and Eric Winterling. Millinery by Rodney Gordon and Lynne Mackey. Shoes by T.O. Dey, Frederick Longtin, Pluma, LaDuca Shoes NYC, and J.C. Theatrical. Flatheads and monkey wings built by Michael Curry Design Inc. Masks and prosthetics by W.M. Creations, Inc., Matthew W. Mungle and Lloyd Matthews; lifecasts by Todd Kleitsch. Fur by Fur & Furgery. Undergarments and hosiery by Bra*Tenders, Inc. Antique jewelry by Ilene Chazanof. Specialty jewelry and tiaras by Larry Vrba. Custom Oz accessories by LouLou Button. Custom screening by Gene Mignola. Certain props by John Creech Designs and Den Design Studio. Additional hand props courtesy of George Fenmore. Confetti supplied by Artistry in Motion. Puppets by Bob Flanagan. Musical instruments from Manny's and Carroll Musical Instrument Rentals. Drums and other percussion equipment from Bosphorus, Black Swamp, PTECH, D'Amico and Vater. Cough drops supplied by Ricola, Inc. Emer'gen'C provided by Alacer Corp. Rehearsed at the Lawrence A. Wien Center, 890 Broadway, and the Ford Center for the Performing Arts.

NEDERLANDER

Chairman ....**James M. Nederlander**
President ....**James L. Nederlander**

Executive Vice President
Nick Scandalios

Vice President Corporate Development
Charlene S. Nederlander

Senior Vice President Labor Relations
Herschel Waxman

Vice President
Jim Boese

Chief Financial Officer
Freida Sawyer Belviso

STAFF FOR THE GERSHWIN THEATRE
Manager ....**Richard D. Kaye**
Assoc. Manager ....Dwayne Mann
Treasurer ....John Campise
Assistant Treasurer ....Anthony Rossano
Carpenter ....John Riggins
Electrician ....Henry L. Brisen
Property Master ....Mark Illo
Flyman ....Dennis Fox
Fly Automation Carpenter ....Michael J. Szymanski
Head Usher ....Martha McGuire Boniface

Wicked

Scrapbook

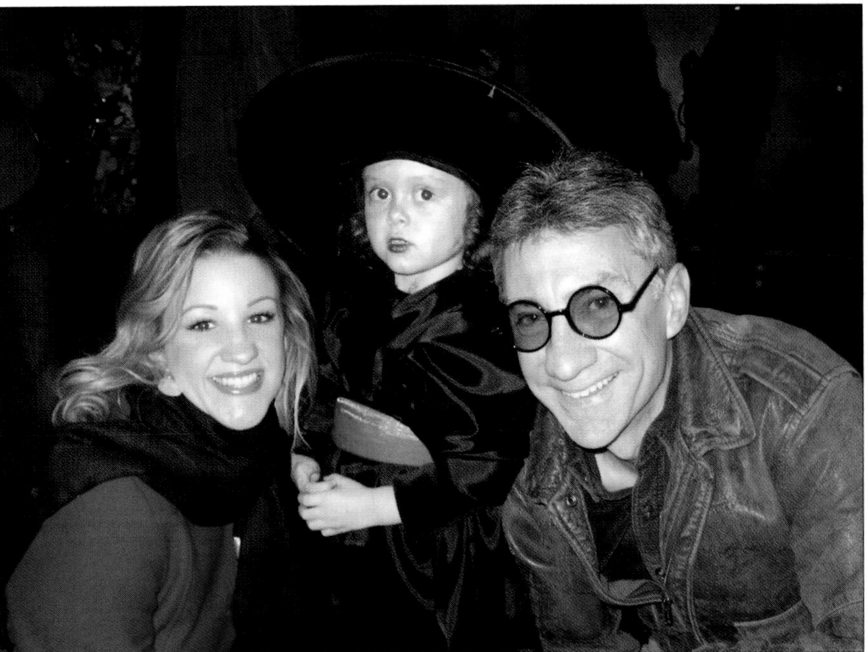

(L-R): Cast member Katie Adams, with a little witch named Grace and David Garrison at the third anniversary *Wicked* Block Party outside the Gershwin Theatre October 29, 2006.

Correspondent: Jason Viarengo, Star Dresser to "The Wizard"

Record Breakers and Milestones: *Wicked* celebrated its third anniversary on Broadway, October 30, 2006.

On January 23, 2007, *Wicked* became the 60th longest running show, passing *Funny Girl.*

On February 15, 2007 *Wicked* became the 59th longest running show, passing *The Music Man.*

On March 24, 2007 *Wicked* became the 57th longest running show, passing *How to Succeed in Business Without Really Trying.*

On April 15, 2007 *Wicked* became the 55th longest running show, passing *The Sound of Music.*

For the week ending December 31, *Wicked* once again broke box office records by grossing $1,800,310 in ticket sales. That's the highest gross for an eight-performance week of any show in the history of Broadway.

Wicked was the top grossing Broadway show of 2006 with $73,119,309 in ticket sales.

Wicked was #1 on Ticketmaster's list of most-requested events in 2006, marking the first time a theatrical production has made the list and certainly the first time that one has held the #1 position, which is otherwise comprised of rock concerts and sporting events.

On November 8, 2006, the original Broadway cast recording of *Wicked* received platinum certification by the Recording Industry Association of America, meaning that the cast recording had sold at least one million copies.

Parties and/or Gifts: On Sunday, November 12, Carol Kane threw a catered brunch from The Palm to celebrate her final performance as Madame Morrible.

On Sunday, January 8, the producers threw the company a holiday party at Charlie Palmer's Metrazur restaurant in Grand Central Station. Cast & crew celebrated by eating and drinking on the balcony of Metrazur while enjoying the spectacular interior view of this legendary New York City landmark.

The 2006 Holiday gift to the cast and crew from our producers was a canvas tote bag printed with the *Wicked* logo and all the cities that *Wicked* has played.

On April 8th, Jayne Houdyshell had The Palm restaurant cater our weekly brunch to celebrate Easter Sunday. The delicious spread included a variety of bagels and cream cheeses, fresh fruit, smoked salmon, danish, and various cheeses.

Celebrity Visitors: Some of our celebrity visitors this past year were Broadway star Tom Hewitt; screen and stage actresses Julianne Moore; Lois Smith; Jennifer Grey; Nancy Dussault; Tony Award-winning actor John Glover; singer and actress Maureen McGovern; Legendary Dreamgirl Diana Ross; Ringling Brothers, Barnum and Bailey Circus's Bello The Clown; Grammy Award-winning singer Lenny Kravitz; "Everybody Loves Raymond" star Patricia Heaton; and Amanda Bearse who came to cheer on her "Married…with Children" co-star David Garrison.

Fundraising: For the 18th annual "Gypsy of the Year" contest, *Wicked* raised $192,900 for Broadway Cares/Equity Fights AIDS.

"Easter Bonnet" Skit: "Weekeed, Live From The Grand Ole Opry!"directed by Anthony Galde, choreographed by Galde and Kristina "Cha-Cha" Fernandez.

"Carols for a Cure" Carol: "The First Noel."

Special Backstage Rituals: Derrick Williams, who played Fiyero, and his dresser Michael Michalski came up with "Derrick's Dessert Wednesday." Every week Michael would bake Derrick a cake of his choosing. Some of the tasty treats included German chocolate cake, lemon bundt cake, red velvet cake and banana pudding pie.

Every Thursday the principal hallway dressers and actors participate in "Cookies & Cash" in which everyone alternates bringing in some cookies to share. The cash comes in the form of our paychecks, courtesy of Company Management. The favorite cookie flavor is chocolate chip. Madame Morrible dresser Bobbye Sue Albrecht came up with this wonderful Thursday tradition.

Every Friday, Steven Skybell, who plays Doctor Dillamond, brings in Entenmann's Chocolate Donuts, pretzels filled with peanut butter and Little Debbie snack cakes.

On Saturdays we have "Dollar Friday on Saturday." Katie Adams, who is the Glinda standby, goes around the theater and collects the dollars for the pot. At intermission she gets on the intercom system, does a little skit and announces the lucky winner.

"Saturday Night On Broadway" takes place during "For Good" in the Male Ensemble Dressing Room. It is hosted by ensemble cast member Charlie Sutton. Every week Charlie comes up with a different theme to celebrate the end of the work week. Some past themes have included "Mexican Night" in which chips and salsa are served and "Hawaiian Night" which includes pineapple, sliced oranges and whipped cream.

Female Ensemble Dresser Barbara Rosenthal reads the horoscope from *The New York Post* to the girls in the dressing room out loud every day.

Kendra Kessebaum who plays Glinda, listens to record albums from her childhood on her record player that she grew up with while she puts on her makeup and gets ready for the show. Some of the albums that Kendra listens to are Billie Holiday's "Greatest Hits Volume 1," Judy Garland, Frank Sinatra's "That's Life" and Lawrence Welk's "Favorites."

Favorite In-Theatre Gathering Places: The Elphaba dressing room always seems to be a favorite place to hang out during the show. Julia Murney always keeps her door open, and cast and crew are welcome to stop in. Julia is always baking and bringing in her baked goods to share. If there aren't any bakery items, Julia also keeps a large bowl full of chocolate in her dressing room for anyone who is need of a sugar rush.

During the Christmas holidays David Garrison

Wicked
SCRAPBOOK

Photo by Aubrey Reuben

Photo by Kathe Mull

Photo by Jason Viarengo

Photo by Aubrey Reuben

1. Composer Stephen Schwartz poses with his portrait and radio host Valerie Smaldone for the Broadway Wall of Fame at Tony's Di Napoli restaurant.

2. David Garrison playing with his dressing room train set at Christmas.

3. Kate Reinders, Jenna Leigh Green and Derrick Williams pose with the *Wicked* tote bags the producers gave them for Christmas.

4. (L-R): Michele Pawk, son Jack and husband John Dossett at the third anniversary *Wicked* Block Party.

decorated his dressing room complete with a big white Christmas tree and toy train set. Cast and crew were welcome to come by and look at the tree and enjoy some hot apple cider and holiday cookies during the holiday season.

The greenroom is a favorite hangout among cast and crew to relax between shows, and where we have all our birthday cake celebrations.

Sunday Brunch is held in the Male Ensemble Dressing Room, hosted by Anthony Galde. Some of the yummy favorites are bagels, Krispy Kreme doughnuts, fresh fruit, salsa and chips, Entenmann's cakes and macaroni & cheese.

The crew room offstage right. There is a big television in the room courtesy of producer Marc Platt. Against the wall where the TV is best viewed is a sign that reads "Reserved for Marc Platt."

Sweethearts Within the Company: Female Swing Tiffany Haas and Concertmaster Christian Hebel have been dating for over a year. One of their traditions since they began seeing each other is that, right before the show starts, Tiffany taps on the number ten on stage which is directly above where Christian sits in the orchestra pit, to let him know she's at places and ready to begin the show.

Most Colorful Dressing Room: When you enter Sebastian Arcelus's dressing room you get the feeling you are entering an oasis of multiculturism consisting of Russian, Uruguayan and Italian family heirlooms. When Sebastian chose to paint his room he felt his eclectic belongings would look best with the color Monticello Rose. However when it went up on the wall it turned out to be an unsatisfying pink.

Favorite Therapies: Ricola, Throat-Coat tea, Entertainers Secret throat spray, and physical therapy with Marc Hunter-Hall.

Favorite Off-Site Hangouts: Cast and crew frequently go to House of Brews, The Palm, Arriba Arriba, Sosa Borella, and Sardi's on Wednesdays between shows. The stage managers head to Harmony View Grill.

Favorite Snack Foods: The principal hallway candy jar is always filled with M&M's, Hershey's Kisses and cookies. The stage managers always have pretzel rods on hand. Norman Weiss of *Phantom of the Opera* drops off baked goods to the principal hallway.

Coolest Thing About Being in This Show: Two words: Steady Employment!

Remembrance: In October we lost our beloved publicist Bob Fennell to cancer. Bob would visit the theatre at least once a week to check on everyone. He was a true gentleman who loved life and loved Broadway. When Bob's illness was announced to the company, producer David Stone organized a card-writing campaign. David even contacted press industry people and *Wicked* alumni to be a part of the project, to let Bob know how much the *Wicked* family was thinking of him, and let his family know what Bob meant to the entire Broadway community.

The Year of Magical Thinking

First Preview: March 6, 2007. Opened: March 29, 2007.
Still running as of May 31, 2007.

PLAYBILL

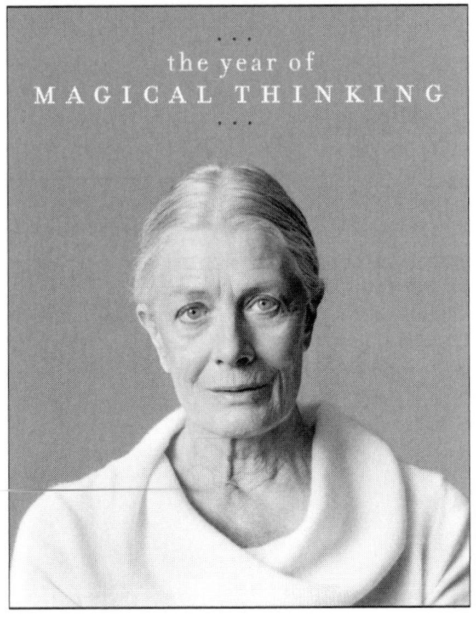

BOOTH THEATRE
222 West 45th Street
A Shubert Organization Theatre
Gerald Schoenfeld, *Chairman* **Philip J. Smith**, *President*

Robert E. Wankel, *Executive Vice President*

SCOTT RUDIN
ROGER BERLIND DEBRA BLACK DARYL ROTH
THE SHUBERT ORGANIZATION

Executive Producers
STUART THOMPSON JOHN BARLOW

present

VANESSA
REDGRAVE

...

the year of
MAGICAL THINKING

...

a play by
JOAN DIDION
based on her memoir

Scenic Design BOB CROWLEY
Costume Design ANN ROTH
Lighting Design JEAN KALMAN
Sound Design PAUL ARDITTI
Production Stage Manager KAREN ARMSTRONG
Associate Director BT MCNICHOLL
Press Representative BONEAU/BRYAN-BROWN
Marketing ERIC SCHNALL
Production Management AURORA PRODUCTIONS
General Management STP/JAMES TRINER

Directed by
DAVID HARE

LIVE BROADWAY

3/29/07

CAST

Joan Didion .... VANESSA REDGRAVE

STANDBY

MAUREEN ANDERMAN

Vanessa Redgrave is appearing with the permission of Actors' Equity Association.

Vanessa Redgrave as Joan Didion.

(L-R): Joan Didion and Vanessa Redgrave

Photos by Brigitte Lacombe

The Year of Magical Thinking

Vanessa Redgrave
Joan Didion

Joan Didion
Playwright

David Hare
Director

Bob Crowley
Scenic Design

Ann Roth
Costume Design

Jean Kalman
Lighting Design

Naomi Donne
Hair & Makeup Design

Maureen Anderman
Standby for Ms. Redgrave

James Triner
General Manager

BT McNicholl
Associate Director

Scott Rudin
Producer

Roger Berlind
Producer

Daryl Roth
Producer

Debra Black
Producer

Gerald Schoenfeld, Chairman, The Shubert Organization
Producer

Stuart Thompson
Executive Producer

John Barlow
Executive Producer

2006-2007 AWARD

Drama Desk Award
Outstanding Solo Perfomance
(Vanessa Redgrave)

BOX OFFICE
(L-R): Eddie and Vinnie Whittaker.

HAIR AND WARDROBE
(L-R): Aleksandra Nesterchuk (Hairdresser) and Laura Beattie (Wardrobe Supervisor/Dresser).

Photos by Ben Strothmann

The Year of Magical Thinking

STAGE CREW
Front Row (L-R): Tim McDonough (Carpenter), Aleksandra Nesterchuck (Hairdresser), Maureen Anderman (Standby for Ms. Redgrave), R.J. Burns Sr. (House Electrician).

Middle Row (L-R): Ronald Fogel (Head Electrician), Laura Beattie (Wardrobe Supervisor), Martha Donaldson (Stage Manager).

Back Row (L-R): Kenny McDonough (House Carpenter), Jimmy Keane (House Properties) and Bill Lewis (Production Sound Operator).

DOORPERSON
Amanda Tramontozzi

Photos by Ben Strothmann

STAFF FOR *THE YEAR OF MAGICAL THINKING*

GENERAL MANAGEMENT
STUART THOMPSON PRODUCTIONS
Stuart Thompson Caroline Prugh James Triner

COMPANY MANAGER
Cassidy J. Briggs

PRODUCTION MANAGEMENT
AURORA PRODUCTIONS INC.
Gene O'Donovan W. Benjamin Heller II
Bethany Weinstein Melissa Mazdra
Meghan VonVett

GENERAL PRESS REPRESENTATION
BONEAU/BRYAN-BROWN
Chris Boneau Steven Padla Heath Schwartz

CASTING
Daniel Swee, C.S.A.

HAIR & MAKEUP DESIGN
Naomi Donne

COVER PHOTO & PRODUCTION PHOTOGRAPHY
Brigitte Lacombe

DIALECT COACH
Deborah Hecht

Production Stage Manager ....Karen Armstrong
Stage Manager ....Martha Donaldson
Associate Scenic Designer ....Bryan Johnson
Associate Scenic Designer ....Jeffrey Hinchee
Associate Costume Designer ....Michelle Matland
Associate Lighting Designer ....Bobby Harrell
Associate Sound Designers ....Walter Trarbach, Tony Smolenski IV
Production Electrician ....Michael Pitzer
Head Electrician ....Ronald Fogel
Production Sound Operator ....Bill Lewis
Wardrobe Supervisor/Dresser ....Laura Beattie
Hairdresser ....Aleksandra Nesterchuk
Production Carpenter ....Kenneth McDonough
Assistant Carpenter ....Ed White
Production Properties ....Jimmy Keane
House Electrician ....Ronnie Burns Sr.
Props Fabrication ....Craig Grigg
Production Assistant ....Johanna Karlin
Assistants to Mr. Rudin ....Mark Rothman, Nathan Kelly
Assistant to Mr. Berlind ....Jeffrey Hillock
Assistant to Ms. Black ....Ana Pilar Camacho
Assistant to Ms. Roth ....Greg Raby
Assistant to Ms. Didion ....Sharon Lieberman
Assistant to Mr. Hare ....Erica Lipez
Assistant to Ms. Redgrave ....Eamonn Burke
General Management Assistant ....Megan Curren
Management Interns ....Aaron Thompson, Diane Alianiello
Press Representative Staff ....Adrian Bryan-Brown, Ian Bjorklund, Jim Byk, Brandi Cornwell, Danielle Crinnion, Jackie Green, Juliana Hannett, Hector Hernandez, Allison Houseworth, Jessica Johnson, Kevin Jones, Amy Kass, Aaron Meier, Christine Olver, Joe Perrotta, Linnae Petruzzelli, Matt Polk, Matt Ross, Susanne Tighe
Banking ....JP Morgan Chase/Michelle Gibbons
Payroll ....Castellana Services, Inc.
Accountant....................Fried & Kowgios CPA's LLP/ Robert Fried, CPA
Controller ....Anne Stewart FitzRoy
Insurance ....DeWitt Stern Group
Legal Counsel ....Loeb & Loeb Inc./ Seth Gelblum, Esq.
Advertising ....SPOTCO/ Drew Hodges, Jim Edwards, Jim Aquino, Y. Darius Suyama
Immigration ....Traffic Control Group, Inc./ David King

Theatre Displays ....King Displays, Inc.

CREDITS
Scenery and automation from Hudson Scenic Studio, Inc. Soft goods by I. Weiss. Lighting equipment from PRG Lighting. Sound equipment from PRG Audio. Rehearsed at the New 42nd Street Studios.

The producers would like to express their thanks to Michael Weber for his contribution to this production.

www.MagicalThinkingonBroadway.com

THE SHUBERT ORGANIZATION, INC.
Board of Directors

Gerald Schoenfeld Chairman
Philip J. Smith President
Wyche Fowler, Jr.
John W. Kluge
Lee J. Seidler
Michael I. Sovern
Stuart Subotnick

Robert E. Wankel
Executive Vice President

Peter Entin Vice President Theatre Operations
Elliot Greene Vice President Finance
David Andrews Vice President Shubert Ticketing Services
John Darby Vice President Facilities

D.S. Moynihan
Vice President – Creative Projects

House Manager ....Laurel Ann Wilson

The Year of Magical Thinking
Scrapbook

Correspondent: Martha Donaldson, Stage Manager
Memorable Opening Night Fax: We loved all the faxes from the other Broadway shows.
Opening Night Gifts: From the Producers—A candid photo by Brigitte Lacombe of David, Vanessa and Joan talking, sealed in a Lucite block with the opening night "Show Poster" on the back.
From Aurora Productions (our Production Management Team)—A little silk "drop" in a small wooden box that is the same wood as the stage deck. On the drop is printed "Happy Opening—*Year of Magical Thinking* from Aurora Productions."
From our standby, Maureen—Pamplemousse-scented incense rocks.
From Vanessa—Many, many beautiful flowers.
Most Exciting Celebrity Visitor and What They Did/Said: Lauren Bacall, as she was being taken up the stairs to Vanessa's dressing room after the show, she balked at the stairs. So Vanessa's assistant offered for her to stay downstairs and Vanessa would come down to her—to which she replied "If she can do it, I can do it," and up the stairs they went.
Actor Who Performed the Most Roles in This Show: Vanessa Redgrave.
Who Has Done the Most Shows in Their Career: Vanessa Redgrave.
Who Wore the Heaviest/Hottest Costume: Vanessa Redgrave.
Who Wore the Least: Vanessa Redgrave.
Company Legend: Vanessa Redgrave.
Special Backstage Ritual: Saturday "Sundaes"—Ice cream and yummies provided weekly by Ms. Redgrave.
Company Traditions: They are all food-based: eating Piece O' Chicken and Edison's Matzoh Ball Soup. We also made almost daily trips to the soup counter at "Dishes."
Favorite Moment During Each Performance: The opening of the show as the first drop drops.
Favorite In-Theatre Gathering Place: Café Didion backstage right.
Favorite Off-Site Hangout: Joe Allen's restaurant.
Favorite Snack Food: Morello Cherry Jam.
Favorite Therapy: Post-show: One whiskey-soaked Maraschino cherry, courtesy of our house electrician Ronnie Burns, Sr.
Record Number of Cell Phone Rings During a Performance: 5?
Memorable Press Encounter: CBS Sunday morning interviews.
Catchphrase Only the Company Would Recognize: "Never Better."
Memorable Directorial Notes: "Savage Gear Changes. Double D Clutch."
Company In-Joke: Spritzing.
Understudy Anecdote: People mistake Maureen for Joan Didion.
Sweethearts Within the Company: Ice Cream and Cherry Jam.
Coolest Things About Being in This Show: Vanessa Redgrave, Joan Didion, David Hare, Bob Crowley, Ann Roth, Jean Kalman, Paul Arditti, Scott Rudin and Magic Tricks—need we say more?

Photo by Ben Strothmann

Photos by Aubrey Reuben

Photo by David Gewirtzman

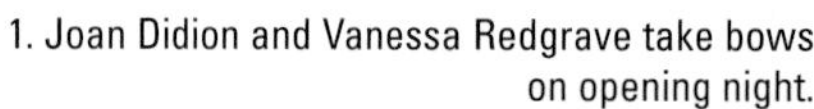

1. Joan Didion and Vanessa Redgrave take bows on opening night.
2. Café Didion, created just offstage by the crew.
3. Director David Hare and wife Nicole Farhi at the first performance.
4. One of the window cards outside the Booth.
5. Guests Lynn Redgrave and Joseph Hardy arrive at the Booth Theatre.
6. Guest Jane Fonda on opening night.

Events

Events

Stars in the Alley

June 7, 2006 in Shubert Alley

An impressive collection of Broadway's current leading players toughed out a dreary day to be a part of the annual "Stars in the Alley" concert in Shubert Alley. The event offers theatre fans a chance to see their favorites up-close, in-person and free.

Among those who braved the rain: Lucie Arnaz, Kate Burton, Sutton Foster, David Garrison, Jonathan Hadary, Cherry Jones, Carol Kane, Judy Kaye, Cynthia Nixon, Ian McDiarmid, Oliver Platt, Jonathan Pryce, Pablo Schreiber and David Wilmot. Sponsored by Continental Airlines and The League of American Theatres and Producers, the event featured performances from *Avenue Q, Chicago, The Color Purple, The Drowsy Chaperone, Hairspray, Jersey Boys, The Light in the Piazza, Mamma Mia!, The Phantom of the Opera, The Producers, Rent, Spamalot, Sweeney Todd, The Wedding Singer* and *The 25th Annual Putnam County Spelling Bee*, plus appearances by cast members of *Awake and Sing!, Dirty Rotten Scoundrels, Doubt, The History Boys,* and *Wicked*. Arnaz and Pryce presented the Star Award to Christine C. Quinn, Speaker of the New York City Council, recognizing "an individual in public or government service who has demonstrated significant support for Broadway."

Photos by Aubrey Reuben

1. (L-R): Ian McDiarmid and Cherry Jones of *Faith Healer* wait out the raindrops backstage.
2. (L-R): Kenita R. Miller and Angela Robinson of *The Color Purple*.
3. (L-R): Kate Burton of *Constant Wife* and Jed Bernstein, retiring president of the League of American Theatres and Producers.
4. (L-R): Amy Spanger (*The Wedding Singer*), Michael Cerveris (*Sweeney Todd*) and Angie Schworer (*The Producers*).
5. (L-R): *The Drowsy Chaperone*'s Bob Martin, Beth Leavel and Sutton Foster.
6. Cynthia Nixon of *Rabbit Hole*.

Events

Broadway Bares 16

June 18, 2006 at the Roseland Ballroom

"Broadway Bares 16," the annual fundraiser for Broadway Cares/Equity Fights AIDS brought in a record-breaking $659,500 in two shows on June 18.

Executive-produced by 2005 Tony Award winner Jerry Mitchell and directed by *The Full Monty*'s Denis Jones, this year's event was titled "New York Strip" and featured Barrett Foa and Andrew Rannells as a midwestern gay couple sightseeing in the Big Apple. The boys got quite an eyeful, with 200 chorus guys and gals portraying New York's hottest policemen, firefighters, construction workers, delivery men, the transit strike, "Sex in the City," the Statue of Liberty, Studio 54 and the "Rock-hard-ettes."

Special guest stars included Cyndi Lauper (singing "True Colors"), Mario Cantone (singing "New York, New York"), Fran Drescher, Sara Gettelfinger (singing the title song written by Gary Adler) and *Jersey Boys*' Dominic Nolfi, Daniel Reichard, J. Robert Spencer and John Lloyd Young. Sandra Bernhard and Rita Wilson helped present a BC/EFA with a $100,000 check from MAC Cosmetics.

1. (L-R): Jerry Mitchell (executive producer) and Josh Strickland (*Tarzan*) backstage at Roseland.
2. (L-R): Ariel Reid (*Spamalot*) and Nicole Winhoffer (*Wicked* tour).
3. (L-R): Lorin Latarro and Holly Cruz.
4. Mitchell and Latarro.
5. (L-R): Mario Cantone and Marissa Jaret Winokur.
6. (L-R): Sandra Bernhard and Rita Wilson.

Photos by Aubrey Reuben

Broadway Under the Stars

June 26, 2006 in Central Park

The fifth annual "Broadway Under the Stars" concert was a salute to 21-time Tony Award winner Harold Prince. Nearly 30,000 people attended the free outdoor event, held for the first time on Central Park's Great Lawn. The show, directed by Jeff Calhoun, featured current Broadway stars and a live orchestra performing numbers from musicals directed or produced by Hal Prince. Chase Brock and Phil Reno handled choreography and music direction.

Kelli O'Hara and Matthew Morrison performed the balcony scene from *West Side Story*, Bebe Neuwirth sang "Cabaret," Carolee Carmello led a rendition of "Buenos Aires" and Anika Noni Rose performed "Can't Help Lovin' Dat Man."

Also performing were Michael Cerveris and Manoel Felciano (*Sweeney Todd*), Christine Ebersole (*Grey Gardens*), Renée Elise Goldsberry (*The Color Purple*), Donna McKechnie, Shuler Hensley (*Tarzan*), Brian d'Arcy James (*Dirty Rotten Scoundrels*) and Rebecca Luker (*Mary Poppins*). Liza Minnelli made a surprise guest appearance. Highlights from the concert were televised by WCBS on July 15.

Photos by Aubrey Reuben

1. Sutton Foster (C) and her Boys performed "You've Got Possibilities."
2. Elaine Stritch sang "Why Do I Love You?"
3. Jane Krakowski vamped "Don't Tell Mama."
4. (L-R): Michael Longoria, Dominic Nolfi, Christian Hoff and J. Robert Spencer sang *Phantom*'s "All I Ask of You" in *Jersey Boys* style.
5. (L-R): Manoel Felciano (*Sweeney Todd*) with Bebe Neuwirth.

Events

Broadway on Broadway 2006

September 10, 2006 in Times Square

Martin Short, star of *Martin Short: Fame Becomes Me*, served as ringmaster of Broadway shows old and new at the 15th annual "Broadway on Broadway" free concert in the heart of Times Square.

Several Tony winners (including Short himself), a few "American Idol" finalists and a slew of Broadway favorites joined the parade offering free samples of their shows to a crowd estimated at 50,000. Among them were LaChanze, Constantine Maroulis, Diana DeGarmo, Frenchie Davis, Christine Ebersole, Josh Strickland, Hunter Foster, John Treacy Egan, Eden Espinosa, Kate Reinders, Bob Martin and Beth Leavel.

Attendees caught performances from the casts of ongoing favorites *Avenue Q, Beauty and the Beast, The Color Purple, The Drowsy Chaperone, Hairspray, Jersey Boys, The Lion King, Mamma Mia!, The Producers, Rent, Spamalot, Tarzan, The 25th Annual Putnam County Spelling Bee, The Wedding Singer* and *Wicked* plus the soon-to-open productions of *Les Misérables, High Fidelity, Grey Gardens, Jay Johnson: The Two and Only!* and *The Times They Are A-Changin'.*

Photos by Aubrey Reuben

1. Christine Ebersole of *Grey Gardens* embraces Martin Short of *Fame Becomes Me* in the middle of Times Square.
2. Jay Johnson and friend from *Jay Johnson: The Two and Only!* limber up before their appearance.
3. Jenn Colella and Will Chase of *High Fidelity*.
4. (L-R): Haylie Duff, Michelle Dowdy and Diana DeGarmo of *Hairspray*.
5. Norm Lewis of *Les Misérables*.

20th Annual Broadway Flea Market and Grand Auction

September 24, 2006 in Shubert Alley

The 20th Annual Broadway Flea Market and Grand Auction—held September 24 in Shubert Alley—raised $505,832 for Broadway Cares/Equity Fights AIDS. The outdoor theatrical extravaganza featured several fundraising events, including a Celebrity Table, a Silent Auction, a Grand Auction and various booths manned by theatre performers and theatre lovers selling memorabilia and other merchandise.

The booth that raised the most money this year ($24,311) was hosted by the United Scenic Artists. That organization also brought in the most funds in 2005 ($23,865). The show booth that raised the most money was *The Phantom of the Opera* which took in $13,230.

Highlights of the Silent Auction: The Nederlander Theatre stage door, which was autographed by the original cast of *Rent*, sold for $2,300. A backstage celebrity autograph book donated by the *Avenue Q* cast sold for $1,300. A "Trekkie Monster" puppet, created by Rick Lyon for *Avenue Q*, brought in the most money during the Grand Auction, $10,500. Other notables: two pair of tickets to the opening night performance and party for the *Les Misérables* revival went for $9,500 each, while walk-on roles in *Jersey Boys* and *Rent* brought in $8,500 apiece.

Photos by Aubrey Reuben

1. (L-R): Melissa Gallo ("One Life to Live") and Felicia Finley (*The Wedding Singer*) smile for visitors in Shubert Alley.
2. (L-R): John Driscoll ("The Guiding Light") poses with Bebe Neuwirth (*Chicago*).
3. (L-R): Jill Haworth (the original Sally Bowles in *Cabaret*) autographs posters with Nicole Forester ("The Guiding Light").
4. (L-R): John Lloyd Young and Daniel Reichard of *Jersey Boys* flank Edie Falco.
5. (L-R): Stephanie D'Abruzzo (*Avenue Q*) and Kevin Cahoon (*The Wedding Singer*).

Actors' Fund *Best Little Whorehouse in Texas*

October 16, 2006 at the August Wilson Theatre

An all-star concert performance of *The Best Little Whorehouse in Texas* helped raise money for the Actors' Fund of America October 16 at the August Wilson Theatre.

Side Show's Emily Skinner and *Beauty and the Beast*'s Terrence Mann co-starred as (respectively) Mona Stangley and Sheriff Ed Earl Dodd in the sixth annual fundraiser. The event also boasted Harry Groener as the Governor, Andrea McArdle as Doatsy Mae, Felicia Finley as Angel, Mary Faber as Shy, Richard Kind as Senator Wingwoah, Jennifer Hudson as Jewel, "American Idol" finalist Constantine Maroulis as an Aggie soloist, Bob Martin as Melvin P. Thorpe and the cast of *[title of show]* as The Melvin P. Thorpe Singers as well as Daniel Reichard, Peter Gregus, Matt Scott and Tony Award winner Christian Hoff.

In the ensemble: Roxane Barlow, Ed Carlo, Jen Cody, Amber Efe, Phil Fabry, Rick Faugno, Sue Goodman, Justin Greer, Nina Hennessey, MaryAnn Hu, Trent Armand Kendall, Michelle Kittrell, Jeff Lewis, J. Elaine Marcos, Val Moranto, Naomi Naughton, Darius Nicols, Christina Marie Norrup, Kate Pazakis, Rachelle Rak, Matt Rossoff, Jason Patrick Sands, Charlie Schwartz, Angie Schworer, Bret Shuford, Giovanni Stella, Dennis Stowe and Will Taylor.

Photos by Aubrey Reuben

1. The cast and artistic producer/music director Seth Rudetsky (front) take bows.
2. Jen Cody and husband (and former *Urinetown* co-star) Hunter Foster at the afterparty at John's Pizzeria.
3. (L-R): Missy Goldberg, Donna McKechnie and Rudetsky.
4. Cast members (L-R) Christina Marie Norrup, J. Elaine Marcos, Rachelle Rak, Michelle Kittrell and Roxane Barlow.
5. Constantine Maroulis and Jennifer Hudson.

2006 Tony Honors

October 24, 2006 at Tavern on the Green

Photos by Aubrey Reuben

Tony Award winner Cynthia Nixon hosted the 2006 Tony Honors for Excellence in the Theatre celebration October 24, 2006 at Tavern on the Green. The Tony Honors recognize contributions to the field of theatre for individuals and organizations not eligible in any of the established Tony categories. The 2006 honorees were the BMI Lehman Engel Musical Theatre Workshop, *Forbidden Broadway* and its creator Gerard Alessandrini, talent agent Samuel ("Biff") Liff and Ellen Stewart of La MaMa Experimental Theatre Club.

The BMI Workshop has nurtured new musical theatre talent for more than 45 years. Writers who were trained at the workshop include Maury Yeston, Stephen Flaherty and Lynn Ahrens.

Liff is a senior vice president of the William Morris Agency. Throughout his lengthy career he has been an associate producer to David Merrick, the Broadway stage manager of *My Fair Lady*, and he currently represents such theatre icons as Jerry Herman and Chita Rivera.

Gerard Alessandrini created the long-running Off-Broadway revue *Forbidden Broadway*, which pokes fun at the theatre and its stars.

Ellen Stewart is the founder/director of La MaMa E.T.C., which has presented more than 2,000 productions since its launch in 1961.

Presenters included Tony winners Angela Lansbury, Manny Azenberg, Andre DeShields, Lynn Ahrens and Stephen Flaherty.

1. (L-R:) Presenter Angela Lansbury with honoree Gerard Alessandrini of *Forbidden Broadway*.
2. Host Cynthia Nixon.
3. Honoree Samuel "Biff" Liff and Chita Rivera.
4. (L-R:) Doug Leeds, President of the American Theatre Wing Sondra Gilman, and presenters Maury Yeston and Lynn Ahrens.
5. (L-R:) Presenter André DeShields, Ellen Stewart and Executive Director of the League of American Theatres and Producers Charlotte St. Martin.

Broadway Show League Softball Championship

August 31, 2006 at North Meadow Field in Central Park

The team from *The Producers* reclaimed the championship of the Broadway Show League, beating the team from the Atlantic Theatre Company by a score of 4-1, giving *The Producers'* team its fourth championship since 2002.

The 2006 season was played on the Great Lawn and North Meadow fields while the Heckscher fields were being restored.

The Broadway Show League consists of teams from more than two dozen Broadway shows and organizations that play Thursday afternoon games in Central Park.

Photo by David Zukerman

The 2006 Champions: The team from *The Producers.*

Inside Broadway's 25th Anniversary Concert

November 2, 2006 at the Cadillac Winter Garden Theatre

Photo by Aubrey Reuben

Cast members from *Hairspray, The Lion King, Wicked, Mamma Mia!, Tarzan* and the Inside Broadway production of *Cinderella* celebrated Inside Broadway's 25th anniversary with a free event at the Cadillac Winter Garden. The not-for-profit educational organization brings Broadway to young audiences through a student ticket program, Broadway show study guides, educational videos about the behind-the-scenes operations at a Broadway theatre and 50-minute versions of classic Broadway musicals.

(L-R): Elizabeth Daniels (*Cinderella*), Kearran Giovanni (*Tarzan*), Katie Adams (*Wicked*), Josh Strickland (*Tarzan*), Brandi Chavonne Massey (*Wicked*), Chester Gregory (*Tarzan*) and Kenyon Adams (*Cinderella*) backstage at the Cadillac Winter Garden Theater.

A Tribute to Mary Rodgers

October 23, 2006 at the Manhattan Penthouse

Tony-winners Donna Murphy and Faith Prince were among performers at Music-Theatre Group's annual gala, this year honoring Mary Rodgers, composer of the Broadway musicals *Once Upon a Mattress* and *Hot Spot,* who also contributed songs to *From A to Z* and *The Madwoman of Central Park West.* She is also the author of the book "Freaky Friday" and the screenwriter of the Disney film of the same name.

Photo by Aubrey Reuben

(L-R): Robert Hurwitz of Nonesuch Records, Mary Rodgers, Ted Chapin (President of the Rodgers & Hammerstein Organization) and MTG President Diana Wondisford at the Manhattan Penthouse.

Gypsy of the Year

December 4-5, 2006 at the Neil Simon Theatre

The Color Purple was named the top fundraiser and also won the prize for best presentation at the 18th annual Gypsy of the Year competition, December 4-5.

The musical raised $194,500 of the $2,992,800 gathered by fifty-eight participating Broadway, Off-Broadway, and national touring companies, which spent six weeks appealing to audiences during curtain calls for funds for the charity Broadway Cares/Equity Fights AIDS. The total edged past last year's take of $2,972,721.

The Broadway fundraising runners-up were *Wicked* ($192,900), *The Drowsy Chaperone* ($185,900), *The Phantom of the Opera* ($153,800) and *Jersey Boys* ($133,250). The top touring company was the *Wicked* Chicago company with $175,000. *The Little Dog Laughed* was the top play with $44,330 and *The Clean House* won the Off-Broadway award with $26,700.

The Color Purple's presentation—a rendition of the Stevie Wonder song "They Won't Go When I Go"—won top honors at the competition's benefit event at the Neil Simon Theatre involving skits and songs written and performed by cast members from some of the participating shows.

Photos by Ben Strothmann

1. (L-R): The gypsies of *The Color Purple* celebrate their double win.
2. Tom Jones, lyricist and co-star of *The Fantasticks*, sings "Mister Off-Broadway."
3. Hosts (L-R): Martin Short of *Fame Becomes Me*, Christine Ebersole of *Grey Gardens*, and Marin Mazzie and Jonathan Hadary of *Monty Python's Spamalot.*
4. The cast of *The Little Dog Laughed* in terrycloth (L-R): Tom Everett Scott, Ari Graynor, Julie White and Johnny Galecki.
5. (L-R): Jimmy Smagula and Sally Williams of *The Phantom of the Opera* riff on the stars of *Grey Gardens* in their skit.
6. Cast members from *Mamma Mia!* perform the skit "Calling In Sick."

Theater Hall of Fame Ceremony

January 29, 2007 at the Gershwin Theatre

Photos by Aubrey Reuben

Phylicia Rashad hosted the 36th annual Theater Hall of Fame ceremony at the Gershwin Theatre, inducting actors Patti LuPone, George Hearn and Elizabeth Wilson; playwright Brian Friel; and designers Willa Kim and Eugene Lee.

Playwrights Wendy Wasserstein and August Wilson were inducted posthumously.

Among the guest presenters were the stars of the Terrence McNally play *Deuce*, Angela Lansbury and Marian Seldes. Also presenting were George Grizzard, William Ivey Long, Peter Weller, Jack Viertel and Oskar Eustis. Constanza Romero Wilson accepted the honor for her late husband, August Wilson; Pamela Wasserstein accepted for her aunt, the late Wendy Wasserstein.

Nominees for the Theater Hall of Fame must have a minimum of five major credits and twenty-five years in the Broadway theatre. The inductees are voted on by the American Theatre Critics Association and the members of the Theater Hall of Fame.

1. Presenter William Ivey Long and honoree Willa Kim.
2. Presenters Angela Lansbury and George Hearn.
3. Host Phylicia Rashad.
4. Honoree Eugene Lee.
5. Honoree Elizabeth Wilson and previous honoree Frances Sternhagen.
6. Lee, Kim, presenter Peter Weller and Wilson.

Kids' Night on Broadway

January 30 and 31, 2007

"Kids' Night on Broadway," the annual event in which kids can attend a show for free if they come with a paying adult, took place January 30 and 31, 2007, with more than two dozen Broadway and Off-Broadway shows participating. Julie Andrews, the stage and screen actress, and her daughter Emma Walton Hamilton, the co-founder of the Bay Street Theatre, served as National Ambassadors for this year's event.

Photo by Aubrey Reuben

Broadway child actors join Emma Walton Hamilton (3rd from L) and her mom, Julie Andrews (3rd from R) at a press launch for "Kids' Night on Broadway" at Sardi's restaurant.

Broadway Bears 10

February 11, 2007 at B.B. King Blues Club & Grill

Photos by Aubrey Reuben

1. Christopher Sieber with the dismembered *Spamalot* bear.
2. Stephanie D'Abruzzo with *Avenue Q*'s puppet bear
3. Marge Champion with the Minnie Fay (*Hello, Dolly!*) bear.

The 10th anniversary "Broadway Bears" event, hosted by Bryan Batt, raised $131,000 for Broadway Cares/Equity Fights AIDS with its traditional auction of theatre-themed teddy bears. Top bids were for the *Mary Poppins* bear ($8,000), which was signed by Julie Andrews and Ashley Brown, and the *Phantom of the Opera* bear ($6,500) signed by director Harold Prince. The *A Chorus Line* bears (17 small bears in total) brought in $6,000 and were signed by the entire cast of the musical revival.

Others among the forty bears auctioned this year included bears dressed as characters from *Jersey Boys, Martin Short: Fame Becomes Me, Grey Gardens, Spamalot, Wicked, Avenue Q, The Color Purple, Sweeney Todd, The Boy From Oz* and *The Pajama Game.*

Leading Men II

February 5, 2007 at Birdland

"You've got male" could've been the catchphrase at "The Leading Men II" concert, hosted by John Tartaglia, at Birdland. The benefit for Broadway Cares/Equity Fights AIDS was a sold-out celebration of theater and cabaret crooners singing everything from Loesser to *Lestat*. Directed by Alan Muraoka, the lineup featured Tom Andersen, Jim Caruso, Matt Cavenaugh, Tim Di Pasqua, David Gurland, Adam Jacobs, Telly Leung, Norm Lewis, Perry Ojeda, Hugh Panaro, Daniel Reichard, Seth Rudetsky, Jason Michael Snow and Ben Strothmann. It was created and produced by Wayman Wong, who originated "The Leading Men" column and wrote it for four years at Playbill.com.

Photo by Linda Lenzi

(L-R): Matt Cavenaugh, John Tartaglia and Daniel Reichard.

Vincent Sardi, Jr. Memorial

March 3, 2007 at the Schoenfeld Theatre

Photo by Aubrey Reuben

The stage of the Schoenfeld Theatre was turned into a makeshift version of Sardi's Restaurant as a near-capacity crowd gathered to remember restaurateur Vincent Sardi, Jr., who passed away January 4 at age 91. Shubert Chairman Gerald Schoenfeld pretended to be an impatient diner at Sardi's eatery. Actor and choreographer Donald Saddler played a tap-dancing waiter trying to impress Schoenfeld and his guest, director Harold Prince, as they introduced speakers and a slide show covering Sardi's long life.

(L-R): Donald Saddler, Gerald Schoenfeld and Harold Prince at a recreation of a Sardi's table on the stage of the Schoenfeld Theatre.

125th Anniversary Gala of the Actors' Fund of America

April 30, 2007 at the Waldorf-Astoria Hotel

The Actors' Fund held its annual gala on April 30, 2007, which New York City mayor Michael Bloomberg declared Actors' Fund Day in honor of the Fund's 125th anniversary. Unlike years past, when the gathering honored an individual, this year's party was held to celebrate The Actors' Fund itself. Stars came out in droves to fete an organization that helps needy members of the entertainment industry.

Photo by Aubrey Reuben

(L-R): Josh Strickland of *Tarzan*; Rebecca Luker, Gavin Lee and Ashley Brown of *Mary Poppins*.

Nothing Like a Dame

March 19, 2007 at The Marquis Theatre

A host of the theatre's leading ladies took part in the 12th Annual Nothing Like a Dame concert March 19 at the Marquis Theatre, raising $300,000 for The Phyllis Newman Women's Health Initiative of The Actors' Fund of America.

The event featured performances by Shoshana Bean, Liz Callaway, Paul Castree, Kate Clinton, Joyce DiDonato, Jill Eikenberry, Jenn Gambatese, Ana Gasteyer, Milena Govich, Jennifer Holliday, Beth Leavel, Jose Llana, Tshidi Manye, Maureen McGovern, Tiler Peck, Lynn Redgrave, Barbara Rubenstein, Lea Salonga, Jennifer Smith, Jason Michael Snow, Brooke Tansley, Barbara Walsh, the Westchester Academy of Dance, the women of the Broadway cast of *Company* and "One Life to Live" co-stars Renee Goldsberry and Tika Sumpter.

Photos by Aubrey Reuben

1. Lynn Redgrave at the Marquis Theatre.
2. Jennifer Holliday and opera mezzo soprano Joyce DiDonato.
3. Jason Michael Snow, Jose Llana and Paul Castree present a check for $300,000 to Lynn Redgrave and choreographer Rhonda Miller.
4. Ana Gasteyer.
5. Members of the Westchester Academy of Dance.

The 21st Annual Easter Bonnet Competition

April 23 and 24, 2007 at the Minskoff Theatre

Photos by Aubrey Reuben

Showing that theatergoers' generosity knows no geographical bounds, the national touring company of *Jersey Boys* staged an upset April 24, 2007, winning the grand prize at the Broadway Cares/Equity Fights AIDS 21st annual Easter Bonnet Competition by raising $236,844 for the fight against the deadly disease. It's the first time a show other than a musical on Broadway won the top prize.

In another upset, the prize for best bonnet presentation went to non-musical *Journey's End* for a comedy skit—a musical adaptation of their World War I drama, retitled *Journey's End: The Underdogs of War*. The macabre *Journey's End* bonnet consisted of a doughboy helmet pierced by a comically large shell and surmounted by a recruiting poster, saying "We Want YOU."

All told, $3,345,998 was raised by more than 60 participating shows in six weeks of post-show appeals from their respective stages, nearly equalling the previous record, 2004's $3.4 million.

Special guests Vanessa Redgrave (*The Year of Magical Thinking*) and David Hyde Pierce (*Curtains*) presented the awards at the Minskoff Theatre following two days of performances April 23 and 24, 2007

Other awards:

The Broadway *play* that raised the most money: *The Coast of Utopia*— $18,412.

The Off-Broadway show that raised the most: *In the Heights*— $26,659.

Runners-up for fundraising (all Broadway musicals): *Wicked* ($227,769), *The Color Purple* ($168,621), *Mary Poppins* ($164,373) and *The Lion King* ($163,175).

Runners-up for best bonnet and skit: *Hairspray*, *In the Heights* (tie) and *The Lion King*.

Special Award for Best Designed and Constructed Bonnet: *The Phantom of the Opera*.

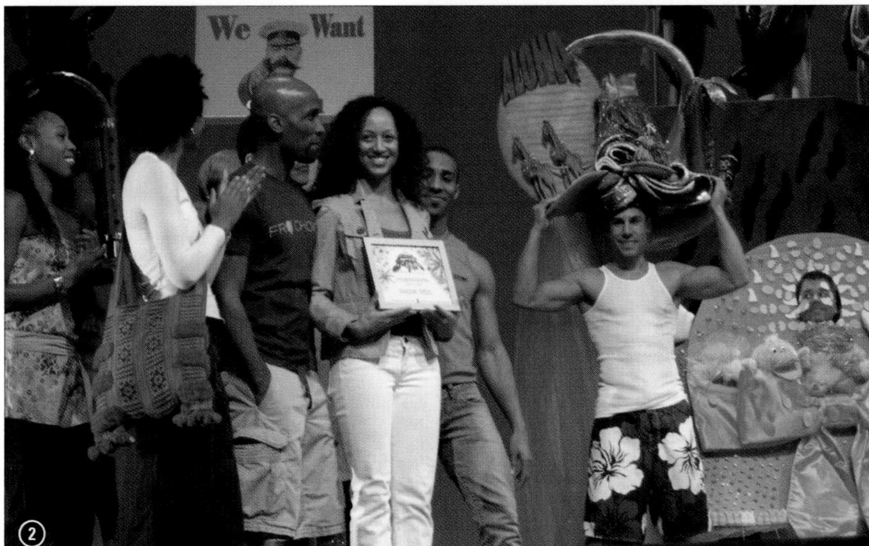

1. Special guests Vanessa Redgrave and David Hyde Pierce (front) read the names of the winners.
2. Actors from the competing shows await the reading of the winners. Bonnets from *The Lion King* and *The 25th Annual Putnam County Spelling Bee* can be seen at right.
3. Dancers reveal the record-breaking total.

Other Theatre Awards

Covering the 2006-2007 Broadway Season

DRAMA DESK AWARDS

Outstanding Play: Tom Stoppard, *The Coast of Utopia*
Outstanding Musical: *Spring Awakening*
Outstanding Revival of a Play: *Journey's End*
Outstanding Revival of a Musical: *Company*
Outstanding Actor in a Play: Frank Langella, *Frost/Nixon*
Outstanding Actress in a Play: Eve Best, *A Moon for the Misbegotten*
Outstanding Actor in a Musical: Raúl Esparza, *Company*
Outstanding Actresss in a Musical (tie): Audra McDonald, *110 in the Shade* and Donna Murphy, *LoveMusik*
Outstanding Featured Actor in a Play: Boyd Gaines, *Journey's End*
Outstanding Featured Actress in a Play: Martha Plimpton, *The Coast of Utopia*
Outstanding Featured Actor in a Musical: Gavin Lee, *Mary Poppins*
Outstanding Featured Actress in a Musical: Debra Monk, *Curtains*
Outstanding Director of a Play: Jack O'Brien, *The Coast of Utopia*
Outstanding Director of a Musical: Michael Mayer, *Spring Awakening*
Outstanding Choreography: Andy Blankenbuehler, *In the Heights* (OB)
Outstanding Music: Duncan Sheik, *Spring Awakening*
Oustanding Lyrics: Steven Sater, *Spring Awakening*
Outstanding Book of a Musical: Rupert Holmes and Peter Stone, *Curtains*
Outstanding Music for a Play: Mark Bennett, *The Coast of Utopia*
Outstanding Orchestrations (tie): Mary-Mitchell Campbell, *Company* and Jonathan Tunick, *LoveMusik*
Outstanding Set Design of a Play: Bob Crowley and Scott Pask, *The Coast of Utopia*
Outstanding Set Design of a Musical: Bob Crowley, *Mary Poppins*
Outstanding Costume Design: Catherine Zuber, *The Coast of Utopia*
Outstanding Lighting Design: Brian MacDevitt, Kenneth Posner and Natasha Katz, *The Coast of Utopia*
Outstanding Sound Design: Gregory Clark, *Journey's End*
Outstanding Solo Performance: Vanessa Redgrave, *The Year of Magical Thinking*
Unique Theatrical Experience: *Edward Scissorhands* (OB)

(L-R): Donna Murphy, Raúl Esparza and Audra McDonald all won Drama Desk Awards.

OUTER CRITICS CIRCLE AWARDS

Outstanding Broadway Play: *The Coast of Utopia*
Outstanding Broadway Musical: *Spring Awakening*
Outstanding Off-Broadway Play: *Indian Blood*
Outstanding Off-Broadway Musical: *In the Heights*
Outstanding New Score: *Spring Awakening*
Outstanding Revival of a Play: *Journey's End*
Outstanding Revival of a Musical: *Company*
Outstanding Actor in a Play: Frank Langella, *Frost/Nixon*
Outstanding Actress in a Play: Eve Best, *A Moon for the Misbegotten*
Outstanding Actor in a Musical: Raúl Esparza, *Company*
Outstanding Actress in a Musical: Donna Murphy, *LoveMusik*
Outstanding Featured Actor in a Play: Boyd Gaines, *Journey's End*
Outstanding Featured Actress in a Play: Martha Plimpton, *The Coast of Utopia*
Outstanding Featured Actor in a Musical: David Pittu, *LoveMusik*
Outstanding Featured Actress in a Musical: Karen Ziemba, *Curtains*
Outstanding Solo Performance: Nilaja Sun, *No Child...* (OB)
Outstanding Direction of a Play: Jack O'Brien, *The Coast of Utopia*
Outstanding Direction of a Musical: Michael Mayer, *Spring Awakening*
Outstanding Choreography: Andy Blankenbuehler, *In the Heights* (OB)
Outstanding Set Design: Bob Crowley and Scott Pask, *The Coast of Utopia*
Outstanding Costume Design: Catherine Zuber, *The Coast of Utopia*
Outstanding Lighting Design: Brian MacDevitt, Kenneth Posner and Natasha Katz, *The Coast of Utopia*
Special Achievement Awards: Angela Lansbury and Marian Seldes, *Deuce*
John Gassner Award (presented for an American play, preferably by a new playwright): Nilaja Sun, *No Child...* (OB)

THE PULITZER PRIZE FOR DRAMA

Rabbit Hole by David Lindsay-Abaire

NY DRAMA CRITICS' CIRCLE AWARDS

Best Play: Tom Stoppard, *The Coast of Utopia*
Best American Play: August Wilson, *Radio Golf*
Best Musical: Duncan Sheik and Steven Sater, *Spring Awakening*
Special Citation: *Journey's End*

THE DRAMA LEAGUE AWARDS

Distinguished Production of a Play: *The Coast of Utopia*
Distinguished Production of a Musical: *Spring Awakening*
Distinguished Revival of a Play: *Journey's End*
Distinguished Revival of a Musical: *Company*
Distinguished Performance Award: Liev Schreiber, *Talk Radio* and *Macbeth*

THEATRE WORLD AWARDS

For outstanding Broadway or Off-Broadway debuts:
Fantasia Barrino, *The Color Purple*
Eve Best, *A Moon for the Misbegotten*
Mary Birdsong, *Martin Short: Fame Becomes Me*
Erin Davie, *Grey Gardens*
Xanthe Elbrick, *Coram Boy*
Johnny Galecki, *Little Dog Laughed*
Jonathan Groff, *Spring Awakening*
Gavin Lee, *Mary Poppins*
Lin-Manuel Miranda, *In the Heights* (OB)
Bill Nighy, *The Vertical Hour*
Stark Sands, *Journey's End*
Nilaja Sun, *No Child...* (OB)

Photos by Aubrey Reuben

Designers William Ivey Long and Catherine Zuber at the Drama Desk nominees' reception.

THE CLARENCE DERWENT AWARDS

From Actors' Equity for "most promising female and male performers on the New York metropolitan scene":
Leslie Kritzer, *Legally Blonde*
Lin-Manuel Miranda, *In the Heights* (OB)

THE RICHARD SEFF AWARDS

From Actors' Equity, to female and male character actors 50 years of age or older:
Mary Louise Wilson, *Grey Gardens*
David Margulies, *All That I Will Ever Be* (OB) and *The Accomplices* (OB)

THE IRENE SHARAFF AWARDS

From the Theatre Development Fund, for outstanding theatrical design:
Robert L.B. Tobin Award for Lifetime Achievement: Santo Loquasto
Lifetime Achievement Award: Bob Mackie
Young Master Award: Murell Horton
Artisan Award: Kermit Love
Posthumous Award: Rouben Ter-Arutunian

The Tony Awards

June 10, 2007 at Radio City Music Hall

Photos by Aubrey Reuben

Spring Awakening, The Coast of Utopia, Company and *Journey's End* won the major production categories of the 2007 Tony Awards.

The 61st annual awards, representing excellence in Broadway theatre for the 2006-07 season, were presented at Radio City Music Hall. In lieu of a single host, some 40 presenters introduced portions of the show and handed out the awards.

Youth and history seemed to dominate the proceedings as *Spring*, about the sexual awakening of a group of repressed German teenagers, took home eight Tonys, including Best Musical, Best Score, Best Book, Best Director of a Musical, Best Featured Actor in a Musical and several technical awards. Composer Duncan Sheik earned two awards, for Score and Orchestrations. His collaborator, Steven Sater, also won two: sharing the Score Award and winning Best Book in his own right.

Tom Stoppard's *The Coast of Utopia*, which was presented in three parts, *Voyage, Shipwreck* and *Salvage,* at Lincoln Center Theater, earned seven Tonys, the most ever for a single play. Because of its limited subscription run, the drama about European revolutionaries in the 19th century was already closed by the time it was named Best Play.

Journey's End's win as Best Revival of a Play was bittersweet, as the show about World War I played its final performance earlier the same day.

Frank Langella's performance as President Richard Nixon in *Frost/Nixon* earned him the Tony as Best Leading Actor in a Play. Julie White's performance as a stop-at-nothing talent agent in *The Little Dog Laughed* won her the Tony as Best Leading Actress in a Play over powerhouse performances like Vanessa Redgrave's in *The Year of Magical Thinking* and Angela Lansbury's in *Deuce.*

The heralded stage adaptation of Disney's *Mary Poppins* earned just a single award, Best Scenic Design for a Musical.

Here are all the nominees, with the winners listed in **bold**.

Best Play
The Coast of Utopia
Frost/Nixon
The Little Dog Laughed
Radio Golf

1. Winners (L-R): Christine Ebersole of *Grey Gardens*, Frank Langella of *Frost/Nixon*, Julie White of *Little Dog Laughed* and David Hyde Pierce of *Curtains*.
2. *Spring Awakening* writers (L-R) Duncan Sheik and Steven Sater won two Tonys each.
3. Nominee and presenter Angela Lansbury (*Deuce*) arrives at Radio City Music Hall.
4. *Coast of Utopia* author Tom Stoppard (C) with (L) André Bishop and (R) Bernard Gersten of Lincoln Center Theater.

The Tony Awards

Best Musical
Curtains
Grey Gardens
Mary Poppins
Spring Awakening

Best Revival of a Play
Inherit the Wind
Journey's End
Talk Radio
Translations

Best Revival of a Musical
The Apple Tree
A Chorus Line
Company
110 in the Shade

Best Performance by a Leading Actor in a Play
Boyd Gaines, *Journey's End*
Frank Langella, *Frost/Nixon*
Brían F. O'Byrne, *The Coast of Utopia*
Christopher Plummer, *Inherit the Wind*
Liev Schreiber, *Talk Radio*

Best Performance by a Leading Actress in a Play
Eve Best, *A Moon for the Misbegotten*
Swoosie Kurtz, *Heartbreak House*
Angela Lansbury, *Deuce*
Vanessa Redgrave, *The Year of Magical Thinking*
Julie White, *The Little Dog Laughed*

Best Performance by a Leading Actor in a Musical
Michael Cerveris, *LoveMusik*
Raúl Esparza, *Company*
Jonathan Groff, *Spring Awakening*
Gavin Lee, *Mary Poppins*
David Hyde Pierce, *Curtains*

Best Performance by a Leading Actress in a Musical
Laura Bell Bundy, *Legally Blonde The Musical*
Christine Ebersole, *Grey Gardens*
Audra McDonald, *110 in the Shade*
Debra Monk, *Curtains*
Donna Murphy, *LoveMusik*

Best Performance by a Featured Actor in a Play
Anthony Chisholm, *Radio Golf*
Billy Crudup, *The Coast of Utopia*
Ethan Hawke, *The Coast of Utopia*
John Earl Jelks, *Radio Golf*
Stark Sands, *Journey's End*

Best Performance by a Featured Actress in a Play
Jennifer Ehle, *The Coast of Utopia*
Xanthe Elbrick, *Coram Boy*
Dana Ivey, *Butley*
Jan Maxwell, *Coram Boy*
Martha Plimpton, *The Coast of Utopia*

Photos by Aubrey Reuben

1. Mary Louise Wilson of *Grey Gardens* brandishes her Tony for Best Featured Actress in a Musical.
2. (L-R): Nominees Rupert Holmes and John Kander, authors of *Curtains*.
3. The cast of *Spring Awakening* enjoys the spotlight.
4. Nominee Orfeh (*Legally Blonde*) on the red carpet.
5. (L-R): Nominees John Earl Jelks and Anthony Chisholm (*Radio Golf*) enter Radio City.
6. Judith Blazer with *LoveMusik* co-star and nominee David Pittu.

The Tony Awards

Best Performance by a Featured Actor in a Musical
Brooks Ashmanskas, *Martin Short: Fame Becomes Me*
Christian Borle, *Legally Blonde The Musical*
John Cullum, *110 in the Shade*
John Gallagher, Jr., *Spring Awakening*
David Pittu, *LoveMusik*

Best Performance by a Featured Actress in a Musical
Charlotte d'Amboise, *A Chorus Line*
Rebecca Luker, *Mary Poppins*
Orfeh, *Legally Blonde The Musical*
Mary Louise Wilson, *Grey Gardens*
Karen Ziemba, *Curtains*

Best Book of a Musical
Rupert Holmes & Peter Stone, *Curtains*
Doug Wright, *Grey Gardens*
Heather Hach, *Legally Blonde The Musical*
Steven Sater, *Spring Awakening*

Best Original Score (Music and/or Lyrics) Written for the Theatre
Music: John Kander, Lyrics: Fred Ebb, John Kander and Rupert Holmes, *Curtains*
Music: Scott Frankel, Lyrics: Michael Korie, *Grey Gardens*
Music & Lyrics: Laurence O'Keefe & Nell Benjamin, *Legally Blonde The Musical*
Music: Duncan Sheik, Lyrics: Steven Sater, *Spring Awakening*

Best Direction of a Play
Michael Grandage, *Frost/Nixon*
David Grindley, *Journey's End*
Jack O'Brien, *The Coast of Utopia*
Melly Still, *Coram Boy*

Best Direction of a Musical
John Doyle, *Company*
Scott Ellis, *Curtains*
Michael Greif, *Grey Gardens*
Michael Mayer, *Spring Awakening*

Best Choreography
Rob Ashford, *Curtains*
Matthew Bourne & Stephen Mear, *Mary Poppins*
Bill T. Jones, *Spring Awakening*
Jerry Mitchell, *Legally Blonde The Musical*

Best Orchestrations
Bruce Coughlin, *Grey Gardens*
Duncan Sheik, *Spring Awakening*
Jonathan Tunick, *LoveMusik*
Jonathan Tunick, *110 in the Shade*

Best Scenic Design of a Play
Bob Crowley & Scott Pask, *The Coast of Utopia*
Jonathan Fensom, *Journey's End*
David Gallo, *Radio Golf*
Ti Green & Melly Still, *Coram Boy*

Photos by Aubrey Reuben

1. The cast of *Company* on their way to a win for Best Revival of a Musical.
2. The cast of *Journey's End,* named Best Revival of a Play.
3. Original *Oklahoma!* cast member Celeste Holm.

Best Scenic Design of a Musical
Bob Crowley, *Mary Poppins*
Christine Jones, *Spring Awakening*
Anna Louizos, *High Fidelity*
Allen Moyer, *Grey Gardens*

Best Costume Design of a Play
Ti Green & Melly Still, *Coram Boy*
Jane Greenwood, *Heartbreak House*
Santo Loquasto, *Inherit the Wind*
Catherine Zuber, *The Coast of Utopia*

Best Costume Design of a Musical
Gregg Barnes, *Legally Blonde The Musical*
Bob Crowley, *Mary Poppins*
Susan Hilferty, *Spring Awakening*
William Ivey Long, *Grey Gardens*

Best Lighting Design of a Play
Paule Constable, *Coram Boy*
Brian MacDevitt, *Inherit the Wind*
Brian MacDevitt, Kenneth Posner and Natasha Katz, *The Coast of Utopia*
Jason Taylor, *Journey's End*

Best Lighting Design of a Musical
Kevin Adams, *Spring Awakening*
Christopher Akerlind, *110 in the Shade*
Howard Harrison, *Mary Poppins*
Peter Kaczorowski, *Grey Gardens*

Regional Theatre Tony Award
Alliance Theatre, Atlanta, Georgia

Autographs

Faculty

The Shubert Organization

Photos by Ben Strothmann

Gerald Schoenfeld
Chairman

Philip J. Smith
President

Robert E. Wankel
Executive Vice President

Jujamcyn Theatres

Photos courtesy Jujamcyn Theatres

Rocco Landesman
President

Paul Libin
Producing Director

Jack Viertel
Creative Director

Faculty

The Nederlander Organization

File Photo

James M. Nederlander
Chairman

Freida Belviso

Jim Boese

Susan Lee

Jack Meyer

Photos by David Gewirtzman

Photo by Ben Strothmann

James L. Nederlander
President

Photo by Ben Strothmann

Kathleen Raitt

Photo by Ben Strothmann

Nick Scandalios

Photo by David Gewirtzman

Herschel Waxman

Photo by Ben Strothmann

NEDERLANDER STAFF
Front Row (L-R): Rachel Jukofsky (Group Sales), Tracey Malinowski, Phyllis Buono (Account Manager), Rina Beacco (Assistant Comptroller), Kim Jugmohan (Accounting).
Second Row (L-R): Thuy Dang (Accounting), Marjorie Stewart (Assistant to Nick Scandalios), Maria Manduca (Accounting), Maleka Musliwala (Accounting), Alyce Cozzi (Assistant Comptroller), Renee Pressley (Accounting), Alice Gold (Reception).
Third Row (L-R): Ken Happel (Assistant to James L. Nederlander), David Vaughn (Operations), Julia Barr (Accounting), Blair Zwillman (Assistant to James M. Nederlander), Rick Kaye, Susan Knoll (House Seats), Lisa Lent (Accounting), Nancy Santiago (Accounting), Josh Salez, Brian Harasek (Group Sales) and Rebecca Velazquez (Group Sales).

Faculty

Disney Theatricals

Front Row (L-R): Michele Steckler, Jonathan Olson, Barbara Toben, Isander Rojas, Nick Judge, Juil Kim, Shillae Anderson, Jessica Doina, Jay Kimbro, Kerry McGrath, Francesca Panagopoulos, Janine McGuire.

Second Row (L-R): Gregory Hanoian, Dusty Bennett, Tivon Marcus, Nick Falzon, David Scott, Eric Kratzer, Cara Moccia, Kyle Young, Andy Singh, Ryan Pears, Dana Torres, Craig Buckley, Jason Zammit, Liz Jurist.

Third Row (L-R): Joe Doughney, Karl Chmielewski, Kevin McGuire, Cynthia Young, Michael Giammatteo, Melanie Montes, Shawn Baker, Violeta Burlaza, Marshall Purdy, Todd Lacy, Randy Meyer, Tom Kingsley, Roseann Warren, Lauren Daghini.

Fourth Row (L-R): Michael Height, Tara Engler, Dana James, Tatiana Bautista, Cristi Finn, Dayle Gruet, Justin Gee, Joe McClafferty, Seth Stuhl, Thomas Schlenk, Suyin Chan, Allan Frost, Alan Levey, Canara Price.

Back Row (L-R): Kymberly Tubbs, Thomas Schumacher, Amy Caldamone, Laura Eichholz, Jane Abramson and Jonathan Hanson.

Not Pictured: Dana Amendola, Peter Avery, Scott Benedict, David Benken, Chris Berger, Manisha Brahmbhatt, Michael Buchanan, Brian Bustos, Michael Cassel, Eduardo Castro, Ken Cerniglia, Stephanie Cheek, Tracy Christensen, Amy Clark, Keith Cooper, Steven Downing, Peter Eastman, Rick Elice, Steve Fickinger, Andrew Flatt, Cristina Fornaris, Harry Gold, Marey Griffith, Michele Groner, Lance Gutterman, June Heindel, Scott Hemerling, Suzanne Jakel, Bryan Johnson, Jeff Knizner, Ron Kollen, Jeff Lee, John Loiacono, Shaina Low, Anthony Lyn, Aubrey Lynch, Lisa Mitchell, Denny Moyes, Tanya Noginova, Kelli Palan, Mary Peterson, Anne Quart, Mark Rozzano, Jen Rudin Pearson, Kisha Santiago, David Schrader, Clifford Schwartz, James Thane, Fiona Thomas, John Tiggeloven, Reena Vadehra, Brian Webb and Doc Zorthian.

(L-R): Laura Eichholz, Dave Ehle, Verity Van Tassel and Jeff Parvin.

Faculty

Roundabout Theatre Company

Photo by Ben Strothmann

Front Row Sitting in Chairs (L-R): Harold Wolpert (Managing Director), Todd Haimes (Artistic Director), Julia Levy (Executive Director).
Second Row Sitting in Chairs (L-R): Jeffory Lawson (Director of Development), David Steffen (Director of Marketing & Sales Promotion), Rebecca Habel (General Manager/Laura Pels Theatre), Greg Backstrom (Associate Managing Director), Sydney Beers (General Manager/AA, Studio 54), Stephen Deutsch (Human Resources Manager), Jim Seggelink (Director of Sales Operations), Susan Neiman (Director of Finance), Nancy Hirschmann (General Counsel).
Third Row Sitting in Chairs (L-R): Kate Schwabe, Nicholas Caccavo, Julie D'Andrea, Steve Schaeffer, Monica Sidorchuk, Elisa Papa, Robert Weinstein, Doug Sutcliffe, Josh Cohen, Yonit Kafka, Matt Armstrong.
Fourth Row Sitting in Chairs (L-R): Lillian Soto, Nalane Singh, Elisa Mala, Catherine Fitzpatrick, Katrina Foy, Dollye Evans, Jessica Nash, Gavin Brown, Tova Heller, Lindsay Ericson.
Fifth Row Sitting in Chairs (L-R): Stefanie Schussel, Sari Abraham, Erica Rotstein, Ashley Turner, Jill Rafson, Mike DePope, Daniel Gabriel, Joe Clark, DJ Thacker, Frank Surdi.

Sixth Row Standing (L-R): Erica Ruff, Kara Kandel, Sarah Krasnow, Deanna Cirino, Sarah Malone, Jennifer DeBruin, Tina Bishko, Charlie Garbowski, Ethan Ubell, Thom Walsh, Pam Unger.
Seventh Row Standing (L-R): Steve Ryan, Darnell Franklin, Micah Kraybill, Robert Traille, Jeff Goodman, Jillian Brewster, Caroline Patterson, Glenn Merwede, Ellen Holt, John Haynes, Jeff Monteith, David Pittman, Willie Phillips, Magali Western, Abraham David, Jacob Burstein-Stern, Robert Morgan, Adam Elsberry, Mead Margulies.

Sitting on Floor (Left, Front to Back): Kate Bartoldus, Ashley Firestone, Allison Baucom, Tania Camargo, David Solomon, Maggie Cantrick, Christopher Taggart, Margaret Casagrande.
Sitting on Floor (Right, Front to Back): Trina Cox, Robert Kane, Edwin Camacho, Zipporah Aguasvivas, John LaBarbera, Dorothea Kenul, Nichole Jennino, Kaia Rafoss, Hannah Weitzman and Scott Kelly.

Faculty

League of American Theatres and Producers

Photo by Ben Strothmann

Gerald Schoenfeld
Chairman

Photo by Connie Ashley

Charlotte St. Martin
Executive Director

Photo by Ben Strothmann

Back Row (L-R): Alan Cohen, Roger Calderon, Lindsay Florestal, Laura Fayans, Roxanne Rodriguez, Joy Axelrad, Ed Sandler.
Third Row (L to R): Robert Davis, Jim Lochner, Jennifier Stewart, Karen Hauser, Zenovia Varelis, Robin Fox, Colin Gibson, Jim Echikson, Ben Pesner.
Second Row: (L to R): Charlotte St. Martin, Erica Ryan, Patty Casterlin, Rachel Reiner, Jan Svendsen.
Front Row: (L to R): Jean Kroeper, Seth Popper, Britt Marden, Amy Steinhaus, Neal Freeman, Ed Forman.

Not Pictured: Irving Cheskin, Barbara Janowitz, Shoshana Parets and Harriet Slaughter.

Live Nation

Photo by David Gewirtzman

Front Row (L-R): Paul Dietz, Alison Spiriti, Jennifer Costello, David Anderson.
Back Row (L-R): Steve Winton, Susie Krajsa and Steve Winton.

Faculty

Manhattan Theatre Club

Front Row (L-R): Jill Turner Lloyd, Mandy Greenfield, Paige Evans, Lynne Meadow, Barry Grove, Florie Seery, Jeffrey Bledsoe, Debra Waxman, David Shookhoff.

Second Row (L-R): Emily Shooltz, Annie MacRae, Amy Loe, Charles Graytok, Stephanie Madonna, Andrea Paul, Lindsey Brooks Sag, Tom O'Connor, Mark Bowers.

Third Row (L-R): Nancy Piccione, Kacy O'Brien, Ashley Dunn, Jessica Sadowski, Andrea Gorzell, Ann Mundorff, Allison Gutstein, Antonello DiBenedetto, Adam Cook.

Fourth Row (L-R): Jon Haddorff, Rebecca Stang, Sage Young, Amy Harris, Rebekah Dewald, Rebecca Atwood, Laura Roumanos, Kristin Svenningsen, Sarah Ryndak.

Back Row (L-R): Avishai Cohen, Karen Zornow Leiding, Liz Halakan, Alexis Allen, Joshua Jacobson, Holly Kinney, Erin Moeller and Lisa McNulty.

Faculty

American Theatre Wing

Photo by Kristen Luciani

BOARD OF DIRECTORS AND STAFF

Back Row Standing (L-R): Robb Perry (Staff), Howard Sherman (Staff), Jeffrey Eric Jenkins (Board), Mallory Factor (Board), David Brown (Board), Jay S. Harris (Board), Theodore S. Chapin (Board), William Craver (Board), Ronald S. Konecky (Board), Randy Ellen Lutterman (Staff), Matt Jarrett (Staff), Raisa Ushomirskiy (Staff).

Seated (L-R): Michael P. Price (Board), Dasha Epstein (Board), Lucie Arnaz (Board), Sondra Gilman (Board), Douglas B. Leeds (Board), Enid Nemy (Board), Pia Lindström (Board), Anita Jaffe (Board).

Kneeling (L-R): Joanna Sheehan (Staff), Myra Wong (Staff), Jeremy Desmon (Staff), Lexie Pregosin (Staff).

Not Pictured: Marlene Hess, Jo Sullivan Loesser, Jane Safer, Peter Schneider, Alan Siegel, Howard Stringer.

ATW Theatre Intern Group

Photo by Ben Strothmann

Theatre Intern Group Manager Lexie Pregosin (standing, far right) of the American Theatre Wing with a contingent of 2006-2007 Theatre Intern Group members.

Faculty

Tony Award Productions

Don't Say "Break a Leg!"

Kit Ingui, Sue Wagner, Elizabeth I. McCann, John Johnson and Steve Sosnowski.

Photos and layout by Tony Award Productions

Yonkers Meets *Jersey*

Joey Parnes with John Lloyd Young.

Ladies and Gentlemen, the TAPettes!

Trini Huschle, Sue Wagner, Kit Ingui and Emily Campbell.

Our Little Shutterbug

Anthony Chisholm and Gaydon Phillips

You Wouldn't Recognize Him Without It.

John Johnson

You Wouldn't Know It To Look at Them But These Gorgeous Girls Spend Their Days Doing Manual Labor

Katrina Dibbini, Maddie Felix and Caryn Morrow.

There's Got to Be a Morning After

Michelle Perna

TonyAwards.com

(L-R): Andrew McGibbon and Ben Pesner.

Photos courtesy of TonyAwards.com

Producing Companies

Photo by David Gewirtzman

RICHARD FRANKEL PRODUCTIONS and THE FRANKEL GROUP
Bottom Row (L-R): Richard Frankel, Steven Baruch, Marc Routh, Tom Viertel.
Second Row (L-R): Denise Cooper, Michael Sinder, Rod Kaats, Michael Naumann, Roddy Pimentel, Jo Porter, Sara Schatz.
Third Row (L-R): Lori Steiger-Perry, Kristi Bergman, Leslie Anne Pinney, Myriah Perkins, Tracy Geltman, Jason Pelusio, Susan Keappock, Aliza Wassner, Tim Grassel.
Fourth Row (L-R): Stephanie Adamczyk, Jia Liu, Maia Sutton, Melissa Marano, John Retsios, Rachel Kiwi, Tanase Popa, Heidi Libby, Amy Clarke
Top Row (L-R): Heather Allen, Dara Messing, Ashley Pitman, Nicole O'Bleanis, John DiMeglio, Robert Sherrill, Allison Engallena, Josh Saletnik and Megan Fortunato.

Photo by Ben Strothmann

BARRY AND FRAN WEISSLER

Photo Courtesy Cameron Mackintosh

CAMERON MACKINTOSH

Photo Courtesy Waxman and Williams

WAXMAN/WILLIAMS ENTERTAINMENT
(L-R): Anita Waxman and Elizabeth Williams.

Faculty

Producing Companies

Photo by Ben Strothmann

LINCOLN CENTER THEATER
(L-R): André Bishop (Artistic Director) and Bernard Gersten (Executive Producer).

Photo by Ben Strothmann

VIENNA WAITS PRODUCTIONS
John Breglio

Photo by Ben Strothmann

THE COOPER COMPANY
Front Row (L-R): Amanda Rhodes Taylor (Executive Assistant), Mink Chu (Executive Assistant).

Back Row (L-R): Jason Viarengo (Theatre Development Associate), Pamela Cooper (President), Robert Sherrill (Booking Agent).

Photo courtesy of Arielle Tepper

ARIELLE TEPPER

Photo by Aubrey Reuben

ROGER BERLIND

Faculty

Theatre Development Fund and TKTS

Front Row (L-R): Charles James Parks, Joy Cooper, Ann Mathieson, Veronica Claypool, Victoria Bailey, Eric Sobel, Terry Erkkila.
Second Row (L-R): Campbell Ringel, Katya Andreiev, Joe Cali, Tymand Staggs, Lisa Carling, Marianna Houston, Doug Smith, David LeShay.
Third Row (L-R): Cheryl Schoonmaker, Paula Torres, William Castellano, Julian Christenberry, Gregory Poplyk, George Connolly.
Fourth Row (L-R): Costas Michalopoulos, Tina Kirsimae, Fran Polino, Tom Westerman, Lawrence Paone, Michelle St. Hill.
Fifth Row (L-R): Christophe Mentor, Rob Neely, Michael Yaccarino, Branden Huldeen, Eve Rodriguez, Richard Price.
Sixth Row (L-R): Patty Allen, Catherine Lizima, Howard Marren and Jessica Wells.

TKTS TREASURERS
Front Row (L-R): Sherry Teitelbaum, Lawrence Paone, Laura Turcinovic, Michael Campanella, Tony Heron, Rajesh Sharma.
Back Row (L-R): Robert Kitson, John Palumbo, Brian Roeder, William Castellano, Wesley Heron and William Holze.

Faculty

Actors' Equity Association

Mark Zimmerman
President

John Connolly
Executive Director

Photos by Ben Strothmann

NATIONAL COUNCIL
Front Row (L-R): Paige Price (1st Vice President), Mark Zimmerman (President), Jean-Paul Richard (2nd Vice President).
Back Row (L-R): Ira Mont (3rd Vice President), Arne Gundersen (Eastern Regional Vice President), Conard Fowkes (Secretary Treasurer).

Front Row (L-R): David Thorn, Helene Ross, Christopher LaGalante, Debbie Johnson, John Fasulo.
Back Row (L-R): Stacey Maya, Matthew Summersgill, Lauren Keating, Allison Plotkin, Courtney Godan and Karlene Laemmie.

Front Row (L-R): Cara Kossman, Beverly Sloan, Kathryn Herrera, Christopher Williams, Nancy Fattorini, John Baron.

Second Row (L-R): Barry Rosenberg, Duane Upp, Catherine Jayne, Dawn Campbell, Mandi LeBlanc, Valerie LaVarco.

Third Row (L-R): Gisela Valenzuela, Joel Solari, Maria Cameron, Karen Masters, Gretchen Souerwine, William Adriance.

Fourth Row (L-R): Thomas Kaub, Kevin Pinzon, Jessica Palermo, Melissa Colgan, Sylvina Persaud, Tatiana Kouloumbis, Diane Raimondi, Gary Dimon, Joe Erdey, Naomi Major, Walt Kiskaddon, Louise Foisy, Russell Lehrer and Zalina Hoosein.

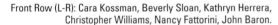

EXECUTIVE WING, 16th FLOOR GROUP
Front Row (L-R): Spring Streetman, Marie Gottschall, Steve DiPaola, John Fasulo, Diana Previtire.

Middle Row (L-R): Flora Stamatiades, Doug Beebe, Ann Fortuno, Karen Nothman, Stephanie Masucci.

Back Row (L-R): Joseph De Michele, Stuart Levy, Elly Deutsch, Robert Fowler, Megann McManus, Julie Coppola and Frank Horak.

IATSE Local 306 Motion Picture Projectionists, Video Technicians and Allied Crafts (Ushers)

Photos by Ben Strothmann

Seated (L-R): Lulu Caso, Dotty Rogan and Rita Russell.
Standing (L-R): Arlene Reilly, Ken Costigan, Mim Pollock, Hugo Capra, Mike Terr, Joe Rivierzo, Lea Lefler and Larry Aptekar.

United Scenic Artists, IATSE Local 829

(L-R): Cynthia Parker-Frye, Susan Abbott, Michael McBride, Beverly Miller, Patrick Langevin, Cathy Santucci-Keator, Carl Baldasso and Cecilia Friederichs.

Faculty

Association of Theatrical Press Agents and Managers

Photos by Ben Strothmann

Seated (L-R): Rick Miramontez, Susan Elrod, Maria Somma, Lauri Wilson, Jeremy Shaffer.
Standing (L-R): David Calhoun, Dick Seader, Bruce Cohen and Gordon G. Forbes.

Society of Stage Directors and Choreographers

Front Row (L-R): Tisa Chang (Executive Board), Ronald H. Shechtman (Counsel), Pamela Berlin (Executive Board President), Barbara Hauptman (Executive Director), Walter Bobbie (Executive Board), Barbara Wolkoff (Staff).
Middle Row (L-R): Larry Carpenter (Executive Board), Gretchen M. Michelfeld (Staff), Michele Holmes (Staff), Richard Hamburger (Executive Board), Sheldon Epps (Executive Board), Sue Lawless (Executive Board Secretary), Mary B. Robinson (Executive Board), Randy Anderson (Staff).
Back Row (L-R): Tracy Mendez (Staff), Evan Shoemake (Staff), Kim Rogers (Staff), Daniel Sullivan (Executive Board), Edie Cowan (Executive Board), Ethan McSweeny (Executive Board), Lonny Price (Executive Board), Rob Ashford (Executive Board), Julie Arenal (Executive Board), Renée Lasher (Staff), Karen Azenberg (Executive Board Executive Vice President), Samuel J. Bellinger (Staff), Mauro Melleno (Staff).
Executive Board Not Pictured: Mark Brokaw (Vice President), Gerald Freedman, Michael John Garcés, Wendy C. Goldberg, Doug Hughes (Treasurer), Paul Lazarus, Kathleen Marshall, Tom Moore, Amy Morton, Sharon Ott, Lisa Peterson, Susan H. Schulman, Oz Scott, David Warren and Chay Yew.

Treasurers & Ticket Sellers Union, IATSE Local 751

Front Row (L-R): Matthew Fearon, Vice President; Gene McElwain, Secretary-Treasurer/Business Manager.
Back Row (L-R): Kathy McBrearty; Patricia Quiles; Joseph Scanapicco, Jr., President; and Jim Sita.

Front Row (L-R): Matthew Fearon, Vice President; Joseph Scanapicco, Jr., President; Gene McElwain, Secretary-Treasurer/Business Manager.
Middle Row (L-R): Karen Winer, Noreen Morgan, Diane Heatherington, Greer Bond.
Back Row (L-R): Lawrence Paone, Michael Loiacono, Peter Attanasio, Jr. and John Nesbitt.

Photos by Ben Strothmann

Theatrical Wardrobe Union, IATSE Local 764

Front Row (L-R): Trustee Margaret Kurz, Members Thomas M. Slack, Barbara Hladsky, Zinda Williams, Jennifer Molloy and R.J. Malkmus.
Second Row (L-R): Members Richard Zimmer, Kevin Ritter, Haley Lieberman, Lisa Marie Grosso and Rose Mary Taylor, Trustees Veneda Truesdale and Rochelle Friedman.
Third Row (L-R): Business Representative James Hurley, Members Andrea Ross, Micheline Brown and Heidi Shulman, Trustee Shannon Koger, Member Sonya Wysocki, Trustee Patricia Sullivan, Member James Kabel.
Fourth Row (L-R): Trustee Charles Catanese, Members Paul Nicks, Kathryn Guida, Dwayne Trotman, Gregory Young, Marilyn Knotts and Suzanne Sponsler, Vice President Kristin Gardner
Fifth Row(L-R): Fund staff Michael Gemignani, Union staff Joan Boyce, Fund staff Binh Hoong, Secretary-Treasurer Jenna Krempel, Union staff Rosemary McGroarty, President Patricia A. White, Business Representative Frank Gallagher
Back Row (L-R): Chair of Trustees Danajean Cicerchi and Sergeant-at-Arms Terry La Vada.

Theatrical Teamsters, Local 817

EXECUTIVE BOARD
Front Row (L-R): Francis J. Connolly, Jr. (Business Agent & Union Trustee), Jim Leavey (Recording Secretary), Ed Iacobelli (Vice President).
Back Row (L-R): Mike Hyde (Union Trustee), Thomas R. O'Donnell (President), Thomas J. O'Donnell (Secretary-Treasurer), Kevin Keefe (Union Trustee).

STAFF
Front Row (L-R): Christine Harkerss (Human Resources), Tina Gusmano (Union Secretary).
Back Row (L-R): Terry Casaletta (Casting Director Organizer), Marge Marklin (Fund Secretary).

Not Present: Kathy Kreinbihl (Fund Administrator), Margie Vaeth (Union Secretary).

Service Employees International Union Local 32BJ

Photos by Ben Strothmann

EXECUTIVE OFFICERS
(L-R): Kevin Doyle (Executive Vice President), Héctor J. Figueroa (Secretary-Treasurer) and Michael P. Fishman (President).

International Union of Operating Engineers Local 30

Photo Courtesy Local 30

BUSINESS MANAGER
Jack Ahern

Faculty

Coalition of Broadway Unions and Guilds

Photo by Ben Strothmann

Seated (L-R): Mim Pollock (IATSE Local 306), Barbara Hauptman (Society of Stage Directors and Choreographers), Tracy Mendez (Society of Stage Directors and Choreographers), Gene McElwain (IATSE Local 751), Anthony De Paolo (IATSE), John P. Connolly (Actors' Equity Association), Mark Zimmerman (Actors' Equity Association), Cecilia Friederichs (IATSE Local USA 829), Carol Waaser (Actors' Equity Association).

Standing (L-R): Joseph Scanapicco (IATSE Local 751), Bill Dennison (Local 802 AFM), Bruce Cohen (IATSE Local 18032 ATPAM), Mary Landolfi (Local 802 AFM), Gordon G. Forbes (IATSE Local 18032 ATPAM), Frank Connolly (Teamsters Local 817), Mike Wekselblatt (IATSE Local One), Ken Greenwood (Actors' Equity Association), Joe Eisman (Local 802 AFM), James J. Claffey, Jr. (IATSE Local One), Patrick Glynn (American Federation of Musicians), Ira Mont (Actors' Equity Association), Pat White (IATSE Local 764), Mauro Melleno (Society of Stage Directors and Choreographers), Frank Gallagher (IATSE Local 764), Ralph Sevush (Dramatists Guild), Deborah Alton (AGMA), Alan Gordon (AGMA) and Paige Price (Actors' Equity Association).

Tobak Lawrence Company

Photo by Ben Strothmann

(L-R): Michael Lawrence, Joanna B. Koondel and Richard Fromm.

Faculty

IATSE Local One, Stagehands

Seated (L-R): Robert "Toby" McDonough (Treasurer), Robert C. Score (Recording-Corresponding Secretary), James J. Claffey, Jr. (President), William J. Walters (Vice President), John M. Diaz, Sr. (Chairman, Board of Trustees).

Standing (L-R): William Ngai (Trustee), Kevin McGarty (Theatre Business Manager), Michael Wekselblatt (Theatre Business Manager), Robert C. Nimmo (Television Business Manager), Edward J. McMahon III (Television Business Manager) and Daniel Thorn (Trustee).

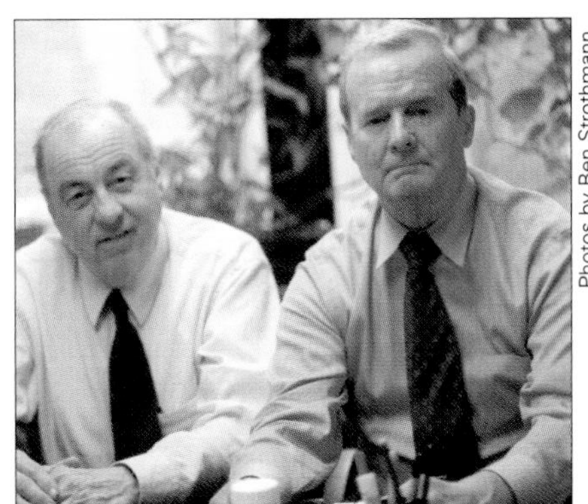

Photos by Ben Strothmann

(L-R): Paul F. Dean, Sr. (Replacement Room Chairperson) and Edmond F. Supple, Sr. (Administrative Secretary).

American Federation of Musicians, Local 802

Mary Landolfi
President

Bill Dennison
Recording Vice President

Photos by Walter Karling

Back Row (L-R): Bud Burridge, Maxine Roach, Andy Schwartz, Al Hunt, Ethan Fein, Maura Giannini, Jay Schaffner, Ken Rizzo and Mark Johansen.
Front Row (L-R): Financial Vice President Jay Blumenthal, President Mary Landolfi and Recording Vice President Bill Dennison.

Faculty

Dramatists Guild

Photos by Ben Strothmann

DRAMATISTS GUILD COUNCIL - STEERING COMMITTEE
(L-R): Arthur Kopit (Secretary), Jonathan Reynolds (Treasurer), John Weidman (President), Stephen Schwartz, Marsha Norma (Vice President) and Jeanine Tesori.

THE DRAMATISTS GUILD STAFF
Seated (L-R): Tari Stratton (Director of Education, Events & Outreach), Gary Garrison (Executive Director of Creative Affairs), Ralph Sevush (Executive Director of Business Affairs), David Faux (Director of Business Affairs), Doug Green (Director of MIS).

Standing (L-R): Tom Epstein (Director of Membership), John Minore (Executive Assistant), Greg Bossler (Director of Publications), Susan Drury (Administrator Dramatists Guild Fund) and Abby Marcus (General Manager).

Faculty

Hudson Scenic Group

Photo by Ben Strothmann

Front Row (L-R): Carrie Silverstein, Jose Ortiz, Louise Krozek, Pat Bases, Phil Giller, Gabriel Tepoxteco, Jim Starr, Dave Rosenfeld.

Second Row (L-R): Chris Costa, Beth Lieberman, Mary Burt, Maggie Ryan, Grace Brandt, Flo Frintzilas, Bruce Knechtel, Walter Murphy.

Third Row (L-R): Dana Heffern, Midge Lucas, Ann Sherill, Diane Rich, Chris Cuccia, Richard Chebetar, Dana Gracey, Matt Saide, Dom Godfrey.

Fourth Row (L-R): Hector Roman, Rise Abramson, Joyce Kubalak, Jess Stevens, Jim Curry, Russ Stevens, Karl Schuberth, Don Cafaro, Kevin Fedorko.

Fifth Row (L-R): Riccardo Valentin, Fernando Colon, Leo Drondin, Clare Hines, Chris Clarence, Joyce Liepertz, Jim Gilmartin, Marc Schmittroth, Drew Lanzarotta, Mike Leston, Neil Mazzella.

Sixth Row (L-R): Pat Fitzpatrick, Susan Blume, Brandon Forbono, Angela Dufrensne, Jim Geyer, Jeff Glave, Dean Sorenson, Carlos Ramos, Sty Tygert, Ishmael Gerena, Jordan Gable, Doug Mestanza, Chuck Adomanis, Jerry Valenzuela, Shawn Larkin, David Steiner.

Seventh Row (L-R): Barbara Bloomfield, Richie Fuggetta, Grace Uffner, Wayne Alfano, Joseph Trainor, Oleg Levin, Tommy Devitt, Chris Pravata, Matt Coviello, Rick Lebrenz, Eric Cooper, Eric Czarnecki.

Eighth Row (L-R): Delia Washington, Daryl Haley, Jo Ann Veneziano, Carrie Irons, Nancy Branton, Chris Doogan, Will Ball, Elisio Rodriguez, David Kidd, Bart Coviello, Bobby Cox, Mike Testa, Ian Stell, Gary Deluca, James Bolar, Josh Braun.

Ninth Row (L-R): Job Guzman, Eleni Friscia, Bruce Kessner, Freddie Sanchez, Bob Braun, Renee Kildow, David Berendes, Tony Goncalves, Tony Tallarico, Mike Stone, Robert Paternoster, Brian Chebetar, Roger Bardwell.

Tenth Row (L-R): Matt Jones, Sam Ellis, Josh Coakley, Will Wells, Bob Arietta, Chris Labudde, Gerhard Brandner Adam Cohan, John Sisilli, Sean Farrugia, Pete McGovern, Brant Underwood, Drew Williamson.

Back Row (L-R): Irene Wang, Corky Boyd, David Howe, Tom Sullivan, Mike Madravazakis, Rick Mone, Mike Banta, Brian Griffin, George Sibbald, Kurt White and Dean Kozeleck.

Faculty

Broadway Cares/Equity Fights AIDS

Photos by Ben Strothmann

Front Row (L-R): Michelle Abesamis, Anthony LaTorella, Ariadne Villarreal, Ngoc Bui, Dennis Henriquez.
Second Row (L-R): Janice Mayer, Brian Schaaf, Wendy Merritt Kaufman, Scott Tucker, K.T. Baumann, Andy Smith, Chris Davis.
Third Row (L-R): Frank Conway, Cat Domiano, Janie Smulyan, Carol Ingram, Yvonne Ghareeb, Denise Roberts Hurlin, Trisha Doss.
Fourth Row (L-R): Chris Kenney, Skip Lawing, Rose James, Producing Director Michael Graziano, Michael Clarkston, Scott Stevens, Chris Economakos, Joe Norton, Jody O'Neil, Ed Garrison, Executive Director Tom Viola, Director of Finance and Administration Larry Cook.
Back Row (L-R): Peter Borzotta, Andy Halliday, Charles Hamlen, Nathan Hurlin.

Dodger Theatricals

Back Row (L-R): Michael David, Sandra Carlson, James Love, Gordon Kelly, Tim Sulka, Lauren Mitchell, Edward Strong.
Middle Row (L-R): Jessica Ludwig, Andrew Serna, Jennifer Vaughan, Ashley Zimmerman, Nefertiti Warren, Paula Maldonado.
Front Row (L-R): Pamela Lloyd, Laurinda Wilson and Sally Campbell Morse.

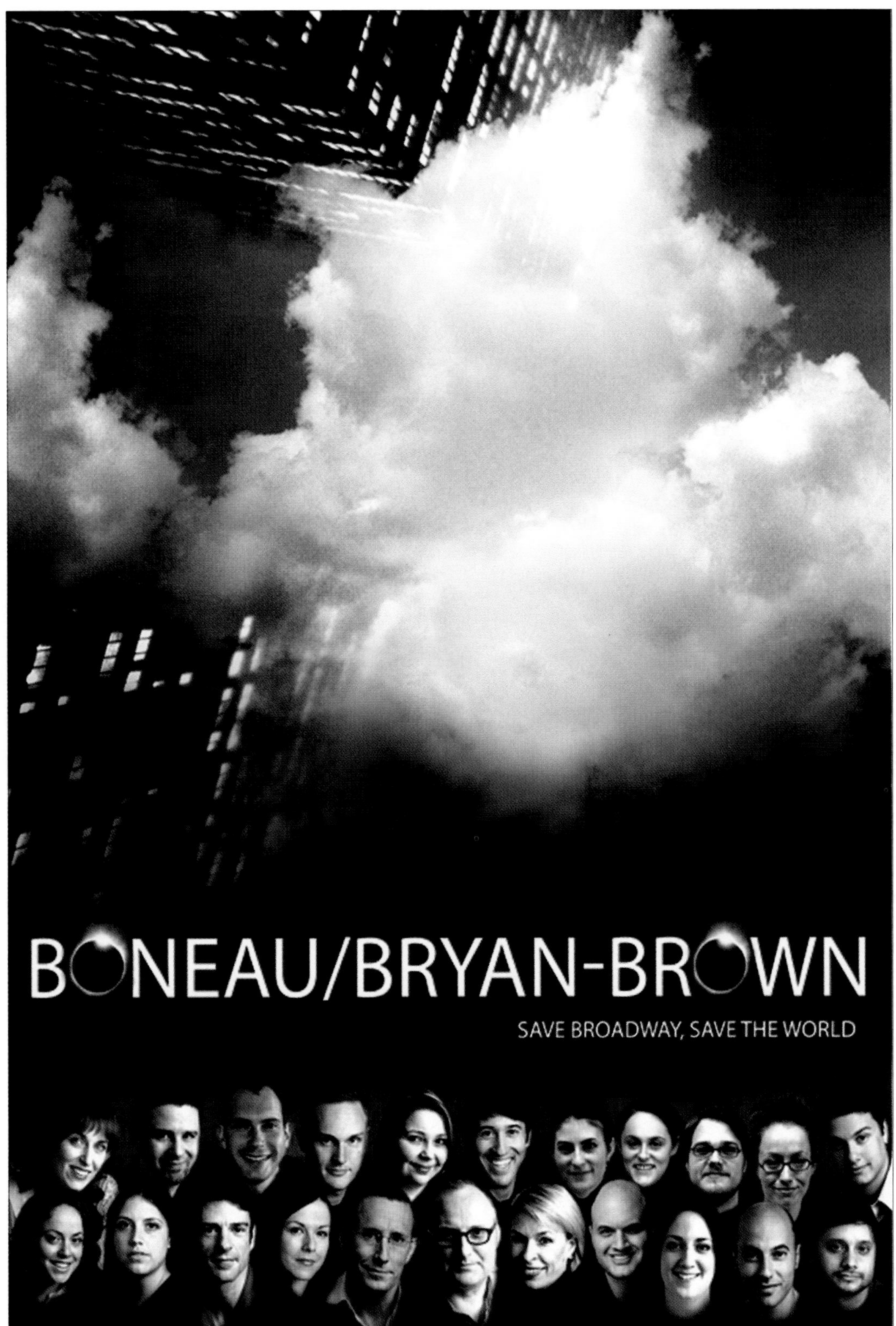

Top Row (L-R): Jackie Green, Jim Byk, Steven Padla, Aaron Meier, Juliana Hannett, Matt Polk, Danielle Crinnion, Amy Kass, Ian Bjorklund, Allison Houseworth and Matt Ross.
Bottom Row (L-R): Jessica Johnson, Linnae Petruzzelli, Kevin Jones, Brandi Cornwell, Chris Boneau, Adrian Bryan-Brown, Susanne Tighe, Heath Schwartz, Christine Olver, Joe Perrotta and Hector Hernandez.
Page designed by Boneau/Bryan-Brown.

Faculty

Barlow•Hartman Public Relations

Photos by Ben Strothmann

Standing (L-R): Bethany Larsen, John Barlow, Kevin Robak, Ryan Ratelle, Michael Hartman, Carol Fineman, Dennis Crowley, Tommy Prudenti and Wayne Wolfe.
Front (L-R): Tom D'Ambrosio and Leslie Baden.

Not pictured: Michelle Bergmann and Matt Stapleton.

Springer Associates Public Relations

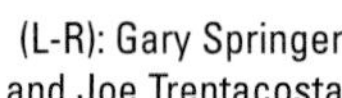

(L-R): Gary Springer and Joe Trentacosta

Faculty

Richard Kornberg & Associates

Richard Kornberg

Don Summa

Carrie Friedman

Tom D'Ambrosio

Photos by Ben Strothmann

Laura Kaplow-Goldman

Billy Zavelson

Alyssa Hart

The Pete Sanders Group

Pete Sanders

Jeffrey Richards Associates

Irene Gandy

The Publicity Office

Michael Borowski

Faculty

G. ANDERSON — ART CLUB
B. AQUART — BASKETBALL
J. AQUINO — TRACK & FIELD
M. BARRY — BADMINTON
J. COOPER — 4-H
T. COPPOLA — CHORUS
D. COX — HISTORICAL SOCIETY
T. CREWS — TECHNOLOGY CLUB

A. CRUZ — GLEE CLUB
A. DAVIS — BLACK HISTORY CLUB
B. DOWNING — BOWLING TEAM
P. DUFFY — BALLET
D. EDWARDS — FOOTBALL
S. FITZPATRICK — CHEERLEADING
T. FRANCIS — STUDY CLUB
F. GARGIULO — DUNGEONS & DRAGONS CLUB

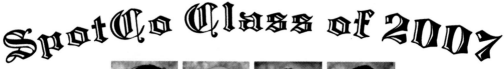

SpotCo Class of 2007

D. HODGES — PRINCIPAL
J. EDWARDS — VICE PRINCIPAL
B.BERK — DEAN OF STUDENTS
T. GREENWALD — AV SQUAD

G. GREEN — PEP SQUAD
K. HALL — WEIGHTLIFTING
L. HUNTER — ICE HOCKEY
L. JOHNSON — DANCE TEAM
L. KAISER — YEARBOOK
H. LEE — DRILL TEAM
N. LINDEMAN — PING PONG
M. LITTELL — COLOR GUARD

T. MCCANN — EQUINE CLUB
J. MCNICHOLAS — BROADCAST CLUB
P. MILANO — GOLF
W. MITCHELL — DRAMA SOCIETY
D. PRESTON — MATHLETE
L. PRICE — PROM COMMITTEE
M. RHEAULT — WRESTLING
A. ROTHENBERG — HALL MONITOR

V. SAINATO — DEBATE
S. SOSNOWSKI — FENCING
D. SUYAMA — SOCCER
E. VICIOSO — BAND
J. WALTERS — DRUMLINE
M. WILSTEIN — ASTRONOMY CLUB
G. WINGFIELD — CREATIVE WRITING

Text and page designed by SpotCo

Serino Coyne, Inc.

Nancy Coyne
Class Co-President

Class of 2006-07

Matthew Serino
Class Co-President

Andy Apostolides

David Barrineau

Sandy Block

Tom Callahan

Greg Corradetti

Angelo Desimini

Joaquin Esteva

Noriko Ishikawa

Scott Johnson

David Kane

Burt Kleeger

Caroline Lenher

Roger Micone

Jim Miller

Catherine Reid

Ruth Rosenberg

Jim Russek

Beth Schefflan

Ginger Witt

Scott Yambor

Text and page designed by Serino Coyne Inc.

Faculty

From top left: DeWayne Snype Richard Robertson Adam Neumann Lucy Lamela Sasha DeFazio Ryan Klink Suzanne Hereth Frank Verlizzo Jeronimo Sochaczewksi Denise Ganjou Kara Eldridge Taliah Weiss Jon Bierman Martha Magnuson Clint White Jovan Villalba Taryn O'Bra Pamela Bush Elizabeth Findlay Heather Liebling Davlynn Gundolff Janice Brunell Ann Murphy Barbara Eliran Erika Creagh Marshall Vickness John Zontini Al Garcia Lianne Ritchie Simona Tanasescu Li Zhang Patrick Flood Terry Newberry

Text and page designed by Eliran Murphy Group

Faculty

The Actors' Fund of America

Photos by Ben Strothmann

Seated (L-R): Icem Benamu, Stephanie Linwood Coleman, Patch Schwadron, Lucy Seligson, Liz Lawlor, Erica Chung, Josh Levine, Ryan Dietz.
Second Row (L-R): Debbie Schaum, Judy Fish, Belinda Sosa, Joe Benincasa, Sue Composto, Tamar Shapiro, Sara Meehan.
Third Row (L-R): Victor Mendoza, Jose Delgado, Gloria Jones, Dave Gusty, Billie Levinson, Wally Munro, Catherine Cooke, Ruth Shin.
Fourth Row (L-R): Melissa Haslam, Sylvian Underwood, Lorraine Chisholm, Lisa Naudus, Helene Kendler, Thomas Pileggi.
Fifth Row (L-R): Barbara Davis, Sam Smith, Charlene Morgan, Vicki Avila, Carol Wilson, Rick Martinez, Tim Pinckney, Israel Duran, Janet Pearl.
Back Row (L-R): Dr. Jim Spears, David Engelman, Jonathan Margolies, Keith McNutt and Bob Rosenthal.

Binder Casting

(L-R): Jack Bowdan C.S.A.Nikole Vallins, Jay Binder C.S.A., Megan Larche, Mark Brandon, Allison Estrin and Jonathan Mills.

Faculty

Playbill / Manhattan Office

Philip S. Birsh
Publisher

Clifford S. Tinder
Senior Vice President/ Publisher, Classic Arts Division

Photos by Ben Strothmann

MANHATTAN OFFICE
Front Row (L-R): Natasha Williams, Wanda Young, Jane Katz, Ruthe Schnell, Clifford S. Tinder, Melissa Merlo, Oldyna Dynowska.
Second Row (L-R): Orlando Pabon, Ari Ackerman, Ira Pekelnaya, Arturo Gonzalez, Maude Popkin, Terry Wilson, Theresa Holder, Jan Meiselman, Silvija Ozols.
Third Row (L-R): Anderson Peguero, Glenn Asciutto, Erica Rubin, Alex Near, Clara Tiburcio, Judy Samelson, Amy Asch, Esvard D'Haiti.
Fourth Row (L-R): Michael Rafael, Harry Haun, Bruce Stapleton, Susan Ludlow, Timothy Leinhart, Philip S. Birsh, Robert Viagas, David Gewirtzman, Andy Buck.
Not Pictured: Jolie Schaffzin, Glenn Schaevitz, Kesler Thibert, Joel Wyman, Louis Botto and Irv Winick.

EDITORIAL
Front Row (L-R): Silvija Ozols, Judy Samelson, Clifford S. Tinder, Ira Pekelnaya.
Back Row (L-R): Harry Haun, Robert Viagas and Andy Buck.

Not Pictured: Louis Botto.

ADVERTISING
Front (L-R): Theresa Holder and Clifford S. Tinder.
Middle Row (L-R): Wanda Young, Maude Popkin, Jane F. Katz, Terry Wilson, Alex Near.
Back Row (L-R): Glenn Asciutto, Timothy Leinhart, Ruthe Schnell, Susan Ludlow, Ari Ackerman.

Not Pictured: Jolie Schaffzin, Glenn Shaevitz, Joel Wyman and Irv Winick.

Faculty

Southern Playbill / Miami

Arthur T. Birsh
Chairman

Joan Alleman
Corporate Vice President

Leslie J. Feldman
Publisher/ Southern Division

Photos by Alex Matschick

PUBLISHING AND ADVERTISING STAFF
Front Row (L-R): Sara Smith, Arthur T. Birsh, Leslie J. Feldman, Donald Roberts.
Back Row (L-R): Tom Green, Jeff Ross and Ed Gurien.

Nubia Robo

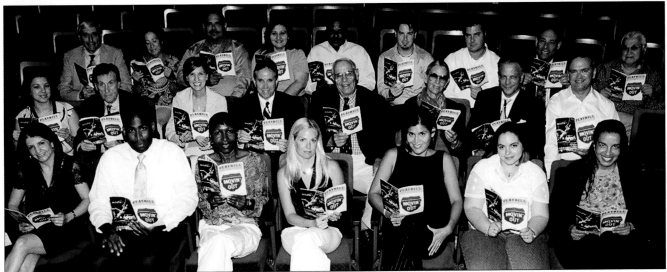

SOUTHERN PLAYBILL STAFF
First Row (L-R): Sara Smith, Mark Hamilton, Ruth Ingram, Laura Goldman, Maria Chinda, Maritza Lopez, Sally Coscia.
Second Row (L-R): Raquel Romero, Jeff Ross, Michelle Campos, Leslie J. Feldman, Arthur T. Birsh, Joan Alleman, Donald Roberts.
Third Row (L-R): Tom Green, Silvia Cañadas, Christopher Diaz, Carolina Diaz, Milton McPherson, Eric Schrader, Lance Lenhardt, Ed Gurien and Baldemar Albornoz.
(Photos taken at the Jackie Gleason Theatre in Miami Beach.)

ART STAFF
Front Row (L-R): Maria Chinda, Carolina Diaz, Joan Alleman (Vice President), Maritza Lopez, Silvia Cañadas.
Back Row (L-R): Lance Lenhardt, Christopher Diaz, Milton McPherson, Sally Coscia, Baldemar Albornoz.

PRODUCTION STAFF
Front Row (L-R): Raquel Romero, Laura Goldman, Linda Clark, Ruth Ingram.
Back Row (L-R): Mark C. Hamilton, Eric Schrader, Michelle Campos and Kevin Keegan.

Faculty

Playbill / Woodside

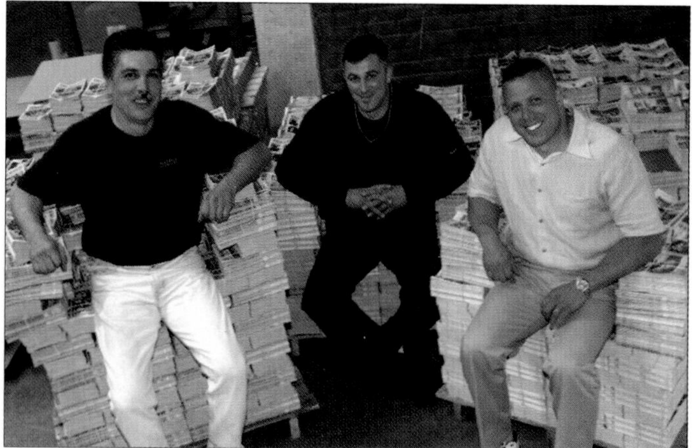

PRODUCTION CHIEFS
(L-R): Louis Cusanelli, Robert Cusanelli and Patrick Cusanelli.

PRINTERS
Front Row (L-R): Thomas Pagliaro, Domingo Pagan, Louis Cusanelli.

Middle Row (L-R): Valerie Timmerman, Nancy Galarraga, Maheshwari Moti, Mary Roaid, Carlos Moyano, Fabian Cordero, Gilberto Gonzalez, Joseph Luciana, Ana Rincon.

Back Row (L-R): Elias Garcia, Carlos Robinson, Frank Dunn, John Matthews, Manuel Guzman, Lennox Worrell, Wilfredo Lebron, David Rodriguez Jr., Ramdat Ramlall, Sadu Greene and Scott Cipriano.

PRODUCTION
(L-R): Sean Kenny, David Porrello, Benjamin Hyacinthe and Patrick Cusanelli.

Faculty

Playbill / Woodside

Photos by Ben Strothmann

PLAYBILL.COM and PLAYBILLARTS.COM
(L-R): Kenneth Jones, Zachary Pincus-Roth, Greg Kalafatas, Matthew Westphal, Andrew Gans, David Gewirtzman and Andrew Ku.

CLASSIC ARTS DIVISION PROGRAM EDITORS
(L-R): Scott Sepich, Kristy Bredin, Tom Nondorf, Claire Mangan and William Reese.

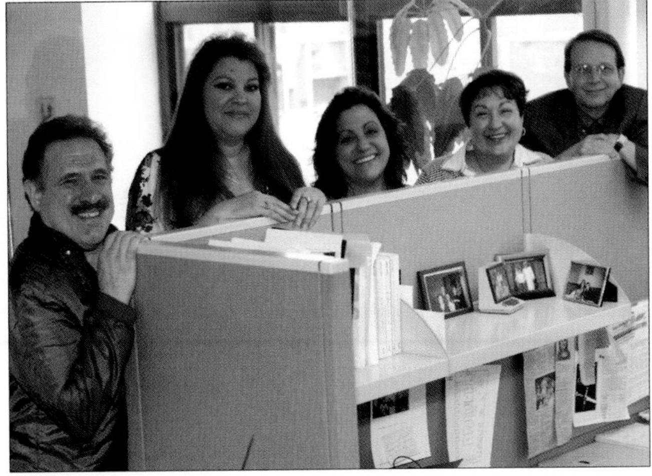

ACCOUNTING
(L-R): John LoCascio, Beatriz Chitnis, JoAnn D'Amato, Theresa Bernstein and Lewis Cole.

Robert Simonson
Columnist

Michael Buckley
Columnist

Harry Haun
Columnist

Steven Suskin
Columnist

Matt Windman
Contributor

Not Pictured: Seth Rudetsky.

Faculty

Playbill / Woodside

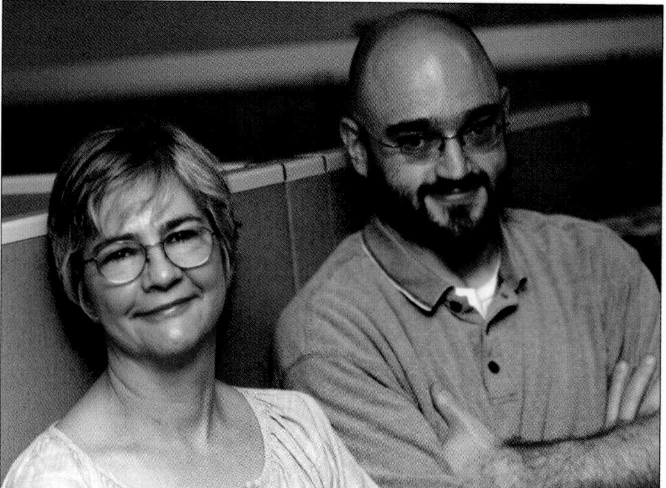

Photo by Ben Strothmann

PROGRAM EDITORS
(L-R): Pam Karr (Broadway) and Scott Hale (Off-Broadway).

Playbill Broadcast

Photo by Ben Strothmann

PLAYBILL RADIO
(L-R): Melissa Merlo, David Gewirtzman, Robert Viagas and Amy Asch.

Photo by David Gewirtzman

VIDEO INTERNS
(L-R): Lindsey Kremer, Noah Siegel and Alex Birsh.

Faculty

Playbill Yearbook Staff

EDITORIAL
(L-R): Amy Asch, David Gewirtzman, Robert Viagas, Ben Strothmann and Melissa Merlo with the 2005 and 2006 Yearbooks, plus the working manuscript for 2007.
Not Pictured: Kesler Thibert.

PHOTOGRAPHER
Aubrey Reuben

INTERNS
(L-R): Julie Cohen and Kristen Luciani

Playbill / Regional Advertising Salespersons

Kenneth R. Back
Sales Manager
Cincinnati

Abigail Bocchetto
Sales
Houston

Elaine Bodker
Sales
St. Louis

Carol Brumm
Sales
St. Louis

Bob Caulfield
Sales
San Francisco

Margo Cooper
Sales Manager
St. Louis

Ron Friedman
Sales Manager
Columbus

Betsy Gugick
Sales Manager
Dallas

Ira Kamens
Sales Manager
Philadelphia

Michel Manzo
Sales Manager
Philadelphia

Marilyn A. Miller
Sales Manager
Minneapolis

Judy Pletcher
Sales Manager
Washington, DC

John Rosenow
Sales Manager
Phoenix/Tucson

Kenneth Singer
Sales Manager
Houston

Not Pictured: Jennifer Allington, Dory Binyon, Megan Boles, Dick Coffee, Nancy Hardin, Dave Levin and Donald Roberts.

In Memoriam

May 2006 to May 2007

Hope Abelson
Bret Adams
Timothy Albrecht
Elizabeth Allen
Jay Presson Allen
June Allyson
Robert Altman
Tige Andrews
Ernest Austin
Jerry Belson
Isabel Bigley
John Bishop
Hendrik Booraem
Frank Bouley
Peter Boyle
Brian Brolly
Ruth Brown
Roscoe Lee Browne
Red Buttons
Frank Campanella
Deborah Coleman
Betty Comden
John Conte
Alvin Cooperman
Caris Corfman
Pat Corley
Richard Curnock
Mark Dawson
Yvonne De Carlo
Curt Dempster
Joan Diener
Katherine Dunham
Vilma Ebsen
Gino Empry
Ray Evans
Robert Fennell
Eddie Firestone
Arthur Franz
Ben Gannon
Lovette George
Richard Gilman
Abram S. Ginnes
Frank Goodman
Murray Grand
Timothy Gray
Richard Grayson
Ellen Hanley
Jay Harnick
Kitty Carlisle Hart
Melissa Hayden
Joseph Hayes
Benjamin Hendrickson
Henry Hewes
Arthur Hill
Barnard Hughes
Gareth Hunt
Betty Hutton
Lois January
Tony Jay
Robert Earl Jones
Norman Kelley
Bruno Kirby
Florence Klotz
Virginia Kolmar
Philip Kraus
Arthur Lewis
Salem Ludwig
Mako
Arthur Malvin
Alan Martin
Sophie Maslow
Daniel McDonald
Robert McFerrin
Barbara McNair
Ulpio Minucci
Robert D. Mitchell
Mavor Moore
Eric Muratalla
Rupert Murray
Carrie Nye
Mary Orr
Edwin C. Owens
Jack Palance
Chris Parry
Margaret Perry
Taliep Petersen
Tom Poston
Robert Prince
Richard Warren Pugh
Patrick Quinn
Charles Nelson Reilly
Lloyd Richards
Ian Richardson
Howard Rosenstone
Herbert Rudley
Lanna Saunders
Harold Scott
J.C. Sheets
Sidney Sheldon
Vincent Sherman
Michael Shurtleff
Edgar Small
Robert Sterling
Victoria Stevenson
Arnold Sundgaard
Glen Tetley
Jose Vega
Kurt Vonnegut, Jr.
Dick Vosburgh
Jack Warden
Ruth Webb
Lennie Weinrib
Eddie Weston
Tudi Wiggins
Darlene Wilson
John Wilson
Jane Wyatt
Gretchen Wyler

Index

Index

Index

Index

Index

Index

Index

Index

Index

Index

Index

Index

Index

Index

Index

Index

Index

Index

Index

Index

Index

Index

Index

Index